Paul and Palestinian Judaism

E. P. SANDERS

PAUL AND PALESTINIAN JUDAISM

A Comparison of Patterns of Religion

FORTRESS PRESS

PHILADELPHIA

First American Edition by Fortress Press 1977

Second printing 1983

Library of Congress Catalog Card Number 76-62612
ISBN 0-8006-0499-7

794K83   Printed in the United States of America   1-1899

In memory of
Susan Phillips
July 2 1947 – September 26 1975

CONTENTS

PART TWO PAUL

PREFACE

The present work is the result of rather a long period of research and thought, during which there was at least one major change in the precise focus of the research. I first started trying to work seriously on what I then thought of as the Jewish 'background' of the New Testament in 1962–63, when I studied Rabbinic and modern Hebrew in Oxford and Jerusalem. Since I thought that comparative studies should not be undertaken too early, nor under the time pressure of a doctoral program, my thesis was not a comparative study, although I did continue course work on aspects of Judaism. In 1966 I set myself to consider Goodenough's theory of Judaism – a small island of Rabbinic Judaism set in a vast sea of mystical, strongly Hellenized Judaism. I worked on Goodenough's materials for two years and then, during a year's leave, returned to the Hebrew language sources. During this period I not only came to the obvious conclusion that Judaism must be studied in its own right, but, as I became increasingly immersed in the study of Rabbinic religion, I also began to focus on a somewhat different project from the one first outlined: a comparative study limited to Palestinian Judaism and the most obvious New Testament writer, Paul. The present work is the result of that study.

The more I studied Jewish sources, the more it became apparent that it would be wrong and futile to try to write as if I were not primarily a student of the New Testament. New Testament scholars who have written on Judaism have sometimes pretended to an indifferent 'history of religions' viewpoint and educational background which they have not had, and I have tried not to make that mistake. On the other hand, I have tried to avoid the opposite pitfall of limiting the description of Judaism to individual motifs which are directly parallel to a motif in Paul or which are seen as directly relevant to his 'background'. I have attempted to compare Judaism, understood on its own terms, with Paul, understood on his own terms. I hope that this effort will prove to make a contribution not only to the understanding of Paul and his relationship to Judaism, but to the study of Judaism itself. If I cannot teach a Talmudist anything about Rabbinic religion, I hope at least that the argument about the structure and functioning of that religion and the way in which it is compared to other forms of Judaism will prove useful.

The present study may present the reader with the problem of the forest and the trees, and a word about that problem should be said in advance. The 'forest' in this case is really two forests, each one of which is, dropping the metaphor, a comparison. In the first part of the book there is a comparison of the various forms of Judaism, and a hypothesis as to the nature of Palestinian Judaism is argued. In the second there is a comparison between Paul and Palestinian Judaism, and a further hypothesis is presented. Along the way there are quite sizeable accounts of religion as reflected in the different bodies of literature considered. In each chapter I end up arguing for a certain view: religion as reflected in each of the bodies of literature dealt with – early Rabbinic literature, the Dead Sea Scrolls, several of the apocryphal and pseudepigraphical works, Paul's letters – should, it is argued, in each case be understood in one way rather than another. All of these arguments are important for the larger theses, and I have tried to make each chapter and section worthy of careful consideration as a discrete account of the material under discussion. On the other hand, the overall aim of the work is to carry out the two comparisons named. Thus I need to be right about both the trees and the forests. The reader who is interested primarily in the comparisons will need to bear in mind that we need well-described entities to compare, and be patient while reading through a few hundred pages of descriptions of those entities before I undertake to compare them. The reader who is primarily interested in my account of religion as it appears in the body of literature which most interests him or her will need to bear in mind the limitations imposed by the comparative aim of the book as a whole. I do not intend by these remarks to avoid criticism from either side, but only to inform the reader about the relationship of the parts and the whole.

Another way of stating the matter is to explain that I am trying to accomplish at least six things. The chief aims are these:

— to consider methodologically how to compare two (or more) related but different religions;
— to destroy the view of Rabbinic Judaism which is still prevalent in much, perhaps most, New Testament scholarship;
— to establish a different view of Rabbinic Judaism;
— to argue a case concerning Palestinian Judaism (that is, Judaism as reflected in material of Palestinian provenance) as a whole;
— to argue for a certain understanding of Paul;
— to carry out a comparison of Paul and Palestinian Judaism.

These various aims are not contradictory but complementary, and I think that it is reasonable to try to achieve them all in one book. It should be noted that the fourth and sixth constitute the general aim of the book, while I hope to accomplish the others along the way.

In arguing against some positions and for others a certain amount of scholarly polemic is naturally involved, and the reader will find this in the normal proportions in the Introduction and in chapters II, III and V. Chapter I, which deals with Rabbinic religion, deserves special mention, for there the criticism of the positions of other New Testament scholars over several generations becomes pronounced. The chapter was originally written in an almost entirely positive way, and it was only in the third or fourth revision that the argument against a certain understanding of Rabbinic religion was introduced. I hope that a careful reading of section I of chapter I will indicate why I judged it necessary to introduce a tone of sharp rebuttal: milder statements have fallen on deaf ears and are now cited as if they supported views which in fact they opposed. As I read book after book in which the same texts were repeatedly misconstrued, it seemed increasingly necessary to go into the misconstruction at some length, and this involves not only criticism of misunderstandings, but also the full quotation of numerous passages which have often appeared only as references in footnotes. Thus the first chapter turns out to be not only polemical, but also long. Achieving a correct understanding of Rabbinic Judaism, a religion which has been so often misunderstood, is sufficiently important to justify both explicit and detailed criticism and lengthy citation. I intend by all the negative criticism to accomplish a positive goal, the implantation of a better understanding of Rabbinism in New Testament scholarship.

Once the question of polemics in connection with Rabbinic Judaism is raised, the reader may wonder whether or not the topic is anti-Semitism. It is not. A Jewish scholar of my acquaintance offered to tell me which of the older generation of scholars whose views I criticize were in fact anti-Semites, but I declined to find out. As I see it, the view which is here under attack is held because it is thought to correspond to the evidence, and I attack it because I think it does not. The history of the relationship between scholarly representations of Judaism and anti-Semitism is quite complex, but the present work is not a contribution to unravelling it. The charges of misunderstanding should be read as simply that and no more.

Each of the sections of the work has presented its own difficulty, but perhaps only one difficulty involved in writing about Paul needs to be mentioned here. The secondary literature on Paul is vast, and it proved not to be feasible to summarize and discuss all the positions on each point. There are some questions of perennial interest in Pauline studies which are not even mentioned: the question of the identity of Paul's opponents, for example, has been excluded from the discussion, and with the exclusion has gone the omission of references to a large body of secondary literature. The section on Paul is written primarily *vis à vis* three positions: Bultmann and the Bultmann school, Schweitzer, and Davies. The first two were chosen because they are two major ways of understanding Paul which are more or less polar opposites and the third because of the obvious significance of Davies's position for the question of Paul and Judaism. Other scholarly views and contributions are discussed on individual points, but I have systematically tried to set my view of Paul over against (and sometimes in agreement with) the three positions mentioned.

The transliteration of Hebrew is based on the simplified system of the *Jewish Encyclopedia*, with only one or two minor alterations (e.g. *q* instead of *ḳ* for ק). The vowels in particular are not scientifically transliterated (thus *e* represents *seghol, tserę* and vocal *sheva*). In transliterating I have had in mind producing terms which can be conveniently read by the reader who may not know Hebrew, or who may know it only slightly. I do not think that any of the transliterations will mislead those who do know Hebrew, any more than Schechter's transliteration of זכות as *Zachuth* has prevented people from knowing what he was writing about. Worse, from the point of view of some, than the use of a simplified transliteration system will be the appearance of more than one system. When quoting others, I have naturally kept their transliterations. For Rabbinic names and for the titles of the Mishnaic and Talmudic tractates I have used Danby's transliterations as being most familiar to English readers, and for the Mekilta tractates I have followed Lauterbach.

The research for and writing of this book have been supported by generous grants, and I am glad to be able to acknowledge my indebtedness and gratitude to the granting institutions and agencies: to McMaster University for a series of summer grants which supported the research during its early stages; to the Canada Council for a Post-Doctoral Fellowship which provided a year's study in Jerusalem; to the American Council of Learned Societies for a Leave Fellowship; and to the Killam Program of the Canada Council for a Senior Research Scholarship which not only provided the time to complete the study but also provided funds for secretarial help and research assistance, travel to discuss drafts of the various sections with other scholars, visits to other libraries, and all the miscellaneous expenses which are incurred in the production of a manuscript. Without this support the manuscript would still be a bundle of notes and drafts.

As grateful as I am for financial support, I am even more grateful to the scholars who have read and discussed the manuscript with me. I have for years been cornering everyone I could to discuss Paul and Judaism, and this must serve as a general word of thanks to numerous scholars who have answered my questions and discussed my theories. I should single out for special mention my two colleagues, Dr Ben Meyer and Dr Al Baumgarten, and also Professor C. F. D. Moule, Professor John Knox, and Dr J. A. Ziesler, with all of whom I had especially rewarding and detailed conversations. Five scholars read extensive parts of the manuscript in an earlier draft, and I was able to discuss it with four of them. Professors Samuel Sandmel and Wayne Meeks both read chapter I and chapter V and discussed the two chapters with me at some length. Professor W. D. Davies read the Introduction, part of chapter I and all of chapter V. I am grateful both for his strong and unflagging encouragement and for his critique on several points. Professor B. Z. Wacholder read chapter I, and his notes on it saved me from several mistakes. Dr Gerd Lüdemann read the penultimate draft of the entire manuscript. His notes allowed me to correct several errors, and he also made helpful comments with regard to the contents. I am deeply indebted to these scholars, all of whom gave generously of their time. Their notes and suggestions have measurably improved the manuscript, and I am glad to record here my appreciation and thanks to them. In addition to the usual (and perfectly correct) statement that those who have so kindly helped me are not responsible for mistakes that remain, I should say that I have sometimes had to remain in disagreement with some of those who read the manuscript. The disagreements often provided the most fruitful topics in discussion, and I hope that in their written form they will be of interest to a wider audience.

I owe a debt of gratitude of a different kind to the late Dr Mordechai Kamrat. Dr Kamrat, who is best known as the 'father' of the Ulpan system in Israel, was a peerless teacher of Hebrew. Although his academic field was not Talmudics, he had an encyclopedic knowledge of Rabbinic literature (as well as of much else). Although burdened with numerous responsibilities, he undertook my private tutelage in modern and Rabbinic Hebrew both in 1963 and in 1968–69. It will give an idea both of the time he devoted to my education and of the incalculable debt which I owe him when I say that together we read through most of three of the four principal Tannaitic midrashim, several Mishnah and Tosefta tractates, and portions of the minor Tannaitic midrashim. The reading was necessarily rapid, bit it gave me the opportunity of coming to grips with Tannaitic literature in a way which would otherwise have been impossible. Dr Kamrat's untimely death in 1970 deprived the world of a man of great learning and prodigious ability, but of even greater heart and spirit.

My research assistants at McMaster University have made material contributions to the work. Dr Manfred Brauch prepared a survey of research on the phrase *dikaiosynē theou* which has led to an appendix to chapter V. Dr Phil Shuler checked the references to the Dead Sea Scrolls. Dr Benno Przybylski checked the references to Rabbinic literature and also gave me notes on the chapter which clarified some points. He has also spent dozens of laborious hours in proof-reading. Phyllis Koetting made last-minute corrections in the typescript, typed several revised pages, prepared the bibliography, helped prepare the indices, and assisted in proof-reading. I am grateful to them all for their careful work.

The principal burden of preparing the manuscript for the press was carried by Susan Phillips. Between 1969 and late 1975 she helped organize and carry out my administrative duties so that I would have time for research and writing, typed almost countless drafts of various parts of the manuscript, conformed the footnote and manuscript style to the requirements of the press, checked the English language quotations in chapter I and chapter III, and finally prepared, in the first twenty days of September, 1975, an almost flawless typescript of some 1100 pages. For these things alone I would have recorded my warmest admiration, respect and gratitude. But, when she died, we had been looking forward to a long and happy life together; this book is offered as a memorial to her and that hope.

ABBREVIATIONS

AB	Analecta Biblica, Rome
AGJU	Arbeiten zur Geschichte des antiken Judentums und des Urchristentums, Leiden
ATANT	Abhandlungen zur Theologie des Alten und Neuen Testaments, Zürich
BASOR	*Bulletin of the American Schools of Oriental Research*, New Haven, Conn.
BBB	Bonner Biblische Beiträge, Bonn
BWANT	Beiträge zur Wissenschaft vom Alten und Neuen Testament, Stuttgart
BZ	*Biblische Zeitschrift*, Paderborn
BZAW	*Beiheft zur Zeitschrift für die alttestamentliche Wissenschaft*, Berlin
CBQ	*Catholic Biblical Quarterly*, Washington
DJD	*Discoveries in the Judaean Desert*, Oxford
DSS	Dead Sea Scrolls
ET	English translation
EvT	*Evangelische Theologie*, Munich
Exp	*The Expositor*, London
ExpT	*Expository Times*, Edinburgh
FRLANT	Forschungen zur Religion und Literatur des Alten und Neuen Testaments, Göttingen
HNT	Handbuch zum Neuen Testament, Tübingen
HTR	*Harvard Theological Review*, Cambridge, Mass.
HUCA	*Hebrew Union College Annual*, Cincinnati
ICC	The International Critical Commentary, Edinburgh
IDB	*Interpreter's Dictionary of the Bible*, New York
IEJ	*Israel Exploration Journal*, Jerusalem
JBL	*Journal of Biblical Literature*, Philadelphia
JE	*The Jewish Encyclopedia*, New York and London
JJS	*Journal of Jewish Studies*, London
JQR	*Jewish Quarterly Review*, London
JR	*Journal of Religion*, Chicago
JSJ	*Journal for the Study of Judaism*, Leiden

JSS	*The Journal of Semitic Studies*, Manchester
JTC	*Journal of Theology and the Church*, New York and Tübingen
JTS	*Journal of Theological Studies*, Oxford
KD	*Kerygma und Dogma*, Göttingen
NT	*Novum Testamentum*, Leiden
NTS	*New Testament Studies*, Cambridge
PAAJR	*Proceedings of the American Academy of Jewish Research*, New York
RB	*Revue Biblique*, Paris
RHPhR	*Revue d'Histoire et de Philosophie Religieuses*, Strasbourg
RHR	*Revue de l'Histoire des Religions*, Paris
RQ	*Revue de Qumran*, Paris
RSR	*Recherches de Science religieuse*, Paris
SANT	Studien zum Alten und Neuen Testament, Munich
S.-B.	Strack-Billerbeck, *Kommentar*
SBT	Studies in Biblical Theology, London
SJ	*Studia Judaica*, Berlin
SJT	*Scottish Journal of Theology*, Edinburgh
SNT	Supplements to *Novum Testamentum*, Leiden
SNTS	Studiorum Novi Testamenti Societas, Oxford
SNTSMS	Society for New Testament Studies Monograph Series, Cambridge
SPB	Studia Post-Biblica, Leiden
ST	*Studia Theologica*, Lund
STDJ	Studies on the Texts of the Desert of Judah, Leiden
SUNT	Studien zur Umwelt des Neuen Testaments, Göttingen
TDNT	*Theological Dictionary of the New Testament*, Grand Rapids, Michigan
TLZ	*Theologische Literaturzeitung*, Leipzig
TU	Texte und Untersuchungen, Berlin
TZ	*Theologische Zeitschrift*, Basle
USQR	*Union Seminary Quarterly Review*, New York
VT	*Vetus Testamentum*, Leiden
WMANT	Wissenschaftliche Monographien zum Alten und Neuen Testament, Neukirchen
YJS	Yale Judaica Series, New Haven, Conn.
ZAW	*Zeitschrift für die alttestamentliche Wissenschaft*, Berlin
ZNW	*Zeitschrift für die neutestamentliche Wissenschaft und die Kunde des Urchristentums*, Berlin
ZTK	*Zeitschrift für Theologie und Kirche*, Tübingen

References to texts will generally be familiar and self-explanatory. Details are given in the Bibliography.

INTRODUCTION

1. Paul and Judaism in New Testament scholarship

The phrase 'Paul and Judaism' starts more questions than can be dealt with in one book, and perhaps more than we can conveniently list here. Even the phrase itself introduces a problem: should one not say, 'Paul and *the rest* of Judaism', since Paul himself was surely Jewish? He explicitly contrasts himself and Peter with the Gentile sinners (Gal. 2.15). Whatever his perception of his own identity, however, the traditional terminology would seem to be justified by his being engaged in a mission which went beyond the bounds of Judaism. He must himself discuss the fact that the Jews have not accepted his gospel, and he has to redefine 'Israel' so that not all who are descended from Israel belong (Rom. 9.6–8). In any case, the question of Paul's self-identity is not the question before us, and we shall retain the convenient phrase 'Paul and Judaism'.

Far hotter issues are raised by the phrase than whether or not Paul should be called Jew or Christian. There are, to begin with, the polemics of Paul's letters against Jews and Judaizers ('Look out for the dogs . . . , look out for those who mutilate the flesh', Phil. 3.2). Almost as vitriolic have been the scholarly debates of the last several decades on how Paul does or does not relate to Judaism. Is he to be primarily understood as a Jewish apocalypticist, a Hellenistic mystic, a Rabbi who accepted Jesus as the Messiah, a Hellenistic Jew? Or as none of these or as some combination of them? Paul's relationship with the contemporary world has been and remains one of the three or four main preoccupations of New Testament scholarship.

In order to give some immediate focus to the present work, but without yet defining the precise question which is to be raised, it should be said that we shall be dealing with the basic relationship between Paul's religion and the various forms of Palestinian Judaism as revealed in Palestinian Jewish literature from around 200 b.c.e. to around 200 c.e. This restriction does not presuppose that Palestinian Judaism and Hellenistic Judaism have nothing in common, nor does it prejudge the question of whether Paul is closer to Palestinian Judaism, or some form of it, than to Hellenistic Judaism or to Hellenism proper. We do not intend to sort out and weigh 'parallels' and 'influences' in order to determine what part of the ancient world most influenced Paul and in what respects.[1] The limitation to Palestinian Jewish literature as providing a point of comparison is basically practical. One cannot discuss everything at once. We shall, however, in the conclusion raise briefly the question of Paul's relationship to Hellenistic Judaism as known in Philo. In any case, it is not the intention of the present study to find sources and influences, although they will be sometimes discussed along the way, but to *compare* Paul's religion and his view of religion to those which are seen in Palestinian Jewish literature.

It does not seem necessary to attempt a full review of scholarly stances on the question of how Paul and Palestinian Judaism are related. On the other hand, there has been serious disagreement among scholars on the question of the relationship. Without entering into a detailed history, it is possible to discern a few main tendencies. A view which has been very prevalent – it may deserve the adjective 'dominant', at least for certain periods and schools of New Testament research – is seen in H. St John Thackeray's *The Relation of St Paul to Contemporary Jewish Thought*, published in 1900. The view is quickly summarized: Paul's theology was basically *antithetical* to Judaism, but many *particulars* of his thought were *rooted in* Judaism.

Thackeray argued, for example, in discussing 'justification by faith or works', that the topic reveals 'the Apostle's independence of thought and his complete break from Judaism' (p. 80). Thackeray briefly described 'the Jewish idea of righteousness and the means of attaining to it in the time of St Paul', basing his discussion on Weber's systematic theology of Rabbinic Judaism. The latter will occupy us in the next chapter. It suffices here to say that the Jewish view, according to Weber, was that righteousness is earned by works, while Paul's was that righteousness is the gift of God received by faith (pp. 80–7). Nevertheless, despite the antithesis, the various elements that make up Paul's view have their 'roots in the older ideas of Judaism' (p. 87).

It is not our intention to use an old book which (unlike Thackeray's work on the Septuagint and Josephus) has not had much influence on subsequent writers as a foil for the present study. There are, however, two points about Thackeray's book which are interesting and instructive. In the first place, he himself stated that his knowledge of Rabbinic literature was completely derivative (p. 25). He cited several authors, but he made most use of Weber. Secondly, he did not consider the contrast which he sketched between Paul and Judaism to be the creative part of his work. He pointed out the anti-

---

[1] There is a large body of secondary literature which attempts to do this. See, for example, K. L. Schmidt, 'Der Apostel Paulus und die antike Welt', *Das Paulusbild* (ed. Rengstorf), pp. 214–45. Schmidt was also concerned to describe Paul's attitude towards 'the ancient world'. A more recent example is E. Brandenburger, *Fleisch und Geist*, 1968.

thesis partly in order to protect himself from being charged with having eliminated Paul's originality and with having made him too Jewish (cf. pp. 4–6, 80, 97). What he considered original was the attempt to find Jewish *sources* for elements in Paul's thought in a 'connected work dealing with the whole subject' (p. 6). What is instructive about these two points taken together is this: Thackeray's depiction of Judaism – especially Rabbinic Judaism, although the distinction is not sharply drawn – *and* his consideration of Paul's thought as the *antithesis* of Judaism were widely held opinions in his day. On neither point does Thackeray consider himself original, but he simply repeats what he regards either as being the scholarly consensus or as being obvious.

The two elements which constitute Thackeray's view – *on the whole* Paul represents the *antithesis* of Judaism, while being *dependent* on it with regard to *individual motifs* – also constitute the view of many other scholars. In the next chapter we shall show how Weber's view of (Rabbinic) Judaism has lived on in New Testament criticism. Wherever it appears, the antithesis between it and Paul is either explicit or implicit. Once Judaism is described as a religion of legalistic works-righteousness, the contrast with Paul is as obvious as Thackeray took it to be, especially if the heart of Paul's religion is considered to be justification by faith.[2] Thus the works to be dealt with in the next chapter will also serve as examples of the view, even if it is only implicit, that Paul and Judaism, or some form of it, were antithetical. We shall give here only two examples which will indicate how prevalent the attitude reflected in Thackeray's work has been. The point is not that Thackeray has been in any way responsible for this view. The view is, rather, common in New Testament scholarship.

In discussing the term righteousness, Rudolf Bultmann argued that 'there is complete agreement' between Paul and Judaism 'as to the formal meaning of DIKAIOSYNE: It is a forensic-eschatological term'.[3] Nevertheless, on this very point there is direct antithesis between Paul and Judaism:

The contrast between Paul and Judaism consists not merely in his assertion of the present reality of righteousness, but also in a much more decisive thesis – the one which concerns the condition to which God's acquitting decision is tied. The Jew takes it for granted that this condition is keeping the Law, the accomplishing of 'works' prescribed by the Law. In direct contrast to this view Paul's thesis runs – to consider its negative aspect first: '*without works of the Law*'.
. . . .

---

[2] Cf. W. D. Davies, 'Paul and Judaism', *The Bible and Modern Scholarship* (ed. Hyatt), pp. 184f. Davies noted that Schweitzer's relegation of justification by faith to a subsidiary position in Paul's thought opened the way to considering Paul as fulfilling, rather than opposing, Judaism. He granted, however, that probably a majority of New Testament scholars 'still find the essence of Paulinism in justification by faith' (p. 185). The question is treated extensively in Chapter V.
[3] R. Bultmann, *Theology of the New Testament* I, p. 273. Emphasis removed.

The negative aspect of Paul's thesis does not stand alone; a positive statement takes its place beside it: *'by, or from, faith'*.[4]

In a similar way Schrenk, in his article on *dikaioō* in Kittel's *Wörterbuch*, wrote: 'The Rabbinic saying that the soul of the dead achieves expiation by death, and the Pauline statement that he who dies is thereby pronounced free from sin, are fully identical in substance. Paul is thus using here a Rabbinic theologoumenon.'[5] Thus Schrenk finds detailed agreements between Paul and Judaism. On the basic question of how one achieves righteousness, however, Schrenk is at one with Thackeray, Bultmann and countless others: Paul is the antithesis of Judaism.[6]

It is evident that the antithetical contrast, not by works but by faith, is Paul's own. New Testament scholars who accept the contrast, however, do not consider themselves to be simply accepting Paul's polemical description of Judaism as accurate. Rather, they find that description proved and elaborated on in scholarly works on Judaism.[7] Thackeray, as we have seen, used Weber; Bultmann, as we shall see in the next chapter, used Bousset; and Schrenk's description of Judaism relies on numerous quotations and citations of Rabbinic literature culled from Billerbeck.[8] Despite this attempt to base the depiction of the Judaism which is placed in antithesis to Paul on an investigation of Jewish literature, one cannot avoid the suspicion that, in fact, Paul's own polemic against Judaism serves to define the Judaism which is then contrasted with Paul's thought.

It is curious that C. G. Montefiore, in attempting to deflect the criticism of Judaism implicit in the antithesis between Paul and Judaism, himself accepted Paul's negative statements as accurately representing the Judaism which Paul knew.[9] Montefiore argued, however, that the Judaism which Paul knew and to which he objected so strenuously was not main-line Rabbinic Judaism, but a poorer form of Judaism, which he identified as Hellenistic (pp. 92–112). Further, Montefiore argued (following the German *religionsgeschichtliche Schule*) that Paul was strongly influenced by Hellenistic syncretism (pp. 112–29). Montefiore's method was to give in essay form (references to sources are almost non-existent) a description of the Rabbinic

---

[4] *Ibid.*, pp. 279f. Bultmann's position on the point of agreement and the essential contrast is simply repeated by Conzelmann, *An Outline of the Theology of the New Testament*, p. 217.

[5] *TDNT* II, p. 218. I fail to see the identity of the conceptions (see the Conclusion, n. 8), but the point here is only to illustrate a way of using Rabbinic material.

[6] Ibid., pp. 205–7.

[7] One could conceivably argue that the Judaism which Paul attacked must have existed, since he attacked it, even if it cannot be independently recovered from extant Jewish sources. The scholars who take Paul's attack to be accurate, however, have believed that the sort of Judaism criticized by Paul is found in Rabbinic literature. I agree, as will be seen in Chapter I, with the assessment of Montefiore, Moore and others (see immediately below) that it is not. The explanation of Paul's polemic against the law will be discussed in Chapter V, section 4.

[8] See, for example, *TDNT* II, pp. 186f., 196–8, on *dikaios* and *dikaiosynē* in 'the Synagogue'.

[9] Montefiore, *Judaism and St Paul*. See e.g. pp. 21f.

Judaism of, as he put it, 300 or 500 c.e. (p. 15). He left it to scholars to determine whether or not the Judaism of 50 c.e. was the same (p. 17); but he clearly supposed that Palestinian Judaism had at least not greatly improved between 50 c.e. and 500 c.e. (pp. 87–91). Since his summary of the main lines of Rabbinic religion in 300 or 500 did not reveal the kind of legalistic works-righteousness to which Paul objected, and since he had no reason to believe that earlier Rabbinic religion was vastly inferior to later, he concluded that Paul had not known Palestinian (Rabbinic) Judaism (p. 126).

Montefiore did not dwell on detailed motifs which are common to Rabbinic Judaism and Paul. Rather, he went to the large issues on which Paul's description of Judaism cannot be supported from Rabbinic sources (in Montefiore's view, though not in the view of Weber, Bousset, Billerbeck and others). He contrasted, for example, Paul's pessimism with the view of Rabbinic Judaism that the world is good (pp. 69–70). The most telling point of contrast, however, has to do with the way to salvation. In contrast to Paul's depiction of Judaism, for Rabbinic Judaism, as for Jesus, 'God was so good and near and kind, and man, through the Law and through repentance, had such constant, easy and efficacious opportunities of access to Him, that there was no need of a tremendous cosmic and divine event such as was provided by the incarnation and the crucifixion' (p. 74). He then focuses on the main point:

And even from sin and misery there was a way out. That way was constructed by God's forgiveness and man's repentance. Its outward symbol was the Day of Atonement. What neither God nor can could do according to Paul except by the incarnation of the Son, was done according to Rabbinic Judaism constantly, hour by hour, and year by year. Nothing is more peculiar in the great Epistles than the almost complete omission of the twin Rabbinic ideas of repentance and forgiveness (p. 75; cf. pp. 60, 66, 127).

Paul, Montefiore argued, could not 'have ignored the very keynote' of the Palestinian (or Rabbinic) Jewish position if he had known it (p. 76; cf. p. 66). Therefore he knew some other kind of Judaism.

Montefiore's effort was a serious attempt to solve a real problem. Scholars who found in Weber's description of Rabbinic Judaism (often equated simply with Judaism) a convincing depiction of the Judaism which Paul is likely to have known had no problem. The Judaism which Paul attacked is the same as that which emerges from Weber's study.[10] Jewish scholars and Christian scholars more knowledgeable about Rabbinic Judaism, however, found an incongruity between what Paul criticized and the Judaism which they knew. Five years before Montefiore wrote, Schechter had put the problem thus:

[10] Note Montefiore's criticism of relying, in a polemical situation, on one who shares one's own biases for knowledge of the other position; ibid., pp. 7–9.

Either the theology of the Rabbis must be wrong, its conception of God debasing, its leading motives materialistic and coarse, and its teachers lacking in enthusiasm and spirituality, or the Apostle to the Gentiles is quite unintelligible.[11]

Schechter, of course, took the second view. Paul's critique of Judaism was not to the point: therefore Paul could not be understood. In 1936 Parkes took something of the same view:

We have further to admit, on any basis of intellectual honesty, that we know sufficient of the Pharisees and of Rabbinic Judaism of his [Paul's] period to be compelled to allow that if it *is* Rabbinic Judaism which he is attacking, then to a large extent his charges against the Law are unjustified. Judaism can be attacked from various points of view, and much in it can be criticized, but if Paul was really attacking 'Rabbinic Judaism,' then much of his argument is irrelevant, his abuse unmerited, and his conception of that which he was attacking inaccurate.[12]

Like Montefiore, Parkes found the solution in Paul's having imbibed the Hellenistic spirit (p. 123). Paul attacked not Rabbinic Judaism, but Diaspora Judaism (p. 124).

The problem was more perceptively handled by George Foot Moore. In agreement with Montefiore, he posed it thus:

How a Jew of Paul's antecedents could ignore, and by implication deny, the great prophetic doctrine of repentance, which, individualized and interiorized, was a cardinal doctrine of Judaism, namely, that God, out of love, freely forgives the sincerely penitent sinner and restores him to his favor – that seems from the Jewish point of view inexplicable.[13]

Moore did not find the answer in supposing that Paul was attacking some other form of Judaism, however. Rather, he granted that Paul's position, from the point of view of Judaism, *was* inexplicable. Paul's view is to be explained only on the basis of his conviction that salvation comes only through Christ. Hence, Judaism could not in any way provide salvation, either by works *or* by forgiveness. Paul, according to Moore, was not addressing himself to Jews to refute them on their own terms, but to Gentile converts, to prevent their being persuaded by Jewish propagandists that observance of the law was necessary along with allegiance to Christ.[14]

Although the view that Paul is to be understood primarily on the basis of Hellenistic Judaism rather than Palestinian Judaism has found such recent advocates as Sandmel[15] and Goodenough,[16] the point of the question

---

[11] S. Schechter, *Aspects of Rabbinic Theology*, p. 18. Montefiore was attempting to find an alternative to the two possibilities posed by Schechter; see *Judaism and St Paul*, pp. 11f.

[12] J. Parkes, *Jesus, Paul and the Jews*, p. 120.

[13] G. F. Moore, *Judaism* III, p. 151.

[14] Ibid.

[15] S. Sandmel, *The Genius of Paul*; see e.g. p. 59.

[16] E. R. Goodenough, 'Paul and the Hellenization of Christianity', *Religions in Antiquity* (ed. Neusner), pp. 23–68. The article was completed by A. T. Kraabel.

raised by Montefiore, Moore and others has not substantially influenced subsequent scholarship. Their point is that, *on matters which are essential to Rabbinic Judaism*, such as the way to salvation, the description of Judaism implicit in Paul's attack on 'works of law' is wrong. Far from this view prevailing in New Testament scholarship, Paul's criticism of Judaism, as we have seen in the work of Bultmann and Schrenk, is frequently taken to be accurate and to the point. In other words, there are broad and influential spheres of New Testament scholarship which have not taken up, one way or the other, the point raised by Montefiore and Moore.

Montefiore's argument was taken up in some of its aspects by W. D. Davies in a work which marks a watershed in the history of scholarship on Paul and Judaism: *Paul and Rabbinic Judaism.*[17] Davies argued against Montefiore's position in two respects. First, he denied the neat compartmentalization of Hellenistic and Palestinian Judaism, citing the interpenetration of Hellenism and Judaism (pp. 1–16). Next, he argued that many of the motifs in Paul which have been viewed as being most Hellenistic in fact can be paralleled in, and were derived from, Palestinian Judaism as reflected and preserved in Rabbinic literature. Of the elements in Paul's thought which Montefiore was unable to find in Rabbinic literature, Davies mentions as possibly existing in Palestinian Judaism these: 'dissatisfaction with the Law, transcendentalism, pessimism and "mysticism"' (pp. 15f.). Davies did not, however, deal with the essential element which Montefiore found in Rabbinic literature but which is not taken into account in Paul's critique of Judaism: the doctrine of repentance and forgiveness.

Davies's work clearly caught the tide at its turning. One has not seen much on Paul and the mystery religions or on Paul and Hellenism in general since then.[18] If it is not universally conceded that the most pertinent 'background' to study in order to understand Paul is Judaism, that position is at least clearly dominant.[19] It was reinforced by the work of Schoeps in *Paul: The Theology of the Apostle in the Light of Jewish Religious History*. Schoeps's main argument, seen for example on the crucial questions of eschatology[20] and soteriology,[21] is that Paul transformed Jewish views partly by his own genius and partly with the help of Hellenistic categories. The main thrust, however, is that the *origin* of Paul's thought on various points is to be found in Judaism, especially as seen in Rabbinic literature.[22]

[17] Cf. Whiteley, *The Theology of St Paul*, p. 4: Davies's book is 'one of the best books ever written on Paul'. In Conzelmann's short history of Pauline research, however, Davies is not mentioned (Conzelmann, *Theology*, pp. 155–61).

[18] An exception is G. Wagner, *Pauline Baptism and the Pagan Mysteries* (ET of *Das religionsgeschichtliche Problem von Römer 6, 1–11*). Wagner notes (p. 269) the dearth of recent comprehensive studies.

[19] Cf. J. Munck, 'Pauline Research Since Schweitzer', *The Bible in Modern Scholarship* (ed. Hyatt), p. 174.

[20] Schoeps, *Paul*, pp. 88, 112.   [21] Ibid., pp. 126, 180.

[22] On the other hand Schoeps, like Montefiore, appeals to Paul's being a Hellenistic Jew to explain

Although Munck did not explicitly deal with the question of Paul's relation to Judaism, his supposition that Paul's whole activity was dominated by his eschatological outlook helped to drive home the point that Paul is to be understood on the basis of his Jewish background – and Palestinian Jewish at that.[23] Here he followed somewhat in the footsteps of Schweitzer, who saw apocalypticism as the dominating influence in Paul as well as in Jesus.[24] Schweitzer also, however, had not sought to deal thoroughly with the question of the *relation* of Pauline theology to that of Judaism. Jewish apocalypticism serves, rather, as the point of departure for his description of Paul's thought.

Davies's approach has had many followers. The basic method is to take a theme in Paul's letters, preferably a central theme, and to examine Jewish literature to determine whether or not the theme could have been derived from Judaism. One may mention, for example, Dahl's study of the atonement, based on Rom. 8.32,[25] and Scrogg's study of *The Last Adam*. The discovery of the Dead Sea Scrolls opened a wide field for what we may call *motif research*. Paul's central themes of 'justification by faith' and the 'righteousness of God' have been thought to be paralleled in, and perhaps derived from, the Essene community.[26] It is assumed in these studies, and in many more, that there is a positive relationship of some sort between Paul and Judaism, especially Palestinian Judaism. All that needs to be done is to show just which ideas Paul derived from just which stream of Judaism and to determine in what ways Paul differed from his sources.

On the basis of his comparison of central Pauline motifs with Rabbinic statements, Davies came to a substantial conclusion: Paul's thought can be understood as that of a Rabbi who believed that the Messiah had come,[27] the latter belief accounting for all divergences of Paul from Rabbinic Judaism. In his conclusion, Davies puts the matter thus:

Both in his life and thought, therefore, Paul's close relation to Rabbinic Judaism has become clear, and we cannot too strongly insist again that for him the acceptance of the Gospel was not so much the rejection of the old Judaism and the discovery of a new religion wholly antithetical to it, as his polemics might sometimes pardonably lead us to assume, but the recognition of the advent of the true and final form of Judaism, in other words, the advent of the Messianic Age of

---

his lack of knowledge of repentance (Schoeps, p. 196), his misunderstanding of the law (p. 200), and his failure to understand the relation between the covenant and the law (pp. 213–18; 260).

[23] J. Munck, *Paul and the Salvation of Mankind*.

[24] A. Schweitzer, *The Mysticism of Paul the Apostle*; see especially ch. 2.

[25] N. A. Dahl, 'The Atonement – An Adequate Reward for the Akedah? (Ro. 8.32)', *Neotestamentica et Semitica* (ed. Ellis and Wilcox), pp. 15–29.

[26] See, for example, S. Schulz, 'Zur Rechtfertigung aus Gnaden in Qumran und bei Paulus', *ZTK* 56, 1959, pp. 155–85. While individual Pauline themes have been traced to Qumran, no one has ever argued that Paul was an Essene who believed the Messiah had come.

[27] *Paul and Rabbinic Judaism*, p. 16.

Jewish expectation. It is in this light that we are to understand the conversion of Paul.[28]

It is instructive to compare Davies's position with that of what I believe to be the majority of New Testament scholars, the position which we above illustrated with citations from Thackeray, Bultmann and Schrenk: that despite parallels in detail, there is a fundamental antithesis between Paul and Judaism, especially Rabbinic Judaism. Davies argued, rather, that because of the numerous and substantial parallels, there can be no such antithesis. The thing missing from Davies's work is the element which most strongly characterizes the view, for example, of Bultmann: a description of the *essence* of Paulinism and the *essence* of Judaism which can be contrasted with each other. This is partly to be explained by the fact that Davies does not, in contrast to the majority of New Testament scholars, put justification by faith in the centre of Pauline theology; thus the possibility of the facile contrast between justification by works and by faith disappears.[29] Davies regards 'the significance of Jesus of Nazareth as the Messiah' rather than the doctrine of justification by faith as central for Paul,[30] and he identifies the idea of being 'in Christ' as the central soteriological concept.[31] The latter, while the opposite of being 'in Israel',[32] Davies does not see as constituting an antithesis to Judaism. Paul thought rather of a new exodus which established a new Israel (in which one has membership) and a new Torah; Christianity is thus the fulfilment rather than the antithesis of Judaism.[33] In dealing with these and other points, Davies has worked inductively: in point after point there is agreement in conception between Paul and the Rabbis; therefore there is conceptual agreement, the only difference being the question of whether or not Jesus is the Messiah.[34] The more common procedure of New Testament scholars is to be begin with a contrast of the matter as perceived by them – faith versus works – and only then to grant or establish various parallels of detail.

In comparison with Montefiore's book, Davies's does not attempt a description of what is *essential* to Rabbinic Judaism. Thus he did not enquire (as most of his followers in motif research have not enquired) why what is essential to Rabbinic Judaism is *not* referred to by Paul: as Moore put it, ignored and by implication denied. Thus Davies denied the validity of the traditional contrast of *essence* with *essence*, but he did not fully respond to the challenge raised by Montefiore and Moore: a comparison of *essential*

---

[28] Ibid., p. 324.
[29] See n. 2 above; *Paul and Rabbinic Judaism*, p. 222.
[30] *Paul and Rabbinic Judaism*, p. 352.
[31] Ibid., pp. 177, 86–110.
[32] Davies, *Invitation to the New Testament*, p. 349.
[33] *Paul and Rabbinic Judaism*, p. 323.
[34] Ibid., pp. 323f.

elements with *essential elements*. The charge would be untrue that Davies chose minor points in Paul for his study; he did not. But he did not carry out an even-handed *comparison*, for he did not deal with what is essential to Rabbinic Judaism on its own terms. Consequently he did not ask why it is missing from Paul. Davies's view at first seems to imply a positive comparison which leads to the conclusion that Paul's view of religion is structurally similar to Judaism: entrance into the new covenant results in receiving a new Torah, to which obedience is necessary.[35] Despite this implicit comparison, the failure to account for the absence in Paul of key elements of Judaism shows that the comparison was not followed through evenly on both sides.[36]

It must be noted immediately that Davies did not intend to *compare* Paul and Judaism. In common with virtually all other New Testament scholars who have dealt with the question, Davies intended to identify Paul's *background*, not compare *religions*.[37] The only comparison of religions which has been carried out has been the inadequate one based on short descriptions of *essences* and summarized by the phrase 'faith versus works'. Montefiore and Moore raised an interesting question which could lead to a genuine comparison of religions – why what is essential to Rabbinic Judaism is missing from Paul and is not taken account of by Paul – but the question has gone unexploited. Instead, scholars have been content to search through Jewish materials for parallels, preferably early ones, to various motifs in Paul's thought. We have focused on Davies in this regard because of the 'watershed' character of his book, but the same thing is true of subsequent scholars from Schoeps to the present day.

The search for the history of motifs, however, is not mere antiquarianism; rather, it leads, as we saw in the case of Davies, to conclusions about the fundamental nature of Paul's religion. Parallels of detail lead to the conclusion that there is basic agreement. Drawing large conclusions on the basis of parallel motifs has been sharply attacked by Sandmel, and it is worth quoting his opinion of Davies's results:

Davies' book is an admirable book, indeed, a great one – and one with which I disagree almost one hundred per cent. What seemed to me initially to be faulty in Davies was his procedure in setting up Montefiore, *Judaism and St Paul*, as a straw man and attempting to demolish it, and a progression thereafter to an assumption of a similarity in Diaspora and Palestinian Judaism that my work in Philo persuaded me was wrong. On its affirmative side, Davies' case seemed to me to be this at a maximum, that affinities between Paul and the Rabbis were

---

[35] Cf. below, Chapter V, section 5.

[36] Cf. S. Sandmel's remark (*Philo's Place in Judaism*, pp. 19f.) on comparisons which deal with similarities but not differences.

[37] This is true even of Montefiore, who intended to discover the kind of Judaism known by Paul before his conversion, not to compare Pauline thought with Jewish; see *Judaism and St Paul*, pp. 13–16.

limited to some minor and elusive strands, and that Davies, rather than proving his case, had disproved it.[38]

Sandmel, who finds Paul to be at home in Hellenistic Judaism, considers that 'Pauline Christianity and rabbinic Judaism share little more than a common point of departure, the Bible'.[39] He is here referring especially to their views of sin and the remedy for it.

My own judgment of Davies's accomplishment would be considerably more positive than that of Sandmel. I take it that Davies and the many others who have worked in the field have shown that *numerous* and *important* terms and concepts in Paul's letters can be traced to Palestinian Judaism; at least, they have parallels in Palestinian Jewish literature, even if some of it is later than Paul. Further, I think that it is an important and valuable matter to trace the historical background of Paul's terms and concepts. Parallels *are* often illuminating, as long as one does not jump from 'parallel' to 'influence' to 'identity of thought'. Thirdly, I am much more in sympathy with Davies's judgment that Paul and Rabbinic Judaism are not antithetical than to the quick conclusion that they are, based on a misleading and inadequate comparison of essences.

Despite these points of agreement and appreciation, however, there is something unsatisfying about Davies's conclusion. It would seem that before anyone could conclude that Paul was a Rabbinic Jew who differed from the rest of Rabbinic Judaism only in thinking that the Messiah had come (a point which influences several other points), he would have to carry out more of a *comparison* than Davies has done. The comparison would have to take into account disagreements as well as agreements and important aspects of Judaism which one does not see in Paul as well as the important elements of Paul's thought: in short, both the whole and the parts as seen from both sides.

It is not only Davies's conclusions which are unsatisfactory, but the entire state of the question. There are basically three positions on the question of Paul's fundamental relationship with Palestinian Judaism: that, because of numerous and important detailed agreements, Paul should be seen as essentially a Rabbi who thought that the Messiah had come (Davies); that, in spite of some agreements in detail, Paul's religion is basically antithetical to that of Palestinian Judaism (probably the majority view); and that Paul had little relationship to Palestinian Judaism one way or another (Sandmel). With regard to Paul's polemical statements about Judaism, there are also basically three positions: that they do not represent his fundamental view

---

[38] Sandmel, *The Genius of Paul*, p. 223; cf. 'Parallelomania', *JBL* 81, 1962, p. 4: even 259 parallels (Sandmel's hypothetical number) would not suffice to show that Paul and Rabbinic Judaism were in agreement. Sandmel finds no 'genetic connection' between Paul and Rabbinic literature.

[39] *The Genius of Paul*, p. 59.

and should be discounted as the polemics of the moment (Davies); that they are to the point and represent the basic antithesis of Paul and Judaism (the majority); and that they do not really touch the Judaism which is known from Rabbinic sources, and so must be explained as referring to some other form of Judaism or as arising from an immediate apologetic need (Montefiore, Moore).

What is unsatisfactory about the state of the question is that all of these views have something to be said for them. Scholarship is stuck between the agreements between Paul and Palestinian Judaism and the patent differences, whether for the differences one points to the problem of faith versus works or to Paul's neglect of the Jewish understanding of atonement and forgiveness. Reading Schechter and Montefiore, one wonders what Paul found in Judaism to attack; yet attack it he did. Reading Davies, one sees such close agreements between Paul and Judaism that again one wonders how to account for Paul's own statements of his disagreement with Judaism: not whether or not the Messiah had come, but how one gains righteousness. What is needed is a comparison which takes account of both the numerous agreements and the disagreements – not only the disagreements as stated by Paul, but those evident from the Jewish side, the discrepancy between Paul's depiction of Judaism and Judaism as reflected in Jewish sources. What is needed, in other words, is to compare Paul on his own terms with Judaism on its own terms, a comparison not of one-line essences or of separate motifs, but of a whole religion with a whole religion. It is this task which we wish to undertake here, and which now needs to be methodologically described.

2. The holistic comparison of patterns of religion[1]

I shall try to avoid too abstract a description of the method to be followed here, since the method will be immediately applied and can be tested in its application. I am of the view, however, that the history of the comparison of Paul and Judaism is a particularly clear instance of the general need for methodological improvement in the comparative study of religion.[2] What is difficult is to focus on *what* is to be compared. We have already seen that most comparisons are of reduced *essences* (faith versus works; cf. liberty versus law, a spiritual religion versus a materialistic and commercial religion and the like) or of *individual motifs*. Neither of these constitutes an adequate category of comparison.

---

[1] Cf. my summary article, 'Patterns of Religion in Paul and Rabbinic Judaism: A Holistic Method of Comparison', *HTR* 66, 1973, pp. 455–78.

[2] There is no intention here to discuss theoretical works which deal with comparative religious studies, but only the problem as it appears in the history of comparing Paul and Judaism.

It is not necessary to say much about the comparison of essences. Supposing that a religion can be accurately summarized in a phrase or line is dubious on the face of it. A briefly stated essence can never do justice to an entire religion. Further, when Judaism and Christianity have been so compared by Christian scholars, the point of the comparison has been polemical in intent. The point is universally to show how Paul (or Jesus or Christianity in general) is superior to Judaism. Such a contrast may be made even when there is no real intention to denigrate Judaism, but only the desire to set off sharply what appears to be distinctive about Paul (or Jesus or Christianity). In any case, however, it is clear that the use of reduced essences as the point of comparison is inadequate if one is seriously interested in comparing two religions.

The case is not quite so clear when one considers the comparison of individual motifs. The notion that a religion is the sum of its parts is not a ridiculous one, and therefore the comparison of numerous parts is not so obviously inadequate as the comparison of reduced essences. Nevertheless, it is inadequate for the true comparison of religions, for two reasons. In the first place, it is usually the motifs of *one* of the religions which are compared with elements in the second religion in order to identify their origin. The two religions are not treated in the same way. The history of the comparison of Paul and Judaism shows this clearly. One starts with Pauline motifs and looks for their origins in Judaism, but the various elements of Judaism are not taken up for their own sake. It follows that there is no true comparison of the two religions. In the second place, motif research often overlooks the context and significance of a given motif in one (or sometimes both) of the religions. It is conceivable for precisely the same motif to appear in two different religions but to have a different significance. One may consider the analogy of two buildings. Bricks which are identical in shape, colour and weight could well be used to construct two different buildings which are totally unlike each other. One could knock down a building and build another, unlike the first, from the same bricks. In motif research, one must consider *function* and *context* before coming to an overall conclusion as to similarity or dissimilarity. Thus, for example, in comparing righteousness in Paul and Judaism, one must consider the *function* and *significance* of righteousness in the overall scheme in both places, which means that there must *be* an overall scheme both in Paul and in Judaism and that one must understand both schemes as wholes.

Motif research is so common in New Testament research, and the supposition that identity of motifs indicates identity or similarity of viewpoint is so widespread, that we shall pause to give two examples of how false conclusions can readily be drawn on the basis of similarity of themes.

Although in his book *The Consequences of the Covenant* G. W. Buchanan did not explicitly raise the question of how Paul relates to Judaism, Paul is worked into the discussion in such a way as to make Buchanan's position clear. His general view is seen in his conclusion: despite differences 'from the time of Moses to Bar Cochba', the alterations introduced by time

> did not change the structure or theology so much that the consequences of the covenant that was introduced by the early Israelites could not be faithfully understood and practiced by later sects in Judaism and Christianity. It was because of the covenant that the practices and beliefs continued as steadily as they did in the face of a changing world (pp. 314f.).

Thus Buchanan brings the different types of Judaism *and* Christianity under the same blanket of covenantal theology.

There is much to be agreed with in Buchanan's book. He has seen that the concept of the covenant dominates Jewish thought. He has further perceived the sequence of covenantal election, transgression, atonement and reconciliation which typifies much of Jewish literature, even though it is not worked out precisely (see e.g. pp. 192f.) as it will be here. The book's weakness is its superficiality, evidenced by the way given themes are established by the apparently random citation of passages from the Old Testament, the Apocrypha and Pseudepigrapha, Rabbinic literature, the New Testament and the early church fathers.[3] The supposition is obviously that the existence of similar motifs in all these bodies of literature proves that they all shared the same basic view of religion, that of covenantal theology. The weakness of the method becomes clear when Buchanan assumes that the presence of certain common motifs in Paul and Jewish literature means that Paul fits without further ado into the neat covenantal scheme. Thus, for example, he simply lists Paul's discussions of baptism in sequence with references from a wide range of Jewish and Christian literature to purificatory washings in the section on 'Covenantal Provisions for Forgiveness and Reconciliation' (pp. 206f.), without inquiring whether or not baptism actually has the same *function* in Paul's thought as ritual washings do in Judaism. Apart from the question whether Paul's terminology is closer to Hellenistic mystery cults than to Judaism, and granting that some of the terms used by Paul in discussing baptism derive from Judaism, the conclusion still does not follow that the *meaning* and *interpretation* of baptism in Paul is the same as that of ritual washings in Judaism.[4] In fact, I would argue that baptism has quite a different place in the Pauline pattern of religion from its place in Judaism. With the change in the function of

---

[3] It should be noted, however, that Buchanan planned the book as a sketch of his view and that he intends subsequent publications to establish the argument in detail.

[4] The equation of Pauline thought on baptism with Jewish views on cleansing is aided by using Colossians as Pauline; see Buchanan, p. 207.

baptism within the total structure, there must come a change in understanding and meaning.

With a good deal more self-consciousness about methodology, David Flusser undertook a comparison of the religion of Qumran and pre-Pauline Christianity.[5] He pointed out his intention to deal not 'with all the theological motifs of this assumed stratum of Christianity', but only those common to pre-Pauline Christianity and Qumran (p. 217). He explicitly stated that 'the meaning of these features in their new Christian context' would not be considered. Rather, 'the individual *theologoumena* will be arranged according to their structural function in the Qumran theology, not according to their context in Christian thought' (p. 217).

Flusser's article is interesting, not only because of his sensitivity to the method which he was employing, but also because the method is the reverse of that usually employed in comparisons of Judaism and Christianity. Flusser's procedure was to begin with motifs in their Jewish (Qumran) framework and to find parallels from here and there in Christianity. The conclusion is that 'the whole body of ideas' which he discussed, including many central Christian doctrines, 'could have come into Christianity only from the Qumran sect' (p. 265). Any New Testament scholar reading the article will be struck by how strange Christianity looks when the elements which make it up are viewed in light of their place in the religious pattern of the Dead Sea sect. It must be remembered that Flusser treats Christianity the way that most New Testament scholars treat Judaism, except that he was aware of the differences of overall structure, even if he did not deal with the structures as such.

The weakness of the method can be seen in the most striking parallel between Paul and the Scrolls[6] – what Flusser calls 'Election of Grace' (pp. 222–7). There are some striking parallels of a sort (see p. 226), but Flusser has to combine Paul's statements on predestination with his statements on salvation by faith and grace in order to make a real parallel. The appearance of the former is an interesting phenomenon in Paul, but it may be doubted if Paul's occasional predestinarian statements are organically connected in his own thought with his statements on salvation by grace; the organic connection *is* clear in the Scrolls, where God's grace is that he predestines. Thus grace has a different place in the total scheme in Qumran from its place in Paul's thought. When Flusser (p. 227) says that the conviction that

[5] David Flusser, 'The Dead Sea Sect and Pre-Pauline Christianity', *Scripta Hierosolymitana* IV (ed. Rabin and Yadin), pp. 215–66; cf. also his 'The Jewish Origin of Christianity', *Yitzhak F. Baer Jubilee Volume* (ed. S. W. Baron and others), 1960, pp. 75–98; English summary, pp. x–xi. Page references in the text are to the first essay cited.

[6] Despite the intention to deal with pre-Pauline Christianity, the article often deals with themes which are characteristic of one part of the New Testament and which may not be pre-Pauline. In this case, Flusser argues that the idea of election by grace came to Paul from Qumran *via* pre-Pauline Christianity (pp. 226f.).

works are useless is a 'possible consequence' of the view of grace which he believes Paul to have derived from Qumran, a conclusion that Paul but not the authors of the Scrolls drew, he shows his fundamental misunderstanding and the weakness of the methodology. For Paul, grace and the uselessness of works for salvation are *essentially* connected; granted *his* understanding of grace, his conclusion was not 'possible' but inevitable. For the sect, the understanding of grace is also *essentially* connected with the requirement to keep the law. The sectarians have been predestined explicitly to keep the law, and this predestination constitutes God's grace. It is difficult to know how Paul could have pulled out of Qumran one element – grace – while completely reversing its meaning and significance.

It should be emphasized that Flusser recognized that 'the doctrine of the Qumran covenanters did not retain its original function when assimilated by Christianity' (p. 265). He argued, rather, that 'the theological structure of the Sect was taken apart and the stones reused by early Christian thinkers to build a new and different house' (pp. 265f.). Yet even this insight did not prevent him from making a misleading equation between Paul's conception of grace and that of Qumran.

What is clearly desirable, then, is to compare an entire religion, parts and all, with an entire religion, parts and all; to use the analogy of a building, to compare two buildings, not leaving out of account their individual bricks. The problem is how to discover two wholes, both of which are considered and defined on their own merits and in their own terms, to be compared with each other. I believe that the concept of a 'pattern of religion' makes this possible. We should first consider what a pattern of religion is not.[7]

1. By 'pattern of religion', I do not mean an entire historical religion – all of Christianity, Judaism, Islam, Buddhism and the like – but only a given, more or less homogeneous, entity. For our purposes, 'Paulinism' is a religion. A religion in this sense need not be restricted to one figure, but could embrace millions of people over hundreds of years, as long as the same basic understanding of religion and the religious life obtains. It would probably be possible to describe Lutheranism as a 'religion' in this sense. In such a large entity, one would have to take account of differences on individual points and even major divergences here and there, but presumably (I am no scholar of Lutheranism) there is enough agreement on essentials and enough coherence to consider Lutheranism to be a 'religion' in the sense in which the term is used here.

2. A pattern of religion does not include every theological proposition

---

[7] Others have pointed out the need to consider parallels in context. See, for example, Cross, *The Ancient Library of Qumran*, p. 206; Sjöberg, *Gott und die Sünder*, pp. xx, 2. The latter comments that what is necessary is to compare on the basis of a *Gesamtstruktur* (p. xx). Sjöberg's *Gesamtstruktur* for Rabbinic Judaism, however, consists in the tension between justice and mercy (pp. 6–11), not in a pattern of religion as defined here.

or every religious concept within a religion. The term 'pattern' points toward the question of how one moves from the logical starting point to the logical conclusion of the religion. Excluded from the pattern proper are such speculative questions as how the world was created; when the end will come; what will be the nature of the afterlife; the identity of the Messiah; and the like. A great deal of the research which has investigated the relationship of Paul and Judaism and the relationships among the various parties within Judaism has focused on just such questions. It is my hypothesis that the pattern of religion, the sequence from its starting point to its conclusion, does not necessarily vary according to the answers given to such speculative questions. This does not mean that a speculative question *could* not affect the pattern of religion. The absence of the view that history begins and ends, for example, might well prohibit the kinds of religion which are most common in Judaism and Christianity. Precisely what happens at the beginning and end of history, however, need not be a decisive point for the pattern of religion.

A pattern of religion, defined positively, is the description of how a religion is perceived by its adherents to *function*.[8] 'Perceived to function' has the sense not of what an adherent does on a day-to-day basis, but of *how getting in and staying in are understood*: the way in which a religion is understood to admit and retain members is considered to be the way it 'functions'. This may involve daily activities, such as prayers, washing and the like, but we are interested not so much in the details of these activities as in their role and significance in the 'pattern': on what principles they are based, what happens if they are not observed and the like. A pattern of religion thus has largely to do with the items which a systematic theology classifies under 'soteriology'. 'Pattern of religion' is a more satisfactory term for what we are going to describe, however, than 'soteriology'. For one thing, it includes more than soteriology usually does: it includes the logical beginning-point of the religious life as well as its end, and it includes the steps in between. For another, the word soteriology has certain connotations which may not always be entirely appropriate. It may connote a preoccupation with other-worldliness, for example; or it may imply that all are in need of a

---

[8] For the emphasis on understanding the parts in terms of their function in a whole, the structure of which must itself be grasped, one may compare several of the studies of C. Lévi-Strauss. See, for example, 'Structural Analysis in Linguistics and in Anthropology' and 'Social Structure', in *Structural Anthropology*, pp. 31–54 and 277–323 respectively. While the comparison may be instructive for those interested in methodology *per se*, there has been no attempt here to apply the method of structural anthropology systematically to the question of Paul and Judaism. Some of the methodological points are the same – the relationship between the whole and the parts and the need to limit the 'structure' (here called a 'pattern') to a meaningful entity in which the parts actually are interrelated. The methodology employed in the present study is basically *ad hoc*, however, designed to meet the specific problems which have arisen in attempts to compare Paul and Judaism. On structuralism as a technique of literary analysis, see Spivey, 'Structuralism and Biblical Studies: The Uninvited Guest', *Interpretation* 28, 1974, pp. 133–45, and other essays in the same number of *Interpretation*.

salvation which they do not possess, thus further implying a concept of original sin. Since much of Judaism is not other-worldly, and since a concept of original or even universal sin is missing in most forms of Judaism, such connotations would be unfortunate. It may occasionally be appropriate or useful to use the term 'soteriology', but one should bear in mind the above restrictions. The better descriptive term is 'pattern of religion'. A religion will function in some way or other even if the end is not salvation from perdition. We shall see this especially clearly in the case of Ben Sirach.

A pattern of religion, while not being the same as systematic theology and while not having to do with many of the speculative questions of theology, *does* have to do with *thought*, with the *understanding* that lies behind religious behaviour, not just with the externals of religious behaviour. Thus from cultic practice one may infer that the cult of a given religion was *perceived by its adherents to have a certain function* in their religious life. It is the adherents' *perception* of the significance of cult that is important, as well as the fact that the cult was observed. To reiterate, this does not necessarily mean that the adherents themselves articulated a systematic theology in which the cult has a logical place. Even without this, the cult may be perceived to stand in a coherent relationship with other elements in the religion in such a way that a whole pattern consisting of interrelated elements may be seen.

The point of comparison, then, will be patterns of religion. A pattern does consist of separate motifs, but we are more concerned with getting the motifs within the proper framework of each religion than in comparing a motif in some part of Judaism with a similar motif in Paul. Once the various entire patterns clearly emerge, the comparison can take place, and not before.

It is not presupposed that there is only one pattern of religion in Palestinian Judaism. The discussion of the method of comparing one pattern of religion with another does not presuppose that at the end of the study we shall have precisely two patterns; it only indicates the method. There could be numerous patterns of religion which are reflected in Palestinian Jewish literature. Paul's pattern of religion could agree with one of these or with none. Indeed, even within Paul's thought there could be a major inconsistency which would indicate that he did not have one clear pattern of religion. All of these questions are reserved for the subsequent discussion.

Purpose of the study

It is not my intention in Part I to give a history of the Jewish religion, although we shall cover the great bulk of the surviving Palestinian material dating from the period 200 b.c.e. to 200 c.e., so that it will be possible in the conclusion to Part I to draw some conclusions about Judaism in Palestine in the first century and some of its characteristics at the time of Paul. It should be borne in mind, however, that a formal and comprehensive history is not the aim of the study. Nor is the primary intention to discover the sources of Paul's ideas; although, as I indicated above, the subject may occasionally come up. Further, I am not primarily concerned to deal simply with whether or not Paul agreed or disagreed with Jewish conceptions and terminology and whether or not he understood or misunderstood Judaism. The intent, rather, is to answer the question of the basic relationship between Paul's religion and the forms of religion reflected in Palestinian Jewish literature. We have to go behind terminology to determine whether or not Paul and the Rabbis (for example) had the same *type* of religion. In Davies's terms, is Paul's religion that of a Rabbi (or some other Palestinian Jew) who thought that the Messiah had come? It is assumed that the analysis of Paul's relationship with Palestinian Judaism in terms of the pattern(s) of religion will be illuminating for both Paul and Palestinian Judaism, in the way that any comparison is illuminating: we learn by perceiving agreements and dissimilarities. The intention is to make a contribution both to the understanding of Paul and to the understanding of Palestinian Judaism, as well as to clarify how they stand *vis à vis* each other. As will be seen in the discussions in each section and the conclusions, the present investigation has led to definite and perhaps controversial hypotheses concerning the various types of Palestinian Judaism known to us, Paul, and their relationships. I hope, naturally, that all of these hypotheses are persuasive. Even if they are not, I trust that the attempt to carry out a full-scale comparison in the terms described will prove useful.

Difficulties of the comparison

We shall encounter two principal difficulties, summarized by the words *imbalance* and *imposition*. Comparing an individual on the one hand with the large bodies of Palestinian Jewish literature on the other creates obvious difficulties of balance. There seems, however, to be no choice. We shall discuss the matter more fully in section 2 of the chapter on Tannaitic literature, but here we may briefly indicate that the nature of Palestinian Jewish literature leads to considering large blocks of it together, while rendering it almost impossible to isolate the thought of individuals comparable to Paul.[9] On the other hand, Christianity was developing so rapidly that we could not reasonably take up 'the New Testament pattern of religion' as a topic. One would become so occupied in distinguishing the different types and patterns of religion in the New Testament that the hope of meaningful conclusions would be lost. We have from Paul's hand (or mouth, if he dictated) a distinctive body of letters, and we had better not confuse the matter by

---

[9] Cf. Sandmel, *Philo's Place in Judaism*, p. 5, on comparing Philo and the Rabbis.

attempting to consider James, Hebrews and the Gospel of John at the same time.

One could hypothetically say that Tannaitic literature, for example, might contain as rich a profusion of views as the New Testament, so that attempting to derive *a* pattern of religion from Tannaitic literature involves imposing an artificial harmony where none exists. I do not think that this is the case, but rather that a pervasive outlook on the nature of religion and the religious life may be seen in Tannaitic literature. This is a hypothesis, however, which can be judged only after a detailed examination. It will suffice here to say that the question of whether or not an artificial pattern is being imposed on each body of literature studied will have to be considered as the study progresses.

Addendum: patterns and trajectories

Although the discussion is not strictly required in order to understand the methodology of the present study, many may find it useful to know why I have not adopted James Robinson's proposal that Christianity, especially when being compared with other religious movements of the Greco-Roman world, should be studied in terms of 'trajectories'.[10] In Robinson's programmatic essay, he accurately notes, in the section titled 'The Crisis of Categories' (pp. 4–8), that the agenda of New Testament studies has, since the initiation of critical-historical scholarship, been set by later accretions ('the patina') around the text of the New Testament. Thus, for example, scholars have written endlessly about the authorship of the Gospel of John, not because the original Gospel poses the question of authorship, but because Christian tradition attributed it to John. In order to get at the text, the overlay of tradition had first to be penetrated. This situation has now resulted, in Robinson's view, in a crisis for scholarship, since the categories of study established by the need to penetrate the patina are not effective for actually studying early Christianity. Robinson proceeds, still accurately, to criticize New Testament scholars for dealing with non-Christian religions in static terms. As he recognizes, this procedure was adopted because of a lack of evidence and research: 'The fragmentary state of the documentation did not permit tracing step by step a series of developments but required the amalgamation of references scattered over half a millenium into one coherent and harmonized picture' (pp. 12f.). When the discoveries at Qumran and Nag Hammadi fully revealed how inadequate such a procedure was, scholars felt unable to achieve a new synthesis, but fell back on 'a disintegra-

---

[10] See 'Introduction: The Dismantling and Reassembling of the Categories of New Testament Scholarship', in J. M. Robinson and H. Koester, *Trajectories through Early Christianity*, pp. 1–19. I speak of Robinson's view, since it is not clear that Koester is of precisely the same view, although several of his essays appear in the joint volume.

ted positivistic caution: rather than risk a generalization, such as describing a view as "Jewish" or "gnostic" or "Hellenistic," one limits oneself to recording that it is present in a particular document at a given place'. The listing of 'unrelated instances of a given term', however, is not history (p. 13).

The dilemma of scholarship and the solution proposed are put this way:

> The Jewish, Greek, or gnostic 'background' or 'environment' cannot be mastered by reducing it to a mass of disorganized parallels to the New Testament; it must be reconceptualized in terms of movements, 'trajectories' through the Hellenistic world (p. 13).

My difficulties begin with the semi-colon in the sentence just quoted. Granted that undifferentiated static descriptions are not desirable and should be avoided whenever the evidence permits, granted that a 'mass of disorganized parallels' does not constitute real knowledge about religious movements, why does it follow that one must begin to think in terms of trajectories? Robinson acknowledges that the term itself may 'suggest too much determinative control at the point of departure', and he hastens to affirm the individual's freedom 'to redefine one's trajectory' (p. 14). But the term trajectory nevertheless implies *sequential development* and *implicit goal*; and, despite the disclaimer just cited, Robinson clearly has both in mind. Thus he mentions two streams of Paulinism, 'with one stream moving via Ephesians to I Peter, Luke-Acts, the Pastorals, and on to orthodoxy, the other via Colossians to Valentinus, Basilides, Marcion, and on to heresy', and he refers to such streams as 'sequences of development' (p. 10). It is certainly true that Paul lived in the first century and that gnostic 'heresies' were opposed by some who considered themselves 'orthodox' (the terms are anachronistic) in the second century, and even that there are some connections of thought between Marcion and gnosticism proper; it is further true that Acts and the Pastorals can best be seen as efforts to domesticate Paul, to bring him into agreement with the developing orthodoxy;[11] these historical developments have been long known; but can we be sure that there is a *sequential, causal* connection from the Pauline school as represented in Colossians to the *goal* or terminal point of heresy? Marcion apparently consciously intended to base some aspects of his thought on the main Pauline letters, especially Galatians and Romans.[12] Was his thought actually influenced by a Pauline stream running through Colossians? Robinson is not simply asserting that, since both orthodoxy and heresy come after Paul, Paul's thought must in some way have led to them. He has also made a stab at selecting which prior event is the cause of which subsequent event. But

---

[11] Even if one does not accept the precise dating of Acts and the Pastorals proposed by J. Knox (*Marcion and the New Testament*, pp. 73–6; 114–39), his characterization of the way in which Acts and the Pastorals 'save' Paul from being taken over by 'heretics' still seems convincing.

[12] See E. C. Blackman, *Marcion and his Influence*, pp. 103–24; Knox, *Marcion*, pp. 14–18, 45f.

here the imponderables enter, for we do not have at our disposal all the prior events (nor all the subsequent ones).[13] Maybe Valentinus was influenced not by Colossians but by Christian thinkers of Alexandria thus far unknown? The question is this: can the actual historical connections which are asserted be demonstrated? Robinson may be attempting to respond to this sort of question when he writes that the connections shown in the essays in *Trajectories through Early Christianity* 'are not only of the usual cause-and-effect kind, where one author necessarily depended upon the preceding one. Rather,' he continues, 'the connections are explored to show how the overarching movement of the trajectory itself comes successively to expression as one moves downstream from the point of departure' (p. 17). This in no way retracts his belief in continuous sequential development; it simply asserts that sequential development will still continue even where definite cause and effect cannot be shown. Thought progresses. In this case the question would be: can one show that Marcion and subsequent heresies represent the development of *the kind* of Paulinism seen in Colossians, *and of no other*? (Although in the present case Robinson did say 'via', indicating a concrete connection.)

We may cite two other examples of Robinson's belief in sequential development leading to a goal or terminal point. In his essay 'LOGOI SOPHON: On the Gattung of Q',[14] he argued that the literary genre of sayings collections has a 'gnosticizing proclivity'. The proclivity of the genre to move toward gnosticism was blocked by Matthew and Luke, both of whom imbedded it 'in the Marcan gospel form',[15] but it still followed out a developmental sequence which ended up in gnosticism.[16] Elsewhere, he argued that the similarity in form between Mark and John can be explained by their being at the same relative point on a developing trajectory within early Christianity. Later in the sequential development from aretalogy through the Marcan-type gospel to the final stage in the development of the orthodox gospel (a conflation of the Marcan and the Q form), Matthew and Luke independently and naturally made the same sort of revisions in the gospel form, since the point had been reached 'where this is the thing to do'.[17]

What is wrong with this is that history is not in fact always composed of sequential developments which lead to terminal points.[18] This is not to say

[13] Cf. Sandmel, *The First Christian Century*, p. 8.

[14] *Trajectories*, 1971, pp. 71–113. An earlier version appeared in 1964 in *Zeit und Geschichte : Dankesgabe an Rudolf Bultmann*. It also appears in the ET of part of the latter book, *The Future of our Religious Past*, 1971.

[15] Robinson, 'The Problem of History in Mark, Reconsidered', *USQR* 20, 1965, p. 135; cf. p. 137.

[16] *Trajectories*, p. 104.

[17] 'The Johannine Trajectory', in *Trajectories*, pp. 235, 266–8; cf. earlier 'The Problem of History in Mark, Reconsidered', p. 137.

[18] Cf. Sandmel, *The First Christian Century*, p. 24.

that there are no sequential developments in the history of thought and institutions. There are doubtless many, and it is certainly worth describing them wherever it is possible to do so. A lot of things do not move in trajectories, however, and the trajectory paradigm may mislead one into attempting to impose sequential development where none exists. We may take one example. I believe that it would be possible to write a fairly complete history of attitudes towards suffering in Palestinian Judaism. Such a history would, I think, reveal that generally human suffering was considered to be divine punishment for transgression, except during the periods of religious persecution. We can see exceptions to the general rule in the period of the Maccabees and at the time of the Hadrianic persecution, although between these periods and after 150 the general connection of suffering with divine chastisement prevailed.[19] Assuming that this is an accurate description, one immediately sees that it is a *history* (or the summary of one), but that there is no *developmental sequence*. The history reveals a stable, persistent view, only occasionally interrupted by external events. I would not even describe the consolidation of Rabbinic Judaism at Jamnia and subsequently at Usha to be the terminal point of a trajectory (beginning where? with Ezra? the *hasidim*? the scribes?), although one can, with some success, trace the historical events that led up to the consolidation. Rabbinic Judaism is not necessarily the terminal point of a sequential development (although in retrospect it could be made to look like one); it is the actual result of concrete historical events, including, among other things, two apparently destructive wars. One can understand historically how Rabbinic Judaism came to be without recourse to the theory of sequential development; and the term trajectory, while it might be employed, adds nothing to the historical reconstruction, while it may obfuscate it by introducing the notion of steady development in a logical as well as chronological sequence.

In the course of Professor Robinson's critique of scholarly categories, he objects to the categories 'Palestinian' and 'Hellenistic', which, he says, presuppose 'a nonexistent correspondence between geographical and cultural boundaries'.[20] It is doubtful if he really means 'nonexistent'. Surely there was some correspondence. Was living in Athens culturally indistinguishable from living in Jerusalem? Presumably he means 'oversimplified', but his term 'nonexistent' oversimplifies the matter as much as does a hard-and-fast distinction between 'Palestinian' and 'Hellenistic'.[21]

[19] See below, Chapter I, section 7; 'R. Akiba's View of Suffering', *JQR* 63, 1973, pp. 332–51. Neither treatment provides a full history, but many of the salient points may be seen.

[20] *Trajectories*, p. 8.

[21] Sandmel has often remarked on the tendency to ignore obvious differences between the Hellenistic world and Palestinian Judaism in the effort to correct the oversimplified view of a hard and fast distinction. See especially his remarks in *The First Christian Century*, p. 46 n. 26 ('a restricted Hellenization'). Cf. further my 'The Covenant as a Soteriological Category and the Nature of Salvation in Palestinian and Hellenistic Judaism', *Jews, Greeks and Christians*, ed. Hamerton-Kelly and Scroggs, 1976.

Having declined Robinson's proposal to study religious history in terms of trajectories (although I hope that I shall be open to history and development), I must now reaffirm, against Robinson, that I think there is some validity to discussing the general character of religion which obtained in a given geographical/cultural milieu. I think that there is some sense in speaking of 'Platonism', for example, when referring to the widespread view in the Hellenistic world that the true is to be identified with the immutable. Robinson might object to this as too essentialist a category and as insufficiently dynamic,[22] and it may be that one can give a history of the conception, but the category of Platonism as just defined does, in my view, point to something real in the ancient world. (It is, by the way, a view which is notable by its absence in most of Palestinian Judaism.) Put another way, it is important to consider not just the possibility of vertical movements down the scale of history, but the horizontal context of religious thought. It is this horizontal context which I am aiming to uncover by searching for the pattern of a given religion within a given geographical and cultural milieu. The term 'pattern' may imply the static view that Robinson so decries; it is not intended to do so. Robinson's work serves as a useful reminder not to reconstruct religious thought by putting all the available ingredients into what Morton Smith has somewhere called 'a timeless stew', and I shall try in each section not to be blind to historical changes. But I do not doubt that the various types of Judaism to be considered here did possess enough stability and homogeneity (not immobility) to permit one responsibly to enquire about the general religious context in terms of a pattern of religion.

3. Sources

We shall here do no more than briefly indicate what material will be used in the study, discussing problems of date and provenance in as much detail as seems necessary in the chapters devoted to each body of material. The sources for Paul are obviously his letters. The problems of authenticity and the use of Acts will be discussed in Part II below. A few comments are necessary here, however, about Palestinian Jewish sources for the years 200 b.c.e. to 200 c.e.

It is my general intention to consider the entire body of material available from this period, although limitations of time and space have imposed some restrictions on the works which receive detailed treatment. We shall begin with the consideration of early Rabbinic (Tannaitic) literature, which I take to be, on the whole, the latest body of literature to be treated here. The reason for beginning with Tannaitic literature is twofold. In the first place,

---

[22] Cf. *Trajectories*, pp. 8f.

this literature has been primarily in mind in most major comparisons of Paul and Judaism which have been carried out by New Testament scholars (for example, Davies and Schoeps). It thus deserves pride of place. In the second place, Tannaitic literature offers a better opportunity of describing a pattern of religion than much of the literature which is presumably much older, such as Jubilees and the various portions of I Enoch. The latter works are relatively short and have specialized concerns. We can best proceed first by investigating the larger and more comprehensive Tannaitic literature and then by enquiring to what extent the pattern of religion which became standard in later material (assuming that a pattern did become standard) was also operative early.

Secondly, we shall study the other relatively large body of material of more or less coherent origin, the Dead Sea Scrolls. The study will be primarily limited to the major Scrolls from Cave I and the Covenant of Damascus.

Thirdly, we shall deal with a selection of works from the Apocryphal and Pseudepigraphical writings, from Ben Sirach to IV Ezra. Several works which probably come from Palestine and which can be dated to the period under consideration have been omitted, however, partly to save time and space and partly to avoid needless repetition. The two principal omissions are the Testaments of the Twelve Patriarchs and II Baruch (the Syriac Apocalypse of Baruch). The Testaments are omitted largely because of the vexing problems of date and Christian interpolations.[1] It would be necessary to carry out a full-scale literary analysis in order to deal with the Testaments, and the potential results, which a preliminary study indicates would be largely repetitive, would not appear to warrant the expenditure of time and space. II Baruch has been omitted primarily because of its close connection with IV Ezra. Although there is no universal agreement on this point, I take II Baruch to be dependent on IV Ezra, rather than vice versa.[2] The viewpoint of the author is not the same, but again a preliminary investigation has indicated that the overall study would not benefit appreciably by including a full discussion of II Baruch.[3] Several of the minor works from the Apocrypha and Pseudepigrapha have also been omitted from direct consideration for the same reason.

I have further left out of consideration the Aramaic Targums which are now sometimes dated to this period.[4] In part, I am not persuaded of the

---

[1] There is a considerable literature on the subject. See especially M. de Jonge, *The Testaments of the Twelve Patriarchs*, and his two articles on Christian influences in *NT* 4, 1960, pp. 182–235, and *NT* 5, 1962, pp. 311–19; J. Becker, *Untersuchungen zur Entstehungsgeschichte der Testamente der zwölf Patriarchen*. On the difficulty of using the *Testaments*, see Longenecker, *Paul: Apostle of Liberty*, pp. 11f.

[2] See the discussion in H. H. Rowley, *The Relevance of Apocalyptic*, p. 119; F. Rosenthal, *Vier apokryphische Bücher*, pp. 72f.; L. Rost, *Einleitung in die alttestamentlichen Apokryphen und Pseudepigraphen*, p. 97.

[3] I have treated the question of the covenant and soteriology in II Baruch briefly in 'The Covenant as a Soteriological Category and the Nature of Salvation in Palestinian and Hellenistic Judaism'.

[4] See M. McNamara, *The New Testament and the Palestinian Targum to the Pentateuch*, p. 35.

antiquity of the Targums as we have them.[5] Even if generally late, the Targums may, to be sure, contain early traditions, but these must now be sought out one by one. In general, the present state of Targumic studies does not permit the Targums to be used for our purposes. At present, the Targums can be used in motif research, in which one can investigate a given theme or idea and attempt to date the Targumic material which is relevant.[6] We are not at the stage, however, of being able to discuss the view of religion and the religious life in the Palestinian Targum to the Pentateuch, and especially not to date a coherent view of religion to the period which falls within our purview.

Having dismissed the Targums from consideration as a primary source for this study, it would be out of place to give a lengthy treatment of the methodology for working with Jewish sources which is dependent on them and which is especially associated with the names of Renée Bloch,[7] G. Vermes[8] and M. McNamara.[9] The importance of the hypothesis which they have put forward, however, does merit some comment. The aim is generally to trace the history of discrete Jewish exegetical traditions, using the Palestinian Targum(s) as the starting point. The ultimate purpose seems to be to provide background information for understanding the exegetical uses of the Old Testament in the New Testament. We should first note a misunderstanding of Rabbinic sources which marks the work of McNamara and Bloch, though not of Vermes. In emphasizing the importance of studying haggadah rather than halakah for the understanding of Judaism, Bloch, in her 'Note méthodologique', twice remarked that there were no critical texts of the midrashic materials available.[10] The article appeared in 1955, and there were then, as there are now, critical texts of all the Tannaitic midrashim except Sifra. It is clear that she had in mind not the Tannaitic midrashim but the later more purely homiletical midrashim. The one example which she gave of her method made use only of such later compilations, such as the

---

[5] See J. Fitzmyer's review of McNamara's work (n. 4 above) in *Theological Studies* 29, 1968, pp. 321–6, and of A. Díez Macho's edition of Neofiti in *CBQ* 32, 1970, pp. 107–12; see further, Fitzmyer, 'The Languages of Palestine in the First Century A.D.', *CBQ* 32, 1970, pp. 524f.; 'The Contribution of Qumran Aramaic to the Study of the New Testament', *NTS* 20, 1974, p. 384 (further references in n. 1); Jonas Greenfield's review of the republication of Etheridge's translation of the Targums to the Pentateuch which were known in the nineteenth century (*JBL* 89, 1970, pp. 238f.); B. Z. Wacholder's review of McNamara's *Targum and Testament* (*JBL* 93, 1974, pp. 132f.); Anthony D. York, 'The Dating of Targumic Literature', *JSJ* 5, 1974, pp. 49–62.

[6] Thus R. Le Déaut, *La nuit Pascale. Essai sur la signification de la Pâque juive à partir du Targum d'Exode XII 42*.

[7] 'Note méthodologique pour l'étude de la littérature rabbinique', *RSR* 43, 1955, pp. 194–227; 'Midrash', *Supplément au Dictionnaire de la Bible* 5, cols. 1263–81.

[8] *Scripture and Tradition in Judaism.*

[9] *The New Testament and the Palestinian Targum*; see p. 28; cf. *Targum and Testament*. On this school of interpretation, which goes back to P. Kahle, see the important and sympathetic bibliographical essay by Merrill Miller, 'Targum, Midrash and the use of the Old Testament in the New Testament', *JSJ* 2, 1971, pp. 29–82.

[10] Pp. 202 and 203 n. 10.

Yalkut Shim'oni, and she did not mention any of the Tannaitic midrashim. In her article on Midrash in the *Supplément au Dictionnaire de la Bible* one sees more clearly her failure to understand the Tannaitic midrashim. The Rabbinic midrash, she wrote, is primarily homiletic. It is popular in character, not a product of the schools.[11] Later, however, she distinguished haggadic from halakic midrash. Halakic midrash, which deals with norms of conduct and related matters, *is* a product of the schools of the 'docteurs'. It is found in the Tannaitic midrashim. The haggadic midrash, on the other hand, the origin of which is popular instruction, is of great religious value, and it gave rise to an immense literature comprised of homilies and commentaries on the text of the Bible.[12] Thus we see that the general discussion of 'Rabbinic midrash' as primarily homiletic was based on an essential equation of midrash with haggadah, and Bloch generally meant 'haggadic midrash' when she wrote about 'midrash'. Since she held it to be fatal for understanding Jewish religion to focus on the Mishnah, which gives halakah but not haggadah,[13] and since she thought of the Tannaitic midrashim as containing only halakah, Bloch effectively excluded from consideration the entire body of Tannaitic literature, which contains material more certainly early than the Targums and the later homiletic compilations. She erroneously and arbitrarily separated halakic from haggadic midrash, not noting that in the Tannaitic midrashim they lie side by side, attributed to the same teachers in a way that does not permit the division of popular and scholastic; she seemed unaware of the large amount of haggadah in Tannaitic literature; and she erred in basically equating midrash with the haggadah of the medieval midrashim, which she held to be of religious value, rather than seeing its intimate connection with the halakah of the second-century schools (which, as we shall see in section 3 of Chapter I, is also of 'religious value').[14] Somewhat similarly, in defining the difference between halakah and haggadah, McNamara remarked that halakic midrash is found in the Mekilta 'and in other midrashim', while 'we have the haggadic midrash in expositional and homiletic commentaries'. He cited Genesis Rabbah as an example.[15] Thus besides our doubts about the Targums as a source of early exegesis, we must note that two of the main proponents of the new method for studying Jewish literature – giving the history of exegetical traditions

[11] 'Midrash', col. 1265.
[12] Ibid., col. 1267.
[13] 'Note méthodologique', pp. 198f.
[14] The equation of midrash and haggadah is still very common. See, for example, Dupont-Sommer, *The Essene Writings from Qumran*, p. 310. The intent here is not to quibble about terms. The objection to the equation is that it results in eliminating from consideration the Tannaitic midrashim, which contain midrash haggadah as well as midrash halakah, both attributed to the same teachers. This criticism of Bloch is not the same as that of Wright (*The Literary Genre Midrash*, pp. 18–25), who objected to using 'midrash' as broadly as did Bloch. The broad use was defended by R. Le Déaut, 'Apropos a Definition of Midrash', ET in *Interpretation* 26, 1971, pp. 259–82.
[15] McNamara, *Targum and Testament*, p. 10.

beginning with the Targums – have held seriously defective views about the nature of Tannaitic literature and its place in the whole body of literature which bears directly on Jewish religion.

It may secondly be noted that the studies of exegetical traditions by McNamara and Vermes do not, thus far, reveal very much about the religion of Judaism. McNamara repeatedly states that the Palestinian Targum is of great importance *for New Testament studies*.[16] The individual studies in his two books do indeed focus on trying to explain New Testament passages, so that one is hardly in a position to learn much about Judaism for its own sake. The same is true of most of the studies in Vermes's *Scripture and Tradition in Judaism*. When he does discuss a matter of importance for Jewish religion, the ground of redemption and atonement,[17] his method takes him astray, in spite of his undoubted knowledge of a wide range of Jewish literature. In focusing on a few brief references connecting God's accepting sacrifices with his remembering the binding of Isaac, Vermes concludes that,

according to ancient Jewish theology, the atoning efficacy of the *Tamid* offering, of all the sacrifices in which a lamb was immolated, and perhaps, basically, of all expiatory sacrifice irrespective of the nature of the victim, depended upon the virtue of the Akedah, the self-offering of the Lamb [Isaac] whom God had recognized as the perfect victim of the perfect burnt offering.[18]

Similarly he writes later that 'the saving virtue of the Passover Lamb proceeded from the merits of that first Lamb, the son of Abraham, who offered himself upon the altar'.[19] He cites a passage from the Mekilta: '*And When I See the Blood*. I see the blood of the sacrifice [aqedah] of Isaac',[20] not noting that this is only one of the interpretative remarks on the biblical phrase 'when I see the blood'. He takes such midrashic interpretations of what blood was seen as establishing a Jewish *doctrine*: 'The firstborn sons of Israel were spared and the people delivered from captivity because the sacrifice of the Paschal lamb reminded God of the sacrifice of Isaac.'[21] Thus he can state that 'the Binding of Isaac was thought to have played a unique role in the whole economy of the salvation of Israel, and to have a permanent redemptive effect on behalf of its people'.[22] This gives the scant references to the binding of Isaac in the Tannaitic midrash a significance far out of proportion to what they actually hold in Rabbinic literature. Vermes has

[16] McNamara, *The New Testament and the Palestinian Targum*, pp. 34f., 253; cf. *Targum and Testament*, p. 13.
[17] 'Redemption and Genesis XXII', *Scripture and Tradition*, pp. 193–227.
[18] Ibid., p. 211.
[19] Ibid., p. 215.
[20] Mek. Pisḥa 7 (24; I, 57; to 12.13); repeated ibid. 11 (39; I, 87f.; to 12.23); Vermes, *Scripture and Tradition*, pp. 215f.
[21] Vermes, p. 216.   [22] Ibid., p. 208.

apparently been misled in part by his method: one focuses on a single tradition and attempts to unravel its history. In unravelling the history of the binding of Isaac, which in part touches on the story of the redemption of Israel from Egypt, Vermes neglects all the other things said in the Tannaitic midrashim about the redemption from Egypt. The midrashim adduce numerous reasons which moved God to bring Israel out of Egypt.[23] Similarly, in seeing the significance of sacrifices for Judaism as depending on their being connected with the binding of Isaac, Vermes makes a doctrinal and single-stranded tie where the Jewish tradition sees only one exegetical/homiletical possibility. The real reason the sacrifices were considered efficacious is that God commanded them to atone for transgression.[24] Thus the new method for Rabbinic studies described by Bloch and the 'new synthesis' proclaimed by Vermes[25] leave something to be desired as means of studying and comprehending the religion of Judaism. *They accurately point to the need for seeing and describing, wherever possible, historical development of exegetical traditions.*[26] It is not the intention of the comments made here to deny that this is an important task, but only to make a few cautionary remarks about 'comparative midrash' and to show the limitations of the method. The tracing out of exegetical traditions one by one, especially to show their significance for understanding a passage or theme in the New Testament, cannot substitute for studying whole bodies of Jewish literature in their own contexts and on their own terms.

It is this study of bodies of Jewish literature which is here undertaken. Despite the sources omitted from direct consideration, the range of material used in the study is quite wide, and, taken together, it should permit fair conclusions as to the main streams of religion in Palestinian Judaism.

[23] Below, Chapter I, section 4.

[24] Below, Chapter I, section 7. The importance of the binding of Isaac in Jewish literature is also overplayed by Schoeps, *Paul*, pp. 144, 256.

[25] See the introduction of *Scripture and Tradition.*

[26] In addition to the studies cited above, see the summary article by R. Le Déaut, 'Targumic Literature and New Testament Interpretation', *Biblical Theology Bulletin* 4, 1974, pp. 243–89. Le Déaut itemizes discrete texts and themes in the New Testament which might be illuminated by the Targums. His conclusions on the use of Targumic exegetical traditions (pp. 287–9) is sober and balanced.

PART ONE

PALESTINIAN JUDAISM

I

TANNAITIC LITERATURE

1. The persistence of the view of Rabbinic religion as one of legalistic works-righteousness

In 1921, in an article which should be required reading for any Christian scholar who writes about Judaism,[1] George Foot Moore commented on a fundamental change which had taken place in the nineteenth century in works by Christian authors about Judaism. Through the eighteenth century Christian literature had primarily tried to show the *agreement* of Jewish views with Christian theology. To be sure, Judaism had been attacked – often viciously – but the overall intent was to convict Jews out of their own mouths: to show, for example, that their statements about intermediaries (*logos, memra*) proved the truth of Christian dogma. With F. Weber, however, everything changed.[2] For him, Judaism was the antithesis of Christianity. Judaism was a legalistic religion in which God was remote and inaccessible. Christianity is based on faith rather than works and believes in an accessible God.[3] Moore then showed the continuation of Weber's picture of Judaism in Schürer[4] and Bousset,[5] and he indicated how inadequate and poorly founded such a construction is.[6]

When Moore followed his apparently devastating analysis with his own constructive presentation of early Rabbinic religion,[7] one would have thought that the question of whether he or Weber and his successors were basically correct would have been closed. In contrast to Weber, Schürer and Bousset, Moore knew the sources in detail and at first hand. In contrast to them, he wished to present a construction of Judaism for its own sake and

---

[1] G. F. Moore, 'Christian Writers on Judaism', *HTR* 14, 1921, pp. 197–254.
[2] F. Weber, *System der altsynagogalen palästinischen Theologie aus Targum, Midrasch und Talmud*, ed. by Franz Delitzsch and Georg Schnedermann, 1880; revised as *Jüdische Theologie auf Grund des Talmud und verwandter Schriften*, 1897. [3] Moore, 'Christian Writers', pp. 228–33.
[4] *Lehrbuch der Neutestamentlichen Zeitgeschichte*, 1874; revised as *Geschichte des jüdischen Volkes im Zeitalter Jesu Christi*, 1886–90. There are subsequent volumes and editions.
[5] W. Bousset, *Die Religion des Judentums im neutestamentlichen Zeitalter*, 1903; revised by H. Gressmann in 1925. The last part of the title was altered to *im späthellenistischen Zeitalter*.
[6] Moore, 'Christian Writers', pp. 237–48.
[7] G. F. Moore, *Judaism in the First Centuries of the Christian Era: The Age of the Tannaim*, 3 vols., 1927–30.

on its own terms, not as part of a 'background to the New Testament' handbook which covers topics of interest to Christianity and leaves out the rest.[8] In contrast to Bousset in particular, he emphasized the Rabbinic material as basic to his construction. Bousset depended mainly on the Apocrypha and Pseudepigrapha, 'with an especial penchant for the apocalypses'.[9] Moore criticized Bousset for calling his book 'the religion of Judaism', while basing it on sources to which, 'so far as we know, Judaism never conceded any authority, while he discredits and largely ignores those which it has always regarded as normative'.[10] Thus we see the historical circumstances in which Moore's much-criticized equation of 'normative Judaism' with Rabbinic Judaism arose.[11]

Moore's critique of Weber and his successors, in which he was joined by many Jewish scholars,[12] should, as we said, have been successful. It was pronounced successful around 1936 by H. Loewe, who considered the false views of Wellhausen, Schürer, Charles, Bousset and Weber to have been sufficiently criticized by Herford, Moore, Schechter, Montefiore, Büchler, Marmorstein, Lauterbach, Finkelstein and others, so that Loewe himself did not see the need of continuing the *apologia* for Judaism.[13] In 1952, R. Marcus gave a similarly optimistic report:

Unpleasant as it is for modern Jews to carry on the long and wearying struggle to exculpate the Pharisees from the charges of hypocrisy and uncharitableness made against them by the Evangelists, it is the more consoling to realize how much modern Christian scholarship has done to correct the popular belief that there was an irreconcilable difference between Jesus and the Pharisees.[14]

---

[8] Cf. Moore, 'Christian Writers', p. 238.

[9] Ibid., p. 243. On Gressmann's additions of Rabbinic material to Bousset, see below, p. 56.

[10] 'Christian Writers', p. 244.

[11] See, for example, E. R. Goodenough, *Jewish Symbols* 12, p. 6: Moore regarded Mishnaic Judaism 'as the norm for all Judaism, even at this earlier period . . . He called it "normative" Judaism, as compared to which apocalyptic Judaism, mystic (or gnostic) Judaism, and Philonic Judaism were aberrations.' Moore (*Judaism* III, pp. v–vi) defended himself against such criticism by pointing out that he intended to describe the Judaism which *became* normative by the end of the second century c.e., but he has repeatedly been criticized for supposing that Rabbinic religion was normative for all Judaism in the first century; and he may have harboured that view, despite his printed denial, since his own student, Goodenough, attributed it to him. It is certainly true that in *Judaism* he did not give sufficient independence to Jewish thought as represented by apocalyptic literature. On the other hand, one must consider the historical circumstances in which he wrote. He was entirely correct in criticizing Bousset for calling *his* book, which relied largely on the apocalypses, 'The Religion of Judaism', and in objecting to defining Jewish piety on the basis of such sources as IV Ezra (also post-70!) and reading that piety into Rabbinic literature, as did Bousset and Köberle, among others. The aim of the present chapter, in any case, is not to try to determine what was the dominant form of Judaism at any given time and place, but what is the correct interpretation of Rabbinic Judaism. Among those who constructed major accounts of Judaism during the late nineteenth and early twentieth centuries – which is when the major constructions now in use in the Western world were made – Moore was clearly the most knowledgeable and perceptive interpreter of Rabbinic religion.

[12] See 'Christian Writers', p. 243.

[13] H. Loewe, 'Pharisaism', in *Judaism and Christianity* I: *The Age of Transition* (ed. W. O. E. Oesterley), p. 105.

[14] R. Marcus, 'The Pharisees in the Light of Modern Scholarship', *JR* 32, 1952, p. 163.

This optimism seems widespread among Jewish scholars especially, and several have remarked to me that it is no longer necessary to argue against Christian biases. One suspects, however, that many Jewish scholars do not perceive the depth of the Protestant critique of Judaism. Marcus was content that the Pharisees are no longer openly accused of hypocrisy by scholars. He seems not to have realized that in his day (and, indeed, to the present day) the weight of New Testament scholarly opinion was behind a view of Judaism which holds it to be at best an inadequate religion and at worst one which destroys any hope of a proper relationship between God and man.

Most Jewish scholars, to be sure, have had other occupations than carrying on the 'wearying struggle' to get Christian scholars to see Rabbinic Judaism (or Pharisaism) in an unbiased light. It is worth pausing before describing how Weber's view has continued in New Testament scholarship to note the more realistic attitude of the one Jewish scholar who has constantly been concerned with the problem of subjective bias in scholarship in this field, Samuel Sandmel. He recently noted that 'the fact must be faced that value judgments on Judaism, as distinct from a detached description of it, constitute an ongoing reality in much of modern New Testament scholarship, despite Moore's valiant effort to correct an infelicitous trend'. He remarked that Jewish scholars sometimes, in reaction, tend to glorify Judaism. There is always the danger of subjective bias. He continued by assessing the present situation in New Testament scholarship:

If I were asked to comment on the chief difference between the attitude toward Judaism in the Christian scholarship prior to Moore's time and that after it, I would say that, prior to Moore's time, there was almost no effort to be fair to Judaism, and since Moore's time, there has been a considerable effort, and considerable attainment, especially in America and Britain. There is still a great distance to go, but I have every confidence, possibly naïvely so, that that ability of scholarship to correct itself will some day bring about the assertion of detachment and objectivity even in this field.[15]

In a footnote to a reference to Schürer on the very page just quoted, however, Sandmel wrote as follows:

It can be set down as something destined to endure eternally that the usual Christian commentators will disparage Judaism and its supposed legalism, and Jewish scholars will reply, usually fruitlessly. I have addressed myself to this topic in three or four essays, and do not intend to pursue this any more beyond this one time, preferring to conclude that with those Christians who persist in deluding themselves about Jewish legalism, no academic communication is possible. The issue is not to bring these interpreters to love Judaism, but only to bring them to a responsible, elementary comprehension of it.[16]

[15] Sandmel, *The First Christian Century*, p. 66.
[16] Ibid., p. 98 n. 10. Cf. the review by Eldon J. Epp, *Central Conference of American Rabbis Journal* 18, 1971, pp. 72–4. On the basis of his own educational experience, Epp inclines more to Sandmel's more optimistic view.

Here we see that one Jewish scholar – a scholar of the New Testament who knows Christian New Testament scholarship intimately, who, unlike many, perceives what has been the dominant trend in New Testament scholarship with regard to Judaism, and who describes and has attempted the task of bringing to that scholarship 'a responsible, elementary comprehension' of Judaism[17] – has finally given up the effort on the grounds that it is fruitless to try to persuade those who refuse to be enlightened.

Despite the optimistic hope for the future, Sandmel accurately attributed the 'infelicitous trend' to 'much of modern New Testament scholarship'. In fact, as we shall see, the view that Moore opposed and that Sandmel decries is very solidly entrenched in New Testament scholarship, appearing in the basic reference works and being held by many of the most influential scholars of the·present and the immediately preceding generations. Weber's general view of Judaism lives on in New Testament scholarship, unhindered by the fact that it has been denounced by such knowledgeable scholars as Moore and the others named by Loewe and despite the fact that many of its proponents, despite Moore's scathing criticism on this point,[18] *still* cannot or do not look up the passages which they cite in support of their view and read them in context. It is necessary to show that this is the case.

So that we may have in mind the view that is going to be traced through successive generations of scholars, it will be useful first to summarize the most relevant points of Weber's attempt to describe Judaism as a systematic theology. We here restrict the summary to the section which Weber entitled 'Der soteriologische Lehrkreis'.[19]

Weber first gives what he considers to be the Jewish view of 'general soteriology'. Under 'Anthropology', Weber describes the universal fall of man, which he recognizes does not constitute a doctrine of inherited sin, but which nevertheless estranges man from God (pp. 218–25). He takes Taanith 11a as evidence that an account was kept of sins and fulfilments, on the balance of which each man would be judged (p. 242). Weber then turns to 'Soteriology'. There are two ways for fallen man to return (*zurückkehren*) to God: repentance and obedience to the law (p. 259). Repentance is above all an accomplishment (*Leistung*) 'through which a previous sin is made good' (p. 261). Repentance is described as 'the first means of salvation' (p. 262). Repentance, however, does not make one righteous, nor does it give one any claim (*Anspruch*) to the Kingdom of Heaven, which was lost through the fall of Adam. For this reason, God has provided a 'second means of salvation', the law, whose fulfilment provides what repentance does not (p. 262).

Having described this general situation, Weber turns to consider the

[17] Cf. Sandmel, 'The Jewish Scholar and Early Christianity', *The Seventy-Fifth Anniversary Volume of The Jewish Quarterly Review*, 1967, p. 476.
[18] 'Christian Writers', pp. 235f.; cf. Montefiore, *Judaism and St Paul*, pp. 7–9.
[19] The page numbers in the text refer to the 1897 revision of Weber's book.

election and the significance of the Exile and the gift of the law on Mt Sinai (pp. 262–73). The acceptance of the covenant removes the consequences of the sin of Adam and restores Israel to the *Herrlichkeit* lost through Adam's fall (p. 271). The restoration, however, is brief. Because of the incident of the golden calf, Israel loses its restored status: as Adam's fall resulted in the separation of mankind from God, the worship of the golden calf results in Israel's separation from God; 'es ist Israels Sündenfall' (p. 274). Thereafter it becomes the goal of the individual Israelite to regain what had been lost through the fall of Israel. This is accomplished by the precise fulfilment of the law and the practice of the sacrificial system: 'Thus it can be concluded that the means of earning salvation are Torah and Aboda [the Temple cultus], the works of the law (*Gesetz*) and repentance' (p. 277).

The individual's relation to God is determined by his relation to the Torah. God judges man by producing his book in which sins and righteous deeds are recorded, and one is righteous who has fulfilled all the commandments. Since, however, no one is truly righteous, man is judged according to whether transgressions or fulfilments weigh more heavily (p. 280). 'Weighing' does not rest solely on enumeration, however, since some commandments weigh more heavily than others. The principle is clear, but it leads to uncertainty: no one can know whether or not his fulfilments outweigh his transgressions (pp. 281 and 282). Theoretically one is judged every day, but the final judgment can be determined only at the end of one's life. Then the account is closed and a final decision rendered (pp. 283f.). The fulfilment of commandments makes man righteous (innocent before God) and meritorious; thus *zekut* has both a forensic and a soteriological meaning (pp. 278f.).

Besides fulfilment of commandments, however, there is a second means of earning righteousness before God: 'good works'. These are almsgiving and acts of kindness (pp. 284–8). Further, one's own fulfilments of commandments and good deeds may be supplemented by those of others, above all the fathers, in a way analogous to that of the Roman *Thesaurus operum supererogationis* (pp. 292–7). Even living righteous men may provide some help in the attempt to compile enough merit (pp. 297–302).

Weber then discusses the 'concept of atonement' (pp. 313–34). It provides another way 'to life' besides the Torah (p. 316). The various means of atonement (sacrifices, repentance, the Day of Atonement, suffering, death, substitutionary suffering, good works) are described. They all have the function of making the sins for which they atone as if they had not happened and restoring man to whatever relationship to God he had had before the transgression (p. 313). Weber does not bring the 'concept of atonement' into strict connection with the idea of weighing transgressions against fulfilments of commandments and good deeds. One supposes, however, that the separate acts of atonement, which deal only with individual sins, serve to reduce the number of transgressions which are weighed in the final judgment. There are two clear results to the matter, however: 1. there is a diversity of means for earning righteousness and achieving atonement; 2. this very diversity leads to the uncertainty of the 'sinner' about his relationship with God (pp. 334–6).

Apart from the curious theory of the two falls – Adam's, in which all men fell, and the incident of the golden calf, in which Israel fell[20] – much of Weber's scheme is still alive and well. It is remarkable that it should be so, since the theory of the second fall from grace is essential to Weber's system. He recognized that the covenant at Mt Sinai was regarded in Jewish literature as establishing (or demonstrating) that the Israelites were God's chosen people and as such were promised by God that he would remain their God and they his people. But since Judaism is the antithesis of Christianity, and since Christianity is based on grace and faith, what is to be done with this clear evidence of the electing grace of God? It becomes inoperative because of the second fall. Weber obviously attributes to the golden calf story a systematic place in the history of God's dealing with Israel which it never occupied in Jewish literature; indeed, which it never could have occupied, since that literature does not offer a systematic theology which could dogmatically incorporate such a story as part of a system. It permitted him, however, to get past the worrisome problem of the grace of God made manifest at Sinai and on to the heart of his scheme, the theory which has dominated subsequent discussion: that Judaism is a religion in which one must *earn* salvation by compiling more good works ('merits'), whether on his own or from the excess of someone else, than he has transgressions. The theory that individuals must *earn* salvation rests on the view that Israel 'fell' from the relationship with God established on Mt Sinai; thus the covenant itself is viewed as not retaining its efficacy: the promises of God are made void.

Although not covered in the section on soteriology, equally important was Weber's theory that God in Judaism was inaccessible. According to Moore, this theory constitutes Weber's primary original contribution to the misunderstanding of Judaism.[21] We shall return to this point in section 10 below and shall mention it only occasionally in the present survey, which will focus on the view that weighing merits and transgressions constitutes Jewish soteriology.

By the end of the nineteenth century, Weber's soteriology was widely considered to be an accurate presentation based directly on the original

---

[20] Recently Smolar and Aberbach, without mentioning Weber's use of the golden calf story, have denied that it was taken as meaning that God rejected Israel. See 'The Golden Calf Episode in Post-biblical Literature', *HUCA* 39, 1968, pp. 91–116'

[21] 'Christian Writers', p. 233.

sources. In 1896 R. H. Charles summarized Rabbinic soteriology in his commentary on II Baruch. He acknowledged that the summary is taken from Weber, although he left out the theory of two falls:

Every good work . . . established a certain degree of merit with God, while every evil work entailed a corresponding demerit. A man's position with God depended on the relation existing between his merits and demerits, and his salvation on the preponderance of the former over the latter. The relation between his merits and demerits was determined daily by the weighing of his deeds. . . . But as the results of such judgments were necessarily unknown, there could not fail to be much uneasiness, and to allay this the doctrine of the vicarious righteousness of the patriarchs and saints of Israel was developed. . . . A man could thereby summon to his aid the merits of the fathers, and so counterbalance his demerits.

It is obvious that such a system does not admit of forgiveness in any spiritual sense of the term. It can only mean in such a connection a remission of penalty to the offender, on the ground that compensation is furnished, either through his own merit or through that of the righteous fathers.[22]

Charles never purported to be expert in Rabbinic religion, and the above quotation simply shows that Weber's work was widely accepted, while further serving as a succint summary of the principal points of his soteriology.

Bousset's acceptance of Weber's theory, however, had a much more far-reaching effect. For one thing, Bousset's view, which depended on Weber, was, as we shall see, appropriated and disseminated to generations of New Testament scholars by his student, Rudolf Bultmann. Further, Bousset's work itself, unlike that of Weber, has remained in print and has been directly influential in New Testament scholarship.[23] As we shall see when we discuss the topic (section 10 below), the idea that God is remote and inaccessible became a dominating theory in Bousset's work. His principal alteration with respect to Weber's soteriology was to deny that the merits of one person could be transferred to another. This is a curious aspect of Bousset's construction. He repeated the general view about a treasury of merits established by the works of supererogation of the pious and the guiltless suffering of the righteous, but he argued that this treasury really provided no security for the *individual*. The 'Jewish church' was deficient in that it lacked sacraments, and it thus had no means for transferring its store of works of supererogation to individuals.[24] Thus, in Bousset's view, the one hope of Jews – the transfer

---

[22] R. H. Charles, *The Apocalypse of Baruch*, pp. lxxxiif. In 1900 Thackeray similarly adopted Weber's soteriology without reservation. See *The Relation of St Paul to Contemporary Jewish Thought*, pp. 80–7. Similarly Albert Schweitzer, *Paul and His Interpreters*, p. 45 (the reliability of Weber and Schürer on Jewish religion), p. 48 (Rabbinic religion was 'a sun-scorched plain').

[23] See, for example, from the older literature Schweitzer, *Paul and His Interpreters*, p. 162; from the more recent literature Koch, *The Rediscovery of Apocalyptic*, pp. 13, 58: Bousset's *Religion* is a standard work and is still indispensable. The point is returned to later in this section.

[24] Bousset, *Die Religion des Judentums*, pp. 179–82 in the first edition of 1903; pp. 177–9 in the fourth edition of 1966.

of the merits of the fathers – was doomed to frustration, and Judaism was consequently judged to be an inadequate and non-functional religion.

Shortly after the publication of the first edition of Bousset's book, Köberle examined the history of soteriology in Jewish thought.[25] He recognized that the election of Israel is the basis of Jewish religion (p. 408), but he did not describe the election as being salvific; rather, it is a regrettable form of nationalism (pp. 408–15).

The Pharisaic view of the centrality of the law has as its motivating force the racial instinct. The perception of the election which is bound up with the commitment to the law is based on narrow nationalism: 'One must recognize above all that the entire so-called piety of the Pharisees developed in opposition to heathen *Nivellierung* ("levelling")' (pp. 482f.). It is thus elitist.

The commitment to the law implies that sin is transgression of commandments. Despite the numerous passages concerning the joy of keeping the law, especially the Sabbath commandments (p. 485), 'on the whole the Sabbath commandment remained a yoke' (p. 486). The privileges achieved by Israel by the election must be confirmed for the individual by his absolute obedience to the law (p. 489). Obedience and disobedience are always conceived as individual acts, so that sin is the sum of individual sinful acts (pp. 493–6). This leads to the result that one's self-assessment is necessarily divided. 'Individual acts of commandment-fulfilments stand over against individual sins; other deeds exceed the requirement of the commandment and can therefore be reckoned as merit' (p. 496).

This creates a religious situation to which different individuals will respond in different ways, according to their character. The self-satisfied man will find many instances in which he will feel that he has done more than is necessary. One who is anxious, strict or conscientious, however, can never be content (p. 509). Köberle states the impossibility of the individual's situation like this: in general the avoidance of evil in any particular case is possible, and as the fulfilment of a positive ideal, it may appear achievable. But what happens when in fact evil is not avoided? It is the presupposition of the entire system that by an effort of the will which is sufficient to what is required, one could actually be justified (*gerecht*). But if a man should not want to avoid evil in some particular case, how much less would he always desire sufficiently strongly to achieve the good! 'Who can set one free from this situation (cf. Rom. 7.14ff.)' (pp. 509f.). Or again: 'What a torment it must have been, always to hold this ideal before oneself and always to discover that it cannot be achieved' (p. 516). The difficulty is heightened by the fact that there is no other path to the future world than obedience to the law (cf. p. 518).

[25] J. Köberle, *Sünde und Gnade im religiösen Leben des Volkes Israel bis auf Christum. Eine Geschichte des vorchristlichen Heilsbewusstseins*, 1905.

Köberle was aware of many of the statements about the efficacy of repentance and God's grace (pp. 611–37), but they do not change his evaluation of the situation of the individual. What did it help, he asks, to believe
in the forgiving grace of God in respect to individual sins, when the menac-
ing judgment was always suspended over one's head? No matter how much
a man desired forgiveness, no matter how certain he was of the forgiving
grace of God, he could know no joy, for no decisive decision was taken in this
life. A man could experience grace in this life, but have no guarantee that
he would be found to have achieved righteousness before God at the time of
judgment: '*no firm certainty of salvation for the future, no certain possession
of salvation in the present, no guarantee of the first by the second*'. The best
one can say is *spem miscet cum timore*, hope mixed with apprehension. How
can one have certainty of salvation when faced with the doctrine of strict
recompense for deeds as determining the future? (p. 638).

Köberle then pursues further the question of the search for *Heilsgewissheit*.
He gives a penetrating and accurate presentation of the problem as seen by
the author of IV Ezra (pp. 651–5). IV Ezra does not stand alone, however,
in his fear of the future judgment and his anxiety about the impossibility of
salvation. The same view was held by Johanan b. Zakkai (Berakoth 28b) and
Eleazar b. Azariah (Hagigah 4b) and others (Ber. 4a; Hag. 4bff.) (pp. 655f.).
'On the whole . . . the author of IV Ezra without doubt gives us a correct
presentation of the repercussion of the belief in the future judgment on the
religious expressions of individual Jewish piety. *All the many expressions of
belief in God's grace and mercy appear to be denied*' (p. 657).

Jewish piety could not remain, however, where it was left by IV Ezra.
Further, few thought through the logical consequence of the fundamental
views of the Jewish religion as thoroughly as did the author of IV Ezra.
The view of a juristic relation between God and man did not provide
Heilsgewissheit, but it did moderate the inner agitation of the quest for it.
This juristic view provided for the balancing of fulfilments of the law with
transgressions. One who had one merit in excess of his transgressions would
be saved at the final judgment, while an excess of transgressions would lead
to damnation. Further, Israel possessed a rich treasury in the merits of the
fathers, and the good deeds of one generation could supplement those of
another (pp. 663f.).

In addition to this juristic view, Jewish piety relied on a still cruder means
of assuring salvation, one which is connected with the concept of the
election: one who lives in Palestine and teaches his son the Torah, etc., will
be saved. But the truth is that the author of IV Ezra presents the conclusion
of the development of the Jewish religion as it affects the individual (pp.
664f.).

'The conclusion of the history of Jewish piety is a series of unresolved questions' (p. 665). It presented a requirement that should be met, but supplied no means of fulfilling it. It neither provided a guarantee of atonement nor supplied a substitute for it. The fundamental mistake of the entire religion resides in the fact that the theory that the future world could be earned only by fulfilment of commandments was never broken (pp. 665f.).

Besides Bousset, the two individual authors who have had the most to do in implanting Weber's theory of Jewish soteriology deeply in New Testament scholarship have been Paul Billerbeck and Rudolf Bultmann.[26] Billerbeck, who carefully compiled countless 'parallels' to New Testament passages from Rabbinic literature, more than any other passed on Weber's soteriological scheme to the present generation. Here every sentence is documented with numerous quotations from Rabbinic literature, and the weight of the quotations lends the air of scientific proof to statements which may or may not accurately reflect some consensus of Rabbinic thought. The fact that many New Testament scholars, when writing about Rabbinic literature, can refer only to Billerbeck indicates that they do not perceive a theory operating in the selection of passages which may itself be suspect. For them, Billerbeck simply presents in a convenient form the Rabbinic sources, with the result that, in referring to Billerbeck, they see themselves not as referring to one scholar's opinion, but as appealing directly to the sources.[27] We shall subsequently have occasion to note with regard to specific points how Billerbeck has distorted the clear meaning of a text or has prejudiced a question by his selections.[28] We shall here, however, only summarize his own statement of 'the soteriological system of the old synagogue', which presents a view which governs many other parts of his commentary.[29]

God gave Israel the Torah so that they would have the opportunity to earn merit and reward. Individuals have the capability of choosing the good, and the entire system of 'Pharisaic soteriology' stands or falls with man's

[26] An important work in this regard is Kittel's *Theologisches Wörterbuch zum Neuen Testament*, ET *Theological Dictionary to the New Testament*. As we shall note with regard to particular topics below, many of the articles incorporate elements of Weber's scheme, and thus dignify them by placing them in a standard 'Dictionary'. See e.g. Schrenk's article on the *dik-* word group. The repetition of Weber's view in the articles of *TDNT* is presumably the responsibility of no one person, however, and simply shows how widespread the Weber/Bousset/Billerbeck view has become.

[27] Even Sjöberg, who knew the inadequacy of the view of Weber, Bousset and Schürer, nevertheless regarded Billerbeck as having 'set forth the material clearly' (*Gott und die Sünder*, p. xx). More recently, note the optimism of Stephen Neill in *The Interpretation of the New Testament*, p. 292: 'In the dark days before Strack-Billerbeck we referred to Rabbinic matters cautiously, if at all; in this bright post-Strack-Billerbeck epoch, we are all Rabbinic experts, though at second hand.' Unfortunately, the statement is not meant sarcastically. Neill regards Billerbeck's *Kommentar* as a 'resounding success' (p. 296).

[28] In 'Parallelomania' (*JBL* 81, 1962, pp. 8–10), Sandmel gives a devastating critique of Billerbeck's *Kommentar*. The only reasonable conclusion from Sandmel's remarks is that one should not use it unless one can work with the sources independently of it; but I do not note that this has deterred anyone from relying solely on Billerbeck for his knowledge of Rabbinic literature.

[29] Strack-Billerbeck, *Kommentar zum Neuen Testament aus Talmud und Midrasch* IV, 1928, pp. 3–13. On the role played by Strack, see Billerbeck's 'Foreword' to vol. IV and Jeremias's 'Foreword' to vol. V.

capability to fulfil the law (p. 4). Every fulfilment of a commandment earns for the Israelite a merit (*zekut*), while every transgression earns a debt or guilt (*Schuld, ḥobah*). God keeps a record of both merits and demerits. When a man's merits are more numerous he is considered righteous (*gerecht*), but when transgressions outnumber[30] merits he is considered wicked (*ein Gottloser oder Frevler, rasha'*). If the two are balanced, he is an intermediate (*Mittelmässiger, benoni*). Man does not know how his reckoning with God stands; consequently he has no security on earth (no *Sicherheit* or *Heilsgewissheit*). The balance of his account may alter at any moment. At the end, his final destiny is decided on the basis of the account. One with more fulfilments goes to Gan Eden, one with more transgressions to Gehinnom, while for one in the intermediate position God removes a transgression from the scale so that his fulfilments will weigh more heavily. Billerbeck notes that on this last point the school of Shammai differed with the school of Hillel and did not accept 'diese Erleichterung für die Mittel-mässigen' p. 5).

A man's effort, then, is to see that his fulfilments outweigh (outnumber) his transgressions. There are two ways of doing this. One is by the positive activity of piling up fulfilments, supplemented by 'good works' (good deeds which are not strictly commanded by law). Further, he can draw on the merits of the fathers to supplement the number of his merits. In the second place, one can reduce the number of transgressions by acts of atonement, each of which cancels sin and consequently some of the debts or guilts. Billerbeck summarizes: 'the old Jewish religion is thus a religion of the most complete self-redemption (*Selbsterlösung*); it has no room for a redeemer-saviour who dies for the sins of the world' (p. 6). The last clause indicates what is *really* wrong with Judaism.

Bultmann's most succinct presentation of his view of Judaism at the time of Jesus is in his *Das Urchristentum im Rahmen der antiken Religionen*.[31] As far as I can determine, not only from this work, but also from his articles in Kittel's *Wörterbuch*[32] and his use of Rabbinic material in *The History of the Synoptic Tradition*, Bultmann had no substantial independent access to the literature of 'late Judaism', and particularly not to Rabbinic sources. He cites as the principal authority for the history, literature *and religion* of Judaism the work of Schürer,[33] having apparently not noted or not heeded the attacks of Judaic experts on Schürer's presentation of Jewish religion as distinct from his account of the history of the period.[34] Bultmann cites

---

[30] Weber's care not to equate *outweighing* with simple *numerical* majority has been lost. Billerbeck (p. 5) speaks of 'das zahlen- und wertmässige Verhältnis' between merit and demerit, and he says that a man's fate is determined 'nach der Menge (Mehrzahl) der Taten'. The equation of number and weight becomes standard.

[31] Published in 1949. ET, *Primitive Christianity in Its Contemporary Setting*, 1956.

[32] See e.g. the article on *pisteuō*, *TDNT* VI, pp. 199–201.

[33] *Primitive Christianity*, p. 212; *Urchristentum*, p. 238.   [34] See Moore, 'Christian Writers', p. 238.

Bousset and Moore as the most useful studies next to Schürer, not noting that Moore's work is antithetical to those of Schürer and Bousset. Throughout the section Moore is referred to in footnotes, but the argument of his work as a whole, which is directly contradictory to Bultmann's own presentation, seems to have been missed. Despite the citing of Schürer as the primary authority, much of Bultmann's survey seems to derive rather from Bousset. The work of Sjöberg is occasionally referred to.

It is a testimony to Bultmann's mental prowess and theological sophistication that his presentation of Judaism, though derivative, is often more acute and better nuanced than the works of those from whom he derived his information. This point is best seen in the earlier work on Jesus, where his discussion of *obedience* ('the unconditional obedience of the religious man' to the law) and *hope* and their interrelations would seem to offer the real possibility for a constructive analysis of Judaism.[35] Similarly, in his section on 'the remoteness and nearness of God', he was not insensitive to the positive possibilities of Judaism.[36] The final judgment is negative, however, and Judaism is the foil over against which the superiority of Jesus is presented.[37]

This motif is even clearer in *Primitive Christianity*. Here we find the Weber/Schürer/Billerbeck/Bousset outline, and Bultmann's primary contribution is to punctuate the presentation with some existentialist analysis.[38]

Bultmann begins by recognizing the strong sense of history and election in Judaism. But the idea of the election contains 'a curious inner contradiction' which 'is the clue to our whole understanding of Israel': 'By binding herself to her past history, Israel loosened her ties with the present, and her responsibility for it' (p. 60). God was 'no longer a vital factor in the present' (p. 60). Even the hoped-for future redemption was not understood as really connected with the present; it is simply a 'fantastic affair' of the remote future (p. 61). The contrast implied with Jesus' eschatology as depicted by Bultmann[39] is clear: the future in Judaism does not determine the present. God was regarded as so transcendent that he 'was no longer bound to his people' (p. 61). Although the law commands both ethics and ritual, 'ritual became the more important of the two' (p. 62). The 'whole of life was covered by ritual observances' which were elaborated 'to the point of absurdity' (p. 65). The law as a whole, broken down into 613 regulations, most of which were negative, became a charade. 'To take them [the commandments] seriously meant making life an intolerable burden. It was almost impossible to *know* the rules, let alone put them into practice.' Having come to this

---

[35] Bultmann's *Jesus* was published in 1926. For the present point, see *Jesus and the Word*, ET (1958 reprint), pp. 16–20.

[36] Ibid., pp. 133–40.   [37] Ibid., pp. 141, 146, 151.

[38] See, for example, *Primitive Christianity*, pp. 68f. The page numbers cited in the following text refer to the English translation.   [39] See *Jesus and the Word*, p. 51.

judgment, Bultmann proceeds to retract it, concluding that the ordinary Jew 'would not have felt [the commandments] to be a burden at all' (p. 66). The first statement, however, seems to convey Bultmann's true opinion of Jewish legalism.

The emphasis on observing complex and (to Bultmann) often unintelligible laws led to a perversion of the fundamental relation between God and man: 'man's relation to God was inevitably conceived in legalistic terms' (p. 68). Despite his earlier having written about 'unconditional obedience' in Judaism, Bultmann now concludes that 'radical obedience' (the hallmark of Jesus' call) was not possible in Judaism. 'The kind of obedience produced was formal rather than radical.' 'The Law failed to claim the allegiance of the *whole* man' (p. 68). It was possible for a man to fulfil the whole law but still not to feel wholly dedicated to God. Once the law was satisfied, 'a man was free to do what he liked. There was thus scope for works of supererogation, "good works" in the technical sense of the term.' Bultmann continues: 'These provided a basis for merit in the proper sense of the word. The accumulation of merits might serve to atone for breaches of the Law' (p. 69).

The legalistic conception of man's relation to God led to the view that at the judgment all of one's works would be counted and weighed, the verdict on a man's fate being determined by the balance of merits and demerits. As a result, 'the prospect of salvation became highly uncertain. Who could be sure he had done enough in this life to be saved?' (p. 70). An example is provided by the death-bed scene of R. Johanan ben Zakkai, who wept because he was uncertain of his fate. Thus coupled with uncertainty there developed an acute consciousness of sin and a 'morbid sense of guilt' (p. 70).

But Jewish legalism led not only to an unhealthy anxiety, but also to smug self-righteousness: 'It is a remarkable fact that side by side with this sense of sin and urge to repentance we find the "righteous" proud and self-conscious' (p. 71). From a passage in IV Ezra Bultmann concludes that even repentance was not a valid religious impulse; rather, it became simply another good work which could secure merit in God's sight. 'In the end the whole range of man's relation with God came to be thought of in terms of merit . . .' (p. 71).

At the beginning of this summary of Bultmann's view, we noted that Bultmann cited Moore alongside Bousset without noting that Moore contradicts Bousset at point after point. It is even more revealing of how Weber's view continued despite the objections of experts in Rabbinics to note Bultmann's treatment of Sjöberg's work, *Gott und die Sünder im palästinischen Judentum*.[40] We shall subsequently have occasion to deal

[40] Published in 1939.

with some of Sjöberg's principal views. It will suffice here to note that he consciously based his work on Moore's 'fundamental book', while hoping in some respects to correct and go beyond Moore.[41] Sjöberg also cited as works which viewed Rabbinic Judaism in the correct light those of such authors as Herford, Büchler, Marmorstein, Bonsirven and Montefiore.[42] He explicitly noted that the three works which were most in use by Christian theologians – those by Weber, Schürer and Bousset – although they contain much useful material, present 'kein richtiges Bild des Judentums'.[43] He was further of the view that this negative evaluation of those works was becoming increasingly widespread.[44]

When Bultmann writes that Judaism held a 'legalistic conception of divine retribution', he cites Sjöberg, pp. 21–5 and 95–109. In these pages Sjöberg does describe the Rabbinic view of God's justice. Sjöberg's view of Tannaitic religion, however, was that it was *principally characterized by the ability to maintain at the same time God's justice and his mercy*.[45] Thus p. 25, which concludes the section on the obligation to obey and punishment for disobedience, also contains the beginning of the section on God's *unmerited mercy* to Israel. Similarly, after the section on 'the punishment of sinful Israelites' (pp. 95–109), Sjöberg has a section on 'the goodness of God to sinful Israelites' (pp. 109–24). Bultmann has in fact cited only one half of Sjöberg's evidence on the question of legalism and strict retribution and has thus completely distorted Sjöberg's view.

An even more striking case is Bultmann's statement that 'repentance itself became a good work which secured merit and grace in the sight of God'. He continues that faith also came to be included in the overall scheme of merit.[46] He refers to Schlatter[47] and to Sjöberg, pp. 154–69. The section referred to in Sjöberg is entitled 'the tendencies toward the transformation of repentance into a meritorious achievement (*Leistung*) of man'. It may be that Bultmann was misled by the title of the section, for in it Sjöberg launches an attack on the view to that effect presented in Weber and Bousset and held, as he notes, as the common opinion of (Christian) theologians (p. 154). There may be a few traces of the view that repentance is a meritorious achievement in Rabbinic literature, but essentially it is not; and that description of it, writes Sjöberg, must be given up (p. 157; cf. pp. 168, 189). Bultmann cited Sjöberg, but simply ignored his position in favour of that of Weber and his teacher Bousset,[48] who are not, however, cited

---

[41] *Gott und die Sünder*, p. xxii.
[42] Ibid., p. xxii n. 1.
[43] Ibid.
[44] Ibid.
[45] Ibid., pp. 2–11; 184–90.
[46] *Primitive Christianity*, p. 71.
[47] The reference is to *Der Glaube im Neuen Testament*, ⁴1924, pp. 29–32.
[48] Bousset, *Die Religion des Judentums*⁴, pp. 389f.

on the point. We shall subsequently see that as recently as 1970 Thyen employed Sjöberg in the same way.

Although Bultmann did not cite Sjöberg on the question of works of supererogation and the treasury of merits, it is worth noting that Sjöberg seconded Moore's view that the phrase *zekut 'abot* (and related phrases) cannot be so construed and, in fact, added further evidence from Rabbinic literature.[49] Thus Bultmann had before him the works of two scholars, both of whom had the advantage of having examined the passages in the original sources, but he again paid them no heed. Weber's view is simply repeated.

We noted that Bultmann's short summary of Palestinian Judaism was important in ensuring the continuation of the Weber/Schürer/Bousset description of Judaism. It is important in quite a different way from Billerbeck's commentary. Present-day scholars do not cite Bultmann on Judaism, as they do Billerbeck, to support points. Bultmann is significant because he lent his enormous prestige to Bousset's work in particular and thus made it acceptable for New Testament scholarship to overlook, for example, Moore's evaluation of Bousset and the arguments of such scholars as Büchler and Schechter and, more important, *to use the opponents of Bousset as source books which provide the quotation of passages which are read in the light of Bousset's view.* To understand Bultmann's importance, one must try to imagine what would have been the case if he had accepted, as Sjöberg did, Moore as representing the Rabbis more faithfully than did Schürer and Bousset. One can readily imagine that we would not today see New Testament scholars complacently repeating Weber's view (now based on quotations from Billerbeck) as if it were the universally accepted picture of Rabbinic Judaism and as if it had never been countered by scholars more knowledgeable and more perceptive.

With the discovery of the Dead Sea Scrolls, New Testament scholars discovered a new use for Weber's picture of Judaism: it is now clearly specified that that picture applies to Rabbinic Judaism (or to Pharisaism, or to both undifferentiated), and Rabbinic Judaism is used as the foil over against which other forms of Judaism are described. Writers no longer (or at least only occasionally) mix quotations indiscriminately from the Apocrypha and Pseudepigrapha and Rabbinic literature, as did Bousset, to build a composite picture of 'the religion of Judaism'. Instead, Bousset's view, built primarily on the apocalypses, has been transferred back to apply only to Rabbinic religion, as Weber originally had it. The discovery of the Scrolls did not lead to a fundamental re-evaluation of Judaism, but to a differentiation of types within it. In this differentiation Rabbinic Judaism, without re-examination, continues to play the role of the kind of religion

[49] *Gott und die Sünder*, pp. 42–55.

which should be avoided. We shall consider five examples of this use of Rabbinic Judaism.

In his article on 'Tora-Verschärfung' in Judaism,[50] H. Braun compares the religion of Qumran with that of the Rabbis. In Rabbinic Judaism God *weighs* transgressions against fulfilments to determine a man's fate, while in Qumran he is lost (*verloren*) if he does not do *all*. Merely having the balance in one's favour is not enough. Braun's view of Rabbinic Judaism is more clearly worked out in the first volume of *Spätjüdisch-häretischer und früh-christlicher Radikalismus*.[51] Braun notes the passages in Aboth which oppose working for a reward (p. 6). Yet he concludes that in Rabbinic Judaism belief in retribution (*Vergeltungsglaube*) motivates behaviour. Good works are seen as overcoming a possible deficit and they are thus capable of being supererogatory (*überpflichtmässig*) (p. 6).

In posing the question of how man stands before God in Rabbinic Judaism, Braun sees only two possibilities: he is full of anxiety or confident of his achievement (p. 10). His conclusion on Rabbinic Judaism as a religion is that it is 'ein temperierter Werkoptimismus' (p. 13). The basis of this optimism is the lightness of the requirement. Rabbinic Judaism requires 'not the totality, but the majority of deeds'; he cites Aboth 3.15, which he takes to be doctrinal (p. 13; cf. pp. 27, 31). He repeats Bultmann's view that, since total obedience is not required, supererogation is possible (p. 33).

In 1960 Rössler published a study entitled *Gesetz und Geschichte* in which he purported to compare the relationship between history and law in apocalyptic literature and Rabbinic literature.[52] The book seems to have been influential,[53] although it has also been sharply criticized.[54] We shall summarize the main lines of Rössler's description of Rabbinic Judaism, leaving aside his particular (and ill-founded) theory on law and history.[55]

Only the abundance of fulfilments of commandments grounds righteousness and secures salvation for the pious (p. 20). What is necessary for salvation is revealed in the law (p. 18), and thus interpretation is required in order

---

[50] H. Braun, 'Beobachtungen zur Tora-Verschärfung im häretischen Spätjudentum', *TLZ* 79, 1954, cols. 347–52.

[51] Published in 1957.

[52] Second edition, 1962, to which page numbers refer.

[53] See Harnisch, *Verhängnis und Verheissung der Geschichte*, p. 12 n. 1. Kertelge ('*Rechtfertigung' bei Paulus*), while criticizing Rössler's overly schematic division of apocalyptic and Rabbinic literature (p. 34 n. 83), nevertheless accepts his general hypothesis (p. 43 n. 122). So also Roetzel, *Judgement in the Community*, p. 66 n. 1. Rössler's view was accepted by Wilckens, 'Die Bekehrung des Paulus', *Recht-fertigung als Freiheit*, p. 16. On the debate, see in addition to Harnisch, Wilckens, ibid., p. 20 n. 9; Koch, *Apocalyptic*, pp. 41, 85, 86–93.

[54] There is a point-by-point critique in A. Nissen, 'Tora und Geschichte im Spätjudentum', *NT* 9, 1967, pp. 241–77. Nissen does not note, however, that Rössler was apparently unable to use Rabbinic sources directly in his discussion of 'Pharisaic orthodoxy'. Cf. also Harnisch, *Verhängnis und Verheissung*, pp. 12f. There is a critique of Nissen in Koch, *Apocalyptic*, p. 87.

[55] On this see further Thyen, *Studien zur Sündenvergebung*, p. 55 n. 3; cf. p. 60. Rössler's sharp distinction of 'Pharisaism' from apocalyptic literature simply ignores the arguments of such scholars as W. D. Davies. See 'Apocalyptic and Pharisaism', *Christian Origins and Judaism*, pp. 19–30.

to know what is necessary for salvation (p. 19). Participation in the world to come is the particular *Heilsgut* which the pious man hopes to *earn* by his righteousness (p. 26). He has, however, no certainty of being able to do so. Thus Jacob was said to have feared despite the promise of God and even David was uncertain of his salvation (p. 27).[56]

The efficacy of the covenant is explicitly denied: the *promises* to the fathers are not eternally valid, and the only connection between the fathers and subsequent generations is the *thesaurus meritorum* (p. 28).

Rabbinic theology is dominated by the theory of keeping account of fulfilments and transgressions. The fulfilment of a commandment earns for the pious a merit, while every transgression constitutes a guilt. 'Participation in salvation is decided by settling the accounts.' 'One of the most significant consequences of this theory is that there is never a certainty of salvation (*Heilsgewissheit*) for the pious' (pp. 32f.).

As I indicated, Rössler's overall hypothesis has been criticized, and he · has also been criticized for using I Enoch, IV Ezra and II Baruch without differentiation as representing an entity called 'apocalypticism'.[57] Now we must also remark on his use of Rabbinic sources. Almost one-half of Rössler's work is devoted to establishing a theory about Rabbinic thought, yet he refers directly to Rabbinic sources, and especially to early Rabbinic sources, almost not at all. There are a few references to Genesis Rabbah and other late midrashim, and a few to secondary literature, but the vast majority of references are simply to Billerbeck, who is here taken to *be.* Rabbinic literature. Many of the references are to the section on soteriology which we analysed above. It is clear that Rössler does not consider himself to be doing new research in Rabbinic literature, only spelling out the consequences of what is universally known. And what is universally known is deposited in Billerbeck. There is no hint in Rössler that Billerbeck's view and selections are suspect.

In his work on the conception of salvation and sin in Qumran and the New Testament, which was published in 1964, Jürgen Becker includes a two-page summary of the 'theory of retribution of the Tannaim' (*Vergeltungslehre der Tannaiten*).[58] There are no specific references in the two pages, but the reader is referred at the beginning to several passages in Billerbeck (including the section on 'soteriology'), to Sjöberg's *Gott und die Sünder*, and to Mach's *Der Zaddik*. However, it is clearly the first which has been followed. Becker's scheme runs like this: the fundamental presupposition is that God loves only Israel and therefore has given them the Torah. This is a *Heilsgabe*, since thus Israel learns what God requires.

---

[56] Citing Genesis Rabbah 76 and Berakoth 4a. The first reference is inappropriate, since it refers only to this world, not to salvation.

[57] See, for example, Nissen. See n. 54 above.

[58] J. Becker, *Das Heil Gottes*, pp. 19–21.

Israel thus has the opportunity of gaining merit by fulfilling command-ments. The essence of human righteousness consists in 'meritorious obedience *vis à vis* the divine will'. The righteousness of God is not his gift, but a judgment of God on the situation of man (p. 19). At the judgment, 'the sum of the individual good deeds ... with their meritorious character will be compared with the group of transgressions of commandments with their guilt character. If the first are heavier by so much as one individual deed, then the man is צדיק and gains eternal life as a well-merited reward' (p. 20). God's mercy can be applied only within this scheme. God cannot by grace make the wicked man righteous, but can only reward the man already righteous more than he strictly merits (p. 21).

Becker's phrase 'by so much as one individual deed' is especially striking, since Sjöberg had explicitly denied that the theory of retribution was so mechanically applied.[59] This gives a clear indication of the degree to which Becker's thought was affected by anyone but Billerbeck.

In her extended treatment of the conception of the covenant in Judaism at the beginning of the Christian era, Jaubert deals only briefly with Rabbinic literature, citing the difficulty of establishing what is and is not before 70 c.e.[60] She settles on basing her discussion on Pirke Aboth, which she curiously characterizes as 'a tractate which collects sayings of ancient Rabbis, gathered in the Pharisaic schools from before the Christian era' (p. 289). Despite her intention to employ Aboth, however, I cannot tell that she has actually done so. She seems instead simply to repeat the common Christian view of Rabbinic Judaism as it would be applied to the conception of the covenant.

With regard to the grace of God in the election, she states that 'it would be unjust to say that the Synagogue abandoned the free and merciful aspect of the election of Israel', but it is nevertheless certain that it was no longer the covenant 'which embraced the law, but the law which was the reason for the covenant' (p. 291). She points especially to 'the entire stream of Pharisaic theology which was oriented towards the conception of the merits of the patriarchs, or even towards the merits of Israel which had chosen and accepted the law' (pp. 291f.). The Pharisaic view was that Israel had earned the *right* to the covenant (pp. 128–38).

Jaubert notes (p. 292 n. 160) that this description of the Pharisaic view is strongly disputed by Schoeps,[61] but his objection does not in any way influence her conclusion: the idea of the election in Pharisaism is tied to the merit earned by works (p. 294). Thus we see that the traditional line of Christian scholarship on this point continues unchecked in Jaubert's work, even though Schoeps had firmly shown that the supposed link of

---

[59] *Gott und die Sünder*, pp. 106–8.
[60] A. Jaubert, *La notion d'alliance dans le judaïsme*, pp. 289–92.
[61] In 'Haggadisches zur Auserwählung Israels', *Aus frühchristlicher Zeit*, pp. 184–200; cf. 201–11.

election with works is not anchored in the texts and that election depends on grace.

Under the general heading of works which compare Rabbinic religion with that of other Jewish groups, we may also consider Matthew Black's essay on the Pharisees in *The Interpreter's Dictionary of the Bible*.[62] Black's contrast is between the *early Pharisees* and the early *Rabbis* (the Tannaim). He assumes, however, that the later Pharisees (those of Jesus' time) had a religion like that of the Tannaim, so that the contrast is rather between early and late Pharisaism; but the latter is defined by Rabbinic literature. This late Pharisaic/Rabbinic religion, writes Black, was 'arid and sterile'.[63] 'It is a sterile religion of codified tradition, regulating every part of life by a halachah, observing strict *apartheid* . . .' Black does not repeat the general view of the soteriology of this sterile legalism, but the charge is clear: late Pharisaic/Rabbinic religion was marred by legalism.

To conclude this survey of the persistence of Weber's view, we now turn to consider its preservation in three general books of New Testament scholarship. This will by no means exhaust the list; and, as we deal with specific topics below, we shall give occasional instances of the adherence of contemporary New Testament scholars to various parts of Weber's systematic theology. Further, we are not attempting to cite here recent opponents of Weber's view. The intention is to show the persistence of the view that Rabbinic soteriology is dominated by the theory that salvation is earned by the merit of good works.

In the widely-circulated *The Book of the Acts of God*, Reginald Fuller wrote as follows concerning 'Pharisaism and Rabbinic Judaism':

The two great commandments, love of God and love of the neighbour, were of course part of the law, but even in combination they were not accorded that central and unifying position which they were given in the New Testament. All this naturally led to legalism and scrupulosity, to a belief in the saving value of good works, and the consequent sense of pride which a doctrine of merit inevitably entailed.[64]

Fuller denies that 'the rabbis completely abandoned the idea of sacred history' and even grants that 'they did not altogether ignore the crucial fact that the observance of the law was meant to be Israel's grateful response to the prior action of God'. Regrettably, he did not see that this last phrase

---

[62] Vol. 3, pp. 774–81, especially p. 781. Cf. J. Neusner, *The Rabbinic Traditions about the Pharisees Before 70* III, pp. 360–2.

[63] Cf. Sandmel ('Parallelomania', *JBL* 81, 1962, p. 9): Rabbinic Judaism in 'pseudo scholarship' is described 'as merely dry and arid legalism – it is never dry *or* arid, but always dry *and* arid'. Black has at least found a new turn of phrase. For the full offensiveness of this unscholarly and prejudicial way of describing Judaism, see Sandmel's comment on Black's article in *The First Christian Century*, pp. 101f.: 'I am personally a descendant of the Rabbinic religion, the sterility of which was not so complete as to prevent my being born. Black's article is not only unreliable, it is disgraceful that it should have appeared in the same dictionary to which I and some dozen other Jews contributed.'

[64] In G. E. Wright and R. Fuller, *The Book of the Acts of God*, 1960, pp. 229f.

would have been correct if he had changed 'did not altogether ignore' to 'emphasized above all'. Instead, he relegated doing the law as the response to grace to the status of a 'peripheral' belief.[65] Good works were primarily thought of as *earning* salvation.

Bultmann's description of 'Jewish legalism' in *Primitive Christianity* is repeated only slightly altered by H. Conzelmann in *An Outline of the Theology of the New Testament*.[66] For his purpose of giving a short account of 'Judaism' in the time of Jesus, Conzelmann returns to the practice of giving a composite picture based on the apocalypses and Rabbinic literature, although now some references to Qumran are added. The description does not change, however: 'The way to salvation is the fulfilment of the law' (p. 20). The law is primarily understood as a formal requirement 'and is therefore not comprehensible in itself' (p. 21). Conzelmann recognizes that the law is 'the sign of the election of Israel', but this does not govern the understanding of the law. Despite this, 'man's relationship with God is necessarily a legalistic one' (p. 21). It is possible to fulfil the demand of the law and 'for the moment' to 'have settled accounts with God'. Doing anything more results in the acquisition of merit. Thus law 'becomes a means by which a man can stand before God through his own efforts. This makes certainty of salvation impossible.' Men are conscious of sin and recognize the preponderance of transgressions. Sin is compensated for by good works. If these do not suffice to compensate, one can turn to the cult. Even the cult, however, 'is primarily directed towards the nation, and not towards the individual'.[67] One can only appeal for mercy (p. 22). Curiously, Conzelmann does not say whether or not Judaism considered such appeals to be effective. Conzelmann omits from Bultmann's description the theory that repentance itself becomes only another good work, but Conzelmann gives it no new interpretation.

That Weber's view is still alive and well (though Weber himself is no longer cited) can, finally, be seen in the recent work of Thyen on the forgiveness of sins:[68] Rabbinic soteriology consists of weighing merits and demerits (p. 72). Thyen makes extensive use of Sjöberg and, apparently following him, writes that the most distinctive characteristic of post-biblical (and especially Rabbinic) Judaism is the tension between recompensing righteousness and free grace. He does not struggle, however, as did Sjöberg, to keep the two in balance. He applies to 'the totality of this Judaism' H. Braun's verdict on the Psalms of Solomon:[69] the idea of mercy

---

[65] Ibid., p. 230.

[66] Quotations are from the ET of the second German edition of 1968.

[67] Thus Bousset's denial of sacraments in Judaism is continued.

[68] H. Thyen, *Studien zur Sündenvergebung im Neuen Testament und seinen alttestamentlichen und jüdischen Voraussetzungen*, 1970.

[69] To be considered below, pp. 394–7.

is perverted through the theory of merit and trivial group egotism. God's mercy is no more than a supplement to human achievement (*Leistung*) (pp. 76f.). This way of finding a simple formula to accommodate justice and mercy, by making 'mercy' the earned reward of righteousness, was explicitly rejected by Sjöberg.[70]

In a similar way, Thyen cites page numbers in Sjöberg on the question of the perversion of repentance into a human achievement, without noting that his statement diametrically opposes the carefully considered conclusion of Sjöberg. The passage is worth quoting at length, since it indicates the real grounds for the evaluation of Judaism: it is not Lutheranism:

Aber da wir, durch unser reformatorisches Erbe verpflichtet, wissen, wie sehr auch die geringste Spur von Verdienstgedanken und Synergismus die Idee der Gnade in ihrer Wurzel korrumpiert, nimmt es nicht wunder, wenn hier gelegentlich selbst die Umkehr in das kleinliche System der Verrechnung eingespannt und das Bekenntnis zur eigenen Schuld und Verderbtheit als verdienstlich angerechnet wird.... Vollends ist die Umkehr da, wo ihre Gültigkeit an bestimmte gute Werke als 'Bussleistungen' geknüpft wird, dem Vergeltungsdogma unterworfen.[71]

It is noteworthy that in Thyen's work, as in Rössler's, there are seldom references to Rabbinic passages, although a substantial section is given over to the discussion of Rabbinic literature. On the question of repentance as a good work, as we have just noted, he cites Sjöberg and Bousset. It is evident that Thyen has not reworked the question in the texts. What is most striking, however, is that he prefers, without any explanation and even without noting the opposition, Bousset's view to that of Sjöberg. This is so even though Sjöberg's discussion was explicitly directed against the view of Weber and Bousset and provides a thorough and conscientious canvassing of the material – something that is missing in Bousset. We see here that the Weber/Schürer/Bousset view of Rabbinic Judaism has become so widely accepted in influential New Testament circles that a writer need not even explain why he prefers it to an opposing point of view, but can simply cite Bousset *and* his opposition and agree with Bousset without even noting the disagreement.

Thus we see that the principal elements of Weber's view of Rabbinic soteriology have endured to the present day in New Testament scholarship, even though one would have thought that his view was long since discredited

---

[70] *Gott und die Sünder*, pp. 187f.

[71] 'But as the heritage of the Reformation obliges us to remember how much even the slightest trace of the notion of merit and synergism strikes at the very roots of the idea of grace, we cannot be surprised that from time to time even repentance is involved in a petty system of calculation, and the confession of a man's guilt and wickedness is counted as meritorious ... Repentance is completely subordinate to the doctrine of retribution where its validity is associated with particular good works as "signs of penitence".' Thyen, p. 75, citing Sjöberg, pp. 158ff., and Bousset, pp. 389ff. The view is refuted by Sjöberg, p. 168, cf. p. 189.

in all its aspects. The principal element is the theory that works *earn* salvation; that one's fate is determined by *weighing* fulfilments against transgressions. Maintaining this view necessarily involves *denying* or getting around in some other way *the grace of God in the election.* Weber's theory that there was a fall after the election of Israel has not been followed, but the general denial of the election as a *gracious, saving* event has been kept. Some would deny that the election rests on God's grace: it was earned (e.g. Jaubert). Others simply deny that the election was regarded as establishing salvation (e.g. Rössler: contact with history has been lost). As we shall subsequently see, Sjöberg was of the view that the election was effective to save Israel as such, but was not effective for individuals within Israel: it only guarantees the preservation of the chosen people.[72] A third aspect of Weber's view, which is also tied to the theory of salvation by works, is that of establishment of *merit* and the possibility of a *transfer of merit* at the final judgment. The fourth element has to do with the attitude supposedly reflected in Rabbinic literature: *uncertainty* of salvation mixed with the self-righteous feeling of accomplishment. This too depends on the view that a man is saved by works. He will either be uncertain that he has done enough or proud of having been so righteous. Besides these main elements of Weber's soteriology, his view that God was *inaccessible* has also been maintained to the present day. Our preceding survey has not always had this point in view, but we shall return to the topic in section 10 below.

When we say that Weber's view of Rabbinic Judaism as a religion of legalistic works-righteousness has persisted, we do not imply that all New Testament scholars hold such a view. Many doubtless do not; yet the view continues to flourish and to be propounded virtually without objection. It is necessary to consider further the present state of New Testament scholarship in this regard.

We should first observe that the descriptions of Rabbinic Judaism given by Bultmann, Braun, Rössler, Becker, Jaubert, Fuller, Black and Thyen are not simply eccentric examples. What is striking about all these works is that the authors feel no need to *defend* their view of Rabbinic Judaism or even to turn to the sources to verify it. This illustrates that there is a very large community of scholars – not only these authors, but also their reviewers and readers – which is prepared to accept this view of Rabbinic Judaism as *the standard* view. In some mysterious way Bousset has been accepted and Moore rejected, without anyone ever arguing the case. I do not pretend to have read all the reviews of all the books surveyed above, but I have not noted that any of these authors has been called to task for having accepted *without discussion or rationale* the Weber/Schürer/Billerbeck/Bousset depiction of Rabbinic Judaism rather than that of Schechter/Moore/Büchler and others.

[72] *Gott und die Sünder*, pp. 106–9, 118–24.

One important aspect of the present situation – and it must be faced squarely, if only to be dismissed – is the language barrier. Most of the proponents of the main elements of Weber's view have been Lutheran German scholars, while the best constructive accounts which differ from Weber's are in English.[73] Even Büchler, who to begin with wrote in German, moved to England and wrote his two best constructive analyses in English.[74] It is noteworthy that all of the major treatments of Judaism which Sjöberg listed as being reliable were either by Jews or in English, except one – Bonsirven's *Le judaïsme palestinien aux temps de Jésus Christ*.[75] Bonsirven repeated the view that merits and demerits are counted at the last judgment and determine God's verdict (*Judaïsme palestinien* II, p. 58), that there is a treasury of merits (pp. 57f.), and that the theory of judgment according to deeds led to anxiety on the one hand and to self-righteousness on the other (p. 62). He cited some mitigations of the theory of strict retribution, however (pp. 62–4), and he did not call this theory 'Rabbinic soteriology', but placed it within the discussion of the motivations for moral behaviour (see pp. 67–9). It is nevertheless the case that English-speaking New Testament scholars have often accepted Weber's view (so e.g. Charles and Fuller). More frequently, they have simply let it stand unchallenged, thus at least acquiescing. Even when they have not accepted it in all its main points, they have accepted some, as we shall see in the subsequent chapters. Thus in speaking of the continuation of Weber's view we are not describing an isolated phenomenon in Germany.[76]

A final aspect of the current situation which must be mentioned is the disappearance of the perception that the main constructions of Judaism which were made in the late nineteenth and early twentieth centuries were and are in sharp conflict. We may note especially Lohse's introduction to the latest edition of Bousset-Gressmann, an edition prepared to serve as a basic textbook on 'the religion of Judaism' in the series *Handbuch zum Neuen Testament*.[77] Bousset's intention, according to Lohse, was not simply to contrast Jewish and Christian piety. He wished to set Judaism in its context in the Hellenistic world and to show how Christianity took up the inherit-

[73] There is now a major constructive account of Rabbinic Judaism in Hebrew: E. E. Urbach, *Hazal* (*The Sages – Their Concepts and Beliefs*), 1969. The ET appeared too late to be used in this study, but page numbers have been added in parentheses.

[74] *Studies in Sin and Atonement* and *Types of Jewish-Palestinian Piety*.

[75] Sjöberg, *Gott und die Sünder*, p. xxiii: one should use above all Moore's fundamental work for the correct understanding of Judaism, then those of Herford, Bonsirven, Dietrich (on repentance, not a general account of Judaism), Büchler, Marmorstein, Abelson, Schechter, Montefiore, Friedlaender, Kohler and Baeck.

[76] On the continuation of the denigrating view of Judaism in English-speaking New Testament scholarship, see Lloyd Gaston's review of F. W. Danker, *Jesus and the New Age According to St Luke*, *JBL*, 94, 1975, pp. 140f. For an example of how the view appears in popular homiletical dress, see Sandmel's citation of Harry Emerson Fosdick (Jews neglected the weightier matters in favour of trivia) in 'The Need of Cooperative Study', p. 33.

[77] Citations are from the 4th ed. of 1966 of *Die Religion des Judentums*.

ance of Judaism. Gressmann's contribution was to pay greater attention to the Pharisaic-Rabbinic tradition. His reworking of Bousset did not result in a change of the overall theme; but by incorporating a quantity of material which had been carefully worked through, he improved the book so that it won its place as a 'standard work' (pp. v–vi). Subsequent works have *supplemented* and *taken further* the accomplishment of Bousset-Gressmann. Of primary importance is Billerbeck's commentary. G. F. Moore, in his 'distinguished work on Judaism in the first Christian centuries', which was based on the sayings of the Tannaim, established many connections between Judaism and Christianity (p. vi). Three pages later Moore is again cited as the author of one of the works which 'supplements' Bousset-Gressmann (p. ix). One can only conclude that Lohse did not understand Moore's intention or his book at all. Moore did not attempt to establish connections between Judaism and Christianity, but to present a composite and constructive view of Judaism in its own terms. Further, his work was directly antithetical to that of Bousset. To describe it as a 'supplement' is to mislead the reader into thinking that Bousset's work has been accepted by experts in Rabbinics as being basically along the right lines, needing only further citations, and erroneously to suggest that the path of *Wissenschaft* is flowing smoothly – from Bousset's description of Judaism in the Hellenistic world on the basis of the Apocrypha and Pseudepigrapha, through the additional working out of Bousset's view in the Rabbinic sources by Gressmann and Billerbeck, to Moore's establishment of that same view on the basis of Tannaitic sayings and the comparison of *the one standard view* of Judaism with Christianity. No history of scholarship could be further from the truth. If there is knowledge of this world after death, Moore is turning over in his grave.[78]

Even when there is a perception that there is a serious dispute about the basic nature of Rabbinic Judaism, scholars are frequently unable to resolve the dispute except by compromise: both views must be partly right. One may see this, for example, in Longenecker's *Paul, Apostle of Liberty*. Longenecker first cites 'expressions that reveal a purely commercial view of righteousness' (p. 67). Here he is simply repeating the dominant view of Pharisaic Judaism as a religion of legalistic works-righteousness. He is aware of another view, however, and subsequently states that 'in all fairness it must be noted that the Judaism of the predestruction period was not all externalism' (p. 70). There is 'evidence from several sources of a realization in predestruction Judaism that one must start from the mercy and love of God' (p. 71). He thus notes the two elements – justice and mercy – which

---

[78] For another example of the loss of the perception that Moore's view was antithetical to Bousset's, see M. Simon and A. Benoit, *Le Judaïsme et le Christianisme antique*, pp. 24f., where Bousset's work is characterized as 'fundamental' and Moore's as 'important'. If Bousset's book is actually fundamental, Moore's can be only a sustained but unsuccessful attempt to refute it.

Sjöberg dealt with extensively and which Thyen noted. Longenecker, however, unlike Thyen, inclines more to the side of leniency. He argues that both types must have existed within Pharisaism, some who were governed by the legalistic view ('acting legalism') and some by a nobler view ('reacting nomism') (p. 78). Both tendencies existed, and Longenecker views legalism as being just as bad as it is usually thought to be (p. 79). There was also the nobler 'reacting nomism', however, a 'truly spiritual and noble' religion (p. 82), which existed alongside the legalistic Judaism so often described (p. 84). It may be seen especially in Qumran, but it must have characterized some Pharisees as well (pp. 80–3).

One does not have the impression that Longenecker has won through to a new view of Judaism on the basis of a detailed and fresh study of the sources. He accepts the Weber/Bousset/Billerbeck view as being accurate for what it covers, only observing that there is evidence of a better form of Judaism. Here, as we indicated, the debate over which view of Judaism is correct is simply compromised. Weber's view is confirmed, but set within limits: it does not cover all of Judaism, nor even all of Pharisaism.

One of the most remarkable things about Weber's view is how it has endured so many alterations in what it refers to. It often refers simply to Palestinian Judaism in the time of Jesus, and it is established by references both to intertestamental and to Rabbinic literature (so, for example, Bousset, Bultmann and Conzelmann). It may refer to one form of Palestinian Judaism in contrast to other forms, such as apocalypticism (Rössler) or Qumranism (Braun, Becker). In this last case, the group to which Weber's description applies may be called the Pharisees (Rössler) or the Tannaites (Becker), but in any case the description depends on Rabbinic literature as presented by Billerbeck. Legalistic Judaism may even be restricted in terms of time: it represents the later deterioration of early Pharisaism (Black).

The supposed legalistic Judaism of scholars from Weber to Thyen (and doubtless later) serves a very obvious function. It acts as the foil against which superior forms of religion are described. It permits, as Neusner has said, the writing of theology as if it were history.[79] One must note in particular the projection on to Judaism of the view which Protestants find most objectionable in Roman Catholicism: the existence of a treasury of merits established by works of supererogation.[80] We have here the retrojection of the Protestant-Catholic debate into ancient history, with Judaism taking the role of Catholicism and Christianity the role of Lutheranism.

The great usefulness of Weber's legalistic Judaism and the temptation to retroject more recent arguments into the New Testament period do not, however, completely account for the persistence of Weber's view. *It persists*

---

[79] *Rabbinic Traditions* III, pp. 359–63.
[80] So also Moore, 'Christian Writers', p. 231.

because it appears to rest on solid evidence. The view that weighing fulfilments
and transgressions constitutes Rabbinic (or Pharisaic or Jewish) soteriology
can apparently be supported by actual texts concerning weighing. In
support of the doctrine of a treasury of merits which can (or cannot) be
transferred at the judgment, it is possible to cite passages containing the
phrase *zekut 'abot,* 'merit of the fathers'. And so it goes on. As we noted
above, Billerbeck's work, with its thousands of quotations and citations,
appears to provide hard proof that *someone* held the view which Billerbeck
himself called 'Pharisaic soteriology'. Quibbling over terms (he should have
said Rabbinic) and dates (the material is mostly after 70 c.e.) does not
really help.[81] The view is there in Billerbeck (=Rabbinic literature);
it was held by the Rabbis of some period or other; they did not make it up
de novo; therefore it may be safely applied to some group or other of Jews
around the time of Jesus, give or take a few decades.

Nor is it responsive to the situation of New Testament scholarship to
dismiss the view of Judaism which we have been describing as resting on
'pseudo scholarship'[82] or as being 'beneath criticism'.[83] Such opinions are
accurate and the attitude is understandable, but they will in no way deflect
the continuation of the view in New Testament criticism, since they do not
refute the evidence on which the dominant Christian assessment of Rabbinic
Judaism rests. The perception of New Testament scholars who hold some
variant of Weber's view is that they hold the only view of Rabbinic Judaism
which is permitted by the evidence before them, and they regard their
position as well-founded, frequently tested and widely consented to. As we
saw in discussing Lohse's foreword to the current edition of Bousset, the
view is that Bousset's view has been steadily confirmed and further elaborated, and even Moore can be worked into that picture. Since the Weber/
Bousset/Billerbeck view can now be cited without opposition, Lohse's view
of the situation seems to be widespread. Their view is perceived to rest on
solid evidence, and this perception will not be altered by sarcasm, however
justified.

The early 'apologists' for Judaism, who were critical of the theological
construction which lies behind Billerbeck's *Kommentar,* stated that it was
not right and provided different constructions, but they did not directly
refute the construction on its own terms or in a polemical way. Moore hid
his polemics in an article and wrote his three-volume work with virtually no

---

[81] Neusner's criticism that the dominant Christian view of Pharisaism does not rest on evidence about
Pharisaism (*Rabbinic Traditions* III, pp. 361, 363) is correct, but it will not arrest the view. The scholars
do have in mind certain Rabbinic passages, and Weber's description of legalistic Judaism can readily
be switched from the Pharisees to their presumed successors, the Rabbis.

[82] Sandmel, above, n. 63. Sandmel elsewhere and more usually recognizes, however, the need 'not
to retort in pique, but rather to set the record straight in terms of responsible and tenable scholarship'
(*The First Christian Century,* p. 4; cf. n. 17 above).

[83] Neusner, *Rabbinic Traditions* III, p. 359.

reference to the view which he opposed. His own construction is presented, but Bousset's is not argued against. He thus, in a way, permitted his work to be used as a source book which can be read in the light of Bousset. The impact of his work would have been greater had his article on 'Christian Writers on Judaism' been attached to the book. Then New Testament scholars would at least have known that he opposed Bousset.

Thus the general Christian view of Judaism, or of some part of it, as a religion of legalistic works-righteousness goes on, unhindered by the fact that it has been sharply – one would have thought, devastatingly – criticized by scholars who have known the material far better than any of its proponents. One of the intentions of the present chapter, to put the matter clearly, is to destroy that view. This will be accomplished, it is hoped, not by an appeal to greater charitableness toward Judaism nor by simply bringing forward other passages than those on which Weber's view was based and claiming that they provide a truer account of Rabbinic Judaism, but by showing that the Weber/Bousset/Billerbeck view, as it applies to Tannaitic literature, is based on a massive perversion and misunderstanding of the material. Before we proceed, however, we must establish how the material will be used and what it will be taken to apply to.

2. The use of Rabbinic material[1]

The preceding discussion will have made it clear that the same material which has been used to support the Weber/Billerbeck/Bousset view of Rabbinic (or Jewish or Pharisaic) religion needs to be reassessed. This in part determines the material which will be employed. There are, however, other and more compelling factors which would determine our use of the Tannaitic literature even if there were no apologetic need to deal eclectically with a large body of Rabbinic material. It will be simplest if we first summarize the way in which the material will be used and then deal with individual points and possible objections in more detail.

The material employed is that which is traditionally considered Tannaitic, that is, coming from the period between the fall of Jerusalem (70 c.e.) and the compilation of the Mishnah by R. Judah ha-Nasi (ca. 200 c.e.). Of primary importance are the works which are predominantly Tannaitic: the Mishnah, the Tosefta and the Tannaitic or halakic midrashim (the Mekilta on Exodus, Sifra on Leviticus and Sifre on Numbers and Deuteronomy; the supposed Tannaitic midrashim which have been reconstructed out of later sources have been used with caution. These are the Mekilta of R. Simeon b. Yohai to Exodus, Sifre Zuṭa to Numbers and the Midrash Tan-

---

[1] For texts, translations and the system of reference, see the bibliography.

naim to Deuteronomy.) I have also made some use of traditions which are attributed to Tannaim in the two Talmuds and the later midrashim, such as Midrash Rabbah.

In using the material, I assume that it provides an accurate presentation of Rabbinic discussions during the 130-year period mentioned above, and especially (as we shall see below) during the last two-thirds of the second century c.e. I do not suppose that it provides an accurate picture of Judaism or even of Pharisaism in the time of Jesus and Paul, although it would be surprising if there were no connection.

Perhaps most controversial is using the material eclectically, rather than focusing on the sayings of one Rabbi or a small group which can be named and specified as to time and place. The justification for this procedure will be given below. We should now discuss some of the principal points in more detail.

Pharisees and Rabbis

As we saw in our discussion of the continuation of Weber's view in New Testament scholarship, there is a long tradition of citing Rabbinic passages as evidence for Pharisaism.[2] The view rests on the supposition that the Rabbis continued Pharisaic traditions. To take two examples, Billerbeck, while citing Rabbinic passages, considers himself to be discussing 'Pharisaic soteriology', and Rössler calls his section which depends primarily on Rabbinic passages from Billerbeck a treatment of 'Pharisaic orthodoxy'.[3] The equation of Pharisees and Rabbis is by no means unique to Christian scholars, however, but has also been made by many prominent Jewish scholars. Thus in 1935 Belkin noted with approval Thackeray's view that Tannaitic literature represents the views of the Pharisees.[4] Similarly, Zeitlin is fairly sanguine about the possibility of establishing Pharisaic views from Rabbinic material. In his discussion, he clearly has primarily in mind many anonymous halakot which appear to have passed into law before the fall of the Temple.[5] Finally, Finkelstein has repeatedly argued for the great antiquity not only of the Pharisaic party, but also of substantial portions of Rabbinic literature. It is clear that he, too, is of the view that Rabbinic

---

[2] The usual view is that one speaks of Pharisaism up until 70 c.e. With the demise of the parties consequent upon the destruction of Jerusalem, the name becomes inappropriate. Those who reconstituted Judaism at Jamnia and their successors are Rabbis (if ordained, as most of the leaders were). It is noteworthy that sages from before 70 c.e. are not called 'Rabbi' in Rabbinic literature; thus 'Hillel' rather than 'R. Hillel'.

For a brief summary of theories on the origins and nature of the Pharisees, see Wolfgang Beilner, 'Der Ursprung des Pharisäismus', *BZ* 3, 1959, pp. 235–51.

[3] See section 1 above.

[4] Belkin, 'The Problem of Paul's Background', *JBL* 54, 1935, p. 41, referring to Thackeray's *The Relation of St Paul to Contemporary Jewish Thought*.

[5] S. Zeitlin, *The Rise and Fall of the Judaean State* II, pp. 344–6.

literature, including some anonymous halakot, can, if examined with care, be used to establish the main lines of Pharisaism.[6]

Recently many scholars have shown themselves sceptical about the possibility of simply establishing Pharisaism on the basis of Rabbinic literature. Some of the scepticism springs from a perception of how difficult it is to date Rabbinic materials. Thus Maier, in his study of free will and predestination, turns to the Psalms of Solomon for his discussion of the Pharisaic view, citing the problems involved in dating Rabbinic material as grounds for ignoring it.[7] As we saw above, Jaubert refrains from more than a cursory discussion of Rabbinic material in her study of the covenant, since she wished to deal only with sources from before 70 c.e.[8] Similarly, Buchanan has shown himself to be dubious – one may say overly sceptical[9] – about the connection between Pharisaism and Rabbinism.[10] His mention of the 'anti-Pharisaic' passages in Rabbinic literature as reason for caution[11] is not well founded, however; these passages (which he does not cite) seem to refer not to the great historical party of the Pharisees, but to overly-ascetic groups known to the later Rabbis.[12] They date from a period after the party names had lost their significance.

Very recently, two scholars have attempted, from different points of view, to determine what can be surely known about the Pharisees based on Rabbinic evidence. On the basis of an examination of every mention of *perushim* in the Tannaitic literature, Rivkin has attempted to re-define the Pharisees.[13] They are not to be connected with the *haberim* as is traditionally done; individual Pharisees may or may not have been *haberim*, and vice versa, but there is no definite equation of the two.[14] Rather, the Pharisees were 'that scholar class that created the concept of the twofold Law, carried it to triumphant victory over the Sadducees, and made it operative in society'.[15]

---

[6] See Finkelstein's *The Pharisees* and the discussion of his view of the date of the material in the next sub-section.

[7] G. Maier, *Mensch und freier Wille*, p. 23.

[8] Jaubert, *La notion d'alliance*, p. 289.

[9] Cf. Neusner, *Rabbinic Traditions* III, pp. 356f.

[10] G. W. Buchanan, *The Consequences of the Covenant*, pp. 259–67.

[11] Ibid., p. 261.

[12] Cf. E. Rivkin, 'Defining the Pharisees: the Tannaitic Sources', *HUCA* 40–41, 1969–70, pp. 234–8. Rivkin notes that *perushim* in T. Sotah 15.11f. // Baba Bathra 60b; Pesahim 70b; and T. Berakoth 3.25 means 'heretics', not 'Pharisees'. It would seem that *perushim* in the main 'anti-Pharisaic' text, Sotah 22b, should also not be translated 'Pharisees'; see Rivkin, pp. 240f. One may further observe the *date* of the groups referred to: after the destruction of the Temple in T. Sotah 15.11; contemporary with Rab Ashi in Pesahim 70b (352–427 c.e.; see the *JE*, s.v. Ashi). In T. Berakoth 3.25 the *perushim* are identical with the *minim* (heretics) who are cursed (euphemistically, 'blessed') in the *birkat ha-minim*, which dates from after the destruction of the Temple. The discussion of the seven types of *perushim*, all bad, in Sotah 22b is attached to a phrase in the Mishnah (Sotah 3.4) which is attributed to R. Joshua. In no case is there any reason to suppose that any of these anti-*perushim* passages refers to a group which existed before 70 c.e. On the need for caution in identifying the *perushim* of Rabbinic literature with the Pharisees, see further J. Bowker, *Jesus and the Pharisees*, pp. 1–37.

[13] In the essay cited in the preceding note and in other essays referred to there.

[14] 'Defining the Pharisees', pp. 445f.   [15] Ibid., p. 248.

Jacob Neusner, on the basis of his study of all the references in early Rabbinic literature to a group (such as the House of Hillel) or an individual presumed to be Pharisaic, has arrived at a different definition of the concerns of Pharisaism. The Rabbinic material about the Pharisees, according to Neusner, relates mostly to the internal life of the party,[16] to such matters as purity and dietary regulations especially. 'Of the 341 individual pericopae alluded to above, no fewer than 229 directly or indirectly pertain to table-fellowship.'[17] When he contrasts this depiction of Pharisaism with that of Josephus, in which the Pharisees play an active part in the governance of the country, he concludes that a change took place in the character of Pharisaism, a change 'from a political party to a sect'.[18] He views Hillel as having been 'responsible for directing the party out of its political concerns and into more passive, quietistic paths'.[19] It is evident that Neusner's picture of the Pharisees is almost diametrically opposite that of Rivkin, who finds in the Tannaitic material evidence that the Pharisees (including the post-Hillel Pharisees)[20] were interested in establishing their view in society and were not interested in purity laws for their own sake, although they did rule on what was appropriate for one who considered himself a *ḥaber*.[21]

We have given this brief summary in order to indicate how complicated the question of the relationship between the Pharisees and the Rabbis is.[22] The question of who the Pharisees were and of how they saw themselves *vis à vis* the rest of Judaism appears quite wide open. One must welcome the attempts of Rivkin and Neusner to pursue the question *de novo* and to try to establish rigorous academic standards for answering it. What should be emphasized here is that it is not our intention to discuss 'the religion of the Pharisees', or that of any other party or sect *qua* party or sect. Our discussion focuses on bodies of literature, not on parties or sects which must be reconstructed from disparate sources. It is supposed here that a discussion of Tannaitic literature will be informative for the religion of the Tannaim. How that may relate to the Pharisees or to common Jewish piety before 70 c.e. is another question, one which will occupy us in the conclusion to Part I. This does not imply, however, that we are not at all concerned with questions of dating. We may now turn to some general observations on the date of the material traditionally ascribed to the Tannaim.

---

[16] *Rabbinic Traditions* III, p. 287; cf. p. 290.
[17] Ibid., p. 297.
[18] Ibid., p. 305.
[19] Ibid.
[20] Rivkin, 'Defining the Pharisees', p. 232.
[21] Ibid., pp. 233, 245.
[22] See further Neusner, *Eliezer Ben Hyrcanus* II, pp. 295, 298–307: Rabbinism was composed of various groups, of which Pharisaism was one. Neusner gives a popular presentation of his view of the Pharisees and the Rabbis in *From Politics to Piety*, 1973, and a short summary in the introduction to *Understanding Rabbinic Judaism*, 1974.

Date and authenticity

With regard to the date and reliability of attributions, I make two large assumptions. In the first place, following Epstein, I assume that most of the anonymous material of the halakic midrashim stems from the period between R. Akiba and R. Ishmael (both apparently died around the time of the Bar Cochba revolt, or at the end of the first third of the second century c.e.) and R. Judah ha-Nasi (ca. 200 c.e.; he is usually called simply 'Rabbi').[23] In the second place, following Neusner, I assume that attributions to named Rabbis of the Jamnian period or later (from 70 c.e. on) are, by and large, reliable. In his *Rabbinic Traditions* (vol. III, p. 3), Neusner gives two rules of thumb with regard to traditions attributed to named Rabbis: he 'takes seriously' attributions to post-70 Rabbis and regards 'post-140 attributions as absolutely reliable'. In his more recent work on *Eliezer Ben Hyrcanus* there is further refinement: material which occurs in works which are on the whole early is more reliable than material which first appears in the Talmuds and later midrashim, the general order of reliability being (1) Mishnah-Tosefta, (2) Tannaitic midrashim, (3) baraitot in the Palestinian Talmud, (4) baraitot in the Babylonian Talmud, (5) traditions in later midrashim (cf. vol. II, p. 226); discussion of a saying by a slightly later Rabbi helps prove the authenticity of the substance of a saying (II, pp. 92–4), as does a chain of tradition (II, p. 87); materials attributed to a Rabbi which cohere with other material attributed to the same Rabbi but differently transmitted are likely to be genuine; and the like.[24] It has long been known that not all attributions are reliable, since sometimes the same material is differently attributed. As long, however, as we confine ourselves generally to the Tannaitic literature, some of the uncertainties of attribution are relatively unimportant, since we shall only seldom have occasion to pursue the question of what a particular Rabbi thought (see the next sub-section on the 'eclectic' use of the material). Our principal concern will be to deal with material from the Tannaitic period, and for convenience attributions will be considered as generally reliable. For the rest of the material, such as the anonymous material in such old tractates as Tamid, I intend always to follow Epstein's dating.[25] It will thus occasionally be possible to give a history of a certain conception, extending from before 70 c.e. to Rabbi (R. Judah ha-Nasi).

At this point we should clarify one aspect of Neusner's view. When he argues that there are relatively few Rabbinic traditions *about the Pharisees*

---

[23] J. N. Epstein, *Mebo'ot le-Sifrut ha-Tannaim*, p. 521; see further below, pp. 68f. and nn. 56–60. Epstein points out, however, that some of the traditions in the Tannaitic midrashim are earlier, going back to the period before 70: ibid., pp. 512f.

[24] See further *Eliezer* I, pp. 1–3. These principles are applicable to material attributed to named Rabbis. Neusner is now beginning the study of the anonymous laws concerning purity, but these volumes began appearing as the present work was being concluded and could not be taken fully into account.

[25] See Epstein, *Mebo'ot*, pp. 25–58.

which stem from before 70 c.e.,[26] he is not arguing that there is no other material from before 70 to be found in Rabbinic sources.[27] He seems not to question Epstein's view that a considerable body of several tractates in the Mishnah comes from before 70. He doubts only that such material is distinctively Pharisaic. Thus he asks how we should account for 'those Mishnaic laws which probably come from the period before 70, but deal with areas of public life not then subject to Pharisaic control'.[28] Much of this material has to do with the Temple and its cult, and from it we can learn a great deal about the understanding of atonement, an important element in our inquiry. Its presence in Rabbi's Mishnah seems to indicate that the Rabbis accepted such material as authoritative, but I should agree that it may not reveal a distinctively Pharisaic view.

In comparison with the position on the dating of the material taken here, there are two extreme views: that the material is much older and that it is much later. One of the major proponents of the former approach has been Louis Finkelstein, whose view we may briefly consider.

In his 1938 work on the Pharisees, Finkelstein put his opinion thus:

Much of the Mishnah was apparently formulated during the Persian and Hellenistic ages, but the controversies between Sadducism and Pharisaism had developed far earlier, in the later generations of the First Commonwealth, or even before.[29]

Finkelstein's subsequent publications have pursued the same theme, and he has recently argued for an even earlier dating of some of the material.[30] It is not our purpose here to evaluate Finkelstein's position. One may, however, wonder about his use of evidence when he cites as 'documentary evidence' for the pre-exilic origin of the Synagogue service a statement to that effect from Sifre Deut. 343 (Finkelstein's edition, p. 395): an early version of the 'amidah was composed by 'the early prophets'.[31] This attribution of historical accuracy to a Tannaitic midrash[32] does not seem to be the correct way to decide questions concerning the period before Ezra. It cannot, on the other hand, be doubted that Finkelstein and others have succeeded in showing the existence of some early traditions[33] and in finding instances of early halakot which are in agreement with later Rabbinic halakot.[34] I am not

---

[26] *Rabbinic Traditions*, passim.   [27] *Rabbinic Traditions* III, pp. 301f.

[28] J. Neusner, *The Modern Study of the Mishnah*, p. xv.

[29] Finkelstein, *The Pharisees* I, p. lxv.

[30] Finkelstein, *New Light from the Prophets*, 1969. Finkelstein argues, among other things, that some portions of Sifre Deut. are from the exilic or pre-exilic period and that the Mekilta's discussion of the Ten Commandments is pre-exilic.

[31] Finkelstein, *Pharisaism in the Making*, p. vi.

[32] Finkelstein, to be sure, considers the midrashic statement itself to be exilic; *New Light from the Prophets*, pp. 37–41.

[33] See, for example, the discussion of Sanhedrin 10.1 below, the beginning of section 7.

[34] Cf. L. I. Rabinowitz, 'The Halakah as reflected in Ben-Sira', p. 264: 'Although in general the legal pattern [in Ben Sirach] is that of the Written Law, here and there signs of the *halakah* belonging to the Oral Law can be detected.'

persuaded by Finkelstein's overall hypothesis as to the early date of the material and the party disputes. His view, if correct, however, would be no impediment to our present study. We need only maintain that the Tannaitic material represents the attitude of the Tannaim, regardless of whether or not some of it may have originated long before them.

Much more serious for our use of the material is the view of Wacholder. He has argued that the Mekilta of R. Ishmael is to be dated in the eighth century c.e., after the conclusion of the Babylonian Talmud.[35] He also seems to regard the other halakic midrashim as being post-Tannaitic.[36] How sharp the controversy is with regard to the question of the date and reliability of Rabbinic material can be seen from an exchange between Wacholder and Morton Smith which was occasioned by Wacholder's review of Neusner's *Development of a Legend*, an analysis of the traditions concerning R. Johanan b. Zakkai. In his review, Wacholder wrote:

This book suggests that the science of Talmudics has a long distance to go before it reaches the present state of NT scholarship. There is an urgent need for basic chronological, historical, and literary studies of early rabbinic literature before ambitious monographs such as Neusner's could be productive.[37]

Wacholder especially referred to Neusner's failure to recognize late features in the halakic midrashim.[38] Morton Smith replied to the review, suggesting, among other things, that Wacholder's late dating of the midrashim is idiosyncratic.[39] In the same number, Wacholder responded. He cites in favour of a late date for the halakic midrashim the view of E. Z. Melamed:

E. Z. Melamed, Epstein's disciple and the editor of his master's *Introduction*, in an exhaustive study of his own, concludes that the earliest compilation of the halakic midrashim (he too avoids labelling them 'Tannaitic') took place two generations after Rabbi Judah Hanasi, long after the Mishnah and the Tosephta had become authoritative rabbinic works.[40]

Yet it must be noted that Melamed is not of the view that the halakic midrashim were *composed* two generations after Rabbi; that simply indicates the date of the final redaction. He generally accepts Epstein's position on the composition of the halakic midrashim, both as to the Tannaitic date of the main composition and as to the distinction between the schools of R. Akiba and R. Ishmael.[41] Melamed's position is worth a slightly fuller description.

---

[35] B. Z. Wacholder, 'The Date of the Mekilta de-Rabbi Ishmael', *HUCA* 39, 1968, pp. 117–44.

[36] See 'A Reply', *JBL* 92, 1973, pp. 114f.

[37] *JBL* 91, 1972, p. 124.   [38] Ibid., pp. 123f.

[39] 'On the Problem of Method in the Study of Rabbinic Literature', *JBL* 92, 1973, pp. 112f.

[40] 'A Reply', *JBL* 92, 1973, p. 114. The reference is to E. Z. Melamed, *The Relationship between the Halakhic Midrashim and the Mishna and Tosefta* (in Hebrew), 1967.

[41] Wacholder (*JBL* 91, 1972, p. 124) regards the view that the schools of R. Akiba and R. Ishmael are 'now traceable in the halakic midrashim' to be 'unacceptable'. For Melamed's view, see *Relationship*, p. 105: Epstein has previously proved that the tractates of the Mekilta of R. Ishmael were redacted in different branches of the school of R. Ishmael and that one editor was not responsible for all of them.

The basic method is to note passages in the midrashim which are identifiable as quotations and to determine whether or not they derive from the Mishnah or the Tosefta as known to us or from some variant tradition. We may take two examples. The first category cited by Melamed in his analysis of Sifra is the group of passages beginning 'hence they said'. The phrase is used in the Mishnah usually to refer to an earlier mishnah collection (occasionally to itself), but in Sifra it usually refers to a passage from the Mishnah or Tosefta as we have them.[42] Thus Sifra Nedabah parasha 9.9 begins 'Hence [i.e. on the basis of Lev. 2.2, the passage under discussion] they said: If two Meal-offerings from which the Handful had not been taken were mixed together, but the Handful can still be taken from each by itself, they remain valid; otherwise they become invalid.'[43] Mishnah Menahoth 3.3 has the very same sentence, lacking the introductory 'hence they said'. Thus it is clear that the passage in Sifra quotes the Mishnah. There are other instances in which the wording of Sifra differs from that of the Mishnah, however, although the phrase 'hence they said' introduces a halakah which is similar to one in the Mishnah. In these cases, Melamed comments that it is difficult to determine whether the Tanna of Sifra rephrased the wording of the Mishnah, or whether the Mishnah as we have it has had another text incorporated after the principal redaction.[44] Sifra is not regarded as necessarily secondary to the Mishnah.

The second example given here is more complex and shows Melamed's view more clearly. The texts being compared are Sifra Nedabah parasha 8.7 and Menahoth 12.5. The passage in Sifra opens with an anonymous opinion that an individual *may* bring oil as a free-will offering. It then quotes virtually verbatim from the Mishnah a debate between R. Akiba and R. Tarfon on that point, with R. Akiba taking the position that free-will offerings of wine but *not* of oil may be made. Melamed comments that the anonymous (*stam*) author of Sifra, *R. Judah* (ben Ilai, a student of R. Akiba and predecessor of Rabbi), cited the words of R. Tarfon anonymously (*stam*), but the later editor of Sifra introduced the debate between Rabbi Tarfon and R. Akiba from the Mishnah, citing the Rabbis by name.[45]

It is noteworthy that in this example (and the many others given by Melamed) the later editor did not introduce *post-Tannaitic* material into Sifra; he simply added Tannaitic material to the other Tannaitic material already before him. The result is that what appears to have been the Sifra's original position on oil as a free-will offering (R. Judah anonymously quoting R. Tarfon) is modified by introducing the contrary view of R. Akiba from the Mishnah. This certainly supports Melamed's argument that the final redaction of Sifra was made after the Mishnah became authoritative, but it in no way denies the general Tannaitic character of Sifra or its basic composition by one of the leading Tannaim, R. Judah.

The overall impression of Melamed's work given by Wacholder seems not to be correct. Melamed did not, as Wacholder asserts, argue that 'the earliest compilation' of the halakic midrashim is to be dated two generations after Rabbi;[46] Melamed speaks rather of the 'final redaction'.[47] Further, it is clear that Melamed's work will not support Wacholder's implication that the material of the midrashim is post-Tannaitic. The post-Tannaitic redactors' work seems to have consisted largely in quoting the Mishnah and the Tosefta (and other Tannaitic collections now lost)[48] in appropriate places, and Wacholder grants that the Mishnah and Tosefta are largely Tannaitic. Further, Melamed argued that the differences between parallel passages in the halakic midrashim on the one hand and the Mishnah and Tosefta on the other sometimes show that the Mishnah as we have it contains additions unknown to the final redactor(s) of the midrashim. He further suggests that it may be possible to complete some defective passages in the Mishnah on the basis of Sifra.[49]

Wacholder's longer article on the date of the Mekilta[50] cannot be evaluated here in detail. It is beyond doubt that he has noted at least some discrepancies and additions of late date. The evidence does not seem, however, to compel dating the entire midrash late. One may note that some of the evidence for a late date in the Mekilta can be paralleled even in the Mishnah. Wacholder cites the appearance in the Mekilta of 'controversies' between Rabbis who were not actually contemporaries.[51] In Kelim 27.12 one sees the same sort of anachronistic 'debate', in which the disputants are R. Eliezer and R. Simeon (b. Yohai), who were not contemporaries. Bokser explains the anomaly thus: 'At a later date, R. Simeon, in reviewing the older law, expressed dissent. The compiler of the Mishnah put these views in juxtaposition.'[52] This case is not so extreme as those cited by Wacholder in the Mekilta, but the latter can still be seen as the work of a clumsy later compiler, rather than as proving that the traditions themselves are late and that the names and debates are fictional contrivances. The general consensus of Rabbinic scholars on the date of the Mekilta, following Epstein, considers the bulk of the material to be Tannaitic, while allowing for subsequent redaction.[53] Thus Goldin, for example, takes it that the various tractates of

---

[46] Wacholder, 'A Reply', p. 114.
[47] *Relationship*, p. 181.
[48] Ibid., p. 105, on the quotations in the Mekilta.
[49] Ibid., p. 180.   [50] N. 35 above.
[51] 'The Date of the Mekilta', pp. 129f.; 132f.
[52] B. Z. Bokser, *Pharisaic Judaism in Transition*, pp. 121f. n. 9.
[53] Epstein's view of the redactional history of the Mekilta is quite complex, and we can give only a few main points. The Mekilta as it stands consists of originally independent sections simply put together.

the Mekilta are Tannaitic, while holding that the compilation of the tractates into one commentary was done in the post-Tannaitic period.[54] He further regards the attribution of the bulk of the material to the school of R. Ishmael, especially with regard to halakah, to be well-founded.[55]

It is this general scholarly consensus, which is supported by the enormous erudition and prestige of J. N. Epstein, that we shall attempt to follow with regard to the date and reliability of the material used. It has not been my intention, with regard to these matters, to offer new hypotheses, but to follow what I perceive to be the main line of professional Rabbinic scholarship.

The achievement of Epstein's principal works has now been summarized by B. M. Bokser, and so it is unneccessary to sketch his overall position.[56] We should, however, give at least one example of how one of our primary assumptions with regard to date is supported: the assumption that the bulk of the anonymous material in the halakic midrashim stems from the period between R. Akiba and R. Ishmael on the one hand and Rabbi on the other. We earlier noted that Melamed accepts Epstein's view that the anonymous author (*stam*) of Sifra is R. Judah b. Ilai, a disciple of R. Akiba. There is, of course, a simple statement to that effect in Sanhedrin 86a:

... R. Johanan said: [The author of] an anonymous Mishnah is R. Meir; of an anonymous Tosefta, R. Nehemiah; of an anonymous [dictum in the] Sifra, R. Judah; in the Sifre, R. Simeon; and all are taught according to the views of R. Akiba.

Epstein takes the statement with regard to Sifra seriously: 'this means that the majority of the anonymous material in the Sifra is the midrash of R. Judah.'[57] Epstein does not simply rely on the traditional account, however, but undertakes to show that it is accurate by an examination of the anonymous material of Sifra, especially by noting that it is often elsewhere attributed to R. Judah. Thus, for example, the anonymous opinion of Sifra Shemini parasha 3.2 to the effect that no sea but the Mediterranean is valid

---

In its final version it is a compilation rather than the work of a redactor or editor (*Mebo'ot*, p. 572). The *stam* (anonymous opinion) in some of the tractates is elsewhere attributed to R. Ishmael, but the redaction of some traditions shows the work of the school of Rabbi, others have passed through the school of R. Simeon b. Yohai, and there are traditions which reflect the system of R. Akiba (p. 581; cf. pp. 550, 554, 566). He still, however, regards the Mekilta as being basically from the school of R. Ishmael (pp. 564, 568, 570).

For a bibliography on the consensus view that the Mekilta is Tannaitic, see Wacholder, 'The Date of the Mekilta', p. 117 n. 1. See further W. S. Towner, *The Rabbinic 'Enumeration of Scriptural Examples'*, 1973, and 'Form-Criticism of Rabbinic Literature', *JJS* 24, 1973, pp. 101–18. In attempting to develop laws of transmission for Rabbinic literature, Towner in part presupposes and in part gives evidence for the relative antiquity of the traditions in the Mekilta in comparison with other Rabbinic literature.

[54] J. Goldin, *The Song at the Sea*, p. x.
[55] Ibid., p. 11.
[56] In *The Modern Study of the Mishnah* (ed. J. Neusner), pp. 13–55.
[57] *Mebo'ot*, p. 656.

as an immersion pool, citing Gen. 1.10 as a proof text, is attributed by name
to R. Judah twice in the Mishnah, in Parah 8.8 and in Mikwaoth 5.4.[58] It is
on the basis of this sort of evidence, multiplied many times, that Epstein
bases his views concerning the anonymous material in the midrashim.[59] It
leads him to a general view concerning the midrashic material: the flowering
of midrashic commentaries on the legal parts of the Pentateuch stems from
R. Akiba and R. Ishmael.[60] It is on the basis of this view that we take the
bulk of the anonymous material in the Tannaitic midrashim to be an
appropriate source for the study of Rabbinic Judaism in the last two-thirds
of the second century c.e. Some of the interpretations are doubtless traditional, but we have them as they passed through the schools of the second
century.

The eclectic use of Tannaitic material

The term 'eclectic' may be a little misleading, since it is not proposed to use
the material in such a way as to obscure differences in opinion, time and
place. Nevertheless, it is an important aspect of the present study to argue
that there is a general understanding of religion and the religious life which
informs and underlies all of Tannaitic literature. It is evident that there are
difficulties about considering any large body of literature to reflect one view
of religion. Further, recent trends in the study of early Rabbinic literature,
which involve breaking it down into as many substrata as possible, would
seem especially to argue against a large constructive hypothesis covering
more or less all of it. An objection from such a viewpoint would be fatal if we
wished to show that there was one *systematic theology* operative in the entire
period (as did Weber, Billerbeck and others surveyed above); or if we wished
to argue for one *point of view on any given point*, whether of halakah, ethics
or some such speculative question as the coming of the Messiah; or if we
wished to argue for some *overarching philosophical or sociological* point of
view. In all these respects, Tannaitic literature is very varied. It is my
contention, however, that with regard to the question of how religion and

---

[58] Ibid., p. 657.

[59] We cannot give a complete list of Epstein's conclusions on the anonymous portions of the midrashim
here. As indicated in n. 53 above, these are sometimes quite complex. Even Sifra, basically from the
school of R. Akiba (the *stam* is R. Judah), contains sections from the school of R. Ishmael (Epstein,
Mebo'ot, pp. 639–41). The main conclusions on Sifre Num. and Deut. are these: Sifre Deut. is from the
school of R. Akiba and the principal *stam* is R. Simeon b. Yohai (pp. 703–7); Sifre Num. is from the
school of R. Ishmael and the *stam* is at least sometimes R. Ishmael (pp. 588f.), although there are some
substantial portions from other sources, including the school of R. Simeon (pp. 597–608). Cf. Finkelstein, 'Studies in the Tannaitic Midrashim', *PAAJR* VI, 1934–5, p. 220: the haggadic portions of Sifre
Num. and Sifre Zuta, which are similar and often identical, seem to come from R. Simeon, since anonymous statements in Sifre are often attributed to him elsewhere.

[60] Epstein, *Mebo'ot*, p. 521. He comments that they needed to connect the halakah to the Torah (in
distinction from the Mishnaic method, in which halakah is usually given without reference to the
biblical text).

the religious life *worked*, how the religion *functioned* (how one gets in and stays in), a common pattern can be discerned which underlies otherwise disparate parts of Tannaitic literature. This is a contention which cannot be proved in advance, but only by actually carrying out the requisite analysis. Throughout the subsequent sections we shall be concerned with the question of whether or not a pattern is artificially being imposed on the thought of the Rabbis, and the question will be returned to directly in the conclusion. Here, however, we should point out several factors which lend support for seeking a common pattern of religion in Tannaitic literature.

1. As we observed above, there is an apologetic reason for studying a large body of Rabbinic literature: to show that the systematic Rabbinic soteriology which is widely believed to be based on Rabbinic sources actually rests on a misunderstanding of them. The apologetic motive is not justification for our use of the material, but it is a point which has been borne in mind.

2. More to the point, Rabbinic literature is by its nature, to use Neusner's term, 'a "collective literature"'. He continues by noting that, while individual elements may have begun with individual authors, the material 'was publicly transmitted, and rapidly made the property of the community of the schools. Whatever the role of individuals, it was rapidly obliterated and therefore does not matter. . . . This must mean that conventionality takes precedence over style, formulaic routine over unusual expression, the public consensus over the private insight.'[61] This consideration has a negative and a positive implication. We shall consider the former first.

The collective character of the literature means that it is difficult to identify a distinctive theology or even 'pattern of religion' for any given individual. There have been numerous studies of individual Rabbis, and these are continuing,[62] but they do not lead to a picture of an individual thinker who may be readily compared with, for example, Paul. Many of the great Rabbis may well have had the comprehensiveness of view which would enable them to be compared with Paul; but, if so, it can no longer be recovered. One may consider, for example, the question of motivation. While one may debate the question of what drove Paul to do what he did, there is material in Paul's letters to inform the debate. It would be difficult to establish a clear motivation, except by inference and hypothesis, for a single individual Rabbi. Thus, to take one controverted point, it has been traditionally thought that R. Akiba not only sanctioned but encouraged the Messianic revolt led by Bar Cochba. Finkelstein, on the other hand, has

---

[61] *Rabbinic Traditions* III, p. 3. For another statement by Neusner on the unity and coherence of Rabbinic religion, see *Understanding Rabbinic Judaism*, p. 1.

[62] Some of the principal studies in English are those of R. Akiba by Finkelstein, of R. Joshua by Podro, of R. Eliezer by Bokser, of R. Johanan b. Zakkai by Neusner and of R. Eliezer by Neusner. See the bibliography for details.

argued that R. Akiba resisted the militaristic movement and finally sanctioned Bar Cochba as Messiah only reluctantly.[63] The point is that, despite
the numerous sayings in Rabbinic literature attributed to R. Akiba, we do
not have one clear saying about what he thought concerning the most
important issue to confront the Jewish community in his time. We generally
lack sayings in which Rabbis explain *why* they do what they do. In contrast
to this, it is relatively easy to find strong motivating factors for the Rabbinic
movement as a whole. One may not be able to determine why an individual
Rabbi undertook to give halakah on a given point, but, as we shall discuss
further below, the overall motivation for halakah is quite clear. Thus,
negatively speaking, the collective nature of the material, while not making
it impossible to study individuals from certain points of view, does make it
impossible to find out about them what we wish to know: how they viewed
the nature of religion and the religious life on the whole.[64] Further, the
apologetic motive enters here again. Even if we could show that some one
Rabbi held a view of religion completely different from that ascribed to the
Rabbis by Bousset, Billerbeck and their followers, this would not show that
the Bousset/Billerbeck view is wrong. That view would then simply be
attributed to the rest of the Rabbis, with the footnote that it may not apply
to one.

3. Before returning to the positive aspects of a collective literature for the
purpose of our study, we should at least briefly refer to another characteristic
of the literature which makes a small-scale analysis of basic religious principles impossible: they are not discussed as such. Rabbinic discussions are
often at the third remove from central questions of religious importance.[65]
Thus the tractate Mikwaoth, 'immersion pools', does not consider the
religious value of immersion or the general reason for purity, much less such
a large topic as *why* the law should be observed. It simply begins with the
classification of the grades among pools of water. This does not mean that
there were no religious principles behind the discussion; simply that they
(*a*) were so well understood that they did not need to be specified and (*b*) did
not fall into the realm of halakah. We shall enlarge on this point below, but it
deserves separate mention here. This sort of literature, which deals with
questions of detail rather than principle, makes the analysis of the principles
of religion which govern an individual very difficult, while permitting
inferences as to what principles lie behind the discussions as a whole.

4. Positively, the collective character of the literature means that there is,
on certain kinds of issues, consensus if not uniformity. This has been widely

---

[63] Finkelstein, *Akiba*, pp. 200–2; 260–9; see now G. S. Aleksandrov, 'The Role of 'Aqiba in the Bar
Kokhba Rebellion', ET in Neusner's *Eliezer* II, pp. 422–36.

[64] For a discussion of the lack of information about individual Rabbis' views on important issues, see
Neusner, *Eliezer* II, pp. 129, 326.

[65] Cf. Neusner, *Rabbinic Traditions* III, pp. 235, 238; see further, section 3 below.

recognized with regard to haggadah, but there is also a type of consensus – in fact, in this case, uniformity – with regard to halakah: while Rabbis disputed what the halakah on any particular point should be, they believed *without exception that there should be halakah*. This is a fact that will tell us, as we shall see, a great deal about their understanding of religion.

Any construction of the principles of Rabbinic religion, however, must ultimately rely a great deal on haggadah – that large body of material which covers everything which the Rabbis did not consider law. It is in haggadah that one finds whatever statements there are about the significance of the Torah, the understanding of the covenant, what one must do to be saved and the like. And it is haggadah that many Rabbinic scholars have singled out as especially revealing a general consensus. Thus, for example, Goldin, in his discussion of Rabbinic commentaries on the Song at the Sea, confirms the traditional attribution of the Mekilta of R. Ishmael to the school of R. Ishmael and the Mekilta of R. Simeon b. Yohai to the school of R. Akiba.[66] Then he notes, 'As regards nonlegal substance, the haggadic . . . contents, both Schools are more or less at one.' In the tractate on the Song at the Sea, Shirta (so Goldin; Lauterbach: Shirata), which is haggadah, the two Mekiltas are in close agreement:

This very agreement within the haggadic materials is particularly noteworthy. One is here in the presence of rabbinic *consensus*: not unanimity, but a hospitality on the part of both Schools to the same corpus of various teaching for further study and reflection.

Goldin continues by speaking of Shirta as reflecting 'the overall tannaite understanding of the Song at the Sea'.[67]

The principal and by far the most ingenious proponent of coherence in Rabbinic thought, however, is Max Kadushin. He has worked out his view of Rabbinic thought in several works, but we may best summarize it on the basis of his early major work, *Organic Thinking*.[68]

Kadushin points out that any attempt such as Weber's to represent Rabbinic thought (Kadushin says 'theology', but he subsequently shows that the term is incorrect; see p. 185) as a logical *system* must be wrong, since Rabbinic thought is not logical or systematic in the way that permits the construction of a systematic theology. Yet there is coherence and unity to Rabbinic thought, as may be seen, for example, by the fact that 'disparate passages drawn from rabbinic sources that were composed at different

---

[66] Goldin, *The Song at the Sea*, p. 11.

[67] Ibid., p. 12. Finkelstein had earlier made a similar observation with regard to the sections Beshallah and Jethro in the two Mekiltas and the sections on Num. 10.29–11.35 in Sifre Num. 78–98 (pp. 72–97) and Sifre Zuta (pp. 262–74) (Finkelstein, 'Studies in the Tannaitic Midrashim', p. 201).

[68] Published in 1938. See further *The Rabbinic Mind*, 1952 ([2]1965), and *A Conceptual Approach to the Mekilta*, 1969. Page numbers in the text are to *Organic Thinking*. For a generally favourable assessment of Kadushin's work, see Goldin, 'The Thinking of the Rabbis', *Judaism* 5, 1956, pp. 3–12.

periods and under divergent circumstances can yet be brought together so as to elucidate a rabbinic concept' (p. 2). The coherence is of a sort, however, that permits differences according to the circumstances and individual proclivities (p. 3). The differences are not doctrinal, since doctrine implies credal and philosophical thought (p. 22), nor is the coherence dogmatic (pp. 210f.). As he puts it in another work, Rabbinic concepts form an 'integrated pattern' which is not, however, 'the result of logical, systematic thought'.[69]

The coherence, according to Kadushin, resides in an organic complex[70] which consists of a multitude of concepts which interweave with one another. There are four 'fundamental' concepts: 'God's loving-kindness, His justice, Torah, and Israel' (p. 6). The fundamental concepts are not the only *important* concepts – others are as important – but they are the concepts which are always woven into other concepts. They may further be inter-woven among themselves, and they have no hierarchical value *vis à vis* one another (pp. 6f., 16, 183).

Kadushin defines an organic complex thus:

Organic concepts are concepts in a whole complex of concepts none of which can be inferred from the others but all of which are so mutually interrelated that every individual concept, though possessing its own distinctive features, nevertheless depends for its character on the character of the complex as a whole which, in turn, depends on the character of the individual concepts. Each organic concept, therefore, implicates the whole complex without being completely descriptive of the complex, retaining, at the same time, its own distinctive features (p. 184).

Since any concept can be combined with any of the four, or with any combination of them, 'it happens not infrequently that the same or a similar situation may be given several interpretations "contradictory" to each other' (p. 13). Rabbinic thought is based on human experience, and the interpreta-tion of experience by the organic complex renders the Rabbis indifferent to logical contradictions (p. 77). The concepts are not defined by the Rabbis, although distinctions may be drawn between them (pp. 190f.). They do not, however, permit systemization (p. 194). The point that the concepts may yield different interpretations of the same experience, without any attempt to establish a systematic relationship among the interpretations, is so important that we may quote one of Kadushin's examples:

At one time, the Rabbis declare that Adam's sin is responsible for the presence of death (not of sin) 'until the end of all generations', a view determined by the concept of corporate justice; at another, they say that each man dies because of his own sin, a view determined by the concept of individual distributive justice; and at still another time, instead of regarding death as a calamity, they state that it is a moral purgative for the world, a view determined by the concept of chastise-ment (p. 209).

---

[69] *A Conceptual Approach to the Mekilta*, p. 16.

[70] Kadushin later preferred to speak of an 'organismic complex'; see *The Rabbinic Mind*[2], pp. 24f., 31.

The insistence on the non-systematic nature of Rabbinic thought does not mean that logic was never exercised. On the contrary, within the bounds of the organic framework, logic was employed, as may be seen in the interpretation of biblical texts (pp. 202–11). While any given interpretation of a text may be logical and reasonable, it does not exclude some other interpretation, which might also be logical; but there would be no need or inclination to establish a logical relationship between the two interpretations: 'The same verse could be interpreted in any number of different ways, providing the rabbinic methods of interpretation were employed and providing the interpretation embodied an organic concept' (p. 205).

Kadushin especially emphasizes how firmly fixed the Rabbinic concepts were and how enduring they proved: 'Every conceptual term is a stable term, and the terminology as a whole is a fixed terminology. Throughout the entire rabbinic period no valuational term is either altered or displaced by another.'[71] This view may sometimes lead him into a position which is too ahistorical (see, for example, *Organic Thinking*, p. 12), but he himself would attribute this to his desire to establish the organic complex rather than to show how variety and change can take place within it. He allows for the latter (e.g. *Organic Thinking*, p. 199), but emphasizes the stability of the organic complex.[72]

This summary of the formal characteristics of Kadushin's theory does not do justice to the richness of his presentation of Rabbinic thought. We shall have occasion in discussing various points to make use of some of his detailed analyses. The reason for providing so lengthy a summary of some of the main elements of Kadushin's theory here is to indicate one way of dealing with the entire body of Rabbinic literature which is pursued by a scholar whose main field is Rabbinics. Further, some of Kadushin's main points appear to me to be perfectly convincing and to provide the only possible way of relating certain Rabbinic sayings to one another. These points are (*a*) the emphasis on the possibility of differing interpretations of the same text and/or experience, each having its own internal logic and each valid in itself, without the interpretations' being related hierarchically or systematically to one another, and (*b*) the insistence on the coherence of Rabbinic thought. It does not seem necessary to pronounce judgment on his view that there are four and only four 'fundamental' concepts, that all other concepts interweave with these four, and the like. It is enough for our present work that he has shown that it makes sense *for certain purposes* to use the material eclectically.

The present effort at a constructive representation of Rabbinic thought is

---

[71] *The Rabbinic Mind*[2], p. 44.

[72] Kadushin's work applies mainly to haggadah, but he considers that halakah is also 'informed by the organismic complex of rabbinic concepts' (*Conceptual Approach*, pp. 21f.). On halakah and haggadah, see further *The Rabbinic Mind*[2], ch. 4.

not meant to reduplicate or supplant Kadushin's view of an organic complex. For one thing, I cannot bring myself to be quite as ahistorical as Kadushin is. For another, I do not intend to account for all the themes and motifs of Rabbinic literature. It should also be obvious that the present effort will not be directed towards establishing a new systematic theology. Rather, we are seeking the basic pattern of Rabbinic religion, a pattern which gives an account of the basic motivating forces of the religious life and of how the participants perceived the religion to function. The pattern of religion, as we explained in the Introduction, has to do with how one moves from the logical starting point of the religion to the logical end. In this sense, the 'pattern of religion' may be called 'soteriology'.

We earlier noted that the term 'soteriology' may be misleading when applied to Judaism. When applied to Rabbinic thought, it has two drawbacks. In the first place, it may seem to imply just what we have been so concerned to deny, a systematic scheme in which various elements have a hierarchical value *vis à vis* one another. The 'soteriology' which we shall describe does constitute a coherent view, but it is a way of looking at religion and life rather than being a systematic theology or a part of a systematic theology. A second possible objection to the term 'soteriology' with regard to Rabbinic religion is that Judaism in general and Rabbinic Judaism in particular is not a religion which is primarily other-worldly. The query, 'What can I do to be saved?' is one which is not prominent in the literature. As Kadushin correctly noted, the incorrect supposition that the Rabbis were worried over what to do to be saved lies behind such erroneous depictions of Rabbinic (or Pharisaic) soteriology as that of Weber.[73]

In favour of the use of the term 'soteriology' is that it points to a concern which *is* central to Judaism: a concern to be properly rather than improperly religious, to serve God rather than to desert his way, to be 'in' rather than 'out'. When a man is concerned to be 'in' rather than 'out', we may consider him to have a 'soteriological' concern, even though he may have no view concerning an afterlife at all. There does appear to be in Rabbinic Judaism a coherent and all-pervasive view of what constitutes the essence of Jewish religion and of how that religion 'works', and we shall occasionally, for the sake of convenience, call this view 'soteriology'. The all-pervasive view can be summarized in the phrase 'covenantal nomism'. Briefly put, covenantal nomism is the view that one's place in God's plan is established on the basis of the covenant and that the covenant requires as the proper response of man his obedience to its commandments, while providing means of atonement for transgression.

[73] *Organic Thinking*, pp. 83–94.

3. The nature of Tannaitic literature

We can gain an initial insight into the pattern of Rabbinic religion by first considering the nature of Tannaitic literature, especially the halakic portions.[1] All of the Tannaitic works which survive are basically halakic; that is, there are no complete works from the Tannaitic period which can be described as haggadic. The midrashim are commentaries on the legal books of the Bible – Exodus, Leviticus, Numbers and Deuteronomy. The Mekilta begins with Exodus 12.1, omitting the early narrative portion (although the Mekilta of R. Simeon b. Yohai begins with Exodus 3). Other narrative parts of the biblical books are also omitted in the midrashim. The general halakic character of the midrashim is maintained, even though each work may include a great deal of haggadah. This is especially to be noted with regard to the Mekilta, of which Lauterbach has estimated over 50% to be haggadah.[2] This is partly to be explained by the greater amount of narrative material in Exodus even after chapter 12, in comparison with Leviticus and Deuteronomy, and partly by the fact that many events narrated in Exodus – especially the Exodus itself and the giving of the Torah at Mt Sinai – were naturally the occasion for a great deal of haggadah. Further, one of the tractates which comprises the present Mekilta, Shirata, on the Song at the Sea, is entirely haggadic. Despite the appreciable amount of haggadah in the Tannaitic midrashim, however, it is still accurate to call them halakic, since the general arrangement and the biblical material covered indicate the concern to deal with legal matters. It is noteworthy that there are no Tannaitic midrashim on the other books of the Bible.

The Mishnah is the halakic work *par excellence*, although it too contains a certain amount of haggadic material. The very arrangement of the Mishnah, along topical lines, points to its character. It deals with the laws governing different areas of life – civil and criminal cases, agriculture, ritual and the like. The Tosefta contains more haggadah than does the Mishnah, but it is also basically halakic. The purpose of halakah is to determine whether or not a biblical passage does in fact constitute a commandment, if there can be any doubt; to establish the application of a biblical commandment; to define its precise scope and meaning; and to determine precisely what must be done in order to fulfil it.[3] We may take a few examples.

---

[1] In view of recent debates about terminology (Introduction, section 3 n. 14), I shall indicate here how some of the contested terms are used. The usage followed here is that appropriate to Tannaitic literature: by *form*, the literature is in the midrash form (commentary on the biblical text) or the mishnah form (arranged by subject matter). In *content*, it is halakic (legal) or haggadic (non-legal). The midrashim contain both haggadah and halakah, as do the Mishnah and Tosefta (both arranged by topic).

[2] Lauterbach, *Mekilta* I, p. xix.

[3] Cf. Lauterbach, 'Midrash halakah', *JE*, vol. 8, p. 570: 'The early halakah sought only to define the compass and scope of individual laws, asking under what circumstances of practical life a given rule was to be applied and what would be its consequences.' On the nature and function of halakah and some of

Frequently it is discussed whether an action is obligatory (*hobah*) or voluntary (*reshut*). Here the question is whether God has explicitly commanded the performance of a certain action or only commended it. Thus in commenting on Ex. 22.24, 'If thou lend money to any of my people', R. Ishmael argues that ordinarily the word 'if' indicates a voluntary act, but here and in Lev. 2.14 it indicates an obligatory act.[4] The details of the argument are not important here. The point is simply that the Rabbis felt it necessary to decide whether a passage did or did not convey a commandment.

The application is frequently debated. One such question is whether a certain commandment was applicable only at the time it was given (e.g. to the children of Israel in the wilderness) or is always valid. In commenting on Ex. 14.1, R. Simeon b. Yohai says, 'When in any commandment to the people Scripture uses the expression "saying", or "and thou shalt say unto them", that commandment is for all generations (*ledorot*). When neither [expression] is used, it is only for the time being (*lesha'ah*).' Rabbi (Judah ha-Nasi), however, is of a different opinion: 'Even when it does not use [either expression], the commandment is for all generations, with the exception of three instances.'[5]

Often the question concerns the purpose or function of a certain commandment. An example is Sifre Num. 17 (21; to 5.24): ' "And he shall make the woman drink." Why is it said? It had already said, "and afterward he shall make the woman drink", so why does Scripture say "And he shall make the woman drink"? Because if the roll was put into the water and then the woman said, "I do not want to drink", they compel her and force her to drink against her will. So R. Akiba.' Here we see that each commandment was regarded as having a purpose; there are no idle commandments. The question 'why is it said?' is a very frequent one in the Tannaitic midrashim.[6]

Another type of decision is on whom the commandment is laid. Does it apply to men, women and children equally? Does it apply to those of dual or doubtful sex? Are only Israelites included or also Gentiles? If Israelites, does it include proselytes? Thus when the Rabbis note that the command-

---

the motives behind halakic rulings, see E. Berkovits, 'The Centrality of Halakhah', *Understanding Rabbinic Judaism* (ed. Neusner), pp. 65–70.

[4] Mek. Mishpatim 19 (Kaspa 1) (315; III, 147); cf. also Mek. Vayassa' 1 (157; II, 95f.; to 15.26). For other wording, see Sifra Nedabah parasha 2.4 (to 1.2): ' "If any man of you brings an offering": Can it be an ordinance (*gezerah*)? [No; for] scripture teaches, "*If* he brings". It is only voluntary (*reshut*).'

[5] Mek. Beshallah 1 (83; I, 187 [in Lauterbach's edition, ch. 2, since he numbers the introduction ch. 1]).

[6] Indeed, every sentence and word were often regarded as having a specific purpose. In the case of duplications, the Rabbis generally inquired after the meaning of the repetition. R. Akiba was especially noted for deriving meaning from very small points in the biblical text, such as a plene spelling (with a *waw* or *yod*) of a word normally not written plene. See Epstein, *Mebo'ot*, pp. 521–36, esp. 534 and 536, where he gives examples of the traditional view that R. Ishmael tended to follow the simple meaning of the text, while R. Akiba wished to draw a commandment from each passage.

ment to circumcise and to do the things connected with it overrides the Sabbath, the question arises whether this applies to all children: 'They may not profane the Sabbath for the sake of a child about which there is doubt or that is androgynous; but R. Judah permits it for one that is androgynous' (Shabbath 19.3). A clear example of the question of application is to be found in Sifre Num. 39 (42f.; to 6.22f.). The biblical passage is this: 'Thus you shall bless the sons of Israel.' I give here only the first sentence of a series of paragraphs which describe how the blessing is done and who is blessed, omitting the counter-arguments and documentation for each point: 1. 'In the holy language'; 2. 'While standing'; 3. 'With palms raised'; 4. 'With the explicit name'; 5. 'I have only blessing Israel. Whence do we know that blessing proselytes, women and slaves [is also included]? Scripture says: "And I shall bless *them*"' (Num. 6.27); 6. 'Face to face'; 7. 'So that all the congregation may hear.' To give something of the flavour of this passage, I give here one of the paragraphs (no. 2 above) in full:

'Thus you shall bless the sons of Israel': While standing. – You say while standing, or is it not rather either while standing or while not standing? – Scripture says: '[And] these shall stand to bless the people' (Deut. 27.12). Blessing is mentioned here (in Numbers) and blessing is mentioned there (in Deuteronomy). Just as the blessing mentioned there [is given] while standing, so also the blessing mentioned here [is given] while standing. R. Nathan said: It is not necessary [to argue thus], since it was already said: 'And the priests the sons of Levi shall come forward, for the Lord your God has chosen them to minister to him and to bless in the name of the Lord' (Deut. 21.5). It juxtaposes (or makes an analogy between) blessing and ministering (in the Temple). Just as ministering [is done] while standing, so also blessing [is done] while standing.

What one must note in all of this is the concern properly to *define* the commandment (blessing means standing with upraised hands, etc.) and to determine to whom the scriptural blessing was to be applied (proselytes, slaves, etc.).[7]

We may now turn to some examples to show the Rabbinic concern for defining when a commandment has been fulfilled. A phrase which recurs repeatedly in the Tannaitic material is 'he has (or has not) fulfilled his obligation', literally 'he has gone out of the hands of his obligation', *yatsa' yede hobato*. It is frequently abbreviated by the word *yatsa'*, 'he has gone out (fulfilled)'. An example of the full phrase is this passage from Sifra Emor pereq 16.2 (Weiss, 102c; to 23.40). The biblical passage is this: 'And you shall take on the first day the fruit of goodly trees, branches of palm trees ... and you shall rejoice before the Lord your God seven days.' The Midrash comments as follows: '"And you shall take for yourself." – Each individual

[7] For another example, see Mek. Bahodesh 7 (230; II, 255; to 20.10). And see also Sifre Zuta to Num. 5.12, where the commentator asks whether the biblical phrase 'sons of Israel' intends to exclude Gentiles and resident aliens or proselytes.

[must take]. "For yourself" – from what is yours and not from what is stolen. Hence they used to say: "No man may fulfil his obligation on the first day of the festival with his neighbour's lulab"', etc.

But one need go no further than the second chapter of the first tractate of the Mishnah for examples of the expression.

If a man was reading [the *Shema'*] in the Law and the time came to recite the *Shema'*, if he directed his heart he has fulfilled his obligation [to recite the *Shema'*]; otherwise he has not fulfilled his obligation. (Berakoth 2.1)

If a man recited the *Shema'* but not loudly enough for himself to hear, he has fulfilled his obligation. R. Jose says: He has not fulfilled it. If he recited it without clearly pronouncing the letters, R. Jose says: He has fulfilled his obligation. R. Judah says: He has not fulfilled it. If a man recited [the sections] in wrong order, he has not fulfilled [his obligation]. (Berakoth 2.3)

The first of these two passages opens a problem much discussed in Tannaitic literature, that of intention (indicated in Berakoth 2.1 by the phrase 'if he directed his heart'). One may compare Megillah 2.2:

If a man read [the Scroll of Esther] piecemeal or drowsily, he has fulfilled his obligation; if he was copying it, expounding it, or correcting a copy of it, and he directed his heart [to the reading of the Scroll], he has fulfilled his obligation; otherwise, he has not fulfilled his obligation.

The question of one's intention with regard to a specific commandment, whether 'intention' is understood as the opposite of 'accidental' or as equivalent to paying attention to what one is doing, is a complicated one, and one which we do not need to explore fully here.[8] We need only note the concern to define when a commandment has been fulfilled, which often includes discussing the degree to which intention ('directing the heart') is necessary.

The detailed definition of what is required for the commandment to be fulfilled has been seen, as we saw in section 1 above, as the imposition of an enormous burden on the members of the Jewish community who attempted to live by Rabbinic standards. On the other hand, many have seen Rabbinic halakah as an attempt to make the law easier to observe and to modernize it. It is doubtful whether either view will serve as a general principle. Thus Finkelstein has argued that the civil law was consistently made more lenient, while the ritual law was maintained strictly.[9] One may quarrel even with

---

[8] R. Eliezer's views, for example, have been much discussed in this regard. See B. Z. Bokser, *Pharisaic Judaism in Transition*, pp. 120f. (where further bibliography on the general question is given); Neusner, *Eliezer* II, pp. 268, 285 (quoting and disagreeing with Gilat), 290f. (giving his own summary). For the passages, see Neusner's index, s.v. intention.

[9] See Finkelstein's preface to the third edition of *The Pharisees*, pp. li-lxvi, where he argues against the view that the Rabbis consistently made the law more lenient. He does not appear, however, to retract his earlier view that the practice of merging households on the Sabbath ('*erub*) was developed to overcome personal hardships (ibid., p. 137; cf. pp. 718f.). Rivkin ('Defining the Pharisees', p. 228) argues that the Pharisees ameliorated the laws of ritual purity.

this attempt to generalize the result of Rabbinic rulings. I am dubious if the categories of strictness and leniency, imposition and relaxation are fruitful ones for investigating the question of the *nature* and *purpose* of the halakah (although on individual points different opinions can often be classified as strict or lenient). The intention of halakah was to define the law and to help the observant Jew determine when it had been fulfilled. This might sometimes result in adding what appear to be additional restrictions or requirements which are not directly implied in the Bible, or it might result in making the biblical law easier to obey; and there are certainly instances of 'modernization'. The point, however, was to define what was required. It was occasionally necessary to contravene the biblical law directly, but this is far from a major theme in Rabbinic literature.[10] Whether lenient or strict, the Rabbinic definitions of what the biblical law requires, as well as Rabbinic enactments, were always capable of being performed.[11] The legal rulings do not hold up an ideal which is impossible of achievement.

In its task of defining the commandments and the method of fulfilling them, the Mishnah deals largely with special problems which arise. It is not too much to say that the Mishnah deals with possibilities and difficulties. One may cite as an example the tractate Zebahim, 'animal offerings'. Many of the paragraphs in the English translation rightly begin with 'if'. The word 'if' does not actually appear in Hebrew, but this is the correct rendering. Thus, for example, Zebahim 8.3: 'If a Guilt-offering was confused with a Peace-offering they must be left to pasture until they suffer a blemish.' But one should read the tractate to see how many difficulties and possibilities are raised. The principles behind the sacrificial system, or its religious significance, are nowhere discussed. One sees, in fact, that several things are presupposed in the tractate. Knowledge of what the sacrifices are is presupposed. The Mishnah does not, for example, define a guilt-offering or a sin-offering – the biblical base is assumed. It is further assumed that the Israelites are to keep the sacrifices as best they are able. Only the difficulties involved in doing so are discussed. A further assumption is that there is a good religious reason for keeping the sacrifices. But nowhere will one find the sentence, 'We should observe the sacrificial system because. . .'.

Thus in addition to seeing from the halakah that the Rabbis were concerned to define precisely what was required and to determine how the requirements should be fulfilled, we also see that the Rabbinic halakah

[10] R. Ishmael said that 'in three places the halakah overrrides the Bible' (Midrash Tannaim to Deut. 24.1, p. 154; reported by R. Johanan in Sotah 16a; cf. p. Kiddushin 59d [1.2], where 'Torah' is presumably a mistake for 'halakah'; a fragment of the tradition is in Mek. Mishpatim 2 [253]; III, 16 (Nezikin 2); to 21.6; Friedmann, f.77b, top, has a different reading]). See Epstein, *Mebo'ot*, p. 535; Urbach, *Hazal*, p. 262 (ET, p. 294); Moore, *Judaism* I, pp. 259f.

[11] See the principle attributed to R. Simeon b. Gamaliel in T. Sotah 15.10 and to R. Joshua in Baba Bathra 60b: regulations were not imposed (by Rabbinic ordinance) which the majority of the community could not endure (referring to fasting after the destruction of the Temple).

reveals agreement on a vast number of principles, since the discussions and disagreements centre on what are, relatively speaking, small details.[12]

Tannaitic literature and Tannaitic religion

The concern with precise definition of details explains why many scholars, especially Christians, have interpreted Rabbinic religion as narrow, formalistic legalism. Yet we have also seen enough to be able to begin an analysis of Rabbinic religion which will result in a description which is both profounder and truer than that. *One must ask what religious motives drove the Rabbis to such a detailed and minute investigation of the biblical commandments.*

There would appear to be two possible motivations. Either the Rabbis were of the view that salvation depended upon their ability to compile a large number of commandment-fulfilments and that the precise definition of the law would aid in this, or else they were of the view that Israel's situation in the covenant required the law to be obeyed as fully and completely as possible. That is, either they saw their efforts to be directed towards achieving salvation, or else as the only proper response to the God who chose Israel and gave them commandments. A hint as to which is the more likely solution is not far to seek.

We may turn to the first section (*pisqa'*) of Sifre Numbers, which comments on Num. 5.1ff.: 'The Lord said to Moses, Command the people of Israel that they put out of the camp every leper, and every one having a discharge, and every one that is unclean through contact with the dead.' The midrash carefully defines each element in the commandment: it is to be applied both at the time it was spoken and in subsequent generations; the partitions of the camp are defined (in decreasing sanctity: the camp of the Shekinah, of the Levites and of Israel); the problem of whether all three groups of those being expelled are put in one place is dealt with; the question of whether the commandment is to be applied to other groups who were counted unclean is raised and answered (it is not; one does not punish on the basis of an inference *ad maius*); it is noted that the commandment applies to male and female, adult and child, and also to the inevitable *tumtum* and androgynous; further, vessels (utensils) which are unclean in the specified ways are to be put out of the camp, although a piece of cloth less than three handbreadths square is exempted by R. Jose the Galilean.

The argumentation concerning the points which have been briefly outlined here, even though the Hebrew is typically brief and economical almost to the point of obscurity, covers over three pages of Horovitz's text (pp. 1–4). This is one more example of the kind of halakic definition which we have already discussed. But then, in commenting on Num. 5.3 ('Which

[12] Neusner, *Eliezer* II, pp. 309f., comes to the same conclusion with regard to Pharisaism before 70 c.e.

I dwell [*shoken*] in the midst of you'), the anonymous author of the midrash gives us a small glimpse into the religious motivation which lay behind the exact and meticulous definition of the commandments:

Beloved is Israel, for even though they are unclean the Shekinah is among them. And also it says: 'Which dwells (*ha-shoken*) with them in the midst of their uncleanness' (Lev. 16.16). And it says: 'By making unclean my tabernacle (*mishkani*) which is in your midst' (Lev. 15.31). And it says: 'That they may not make unclean their camps in which I dwell in the midst of you' (Num. 5.3). And it says: 'You shall not make unclean the land in which you live, in the midst of which I dwell (*shoken*)' (Num. 35.34).[13]

Here the Rabbi not only makes the great religious claim that God's presence (the Shekinah) is with Israel even in their uncleanness, but also points to the reason for exact observance of the law. Since God dwells with the people, they should not tolerate that which is unclean and abhorrent to God. The last two passages quoted (Num. 5.3 and 35.34) make the point especially clearly. The reason for defining the commandments precisely is to be able to do what God enjoined. The reason for doing what God enjoined is that he dwells with his people.[14]

Although the word 'covenant' has thus far not occurred in Sifre, it is clear that the entirety of Sifre Num. 1 presupposes a firm belief in a covenant between God and Israel.[15] God dwells with his people and they are to keep his commandments precisely. *The bulk of the halakic material deals with the elaboration and definition of Israel's obligation to God under the covenant. This is what accounts for the halakic material in general.* Why are the commandments so narrowly defined and the mode of fulfilment so thoroughly discussed? Because keeping the commandments is Israel's response to the God who has chosen them, who has made a covenant with them, and who dwells with them – even when they are not perfectly obedient. Very seldom is *God's* role in the covenant directly discussed. It is assumed so thoroughly that it need not be mentioned. But that role is nevertheless the presupposition upon which all the halakic material rests. The only reason for elaborating and defining man's obligations under the covenant is that God's faithfulness and justice in keeping his side are beyond question. The haggadic comment on Num. 5.3 is one of the relatively rare instances in which God's side is discussed. The covenant is still presupposed, but it is seen from the point of God's mercy rather than man's obligation.

[13] Horovitz, p. 4. Similarly Lev. 16.16 ('which abides with them in the midst of their uncleanness') is taken to show that God (the Shekinah) is with Israel even when they are unclean in Yoma 56b–57a and Sifra Ahare pereq 4.5; so also Sifra Metsora' pereq 9.7 (to 15.31).

[14] On the Shekinah being with Israel despite sin, see further Abelson, *The Immanence of God in Rabbinical Literature*, pp. 138ff.; Kuhn, *Gottes Selbsterniedrigung*, p. 84. And on the presence of God with Israel, see section 10 below.

[15] The nature of the Rabbinic conception of the covenant will be discussed throughout the balance of this chapter, and especially in section 4. It is not presupposed that the conception is identical with one of the biblical conceptions of the covenant.

The relationship between the covenant, the commandments and the requirement of obedience is one of the focal points of this study, and we shall see that the understanding of the relationship which is expressed in Sifre Num. 1 – the reason for fulfilling the commandments is that God specified obedience as Israel's response to the covenant, to God's presence with his people – is the common understanding of the Tannaim. The precise way in which the Rabbis deal with the covenant, the commandments and obedience or disobedience (and consequently with reward and punishment) will require detailed analysis (sections 4–6), but we may conclude this section by citing two further passages which express especially clearly the Tannaitic understanding of obedience, the commandments and the covenant; and these passages will further demonstrate *why* the Tannaim were so concerned with meticulously defining and obeying the commandments.

A profound insight into the motive for obedience appears in the following passage from Sifre Deuteronomy, commenting on Deut. 6.6:

'And these words which I command you this day shall be upon your heart.' Rabbi says: Why is it said? Because it says (Deut. 6.5) 'And thou shalt love the Lord thy God with all thy heart.' I do not know how one should love God (*ha-Maqom*),[16] and so Scripture says, 'And these words which I command you this day shall be upon your heart.' Place these words upon your heart so that through them you will come to know the one who spoke and the world came into being, and cleave to his ways.[17]

The phrase 'place these words upon your heart' doubtless means that the Israelite should both know and intend to obey the commandments of God in the Torah, and obedience demonstrates that one loves God. By studying the commandments, one comes to know God and to adhere to his will. That this is the goal of religion the Rabbis did not need to say. As we shall eventually see, knowing God and cleaving to his way does entail a reward (since God is just), but the reward is not the goal of religion. That is achieved simply when one knows God and does his will; study of the commandments and the intent to obey them are the proper means towards the goal and the proper behaviour within the covenant.

Being in the covenant is most explicitly related to keeping the commandments in a passage from Sifra which is commenting on Lev. 1.2: ' "Speak to the people of Israel, and say to them, When any man of you brings an offering to the Lord, you shall bring your offering of cattle from the herd

---

[16] On the designation of God as *ha-Maqom* as an indication of early material, see Marmorstein, *The Names and Attributes of God*, pp. 92f., 97, 108ff. Urbach (*Ḥazal*, pp. 53f.; ET, pp. 66–8) has shown that Marmorstein was basically right, although he sometimes forced the evidence by resorting to theories of interpolation and the like, thus making too firm a distinction between the early use of *ha-Maqom* and the late use of 'the Holy One, blessed be he'. For other literature, see Urbach, p. 54 n. 3 (ET, p. 711 n. 3).

[17] Sifre Deut. 33 (59). In Friedmann's edition (f. 74a, top), the passage is anonymous and the term for God in both cases is 'the Holy One, blessed be he'.

or from the flock."' The question concerns who may and should bring an offering, and why. The passage is as follows:[18]

Man. [What is the significance of this word?] To include the proselytes. *From you* (RSV, of you). [This is said] to exclude the apostates.[19] – How can you argue thus? It says *man* to include the apostates and *from you* to exclude the proselytes! [The exigetical rule is that] after a passage includes, it excludes [and not vice-versa]. – [Your argument does not hold; for] scripture says, *sons of Israel* (RSV, people of Israel). Just as [native-born] Israelites accept the covenant, also the proselytes accept the covenant. Apostates are excluded, since they do not accept the covenant. – But could you not argue that just as [native-born] Israelites are the *sons* of those who accept the covenant, also apostates are the *sons* of those who accept the covenant [and therefore should be included]? [In this case], the pro-selytes would be excluded because they are not *sons* of those who accept the covenant. – [Your argument does not hold; for] scripture says *from you*.[20] And now say nothing but this: Just as [native-born] Israelites accept the covenant, also proselytes accept the covenant. Apostates are excluded, for they do not accept the covenant (for they have broken the covenant).[21] And thus it says: 'The sacri-fice of the wicked is an abomination; how much more so when he brings it with evil intent' (Prov. 21.27).

Nothing could show more clearly that fulfilling the commandments (in this passage, those concerning sacrifices) is a privilege and obligation *for those in the covenant.* Those outside, even if they were born *Israelites*, are excluded from both the privilege and the responsibility. The commandments accom-pany the covenant. The question now arises of whether or not the covenant itself is earned by fulfilling the law.

4. The election and the covenant

With the question of the relationship between God's giving the covenant and Israel's obedience to the commandments[1] we enter into a subject on which the haggadah is unusually rich. As we noted in section 2 above,

[18] Sifra Nedabah parasha 2.3 (Friedmann, p. 41; to 1.2).

[19] The *meshumadim*. The traditional text has *mumerim*. The two words are not clearly distinct, and the meaning of either may vary slightly from passage to passage (rebels, opponents etc.). See Jastrow on the two words. In any case, 'apostate' is clearly meant here. *Meshumadim* is the word used in the twelfth benediction in the *Shemoneh 'Esreh*: 'For the *meshumadim* may there be no hope', etc. See Finkelstein, 'The Development of the Amidah', *JQR* n.s. 16, 1925–26, p. 157.

[20] Apostates are not included in the word 'you'.

[21] Friedmann brackets this clause. The meaning of 'breaking the covenant' may be 'effacing circum-cision'. See Jastrow, s.v. *parar*.

---

[1] On the question of the relationship between the covenant and the commandments in the Old Testament, see Baltzer, *The Covenant Formulary*, pp. 1–98, especially p. 91; Hillers, *Covenant*, pp. 50, 105, 112, 147, 154f. On the view of the covenant in the second century b.c.e., see Jaubert, *La notion d'alliance*, pp. 27–66.

different haggadic interpretations of the same passage, event or experience
can be given by various Rabbis at different times, without the intention that
any one of the comments is to be taken as a 'doctrine' or as part of a systematic theology. It would be a mistake either to impose an artificial unanimity
on the various statements about the covenant and the commandments or to
suppose that statements which appear to be in conflict are necessarily
fragments of two (or more) differing systematic theologies. It would also be
a mistake simply to count the appearances of a particular view and to
determine the 'majority' viewpoint, relegating divergent statements to a
minority, peripheral position. Our procedure in this, as in subsequent
sections, is to examine the different types of statement and to determine
whether they reveal an underlying agreement. If they do not, we shall have
to be content simply to let the divergent statements stand as real differences
of opinion.

The theme of gratuity

We may begin by noting several passages in which a Rabbi explicitly states
that entrance into the covenant was prior to the fulfilment of commandments; in other words, that the covenant was not earned, but that obedience
to the commandments is the consequence of the prior election of Israel by
God. Thus, for example, these two statements attributed to contemporary
Rabbis of the middle of the second century, R. Joshua b. Karha and R.
Simeon b. Yohai:

R. Joshua b. Karha said: Why does the section *Hear, O Israel* (Deut. 6.4–9)
precede [the section] *And it shall come to pass if ye shall hearken* [*diligently to my
commandments*]? – so that a man may first take upon him the yoke of the kingdom
of heaven and afterward take upon him the yoke of the commandments. (Berakoth
2.2)

R. Simeon b. Yohai made the same argument, referring to Ex. 20.2f. and
Lev. 18.1–3. In each case the statement 'I am the Lord your God' precedes
and grounds the commandments which follow. 'When it says "I am the
Lord thy God", it means this: Am I not he whose kingship you took upon
yourselves at Sinai?' When the Israelites answer affirmatively, God replies,
'You have accepted my kingship, accept my ordinances.'[2] Accepting God as
king, which means accepting him as protector and defender as well as lawgiver, is followed by explicit commandments. The kingship of God over
his chosen people always involves them in keeping the ordinances of the

---

[2] Sifra Aḥare pereq 13.3 (to 18.1f). This is the beginning of a section which has been added to Sifra
from the Yalkut. The section ('Mekilta of 'Arayot') is not from the school of Akiba, but from that of
Ishmael. See Epstein, *Mebo'ot*, pp. 640f.; Weiss, Sifra, 85d. A partial parallel, also in the name of R.
Simeon b. Yohai, is found in Mek. Baḥodesh 6.

king, for that is the proper relationship between king and people; but the acceptance of God's kingship always precedes the enjoining of the commandments.

The same view of the relationship between the covenant and the commandments is found in two picturesque parables in the Mekilta. We shall quote the first in full:

> *I Am the Lord Thy God* (Ex. 20.2). Why were the Ten Commandments not said at the beginning of the Torah? They give a parable. To what may this be compared? To the following: A king who entered a province said to the people: May I be your king? But the people said to him: Have you done anything good for us that you should rule over us? What did he do then? He built the city wall for them, he brought in the water supply for them, and he fought their battles. Then when he said to them: May I be your king? They said to him: Yes, yes. Likewise, God. He brought the Israelites out of Egypt, divided the sea for them, sent down the manna for them, brought up the well for them, brought the quails for them. He fought for them the battle with Amalek. Then He said to them: I am to be your king. And they said to Him: Yes, yes.[3]

The point of being the people's king is presumably that now God can give commandments, but they are preceded by his acts of mercy. Similarly, in commenting on the passage 'Thou shalt not have other Gods before me', the Mekilta gives a parable in which the king refuses to issue decrees until his reign has been accepted by the people.

> Likewise, God said to Israel: 'I am the Lord thy God, thou shalt not have other gods – I am He whose reign you have taken upon yourselves in Egypt.' And when they said to Him: 'Yes, yes,' He continued: 'Now, just as you accepted My reign, you must also accept My decrees: "Thou shalt not have other gods before Me." '[4]

The point is put succinctly elsewhere in the Mekilta: 'Thou hast shown us mercy, for we had no meritorious deeds.'[5] This view also informs the Mekilta's statement that 'Already before I (God) gave them the commandments I advanced them the rewards for them', referring to the giving of the double portion of manna *before* the Sabbath had been observed. The passage continues to the effect that God habitually acted thus toward Israel.[6] This point is reinforced by the observation that even after receiving benefits from God, Israel continued to disobey: 'R. Joshua says: The Holy One, blessed be He, said to Moses: Say to the Israelites: I have brought you out of Egypt, I have divided the Red Sea for you [a list is given] – how long will you refuse to observe My commandments and My laws?'[7]

---

[3] Mek. Bahodesh 5 (219; II, 229f.).   [4] Mek. Bahodesh 6 (222; II, 238f.; to 20.3).

[5] Mek. Shirata 9 (145; II, 69; to 15.13). The Hebrew lacks 'meritorious'. See further the point that God deals with Israel more mercifully than they deserve, Mek. of R. Simeon b. Yohai to Ex. 6.2 (cited below, n. 65) and Mek. Bahodesh 10 (cited below, section 5, n. 93).

[6] Mek. Bahodesh 1 (206; II, 199; to 19.2).

[7] Mek. Vayassa' 5 (169f.; II, 121 [ch. 6]; to 16.28). For the point that the kingdom implies the commandments as its consequence, see Kadushin, *Rabbinic Mind*, p. 23; Schechter, *Aspects*, p. 219, citing targum Pseudo-Jonathan to Ex. 34.7; Lev. 16.21; Num. 14.18.

Thus we see that the view that God had first chosen Israel and only then given commandments to be obeyed is not lacking in Rabbinic literature. These comments occur especially in the haggadic commentaries on the biblical description of the Exodus and the giving of the Torah at Mt Sinai.

The election and the explanations of it

The Rabbis maintained the biblical attitude of being especially chosen and set aside by God.[8] 'I am God for all those who come into the world, nevertheless I have conferred My name particularly on My people Israel.'[9] It does not seem necessary here to give extensive documentation of the fact that the Rabbis regarded Israel as elect.[10] The point is obvious and will in any case emerge repeatedly in the study. Nor do I wish to defend the Rabbis against the charge of arrogance.[11] The Rabbis were no more plagued by arrogance than any other people who have held a doctrine of election; indeed, the idea that suffering was entailed in the election (to be discussed below) helps to give quite a non-arrogant tone to Rabbinic thought on election. The idea of being privileged as children of Abraham may have been abused, but abuses were criticized by the Rabbis themselves. Smugness was resisted.[12] But leaving such matters aside, we may turn immediately to Rabbinic explanations of the election.

We have already seen passages in which God's election was thought of as being totally gratuitous, without prior cause in those being elected. But the Rabbis regarded God as reasonable, as the just judge who, while he may temper his judgments with mercy, is neither capricious nor arbitrary. Thus one finds that the Rabbis could not rest content with simply saying that God chose Israel, but inquired *why* he did so. They wished to explain that it was not 'odd of God to choose the Jews'. There are basically three kinds of answers given by the Rabbis to the question of why God chose Israel.

One answer is that God offered the covenant (and the commandments attached to it) to all, but only Israel accepted it. The second answer is that God chose Israel because of some merit found either in the patriarchs or in the exodus generation or on the condition of future obedience. The third answer is really not an answer at all; that is, it does not in fact give a reason

---

[8] See especially B. W. Helfgott, *The Doctrine of Election in Tannaitic Literature*. He shows that the conception of being the chosen people remained stable during the period, while varying in the precise form of elaboration and degree of emphasis from one Rabbi to another. He reasons that the Christian challenge caused the doctrine to be insisted on in certain ways, especially between 70 and 135 c.e.

[9] Mek. Mishpatim 20 (Kaspa 4) (334; III, 185; to 23.17).

[10] In addition to Helfgott's study cited above, see especially Schechter, *Aspects*, pp. 46–56. Cf. also Moore, *Judaism* I, pp. 398f.; K. Hruby, 'Le concept de Révélation dans la théologie rabbinique', *Orient Syrien* 11, 1966, pp. 17–50.

[11] See Schechter's comment on Luther, *Aspects*, p. 51 n. 3.

[12] Cf. Marmorstein, *Merits*, p. 38.

beyond God's own will: it is that God chose Israel for his name's sake. We may deal with each of these in turn.[13]

That God offered the covenant to all is sometimes said in such a way as to point out Israel's moral superiority to other nations, but the point also serves to explain why Israel and not the other nations are God's people:

Another interpretation: 'And he said, "The Lord came from Sinai"' (Deut. 33.2). When the Holy One, blessed be he, revealed himself to give [the] Torah to Israel, he revealed himself not to Israel alone, but to all the nations. He came first to the sons of Esau and said to them, 'You accept the Torah'. They said to him, 'What is written in it?' He answered, 'Thou shalt not murder.' They answered that the very nature of their father was that he killed (referring to Gen. 27).

God then offered the Torah to other nations, but they found other parts of it unacceptable. There was no nation which he did not approach and upon whose door he did not knock in order to offer the Torah, but they were unable to keep even the seven Noachian commandments.[14] Only Israel accepted the Torah.[15]

The point that the Torah was offered to all appears frequently, the comment often being occasioned by the fact that Mt Sinai is not in the land of Israel:

They Encamped in the Wilderness (Ex. 19.2b). The Torah was given in public, openly in a free place. For had the Torah been given in the land of Israel, the Israelites could have said to the nations of the world: You have no share in it. But now that it was given in the wilderness publicly and openly in a place that is free for all, everyone wishing to accept it could come and accept it. One might suppose that it was given at night, but Scripture says: 'And it came to pass on the third day when it was morning' (Ex. 19.16). One might suppose that it was given in silence, but Scripture says: 'When there were thunders and lightning'

---

[13] Cf. Schechter, *Aspects*, pp. 57–64; Urbach, *Ḥazal*, pp. 440–2; 466ff. (ET, pp. 496–99; 525–41).

[14] On these, see section 9 n. 28 below.

[15] Sifre Deut. 343 (395f.; to 33.2). There are variants (see Finkelstein's apparatus), but the essential points remain. Earlier in the same section it is said that God revealed himself not in one language but in four, and there are other statements to the same effect. There is a parallel, with some variations, in Mek. Bahodesh 5 (221; II 234f.; to 20.2); and there are numerous parallels, mostly abbreviated, in later literature. H. J. Schoeps ('Haggadisches zur Auserwählung Israels', *Aus frühchristlicher Zeit*, pp. 184–200) has discussed the passage in detail, and further literature is cited there. Schoeps is refuting the theory of Emmerich that Israel chose God, rather than God Israel, in order to have a *Volkskönig*. His primary evidence consists of other passages, some Amoraic, which attribute the election to God's free choice. This is in fundamental agreement with the line taken here. But Schoeps views the present passage as an indirect answer to the charge (in the epistle of Barnabas) that Israel was given the law as a punishment for sin (p. 189). It seems to me that there are more direct answers to such a charge in Rabbinic literature and that the present passage serves primarily to answer the question 'why Israel?' in such a way as to 'protect' God from being accused of caprice. Thus the Mekilta passage opens as follows (Lauterbach II, 234): 'And it was for the following reason that the nations of the world were asked to accept the Torah: In order that they should have no excuse for saying: Had we been asked we would have accepted it.' So also Helfgott, *Election*, p. 67. Urbach (*Ḥazal*, pp. 472f. and n. 28; ET, p. 927 n. 29) has also opposed Schoeps's explanation of the *Sitz im Leben* of the passage. He points out that the passage must be directed against pagans, since Christians could not have been accused of not keeping the Noachian commandments.

(ibid.). One might suppose that they could not hear the voice, but Scripture says: 'The voice of the Lord is powerful,' 'the voice of the Lord is full of majesty,' etc. (Ps. 29.4) . . . But what had those wretched nations done that He would not give them the Torah? 'His ordinances they have not known' (Ps. 147.20) – they were unwilling to accept them. . . .[16]

Now let us turn to passages which attribute God's choosing of Israel at the time of the exodus to the exodus generation's having fulfilled commandments already.[17] The most striking passage is Mek. Pisḥa 5 (to 12.6):[18]

And Ye Shall Keep It until the Fourteenth Day of the Same Month. Why did the Scripture require the purchase of the paschal lamb to take place four days before its slaughter? R. Matia the son of Ḥeresh used to say: Behold it says: 'Now when I passed by thee, and looked upon thee, and, behold, thy time was the time of love' (Ezek. 16.8). This means, the time has arrived for the fulfilment of the oath which the Holy One, blessed be He, had sworn unto Abraham, to deliver his children. But as yet they had no religious duties [*mitsvot*] to perform by which to merit redemption, as it further says: 'thy breasts were fashioned and thy hair was grown; yet thou wast naked and bare' (ibid.), which means bare of any religious deeds. Therefore the Holy One, blessed be He, assigned them two duties, the duty of the paschal sacrifice and the duty of circumcision, which they should perform so as to be worthy of redemption. . . . For this reason Scripture required that the purchase of the paschal lamb take place four days before its slaughter. For one cannot obtain rewards except for deeds.

R. Eliezer [sic; read Eleazar] ha-Kappar says: Did not Israel possess four virtues than which nothing in the whole world is more worthy: that they were above suspicion in regard to chastity and in regard to tale bearing, that they did not change their names and that they did not change their language. . . .

Elsewhere in the Mekilta, R. Nehemiah is reported as saying that Israel was redeemed from Egypt as a reward for 'the faith with which they believed', that is, God found in the Israelites a merit which could be rewarded.[19]

The same idea also crops up often not in connection with the exodus or with the election as such. We may take one example: Sifre Deut. 170 (to 18.9): ' "When (*ki*) you come to the land". – Fulfil the commandment which is mentioned so that as a reward for it you may enter the land.[20] "Which the Lord thy God gives to you" – as your reward.'[21]

[16] Mek. Baḥodesh 1 (205f.; II, 198–200; to 19.2b). The Mekilta of R. Simeon b. Yoḥai on the same passage has a similar comment (p. 137). Cf. Mek. Shirata 5 (133; II, 39; to 15.6). On the universality of God's offer, note Sifra Aḥare pereq 13.13 (to 18.5b): 'The Bible does not say that the Torah is for priests, Levites and (ordinary) Israelites alone, but it is the "Torah of man"' (II Sam. 7.19). See further Schechter, *Aspects*, pp. 80–96; Moore, *Judaism* I, pp. 219–34, 276–9: the offer of the covenant to all was the teaching of both of the great schools of the second century.

[17] It did not escape the Rabbis that some commandments had been given before Moses received the law on Sinai. See e.g. Mek. Mishpatim 4 (263; III, 37 [Nezikin 4]; to 21.14): 'Issi b. Akabyah says: Before the giving of the Torah we had been warned against shedding blood.' Cf. Kiddushin 4.14: Abraham performed the law before it was given.

[18] 14; I, 33f.   [19] Mek. Beshallah 6 (114; I, 253 [ch. 7]; to 14.31).

[20] So also Sifre Deut. 297 (316; to 26.1).

[21] 'As your reward': Finkelstein (p. 217) reads *bizekuteka*; Friedmann (f. 107a) *bisekareka*. 'Reward'

It will be seen immediately that this attitude is in direct conflict with the one which we described earlier, which was that God chose Israel without merit on Israel's part and that he gave the reward for the commandments before they were performed. One may contrast the sentence by Matia b. Ḥeresh (cited immediately above), 'One cannot obtain rewards except for deeds', with the anonymous sentence elsewhere in the Mekilta, 'Thou hast shown us mercy, for we had no meritorious deeds' (above, n. 5). We shall not inquire now whether or not these views can be reconciled, but shall proceed to other explanations of why Israel was chosen.

Just as the Rabbis sometimes say that the exodus from Egypt was merited by the Israelites' having performed a meritorious deed and thus having earned the exodus, they also attribute it to the merit (*zekut*) of the patriarchs. The word *zekut* and the phrase *bizekut* will be fully discussed below. We should note here that *zekut*, especially when prefaced by the preposition *bet* (by, in), does not necessarily bear the full meaning of the English word 'merit'. That is, one should not necessarily suppose that the appearance of *zekut* always implies the full doctrine of stored-up merits which some scholars have found in Rabbinic literature (and compared to the Roman Catholic 'treasury of merits'). *Zekut* is closer to the English word 'virtue' in one way: both can bear a full or a weak meaning. Thus to say that someone is a person of virtue is a significant use of the word; but in the phrase 'by virtue of' the meaning is weakened to little more than 'because of'. One should not, therefore, grow too excited over every appearance of the expression *bizekut* – 'by virtue of' or 'by the merit of'. The word 'merit' should not be underlined.[22] After this caveat, we may proceed to consider some of the instances in which a Rabbi says that the exodus from Egypt was *bizekut* somebody or something. Thus Mek. Pisḥa 16:[23]

R. Eleazar the son of Azariah says: Because of the merit [*bizekut*] of our father Abraham did God bring Israel out of Egypt, as it is said: 'For He remembered His holy word unto Abraham His servant,' and, 'And He brought forth His people with joy' (Ps. 105.42f.). R. Simeon b. Yoḥai says: Because of [*bizekut*] their observing the rite of circumcision did God bring the Israelites out of Egypt.

Even if we do not give full theological meaning to *zekut* in the first line, we nevertheless see that God brought Israel out of Egypt because of Abraham. It might be more accurate to say, because of the oath to Abraham, since this is the point of the proof-text; but the Rabbi said '*bizekut* Abraham'. One may also note that R. Simeon b. Yoḥai attributes the exodus to Israel's strict fulfilment of a commandment.

---

is the usual translation for *sakar*, while 'merit' usually translates *zekut*. In the present case, the meaning is 'as your just due for fulfilling the commandment', whichever reading is adopted.

[22] See further below section 8. On the translation of *bizekut*, see Moore, *Judaism* III, p. 164. For related phrases (e.g. *besakar*, 'as a reward' or 'on account of'), see Marmorstein, *Merits*, p. 11.

[23] 62; I, 140f.; to 13.4.

There is a passage which is perhaps even clearer elsewhere in the Mekilta:[24]

R. Banaah says: 'Because of the merit of the deed which Abraham their father did [*bizekut mitsvah*], I will divide the sea for them.' . . . Simon of Teman says: 'Because of the merit of observing the commandment of circumcision, I will divide the sea for them.' . . . The sages say: For the sake of His name [*lema'an shemo*] He acted thus towards them. . . . Rabbi says: 'That faith with which they believed in Me is deserving that I should divide the sea for them.' . . . R. Eleazar the son of Azariah says: 'For the sake of their father Abraham I will divide the sea for them.' . . . R. Eleazar the son of Judah, a man of Kefar Tota, says: 'For the sake of the tribes I will divide the sea for them.' . . . Shema'yah says: 'The faith with which their father Abraham believed in Me is deserving that I should divide the sea for them.' . . . Abtalyon says: 'The faith with which they believed in Me is deserving that I should divide the sea for them.' . . . Simon of Kitron says: 'For the sake of [*bizekut*] the bones of Joseph I will divide the sea for them . . .'

We have been dealing with the exodus, but the same type of answer is given when the Rabbis are faced with other choices which God made. Why did he make this particular choice? Because of a certain *zekut*. Thus in T. Berakoth 4.17(16) the question is asked why Judah (i.e. the tribe of Judah) merited (*zakah*) the kingship. Some answer that it was because Judah confessed about Tamar. R. Akiba rejoins with the question, 'Does God give a reward for transgression?' He then suggests that Judah merited kingship because he redeemed his brother from death, or again because he was humble; but the final answer is that he 'sanctified the name' of God when he (i.e. the tribe) entered the water of the Red Sea first while the others hesitated. The motive of making God's choice seem non-arbitrary is clear here. If Israel was especially chosen, or if the tribe of Judah was especially favoured, it is because of some action which can explain why God made the choice he did.[25]

This way of explaining God's choosing Israel or acting on behalf of the Israelites appears apart from the expression *bizekut*. Thus in Ex. Rab. 15.4 the Tanna R. Judah is reported to have said: 'The Holy One, blessed be He, said: "If I am to scrutinize the deeds of Israel, they will never be redeemed [from Egypt]; I will therefore fix my regard on their holy ancestors."'[26] His contemporary R. Nehemiah is credited with a similar saying in the same passage. But it is not necessary to adduce further examples to show that the

---

[24] Mek. Beshallah 3 (98f.; I, 218ff. [ch. 4]; to 14.15). For other passages, see Schechter, *Aspects*, p. 174.

[25] For similar discussions, see Mek. Beshallah 5 (104–7; I, 232–7, esp. 236f. [ch. 6]; to 14.22); Sotah 36b–37a. It is interesting to note that *bizekut* does not appear in Sifra. One does, however, find in Sifra the phrase 'Why did they merit?' (מפני מה זכו), which plays the same role as 'by what merit did Judah merit' (באיזו זכות זכה) in Mek. Beshallah 5. Thus Sifra Ahare parasha 9.6: Why did the Canaanites merit (deserve) to dwell in their land 47 years? As a reward (*bishbil sakar*) for honouring Abraham.

[26] Cf. II Baruch 84.10: Pray 'that He may not reckon the multitude of your sins, but remember the rectitude of your fathers'.

Rabbis explained God's choice of Israel by reference to meritorious action by the ancestors.[27]

As I have already indicated, God's choice of Israel was also explained by actions yet to be performed. God foresees that Israel will fulfil the Torah and therefore chooses Israel to receive it:[28]

'When the Most High gave to the nations their inheritance'. – When the Holy One, blessed be he, gave [the] Torah to Israel, he stopped, looked (into the future, *tsafah*)[29] and perceived . . . , and, there being no nation among the nations which was worthy to receive the Torah except Israel, 'he fixed the bounds of the peoples'.

This explains God's choice rationally. The same point can be seen by examining the use of the phrase 'on condition that' (*'al tenai*), which appears in Sifra and occasionally elsewhere. There are several passages which say that the exodus was accomplished by God *on the condition that* Israel would take upon itself some commandment or other. It is necessary to quote in full only one example:[30]

'I am the Lord thy God who brought thee out of the land of Egypt.' – On this condition I brought you out of the land of Egypt: on the condition that you take upon yourselves the commandment concerning just measures (*mitsvat middot*); for everyone who confesses to (i.e. agrees to) the commandment concerning just measures confesses to (confirms) the exodus from Egypt; but anyone who denies the commandment concerning just measures denies the exodus from Egypt.

In other passages, other conditions are named: that one keeps the commandment not to charge interest[31] or that one sanctify God's name.[32] Besides the motive of giving a reason for God's action, one sees here also a rhetorical device aimed at emphasizing the importance of the commandment which forms the condition.[33] This last motivation appears clearly in an Amoraic passage in Leviticus Rabba:[34]

R. Johanan says: Let the commandment of the sheaf never seem as a trifling one in your eyes, for as a result of the commandment of the sheaf Abraham attained

---

[27] For the purpose of our discussion we have focused primarily on the election as exemplified by the redemption from Egypt, leaving aside the question of *when* God's decisive choice of Israel was made. In Sifre Deut. 312 (353; to 32.9), it is said to have been with Jacob, who was a perfect man and all of whose sons were worthy, rather than with Abraham or Isaac. The election of Jacob and his descendants proves that Israel is elect. Though based on merit, the election is subsequently unconditional and permanent. E. Mihaly ('A Rabbinic Defense of the Election of Israel', *HUCA* 25, 1964, pp. 103–35) has analysed the passage, arguing that it is a reply to the Christian denial of the election of all Israel.

[28] Sifre Deut. 311 (352; to 32.8).

[29] On the word *tsafah*, 'foresee', see Taylor, *Sayings of the Jewish Fathers*, p. 160.

[30] Sifra Qedoshim pereq 8.10 (to 19.36b).

[31] Sifra Behar parasha 5.3 (to 25.38).

[32] Sifra Emor pereq 9.6 (to 22.33). Cf. Sifre Deut. 303 (322; to 26.15) and 323 (373; to 32.30): If Israel does not do the Torah, how can God fulfil the promises?

[33] Discussing these passages, Kadushin (*The Rabbinic Mind*, p. 359) correctly comments: 'To strengthen regard for the *Mizwot*, the Rabbis thus taught that accepting or observing them is tantamount to acknowledging the exodus from Egypt.'

[34] Lev. Rab. 28.6, beginning (ET, p. 364).

to the privilege [*zakah*] of possessing the land of Canaan, as may be inferred from the text, *And I will give unto thee, and to thy seed after thee . . . all the land of Canaan* (Gen. 17.8). This was on condition [*àl menat*] that *Thou shalt keep My covenant, thou, and thy seed after thee* (v. 9). And which covenant is it? The commandment of the sheaf.

A more important motive behind the 'on condition that' sayings, however, is to emphasize that 'confessing' a commandment indicates one's acceptance of God's reign – his right to give commandments – while 'denying' a commandment indicates a denial of God's kingship and wilful and intentional disobedience. This comes out especially clearly in two other passages in Sifra:

'I am the Lord your God who brought you up from the land of Egypt' (Lev. 11.45). For this purpose (*'al ken*) I brought you up from the land of Egypt: on the condition that you take upon yourselves the yoke of the commandments; for everyone who confesses the yoke of the commandments confesses the exodus from Egypt, etc.[35]

The rather confusing appearance of 'for this purpose' and 'on the condition that' may indicate that the 'condition' part of the latter phrase should not be emphasized. Perhaps the meaning of the whole is 'with the view to'.[36] In any case, the word 'yoke', as Büchler has pointed out, 'expresses the . . . surrender of the Israelite to the Kingship of the Almighty and his obedience to the will of God manifested in His commandments'.[37] We need not recapitulate Büchler's argument here. But he has shown with great force and clarity that taking the yoke does not mean acceptance of a burden imposed, but voluntary and joyful surrender to the entire will of God.[38] The point is not that obeying a commandment, or even all the commandments, *earned* the exodus, but that God accomplished the exodus so that Israel might obey the commandments and that God *made the condition for remaining in the covenant* the free intent to obey the commandments, not their successful fulfilment.

A good insight into the purpose and meaning of the 'on condition that' passages can be gained by examining Sifra Behar parasha 5.3 (to 25.37f.). We have already noted that this is one of the instances in which it is said that God's delivery of the people from Egypt was conditional on their obeying commandments. We should now note the context of the statement:

'Nor give him your food for profit. I am the Lord' (Lev. 25.37f.). Hence they said: Everyone who accepts the yoke of [the commandment not to charge] interest

---

[35] Sifra Shemini pereq 12.4 (to 11.45).

[36] So Büchler translates it, *Studies in Sin and Atonement*, p. 92. Similarly, one cannot be sure whether Sifre Num. 115 (128; to 15.41) should be translated, 'On this condition (*'al menat ken*) I redeemed you: On the condition (*'al menat*) that I should give decrees and you should keep them' or 'For this purpose I redeemed you: So that I might give decrees and you should keep them'.

[37] *Studies in Sin and Atonement*, p. 93.   [38] Ibid., pp. 1–118.

accepts the yoke of Heaven, and everyone who casts off the yoke of [the command-ment not to charge] interest casts off the yoke of Heaven. 'I am the Lord your God, who brought you forth' (25.38). – On this condition I brought you forth from the land of Egypt, on condition that you should accept the commandment [concern-ing] interest; for everyone who confesses to (accepts) the commandment [con-cerning] interest confesses to (accepts) the exodus from Egypt. And everyone who denies the commandment [concerning] interest denies the exodus from Egypt.[39]

Here it is clear that the 'on condition that' passages indicate the attitude which should govern one who counts himself in the covenant (who 'con-fesses the exodus from Egypt'). He should also confess (intend to obey) the commandments. The intention to obey is the *condition of remaining* in the covenant, while the one who 'breaks off the yoke' indicates his intention not to obey, and denies God's right to command does remove himself from the covenant. Thus the 'on condition that' passages are not so narrowly legalistic as they might at first appear.[40]

Thus we see that the passages in Sifra and Sifre Zuṭa concerning God's deliverance of the people from Egypt on condition that the commandments be observed do not imply that the deliverance was *earned* by future obedience, although they do clearly mean that future obedience was expected. The question of 'conditional' and 'unconditional' is sufficiently important, however, to require further investigation. We may first consider the Mekilta's discussion of conditional and unconditional covenants and then the question of whether disobedience would cause God to cancel the covenant.

In commenting on Ex. 18.27, the Mekilta deals directly with the question of conditional and unconditional covenants, regarding the latter as superior.

R. Nathan says: The covenant with Jonadab the son of Rechab was greater than the one made with David. For the covenant made with David was only conditional ['al tenai], as it is said, 'If thy children keep My covenant,' etc. (Ps. 132.12), and if not: 'Then will I visit their transgression with the rod' (Ps. 89.33). But the covenant with Jonadab the son of Rechab was made without any condition. For it is said: '. . . There shall not be cut off unto Jonadab the son of Rechab a man to stand before Me for ever' (Jer. 35.19).

The midrash continues by stating that three things were given to Israel conditionally – the land of Israel, the Temple and the kingdom of David – while two things – the Torah and the covenant with Aaron – were uncon-

---

[39] 'Who brought you forth from the land of Egypt' (Num. 15.41) is interpreted in precisely the same way in Sifre Zuṭa to 15.41 (p. 290), except that the commandment specified is that concerning fringes and 'al menat is used instead of 'al tenai.

[40] These passages have traditionally been understood by New Testament scholars as showing that the law 'antedates and is the ground for the covenant' (Banks, *Jesus and the Law in the Synoptic Tradition*, 1975, p. 36; apparently depending on S.-B. IV, pp. 487f.). On the contrary, they show that the covenant is prior and that obedience to the law is not the ground for the covenant, but the *condition of remaining in it*. Other aspects of these passages are discussed below. On 'confessing' and 'denying', see section 6, pp. 135–8. On transgression of one commandment as indicating that the covenant is rejected, see section 6, pp. 134–6.

ditional.[41] It is remarkable that *the* covenant, the covenant established by the exodus and the giving of the Torah on Mt Sinai, is not mentioned one way or the other. Nevertheless, it is noteworthy that in the example given of a conditional covenant, that with David, the result of not being obedient is punishment, not the loss of election. The three things itemized as being given on condition in this passage – the land, the Temple and the kingdom – were in fact lost, and the passage doubtless reflects this, while affirming that there are gifts of God to Israel which no amount of disobedience would cancel.

In spite of what might at first appear to be the meaning of the 'on condition that' passages – that God would cancel the covenant if its conditions were not fulfilled – there is in fact no hint of such a view in the entire body of Tannaitic literature. The 'on condition that' passages themselves are not directed toward such a possibility. In part they are hortatory: the named commandment should be observed. The primary intention of the passages, however, is to insist that the *individual* who wishes to deny the implications of the covenant (the obligation to keep its commandments) is considered to reject the covenant itself (he 'denies the exodus'). That such a person may withdraw from the covenant is clear, but this in no way implies cancellation on God's side. The Rabbis never doubted that God would remain faithful to the covenantal promises, even when faced with disobedience. The universal view is stated distinctly by R. Jose (b. Halafta): 'No word of blessing that issued from the mouth of the Holy One, blessed be He, even if based upon a condition, was ever withdrawn by Him.'[42] The point is spelled out very elaborately in the Mekilta. Thus R. Eleazar b. R. Jose said in the name of Abba Jose the son of the Damascene:[43] ' "And God saw the children of Israel", that they would provoke Him in the future; "and God took cognizance of them", that they would in the future blaspheme.' Then why was he so lenient? Because of the power of repentance. Similarly, why does it say that 'He was their Saviour' (Isa. 63.8) when he knew that Israel would deal falsely with him? Because ' "He, being full of compassion, forgiveth iniquity" ' (Ps. 78.38).[44]

The only possible exception to this view – that God maintained the promises of the covenant despite disobedience – is a remark attributed to R. Judah.[45] There are two different versions, and we may cite them both:

'You are the sons of the Lord your God' (Deut. 14.1). R. Judah said: If you behave as sons should, you are sons; but if not, you are not sons. R. Meir said: In either case it is thus: 'You are the sons of the Lord your God.'[46]

[41] Mek. Jethro Amalek 2 (200f.; II, 187f. [Amalek 4]; to 18.27).
[42] Berakoth 7a, ET, p. 34, transmitted by the early Palestinian Amora, R. Johanan.
[43] On these Rabbis, see Epstein, *Mebo'ot*, p. 69.
[44] Mek. Bahodesh 1 (205; II, 197; to 19.2).
[45] See Schechter, *Aspects*, p. 54.   [46] Sifre Deut. 96 (157; to 14.1); cf. Kiddushin 36a.

'They have dealt corruptly with him, they are no longer his children because of their blemish' (Deut. 32.5). – Even though they are full of blemishes they are called sons. So R. Meir; as it is said, 'his sons are [full of] blemishes'. R. Judah said: They have no blemishes, as it is said, 'his sons have no blemishes'.[47]

In the second passage, R. Meir interprets the verse by citing the last two words, and R. Judah by citing the last three. R. Judah simply denies that God's sons have blemishes. In the first passage, however, the view attributed to R. Judah is clearly that transgressions cause one to forfeit the title 'sons'. The same point is made in an anonymous midrash to Num. 15.31: 'When blemishes are on them they are not his sons, but when there are no blemishes on them they are his sons.'[48] Here, however, the context clearly indicates that there are no blemishes on them when they repent, and this may have been the understanding behind R. Judah's comment in Sifre Deut. 96, the first passage quoted. Or, alternatively, the point may have been simply that sonship and obedience are always connected.[49] In any case, it would be erroneous to conclude that R. Judah thought that God would not keep faith with Israelites who sinned or that sinners would be excluded from the covenantal blessings. As we indicated before, it is very difficult to penetrate to what any individual Rabbi thought on any major principle of religion. Assuming for the moment, however, that R. Judah said all the things attributed to him, we may cite this baraita:

R. Judah son of R. Ila'i expounded: What is the meaning of, *Shew my people their transgression, and the house of Jacob their sins* (Isa. 58.1)? [The first phrase] refers to scholars, whose unwitting errors are accounted as intentional faults; [The second phase refers] to the ignorant [*'amme ha-'arets*], whose intentional sins are accounted to them as unwitting errors.[50]

Here R. Judah reserves the term 'my people' for scholars, but the 'house of Jacob' is clearly not excluded from the covenant because of sin. Similarly, R. Judah argued that Manasseh had a share in the world to come since he repented (Sanhedrin 10.2). This would indicate that he did not believe that disobedience as such removes one from the covenant.

Thus we conclude that, although God would punish disobedience and although intentional rejection of God's right to command implied rejection of the covenant, the Rabbis did not have the view that God's covenant with Israel was conditional on obedience in the sense that the covenantal promises

---

[47] Sifre Deut. 308 (346f.; to 32.5).

[48] Sifre Num. 112 (121; to 15.31).

[49] So Köberle, *Sünde und Gnade*, pp. 490f. Helfgott (*Election*, p. 121) misses this point when he writes that 'according to R. Judah, the election depends directly upon Israel's continuously observing its part in the reciprocal arrangement of the loving relationship between God and Israel'. The passages which he cites do not deal with the election, but either with the title 'sons' or simply with God's punishing transgression. Neither point indicates that God withdraws the *election* in response to Israel's sins. So also E. Mihaly, 'A Rabbinic Defense of the Election of Israel', *HUCA* 25, 1964, p. 124 n. 36.

[50] Baba Metzia 33b.

would be revoked by God because of Israel's sin. The covenant is, in this sense, unconditional, although it clearly implies the obligation to obey.

We noted above that Rabbinic statements to the effect that the covenant is conditional on obedience have led Christian scholars to conclude that the Rabbinic view of religion is that the covenant (and salvation) are earned and that the grace of God plays no substantial part.[51] It is somewhat amusing to note that other Christian scholars, having noted the passages in which the covenant is said to be given gratuitously and without condition, have concluded that the Rabbinic conception lacked an ethical viewpoint. As Sanday and Headlam put it, by making the covenant unconditional, the Rabbis caused it to lose 'all its higher side'.[52] Similarly Wicks considered that the apocryphal literature took the 'worthier view' by making the covenant conditional on obedience.[53] This shows the degree to which scholars need an inferior religion to serve as the foil to the 'higher' and 'worthier' view. In fact, the Rabbis seem thus far to have kept the indicative and the imperative well-balanced and in the right order. But this is a question to which we may return below. We should now attempt to summarize the explanations of the covenant which we have thus far considered and to determine to what degree they represent a real conflict.

We have been considering the statements that God chose and redeemed Israel because of the merits of the exodus generation, because of the merits of the patriarchs and because of deeds yet to be done, as sub-categories of one general type of explanation: God chose Israel because of their deeds, either past, present or to be done in the future.[54] Marmorstein has argued, however, that the first two types of explanation represent a doctrinal dispute among schools.[55] One school, following Shema'yah, argued that God acted because of Abraham's merit, while the other agreed with Abtalyon that God acted because of the merit of the exodus generation.[56] It is a dispute between those who believe in imputed merit and those who believe in individual merit. Finkelstein similarly argued that the idea of the merit of the patriarchs, *zekut 'abot*, was maintained by Akiba and his school, while Ishmael and his school insisted on the necessity of individual merit. According to Finkelstein, the plebeians, represented by Akiba, 'held that "everything is determined"', and so trusted to the merits of the patriarchs, while the patricians, represented by Ishmael, 'believed that much depends on the individual'.[57] Marmorstein, it should be noted, thought that Akiba, like

[51] Section 1 above, especially on Jaubert and Fuller.
[52] Sanday and Headlam, *The Epistle to the Romans* (ICC), p. 249.
[53] H. J. Wicks, *The Doctrine of God in the Jewish Apocryphal and Apocalyptic Literature*, p. 253.
[54] Even if '*al tenai* be translated 'with the view to' instead of 'on condition that', there is still a connection between the election and deeds.
[55] Marmorstein, *Merits*, pp. 37ff., esp. 64f.
[56] Marmorstein (ibid., p. 65) lists Rabbis holding each view.
[57] Finkelstein, *Akiba*, p. 204.

Hillel, accepted a compromise on the issue.[58] One should also note that R. Eleazar b. Azariah, a patrician according to Finkelstein, mentioned the merit of Abraham as an explanation for the exodus.[59] Urbach agrees with Marmorstein that there was a dispute between those who attributed the redemption primarily to the merits of the fathers and those who attributed it primarily to the exodus generation. He shows, however, that some combined the two ideas, so that the dispute is not so sharp as it appears in Marmorstein's work. Urbach also notes that there was not a hard distinction between the school of R. Ishmael and the school of R. Akiba on the point.[60] It would thus appear that the dispute seen by Marmorstein and Finkelstein, although present, has been over-emphasized.

But even if one does find in these differing explanations a school dispute, it is not clear that it should be called a dispute about a 'doctrine' (as Marmorstein terms it).[61] It is difficult to imagine a Rabbi who emphasized the merits of the patriarchs denying individual responsibility, and surely no one supposed that obedient individuals could have redeemed themselves from Egypt apart from God's election of the descendants of Abraham. When subsequently Marmorstein discusses 'four trains of thought' which attempt 'to satisfy the curiosity of the contemporaries' on the question of why Israel was redeemed from Egypt, the terminology seems more appropriate.[62] In any case, when one considers the third explanation – that God redeemed Israel because of commandments yet to be fulfilled – the underlying agreement becomes clear. All three statements are explanations of the same conviction, the conviction that God chose Israel, and all three are based on the same logic, that God's choice was not capricious or arbitrary. For our purpose, the underlying agreement is more significant than the dispute.[63] In addition, the third explanation emphasizes the importance of the commandments to be fulfilled and points out the essential connection between being elect and intending to observe the commandments given by the God who elects. We may now turn to another kind of explanation of the election.

We have already seen several passages in which a whole series of sug-

[58] Marmorstein, *Merits*, p. 65.
[59] See Mek. Pisḥa, above n. 23; Mek. Beshallaḥ 3, above n. 24.
[60] Urbach, *Ḥazal*, pp. 440f. (ET, p. 497).
[61] Marmorstein, *Merits*, p. 65. Sjöberg (*Gott und die Sünder*, p. 187 n. 1) was also unconvinced by Marmorstein's two-school theory.
[62] *Merits*, p. 139; cf. pp. 164f.; over-emphasis of either side leads to abuse.
[63] In the following passage, God's choice of Israel on the basis of their merits is explicitly opposed to the charge that he is arbitrary. Whose merits account for election, however, is not stated. That is, the general argument that God is not arbitrary is here seen to be more important than the dispute about the merits of the patriarchs and the merits of the exodus generation: 'A Roman lady addressed a query to R. Jose (b. Halafta). She said to him: "Your God brings near to Himself indiscriminately whomsoever he pleases." He brought her a basket of figs and she scrutinized them well, picking the best and eating. Said he to her: "You, apparently, know how to select, but the Holy One, blessed be He, does not know how to select! The one whose actions He perceives to be good, him He chooses and brings near to Himself."' (Num. Rab. 3.2; ET, p. 68).

gestions is made as to why God brought Israel out of Egypt. We may now cite one more, which will lead us to the last type of explanation, that God did so 'for his name's sake':[64]

R. Jose the Galilean said: 'And God said': The Holy One, blessed be he, said to Moses: Israel deserves extinction in Egypt . . . because they are unclean [through worshipping] the idols of Egypt. . . . But for the sake of my great name and because of (*lema'an*) the merits of the Fathers [I will bring them out], as it is written, 'And God heard their groaning [and God remembered his covenant,' etc. (Ex. 2.24)]; and [I will bring them out] so that my name should not be profaned among them, as it also says, 'But I acted for the sake of my name, [that it should not be profaned in the sight of the nations among whom they dwelt], in whose sight I made myself known to them in bringing them out of the land of Egypt . . .' (Ezek. 20.9).

R. Tarfon said: The Holy One, blessed be he, said: It is revealed and known before me that Israel deserves to go forth from Egypt and to be destroyed by Ammon and Moab and Amalek, but I have sworn an oath to fight their wars, and I will save them, as it is said, 'A hand upon the banner of the Lord', etc. (Ex. 17.16). And it says, 'But I acted for the sake of my name, that it should not be profaned' (Ezek. 20.9). And here I am wanting to bring them out of Egypt, but you say to me, 'Send, I pray', etc.

R. Joshua b. Karha said: 'And God said': The Holy One, blessed be he, said: Israel was not worthy that I should give them manna in the wilderness, but rather they deserved hunger and thirst and nakedness. But I completed [paying] to them the reward of Abraham their father who 'stood' and 'made' before the ministering angels, as it is said, 'And he took the curds and milk . . . [which he made . . . and he stood by them . . .'] (Gen. 18.8). And here I am wanting to bring them out of Egypt and you say to me, 'Send, I pray, some other person.'[65]

The principal point here is that God considered Israel unworthy to be redeemed, but that he wished, for his name's sake, to keep the oaths which he had sworn to the patriarchs. Thus the patriarchs and God's name's sake are closely related.

If we ask what the *doctrine* on *why* Israel was elect was, we get no clear answer. It is clear throughout that *there is a universal conviction that Israel was elect and that election entailed commandments*. But there are differing explanations of why God chose Israel. It was not uncongenial to the Rabbis to say that God chose Israel out of sheer mercy – either before the commandments were given or 'for his name's sake'. Yet it is also apparent that the Rabbis wished to be able to find a *reason* for the election. But not one of the causes suggested can stand scrutiny as a systematic explanation of God's election of Israel. That no one cause is seen as such is clear, since a series of

---

[64] 'For his name's sake' has already appeared above, in the quotation from Mek. Beshallaḥ (n. 24). On the phrase, see Marmorstein, *Merits*, pp. 12ff.

[65] Mek. of R. Simeon b. Yoḥai to Ex. 6.2 (p. 5).

explanations for the same effect can often be listed without the editor's feeling compelled to prefer one explanation over others.[66] To say that Israel was brought out of Egypt because of the merit of Abraham only pushes the problem of election back one stage: why was Abraham chosen? The only answer is that God foresaw that Abraham's descendants would keep the commandments. That Abraham 'stood' and 'made' before the ministering angels is not an explanation of Abraham's election, since God had already called him. At one time the Rabbis can say that Israel merited the reward of the exodus because of fulfilling some commandment or other, while at others they can say that Israel did not have any merits, or that the rewards were given before the commandments were fulfilled.[67] The Rabbis did not have the Pauline/Lutheran problem of 'works-righteousness', and so felt no embarrassment at saying that the exodus was earned; yet that it was earned is certainly not a Rabbinic doctrine. It is only an explanatory device. One might have expected the Rabbis to develop a clear doctrine of prevenient grace,[68] but grace and merit did not seem to them to be in contradiction to each other; and doubtless they had good biblical support here. They could assert the grace of God in bringing Israel out of Egypt, yet at the same time ask by whose *zekut* he did so.[69]

Even saying that other nations were offered the Torah does not constitute an answer to the problem of election which is satisfactory to the systematic mind. God had not, after all, parted the sea for the other nations. Why should they have accepted the Torah? There is, then, no clear doctrine. The Rabbis could not, because of the biblical evidence that God rewards fulfilment of commandments,[70] give up the idea of reward for merit; nor could

[66] For a similar list of the various accounts of the exodus, see Kadushin, *The Rabbinic Mind*, pp. 73f. Kadushin points out that many of the statements do not contradict each other; they are 'simply different from each other'. But 'even contradictory statements lie peaceably side by side' (p. 74). This ability to overlook contradictions does not apply to halakic discussions (p. 75). One should add, however, that serious theological and religious discussions are, in the Rabbinic scheme of things, haggadic.

[67] It is not surprising that one Rabbi could have sayings of both types attributed to him. Thus R. Jose (b. Halafta), in replying to the charge that God is indiscriminate in his choice, replied that 'The one whose actions He perceives to be good, him He chooses and brings near to Himself' (Num. Rab. 3.2, near top; ET, p. 68). It was the same R. Jose who said that God gave to Israel the rewards for the commandments before giving the commandments (above, n. 6).

[68] There are at least a few Tannaitic sayings which seem to imply an idea of prevenient grace in a certain sense; 'God does not let ('they do not let') the righteous come into the hands of a serious transgression'; Sifre Num. 135 (commenting on Deut. 3.26; p. 181); on this portion of Sifre Num., see below, section 5 n. 103. See also the prayer cited below, section 7 n. 157; the saying of R. Gamaliel, section 5 n. 76.

[69] Marmorstein (*Merits*, p. 24) found here another doctrinal dispute between 'schools', one holding that God did everything for his name's sake, the other that he rewarded Israel only for merit. While some Rabbis would emphasize one or the other explanation for Israel's election, they do not seem to have divided into doctrinal schools on the point. The genius of Rabbinic theological discussion is that doctrinal debates – at least in the Christian sense of the term – are avoided. It is doubtful that those who emphasized that God rewards merits would have *denied* that God chose Israel for his name's sake; and those emphasizing God's free grace would not deny that God is just and punishes and rewards people according to their merits.

[70] The point need scarcely be documented, but note Lev. 26.3f.: 'If you walk in my statutes and observe

they accept the capriciousness on God's part that the doctrine of election apart from just cause seems to imply.[71] Yet the exclusivism and arrogance which might accompany the view that God dealt in a special way with Israel because Abraham or the exodus generation fulfilled certain commandments were not satisfactory either, so they stated that God acted before the commandments were given. Despite the attempts to explain it, the cause of election finally goes unexplained, as it always must.[72] But in God's choosing Israel, the Rabbis saw Israel's one claim to greatness: those whom the king loves are greater than those who love the king.[73] This passage at once emphasizes that God's love cannot be earned and the Israelites' feeling of being specially chosen.

Even if the view that God chose Israel only because of some past or present or future merit were Rabbinic doctrine – which it is not – this would still not prove that individual Israelites had to *earn* salvation. Even if the election had been earned in the past, there is no thought that subsequent Israelites must continue to earn their place in the covenant as individuals,[74] or that the covenant must be re-won in each generation. For whatever reason God chose Israel in the past, the *a priori* expectation would be that in subsequent generations the covenant would remain effective, that God would keep his promises to redeem and preserve his people. As we saw in section 1, Weber, in order to prove Rabbinic religion to be one of legalistic works-righteousness, had to invent the theory of a post-election fall. More recently, Rössler has denied that the covenant had continuing validity, and it is to this question that we now turn.

The enduring validity of the covenantal promises

Since Rössler has taken it as one of his main themes that in Rabbinic thought the election was not enduringly valid, but that each individual had *de novo* to achieve his individual place in God's grace by works of law, we may briefly summarize his view. We should first note that he does take it to be the

---

my commandments and do them, then I will give you rains in their season, and the land shall yield its increase, and the trees of the field shall yield their fruit.'

[71] Cf. Marmorstein, *Merits*, pp. 14, 137–9.

[72] Schoeps, *Aus frühchristlicher Zeit*, pp. 196f., properly emphasizes that the idea that God elected Israel to accomplish a special service has no basis in Jewish tradition. He sees the Rabbinic view as basically shaped by Deut. 7.7f.: God chose the people of Israel not because of their greatness, but because he loved them. I have been discussing Rabbinic attempts to *explain* that love.

[73] Mek. Mishpatim 18 (311; III, 138 [Nezikin 18]; to 22.20). The saying is attributed to R. Simeon b. Yohai, who applies it to proselytes: beloved are proselytes, etc. In Sifre Deut. 47 (106; to 11.21), a similar saying is attributed to the later R. Simeon b. Menasya, who applies it to the elders; apparently longevity and honour by the community are taken to indicate God's love. The same Rabbi thought that the righteous are rewarded in this world; see below, section 7 n. 123.

[74] Thus the circumcision of a Jewish boy is a symbol of his membership in the holy people of God, not a soteriological event marking his transfer from the realm of darkness to light. See Sjöberg, 'Wiedergeburt und Neuschöpfung im palästinischen Judentum', *Studia Theologica* 4, 1951–52, pp. 44–85.

case that the election determines salvation in apocalyptic literature. For proof, he cites a sentence from Helfgott's study of the election in Tannaitic literature, curiously applying Helfgott's conclusion to literature which Helfgott did not study, while completely ignoring Helfgott's view of the material with which his book was concerned.[75]

With regard to Rabbinic literature, he undertakes to establish his point by an examination of the noun and verbal forms for 'promise' (בטחה, מבטיח, הבטיח) as they are used with regard to God's promises to the fathers. Rössler cites a total of four passages: Num. Rab. 2.12 (ET, p. 41); Mek. Beshallaḥ 3(97; I, 217 [ch. 4]; to 14.15); Pesikta Rabbati 42; Shebuoth 35b. He observes that in all these cases the promise refers to a definite and concrete item which has already been fulfilled. He then concludes that this is the universal understanding of God's promises to the fathers: they are not 'historical', they are not valid through history and they do not remain open. The only connection between the fathers and subsequent generations is the conception of the treasury of supererogatory merits. There is no conception of *Heilsgeschichte*. Further, the word 'covenant' means exclusively law. Rössler finds only one exception: when God's side of the covenant is in mind, his fidelity is made known only in contingent human history (citing Est. Rab. 8.6, ET, pp. 107f., cited as Est. Rab. 4.15). But this is not the centre of the theological sayings about the covenant.[76]

Rössler's thin and superficial treatment does not of itself merit extensive rebuttal. It is a simple observation that *some* of God's biblical promises were fulfilled within biblical history and do not remain open, and Rössler has simply found a few such cases. The instances cited from the Mekilta, Numbers Rabbah and Pesikta Rabbati have to do with God's promise to bring Israel out of Egypt. The promise was fulfilled by parting the sea. Shebuoth 35b is a statement by R. Joshua, 'What He promised He fulfilled', referring to the war of the other tribes against Benjamin. Since Rössler's treatment of the election and the covenant is only a recent example of a widespread view among Christian scholars, however, it is worth a few pages to point out that the view is erroneous.

Had Rössler examined Rabbinic comments on biblical promises other than those obviously fulfilled in the past, he would have found a different situation from the one he described. Thus, for example, the promise that Israel would become as numerous as the sand of the sea (Gen. 22.17) was clearly believed to remain open. With a reference to Moses's mention of 'ten thousand thousands of Israel' (Num. 10.36) and his blessing that the Israelites should become one thousand times as numerous as they were (Deut.

[75] Rössler, *Gesetz und Geschichte*, p. 63; citing Helfgott, *Election*, p. 1! Rössler (p. 63 n. 3) states that Helfgott's conclusion applies *also* to apocalyptic literature, without noting that he did not accept that conclusion, or even mention Helfgott's book, in his own discussion of Rabbinic literature.

[76] Rössler, pp. 27–9.

1.11), the Israelites are depicted in a Rabbinic comment as taking Moses to task for so restricting their numbers, since God had *promised* (הבטיחנו) that they should be as the stars of the heavens and as the sand of the sea. 'Moses said to them: I am flesh and blood and thus there is a limit to my blessings. . . . But [God] will bless as he said to you: as the sand of the sea,' etc.[77]

That the election itself was considered to be eternally valid is seen frequently in the literature. In commenting on Ex. 15.17 ('Thou wilt bring them in and plant them on thy own mountain'), the anonymous comment in the Mekilta is this:

A planting, not to be followed by a plucking up, as it is said: 'And I will build them, and not pull them down; and I will plant them, and not pluck them up' (Jer. 24.6). And it also says: 'And I will plant them upon their land, and they shall no more be plucked up,' etc. (Amos 9.15).

The mountain in Ex. 15.17 is defined as 'The mountain about which Thou hast made us a promise.'[78] Despite Rössler's view of the limitation of the term 'promise' to past promises and fulfilments, the promise is here clearly considered to be eternal.

Rössler's supposition that the only connection between the fathers and subsequent generations of Jews, in the Rabbinic view, was the establishment by the fathers of a treasury of merits which could later be drawn on, is completely wrong. In the first place, as we shall show in section 8 below, he shares a common misunderstanding of the phrase *zekut 'abot*. We may immediately note, however, that there are numerous passages in Rabbinic literature in which the Rabbis clearly identify themselves as the heirs of *promises* to the fathers, as continuing in the covenant established between God and Israel. A full examination of such terms as 'inherit' (*yarash*), 'trust' (*batah*) and 'promise' (*hibtiah*) would produce numerous examples, but we shall illustrate the point only briefly. For evidence of a relation between the fathers and subsequent generations which is conceived quite otherwise than in terms of a treasury of merits, we may refer to the comments on 'my God' and 'my father's God' in the Mekilta on Ex. 15.2: 'With me He dealt according to the rule of mercy, while with my fathers He dealt according to the rule of Justice.'[79]

The community of Israel said before the Holy One, blessed be He: Not only for the miracles which Thou hast performed for me will I utter song and praise before Thee, but for the miracles which Thou hast performed for my fathers and for me and for that which Thou wilt do for me in every generation. In this sense it is said: 'My father's God, and I will exalt Him.'[80]

[77] Sifre Num. 84 (83; to 10.36).
[78] Mek. Shirata 10 (149; II, 77; to 15.17).
[79] Mek. Shirata 3 (128; II, 28; to 15.2).
[80] Mek. Shirata 3 (128f.; II, 29).

Similarly, one might cite the comment on an earlier phrase in Ex. 15.2, 'and he has become my salvation'. The two possibilities for pointing the verb ויהי lead to the comment that the passage means both 'He was and He is. He was my salvation in the past and He will be my salvation in the future.'[81]

Even when the verb *hibṭiaḥ* is used in the perfect (= past tense in Rabbinic Hebrew), it does not necessarily mean that a promise was fulfilled in the past and is no longer valid. Commenting on Deut. 32.6, 'he made you and established you', R. Simeon b. Judah remarked: 'He settled you upon your foundation, he fed you with the plunder of the seven [Gentile] nations, and he gave you what he swore to you and caused you to inherit what he promised you.'[82] Although, following the biblical text, all the verbs are perfect, the meaning is clearly that Israel still possesses the promises: they have inherited what they were promised.

The best evidence, however, that the Rabbis considered the covenantal promises to be enduring and efficacious comes from considering the themes of God's love for Israel and God's presence with Israel. The theme of God's presence with Israel will be dealt with in section 10 below, but here we may note that the covenant includes blessing as well as commandments; it is not only law (as Rössler supposes), but also promise.

God's side of the covenant: commandments and blessings

We began this section by inquiring about the relationship between God's commandments and the covenant. Did the former earn the latter, or did the latter entail the former? We have seen that the Rabbis' view was that in *their* day obedience to the commandments was the Israelites' response to the God who chose them, although some, when explaining *why* God *initially* chose Israel, justified his choice in terms of merit. We have thus seen that one aspect of God's side of the covenant was to give commandments, as Israel's was to obey them. We have also alluded to the promises of God implied in the covenant. We should now refer more directly to what these promises were perceived by the Rabbis to entail.

A complete catena of passages on God's love for Israel would fill a large volume; it is a constant theme in the literature, and it appears in the midrashim wherever the text gives an opening, often with great elaboration.[83] The main themes seem to be these: simply that God loves Israel and has made known his love (so R. Akiba in Aboth 3.15), that God protects Israel

---

[81] Mek. Shirata 3 (126; II, 24; to 15.2). For the exegesis, see Lauterbach's note, ad loc. We shall return to the question of assurance of salvation in section 10 below. The present point has to do with the Rabbinic view that the promises of God in the past were still in effect.

[82] Sifre Deut. 309 (350; to 32.6).

[83] Such a catena from the Mekilta is given by Kadushin, 'The Rabbinic Concept of Israel', *HUCA* 19, 1945–46, pp. 71–80. He observes (p. 72), however, that 'in the rabbinic view God's love is not limited to Israel'.

from evil, that God abides with Israel, that God will ultimately save Israel, and that God will save the soul of the individual Israelite at the time of death. Many of these themes appear in the commentaries on Num. 6.24–6 ('The Lord bless you and keep you', etc.). The comments in Sifre Zuṭa and Sifre Num. are closely parallel. A selection follows:[84] R. Isaac asks why 'and keep you' is explicitly mentioned, since 'and bless you' should by itself imply 'keeping'. The second phrase means ' "And keep you" from the evil impulse so that it will not take you out of the world.'[85]

Another interpretation of 'and keep you': He will keep you from the demons which surround you. . . . So we see that they were blessed and kept. And whence do we know that also the Shekinah would be among them? Scripture says: 'The Lord make his face to shine upon you.'[86]

The phrase 'and be gracious unto you' is interpreted as this: 'He will give you knowledge so that each would be gracious to the other and each would have compassion on the other.'[87] The midrash then returns to the phrase 'and he will keep you'; the theme is not yet exhausted: '*He will keep with you the covenant of your fathers*, as it is said, "The Lord your God will keep with you the covenant and the steadfast love which he swore to your fathers to keep"' (Deut. 7.12).[88]

Another interpretation of 'and he will keep you'. He will keep for you the [end] time, as it is written: 'The oracle concerning Dumah. One is calling to me from Seir, "Watchman [literally, 'keeper'], what of the night? . . ." The watchman says: "Morning comes, and also the night . . ."' (Isa. 21.11f.).

Another interpretation of 'and he will keep you': He will keep your soul at the time of death, as it is written, 'The life of my lord shall be bound in the bundle of the living' (I Sam. 25.29). Am I to understand [that this is the case] for both the righteous and the wicked? [No, for] it is said, 'and the lives of your enemies he shall sling out as from the hollow of a sling' (ibid.).[89]

The midrash comments equally extensively on the other phrases in the biblical passage, but this is sufficient for the present purpose. That Israel is beloved by God and given special blessings is, as we said, a common theme in the literature. It would be a mistake, however, to suppose that the Rabbis thought that the covenant brought only commandments and blessings. On the contrary. The suffering of God's chosen people is repeatedly emphasized, and suffering comes to play a significant role in Rabbinic theology. Sufferings

---

[84] Sifre Zuṭa to 6.24–6 (247–50); Sifre Num. 40–2 (43–8).
[85] Sifre Zuṭa, p. 247; cf. Sifre Num., p. 44.
[86] Sifre Zuṭa, ibid.; the parallel in Sifre Num., p. 44, lacks the passage on the Shekinah.
[87] Sifre Zuṭa, p. 248.
[88] Sifre Zuṭa, p. 248; Sifre Num., p. 44; my emphasis.
[89] Ibid.

are to be accepted with joy (as are the commandments and blessings) because they are part of God's overall redemptive purpose toward Israel.[90] But whether the Rabbis are discussing Israel's special relationship with God in terms of the detailed commandments to be obeyed, the special blessings of Israel, or the sufferings sent by God to lead to reflection and repentance, they show themselves to be equally conscious of living within the framework of a covenant offered by God and accepted by their ancestors and themselves. They are prepared and eager to fulfil their side of the covenant, and they never doubt that God is fulfilling his.

This last is a very important point, since it stands in contrast to a type of religious concern found in the prophets and in Job. It is a mark of the particular genius of prophetism that it was able to charge God with the responsibility of fulfilling the covenant and thus to imply that he might not have been doing so satisfactorily. But this note is never struck in the surviving Tannaitic literature. God's total faithfulness and reliability are always assumed and often stated. This is frequently indicated by comments on the biblical phrase 'I am the Lord your God'. The Rabbis often interpret this to mean: 'I am faithful to pay a reward; I am a faithful judge to punish.'[91] We shall have to return to these passages in considering the question of legalism; just now we note that God was considered reliably to act as God. But the strongest argument here is the total absence of any indication to the contrary.

We may now summarize the discussion thus far. The very existence of the halakic material led us to inquire what religious motive lay behind the minute and thorough investigation of the biblical law. We saw that the Rabbis were of the opinion that Israel stands in a special relationship to God as a result of God's election of them. God acted on their behalf, and they accepted his rule. It pleased God to give his people commandments, and the fulfilling of them is the characteristic religious act of the Israelite: it is his way of responding to the God who chose and redeemed him. In attempting to give a rationale for the election, the Rabbis appealed to the free grace of God and sometimes to the concept of merit. God's rule entails obedience, and it also brings benefits and suffering upon his people, but even the suffering is beneficial. In any case, the Israelite is to fulfil what he was commanded; he does not question that God is fulfilling his role as king, judge and redeemer.

It will be seen that our investigation of the nature of the material introduced us into the middle of the pattern which characterizes the religion of the Rabbis. We have now reasoned back to the beginning, the election of Israel.

---

[90] See especially A. Büchler, *Studies in Sin and Atonement in the Rabbinic Literature of the First Century*, pp. 119–211. Suffering is discussed more fully below, section 7.

[91] Sifra Aḥare parasha 9.1 (to 18.1f.); ibid., pereq 13.15 (from the 'Mekilta of 'Arayot'); Sifra Qedoshim pereq 8.11 (to 19.37); Sifra Behar pereq 9.6 (to 26.2); Sifra Emor pereq 9.6 (to 22.33). In several of these, only the phrase 'I am faithful to pay a reward (just due)' occurs. See further Sifre Num. 115 (129; to 15.41); Mek. Baḥodesh 4 (218; II, 228; to 20.1); Sifre Zuṭa to Num. 15.41.

We have now to proceed to the consequences of obedience or non-obedience of the commandments which were given with the covenant.

5. Obedience and disobedience; reward and punishment

The requirement of obedience

In consequence of God's election of Israel and Israel's acceptance of God, God gave Israel commandments. He intended, in the Rabbis' view, that the commandments be obeyed:

'If you walk in my statutes and observe my commandments and do them' (Lev. 26.3). [It means] one who learns in order to do, not one who learns in order not to do; the one who learns in order not to do would better not have been created.[1]

Similarly, in a discussion of oaths, the Rabbis represent God as saying that he made an oath to Israel, not on the conditions which they might have had in their hearts, but on those which he had in his.[2] And his conditions, of course, are that the commandments be observed.[3]

The emphasis was frequently on the necessity of *intending* to obey. The subject of intention, of 'directing the heart', is a very important one, and it requires some elaboration. There are at least three possible nuances. In the first place, 'directing the heart' can refer to 'directing the heart to God ("Heaven")'. Thus in connection with offerings, it is said that the size of the offering does not matter; all are called 'an odour of sweet savour'. This is 'to teach that it is all one whether a man offers much or little, if only he directs his mind towards Heaven'.[4] The saying that 'a man may do much or he may do little; it is all one, provided that he directs his heart to Heaven', according to the 'Rabbis of Jabneh', was also applied to the study of the Torah. The scholar who studies much is not superior to his fellow, the common man, provided that the latter 'directs his heart to Heaven'.[5] In very much the same sense it is said that 'the one who prays must direct his heart' (*scil.*, to God).[6] According to R. Meir, in praying the *Shemaʿ*, the value of the words depends upon the intention.[7] In all these instances, the meaning of 'directing the heart' is that one should act with sincere religious devotion. It is not a question of whether or not a man intends that his sacrifice, study or prayer

---

[1] Sifra Beḥuqqotai parasha 1.5 (to 26.3).
[2] T. Sotah 7.4–6.
[3] For biblical support, see e.g. Lev. 19.37.
[4] Menahoth 13.11.
[5] Berakoth 17a.
[6] T. Berakoth 3.4 (Lieberman, p. 12, and in Zuckermandel's second beginning of T. Berakoth; 3.6 in Zuckermandel's first beginning). On the addition of 'to Heaven', see Lieberman, *Tosefta Ki-Fshuṭah, Zeraʿim* I, p. 28.
[7] Megillah 20a.

fulfils the commandments to sacrifice, study and pray, but of whether or not what he does is done from pure religious motives and with a mind fixed on God. If so, the quantity of what a man does is of no account; what matters is his devotion.[8]

A second usage of the phrase occurs in discussing whether or not one can accidentally fulfil a commandment. In the Tannaitic period, these discussions concern commandments of saying and hearing. Thus with regard to the commandment to pray the *Shema'*, the Mishnah rules:

If a man was reading [the verses of the *Shema'*] in the Law and the time came to recite the *Shema'*, if he directed his heart he has fulfilled his obligation; otherwise he has not fulfilled his obligation. (Berakoth 2.1)

The same rule applies to similar commandments:

... if a man was passing behind a synagogue, or if his house was near to a synagogue, and he heard the sound of the *shofar*, or the reading of the *Megillah*, if he directed his heart he has fulfilled his obligation, but if he did not he has not fulfilled his obligation. Though one may have heard and another may have heard, the one may have directed his heart and the other may not have directed his heart. (Rosh Ha-Shanah 3.7)

The point is that a man could accidentally say or hear something which he is commanded to say or hear, but it counts as fulfilling the commandment only if he intends for it to do so and pays attention to it. This use of the phrase 'directing the heart' does not necessarily exclude the first use, since the man who accidentally reads the *Shema'* should not only intend his reading to be a fulfilment of the commandment, but he should also truly fix his mind on God; the precise meaning of the phrase, however, is somewhat different. The Tannaim were generally of the opinion that intention to fulfil the commandment *and* attention to what is being said are necessary. They do discuss, however, how far one must pay attention in reciting or reading the *Shema'* in order for the commandment to be fulfilled.[9] In the Amoraic period there were lengthy discussions of whether or not intention to fulfil the commandment is generally required in order for the commandment to be fulfilled. Some were of the opinion that accidental performance of the commandments would satisfy one's obligation to fulfil them.[10]

---

[8] Urbach (*Hazal*, p. 345; ET, p. 397) has correctly noted that intention when applied to prayer is different from the intention which is required to fulfil commandments (see immediately below): 'The meaning of "intention" here [in prayer] does not refer to fulfilling the obligation to pray but to the intention in the heart toward the substance and content of the prayer.' He did not note, however, that the same meaning of intention is found in connection with bringing sacrifices and studying. Thus with regard to sacrifices, the Tannaitic comment is that all sacrifices are equal in the sight of God if the offerer directs his heart to God, not that the offerer fulfils his obligation to bring a sacrifice only if, in bringing it, he intends to be fulfilling his obligation.

[9] T. Berakoth 2.2; p. Berakoth 4a–b (ET, pp. 29f.); Berakoth 13a–b; see the summary in Urbach, *Hazal*, p. 345 (ET, p. 397).

[10] Rosh Ha-Shanah 28a–29b (ET, pp. 129–33); Pesahim 114b (ET, pp. 587–9); Erubin 95b–96a

In the Amoraic period a third possibility was raised. One might intentionally perform a commanded act, but deny the efficacy of the act which he
performed. As we shall see below, there was a dispute among Amoraim as
to whether or not such an action was in fact efficacious.[11] The Tannaim,
however, do not seem to have considered this possibility.

The Tannaitic emphasis on intention could lead to the view that intention
can actually be a substitute for fulfilment. This obviously applied to the
sacrificial laws after the destruction of the Temple. Study of the laws, which
indicates intention, substituted for performing the sacrifices.[12] The rule
was, however, applied more generally. Thus the Mekilta comments that
'reward is given for setting out to perform a religious duty as well as for
actually performing it'. The commentator continues: 'once they undertook
to do it it is accounted to them as if they had already done it.'[13] In giving
alms, there is a reward both for the intent and the deed. If a man has the
intent but, because of lack of money, cannot fulfil it, he is rewarded for the
intention.[14] The general rule came to be that a good thought is counted as a
good deed ('added to it'), although a bad thought is not counted as a bad
deed. One must actually fulfil the evil intention to be punished.[15]

Despite the emphasis on intention, however, religion as seen by the Rabbis
involved fulfilling the intention. The obligation to obey was laid on each
individual; appeal to the piety of others was no substitute:[16]

'And there is none that can deliver out of my hand' (Deut. 32.39). – Fathers cannot
deliver their children. Abraham could not deliver Ishmael and Isaac could not
deliver Esau. – Thus far I know only that fathers cannot deliver their children.
Whence do we learn that brother cannot deliver brother? – Scripture teaches:
'A man cannot ransom his brother' (Ps. 49.8[7]). Isaac could not deliver Ishmael
and Jacob could not deliver Esau.

A similar point is made in this passage from Sifra: 'Has God (*ha-Maqom*)
not already assured Israel that fathers are not judged by [the deeds of] their
sons, nor sons by [the deeds of] their fathers?' (quoting Deut. 24.16). Then
why does it say, 'and also because of the iniquities of their fathers they shall

---

(ET, pp. 662f.); cited by Urbach, *Hazal*, p. 345 (ET, p. 395f. notes). The passage from Erubin seems to
attribute the view that intention is not required for fulfilment of commandments to a Tanna, but the
Tannaitic discussion is not about intention at all. The question is introduced by the Amoraic commentators.

[11] See the passage cited below, section 7 n. 91.

[12] Below, section 7 nn. 78, 81 and the discussion in the text.

[13] Mek. Pisha 12 (42; I, 96; to 12.28).

[14] And the reward for intention ('saying') is equal to the reward for doing. Sifre Deut. 117 (176; to
15.9).

[15] T. Peah 1.4. For textual variants, see Lieberman's edition, ad loc. For parallels, see Lieberman,
Tosefta Ki-Fshutah, Zera'im I, p. 127; Marmorstein, *The Names and Attributes of God*, pp. 115f. A
possible exception may be the saying of R. Akiba in T. Naziruth 3.14 that one who intends to eat pork
but does not actually do so must nevertheless atone.

[16] Sifre Deut. 329 (380; to 32.39); Midrash Tannaim to Deut. 32.39 (p. 202). Ps. 49.8(7) is translated
differently by modern translators.

pine away' (Lev. 26.39)? It refers to repeating the deeds of their ancestors generation after generation.[17] Such passages as these, especially Sifre Deut. 329, may be polemical against abuse of the conception of the 'merits of the fathers', or they might be seen as in contrast to the view of R. Akiba (Eduyoth 2.9) that a father 'merits' certain blessings for his son.[18] But even Rabbis who spoke of the 'merits of the fathers' did not do so in such a way as to absolve the individual of his responsibility to obey the commandments.[19] A father may 'merit' certain things for his son (e.g. physical beauty, as in Eduyoth 2.9), but he does not perform the commandments for him.

The burden of obedience

As often as New Testament scholars have criticized Rabbinic religion for its multitude of commandments – too numerous to know, let alone to perform, as Bultmann put it[20] – Rabbinic scholars have pointed out that Judaism does not regard the obligations which God imposed upon his people as onerous.[21] They are instead regarded as a blessing, and one should fulfil them with joy. They are accompanied by strength and peace,[22] and they are a sign of God's mercy: 'At Sinai He appeared to them as an old man full of mercy.'[23] This passage in the Mishnah puts the point succinctly:[24]

R. Hananiah b. Aksashya says: The Holy One, blessed is he, was minded to grant merit to Israel; therefore hath he multiplied for them the Law and commandments, as it is written, *It pleased the Lord for his righteousness' sake to magnify the Law and make it honourable* (Isa. 42.21).

From another point of view, the Rabbis could comment that God did not give the (ordinary) Israelite many commandments, although he had given the priests many.[25] In any case, whether the commandments are regarded as being a blessing, because so numerous, or as relatively light, because less numerous than those which govern the priesthood, there is no complaint

---

[17] Sifra Behuqqotai pereq 8.2 (to 26.39).

[18] So Urbach, *Hazal*, pp. 443f. (ET, p. 499).

[19] On individual responsibility versus the view of Ex. 34.7, see below, section 8 n. 62 and the discussion in the text.

[20] Bultmann, *Primitive Christianity*, p. 66.

[21] See Schechter's chapter, 'The Joy of the Law', *Aspects*, pp. 148–69. See also Urbach, *Hazal*, pp. 341ff. (ET, pp. 390–3). Urbach notes (p. 342; ET, p. 393) that the joy of the commandments is always connected with keeping them for their own sake (see below), but the Rabbis were not ignorant of the fact that everyone could not always keep the commandments simply for the joy of doing so. See nn. 89, 90 below.

[22] Sifre Deut. 343 (398; to 33.2).

[23] Mek. Bahodesh 5 (219; II, 231; to 20.2).

[24] Makkoth 3.16; cf. Aboth 6.11. Epstein (*Mabo' le-Nosah ha-Mishnah*, pp. 977f.) regards the saying as an addition in both places. And cf. Ex. Rab. 30.9 (ET, pp. 356f.; cited by Schechter, *Aspects*, pp. 143f.): God especially blessed Israel by giving them all the Torah, while the Gentiles received only a few commandments.

[25] Sifra Emor pereq 1.5 (to 21.5, end).

anywhere in Rabbinic literature about the burden of the commandments, despite the fact that they appear burdensome to New Testament scholars. We should consider why this is so.

To the outsider looking in, reading the Mishnah for the first time, let us say, the laws do seem complex, bewildering, inconsequential, and therefore burdensome. To the Rabbis they could never appear inconsequential, since God had commanded them. Further, for people who lived in a community where many of the commandments were observed by daily routine, the biblical laws as interpreted by the Rabbis would not appear complex or difficult. Thus when R. Joshua says that studying two halakot both morning and evening and seeing to one's business affairs is counted as fulfilling the whole Torah,[26] he does not mean that no other commandments would be fulfilled. Many more would be fulfilled by daily routine. Thus R. Meir said that 'there is no man in Israel who does not fulfil a hundred *mitsvot* every day'.[27] Even if the number is reduced to seven,[28] the general point is the same: the Israelite is surrounded by commandments which he fulfils daily.[29] There are ready analogies in modern life.

The total of international, national, state or provincial, and local laws which govern us all are much more numerous, and if they were all printed, together with some of the juristic arguments about them, they would seem much more bewildering and formidable. The Rabbinic halakah is analogous to modern law in that it aimed at providing regulations for all areas of life. It thus presented no particular burden for its adherents, but only the obligation to know and observe laws which is common in human societies. The Rabbinic laws, to be sure, had the force and sanction of divine command-ments, and in that way are totally unlike modern bodies of law. The only point is that there is no particular problem about learning almost any number of regulations and observing them. We all do it. The Bible, and consequently the Rabbis, brought many things under the head of divine commandments which we should consider part of a civil or criminal code or even simply advice on good manners. These things thus have a certain distinctive character in Judaism, but the number and complexity of the rules and regulations is not especially remarkable. The obligation to obey was not seen by the Rabbis as imposing a heavy burden on observant Jews.

Disobedience as sin and guilt

If Israel's response to the God who chose them is to obey the commandments

---

[26] Mek. Vayassa' 2 (161; II, 103f. [ch. 3]; to 16.4).
[27] T. Berakoth 7.24 (Lieberman's edition, 6.24, p. 40); cf. p. Berakoth, end (ET, p. 173).
[28] See Bacher, *Agada der Tannaiten* II, p. 23 n. 1.
[29] Sifre Deut. 36 (67f.; to 6.9): 'Beloved are Israel, for Scripture surrounds them with *mitsvot*', etc. See Lieberman, *Tosefta Ki-Fshutah, Zera'im* I, p. 125.

entailed in the election, sin must be the failure to do so. That is, sin is disobedience.

In Rabbinic religion, disobedience is what we call sin, whether the disobedience is intentional or inadvertent, whether it is a transgression of a cultic regulation or of one of the ten commandments. Failure to obey what is commanded constitutes sin and, at one level, the circumstances are not significant. The degree to which what might now appear as minor infractions of the rules were in fact considered disobedience of God's commandments can be easily exemplified. In a *qal vaḥomer* argument R. Jose reasoned that, if Adam's transgression caused death to fall to countless future generations because of God's 'quality of punishing', much more will God's 'quality of rewarding', which is greater, cause one's descendants to reap benefits from one's fulfilment of commandments.[30] The particular items which R. Jose used for his argument are these: 'The one who repents of *piggul* and *notar* and who fasts on the Day of Atonement.' Both the words *piggul* (refuse) and *notar* (remnant) refer to sacrifices which have not been dealt with correctly.[31] It is noteworthy that one *repents* of transgressing these cultic regulations. What was considered important was to obey the commandments, and the cure for non-obedience is repentance. Thus one 'repents' of ritual errors; they too constitute disobedience.[32]

This is an aspect of Rabbinic thought which has drawn sharp criticism from Christian theologians. Braun considered the placing of ethical commandments and cultic regulations side by side in Aboth to be 'naïve'.[33] As we have already seen in section 1 above, Bultmann and others have been of the view that cultic regulations came to be more important than 'the weightier matters of the law' (thus turning the polemical charge of Matt. 23.23 into an historical statement) and that this is evidence of the formalism and externalism which purportedly characterized Rabbinic religion. Yet we must note that this does not correspond to the Rabbis' view of the matter. In their view, God had given all the commandments, and they were all to be obeyed alike. It would be presumptuous of man to determine that some should be neglected.

Despite this logic, however, the Rabbis did not simply rest content with insisting that all commandments are equally to be obeyed. They are to be, but it was also possible to inquire, without denying the importance of any of the commandments given by God, whether or not there was a central and essential core within the large body of commandments.[34] The most famous

---

[30] Sifra Hobah parasha 12.10 (to 5.17).

[31] See Maaser Sheni 3.2 and Danby's notes.

[32] On this point, see Moore, *Judaism* I, pp. 116f. He gives a parallel to the Rabbinic attitude from the Westminster Shorter Catechism.

[33] H. Braun, *Radikalismus* I, p. 35.

[34] On reduction of the laws to basic principles, see Alon, *Meḥqarim Be-Toldot Yisra'el* I, pp. 278f.;

story indicating concern with the underlying principle concerns Hillel:

On another occasion it happened that a certain heathen came before Shammai and said to him, 'Make me a proselyte, on condition that you teach me the whole Torah while I stand on one foot.' Thereupon he repulsed him with the builder's cubit which was in his hand. When he went before Hillel, he said to him, 'What is hateful to you, do not to your neighbour:[35] that is the whole Torah, while the rest is commentary thereof; go and learn it.'[36]

One may cite other sayings which reflect a similar attitude: '. . . . if one is honest in his business dealings and the spirit of his fellow creatures takes delight in him, it is accounted to him as though he had fulfilled the whole Torah.'[37] 'Charity (*tsedaqah*) and deeds of loving-kindness (*gemilut ḥasadim*) are equal to all the *mitsvot* in the Torah.'[38] The only instance of a commandment which is not 'ethical' being taken as embodying the entire Torah is that of idolatry.[39]

The core of the Torah was sometimes found in a few commandments rather than one. Thus the ten commandments had special prominence and could serve as the basic elements.[40] Conversely, idolatry, licentiousness and homicide were considered the three cardinal sins.[41] It was sometimes said that many of the commandments were given to refine Israel,[42] to discipline and train the people.[43] These were to be obeyed, but the Rabbis were still able to infer from the large body of commandments the underlying religious and ethical values.

The connection between the many commandments and the search for one underlying principle or a few underlying principles is seen especially clearly in the Amoraic discussion in Makkoth 23b–24a. Since this is the passage which states that the Torah contains 613 commandments, a statement which has been taken as showing the negative and external character of

---

Moore, *Judaism* I, pp. 276, 325, 342, 466f.; II, pp. 86ff. For the relation of the basic principles to the various laws, see Moore, *Judaism* III, pp. 141f. (n. 189): the morally significant laws were recognized as such, and predominated over ceremonial and other laws in cases of conflict; but all laws rested on the same ground of obligation – God's will. See further the discussion by Urbach, *Ḥazal*, pp. 301–19 (ET, pp. 342–64).

[35] A popular proverb. See already Tobit 4.15: 'What you hate, do not do to anyone'.
[36] Shabbath 31a.
[37] Mek. Vayassa' 1 (158; II, 96; to 15.26); Friedmann, f.46a, reads: 'in his business dealings, the spirit of man takes delight in him, and it is accounted . . .'
[38] T. Peah 4.19; p. Peah 15b, bottom.
[39] Mek. Pisha 5 (15; I, 37; to 12.6); Sifre Deut. 54, end (122; to 11.28).
[40] See Gedaliahu Alon, *Meḥqarim* I, p. 278; cf. *JE* IV, p. 496, 'The Decalogue contains all the laws of the Torah', referring to p. Shekalim 46d; p. Sotah 22d; Song of Songs Rabbah to 5.14.
[41] See Moore, *Judaism* I, pp. 466f.
[42] Gen. Rab. 44.1. Urbach (*Ḥazal*, p. 321 n. 84; ET, p. 846 n. 90) has noted that this idea is attributed to R. Akiba in Tanḥuma Tazri'a 5, end: '[God] gave the *mitsvot* to Israel only to refine them.' The context is a discussion of circumcision. The passage in Buber's edition of the Tanḥuma is Tazri'a 7, end (vol. II, p. 35).
[43] See Schechter, *Aspects*, p. 208; Urbach, *Ḥazal*, pp. 321f. (ET, pp. 366f.).

Rabbinic religion, it will be useful to give a summary of it. The Mishnah being discussed is R. Hananiah b. Akashya's statement that God blessed Israel in that, being minded to grant Israel merit, he multiplied the commandments (Makkoth 3.16). R. Simlai made the following exposition, here greatly abbreviated:

Six hundred and thirteen precepts were communicated to Moses. David came and reduced them to eleven [principles]. Isaiah came and reduced them to six [principles]. Micah came and reduced them to three. Again came Isaiah and reduced them to two. Amos came and reduced them to one, as it is said, 'For thus saith the Lord unto the house of Israel, seek ye Me and live' (Amos 5.4). To this R. Nahaman b. Isaac demurred, saying . . . It is Habakkuk who came and based them all on one [principle], as it is said, 'But the righteous shall live by his faith.' (Hab. 2.4)[44]

Attempts to live by one commandment, such as 'love', without any further codification or specification, are not actually likely to lead to the desired result, and Judaism fortunately never renounced the actual fulfilment of the many commandments in favour of freedom to pursue a single principle.[45] But the attempt to draw out a governing principle or a few main principles shows that the Rabbis did not relegate the 'weightier matters of the law' to a subsidiary place by their emphasis on the requirement to fulfil all the commandments given by God. It agrees with this that, as we shall see below, transgressions against one's fellow were considered to be harder to atone for than transgressions against God.[46] The latter would include regulations involving the cult, dietary laws, purity laws and the like. The charge of formalism and externalism seems unfounded.[47]

It is not necessary to discuss here Rabbinic speculation on the origin of sinful disobedience. This sort of theological speculation, like speculation concerning the nature of the world to come, lies outside the scope of the Rabbinic pattern of religion. Yet it is important to note that the Rabbis did not have a doctrine of original sin or of the essential sinfulness of each man in the Christian sense.[48] It is a matter of observation that all men sin. Men have, apparently, the inborn drive towards rebellion and disobedience. But this is not the same as being born in a state of sinfulness from which liberation is necessary. Sin comes only when man actually disobeys; if he were not to disobey he would not be a sinner.[49] The possibility exists that one might

[44] On Makkoth 23b–24a, see Schechter, *Aspects*, pp. 138–40.
[45] See Moore, *Judaism* II, p. 88.
[46] See below, section 7 nn. 160–5, and the discussion in the text.
[47] On the view that all *mitsvot* are equal, the contradictory tendency to make gradations, and the predominance of ethical considerations, see Kadushin, *Organic Thinking*, pp. 107–10.
[48] See Moore, *Judaism* I, pp. 474–8. For recent literature, see Brandenburger, *Adam und Christus*, pp. 44f.
[49] On the origin of sin, see Moore, *Judaism* I, pp. 474–96; Schechter, *Aspects*, pp. 242–63; Mach, *Der Zaddik*, pp. 147ff.

not sin. Despite the tendency to disobey, man is free to obey or disobey.[50] The lack of a doctrine of original sin in the Augustinian sense is an important point to be grasped if one is to understand Rabbinic 'soteriology' or the nature and quality of Jewish religious life.

Sin as disobedience and rebellion has been so thoroughly discussed by others[51] that further discussion is not necessary. We may, however, pause to consider Rabbinic sayings which cast some light on their attitude toward guilt, for here we may gain an insight into how their religion functioned. Guilt, of course, is the concomitant of the conception of sin as disobedience. It may be psychologically related to, but is different from, such other feelings of human inadequacy as shame and uncleanness.[52]

Since the Rabbis conceived man's side of religion to be fulfilling the commandments, and since the biblical commandments, while not necessarily more difficult to fulfil than the laws of some other societies, are nevertheless difficult or even impossible fully to obey, one might expect the Rabbis to evidence severe guilt feelings. Actually, this is not so, for reasons which will become fully apparent only later. We may immediately note, however, that the precise identification of what is obligatory and what not, of what is transgression and what not, of what is sufficient atonement and what not is actually a way not of increasing the neurotic feeling of guilt but of removing it. If a man is in doubt, he can get a ruling and be free of anxiety. If he is guilty he can do what is necessary and be forgiven. If the court rules him not obligated on a certain point, he has no further responsibility. On this point one may best read Mishnah Horayoth. We may give here only a brief example:

If the court gave a decision contrary to any of the commandments enjoined in the Law and some man went and acted at their word [transgressing] unwittingly, whether they acted so and he acted so together with them, or they acted so and he acted so after them, or whether they did not act so but he acted so, he is not culpable, since he depended on the [decision of the] court. (Horayoth 1.1)

Similarly, one who makes a vow but does not foresee the evil results of it is released from his vow. He is not held guilty of breaking it.[53] A Nazirite is forbidden, among other things, to touch a corpse and thus render himself unclean.[54] The rule applies even if a near relative dies.[55] But a man cannot be sure that he is avoiding all contact with the dead, since touching a 'tent peg' can bring uncleanness. (The room in which a corpse lies is a 'tent' and a peg protruding into the room is unclean. It is possible without entering the

---

[50] Below, section 7 n. 155.
[51] Schechter, *Aspects*, pp. 219–41; Moore, *Judaism* I, pp. 460–73; III, p. 141 (n. 187, on terminology).
[52] See e.g. E. R. Dodds, *The Greeks and the Irrational*, pp. 28–63.
[53] Nedarim 9.9.
[54] Nazir 6.1, 5; 7.1. The exception is a neglected corpse, which should be cared for. See the discussion in Sifre Num. 26 (32f.; to 6.6f.).   [55] Nazir 7.1.

'tent' of the corpse to touch the 'peg', which may protrude also into a clean room.) The Nazir who has a near relative dead need not live in a constant state of anxiety about transgressing, since the tent peg was excluded from the prohibition.[56] Similarly one who feared that he might have left some leaven in his home at Passover time, and who was on his way to attend another religious duty, need not be guilty about the leaven, since he could annul it in his heart.[57]

Such instances are numerous, but these are perhaps sufficient for the moment. We shall later see the ground which enabled the Rabbis to avoid excessive feelings of guilt in a religion which emphasized obedience.[58]

It is an interesting question, though one which need not be resolved here, whether the Rabbis *felt* ritual contamination or only felt guilt if they transgressed a commandment which forbade ritual contamination. Was there a real feeling of uncleanness, of contagion or miasma?[59] Scholars seem mostly to believe that the laws of uncleanness were obeyed because they were commanded, and that consequently the feeling of transgressing them would be guilt, not uncleanness as such.[60] This is likely to be correct, and yet how does one account for such statements as that Israel was 'enslaved in the power of the uncircumcised and unclean'[61] in Egypt? Do they point to a feeling of revulsion towards those who were not ritually clean? Certainly sin was very often characterized by terms indicating impurity and defilement. The feeling, however, seems to have been of moral impurity. Put another way, the feeling of 'impurity' was the feeling, not of ritual contamination, but of moral guilt. The vocabulary of defilement and pollution was employed to show the heinousness of transgression.[62]

[56] Sifre Zuṭa to Num. 6.7 (p. 242): '"Neither for his father nor for his mother, nor for brother or sister, if they die, shall he make himself unclean". – To the exclusion of one who touches a [tent] peg.' And on touching the tent peg, see Oholoth 1.3. Even the 'tent' of the corpse confers a lesser degree of uncleanness in the case of the Nazir than touching the corpse: Nazir 7.3.   [57] Pesahim 3.7.

[58] There are examples of what might be considered excessive guilt feelings in the Rabbinic literature: Moore cites the case of a man who brought a conditional guilt-offering every day of the year except after the Day of Atonement, when he was not permitted to do so. See *Judaism* I, p. 499. For a fuller description of this type of piety, see Büchler, *Types*, pp. 73ff.; 114. But Kerithoth 6.3 makes it clear that over-scrupulousness was discouraged by the Rabbis.

[59] On the infectious character of miasma in the archaic Greek world, see Dodds, op cit., pp. 36f., 55.

[60] The principal text is Num. Rab. 19.8 (ET, p. 758), where R. Johanan b. Zakkai says: 'It is not the dead that defiles nor the water that purifies! The Holy One, blessed be He, merely says: "I have laid down a statute, I have issued a decree. You are not allowed to transgress My decree."' Schechter observes (*Aspects*, p. 298) that 'the only *raison d'être* for sacrifices is man's compliance with God's will'. Cf. Marmorstein, *The Names and Attributes of God*: 'The real meaning of purity in the Haggada is a life free from sexual errors and moral stains' (p. 208). 'Impurity stands for sin generally, and sanctification for a life according to the law' (p. 211). And on R. Johanan's saying, see Neusner, *Yohanan ben Zakkai*, p. 62; rev. ed., pp. 91f.

[61] Mek. of R. Simeon b. Yohai to Ex. 6.2 (p. 4, end): 'R. Judah said: "And God said to Moses." [It means this:] The Holy One, blessed be he, said to Moses: "I am a judge in truth; I am full of compassion; I am faithful to pay a reward. Israel is enslaved in the power ('hand') of the uncircumcised and unclean, and I want to bring them out,"' etc.

[62] See Büchler's chapter, 'The Defiling Force of Sin in Post-Biblical and Rabbinic Literature', pp. 270-374 in *Studies in Sin and Atonement*.

Reward and punishment

God rewards successful fulfilment of commandments and punishes transgression. The theme of reward and punishment[63] is ubiquitous in the Tannaitic literature. As Urbach has noted, however much the explanations of reward and punishment might vary from Rabbi to Rabbi – in this world or in the next, a 'real' reward or another *mitsvah* to fulfil – they never doubted that God rewards and punishes. Just judgment is part of the concept of God, and in the Torah which he gave to his people judgment is connected to obeying the commandments.[64] We may present here several examples to see how natural it seemed to the Rabbis that God should reward and punish according to a man's accomplishment before considering the limitations which they put on a strict system of reward and punishment according to merit and the consequences of their view for the ultimate salvation of individual members of the covenant.

We have already noted that the school of R. Akiba was more diligent about finding commandments and rewards in the biblical text than was the school of R. Ishmael.[65] Thus T. Hullin 10.16 cites R. Akiba as saying that there is no *mitsvah* in the Torah which does not have a reward (*matan sakar*) beside it and resurrection of the dead written in it. That God is 'faithful to pay a reward' has already been pointed out.[66] This phrase, common in Sifra especially, is matched in passages attributed to the school of R. Ishmael by the saying that God withholds the reward, or just due, from no creature.[67] The Rabbis, at times, at least, emphasized that the payment of a reward must be justified: 'One does not receive a reward except for a deed.'[68]

We have already noted the tendency to interpret blessings as rewards for accomplishments.[69] This is true even of very small items. Thus the added letter in Abraham's name is the result of good deeds.[70] Why do children come to the Bet ha-Midrash? To get a reward for those who bring them.[71]

[63] 'Reward' is שכר, *sakar*, which means 'wage', 'payment', 'just due' and the like, as well as 'reward'. See, for example, Mek. Mishpatim 20, which is quoted below. 'To punish' is frequently פרע, *para'*, in the *nif'al*, which means 'to collect payment from', 'to call to account', and thus to punish. There is a good discussion of reward and punishment in M. Brocke, 'Tun und Lohn im nachbiblischen Judentum', *Bibel und Leben* 8, 1967, pp. 166–78.

[64] Urbach, *Ḥazal*, pp. 456f. (ET, pp. 514f.).

[65] Section 3 n. 6 above.

[66] Section 4 n. 91.

[67] Mek. Mishpatim 20 (321; III, 159 [Kaspa 2]; to 22.30). The same sentence appears in Sifra Tsav Milu'im 31 (also attributed to the school of R. Ishmael; see Epstein, *Mebo'ot*, p. 641). And cf. also Mek. Beshallaḥ 5 (105; I, 233 [ch. 6]; to 14.22); Mek. Shirata 9 (145; II, 67; to 15.12); Nazir 23b; Pesaḥim 118a.

[68] Mek. Pisḥa 5 (14; I, 34; to 12.6). Cf. Akiba's question (T. Berakoth 4.18 [16]), 'does God give a reward for transgression?' and the statement attributed to R. Simeon (b. Yoḥai), 'God does not give ('they do not give') a reward for a transgression', Sifre Zuṭa to 5.28 (p. 238, top).

[69] Section 4, p. 91.

[70] Mek. Jethro Amalek 1 (189; II, 165 [Amalek ch. 3]; to 18.1).

[71] If men come to the Bet ha-Midrash to learn and women come to listen, why do children come? To gain a reward for those who bring them: T. Sotah 7.9.

Although this is not the general interpretation, even God's favourable attitude toward man is sometimes attached to the fulfilment of his will:

One passage says, 'The Lord lift up his countenance upon you' (Num. 6.26), and one passage says, 'Who does not lift up his countenance' (Deut. 10.17). How can these two passages be reconciled? When Israel does God's will, 'he lifts up'; and when Israel does not do his will, 'he does not lift up'.[72]

Even refraining from committing a transgression merits a reward: 'R. Simeon says . . . to him that sits and commits no transgression is given a reward as to one that performs a religious duty [*mitsvah*].'[73] Similarly, an anonymous Rabbi in the Mekilta, with reference to Ex. 22.23 (ET, v. 24), argues:

Now it is to be reasoned by using the method of *kal vahomer*: If for mere refraining from violating justice your reward will be that your wives will not become widows and your children will not be fatherless (so the biblical passage), how much more so when you actually execute justice, etc.[74]

Often the reward fits the fulfilment or the punishment the transgression. Thus since Moses covered his face, therefore God spoke to him face to face.[75] God is merciful to those who are merciful.[76] Similarly, since the woman who committed adultery and is put to the test prescribed in Num. 5 began transgression with the belly and afterward with the thigh, the punishment is that the belly shall swell and the thigh fall.[77] That small work brings small reward and large work large reward is the point of this story in Sifra:[78]

'And I will have regard for you' (Lev. 26.9). – They told a parable. What is the matter like? It is like a king who hired (*sakar*) many workers. There was one particular worker who had laboured for him many days. The workers came to receive their payment (*sakar*) and this worker entered with them. The king said to that worker, 'My son, I shall have (special) regard for you. These many who laboured with me a little I shall pay a little ('give them a small wage, *sakar*'). But I am about to settle a large account with you.' Thus Israel was seeking their reward in this world before God (*ha-Maqom*). And God said to them, 'My sons, I shall have (special) regard for you. These (other) nations of the world laboured with me a little and I pay them a little. But I am about to settle a large account with you.' Therefore it is said, 'And I will have regard for you.'

---

[72] Sifre Num. 42 (45); Sifre Zuta to Num. 6.26. The RSV translates Deut. 10.17 'who is not partial'.

[73] Makkoth 3.15; cf. Sifre Deut. 286 (305; to 25.3). For modifications of this view, see Schechter, *Aspects*, pp. 166f.

[74] Mek. Mishpatim 18 (314; III, 144f. [Nezikin 18]; to 22.23).

[75] Ex. Rab. 3.1, commenting on Ex. 3.6 and 33.11. Exodus Rabbah has a whole series of such 'rewards'.

[76] R. Gamaliel II: T. Baba Kamma 9.30; Shabbath 151b; p. Baba Kamma 6c (8.10). The exegesis implies, however, that God *makes* a man merciful so that he may be merciful to him; see the note to the ET of Shabbath 151b.

[77] Sifre Num. 18 (22; to 5.27). In Num. 5.21 the order is reversed, and Sifre Zuta, with somewhat more logic, comments on *this* verse, 'from the place where the transgression began, from there the punishment begins'. In agreement with Sifre, however, is Mek. Beshallah 1 (Lauterbach [ch. 2], I, 192; to 14.4). See also the critical apparatus in Horovitz, p. 85; Friedmann, f.26a.

[78] Sifra Behuqqotai pereq 2.5 (to 26.9).

The theory operative in such passages is that of 'measure for measure'. It is clearly stated in the Mekilta: 'The sages said: With what measure a man metes it is meted unto him, as it is said: "Yea, for with the very thing with which they acted presumptuously against them"' (Ex. 18.11).[79] As Goldin has observed, 'measure for measure is one of the principles making intelligible God's governance of the universe'.[80] It points toward his justice.[81]

Despite these clear statements of the idea of measure for measure and the way in which it follows logically from the Rabbinic view of the justice of God, the idea that a man's payment is strictly in accordance with his deserts is by no means a Rabbinic doctrine. Just as often, one finds contrary statements. Thus the fulfilment of a very 'light' commandment may merit a very great reward:

A man may not take the dam and her young (together, see Deut. 22.6f.) even for the sake of cleansing the leper. If then of so light a precept concerning what is worth but an *issar* the Law has said *that it may be well with thee and that thou mayest prolong thy days* (Deut. 22.7), how much more [shall the like reward be given] for [the fulfilment of] the weightier precepts of the Law! (Hullin 12.5)

Or again,

Rabbi said: Which is the straight way that a man should choose? That which is an honour to him and gets him honour from men. And be heedful of a light precept as of a weighty one, for thou knowest not the recompense of reward of each precept. . . .[82]

While it may seem that these two things – that God rewards great service more than small service and that no one knows how God will choose to reward a deed, there being no necessary connection between what appear to us great deeds and God's great rewards – are in contradiction, actually they stem from a common concern. The Rabbis, we must repeat, considered that Israel's side of the covenant was keeping God's commandments. God had commanded, and Israel was to obey. They thus strove to encourage attention to the commandments and the fulfilment of them. And both of what may appear to be contradictory themes actually stem from this common concern. By saying that God pays a great reward for great service, they encouraged great service. By saying that no one knows what value God attaches to even the lightest commandment, they encouraged attention to

[79] Mek. Beshallah Amalek 2 (182; II, 148 [Amalek 2]; to 17.14). The same statement is attributed to R. Meir in Sanhedrin 100a, but a different biblical verse is quoted. There are several similar statements at the beginning of Mek. Beshallah 6 (110; I, 243–5 [ch. 7]; to 14.26); cf. also Sifre Num. 106 (105; to 12.15). On the popularity of the idea that rewards fit achievements and punishments transgressions, see further Urbach, *Hazal*, pp. 385–9 (ET, pp. 436–42).

[80] Goldin, *The Song at the Sea*, p. 18.

[81] Ibid., p. 25.

[82] Aboth 2.1. Cf. Sifre Deut. 79 (145; to 12.28): '"These things which I command you" – That a light commandment should be as dear to you as a heavy one.'

all, and further emphasized that the commandments are to be obeyed because God commanded them. It agrees with this that they especially endeavoured to obey and to have others obey the commandments for which no reason could be seen.[83] Wholehearted obedience to such commandments shows that a man has totally surrendered to God and does his will without trying to bring religion under his own control or make it subject to his own power of reason.[84]

Nothing could show more clearly that all Rabbinic statements on a certain point cannot be considered as having a place in some logical and coherent theological system. Rabbinic comments are *ad hoc*, intending to serve a certain purpose or make a certain point. The Rabbis were not concerned with the internal systematic relationship of their statements. Nevertheless, we can often reason from diverse statements on a certain point to a common concern. These several statements about the relationship between the commandments fulfilled or transgressed and God's reward or punishment reveal the common concern that God's commandments should be obeyed. They do not represent different systematic views on precisely how reward and punishment are related to fulfilment and transgression, although they do reflect the universally held view that there is reward and punishment for obedience and disobedience.

Although the Rabbis emphasize repeatedly that the commandments carry rewards (or punishment for non-fulfilment), they also warn against fulfilling the commandments *in order to* earn payment. Rather, one should perform the required commandments without ulterior motive and because they are in themselves good ('for their own sake') or from love of God ('for the sake of Heaven'):

R. Jose said: Let the property of thy fellow be dear to thee as thine own; and fit thyself for the study of the Law, for [the knowledge of] it is not thine by inheritance; and let all thy deeds be done for the sake of Heaven. (Aboth 2.12)

The emphasis on doing commandments 'for their own sake' may be illustrated by this passage from Sifre Deut.:

R. Eleazar b. R. Zadok said: Do the commandments (only) for the sake of doing them[85] [and] speak of them for their own sake (alone). He used to say: If the life

---

[83] See Moore, *Judaism* I, pp. 273f.; Büchler, *Studies in Sin and Atonement*, p. 118.

[84] Thus R. Eleazar b. Azariah gives two reasons for obeying laws for which no moral justification could be seen, such as those which forbid wearing garments of mixed materials and eating pork: they keep one separate from transgression; and (more important), by keeping them, a man 'accepts upon himself the Kingship of Heaven'. Sifra Qedoshim pereq 9.10 (Weiss, pereq 11.22, f.93d; to Lev. 20.26, q.v.). Contrast Bultmann's interpretation of the 'unintelligible' commandments, *Primitive Christianity*, p. 68: unintelligible commands led to formal and merely externalistic obedience. He leaves out of account the Rabbis' own explanation of the significance of obeying such commandments.

[85] The parallel in Nedarim 62a has 'for the sake of their Maker' (ET, p. 197). Bacher (*Agada der Tannaiten* I, p. 48) explains 'for the sake of doing them' as 'als Selbstzweck', an end in itself. Cf. Schechter, *Aspects*, p. 160; Moore, *Judaism* II, p. 97.

of Belshazzar, who used the vessels of the Temple [as if they were] common vessels (see Dan. 5.2–4), were uprooted from this world and from the world to come, how much more will the life of one who makes [improper] use of the vessel by which the world was created (the Torah) be uprooted from this world and from the world to come![86]

It is difficult to know precisely what the improper use of the Torah was to which R. Eleazar objected – whether for gain here or in the hope of a reward from God –, although the former seems more likely. In any case, the use of the Torah for any but its own sake was sharply condemned. So also R. Banna'ah: 'If you do the words of the Torah for their own sake they are life to you. . . . But if you do not do the words of the Torah for their own sake they kill you.'[87]

The Rabbis especially warned themselves and their students against the danger of studying with less than totally pure motives. There are two related passages in Sifre Deut. on the subject, the first of which immediately precedes the saying of R. Eleazar b. R. Zadok just cited:[88]

'To love the Lord thy God.' – [Why is it said?] Lest you should say, 'I shall study Torah so that I may be called Sage, so that I may sit in the Yeshivah, so that I may extend my days in the World to Come,' Scripture says: 'To love the Lord thy God.' [It means] learn in any case (without secondary motive); and at the end the glory will [also] come. And thus it says, 'For they are life to him who finds them and healing to all his flesh' (Prov. 4.22).

'To love the Lord thy God.' – Lest you should say, 'I shall study Torah so that I may be rich and so that I may be called Rabbi and so that I may receive a reward in the world to come,' Scripture says: 'To love the Lord thy God.' All that you do, do only from love.

The Rabbis were aware that other motives, such as fear, could also move one to obey the commandments, although in the literature which survives love is the clearly preferred motive.[89] The Amoraim noted that one who

---

[86] Sifre Deut. 48 (114; to 11.22).

[87] Sifre Deut. 306 (338; to 32.2); cf. Taanith 7a. On 'for its (the Torah's) own sake', see Schechter, *Aspects*, pp. 159f.; Moore, *Judaism* I, p. 35; II, pp. 95ff.

[88] Sifre Deut. 48 (113; to 11.22) and 41 (87; to 11.13).

[89] Finkelstein has argued (*Mabo le-Massektot Abot ve Abot d'Rabbi Natan*, pp. 18–39; cf. the English summary, p. xiii) that the Shammaites taught that the motive of fear was better than the motive of love. The principal text is ARNB, ch. 10 (Schechter's ed., f.13b), which Finkelstein argues originally read as follows: 'The one who does [the Torah] from love inherits the life of this world, but he does not inherit the days of the world to come; while the one who does [the Torah] in awe and fear inherits the life of this world and the life of the world to come,' etc. This is a comment on Aboth 1.3: 'Be not like slaves that minister to the Master for the sake of receiving a bounty, but be like slaves that minister to the Master not for the sake of receiving a bounty; and let the fear of heaven be upon you.' We should note that the Shammaite view is not that God should be served from self-interest or fear of punishment, but that awe, fear and reverence mark the proper attitude toward God. Urbach (*Ḥazal*, pp. 350–2; ET, pp. 402–4) has correctly pointed out that the distinction of 'love' from 'fear' is a later development. The saying by Antigonos of Soko should not be understood to elevate fear of God over love of him. Urbach cites Ben Sirach 7.29f. (Heb., 7.30f.), in which 'fear' and 'love' of God are paralleled. The Rabbis, how-

begins obeying from a less than totally pure motive may end by obeying only from love, and so the other motives were not totally scorned.[90]

Thus we have seen that although the Rabbis believed that God, being just and faithful, rewarded man for service and punished him for transgression, they did not think that one should serve God either from desire to gain a reward or from fear of punishment, but only from love of God.[91] But in order more fully to understand the Rabbinic ideas of reward, we must proceed to note other ways in which the Rabbis contradicted the idea of strict payment of man's just due.

In the first place, the 'reward' of fulfilling a *mitsvah* is said to be receiving another *mitsvah* to fulfil:

Ben Azzai said: Run to fulfil the lightest duty even as the weightiest, and flee from transgression; for one duty (*mitsvah*) draws another duty in its train, and one transgression draws another transgression in its train; for the reward (*sakar*) of a duty [done] is a duty [to be done], and the reward of one transgression is [another] transgression. (Aboth 4.2)

The saying is repeated in slightly different form by Rabbi.[92] This observation not only shows profound moral insight, but it also reinforces what has already been said: one should obey the law for its own sake (or for God's sake). The 'reward' of obedience should not be looked for outside obedience itself.

Further, the Rabbis recognized that God had not really dealt with Israel according to a strict accounting of their merits. Thus in a discussion of the significance of Israel's suffering, R. Meir comments: 'You should consider in your mind the deeds you have done as well as the sufferings I caused to come upon you. For the sufferings I brought upon you are not at all commensurate with the deeds you have done.'[93] The Rabbis even found in the Bible that a man should work according to his ability but was paid according to his need:[94]

This Is the Thing Which the Lord Hath Commanded: Gather Ye of It, etc. (Ex. 16.16). The sages said: Now, Naḥshon the son of Amminadab and his household

---

ever, did subsequently make the distinction. For the view which prevailed – that God should be served from love – see Moore, *Judaism* II, pp. 98–100; Büchler, *Studies in Sin and Atonement*, pp. 119ff.

[90] See Nazir 23b, where there is a lengthy discussion on the point. Schechter (*Aspects*, p. 161) cites a similar example from Berakoth 17a top. A similar saying is attributed to Rab Huna in p. Ḥagigah 76c (1.7).

[91] Cf. Schechter, *Aspects*, p. 162.

[92] Sifre Num. 112 (120; to 15.30); cited by Moore, *Judaism* I, pp. 470f. See also Mek. Vayassaʻ 1 (157; II, 95; to 15.26): if a man 'hears' (i.e. hears and obeys) one commandment, God causes him to 'hear' many, and vice versa.

[93] Mek. Baḥodesh 10 (240; II, 279; on Ex. 20.20[23]). The saying is not printed in Friedmann's text, f.72b. See the apparatus in the editions of Horovitz and Lauterbach: it was omitted from the early printed editions.

[94] Mek. Vayassaʻ 4 (167; II, 115 [ch. 5]; to 16.16).

went out and gathered much. A poor man in Israel went out and gathered little. But when they came to measure it, 'they did mete it with an omer, he that gathered much had nothing over, and he that gathered little had no lack; they gathered every man according to his eating' (v. 18).

It agrees with this that the Rabbis state that God's mercy predominates over his justice when the two conflict, just as they thought that God's reward is always greater than his punishment.[95] Both statements are standard in the literature, but since Christian scholars have often thought that the Rabbis subordinated God's mercy to a legalistic view of his justice, it will be worthwhile to give a few examples. The older, or at least the commoner contrast in the earlier literature, is between God's 'quality of punishing' (*middat pur 'anut*) and his 'quality of rewarding' (*middah tobah, middat ha-tob*). The standard view, often repeated and never contradicted, is indicated in this saying by R. Eleazar of Modi'im:[96] 'Which is greater, the quality of rewarding or the quality of punishing? You must say: the quality of rewarding.' The very same sentence is attributed to R. Jose in Sifra.[97] The idea that the 'quality of rewarding' is greater than the 'quality of punishing' is frequently stated in the Mekilta in other ways.[98] In Sifra, there is a series of *qal vahomer* arguments which depend on this principle. Thus R. Akiba comments:[99] 'If thus the passage punishes one who merely may have committed a transgression, how much more will it give a reward to one who does a *mitsvah*.' The phrase 'how much more' is based on God's being readier to reward than punish.

After the time of R. Akiba, another terminology became more common: 'the quality of mercy' (*middat rahamin*) and the 'quality of justice' (*middat ha-din*).[100] The former is consistently considered greater than the latter:

[95] The most usual terminology is this: God's (quality of) mercy: *middat rahamim*; his (quality of) justice: *middat ha-din*; his (quality of) rewarding: *middah tobah*; his (quality of) punishing: *middat pur 'anut*. There are variations in the writing of the last two phrases, and synonyms are sometimes used. See e.g. the concordance to the Mekilta, s.v. *middah*. From the Amoraic period, note the saying of R. Huna (Gen. Rab. 9.8) referring to the quality of rewarding (*middat ha-tob*) and the quality of chastising (*middat yissurin*). Both are considered good.

[96] Mek. Vayassa' 3 (166; II, 113 [ch. 4]; to 16.14), my translation. There are other difficulties in the text, but the point is clear. The haggadah is repeated anonymously in Yoma 76a, and a similar passage is attributed to R. Meir in Sanhedrin 100a–b.

[97] Sifra Hobah parasha 12.10 (to 5.17).

[98] E.g. Mek. Pisha 7 (24; I, 54f.; to 12.12): 'There is a *qal vahomer* argument: If with regard to the quality of punishing, which is the lesser, [the rule is that] he who sins first is first punished, how much more [should this be the rule] with regard to the quality of rewarding, which is greater' (my translation). For other examples, see the concordance s.v. *middah*. That the *middat pur 'anut* is lesser is also stated in Sifre Deut. 286 (304; to 25.3).

[99] Sifra Hobah parasha 12.8. There are similar comments in the following four paragraphs. There is a substantive parallel in ARN 30 (ET, p. 123) in the name of R. Meir, where the argument is explicitly based on the principle that the *middah tobah* is greater than the *middat pur 'anut*. The wording is the same as that cited above, n. 96. See further Sifra Tsav pereq 16.10 (R. Simeon b. Yohai).

[100] Marmorstein (*The Names and Attributes of God*, pp. 44f.) argued that this terminology does not occur before the time of R. Meir and R. Simeon b. Yohai. Some of his evidence, however, was forced. See Sandmel, *Philo's Place in Judaism*, pp. 21f. It is nevertheless the case that the former terminology

'Thy righteousness (*tsedaqah*) is like the mountains of God' (Ps. 36.7; ET, 36.6): R. Simeon b. Yohai said: Just as the mountains press down the deep, so that it does not rise up and flood the world, so *tsedaqah*[101] presses down the quality of judgment (*middat ha-din*) and punishing (*ha-pur'anut*), so that it does not come to the world.[102]

'Thy mighty hand' (Deut. 3.24): Thou dost suppress the quality of justice (*middat ha-din*) with compassion (*rahamim*) (referring to Micah 7.18–20, *q.v.*).[103]

'For behold, the Lord is coming forth out of his place' (Isa. 26.21): He comes forth from *middah* to *middah*, from the *middat ha-din* to the *middat rahamim*.[104]

The meaning of the last passage is apparently that God replaces strict justice with mercy.

The view that God is inclined to be merciful to man rather than to hold him strictly to account is, as I have said, the general view. Thus one reads with bewilderment Schrenk's statement, 'That God's clemency was greater than his strict equity was only a flickering hope'.[105] It is rather the case, as Kadushin put it, that 'rabbinic thought is dominated . . . by the idea of God's love rather than by the idea of his justice'.[106]

If one asks how the idea that God is just and pays to each his due is to be reconciled into a doctrinal unity with the statement that God's mercy predominates over his justice, the answer is, as before, that this is not a doctrinal system in which every statement has a logical place. One thing or the other would be said depending on the particular needs of the instance. But there should be no doubt that the latter type of statement – that mercy outweighs justice – reflects the Rabbinic attitude towards God at its most basic level. The statements that God pays what is due are partly for exhortative purposes, but also rest, as we have repeatedly stated, on the firm conviction that God is reasonable and just.[107] But the Rabbis also thought that

---

is much more frequent in the Tannaitic literature; see the concordances. See further Urbach, *Hazal*, pp. 396–400 (ET, pp. 448–52). Kadushin (*The Rabbinic Mind*, p. 219) considers *middah tobah* and *middat pur'anut* to be sub-concepts of *middat ha-din*. This seems to be logical. But one must note (*a*) that similar things are said about *middat rahamim* and *middah tobah*; the latter is not treated as a sub-concept of the former; (*b*) that *middat rahamim* and *middat ha-din* tend to replace the other pair.

[101] *Tsedaqah* is taken here, as elsewhere, to refer to God's charity or mercy toward man. See below, section 8.

[102] Tanhuma Noah 8 (ed. Buber, vol. I, p. 34). Cited, but not quoted, by Marmorstein, *The Names and Attributes of God*, p. 44.

[103] Sifre Num. 134 (p. 180). This section is actually a midrash on Deut. 3.24ff. and is from a different source. See Epstein, *Mebo'ot*, pp. 600f. And see Schechter, *Aspects*, p. 323, on God's right hand (the strong one) representing mercy while the left hand represents strict justice.

[104] P. Taanith 65b (2.1), cited by Marmorstein, ad loc.

[105] *TDNT* II, p. 204. Similarly Roetzel, *Judgement in the Community*, p. 56: the severity of God's judgment 'was tempered by a slight emphasis on mercy'.

[106] *The Rabbinic Mind*, p. 219.

[107] Brocke ('Tun und Lohn', p. 168) argued that the insistence on God's being a just judge was a response to Epicurean popular philosophy, according to which the gods are indifferent to man's action, and also to Sadduceanism. He cites Aboth 2.1; 2.15; 4.22.

God was unfailingly merciful. The Rabbis never said that God is merciful in such a way as to remove the necessity of obeying him, but they did think that God was merciful toward those who basically intended to obey, even though their performance might have been a long way from perfect.

6. Reward and punishment and the world to come

God's justice and retribution in the world to come

It was the biblical view, and one that remained influential in Judaism, that God's justice is meted out within this life. One may see the view expressed tenaciously in Ben Sirach, for example, and it never completely disappeared. With the combination of belief in the resurrection and the observation of the suffering of the righteous in this world, especially between 70 and 135 c.e., however, the view arose that the righteous would be rewarded and the wicked punished in the world to come. It is not our intention here to attempt a detailed history of the locale of reward and punishment. We shall return to one aspect of the subject, suffering, in section 7 below. Here we shall give only a few examples which illustrate the continuation of the view that reward and punishment are carried out in this world. In Kiddushin 1.10a, an early mishnah almost certainly to be dated before 70 c.e., it is said that one who obeys the commandments will have a long life and will inherit 'the Land'.[1] Here life is physical life and the land is almost certainly understood literally as the land of Israel, although the phrase was subsequently taken to refer to the world to come. In a later period R. Meir is reported to have said that one who does *tsedaqah* will attain to old age,[2] while R. Nathan, a Tanna of the latter part of the second century, said that 'There is not (even) a light *mitsvah* in the Torah for which there is no reward in this world. And in the world to come, I do not know how great [the reward for each is].'[3] The reward is not 'salvation', but something that is appropriate for what has been done.[4]

The view which is dominant in the literature as we have it, however, is the view which is attributed to R. Akiba and his immediate successors, that punishment and reward are basically carried out in the world to come, a view

[1] Kiddushin 1.10a is discussed further in the next sub-section. On the date, see Epstein, *Mebo'ot.* p. 53. Mach (*Der Zaddik*, p. 32) incorrectly takes 'inherit the land' to refer to the world to come.
[2] Gen. Rab. 59.1; ET, p. 516.
[3] Menahoth 44a, my translation. On the relationship between merit and length of days, see Yebamoth 49b–50a and Urbach's discussion (*Hazal*, pp. 235–7; ET, pp. 264–6). On the tenacity of the popular idea that God rewards the righteous in this world, see Urbach, pp. 388f. (ET, pp. 439–41).
[4] Cf. Kadushin, *Organic Thinking*, pp. 82–94. He argues that the traditional Christian view of Rabbinic soteriology cannot be correct, since the reward of God's justice to those who obey him is not primarily salvation, but specific rewards (material and spiritual) within this world. Cf. Parkes, *The Foundations of Judaism and Christianity*, pp. 201, 285, 298f.

doubtless influenced by the persecutions of the Hadrianic period.[5]

The deferral of punishment and reward to the world to come does not mean that the world to come is *earned* by the performance of a certain number of commandments. Rather, the Rabbinic view of the justice of God meant that God appropriately rewards and punishes for obedience and disobedience. When this was seen not to be the case in this world, the exercise of God's justice was postponed to the next.

That the righteous are rewarded *in* the world to come is often stated. Thus R. Tarfon:

It is not thy part to finish the task, yet thou art not free to desist from it. If thou hast studied much in the Law much reward will be given thee, and faithful is thy taskmaster who shall pay thee the reward of thy labour. And know that the recompense of the reward of the righteous is for the time to come. (Aboth 2.16)[6]

Here it is clear that studying is not considered to earn the world to come; that is simply the locale where the just reward is paid. A similar point is seen in the anonymous statement in Peah 1.1:

These are things whose fruits a man enjoys in this world while the capital is laid up for him in the world to come: honouring father and mother, deeds of loving-kindness, making peace between a man and his fellow; and the study of the Law is equal to them all.[7]

This view is perhaps closer to R. Nathan's (there is reward both here and in the world to come) than to R. Tarfon's, but in all these cases we see that some or all of the just due of obedience is deferred to the world to come.

The passage which most clearly connects reward and punishment in the world to come with the just payment to be expected from a righteous God, which the Bible held to be completed within this world, is Sifre Deut. 307.[8] The passage is too long to quote in full, but we may summarize it. The passage being commented on is Deut. 32.4: 'The Rock, his work is perfect; for all his ways are justice. A God of faithfulness and without iniquity, just and right is he.' There are three paragraphs of a similar structure which present interpretations of the verse. In all three cases, the comment on the phrase 'his work is perfect' concludes by citing the next phrase, 'for all his ways are justice', and commenting, 'he sits with each individual in judgment and gives him what is appropriate'. In all three cases, the point is that God cannot be accused of *unfairness*. 'He conducts himself uprightly with everyone who comes into the world.' The first two paragraphs deal with God's actions in this world, while the third discusses reward and punishment in

---

[5] Below, section 7, p. 171.
[6] Cf. the baraita in the name of R. Jacob in Kiddushin 39b to the effect that the rewards promised in the Torah are dependent on the resurrection – they are not paid in this world.
[7] Similarly R. Nehorai in Kiddushin 4.14.
[8] Pp. 344–6.

the world to come. Thus in the first paragraph the anonymous author states
that the meaning of 'his work is perfect' is that no one may criticize his deeds
on any pretext whatsoever. No one may speculate and say, 'perhaps I
should have had three eyes', and the like, for all his ways are justice; he
gives each what is appropriate. The second paragraph takes up God's
punishments and gifts in biblical history. After the same introductory
formula, the author indicates that the passage proves that one may not ask
why the generation of the flood was drowned (for example) or why Aaron
received the priesthood. All his ways are justice, and he gives each what is
appropriate.

The third paragraph breaks the formula slightly. The commentator
states that neither the reward of the righteous nor the punishment of the
wicked is received entirely in this world, citing biblical proof for each point.[9]
Then how can all his ways be justice; i.e. how can God's justness be maintained? When do they receive their just deserts? 'On the morrow, when he
sits on the throne of judgment, he sits with each individual in judgment and
gives him what is appropriate.' The passage continues:

'A God of faithfulness.' – Just as he pays the completely righteous the reward of
a *mitsvah* which he fulfilled in this world [after he is] in the world to come, so he
pays the completely wicked the reward of a minor commandment which he
fulfilled in this world [while he is] in this world. And just as he punishes the
completely wicked for a transgression which he committed in this world [after
he is] in the world to come, so he punishes the completely righteous for a minor
transgression which he committed in this world [while he is] in this world.
'And without iniquity.' – When a man departs from the world, all his deeds
come before him one by one and say to him: 'Thus and so you did on such a day
and thus and so you did on another day. Do you declare these things to be accurate?' And he says, 'Yes'. They say to him, 'Place your seal', as it is said: 'By the
hand of every man he will seal, so that every man may know his work' (Job 37.7).
'Just and right is he.' – And he declares the judgment just and says, 'You have
judged me well.' And thus it says: 'so that thou art justified in thy sentence'
(Ps. 51.4[6]).[10]

There are several observations to be made on the basis of the passages
which we have quoted thus far. 1. Belief in reward and punishment is
grounded in the conviction that God is just. The opposite of saying that God
is *just* and rewards and punishes would *not* be to say that he is *merciful*, but
to say that he is *arbitrary* and capricious. We have seen above that the Rabbis
sometimes enquired how God's justice and mercy were related. It is now
clear that the two are not opposites, but qualities both of which are maintained, without mercy becoming caprice. This is so important a point that

---

[9] So also Sifre Deut. 324 (376; to 32.34).
[10] There are approximate parallels, all anonymous, in Taanith 11a and elsewhere. See 'R. Akiba's
View of Suffering', *JQR* n.s. 63, 1973, p. 337 n. 15.

we may illustrate it by one more passage.[11] Commenting on Deut. 33.6, 'Let Reuben live, and not die', R. Hananiah b. Gamaliel says: 'God never reverses ('they never reverse') innocence to guilt nor guilt to innocence except in the cases of Reuben and David.' He cites II Sam. 16.13 and I Kings 11.27 to prove the point about David. The passage in Deut. 33.6 is apparently taken to prove the point about Reuben. The 'sages' differ, however: 'God never reverses innocence to guilt nor guilt to innocence, but rather he gives a reward for *mitsvot* and he punishes for transgression. Then why does scripture say, "Let Reuben live and not die"? Because Reuben repented.' It is clear here that the 'sages' do not deny that God is gracious and merciful and forgives sin when they insist that he punishes transgression and rewards obedience. The point, rather, is that he does not *arbitrarily* consider guilt to be innocence, any more than he arbitrarily considers innocence to be guilt. Those who repent, however, no matter how grievous their transgression (and Reuben's was very grievous), are forgiven and restored to a right relationship with God.

2. The theme of reward and punishment *in* the world to come is not a statement of justification by works, but an extension of the theory of the justice of God. Since it is the case that the righteous and wicked are not always dealt with as they deserve in this world, their reward and punishment are reserved for the world to come. *What* the reward or the punishment is is never specified. We are simply assured that God's justice will be maintained, if not here then hereafter.

3. We see already that the theme of book-keeping (testifying to the accuracy of one's recorded deeds by placing one's seal) is also connected to that of theodicy. When a man is judged, he acknowledges the judgment to be just.

In the passages which we have just considered, it is not said that one is rewarded for obedience *by* the world to come, but only *in* it. Yet it is clear that there is a connection between deeds and the world to come. We shall pursue the question of what the connection is by turning to the passages which are taken as proving that life in the world to come is earned *by* performing more commandments than the number of one's transgressions.

Weighing fulfilments and transgressions at the judgment

There are basically three passages which support or which may be taken to support the view that weighing fulfilments against transgressions constitutes Rabbinic soteriology: Kiddushin 1.10a and the material gathered around it in the Tosefta and the Talmuds, part of R. Akiba's saying in Aboth 3.15 (ET, 3.16) to the effect that judgment is by the majority of deeds, and R.

[11] Sifre Deut. 347 (404f.; to 33.6).

Eleazar's saying in Aboth 4.22 that everything is according to the reckoning.[12] We should consider these in turn:[13]

Everyone who fulfils one *mitsvah* – God benefits (they benefit) him and lengthens his days and he inherits the land. And everyone who does not fulfil one *mitsvah* – God does not benefit him nor lengthen his days; and he does not inherit the land. (Kiddushin 1.10a)

The second sentence is euphemistic;[14] the meaning is 'everyone who transgresses one *mitsvah*, God harms', etc., and so Danby takes it.[15] This is a very ancient mishnah, as we have already noted. Later, the promise to inherit the land was taken to apply to the world to come.[16] Further, the Rabbis would later argue that reward was paid to the righteous only in the world to come, while the evil were paid in this world for whatever few good deeds they may have accomplished. The meaning of the ancient mishnah is quite clear: it is an exhortative affirmation that God rewards obedience and punishes transgression: if God gives the land to one who fulfils a commandment, fulfil a commandment! If God denies the land to one who transgresses, avoid transgression! The student of Rabbinic literature comes to expect such non-systematic and exhortative statements. The point is to encourage people to obey and not transgress.

The passage attracted further comments. In the Tosefta, further pertinent sayings were attached to it:[17]

Whoever fulfils one *mitsvah* – God benefits (they benefit) him and lengthens his days and his years, and he inherits the earth.[18] And everyone who commits one transgression,[19] God harms him and shortens his days, and he does not inherit the land. And concerning this one it is said: 'One sinner destroys much good' (Eccl. 9.18): with a single sin this one loses for himself much good. A man should

---

[12] According to Bonsirven (*Judaïsme palestinien* II, p. 58), the principle of weighing is *often* repeated. He cites Kiddushin 39b–40b; p. Kiddushin 61d (1.10); T. Kiddushin 1.14; p. Peah 16b (1.1); Aboth 3.15. We should note that all the references to Kiddushin are comments, largely Amoraic, on Kiddushin 1.10a. The passage in p. Peah is (as Bonsirven also notes) Amoraic. Bonsirven also cites as evidence of the principle of weighing transgressions and fulfilments the *qizai perush* of Sotah 22b, p. Sotah 20c (5.7) and p. Berakoth 14b (9.7). The Palestinian Talmud (Sotah) explains that these balance their fulfilments with transgressions. We should note (1) the word *perush* here does not mean 'Pharisee', but 'ascetic' or 'heretic' (above, section 2 n. 12); (2) all the passages are Amoraic; (3) the interpretation in the Babylonian Talmud ('one who makes his blood to flow against walls') does not lend itself to the 'weighing' theory, which seems to be a still later interpretation.

[13] Pp. 129–43 constitute a revised version of pp. 103–21 of my article 'On the Question of Fulfilling the Law in Paul and Rabbinic Judaism', published in the *Festschrift* for David Daube.

[14] See Albeck's note in his text ad loc. and p. 413 of *Seder Nashim*.

[15] Danby translates: 'If a man performs but a single commandment it shall be well with him and he shall have length of days and shall inherit the Land; but if he neglects a single commandment it shall be ill with him', etc.

[16] Epstein, *Mebo'ot*, p. 53 n. 186; Albeck, *Seder Nashim*, p. 413.

[17] T. Kiddushin 1.13–16, following Lieberman's text.

[18] Lieberman (*Tosefta Ki-Fshuṭah*, Nashim, p. 927) explains that *'adamah* has here replaced *'arets* under the influence of Deut. 5.16.

[19] On the interpretation of the Mishnah's 'does not fulfil one *mitsvah*' as 'commits one transgression', see Lieberman, op. cit., pp. 927f.

always consider himself as if he were half innocent and half guilty.[20] If he fulfils one *mitsvah*, happy is he for weighting himself down in the scale of innocence (*kaf zekut*). If he commits one transgression, [it is as] if he weighted himself down in the scale of guilt (*kaf hobah*). About this one it is said: 'One sinner destroys much good': with a single sin which he committed, he destroyed for himself much good.

14. R. Simeon b. Leazar said in the name of R. Meir:[21] Since the individual is judged according to the majority [and] the world[22] is judged according to the majority, if he fulfils one *mitsvah*, happy is he for weighting himself and the world down in the scale of innocence. If he commits one transgression, [it is as] if he weighted himself and the world down in the scale of guilt. And about this one it is said: 'One sinner destroys much good': with a single sin which he committed he destroyed for himself and for the world much good.

15. R. Simeon said: If a man were righteous (*tsaddiq*) all his days, but rebelled at the end, he would destroy everything, as it is said: 'The righteousness of the righteous shall not deliver him when he transgresses' (Ezek. 33.12). 16. If a man were wicked (*rasha'*) all his days, but repented at the end, God (*ha-Maqom*) would accept him, as it is said: 'And as for the wickedness of the wicked, he shall not fall by it when he turns from his wickedness' (ibid.).

The anonymous comment in T. Kiddushin 1.13 continues the same sort of non-systematic exhortation which is found in the Mishnah passage. A man should consider himself *as if* he were half innocent and half guilty and *as if* his every next act would determine his fate. Clearly, he should always try to obey and not to transgress. This sort of statement is similar in type to the injunction to repent one day before death (Aboth 2.10). It means that one should repent every day. Here, too, one should *always* try to obey and should act *as if* each deed were decisive.

With the saying of R. Simeon b. Eleazar in the name of R. Meir we find the explicit statement that the individual and the Jewish community *are judged* according to the majority, which obviously means according to whether or not they have more fulfilments than transgressions. We may briefly consider to what extent this may represent a systematic theory as to how God judges man. On the assumption that R. Meir is responsible for the saying, we may immediately cite his saying that charity saves from Gehinnom (Baba Bathra 10a). If he could say that the practice of charity is sufficient to save, he can hardly have held the systematic belief that one is judged strictly according to the majority of his deeds. Further, we may note that the editor of the Tosefta placed immediately after the saying of R. Simeon b. Eleazar a contradictory saying by R. Simeon b. Yohai:[23] no

[20] Beginning with this sentence, the passage is paralleled in Kiddushin 40a–b, with minor changes.

[21] Some mss. omit 'in the name of R. Meir'; see Lieberman's apparatus. The Talmud (40b) attributes the saying to R. Eleazar b. R. Simeon.

[22] Lieberman (*Tosefta Ki-Fshutah, Nashim*, p. 928) interprets 'world' as 'community', i.e. the community of Israel.

[23] Paralleled in p. Peah 16b (1.1); Kiddushin 40b. Both Talmuds identify the R. Simeon of the Tosefta as R. Simeon b. Yohai.

matter how many good deeds a man has, he may rebel at the end and be damned, while the wickedest sinner who repents at the end will be saved. Here again the theory of judgment by a majority of deeds is excluded. Before attempting to reach further conclusions, we may consider the comments on Kiddushin 1.10 in the two Talmuds.

In the Babylonian Talmud, Rab Judah takes the mishnah to refer to one whose deeds are otherwise in balance: 'This is its meaning: HE WHO PER-FORMS ONE PRECEPT [*mitsvah*] in addition to his [equally balanced] merits IS WELL REWARDED, and he is as though he had fulfilled the whole Torah.'[24]

In the Palestinian Talmud, the mishnah is first interpreted to refer to one in an intermediary position. His deeds are balanced, and if he fulfils one *mitsvah* it inclines the balance in his favour, and so forth. Then there appears more Tannaitic material:[25]

Ben Azzai gave an interpretation of this verse: 'Dead flies makes the perfumer's ointment give off an evil odour' (Eccl. 10.1). One deduces from the use of the singular verb (though the subject is plural) that just as a single dead fly may infect the perfumer's ointment, so the man who commits only one sin loses thus the merit of his good works. R. Akiba gave an interpretation of this verse: 'Therefore Sheol has enlarged its appetite and opened its mouth beyond ordinance' (RSV, measure) (Isa. 5.14). It is not written here 'beyond ordinances', but 'beyond ordinance'. [It refers to] whoever does not have one *mitsvah* which can prove in his favour [and so make the scales incline] to the side of innocence (*kaf zekut*). This he said with regard to the world to come. But in this world, if even 999 angels declare him guilty and one angel declares him innocent, the Holy One, blessed be he, inclines [the scale] to the side of innocence, etc.[26]

It is apparent that the Amora or later Tanna (who apparently begins commenting with the words 'This he said') understood R. Akiba to mean 'one *mitsvah* more than the number of his transgressions'. He contrasts this system of strict reckoning at the future judgment with God's leniency here. And most modern scholars have followed the later commentator. Thus Schwab[27] translates 'one *mitsvah*' 'une bonne action en excédent sur les mauvaises', while Billerbeck explains 'eine Gebotserfüllung' thus: 'gemeint ist die *eine* Gebotserfüllung, die den auf der Wagschale des Verdienstes liegenden Gebotserfüllungen und guten Werken die Majorität verleiht gegenüber den Übertretungen auf der Wagschale der Schuld'.[28] Similarly, Schechter comments, 'From *Jer. Kiddushin*, 61d, it would seem that this

---

[24] Kiddushin 39b; ET, p. 193.

[25] P. Kiddushin 61d (1.10).

[26] For the continuation, see Moore, *Judaism* I, p. 391, and cf. Shabbath 32a. In Shabbath 32a, however, the saying, 'if 999 argue for his guilt while one argues in his favour, he is saved (*nitstsol*)', may refer to the world to come.

[27] French translation, p. 237.

[28] S.-B. II, p. 560 ('the reference is to the one fulfilment of a commandment, which depresses the balance on the side of fulfilments of the commandments and good works, rather than on the side of guilt').

insistence upon a majority of good actions applies only to the judgement in the next world, but in this world even one good action can save a man.'[29] This is with special reference to Aboth 3.15, which we shall cite below. Bacher, in commenting on the passage, writes, 'In Ies, 5,14 betont er [Akiba] den singular חק und findet darin die Andeutung, dass eine einzige mangelnde gute That beim Gerichte über den Menschen auf der Wagschale der Verdienste fühlbar wird, die Verdammung herbeiführt.'[30] And finally, Montefiore paraphrases Akiba's statement thus: 'The lack of one good deed may prevent the balance going in his favour.'[31]

In support of this interpretation of Akiba's saying, one may cite R. Akiba in Aboth 3.15 (ET, 3.16): 'All is foreseen, but freedom of choice is given; and the world is judged by grace, yet all is according to the majority of works [that be good or evil].'[32] The reading in Aboth is not perfectly clear, since the variant is 'and not according to works'. But if the reading which is generally accepted be considered accurate, the last clause could be seen as supporting the idea that R. Akiba thought that God's judgment is based on balancing one's deeds. Even so, however, it is apparent that the saying intends to hold judgment by grace and by works in balance. Not being a systematic theologian, R. Akiba did not explain how the two parts of the saying fit together.[33]

But leaving Aboth 3.15 aside for a moment, it seems that the view of the Rabbinic commentator on Akiba's saying in the Palestinian Talmud may have unduly influenced later commentators. In the first place, the Hebrew of R. Akiba's saying is quite clear: it refers to any one who does not have one (single) commandment in order that God may incline the scale to the side of innocence. There is no indication that 'one more than the number of transgressions' is meant. Further, R. Akiba's saying is in contrast to that of Ben Azzai, the point of which is that a *single* transgression causes one to lose much good. It seems only reasonable that R. Akiba's saying was to the point that the *fulfilment* of one *mitsvah* produces much good. Sayings of this type are in fact fairly common in the Tannaitic literature, and, although they appear paradoxical, they should occasion no surprise. Such sayings are very important if we are to understand the true significance of the 'weighing' theme, and we may profitably pause to consider them before returning to R. Akiba's remark.

---

[29] *Aspects*, p. 306 n. 4.   [30] *Agada der Tannaiten* I, pp. 325f.
[31] Montefiore and Loewe, *Anthology*, p. 595. We should note that this paraphrase of the passage incorrectly reverses the phrases 'in this world' and 'in the world to come', making God lenient in the final judgment but strict here. This 'improvement' solves the problem and may even be close to the general Rabbinic spirit, but it is not accurate.
[32] In Herford's edition (*Sayings of the Fathers*), 3.19; in Taylor's (*Sayings of the Jewish Fathers*), 3.24. For the variants see their comments on the passage, especially Taylor's notes to the Hebrew text (p. 20) and his additional note on the text (p. 152). Danby has 'excess' for 'majority'.
[33] Cf. Helfgott, *Election*, p. 76.

We have already noted that in Kiddushin 1.10a it is said that the fulfilment of a single commandment lengthens one's days, and the like, and that the transgression of one commandment shortens them. There is a similar saying by R. Hanina b. Gamaliel in Makkoth 3.15: 'If he that commits one transgression thereby forfeits his soul, how much more, if he performs one religious duty [*mitsvah*], shall his soul be restored to him!' The *qal vaḥomer* argument – 'how much more' – is based on the principle that God's quality of rewarding is greater than his quality of punishing. A similar inference on the same grounds is made by R. Jose in a passage already referred to:[34] if Adam's single transgression of a negative commandment led to death for subsequent generations, how much more will a man's action of repenting of *piggul* and *notar* and fasting on the Day of Atonement benefit (מזבה) him and his descendants! R. Jose explicitly refers to the principle that God's 'quality of rewarding' is greater than his 'quality of punishing'.

Sometimes various commandments are singled out which, if a man fulfil, he gains life in the world to come (or something of the sort), but if he break he is damned. The Rabbis duly noted that merely the faith with which Abraham believed was sufficient to merit him life in this world and in the world to come.[35] And similarly, Israel's faith merited that the Holy Spirit should rest upon them. In fact, anyone who accepts even one single commandment with faith deserves having the Holy Spirit rest upon him.[36] It is not surprising that the future world is given to those who keep the Sabbath *only* and that they avoid the great judgment day.[37] Similarly, charity is said to have salvific effect:[38]

It has been taught: R. Meir used to say: The critic [of Judaism] may bring against you the argument, 'If your God loves the poor, why does he not support them?' If so, answer him, 'So that through them we may be saved from the punishment of Gehinnom.'

The point is that the existence of the poor provides an opportunity for charity, which saves one from Gehinnom.[39] Acting mercifully is also sufficient for God's favourable judgment, and this is brought into explicit connection with the weighing motif:[40] 'The one who judges his neighbour

[34] Sifra Hobah Parasha 12.10; above, section 5 n. 30.
[35] Mek. Beshallah 6 (114; I, 253 [ch. 7]; to 14.31). Similarly, one who trusts (*baṭaḥ*) in God has a refuge in this world and the world to come; Menahoth 29b.
[36] Mek., ibid. (Lauterbach, I, pp. 252ff.).
[37] Mek. Vayassa' 4 (169; II, 120 [ch. 5]; to 16.25).
[38] Baba Bathra 10a (ET, p. 45). A story is also told attributing the same saying to R. Akiba. On charity saving, see also the Midrash on Psalm 17 (end).
[39] On charity as saving from (untimely) physical death, see Baba Bathra 10a–b (ET, p. 48); Urbach, *Ḥazal*, pp. 235f. (ET, pp. 264f.). On charity as atoning, see Urbach, p. 428 (ET, p. 484).
[40] An anonymous baraita in Shabbath 127b, near top. Freedman (ET, p. 633) translates: 'He who judges his neighbour in the scale of merit is himself judged favourably.' And cf. the saying by R. Gamaliel II: God will be merciful to those who are merciful; T. Baba Kamma 9.30; Shabbath 151b (ET, p. 774, where the exegesis is explained); p. Baba Kamma 6c (8.10). In the latter two passages, the negative statement that God will not be merciful to those who are not merciful is added.

on the side of innocence (*lekaf zekut*) is judged by God as innocent' (favourably, *lizekut*).[41]

Conversely, breaking a single commandment could be said to lead to the loss of the share in the world to come promised to every Israelite:

And these are they that have no share in the world to come: he that says that there is no resurrection of the dead prescribed in the Law; and [he that says] that the Law is not from Heaven, and an Epicurean. R. Akiba says: Also he that reads the heretical books, or that utters charms over a wound and says, *I will put none of the diseases upon thee which I have put upon the Egyptians: for I am the Lord that healeth thee* (Ex. 15.26). Abba Saul says: Also he that pronounces the Name with its proper letters.[42] (Sanhedrin 10.1; p. Peah 16b [1.1])

Anyone who employs verses from the Song of Songs for secular entertainment has no share in the world to come. (T. Sanhedrin 12.10)

A man who counts out money for a woman from his hand into hers or from her hand into his, in order that he might look at her will not be free from the judgment of Gehenna even if he is [in other respects] like our Master Moses. . . . (Baraita Erubin 18b; ET, p. 125)

R. Eleazar of Modiim said: If a man profanes the Hallowed Things and despises the set feasts and puts his fellow to shame publicly and makes void the covenant of Abraham our father [obliterates circumcision], and discloses meanings in the Law which are not according to the *Halakah*, even though a knowledge of the Law and good works are his, he has no share in the world to come. (Aboth 3.12)[43]

The most important passages in this connection, however, are those which state that those who sin with the intention of denying the God who forbade the sin break or cast off the yoke. That is to say, they exclude themselves from the covenant and consequently from the world to come. Since accepting the covenant meant accepting the commandments, refusal of the commandments is refusal of the covenant. Such phrases as 'he who does so and so casts off the yoke' should be understood in just this way. The particular sin mentioned is *either tantamount to denying God explicitly or is a deliberate sin against one's fellow which violates not only the letter of the law but its basic moral principles and which could only have been committed with calculation and intent.* The main example of the first type of sin is idolatry.

---

[41] Some other examples: Aboth 2.7 (Hillel): One who 'has gained for himself the words of the Law . . . has gained for himself life in the world to come'; Aboth 6.6, end: 'he that tells a thing in the name of him that said it brings deliverance unto the world'. For examples of doing one commandment (not one more than the number of transgressions) and having it count 'as if' one fulfilled the whole Torah, see my article 'On the Question of Fulfilling the Law', pp. 114f. n. 7.

[42] For a discussion of Rabbinic views on the pronunciation of the Tetragrammaton, see Urbach, *Ḥazal*, pp. 106ff. (ET, pp. 127–9). On p. 108 n. 33 (ET, p. 737 n. 30) he corrects the view of Marmorstein, *The Names and Attributes of God*, pp. 17–40.

[43] There are partial parallels in Sifre Num. 112 (121; to 15.31) and p. Peah 16b (1.1).

Just as the transgression of all the commandments breaks off the yoke, annuls the covenant between God and Israel, and misrepresents the Torah, so also the transgressor of this one commandment breaks off the yoke, annuls the covenant between God and Israel, and misrepresents the Torah. Now what can this one commandment be? The one against idolatry.[44]

'From the way which I command you this day to go after other gods' (Deut. 11.28). – On the basis of this passage they said: Everyone who confesses to idolatry denies the entire Torah, and everyone who denies idolatry confesses to the entire Torah.[45]

That transgression of a moral commandment may also be equivalent to denying God is seen in this passage from Sifra:[46]

'You shall not lend him your money at interest, nor give him your food for profit. I am the Lord your God' (Lev. 25.37f.). – On the basis of this passage they said: Everyone who takes upon himself the yoke of [the commandment not to take] interest accepts the yoke of heaven, and everyone who breaks off from himself the yoke of [the commandment not to take] interest breaks off from himself the yoke of heaven.

The passage (which is quoted more fully above, section 4 n. 39) continues by saying that God brought Israel out of Egypt on condition that they observe the commandment concerning interest. We see here the connection between the theme of committing one transgression which is considered to 'break off the yoke', statements that the exodus from Egypt was accomplished 'on condition that' a certain commandment be fulfilled, and the requirement to 'confess' and not 'deny' particular commandments (or all the commandments). The understanding behind these interrelated themes is the same: in giving the covenant, God gave commandments which must be obeyed. One should intend to obey the commandments in order to maintain one's place in the chosen people ('confess the exodus from Egypt'). Wilful rejection ('denial') of one of them is tantamount to denial of the covenant ('denial of the exodus from Egypt') and of God himself ('breaking off the yoke'). These interrelated themes go to the heart of Rabbinic religion: what counts is being in the covenant and intending to be obedient to the God who gave the covenant. Rejection of even one commandment with the intent to deny the God who gave it excludes one from the covenant, while acceptance of a fundamental commandment, such as the commandment not to commit idolatry, may show one's intent to be obedient. Nothing is said, it

[44] Mek. Pisha 5 (15; I, 37; to 12.6). For the translation of the three phrases (breaking, annulling and misrepresenting), see Lauterbach's notes ad loc. There is a verbatim parallel in Sifre Num. 111 (116; to 15.22). On these and other passages and on the three phrases, see Moore, *Judaism* I, p. 325, pp. 465ff.; III, p. 143; Schechter, *Aspects*, pp. 88, 220f.; Büchler, *Sin and Atonement*, pp. 97ff.; Kadushin, *The Rabbinic Mind*, pp. 349f., 342f. (on 'denying the fundamental principle [God]'). The three terms for rebellion are defined in p. Sanhedrin 27c (10.1, top); p. Peah 16b (1.1).

[45] Sifre Deut. 54, end (122; to 11.28). Friedmann (f. 86b) reads 'Everyone who confesses . . . is *like* one who denies', etc.

[46] Sifra Behar parasha 5.3. See Büchler, *Sin and Atonement*, pp. 92, 104ff.

need hardly be observed, about being obedient or disobedient 51% of the time.

The logic behind the view that one transgression may indicate rejection of God is seen in a comment on Lev. 5.21 ('If anyone sins and commits a breach of faith against the Lord and deceives his neighbour. . .'). R. Hananiah b. Hakinai takes the sequence to be causal: 'No one deceives his neighbour until he denies the Root.' In the same passage, another Rabbi comments that 'no one transgresses except one who has denied the one who gave the commandment'.[47] It was not a systematic belief that a single transgression always implies denial of God, although it could do so. The Rabbis could also say, however, that one moves from transgression of particular commandments to denial of God. The principal passage is a comment on Lev. 26.14f. which takes the phrases of the biblical passage as being stages in a sequence which leads from not studying to denying the existence of God. The biblical passage is this: 'But if you will not hearken to me, and will not do all these commandments, if you spurn my statutes, and if your soul abhors my ordinances, so that you will not do all my commandments, but break my covenant, . . .' The commentary is as follows:[48]

'If you will not hearken to me.' – Why does scripture say, 'And will not do'? – Could there be a man who did not study but who did [the commandments]? [No, for] scripture teaches, 'if you will not hearken and will not do'.[49] Thus everyone who does not study does not do. Or could there be a man who does not study and does not do, but who does not despise others? [No, for] scripture teaches, 'And if you despise my statutes.'[50] Thus everyone who does not study and does not do [the commandments] will end by despising others. [Similarly, it is proved that such a man goes on to hate the *ḥakamim*, hinder others from obeying the commandments and deny the *mitsvot* which were given at Sinai.] Or could there be a man who has all these qualities, but who does not deny the Root? [No, for] scripture teaches, 'to break my covenant'. Thus everyone who has all these qualities will end by denying the Root.

Whether wilful transgression be taken as proof that God has already been denied or as the first step in a stage leading to denial, it is clear that the two are closely intertwined. Denial of the obligation to obey commandments given by God implies, as its cause or result, denial of God himself.

[47] T. Shebuoth 3.6, cited by Büchler, loc. cit.; Schechter, *Aspects*, p. 232; Kadushin, *The Rabbinic Mind*, p. 351. Büchler cites also Mek. Mishpatim 19 (316; III, 150 [Kaspa 1]; to 22.24[25]): R. Meir says that one who takes usury has no share in the God who forbade it. Schechter cites also Baba Metzia 71a to the same point (R. Jose) and Sifre Deut. 117 (to 15.9): 'Everyone who withholds mercy from his fellow is like an idolater and has cast off the yoke of heaven.' The last passage is poorly attested, however; see the editions ad loc. Moore, *Judaism* I, p. 467, notes: 'There was . . . a natural disposition, at least for hortatory purposes, to treat all deliberate and wilful transgression as a constructive rejection of God and his Law.'

[48] Sifra Behuqqotai parasha 2.3, cited by Kadushin, *The Rabbinic Mind*, pp. 352f.

[49] Here as elsewhere the sequence is taken as causal: 'Will not hearken and (consequently) not do.'

[50] The statutes are taken to command respect and love for others.

The passages which assert that one who transgresses one commandment loses his place in the covenant or his share in the world to come do not mean that the Rabbis required legal perfection. There is no hint in Rabbinic literature of a view such as that of Paul in Gal. 3.10 or of IV Ezra,[51] that one must achieve legal perfection. This may readily be seen by considering how the Rabbis dealt with certain biblical passages which could be understood as supporting such a view. In Gal. 3.10, Paul quotes Deut. 27.26: 'Cursed be everyone who does not abide by (*emmenei*) all things written in the book of the law, and do them.' This follows the LXX, but the Hebrew word which is translated by *emmenei* in Greek is *yaqim*, which the RSV correctly renders 'confirm'. And so the Rabbis took it. The passage is not, as far as I have noted, commented on in the Tannaitic literature. But the Amoraic literature always emphasizes that one should confirm the law, not keep it without error. Thus in the Palestinian Talmud[52] the verse is interpreted to refer to 'the worldly tribunal which fails in its duty to uphold the law and to protest against crime'.[53] The same interpretation is found in Lev. Rab. 25.1, but applied to the individual.[54] The midrash further observes that 'if the text had read "cursed be he that does not *learn*", he would not have been able to survive, but the reading is "Cursed be he that does not confirm"'.[55] Human perfection was not considered realistically achievable by the Rabbis, nor was it required.

Similarly, Ezek. 18.20 ('The soul that sins shall die. The son shall not suffer for the iniquity of the father, nor the father suffer for the iniquity of the son; the righteousness of the righteous shall be upon himself, and the wickedness of the wicked shall be upon himself') could, by emphasizing the first sentence, have been taken to demand human perfection. But it is taken simply to mean that 'there is no death without sin'[56] or as teaching individual responsibility for sins (in contrast to Ex. 34.7).[57] Ex. 15.26 ('and keep all his statutes') is interpreted to mean those which deal with sexual licentiousness.[58] Deut. 11.22 ('If you will be careful to do all this commandment') is

---

[51] IV Ezra (II Esdras) 7.45ff.; 7.72; 7.88f.

[52] P. Sotah 21d, near top (7.4). The speaker is R. Simeon b. Halafta, a younger contemporary of Rabbi and his student.

[53] Schechter, *Aspects*, p. 193. The discussion concerns the meaning of *yaqim*, which literally means 'cause to stand'. Does it imply that the words of the Torah could fall? No; rather it refers to a temporal court which does not uphold the law. The phrase 'which does not uphold the law' does not actually appear in the text and must be supplied.

[54] This section of Lev. Rab. deals with Deut. 27.26 and Prov. 3.18 ('She is a tree of life to them that lay hold on her'). It is partially paralleled in p. Sotah, loc. cit.

[55] 'Confirm' is taken to include protesting against wrong-doing and supporting scholars.

[56] Shabbath 55a (ET, p. 255). Urbach (*Ḥazal*, p. 237; ET, p. 266; cf. p. 384; ET, p. 435) notes that the opinion that 'there is no death without sin' appears only in the Amoraic period. Here it is attributed to R. Ammi. It may be, however, that R. Judah held such a view. See section 7 n. 128.

[57] Makkoth 24a (ET, p. 173). Ezek. 18.20 is contrasted to Ex. 20.5 ('visiting the iniquity of the fathers upon the children to the third and fourth generation of them that hate me') in Mek. of R. Simeon b. Yohai to 20.5 (p. 148).

[58] Mek. Vayassa' 1 (158; II, 96; to 15.26).

taken to refer to the necessity to *study* the Torah as well as to hear it.[59]

The Rabbis consistently passed up opportunities to require legal perfection. As we have just been seeing, the sayings which indicate that a certain transgression results in being put out of the covenant or in losing the life of the world to come mean something quite different from the kind of legalistic perfectionism which caused the author of IV Ezra to despair. The opposite of denying the commandments (and consequently the God who gave them) is not obeying them with perfect success, but 'confessing' them.[60] What is required is submission to God's commandments and the intent to obey them.[61]

We began by considering the meaning of R. Akiba's statement concerning 'one who does not have one *mitsvah* which can prove in his favour', noting that many have taken it to mean 'one more *mitsvah* than the number of his transgressions', and consequently as supporting the view that weighing fulfilments against transgressions constitutes Rabbinic soteriology. We have now noted that sayings to the effect that fulfilment of one commandment can save and that transgression of one commandment could damn are fairly common, and we have discussed the significance of the latter statements. It thus becomes clear that, if R. Akiba meant that the fulfilment of *only* one *mitsvah* was enough to permit God to tip the scale to the side of innocence, he was saying what many other Rabbis also said. Although one hesitates before disagreeing with such scholars as Bacher and Schechter, this seems the best interpretation of what Akiba said. It is gratifying to be able to quote Finkelstein in support of this view: 'Sometimes [Akiba] asserted God's mercy to be such that a single meritorious act will win a man

[59] Sifre Deut. 48 (107f.; to 11.22; cf. Friedmann, f.83b, where the text differs slightly).

[60] On 'confessing' and 'denying', see especially Kadushin, *The Rabbinic Mind*, pp. 540–67.

[61] H. Hübner ('Gal 3,10 und die Herkunft des Paulus', *KuD* 19, 1973, pp. 215–31) has recently discussed the requirement to do all the law and the statements about good deeds outweighing transgression, and concluded that Paul was a Shammaite rather than a Hillelite. He argues first that, since Paul expected 100% obedience from proper Jews (Gal. 3.10), he could not have been a committed Hillelite, since, as everyone knows, most Pharisees believed in judgment by the majority of one's deeds. He regards this as one systematic theology, which he contrasts with the minority position, that one do all the law, which he attributes to the Shammaites. The latter position he finds in Sifra Qedoshim pereq 8.3 (to 19.34): the proselyte, like the native, should accept all the words of the Torah. Since R. Eliezer, a Shammaite, argued in Yebamoth 46a that proselytes must be circumcised, Hübner concludes that the connection of circumcision with doing all the law (Gal. 3.10) reflects a Shammaite position. Hübner's article seems faulty on every point: 1. The point of Sifra Qedoshim pereq 8.3 is that one should 'accept', i.e. 'agree to' in the sense of 'confess' all the laws, not perform them flawlessly. 2. That one should accept all the Torah and not deny it was a completely standard Rabbinic view. There are no statements to the contrary (that one may accept it selectively!), nor are there any statements parallel to Paul's statement that one must 'keep' all the laws as distinct from 'confessing' them, as we have just shown. The distinction found by Hübner does not exist. 3. The theory that one need be obedient only 51% of the time is not mainline Rabbinic soteriology, nor can 'weighing' statements be especially connected with the school of Hillel. R. Akiba, presumably a Hillelite, said that one fulfilment was sufficient. Nor can the numerous exhortative statements about not transgressing a certain single commandment be connected with Shammaites. This rebuttal of Hübner's argument is not intended to favour the view he argued against, that Paul was a Hillelite (Jeremias). I do not believe we have any information that would enable us to deal with such a question.

admission to the future world. He found support for this view in a fanciful interpretation of Isaiah 5.14.' Finkelstein translates Akiba's statement thus: ' "Only those who possess no good deeds at all will descend into the nether-world." '[62] This interpretation is greatly strengthened by a discussion between R. Gamaliel II and R. Akiba, which is cited by Finkelstein. In discussing Ezek. 18.5–9, which lists numerous sins to be avoided and concludes that one who has observed the ordinances is righteous and will live, the Rabbis comment:[63]

When R. Gamaliel read this verse he wept, saying, 'Only he who does all these things shall live, but not merely one of them!' Thereupon R. Akiba said to him, 'If so, *Defile not yourselves in all these things* [Lev. 18.24]. – is the prohibition against *all* [combined] only, but not against one?' [Surely not!] But it means, *in one* of these things; so here too, for doing one of these things [shall he live].

On the assumption that R. Akiba said the three things attributed to him on this topic (Aboth 3.15: the world is judged by grace, but everything is according to the majority of works; p. Kiddushin 61d: Isa. 5.14 proves that God will incline the scale in favour of one who has performed one *mitsvah*; Sanhedrin 81a: just as Lev. 18.24 means do not defile oneself in any one way, so Ezek. 18.5–9 means that one who does any *one* of the things listed will live), it is clearly impossible to attribute to him the view that God judges by saving those who have one more fulfilment than the number of their transgressions. Aboth 3.15 remains enigmatic. The only clear meaning is that grace and judgment of one's deeds are held in tension. But one cannot derive a systematic soteriology from such an assertion.

Thus we have seen that Kiddushin 1.10a and most of the Tannaitic com-ments gathered around it in the Tosefta and the Talmuds do not support the contention that 'weighing' constituted Rabbinic soteriology. Kiddushin 1.10a itself and T. Kiddushin 1.13 are exhortative statements to encourage obedience and discourage disobedience. They do not work out the logic of weighing one deed against another. The Babylonian Talmud has no unique Tannaitic material on the subject, and the discussion of Ben Azzai and R. Akiba in the Palestinian Talmud does not support the weighing hypothesis. Of the passages which we have thus far considered, there remains in favour of the weighing hypothesis only the saying in T. Kiddushin 1.14 by R. Simeon b. Eleazar in the name of R. Meir to the effect that individuals and

---

[62] Finkelstein, *Akiba*, p. 186. Finkelstein does not bring this passage into connection with Aboth 3.15, which he cites, op. cit., p. 207. There is a parallel to the sayings of Ben Azzai and R. Akiba in Eccl. Rab. 10.1. The English translator (A. Cohen) translates Akiba's saying thus: 'A person who has not [the performance of] one precept [to his credit] which can make the scale of merit incline in his favour' (ET, p. 260). Bonsirven (*Textes rabbiniques*, p. 412) also understood Akiba's saying correctly, as did M. Brocke, 'Tun und Lohn', p. 172.

[63] Sanhedrin 81a (ET, p. 538). The parallel in Makkoth 24a attaches R. Gamaliel's comment to a discussion of Ps. 15, and the answer is prefaced by 'they said' rather than by 'R. Akiba said'. Cf. also Midrash Ps. 15.7 (ET, pp. 194f.), which refers to both biblical passages.

'the world' are judged by the majority of their deeds. But, as we saw, R. Meir can hardly have held such a view as a systematic soteriology, and the editor of the Tosefta placed immediately after it a statement to another effect. To derive from the saying of R. Simeon b. Eleazar in the name of R. Meir a systematic soteriology in which God judges by balancing fulfilments and transgressions is not only wrong, but wrong-headed.

We have yet to discuss R. Eleazar ha-Kappar's saying in Aboth 4.22. It runs as follows:

They that have been born [are destined] to die, and they that are dead [are destined] to be made alive, and they that live [after death are destined] to be judged, that men may know and make known and understand that he is God, he is the Maker, he is the Creator, he is the Discerner, he is the Judge, he is the Witness, he is the Complainant, and it is he that shall judge, blessed is he, in whose presence is neither guile nor forgetfulness nor respect of persons nor taking of bribes; for all is his. And know that everything is according to the reckoning. And let not thy [evil] nature promise thee that the grave will be thy refuge: for despite thyself wast thou fashioned . . . , and despite thyself shalt thou hereafter give account and reckoning before the King of kings of kings, the Holy One, blessed is he.

The intention of the passage is to deny favouritism on God's part and to assure men that they will be punished for their sins, in the hope that they will live in a way that is mindful of that. The reference to 'reckoning' does not naturally refer to a ledger by which it is determined whether or not a man's good deeds outnumber his transgressions.

We can find several statements to the effect that God keeps books on individuals' deeds in the Amoraic literature,[64] but such statements are very rare in Tannaitic literature. We have seen above that one such reference, in which the man at death is commanded to put his seal to testify to the accuracy of the record of his deeds, is motivated by theodicy.[65] A man confesses that God's judgment is just. It is not said that his fulfilments must be more numerous than his transgressions. Rabbi's saying in Aboth 2.1 ('Consider three things and thou wilt not fall into the hands of transgression: know what is above thee – a seeing eye and a hearing ear and all thy deeds written in a book') is exhortative in a way similar to R. Eleazar's saying in Aboth 4.22. A man avoids transgression by remembering that God is a just judge and forgets nothing. Such sayings continue the line which we saw in the preceding sub-section: one may rely on God's justice, and he punishes transgression just as he rewards obedience.[66] The opposite of this view, we may repeat, would not be that God saves by grace, but that one can sin with impudence since there is no requital. The passages which we have been considering, in

---

[64] Nedarim 22a, top; Rosh Ha-Shanah 16b, 32b. Even these passages do not refer to ledgers of debits and credits, however, but to the books of life and death.

[65] Sifre Deut. 307; above, pp. 127f.

[66] Cf. Brocke's interpretation of the two passages, above, section 5 n. 107.

other words, do not represent the view that good works *earn* salvation, although, as we have seen, the wilful intention to disobey does remove one from the covenant and from its promises. Obedience, especially the intention to obey ('confessing') is the *conditio sine qua non* of salvation, but it does not *earn* it.

It is instructive to compare the 'weighing' passages (T. Kiddushin 1.14 and the last phrase of Aboth 3.15) with the statements that the fulfilment of one commandment can save. If we ask which is the doctrine, the answer must be that neither is. The passages indicating that fulfilment of one commandment saves do serve, however, to refute the notion that 'weighing' was a Rabbinic doctrine, even though an even more decisive refutation of that perversely mistaken view will eventually appear. Now we must note, however, that Schechter is also not altogether correct in treating the accomplishment of one law in a perfect manner as a soteriological doctrine.[67] This is, to be sure, much closer to the general spirit of Rabbinic religion than is the idea of weighing. But if there is a 'doctrine' of salvation in Rabbinic religion, it is election and repentance.[68] Sayings about fulfilling one law and being given a share in the world to come are balanced by sayings indicating that damnation is the consequence of one transgression.

The truth is that these three groups of sayings – damnation for one transgression, salvation for one fulfilment and judgment according to the majority of deeds – have a common ground and purpose. All three statements could be made without intellectual embarrassment by anyone but a systematic theologian. Each type of saying is an effective way of urging people to obey the commandments as best they can and of insisting upon the importance of doing so.

How non-systematically sayings connecting life in the world to come directly with the merit acquired here should be regarded can be shown by an additional example. There is a baraita in the name of R. Joshua[69] to the effect that *extending* restrictions in this world (thereby protecting against transgression) *extends* one's days in the world to come. This seems to indicate that a direct correlation exists between deeds and salvation. The better one is at fulfilling the law, the longer one's salvation lasts. But once it is put in this way, the ridiculousness of taking the statement literally becomes apparent. The Rabbis never contemplated individuals' staying in the world to come for a certain period and then leaving if they had only a few good deeds in excess of bad, or something of the sort. The point of R. Joshua's saying is, it is obvious, to encourage 'extending' restrictions, that is, building a fence around the law. He brought home the importance of doing so by a

---

[67] Schechter, *Aspects*, p. 164, where more examples of salvation from the fulfilment of one commandment are listed.
[68] See below, section 7.
[69] Niddah 16b.

play on the word 'extending'. One must be grateful that Billerbeck and others did not seize upon this passage and 'extend' the system which they attribute to the Rabbis by making the *duration* of a man's salvation depend upon the magnitude and number of his deeds.

Before leaving the 'weighing' theme, we should consider the famous controversy between the school of Shammai and the school of Hillel over God's treatment of the 'intermediate' class, that is, those who are neither perfectly righteous nor perfectly wicked:[70]

The School of Shammai say: There are three classes; one for 'everlasting life', another for 'shame and everlasting contempt' (Dan. 12.2) (these are the wholly wicked) [and a third class which is] evenly balanced. These go down to Gehenna, where they scream and again come up and receive healing, as it is written: 'And I will bring the third part through the fire, and will refine them as silver is refined, and will try them as gold is tried; and they will call on my name and I will be their God' (Zech. 13.9). And of these last Hannah said: 'The Lord killeth and the Lord maketh alive, he bringeth down to Sheol and bringeth up' (I Sam. 2.6).

The School of Hillel say: He is 'great in mercy' (Ex. 34.6), that is, he leans in the direction of mercy; and of them David said: 'I am well pleased that the Lord hath heard the voice of my prayer', etc. (Ps. 116.1); and of them, the whole psalm is written.

The two schools apparently agreed that the third class would be redeemed, but the school of Shammai thought that they must first suffer, while the school of Hillel thought that God freely inclined towards mercy and would place the third class together with the first. Nor should we suppose (as some of the Amoraim may have done)[71] that the 'wholly wicked' are those who have only one more evil deed than good. It is an interesting question who the 'wholly wicked' are. They are not those totally devoid of good deeds, just as the 'completely righteous' are not totally devoid of bad deeds, since the wholly wicked are paid here for their few good deeds, while the completely righteous are punished here for their few bad deeds.[72] Probably the 'completely righteous' are those who intend to keep the commandments and are very successful at it, sinning only unwittingly and occasionally, while the 'wholly wicked' are those who renounce the covenant, pay no heed to God's commandments and behave toward their fellows as if God had not commanded love of the neighbour. Perhaps the terms should best be translated 'whole-heartedly wicked' and 'whole-heartedly righteous'. The term

---

[70] T. Sanhedrin 13.3, Danby's translation slightly modified. There is a parallel in Rosh Ha-Shanah 16b. See further Bacher, *Agada der Tannaiten* I, pp. 15f.; Moore, *Judaism* II, p. 318; Neusner, *Rabbinic Traditions* II, pp. 238f. Neusner translates שְׁקוּלִין (which he transliterates as shqwly*h*n) as 'that the least of them' (from *qul*, small) instead of 'evenly balanced' (from *shaqal*). In any case, although the present text of the Tosefta is not as clear as we should like, the point is that the two houses disagreed only about whether or not the third class, neither wholly wicked nor wholly righteous, would be punished before entering heaven.

[71] Rosh Ha-Shanah 17a.

[72] Sifre Deut. 307.

'wholly wicked' does not refer to one who has a simple majority of evil deeds over good, nor even necessarily to one who has a huge majority. Thus we have seen that one Rabbi argued that even if 999 angels argued for a man's guilt and one for his innocence, God would consider him innocent.[73] Similarly, if a man is evil all his life and repents at the end, he is saved.[74] The 'wholly wicked' can only be those who have no intention to obey God. It should be emphasized that not only the 'completely righteous' are saved. As the above controversy shows, all but the 'wholly wicked' are saved. One need not be 'completely righteous' to be judged righteous by God. As we shall see, the righteous are not the sinless, but those who confirm the covenant.[75] In any case, it appears that the controversy between the Shammaites and the Hillelites on the 'three classes' lends no support to the theory that the Rabbinic doctrine of salvation was one of weighing merits.

It is true that there are some sayings which do indicate that God judges strictly according to the majority of a man's deeds. But, as we have seen, this can by no means be taken as Rabbinic doctrine. The saying of R. Akiba in p. Kiddushin 61d and the controversy between the school of Shammai and the school of Hillel, as well as the other sayings to the effect that fulfilling one commandment merits salvation, are simply too well attested, too widespread, too numerous and too strong to permit such a view to stand.[76]

This means that the view that God balances merits and demerits against each other, so that a merit can serve to *annul* or *compensate for* a sin, must also be given up. We have seen above that Bultmann, relying on traditional Christian scholarship, attributed such a view to the Rabbis.[77] It has recently been repeated by Thyen, relying on Sjöberg.[78] This is an instance in which a view in agreement with the Weberian theory of weighing has been read into Rabbinic literature by a fairly gross misreading and mistranslating of passages, and since the view seems to be widespread, we shall examine some of the putative evidence for it.

Thyen states that God 'gives Israel the commandment to eat the paschal lamb as an opportunity to earn merit which outweighs their sins'.[79] The passage which he cites from Sjöberg is this:[80]

R. Jose the Galilean says: Until the last one of them finished his paschal sacrifice, the 'enemies of Israel'[81] were liable to be destroyed in Egypt, as it is said: 'That ye shall say: It is the sacrifice of the Lord's passover,' etc.

---

[73] The passage cited above, n. 25.   [74] T. Kiddushin 1.15f.   [75] Below, section 8.

[76] In the Amoraic period it was also frequently said that the 'weighing' would be 'fixed' by God so that the scale would incline to the side of innocence. In the case of an even balance, God would remove a transgression from the scale of guilt or, in the case of one who lacked good deeds, God would give him some of his own. References in Mach, *Der Zaddik*, pp. 38f.

[77] Above, section 1, p. 45.

[78] Thyen, *Sündenvergebung*, pp. 67, 74; citing Sjöberg, *Gott und die Sünder*, pp. 31, 146.

[79] Thyen, p. 67.   [80] Sjöberg, p. 31. The passage is Mek. Pisha 12 (42; I, 94; to 12.27).

[81] Lauterbach notes that the phrase is a euphemism for Israel.

The passage is difficult. Kadushin takes the relationship between the eating of the paschal lamb and the threatened destruction of Israel to be that the slaughter and eating proved that the Israelites were not idolaters who worshipped lambs.[82] Whether or not this is correct, there is no reference in the passage to earning a merit which annuls or counterbalances a demerit.

The consideration of a second passage cited by Thyen from Sjöberg will require somewhat more discussion. Thyen writes:

Im Geiste von Dan. 9.18 heisst es, dass Mose und David, obwohl sie die Sünden leicht durch gute Werke hätten kompensieren können (!), ausdrücklich darum bitten, Gott möge ihnen *umsonst* vergeben. 'Das ist ein Qalwachomer: Wenn schon diese, die die Übertretung durch ihre guten Werke aufheben konnten, von Gott nur erbaten, dass er ihnen umsonst gebe, – um wievielmehr muss dann der, der nur einer der Tausend der Tausende und der Zehntausend der Zehntausende ihrer Schüler ist, von Gott nur bitten, er möge es ihm umsonst schenken.'[83]

Thyen comments that here the statement of grace is 'sicklied o'er' (*angekränkelt*) by the idea of merit,[84] obviously since David and Moses *could* have compensated for their sins by good deeds and since their good works *could* have removed their transgressions. Thyen takes the passage to refer to the possibility of *compensation* for transgression and to the appeal for gratuitous *forgiveness* of transgression. Actually, however, the ideas of compensation for and forgiveness of transgression do not appear in the text, but have been imported by the translator, perhaps with the slight aid of an inferior text – a text which has now been corrected but which Thyen did not check. The passage runs as follows:

Israel had two leaders, Moses and David the King, who were able to suspend the world by their good deeds; but they only besought God (*ha-Maqom*) that he should give them mercy (*hinam*). Should one not reason *qal vahomer*: If these, who were able to suspend the world by their good deeds, only besought God that he should give them mercy, how much more should one who is no more than one of a thousand of the thousands of thousands . . . of the students of their students do no more than beseech God that he should give them mercy! (Sifre Deut. 26)

It is remarkable that a passage in which the intention is to state that, no matter how numerous a man's good deeds, he should not claim merit before God, but only appeal for mercy, has been taken as indicating the Rabbinic reliance on works and merit. Specifically, the passage is taken as

---

[82] Kadushin, *Conceptual Approach*, pp. 122f.; cf. pp. 78f.

[83] ('In the spirit of Dan. 9.18 we read that although Moses and David could easily have compensated for their sins by good work (!), they explicitly ask God to forgive them *gratuitously*. "This is a *qal vahomer*: If these, who were able to suspend transgression by their good works, only besought God that he should give them gratuitously, how much more should one who is no more than one of the thousands of thousands and ten thousands of ten thousands of their students do no more than beseech God that he should bestow upon them gratuitously!') Thyen, p. 74, citing Sjöberg, p. 146. The passage is Sifre Deut. 26. (38f.; to 3.23).

[84] Thyen, p. 74 n. 7.

supporting the view that good deeds *compensate for* transgressions, a view which fits well into the theory of weighing fulfilments and transgressions, although the passage does not say that at all.[85]

Sjöberg's understanding of the passage naturally depended on Friedmann's text,[86] where the crucial phrase which he and Thyen take to mean 'compensate for transgressions' is *litlot et ha-ʿabirot* (לִתְלוֹת אֶת הָעֲבֵירוֹת), literally, 'to suspend transgressions'. There might be some dispute over the meaning of the phrase, although it may certainly be said that *talah* ('suspend') never means 'compensate for'.[87] The meaning of the passage in Friedmann's text would probably be 'suspend the punishment for their transgressions',[88] in which case 'their transgressions' would refer to the Israelites' transgressions, on account of which Moses was forbidden to cross the Jordan (so Deut. 3.26). The meaning would be that Moses, when praying to be allowed to cross the Jordan (Deut. 3.23–5) (*not* when seeking forgiveness), appealed only to God's mercy, although one would have thought that he had sufficient good deeds to suspend the punishment for the Israelites' transgressions, on account of which God had forbidden him to go over. Finkelstein's more recent text – a text unavailable to Sjöberg but which Thyen might have checked – has a different and better reading, however: 'suspend the world'. This phrase is difficult, and I find no precise parallel elsewhere in Tannaitic literature. There seem to be several possible meanings: 1. To suspend the day of Moses's and David's death. This takes 'the

---

[85] Several misunderstandings appear to have become traditional in the translation of the text. Thus G. Kittel, in his edition of Sifre Deut. (p. 38), translated the first *litlot* phrase: 'Sie hätten nun die Übertretungen durch ihre guten Werke aufheben können' ('they could have suspended transgressions through their good works') and the second one: 'diese, die die Übertretungen auszugleichen durch ihre guten Werke' (those who could offset transgressions by their good works). Translating *litlot* as 'compensate for' or 'offset' (*ausgleichen*) is without justification. Kittel has a dubious translation of another line, which also aids the misunderstanding of the passage. Where my translation given in the text reads 'besought God that he should give them mercy', the concluding Hebrew words are שֶׁיִּתֵּן לָהֶם אֶלָּא חִנָּם. *Hinam* here is best taken as a noun, the object of 'give'. Kittel understands *ḥinam* as if it were adverbial (=ʿal *ḥinam*, *le-ḥinam*, or *be-ḥinam*) and supplies an object in the footnote: 'die Gewährung ihrer Bitte um Vergebung' (the granting of their prayer for forgiveness). Thus Moses and David are depicted as praying for forgiveness, although that is not mentioned in the text and is rendered unlikely by the biblical verse being commented on. The net effect of these alterations (translating 'suspend' as 'compensate for' and supplying 'forgiveness' as the object of 'give') is to make it appear that the kind of interpretation given by Thyen is justified: Moses and David could have *compensated for* transgressions by their good works, but prayed that God gratuitously (Thyen: 'umsonst') *forgive* them. The italicised words represent words or meanings supplied by the translators. Ljungman's edition of Sifre Deut. (pp. 57f.) evidences a similar understanding, even though he had the advantage of a text which read 'world' where the one translated by Kittel read 'transgressions'. His translation of the two *litlot* phrases is this: 'sie konnten die Welt durch ihre guten Werke aufrecht halten' (they could support the world by their good works). The footnote gives this explanation: 'sie konnten durch ihre guten Werke die Übertretung . . . der Welt ausgleichen und die Welt vor dem Gericht schützen' ('they could compensate for the transgression . . . of the world by their good works and protect the world from judgment'). Thus removing 'transgressions' from the text does not remove 'compensate for transgressions' from the interpretation. Ljungman also understands *ḥinam* adverbially: 'umsonst', interpreted as 'aus Gnade'.

[86] Friedmann, 70b. Sjöberg's book and Finkelstein's text were both published in 1939.

[87] See Jastrow, pp. 1670f.

[88] So Weber (*Jüdische Theologie*, p. 313) understood it: 'die Strafe für ihre Sünden hätten abwehren können'.

world' to mean 'the day of death' and depends on the context of Deut. 3.23ff.[89] 'Suspend' is understood as 'postpone', a standard meaning. 2. To suspend the punishment of the world. This relies on the frequent use of *talah without* a direct object to mean suspend or withhold punishment. Thus Sotah 3.4, 5; 8.5; T. Sotah 7.3: *talah l-*, 'suspend [punishment] for'; Sifra Beḥuqqotai pereq 8.7(6) (to 26.42): *talah le-ʿolam*, 'suspend [punishment] for the world'.[90] 3. To support the world. Here the meaning would be similar to that of *talah* in Hagigah 1.8, mountains suspended by a hair. In the Sifra passage last cited the meaning of *talah le-ʿolam* might also be 'support the world'.[91]

None of these suggestions is perfectly satisfactory, and the variants in the text seem to indicate that earlier readers also had difficulty with the phrase. The general sense is in any case clear: Moses and David had a *lot* of good deeds – enough to sustain the world, to suspend God's punishment or to postpone the day of death – but they did not consider that they merited God's favourable reply to their requests, and so they prayed for mercy. In no case can *talah* be taken to mean 'compensate for', however, and especially not 'to compensate for transgression' as the opposite of 'to forgive freely'.

Thus we have seen that Rabbinic soteriology does not consist of balancing merits against demerits. The Rabbis certainly believed that God would punish transgression and reward obedience, but it is not a Rabbinic doctrine that one's place in the world to come is determined by counting or weighing his deeds. Statements to the effect that a man should behave *as if* his deeds were evenly balanced and as if the next act would determine his fate, as well as statements that he is judged by the majority of his deeds, must be seen in the entire context of Rabbinic exhortation to obey the commandments, which includes statements to the effect that one transgression may damn and that one fulfilment may save. 'Weighing' is not Rabbinic soteriology. Further, good deeds are not considered to offset or compensate for transgressions at the judgment, although they may suspend the punishment for transgressions (so Sotah 3.4). Transgressions, as we shall see, are atoned for rather than balanced by a corresponding good deed. Although obedience is required, no number of good deeds can earn salvation if a man acts in such a way as to remove himself from the covenant. Obedience and the intention

---

[89] I am grateful to my colleague Dr. A. Baumgarten for this suggestion.

[90] Some of the texts of the opening lines of Sifre Deut. 26 have basically the same sentence, and the Genizeh fragment there reads *litlot le-ʿolam*. See Finkelstein's apparatus, p. 36 line 20.

[91] So RaSHBa (R. Samson b. Abraham of Sens), commenting on the passage in Sifra: 'the world is maintained (*yitqayyim*) for his sake'. We should further note that the parallel to Sifra Beḥuqqotai pereq 8.7 in Lev. Rab. 36.5 is another instance in which *ʿolam* stands as the direct object of *talah*. Where Sifra reads שיתלה לְעוֹלָם בגינו, Lev. Rab. reads שיתלה כל העוֹלָם בגינו. J. J. Slotki in the Soncino translation of Lev. Rab. (p. 462) correctly translates: 'the deeds of each one alone would suffice for the whole world to be kept suspended in its position. . .'. This seems to confirm understanding Sifre Deut. 26 as meaning 'support the world'.

to obey are required if one is to remain in the covenant and share in its promises, but they do not earn God's mercy.

The decisive evidence against the theory that 'weighing' constitutes Rabbinic soteriology, however, is the fact that the Rabbis held another view, a view which is totally pervasive in the literature and which excludes the possibility that 'weighing' was a Rabbinic doctrine.

7. Salvation by membership in the covenant and atonement

All Israelites have a share in the world to come

The all-pervasive view is this: all Israelites have a share in the world to come unless they renounce it by renouncing God and his covenant. All sins, no matter of what gravity, which are committed within the covenant, may be forgiven as long as a man indicates his basic intention to keep the covenant by atoning, especially by repenting of transgression. Moore has put it this way:

'A lot in the World to come' . . . is ultimately assured to every Israelite on the ground of the original election of the people by the free grace of God . . . [It] is not wages earned by works, but is bestowed by God in pure goodness upon the members of his chosen people, as 'eternal life' in Christianity is bestowed on the individuals whom he has chosen, or on the members of the church.[1]

Similarly Montefiore:

Few Israelites were destined for an abiding hell or for annihilation. Only very high-handed criminals, and very outrageous and unrepentant heretics and apostates, would incur such a doom. And the view of R. Joshua that the righteous of all nations (that is, of all non-Jews) would inherit the world to come became the accepted doctrine of the Synagogue.[2]

The explicit statement that 'all Israelites have a share in the world to come' appears in Sanhedrin 10.1. It is followed by a list of exceptions, which we have already quoted, but which we should now consider at greater length. The first group of exceptions is attached immediately to the anonymous statement concerning every Israelite and may have always accompanied the positive statement.[3] The three groups excluded are these: 'he that says that there is no resurrection of the dead prescribed in the Law, and [he that says] that the Law is not from Heaven, and an Epicurean'. The

---

[1] Moore, *Judaism* II, p. 95.

[2] Montefiore, *Anthology*, p. 582 (the last point refers to T. Sanhedrin 13.2); cf. *Judaism and St Paul*, pp. 44, 77f.

[3] Epstein, however, thinks that the anonymous exclusions belong with Sanhedrin 6.2: 'Every one that makes his confession has a share in the world to come'; *Mebo'ot*, p. 418 n. 8.

statement is then glossed by R. Akiba (excluding those who read heretical books and those who, in healing, claim for themselves the power of God) and by Abba Saul (excluding those who pronounce the Tetragrammaton). The anonymous statement continues (10.2) by saying that in biblical history three kings (Jeroboam, Ahab and Manasseh) and four commoners (Balaam, Doeg, Ahitophel and Gehazi) have no share in the world to come. This saying is glossed by R. Judah's taking exception to the exclusion of Manasseh, who repented, and an anonymous rebuttal of R. Judah.

Further exclusions follow (10.3): the generation of the flood, the generation of the dispersion, the men of Sodom and the spies. This list is further glossed by R. Akiba, who adds the generation of the wilderness, the company of Korah and the Ten Tribes. He is disputed on each point by R. Eliezer. Some texts then add (10.4) the inhabitants of an apostate city to those excluded, but it is best to see the reference to these as continuing the discussion of chapter 9.[4] The statement concerning all Israel and the list of exclusions, then, is confined to 10.1–3 and has been inserted into the discussion of capital punishment in Sanhedrin 7–11.

Billerbeck attributes the entirety of 10.1 to R. Akiba, apparently because his is the first name to appear,[5] and his view seems to have been influential.[6] R. Akiba's comment is clearly a gloss to a preceding statement, however, and the attribution of the anonymous statement to R. Akiba may be safely disregarded. Finkelstein, on the other hand, has argued that the first sentences are the introduction to a proclamation issued by the men of the great synagogue.[7] He takes the first sentence, which he thinks is best translated 'All Israel has a destiny in the future eternity', to be deliberately ambiguous with regard to the nature of the future eternity, whether 'in the world to come' following the resurrection or a future eternity entered by each soul at the time of death.[8] But the general point is clear: 'their primary

---

[4] See the notes in Albeck's text and Danby's translation, ad loc.; see further Epstein, *Mebo'ot*, p. 403 n. 57; pp. 418f. Epstein thinks that 10.4 is an addition from a halakic midrash.

[5] S.-B. IV, pp. 1052–5. He gives an artificial and erroneous systematization of R. Akiba by combining Sanhedrin 10.1–3 with Eduyoth 2.10: the twelve-month punishment of the wicked in Gehinnom refers to atoning punishment (purgatory) for all those not covered by the exclusions of Sanhedrin 10.1–3. Finkelstein (*Akiba*, p. 185) has correctly interpreted Eduyoth 2.10 to mean that God is lenient and so will punish the wicked for only twelve months, after which they are annihilated. Gehinnom does not atone. Cf. Sifre Num. 112 (p. 121). Billerbeck's synthesis also does not take account of the well-attested Akiban view that sufferings in *this* life atone. There *is*, however, an anonymous saying in Sifre Deut. 333 (383; to 32.43) that suffering in Gehinnom atones for the *wicked*.

[6] Schubert (*Dead Sea Community*, p. 109) dates the passage in the first or second century c.e. Professor Jeremias indicated in a seminar that he accepts Billerbeck's dating as well as his theory of Gehinnom as purgatory.

[7] *Mabo'*, pp. 212ff., and p. xxxii of the English summary: 'The basic text ... was formulated no later than the third century, B.C.E.' There is a sketch of his view in 'Introductory Study to *Pirke Abot*', *JBL* 57, 1938, pp. 13–50. For the most recent discussion of Finkelstein's view of the first chapters of Aboth (though not of his connection of Sanhedrin 10 to them), see A. J. Saldarini, 'The End of the Rabbinic Chain of Tradition', *JBL* 93, 1974, pp. 97–106.

[8] *Mabo'*, pp. xxxii–xxxvi.

purpose apparently was to declare that not only the righteous, but also the vast majority of Israelites – neither completely righteous nor utterly wicked – have a share in the future life.'[9]

The negative implication of the document is that 'those who sinned so greatly as to be denied a share in the future life also forfeited the name of Israelite'.[10] Finkelstein thinks that this view was initially directed against the Hellenized apostates who flourished before the Maccabean revolt and who were bitterly opposed by the Ḥasidim.[11] Those who desert the covenant lose the covenant promises.

Whether we accept Finkelstein's precise dating of the text or not, he has performed a valuable service in clarifying its basic intention. Of the three first anonymous exclusions, the second and third obviously refer to those who do not intend to remain in the covenant. Those who deny that the Torah is from Heaven deny that the covenant and its commandments are from God, while 'Epicureans' in Rabbinic parlance are heretics, those who are irreverent towards the law.[12] It is perhaps more natural, however, to take the first exclusion, those who deny that the resurrection of the dead is based on the written Torah, to refer to the Sadducees.[13] We shall return to the question of the Sadducees below.

It is difficult to know precisely how to take the other exclusions, whether as serious statements that the individuals and groups named would not participate in the world to come or as homiletical exercises which show how various texts in the Bible can be used to exclude individuals and groups in Israel's history. Certainly in the later parallels considerable ingenuity was displayed in finding reasons to exclude individuals and groups.[14] It seems likely, however, that the exceptions of 10.2–3 are more seriously meant. We note that only the worst individual sinners and only the most unregenerate generations are named. Those who are *not* excluded are noteworthy: we do not read that one who has not fulfilled more commandments than the number of his transgressions is excluded, nor that the *'amme ha-'arets* have no share in the world to come.

We have repeatedly cautioned against taking one passage from Rabbinic literature to represent a dogma held by all Rabbis at all times, and it is not our intention to use Sanhedrin 10.1 in this way. We have here simply the clearest and most concise statement of a view which in fact seems to have been universal, although it is more often presupposed than stated. We may give two further examples of the view that all Israel will be saved. One is a

[9] Ibid., p. xxxvii.
[10] Ibid., p. xxxviii.   [11] Ibid.
[12] See Jastrow, p. 104.
[13] So Epstein, *Mebo'ot*, pp. 56, 418. The passage is from before 70 c.e. and is anti-Sadducean.
[14] See e.g. ARN 36 (ET, pp. 147–52). As Moore (*Judaism* II, p. 388 n. 4) comments, 'The rabbis are very liberal with homiletical damnation.'

debate between R. Eliezer and R. Joshua about whether or not Israel must repent in order to be redeemed, R. Eliezer taking the position that repentance is necessary and R. Joshua the position that God will in any case redeem his people.[15] The discussion apparently has to do with the physical redemption of Israel, not with the salvation of Israelites in the world to come,[16] but the general point is pertinent: Israel as such will be redeemed. Secondly, we may cite a discussion in which R. Ishmael drew a conclusion about the redemption of Israel in the world to come:[17]

There are sacrifices that can be redeemed and there are sacrifices that cannot be redeemed, there are things forbidden to be eaten which can be redeemed, and there are things forbidden to be eaten which cannot be redeemed. . . . So also in the future world there will be some for whom there will be redemption and there will be some for whom there will be no redemption. For the heathen nations there will be no redemption, as it is said: 'No man can by any means redeem his brother, nor give to God a ransom for him – for too costly is the redemption of their soul' (Ps. 49.8–9). Beloved are the Israelites, for the Holy One, blessed be He, has given the heathen nations of the world as ransom for their souls, as it is said: 'I have given Egypt as thy ransom.' Why? 'Since thou art precious in My sight and honourable and I have loved thee; therefore will I give men for thee, and peoples for thy life' (Isa. 43.3–4).

Although here the attitude toward the Gentiles is not so generous as that expressed by R. Joshua, due allowance must be made for the homiletical use of Isaiah. In any case, however, it is clear that the Israelites will be redeemed. The commentator could have said that those who have one more transgression than fulfilment are not redeemed and that those who have a majority of good deeds are, but he did not say so: all Israelites are redeemed.[18]

The point that all Israelites except unregenerate sinners have a share in the world to come, however, is best proved in two ways: by the absence of any statements to the contrary and by considering the Rabbinic view of repentance and atonement. We may best proceed by considering further those who are or who have been said to be excluded.

The Sadducees

As we saw, the most natural reading of the statement that those who deny

---

[15] See Neusner, *Eliezer* II, p. 418, referring to Tanḥuma (ed. Buber) Beḥuqqotai 5 (vol. II, p. 111); p. Taanith 63d (1.1); Sanhedrin 97b–98a. The traditional text of the Tanḥuma (Beḥuqqotai 3) attributes the debate to R. Judah and R. Simeon. See Buber's notes, ad loc.

[16] See Urbach, *Ḥazal*, pp. 603f. (ET, pp. 668f.); cited by Neusner, *Eliezer* II, p. 259.

[17] Mek. Mishpatim 10 (286; III, 87f. [Nezikin 10]; to 21.30).

[18] For other examples, see ARN 16 (ET, p. 86), where R. Simeon b. Yoḥai tells a parable to show that 'Israel shall never see the inside of Gehenna'; Sifre Deut. 32 (57f.; to 6.5), where the same Rabbi says that the future world is given to Israel; Baba Mezia 33b, where R. Judah b. Ilai argues that all Israelites will see joy, while the idolaters will be ashamed.

that the resurrection of the dead is stated in the Torah do not have a share in the world to come is that it was directed against the Sadducees. This would mean that the statement itself dates from before 70 c.e. It would reflect the view of those who believed that the resurrection can be proved from the Torah, presumably the Pharisees.[19] We appear to have, in other words, a Pharisaic statement to the effect that Sadducees have no share in the world to come. Since it is not the intention here to attempt to describe Pharisaism as such, it will be impossible to determine whether or not the Pharisees systematically held that the Sadducees had no share in the world to come. There is, however, one observation which can be made: the Pharisees continued to participate in the communal life of Judaism, even though the high priesthood was often in the hands of Sadducees. Unlike the Essenes, they did not regard the Temple sacrifices as invalid and did not feel compelled to withdraw from Jerusalem and the Temple. The inference should be that, although they may have thought that the Sadducees were *wrong*, they did not regard them as outside the covenant.

This point is made in a presumably late Rabbinic story about a Sadducean high priest. On the Day of Atonement, the priest prepared the incense outside the Holy of Holies, contrary to Pharisaic and Rabbinic opinion. The Rabbinic story rather gleefully relates that before long the priest died, obviously as punishment for transgressing the law (as the Rabbis defined it).[20] The priest may have been punished for transgressing the law, but it is not said that the offerings on that Day of Atonement were invalid. Although the story can hardly be historical as it stands,[21] it must reflect a continuing attitude: the Sadducees were wrong, but they were still Jews and within the covenant.

We should observe the curious character of the exclusion: it excludes on the basis of a *belief*. This is both striking and odd in a religion which generally insists far more on orthopraxy than on orthodoxy. It seems likely that the exclusion from the world to come of those who deny the resurrection is based on the principle of 'measure for measure': those who deny it will not receive it. As such, the saying may be homiletical rather than dogmatic in intent. On the assumption, however, that the saying is Pharisaic and is directed against the Sadducees, it cannot be denied that it may reflect a widely held Pharisaic view that the Sadducees will not inherit the world to come. It also seems likely, however, that the Pharisees did not exclude the Sadducees

[19] Cf. Josephus, *War* II.8.14 (though he speaks in terms of reincarnation rather than resurrection); Acts 23.6. We should not suppose, however, that only Pharisees believed in an after-life; it may have been only the Sadducees who differed.

[20] Yoma 19b.

[21] The controversy about when the incense was put on the fire is likely to be historical, but the story about the high priest bears all the marks of a fictional narrative. For the halakic dispute, see Sifra Aḥare pereq 3.11 (to 16.12f.). See J. Z. Lauterbach, *Rabbinic Essays*, pp. 51–83.

from 'Israel', since they both continued to participate in the communal life in Jerusalem.[22]

The 'amme ha-'arets

Although the question does not arise out of our consideration of Sanhedrin 10.1, we should deal at least briefly here with the scholarly opinion that the Pharisees (and/or Rabbis) considered themselves the 'true Israel' and that they considered the non-Pharisaic 'amme ha-'arets ('people of the land') to be cut off from Israel, and consequently condemned. Jeremias, for example, has argued that the Pharisees constituted closed societies which were opposed not only to the Sadducees but to the 'amme ha-'arets.[23] In his view, the Jews saw it as their 'supreme religious duty' to 'keep away from sinners'. He quotes with approval O. Betz: 'For the Pharisee, "dealings with sinners put at risk the purity of the righteous and his membership within the realm of the holy and the divine".'[24] This attitude (perhaps needless to say) is contrasted with that of Jesus: 'For Jesus, the love of the Father was directed even towards the despised and lost children.'[25]

Jeremias's view rests on three presuppositions: that every reference to the *haberim* ('associates') in Rabbinic literature indicates a historical fact about or an attitude of the Pharisees before 70;[26] that every use of the word *perushim* in Rabbinic literature refers to the Pharisees before 70;[27] and that the *'amme ha-'arets* are always non-Pharisees.[28] None of these assumptions is correct, and they lead to innumerable confusions in his presentation of the Pharisees.

An attempt to sort out completely all the Rabbinic comments about the 'amme ha-'arets, the *haberim* and the *perushim* would require a monograph,

---

[22] I leave aside here Victor Eppstein's article on 'When and How the Sadducees were Excommunicated', *JBL* 85, 1966, pp. 213–23. It depends on taking T. Parah 3.6 (as reconstructed by Eppstein) as historically accurate for the years 60–61 c.e. (On the passage, see Rengstorf's note, *Die Tosefta*, Rabbinische Texte, vol. 6.2, *Para*, p. 34 n. 74.) Niddah 4.2, which contrasts the daughters of the Sadducees with the daughters of Israelites, would, if it is a Pharisaic halakah, indicate that the Pharisees appropriated to themselves the term 'Israel' to the exclusion of the Sadducees. If it is Rabbinic, it probably only indicates the Rabbinic remembrance of the Sadducees as those who were wrong on numerous points of halakah, and the term Sadducee would not refer to an existing group. In any case, the halakah concerns ritual impurity and by implication limits physical contact. It need not imply anything about soteriology.

[23] J. Jeremias, *Jerusalem in the Time of Jesus*, pp. 246–67. The view is fairly common. Thus J. Schmid stated that the Pharisees regarded the *'amme ha-'arets* as 'godless', citing John 7.49(!) as proof. See 'Sünde und Sühne im Judentum', *Bibel und Leben* 6, 1965, pp. 18f. Similarly Rengstorf, *TDNT* I, p. 328 (*s.v. hamartōlos*, also citing John 7.49).

[24] Jeremias, *New Testament Theology* I, p. 118. The quotation is from O. Betz, *What do we know about Jesus?*, p. 74.

[25] Jeremias, *New Testament Theology*, p. 119.

[26] See *Jerusalem*, pp. 247, 250 (T. Demai ch. 2 refers to *Pharisees* [it actually discusses *haberim*]), 252, et passim.

[27] Ibid., p. 249.

[28] Ibid., p. 249 n. 14. These and similar assumptions have governed the views of numerous scholars, both Christian and Jewish. We deal here with Jeremias because of the influence and systematic character of his account.

perhaps a large one, for the problems are exceedingly complex. One would have, among other things, to do what could be done towards dating the material. It is obviously faulty methodology to use a statement by R. Meir about who an *'am ha-'arets* is in order to establish who were the Pharisees before 70,[29] but many of the passages are anonymous and are difficult to date. I shall briefly attempt, however, some generalizations which I believe to be true. They are at least truer than the presuppositions on which Jeremias's view rests.

1. The *'amme ha-'arets* are never contrasted with the *perushim* when *perushim* clearly means 'Pharisees'.[30] In Hagigah 2.7, for example, the *perushim* are said to be more reliable than the *'amme ha-'arets* about *midras*-uncleanness, but less reliable than the priests. While *perushim* here conceivably could mean 'Pharisees', all it obviously means is a group of *laymen* (and some Pharisees were *priests*) who were more scrupulous than some about *midras*-uncleanness but less scrupulous than the priests.[31] The *'amme ha-'arets* are regularly contrasted, rather, with two groups: with the *haberim* (those who undertake to eat *hullin* in ritual purity and to be strict about tithes)[32] and with scholars.[33] Since scholars are sometimes distinguished from *haberim* (see Bekoroth 30b), we cannot simply equate *haberim* and scholars with Pharisees before 70, especially since virtually all the passages refer to the period after 70.

2. When the word *parush* or the plural *perushim* is used in second-century Rabbinic literature, it virtually never refers to the historical party of the Pharisees.[34] Jeremias's assumption that Sifra's exegesis of the phrase 'be holy (*qedoshim*)' as 'be *perushim*' means that the Pharisees regarded themselves as a holy community, the true Israel, cannot be correct.[35] These passages can hardly be dated before the second century c.e., and, as we have just seen, the Rabbis of that period seem to have had no consciousness of

---

[29] Jeremias (op. cit., p. 265) states that the Pharisees extended the priestly purity laws to the laity, citing as evidence R. Meir's statement (T. Abodah Zarah 3.10) that an *'am ha-'arets* is one who does not eat *hullin* (common food) in ritual purity (p. 265 n. 68). He translates *'am ha-'arets* as 'non-Pharisee', thus making the statement serve to define the Pharisees: Pharisees *do* eat *hullin* in ritual purity.

[30] Despite Moore, *Judaism*, I, p. 60.

[31] On Hagigah 2.7, see Rivkin, 'Defining the Pharisees', pp. 239f. The only other passage contrasting a *parush* and an *'am ha-'arets* is T. Shabbath 1.15, but the meaning of *parush* is not clear. See Rivkin, p. 242.

[32] E.g. Demai 2.3, and often.

[33] E.g. Horayoth 3.8; Pesahim 49a, and often.

[34] For some examples, see section 2 n. 12 above. The only exceptions are such passages as Yoma 19b, where a controversy between the Sadducees and the Pharisees is remembered. Otherwise, in the second century and later, the *perushim* are *always* some group other than the Pharisees *and* other than the Rabbis. On the distinction between the *perushim* of Rabbinic sources and the Pharisees, see further Rivkin, 'Defining the Pharisees'; Bowker, *Jesus and the Pharisees*, esp. pp. 6–15. Bowker's proposed history of the terminology, which places Jesus in opposition to extremist *perushim* (not Pharisees) is not, however, persuasive. I have noted no use of *perushim* in early (pre-70) Rabbinic citations to mean 'extremists' or 'ascetics', and no use of the word in second-century literature to mean 'Pharisees', except when old controversies are discussed.

[35] *Jerusalem*, p. 249 n. 13.

being 'Pharisees'. They are Jews, and the biblical injunction to be holy is taken to mean 'be separate'; i.e. be separate from what God demanded that one be separate from, not from other Jews. Thus be holy = be separate in the comment on Lev. 11.44 means be separate in precisely the sense mentioned in the Bible: 'You shall not defile yourselves with any swarming thing that crawls upon the earth.'[36]

3. The *haberim* are not simply identical with the Pharisees.[37] Jeremias has so thoroughly identified the two that, in paraphrasing a baraita which, at earliest, could date from the period of R. Simeon b. Gamaliel, he replaces the term *haberim* with 'Pharisees'.[38] The use of the term 'Pharisee' for *haber* is dubious enough at any time, but it is clearly impossible in the fourth generation after the destruction of the Temple. Rivkin has dedicated an article to the argument that the Pharisees are not identical with the *haberim*,[39] and we cannot go beyond his evidence here. It is my own view that, in entirely dissociating the Pharisees from the concern to eat *hullin* in ritual purity and to tithe correctly, he has gone too far, but the case that the Pharisees and the *haberim* were not simply identical seems firmly established. I shall cite only one point: the requirements for being a *haber* continued to be debated throughout the second century by the Rabbis, long after there was no longer any Pharisaic party, and there were still disputes as to how one should become a *haber* – surely not a Pharisee! – as well as differences of opinion on what a *haber* should and should not do. Although the Rabbis obviously agreed with the two main positions of the *haberim* (*hullin* should be eaten in ritual purity and tithes should be fully and carefully paid),[40] not even all the Rabbis were *haberim*. Jeremias himself cites the case of R. Simeon b. Nathaniel, purportedly a student of R. Johanan b. Zakkai and a relative by marriage of R. Gamaliel, who was an *'am ha-'arets*.[41] Further, in

---

[36] Sifra Shemini pereq 12.3 (to 11.44).

[37] This could have been learned from Moore. See *Judaism* III, p. 26: 'The common outright identification of the Pharisees with the "associates" [*haberim*] is without warrant in our sources.' Cf. Neusner, 'The Fellowship (חבורה) in the Second Jewish Commonwealth', *HTR* 53, 1960, p. 125 n. 1: not all Pharisees were *haberim*, although all *haberim* were Pharisees.

[38] *Jerusalem*, p. 251 n. 23; citing Bekoroth 30b.

[39] Rivkin, 'Defining the Pharisees'.

[40] See, for example, the anonymous halakot in Tohoroth 7.1,5; 8.1f.; Makshirin 6.3 (ritual purity); Nedarim 20a (tithing). The question of the date at which the Pharisees (or Rabbis) extended the priestly laws of ritual purity to the laity has been much debated, but we need not try to decide the issue here. The passages just cited make it clear that the second-century Rabbis accepted the view as standard. On the question, see A. Büchler, *Types of Jewish-Palestinian Piety*, pp. 76, 102, 132–4; 'The Law of Purification in Mark vii. 1–23', *ET* 21, 1909–10, pp. 34–40; *Der galiläische 'Am-ha'Areṣ des zweiten Jahrhunderts*, especially pp. 131f.; G. Alon, 'Teḥuman shel Halakot Tohorah', *Meḥqarim*, pp. 148–76, especially pp. 158–69; L. Ginzberg, 'The Significance of the Halachah for Jewish History', *On Jewish Law and Lore*, pp. 77–124, especially 79–83; Kadushin, *Organic Thinking*, p. 105.

[41] *Jerusalem*, p. 256; citing T. Abodah Zarah 3.10. The passage is not so clear to me as it is to Jeremias. It says that R. Gamaliel the Elder gave his daughter in marriage to the priest Simeon b. Nathaniel, and that they agreed on the condition that she should not keep ritual purity according to his (Simeon's) principles. Some generations later R. Simeon b. Gamaliel commented that the agreement was not necessary, since a *haber* is never forced to keep ritual purity according to the principles of an *'am ha-'arets*.

a baraita in Bekoroth 30b there is a debate as to whether or not a scholar (*talmid ḥakam*) who wishes to *become* a *ḥaber* must pledge before three *ḥaberim*. Thus not all scholars were *ḥaberim*. (On Jeremias's reading of Bekoroth 30b, this would mean that a Rabbinical scholar who wishes to become a Pharisee must pledge before three Pharisees, a nonsensical statement, especially in the second century.)[42] Perhaps even more striking, R. Judah was of the opinion that a *ḥaber* could not contract uncleanness because of the dead, a point on which he was not followed (Demai 2.3). But the fact that he could hold such a position shows that not all Rabbis (or, presumably, Pharisees in an earlier period) were *ḥaberim*. The requirement to care for the dead (which involves contracting ritual impurity) is a very important commandment in Rabbinic literature.[43] It would be impossible for any Rabbi to maintain that all Rabbis (or, earlier, all Pharisees) should have been exempt from the commandment to care for the dead. R. Judah's remark can only mean that, in his time and place, there were relatively few *ḥaberim*, so few that he could consider it practicable for them all to observe one element of the Nazirite vow.

As to the statements that the Pharisees considered themselves to be the 'true Israel' and considered that contact with the '*amme ha-'arets* caused them to lose membership within the holy community, which imply that the '*amme ha-'arets* were not *in* Israel and were outside the realm of the saved :[44] there is not a shred of evidence for such assertions. We have from Rabbinic literature (the literature on which Jeremias based his description of the Pharisees) no statement to the effect that the '*amme ha-'arets* are not true Israelites nor any to the effect that they have no share in the world to come. The precise sense of Hillel's saying that an '*am ha-'arets* cannot be a *ḥasid* (Aboth 2.5; ET, 2.6) is difficult to recover, but it does not seem to imply that one unlearned cannot be *saved*. Jacobs has suggested that the saying 'means no more than that the ignorant *ḥasid* is far from this teacher's [Hillel's] ideal'.[45] Sandmel's interpretation is perhaps more precise: 'this sentiment is not so much arrogance as merely a statement of fact – that a person who adheres to a Book religion can scarcely be pious if he does not know the Book.'[46] The priest who is an '*am ha-'arets* (unlearned) is not well regarded by the

---

Thus it is R. Simeon b. Gamaliel who called Simeon b. Nathaniel an '*am ha-'arets*, but it is possible that he misunderstood the agreement. The first sentence tells us only that Simeon b. Nathaniel's principles of ritual purity differed from those of his wife's family.

[42] N. 38 above.

[43] Even a high priest and a Nazirite, both ordinarily forbidden to contract corpse uncleanness, may do so in order to care for a neglected corpse: Nazir 7.1.

[44] Jeremias, *Jerusalem*, p. 259; above, nn. 23 and 24.

[45] J. Jacobs, 'The Concept of Ḥasid', *JJS* 8, 1957, p. 152.

[46] Sandmel, *The First Christian Century*, p. 33. On the saying cf. Büchler, *Types of Jewish-Palestinian Piety*, pp. 25–8. Hillel's famed leniency with regard to proselytism (Shabbath 31a) would argue against his excluding the unlearned from *Israel* and *salvation*, although naturally only one knowledgeable in the law could perform it fully.

Rabbis, but he is not excluded from 'Israel'.[47] Relations between the scholar class and the common people were sometimes strained, and periodically there were outbursts of bad feeling, but these do not affect membership in the community and soteriology.[48] Even if the Pharisees (or Rabbis) and the *haberim* were identical, it would still be completely wrong to say that, for the Pharisee, contact with sinners risked his own salvation. On the contrary, R. Judah, one of the leading Tannaim, proposed that the *'amme ha-'arets* should minister to the scholars in the academies (Demai 2.3), which would surely involve some contact. The most one could say would be that contact with ritual impurity was avoided whenever possible, since it led to inconvenience in eating and buying food. Sharing table fellowship was not, for the Rabbis, a soteriological symbol. (Note that a Samaritan can be counted in the number necessary to say the common grace.)[49] We have two explicit sayings, both in the name of R. Judah b. Ilai, to the effect that the *'amme ha-'arets* were counted in Israel. We have already quoted his statement that the intentional sins of the *'amme ha-'arets* are counted as unwitting errors.[50] In the same passage, there is an exegesis of Isa. 66.5, in which he takes the phrase 'that cast you out' to refer to the *'amme ha-'arets*. He continues:

[Yet] lest you say, their hope [of future joy] is destroyed, and their prospects frustrated, Scripture states, *And we shall see your joy.*[51] Lest you think, Israel shall be ashamed, – therefore it is stated, *and they shall be ashamed*: the idolaters shall be ashamed, whilst Israel shall rejoice.

The argument of these two sub-sections has been that from the point of view of soteriology, as far as we can determine from the evidence before us, the Pharisees were not sectarians in the sense that the Essenes were.[52] They did not consider themselves to be the 'true Israel' and everyone else to be outside the covenant. Even though they may have held that those who denied the basic Pharisaic tenet of the resurrection have no share in

[47] Horayoth 3.8. For the priest unlearned in the law, see also Yoma 1.6.

[48] There are several interesting theories on the history of the relationship between the scholars and the common people. See Rosenthal, *Vier apokryphische Bücher*, pp. 25ff., 102f.; Finkelstein, *The Pharisees* II, pp. 754–61; Urbach, *Hazal*, pp. 522–30, 570–2 (ET, pp. 584–8, 632–9). In no case is there reason to think that the scholars (who are not in any event to be neatly equated with Pharisees) considered the unlearned *'amme ha-'arets* to be outside Israel.

[49] Berakoth 7.1.

[50] Baba Metzia 33b; above, section 4 n. 50.

[51] As the English translator, H. Freedman, explained (p. 207), 'we' includes all classes of Israel.

[52] Similarly J. Bowker, *Jesus and the Pharisees*, pp. 13, 21: the Hakamin did not regard themselves as a sect. Morton Smith ('The Dead Sea Sect in Relation to Ancient Judaism', *NTS* 7, 1960–61, pp. 347–60) makes several sound observations about what constitutes a sect: the group has a special covenant (p. 360) and joining requires 'an act of conversion' (p. 358). He regards the Pharisees as originally having been a sect (p. 359), apparently by equating them with the *haberim* (pp. 351–3). It seems to me better to reserve the term 'sect' for those who excluded the rest from Israel and from the covenant promises. On the basis of present evidence, the Pharisees are better called a *party* than a *sect*, and the Rabbis were certainly motivated by the party spirit rather than by sectarianism. A party is a group which believes itself to be right and which wishes others to obey or agree, but which does not exclude dissenters from 'Israel'.

the world to come, they did not exclude the Sadducees from 'Israel'; and they certainly did not exclude the *'amme ha-'arets*. The Rabbis, whose views are more accessible, had no occasion to comment on the status of other parties, but there is no evidence that they excluded the *'amme ha-'arets* from Israel or from the world to come. What evidence there is is to the contrary.[53]

The *individuals* who were excluded from the world to come were, as we have repeatedly seen, those who effectively deny the claims of God. Those excluded from salvation, in other words, are those who exclude themselves from the covenant.

Atonement

That only the most unregenerate sinners were excluded from the covenant and the covenant promises becomes most apparent when we study the passages on atonement for transgression. The universally held view is this: God has appointed means of atonement for every transgression, except the intention to reject God and his covenant. That is, those who are in the covenant will remain in and will receive the covenantal promises (including a share in the world to come), unless they remove themselves by 'casting off the yoke'. No matter how numerous a man's transgressions, God has provided for their forgiveness, as long as he indicates his intention to remain in the covenant by repenting and doing other appropriate acts of atonement.

The passages which indicate this view are very numerous, and there are no opinions to the contrary. We shall give here representative examples in full and then discuss each of the means of atonement. The passages which follow all indicate the view that there is a means of atonement for every transgression, although they differ as to which transgressions are atoned for in which way:

6. For uncleanness that befalls the Temple and its Hallowed Things through wantonness, atonement is made by the goat whose blood is sprinkled within [the Holy of Holies] and by the Day of Atonement; for all other transgressions spoken of in the Law, venial or grave, wanton or unwitting, conscious or unconscious, sins of omission or of commission, sins punishable by Extirpation or by death at the hands of the court, the scapegoat makes atonement.

7. [It makes atonement] alike whether they are Israelites, priests, or the Anointed Priest. Wherein do the Israelites differ from priests and the Anointed Priest? Only

[53] Indirect evidence to the same effect is to be found in J. Heinemann, 'Birkath Ha-Zimmun and Havurah-Meals', *JJS* 13, 1962, p. 26. He points out that the *'amme ha-'arets* could not be counted in for the common grace (*birkat ha-zimmun*; see Berakoth 47b), although there is no such restriction for the communal prayers in the synagogue. The inference is that the meals were *ḥaburah* meals (from which *'amme ha-'arets* were excluded by definition), but the synagogue service was more broadly based. The *'amme ha-'arets* were not members of a *ḥaburah*, but they were in Israel and did participate in the synagogue service.

in that the blood of the bullock makes atonement for the priests for uncleanness that befalls the Temple and its Hallowed Things. R. Simeon says: As the blood of the goat that is sprinkled within [the Holy of Holies] makes atonement for the Israelites, so does the blood of the bullock make atonement for the priests; and as the confession of sin recited over the scapegoat makes atonement for the Israelites, so does the confession of sin recited over the bullock make atonement for the priests. (Shebuoth 1.6f.)

8. The Sin-offering and the unconditional Guilt-offering effect atonement;[54] death and the Day of Atonement effect atonement if there is repentance. Repentance effects atonement for lesser transgressions against both positive and negative commands in the Law; while for graver transgressions it suspends punishment until the Day of Atonement comes and effects atonement.[55]

9. If a man said, 'I will sin and repent, and sin again and repent', he will be given no chance to repent.[56] [If he said,] 'I will sin and the Day of Atonement will effect atonement', then the Day of Atonement effects no atonement. (Yoma 8.8f.)[57]

And thus it says: 'For the Lord will not hold him guiltless that taketh His name in vain.' R. Eleazar says: It is impossible to say: 'He will not clear,' since it is also said: 'And that will clear (*ve-nakeh*)' (Ex. 34.7). But it is just as impossible to say: 'He will clear,' since it is also said: 'He will not clear (*lo yenakeh*)' (ibid.). You must therefore say: He clears those who repent but does not clear those who do not repent.

For four things did R. Matia b. Heresh go to R. Eleazar ha-Kappar to Laodicea. He said to him: Master! Have you heard the four distinctions in atonement which R. Ishmael used to explain? He said to him: Yes. One scriptural passage says: 'Return, O backsliding children' (Jer. 3.14), from which we learn that repentance effects atonement. And another scriptural passage says: 'For on this day shall atonement be made for you' (Lev. 16.30), from which we learn that the Day of Atonement effects atonement. Still another scriptural passage says: 'Surely this iniquity shall not be expiated by you till ye die' (Isa. 22.14), from which we learn that death effects atonement. And still another scriptural passage says: 'Then will I visit their transgressions with the rod, and their iniquity with strokes' (Ps. 89.33), from which we learn that chastisements[58] effect atonement. How are

---

[54] As T. Yom Ha-Kippurim 4(5).5 clarifies, they atone for what scripture says they will atone for. On the atonement effected by individual offerings, see also Sifre Zuṭa to Num. 6.11 (p. 243: 'a sin-offering atones') and Sifra Shemini pereq 2.4 (to 10.17: 'The priests eat and the persons who bring the sacrifices are atoned for').

[55] The Tosefta (ibid.) defines 'heavy' transgressions as those punishable by death at the hands of the court and by extirpation ('cutting off', *karet*), plus transgression of the commandment 'thou shalt not take (the name of the Lord thy God in vain)'. On light and heavy transgressions, cf. Epstein, *Mabo' le-Nosaḥ*, pp. 336f.

[56] This is probably what R. Jose meant in T. Yom Ha-Kippurim 4(5).13: 'If a man sins once, twice and even three times, God forgives ('they forgive') him, [but] the fourth time he does not forgive him.'

[57] The rest of Yoma 8.9 may not be original, but a baraita added later. See Epstein, *Mabo' le-Nosaḥ*, pp. 1306f.; cf. *Mebo'ot*, p. 86 n. 107. Epstein (*Mebo'ot*, p. 86) takes the passage quoted to represent the view of R. Akiba and his school.

[58] *Yissurin*. Without the article, Lauterbach translates the word 'chastisements'. With the article, Lauterbach translates it as 'suffering'.

all these four passages to be maintained? If one has transgressed a positive commandment and repents of it, he is forgiven on the spot. Concerning this it is said:
'Return, O backsliding children.' If one has violated a negative commandment
and repents, repentance alone has not the power of atonement. It merely leaves
the matter pending and the Day of Atonement effects atonement. [This is proved
by reference to the second passage.] If one wilfully commits transgressions punishable by extinction or by death at the hands of the court and repents, repentance
cannot leave the matter pending nor can the Day of Atonement effect atonement.
But both repentance and the Day of Atonement together atone for one half. And
chastisements atone for half. [The third passage is cited.] However, if one has
profaned the name of God and repents, his repentance cannot make the case
pending, neither can the Day of Atonement effect atonement, nor can sufferings
cleanse him of his guilt. But repentance and the Day of Atonement both can
merely make the matter pend. And the day of death with the suffering preceding
it cleanses him. To this applies: 'Surely this iniquity shall not be expiated by
you till ye die.' And so also when it says: 'That the iniquity of Eli's house shall
not be expiated with sacrifices nor offering' (I Sam. 3.14) it means: With sacrifice
and offering it cannot be expiated, but it will be expiated by the day of death.
Rabbi says: I might have thought that the day of death does not effect atonement.
But when it says: 'When I have opened your graves,' etc. (Ezek. 37.13), behold we
learn that the day of death does bring atonement.

Rabbi says: For violations of laws, such as those preceding the commandment:
'Thou shalt not take', repentance alone effects atonement. In cases of violations
of laws such as follow the commandment: 'Thou shalt not take' – including the
commandment: 'Thou shalt not take' itself – repentance makes the matter pend
and the Day of Atonement effects atonement, etc.[59]

R. Judah said: [For the transgression of] every [commandment] following 'Thou
shalt not take [the name of the Lord thy God in vain'], repentance atones. And
[for the transgression of] every [commandment] preceding 'Thou shalt not take',
including 'Thou shalt not take', repentance suspends [punishment] and the Day
of Atonement atones. (T. Yom Ha-Kippurim 4[5].5)

The only transgression about which there was any doubt as to whether
or not there was an appropriate means of atonement was the transgression of
the commandment 'Thou shalt not take the name of the Lord thy God in
vain' (Ex. 20.7). The difficulty was based on the rest of the verse, 'the Lord
will not hold him guiltless (or will not clear, לא ינקה) who takes his name
in vain'. The Tosefta comments that concerning every other transgression
it is said 'and he will clear', but concerning this one it says, 'he will not
clear'.[60] Similarly in ARN 39, the one who takes the name of the Lord in

---

[59] Mek. Bahodesh 7 (227–9; II, 249–51; to 20.7). Cf. ARN 29 (ET, pp. 121f.); Yoma 86a; p. Yoma
45b, c (8.8); T. Yom Ha-Kippurim 4(5).6–8. I have followed Lauterbach's translation, altering it to
conform his various translations of *kipper* ('bring forgiveness', 'secure a pardon' and the like) to Danby's
terminology ('effect atonement').

[60] T. Sotah 7.2. The seriousness of profaning God's name is emphasized in this and several other
ways in T. Sotah 7.2f.

vain is listed among those who will not be forgiven (along with those who sin with the intention of repenting and the like).[61] We have seen three ways of handling the problem. The cleverest, since it is based on the exegesis of a related phrase, is that of R. Eleazar in the Mekilta passage just quoted. Commenting on Ex. 20.7 ('he will not clear'), he notes the phrase ונקה לא נקה in Ex. 34.7. The RSV correctly translates 'who will by no means clear the guilty'. The word translated 'by no means' is the infinitive absolute of 'to clear' and serves to emphasize the finite verb. By taking ונקה to be a finite verb, however, R. Eleazar has the verse say 'and he will clear, he will not clear': he clears when one repents, but not when one does not. Applied to the phrase 'he will not clear' in Ex. 20.7, this means that God *will* forgive taking his name in vain if there is repentance.

R. Ishmael takes profanation of the name to be the sin most difficult to atone for; it requires not only repentance and the Day of Atonement, but also the day of death with the sufferings preceding it. But it can be atoned for. R. Judah and Rabbi consider that transgression of 'thou shalt not take' requires only repentance and the Day of Atonement. This was also apparently the view of the school of Akiba, assuming that 'thou shalt not take' is a grave transgression and is thus covered by repentance and the Day of Atonement (Yoma 8.8). There were apparently some, then, who would add those who profaned God's name to those who 'broke off the yoke', but by far the dominant view was that transgression of any commandment could be atoned for.

In all of these passages, the Rabbis are employing a kind of terminological short cut by using the word 'atone' to include both man's act of atonement and God's act of forgiveness. The two are definitely distinguished in several passages in Leviticus, such as Lev. 19.22: 'And the priest shall make atonement for him with the ram of the guilt offering before the Lord for his sin which he has committed; and the sin which he has committed shall be forgiven him.' The priest 'atones', but the passive 'shall be forgiven' (*nislah*) indicates that God forgives. Sifra, in commenting on such passages in Leviticus, however, does not make anything of the distinction.[62] On the contrary, at least once the term 'atone' is used to explain the biblical 'forgive'. ' "And he did not know and he shall be forgiven" – Thus if he did know, it does not atone (*mitkapper*) for him.'[63] In a similar way, the other word which primarily means 'forgive', *mahal*, is used more or less as an equivalent of 'atone'. In the passage quoted above from the Mekilta in which R. Ishmael's four means of atonement are discussed, it is said that 'suffering *atones*'. But later in the Mekilta one reads this sentence: 'what

[61] ET, p. 161.
[62] See Sifra Ḥobah pereq 6.7 (to 4.20); ibid., pereq 9.5//pereq 10.8//pereq 20.9; ibid., pereq 23.1 (to 5.26; [ET, 6.2]).
[63] Sifra Ḥobah pereq 21.2 (to 5.18).

forgives one [his transgressions]? You must say, suffering.'[64] It would have been more accurate to say 'what means of atonement is appointed for transgressions and brings God's forgiveness?', but the Rabbis more economically said that suffering atones or that suffering forgives, without always nicely distinguishing the two acts. In the case of repentance, the terminological distinction was naturally maintained: man repents and God forgives. Thus in R. Ishmael's discussion quoted above, one reads that 'repentance *atones*'. It is then explained that 'whoever transgresses a positive *mitsvah* and repents – he does not move thence until God *forgives* ('they forgive') him'.[65] In general, however, the Rabbis did not maintain the distinction made in Leviticus between atonement and forgiveness.[66]

It appears, then, that God's forgiveness was included under the general term 'atonement'. The Rabbis did not go to the trouble of saying that man, by confessing, fasting and praying on the Day of Atonement, makes atonement *and* God forgives him. They simply said, 'The Day of Atonement atones'. That they understood that atonement includes God's forgiveness is clear from the way in which 'atone' and 'forgive' can interchange.[67] But their way of phrasing the sentences about atonement may mislead readers into thinking that they conceived the process of atonement to be automatic. The Rabbis doubtless had confidence that God would forgive those who did what was appropriate for atonement, but they did not suppose that atonement would be effective apart from the reconciling forgiveness of God. They pictured God as always ready to forgive, and so had no need of saying 'repentance atones if God chooses to forgive'. As is usual, the Rabbis did not dwell on God's side, and forgiveness was not singled out for special attention as part of the overall reconciling process. They could use simply 'atonement', which properly should refer only to man's action, to indicate the entire reconciliation.

It is clear that the statements about atonement quoted above, and others which might be adduced, are not in perfect accord with one another. We may note that in the passage quoted above from Mek. Baḥodesh 7, R. Ishmael said that repentance alone atones for transgression of positive commandments, while for transgression of negative commandments it has only the power to suspend the matter until the Day of Atonement. Rabbi,

---

[64] Mek. Baḥodesh 10 (240; II, 278; to 20.20). Lauterbach translates 'But what is it that does bring a man forgiveness?'

[65] As Lauterbach words it in the translation quoted above, 'If one has transgressed a positive commandment and repents of it, he is forgiven on the spot.'

[66] Büchler has argued, not altogether persuasively, that R. Akiba did maintain the biblical distinction. See *Studies in Sin and Atonement*, p. 449. In any case, it was not generally maintained. We may also note that the passage in p. Yoma 45c (8.8) which deals with the four types of atonement once uses the word 'cleanse' where the Mekilta has 'atone': 'Thus we learn that death cleanses.' There is no real distinction.

[67] It is noteworthy that one of the eight things for which the high priest says a blessing on the Day of Atonement is forgiveness. See Yoma 7.1; Sotah 7.7.

on the other hand, said that repentance alone atones for violations of laws which are like those preceding the commandment 'Thou shalt not take'.[68] One of the commandments preceding 'Thou shalt not take' is 'Thou shalt not make any graven image', a negative commandment. According to R. Ishmael, transgression of this commandment would require repentance *and* the Day of Atonement.[69] R. Judah and Rabbi have precisely opposite statements on which group of sins repentance alone atones for, although they agree on what atones for transgression of 'thou shalt not take'. They also agree that two means of atonement (repentance and the Day of Atonement) cover all transgressions, against the 'four means' view attributed to R. Ishmael. These and other controversies spring from the desire to take the biblical statements about means of atonement seriously and to harmonize them.[70] They should not deter us from seeing the underlying Rabbinic view: there is no sin, no matter how grievous, for which atonement could not be made. This can be best understood if we consider, at least briefly, the means of atonement specified by R. Ishmael. We shall reserve repentance until last, considering cultic rites, sufferings and death first.

Although the Rabbis were greatly indebted to the prophets – the emphasis on repentance, for example, is in line with the religious attitude of the prophets – they took the Pentateuch, especially the last four books, to be authoritative on matters covered there.[71] These books prescribe various and sundry cultic acts, especially sacrifices and offerings, connected with the Temple. One will look in vain in the Rabbinic literature for any attack on these cultic acts; they were instituted by God and not to be questioned by man. Thus Amos 5.21–2 is not quoted in the Tannaitic literature, as far as I have observed. (V. 22 reads: 'Even though you offer me your burnt offerings and cereal offerings, I will not accept them', etc.). Amos 5.25 ('Did you bring to me sacrifices and offerings the forty years in the wilderness, O house of Israel?') is cited, but it is not used against the sacrificial system. Thus the Rabbinic comment on Num. 9.5, which mentions the first Passover, cites Amos 5.25 as evidence that the Israelites kept only the first Passover, but says that this was to the shame of Israel. Amos is not taken as justifying not making the required sacrifices.[72] Similarly, we may note this story from Num. Rab. 21.25 (ET, p. 852):

---

[68] Yoma 85b (ET, p. 424) attributes another view to Rabbi. See n. 93 below.

[69] In p. Yoma 45c (8.8), a discrepancy between various 'systems' of atonement is noted. After the passage giving R. Ishmael's categories, this comment follows: 'Rab Johanan said: This is the opinion of R. Eleazar b. Azariah, R. Ishmael and R. Akiba. But the opinion of the sages is that the scapegoat atones (cf. Shebuoth 1.6). If there is no scapegoat, the Day atones [in any case].'

[70] So also Moore, *Judaism* I, pp. 546f.

[71] Naturally they did not admit contradictions among various parts of the Bible. This is not to say that they did not see conflicts and difficulties; they did, and sought to harmonize them.

[72] Sifre Num. 67 (62; to 9.5).

A heathen addressed a question to R. Akiba. He said to him: 'Why do you celebrate festive seasons? Did not the Holy One, blessed be He, say to you: *Your new moons and your appointed seasons My soul hateth*' (Isa. 1. 14)? Said R. Akiba to him: 'If He had stated, "*My* new moons and *My* appointed seasons My soul hateth" you might have spoken as you did. But He only said, "Your *new moons and* your *appointed seasons*"!' That was in reference to those festive seasons which Jeroboam ordained. . . .

One could go through passage after passage which in the Bible seems to bear an anti-cultic meaning without finding one which the Rabbis used in such a way.

The Rabbis were aware that the sacrificial system could be seen as encouraging a false view of God, but this did not move them to urge abandonment of it. Thus in Sifre Num. 143, in commenting on Num. 28.8b ('an offering by fire, a pleasing odour to the Lord'), one Rabbi observes that it is not the case that God eats and drinks ('there is no eating and drinking before him'), but God spoke and his will was done. It is that which is pleasing to him.[73] Thus despite the prophetic passages which attack, or seem to attack, the sacrificial system and the obvious potential for misunderstanding which it creates, the Rabbis never opposed it.[74]

On the contrary, they attempted to give to each sacrifice some specific atoning function. That is, sacrifices which are not said to atone for any particular sin in the Bible acquire a specific atoning function in Rabbinic literature.[75] This development is remarkable when one considers that during the entire Rabbinic period the Temple was destroyed. That Judaism could withstand this event indicates that the sacrificial system was not in fact regarded as the necessary condition for the survival of the true worship of God, at least in the eyes of the Rabbis.[76] Indeed, the long existence of the Diaspora shows that this must have been the case. Although the rites of the Day of Atonement would cover the Jews both in and out of the Land, those in the Diaspora obviously could not comply with requirements to bring certain offerings for specified offences.[77]

Thus there is a certain ambiguity in the Rabbinic attitude towards the

---

[73] Sifre Num. 143 (191; to 28.8). See Schechter, *Aspects*, p. 298.

[74] A somewhat more negative attitude toward sacrifices may appear in T. Menahoth 7.9, cited by Kadushin, *The Rabbinic Mind*, pp. 343f. But the disparagement is actually directed toward false ideas about sacrifice: 'Does God get hungry?'

[75] Examples are given by Schechter, *Aspects*, p. 300, and Moore, *Judaism* I, p. 497; III, 151f.

[76] Moore, *Judaism* I, p. 114: 'Long before the *sacra publica* in behalf of all Jews everywhere came to an end, the synagogue had become for the vast majority the real centre of the common religious life, and the cessation of sacrifice, however deeply it was deplored, caused no crisis.' Cf. Schechter, *Aspects*, p. 298 n. 3 (on p. 299).

[77] The significance of the loss of the Temple is discussed in ARN 4 (ET, p. 34). Note especially that R. Johanan b. Zakkai cites Hosea 6.6 ('I desire mercy and not sacrifice') to show that means for atonement exist even without the sacrificial system. On the views of R. Johanan, R. Joshua and R. Eliezer, see Helfgott, *Election*, pp. 46, 61, 64. And see further Neusner, *Yohanan ben Zakkai*, pp. 142–6; rev. ed., pp. 188–92.

sacrificial system and the Temple cultus. On the one hand, the role attached to it in the Pentateuch was never challenged by the Rabbis; it was, if anything, amplified. On the other hand, true religion did not actually depend upon the sacrificial system. In place of sacrifices, the Rabbis began to encourage the study of the laws regarding sacrifice;[78] the activities of the Day of Atonement changed;[79] but Judaism continued as an operative religion with means of atonement appointed by God. This is not to say that every Rabbi was of the view that Judaism could continue as well without the Temple as with it. Neusner has noted that R. Eliezer, for example, seems to have made no provisions for substitutions for the sacrificial system. It would appear that he expected its speedy restoration.[80] Other Rabbis, especially as years went on, may have come to see an actual advantage in substituting study for sacrifice.[81] In either case, however, the value of the sacrificial system was never denied, but Judaism continued to function without it.

An old misunderstanding of the Rabbinic view of sacrifices has recently been repeated by Klinzing in his excellent study of the attitude towards sacrifices in the Dead Sea Scrolls, and we may briefly comment on it. In discussing the view in the Dead Sea Scrolls that prayer, good deeds and the like may substitute for sacrifices, Klinzing refers to the theory of the Rabbis. He cites Bousset to the effect that in late Judaism the cult was used not for its own sake but only because it was commanded.[82] (Klinzing notes that it is difficult to fit the Scrolls into Bousset's history at this point, since the Essenes were obedient to the law and *also* had a living interest in the cult, but he does not challenge Bousset's general view.)[83] The Rabbinic theory is that a sacrifice commanded in the law can be 'fulfilled' by substituting something else commanded in the law.[84] The Essenes, however, posed another question than how the law could be fulfilled: how can atonement be accomplished? The Essenes did not proceed from a desire to achieve a formal obedience to the law, as did the Rabbis, but from a desire to achieve

---

[78] Moore, *Judaism* I, pp. 273, 505; III, p. 155.

[79] See Sifra Ahare pereq 8.1 (to 16.30): ' "For on this day shall atonement be made for you" – by sacrifice. And whence do we know that even if there is no sacrifice and no [scape]goat the Day still atones? Scripture teaches, "For on this day shall atonement be made for you".' And cf. p. Yoma 45c, n. 69 above.

[80] Neusner, *Eliezer* II, pp. 298–301.

[81] Neusner, ibid.; cf. ARN 4 (ET, p. 32): 'the study of Torah is more beloved by God than burnt offerings'; the discussion of Raba and Abaye in Rosh Ha-Shanah 18a (ET, p. 71).

[82] Klinzing, *Die Umdeutung des Kultus*, p. 152; citing Bousset, *Religion des Judentums*, p. 117. Here again we see the use of Bousset as *the* standard text book on Judaism. Klinzing not only did not find it necessary to consult such scholars as Büchler and Moore – scholars intimately acquainted with the material – on the significance of atonement in Rabbinic Judaism, he seems unaware that there is a difference of view. His own perceptive and independent work on the Scrolls stands in sharp contrast to his use of Bousset for Rabbinic Judaism.

[83] Klinzing, pp. 152–5.

[84] Ibid., p. 95.

atonement.[85] As final proof of the Rabbinic view, he cites Kuhn's comment on Sifre Num. 143 (the passage is quoted just above): the only significance of the sacrifices is to achieve fulfilment of the law.[86]

The point of Bousset's view, which is reflected in Kuhn's note and repeated by Klinzing, is that Rabbinism was a religion in which the only concern was the compilation of commandment-fulfilments so that one could earn salvation. The Rabbis had no living interest in atonement, only the desire to achieve more fulfilments than they committed transgressions. It is apparent from all the passages quoted thus far that, on the contrary, the Rabbis had a real concern for how transgressions could be *atoned* for (not simply offset by more fulfilments). They were *also* concerned about how the commandments to carry out sacrifices could be fulfilled, as they were concerned about how all the commandments in the Torah could be fulfilled, but that concern does not lead to Bousset's conclusion. The particular passages cited to show that the Rabbis were concerned only with surface, formal obedience have been misinterpreted. The Rabbis wished to deny crass anthropomorphism and a view of sacrifices as magical. Thus Sifre Num. 143 ('there is no eating and drinking before him', but God spoke and his will was done; it is *that* which is 'a pleasing odour') obviously intends to cut off the possible interpretation that the phrase 'a pleasing odour' indicates that God eats and drinks. Similarly R. Johanan b. Zakkai's statement that 'It is not the dead that defiles nor the water that purifies! The Holy One, blessed be He, merely says: "I have laid down a statute, I have issued a decree. You are not allowed to transgress My decree" '[87] is explicitly said to have been occasioned by a charge that the sacrifices represent witchcraft. To deduce from such statements that the Rabbis had no living concern with atonement and were interested only in an externalistic obedience is gross eisegesis.

Moore, as we have seen, was of the view that none of the prescribed sacrifices were considered by the Rabbis as being efficacious without repentance.[88] It might be possible to construct an argument to the contrary. Thus Mishnah Yoma 8.8 specifically attached repentance to death and the Day of Atonement, but not to the sin-offering and the unconditional guilt-offering. The Tosefta explicitly joined repentance also to the last two.[89] But as Moore has pointed out, confession is implied in bringing the offerings.[90] It is doubtful if the author of Mishnah Yoma 8.8 thought of the possibility raised in the controversy between the Amoraim Abaye and Raba,

---

[85] Ibid., p. 105.

[86] Ibid., p. 166; citing Kuhn's edition of Sifre Numbers, p. 591 n. 53.

[87] Num. Rab. 19.8 (ET, p. 758).

[88] Moore, *Judaism* I, p. 505. This is the general view.

[89] T. Yom Ha-Kippurim 4(5).9. For parallels, see Lieberman, *Tosefta Ki-Fshuṭah, Mo'ed*, p. 825.

[90] Moore, *Judaism* I, p. 498 n. 2. That confession must accompany sin- and guilt-offerings is explicitly stated in Sifre Num. 2 (6; to 5.7). And see Büchler's description, *Sin and Atonement*, pp. 410, 416f.

that one might bring the offering but deny the intention implied in bringing it.[91] This is a theoretical possibility, and the Rabbis eventually got around to considering virtually every theoretical possibility; but it is dubious if such a possibility was in mind when Yoma 8.8 was written.

There are other passages, however, which mention atonement by the appointed rites without mentioning repentance. We have already quoted Shebuoth 1.6, which provides for the atonement of every transgression without mentioning repentance. Moore's comment follows:[92]

This Mishnah is solely concerned with the particular application of the several piacula, not with the conditions of their effectiveness. In a corresponding passage in the Mishnah on the Day of Atonement it is made clear that the effect of the piacula is not *ex opere operato* [referring to Yoma 8.8f.].

It may well be that Shebuoth 1.6 and Yoma 8.8f. should be harmonized in just this way, although I am not so convinced as Moore. If in fact there was, during the course of the Tannaitic period, a view that certain cultic acts, especially the Day of Atonement, were effective in and of themselves, it would help to explain Rabbi's insistence on the point in a saying preserved in the Talmud:[93]

Rabbi said: For all transgressions of the Torah, whether he repented or not, the Day of Atonement brings atonement, except in the case of one who throws off the yoke, perverts the teachings of the Torah, and rejects the covenant in the flesh [circumcision] – [in these cases,] if he repented, the Day of Atonement brings atonement, and if not, the Day of Atonement does not bring atonement.

While generalizations on the basis of character are dangerous, one must note that it does not seem characteristic of Rabbi to occupy a position entirely by himself. That there was some controversy on the point is indicated by the argument of the anonymous author of Sifra (usually assumed to be R. Judah),[94] which is cited by the Amoraim in discussing Rabbi's view:[95]

I might assume that the Day of Atonement atones alike for them who repent and them who do not repent. But is there not an argument [to the contrary]: Sin- and guilt-offerings effect atonement, and the Day of Atonement effects atonement. Just as sin- and guilt-offerings atone only for them that repent, so shall also the Day of Atonement atone only for them that repent? No, [this is not conclusive]. You can rightly say that such is the case of sin- and guilt-offerings, since they do not atone for wilful sins as they do for those in error; will you apply the same to the Day of Atonement which atones alike for wilful sins as well as for those in

---

[91] Kerithoth 7a.

[92] *Judaism* I, p. 498.

[93] Shebuoth 13a; cf. Kerithoth 7a; Yoma 85b. The Hebrew is the same in all three places.

[94] See Epstein, *Mebo'ot*, p. 656; Sanhedrin 86a; Shebuoth 13a; Kerithoth 7a; and elsewhere.

[95] Quoted from the English translation of Kerithoth 7a (ET, p. 49). It appears with only slight verbal differences in Shebuoth 13a. The passage in Sifra is Emor pereq 14.1–2 (to 23.27).

error? I might therefore have thought since the Day of Atonement atones for wilful sins as well as those in error, so it would atone for them that repent as well as them that do not repent, therefore it is written, 'howbeit' [Lev. 23.27], to establish a distinction [between then that repent and them that do not repent].[96]

The point is that argument could have shown that the Day of Atonement atoned without repentance, but scripture refutes that notion with the word 'howbeit'.[97] It is possible that R. Judah's statements 'I might have thought' introduce, for purely rhetorical reasons, hypothetical possibilities held by no one and that he is constructing counter-arguments simply in order to make his own point clearer and surer. On the whole, however, it seems best to grant that there were those who thought that the Day of Atonement was effective apart from repentance. This seems to be confirmed, at least for the Amoraic period, by R. Joḥanan (b. Nappaḥa?), who finds a distinction between the means of atonement listed by R. Ishmael (all of which include repentance) and atonement simply by the Day of Atonement.[98] The argument might appear to be entirely academic, since observing the Day of Atonement includes confession. (See the baraita in Yoma 87b.) The point at issue may only be whether a man should be able to enumerate his sins and repent specifically of them. But it seems more likely that the Rabbis had in mind the *balance* between repentance and the divinely appointed institutions of atonement. If repentance alone suffices, and if one can repent at any time, why have a Day of Atonement at all? The question 'why the scapegoat' is explicitly raised in Shebuoth 12b, end.

In any case, we see how far the Rabbis were from denying the biblically appointed means of atonement or the genuine efficacy of those means. If there was a dispute, it was not over the question of whether or not one's sins would be forgiven, but over what were the conditions to which God attached his promise of forgiveness.[99] The Rabbis tried to take all the biblical material on the matter into account, and they harmonized it and assigned the efficacy of the various appointed means in different ways; but they all agreed that there was an efficacious means for atoning for every sin.[100]

A further clarification of Rabbi's view (above n. 93) may be in order, lest he be understood as advocating a mechanical view of atonement. In saying

---

[96] Sifra has a concluding sentence: 'Thus it does not atone except with repentance.'

[97] R. Judah maintains, however, that the other conditions stated in Lev. 23.27f. – the calling of a religious assembly, humbling oneself by fasting, performing no labour, making sacrifices and sending out the scapegoat — do *not* have to be observed for the Day of Atonement to atone. See Sifra Emor pereq 14.1, immediately before the passage just quoted.

[98] See p. Yoma 45c, cited above, n. 69.

[99] Death alone without repentance could also be said to atone for sins less serious than idolatry. See below, nn. 138, 139.

[100] I have been following the Rabbinic mode of speech in speaking of the efficacy of means of atonement. It is, of course, God who pardons sins, and his pardon is always efficacious. God attached his promise of pardon especially to the Day of Atonement; but it is God who pardons, not the Day. Cf. Büchler, *Sin and Atonement*, p. 351.

that the Day of Atonement covered all sins but explicit rejection of God, and that repentance covered that, he further emphasized the universal efficacy of the various means of atonement – absolutely no sin, not even 'casting off the yoke', is beyond God's forgiveness. Of course, if a man repents of throwing off the yoke of the covenant, he has not finally and definitely thrown it off. The prodigal can always return. Rabbi's view might be stated thus: as long as one's intention is to remain within the covenant, the biblically appointed means of atonement are effective – repentance is, as it were, assumed unless there is definite evidence to the contrary. If one rejects the covenant, it is necessary to return before the means of atonement which are part of the covenant become effective.

In any case, it should be emphasized that sacrifices and other cultic acts were not considered efficacious by themselves in a magical way, as if they had power.[101] The question, as I said above, was to what conditions God attached the promise of forgiveness. It is God who forgives and effects atonement. If he chooses to command sacrifices and other cultic acts, man is to seek atonement through those means.

Suffering as a means of atonement may be discussed somewhat more briefly, thanks largely to Büchler's extensive treatment of it.[102] We have already seen R. Ishmael's view, but we may cite one other passage on the point which is also attributed to R. Ishmael:[103]

R. Ishmael says: A Canaanitish slave can have no redemption, he can go out free only at the pleasure of his master. For it is said: 'And ye may make them an inheritance for your children after you, to hold for a possession' (Lev. 25.46). And by our method we learn from this that the Canaanitish slave is a permanent possession like inherited land. Yet, if the master in punishing him knocks out his tooth or blinds his eye or injures any other of his chief external organs, the slave obtains his release at the price of these sufferings. Now, by using the method of *kal vaḥomer*, you reason: If a person can at the price of suffering obtain his release from the hands of flesh and blood, all the more should it be that he thus can obtain his pardon from Heaven.[104] And thus it says: 'The Lord hath chastened me sore: but He hath not given me over unto death' (Ps. 118.18).[105]

The idea is by no means limited to the school of Ishmael, however, as a series of sayings preserved in a similar form in Sifre Deuteronomy and the Mekilta makes clear. The principal saying is attributed to R. Akiba in the Mekilta[106] and in Finkelstein's edition of Sifre Deut., but to R. Jacob in the early

[101] Cf. the discussion of Rabbi's opinion in Kadushin, *The Rabbinic Mind*, p. 182.
[102] *Sin and Atonement*, pp. 119–211; and especially 337–74.
[103] Mek. Mishpatim 9 (280; III, 73f. [Nezikin 9]; to 21.27).
[104] The general principle is that God pardons more readily than does man, thus the phrase 'all the more'.
[105] As we have frequently seen, the sequence is taken to be causal: God has chastened me; therefore I am not given over to death.
[106] Mek. Baḥodesh 10 (239f.; II, 277–80; to 20.20).

printed editions of Sifre Deut. and in Friedmann's edition.[107] In any case, the second saying quoted below is assigned in three different sources[108] to R. Simeon b. Yohai, who is considered to have belonged primarily to the school of Akiba. The following is from the Mekilta and omits sayings in between those of Akiba and Simeon:

R. Akiba says: *Ye Shall Not Do with Me*. Ye shall not behave towards Me in the manner in which others behave toward their deities. When good comes to them they honour their gods, as it is said: 'Therefore they sacrifice unto their net,' etc. (Hab. 1.16). But when evil comes to them they curse their gods, as it is said: [quotes Isa. 8.21]. But ye, if I bring good upon you, give ye thanks, and when I bring suffering upon you, give ye thanks. [A series of passages is quoted to establish the point.] Furthermore, a man should even rejoice when in adversity more than when in prosperity. For even if a man lives in prosperity all his life, it does not mean that his sins have been forgiven him. But what is it that does bring a man forgiveness? You must say, suffering.

. . . .

R. Simon b. Johai says: Precious are chastisements, for the three good gifts given to Israel which the nations of the world covet were all given only at the price of chastisements. And they are these: the Torah, the land of Israel, and the future world. . . . How do we know it about the future world? It is said: 'For the commandment is a lamp and the teaching is light and reproofs by chastisement are the way to life' (Prov. 6.23). You interpret it thus: Go out and see which is the way that brings man to the life of the future world? You must say: Chastisement. R. Nehemiah says: Precious are chastisements. For just as sacrifices are the means of atonement, so also are chastisements. . . . And not only this, but chastisements atone even more than sacrifices. For sacrifices affect only one's money, while chastisements affect the body. And thus it says: 'Skin for skin, yea, all that a man hath will he give for his life' (Job. 2.4).

In a story which follows immediately, R. Akiba makes the point that chastisements lead one to repent and seek God.[109] The story goes as follows: when R. Eliezer was sick, R. Akiba and three others came to comfort him. All but R. Akiba spoke in extravagant praise of R. Eliezer. R. Akiba, however, said: 'Precious are chastisements.' In explanation, he argued that Manasseh was led to call upon God only through chastisements.[110]

This last point, which has been especially elaborated by Büchler,[111] is one of the two principal motives behind assigning suffering an atoning

---

[107] Sifre Deut. 32 (55f.; f.73a–b; to 6.5). The first part of the saying is different in Sifre from the version in the Mekilta. A form close to that of the Mekilta appears anonymously in Tanhuma Jethro 16 (ed. Buber, vol. II, p. 79), while a precise parallel to the version which is found in Sifre appears in Yalkut I, remez 837, near beginning. The Yalkut attributes the saying to R. Akiba. Billerbeck (S.-B. I, p. 906) thinks Akiba should be read in Sifre.

[108] In the Mek. and Sifre Deut. as cited in the preceding two notes, and in Berakoth 5a, near end.

[109] Mek. Behodesh 10 (240f.; II, 280–2). Most of the story was omitted in the early printed editions. And see the parallels in Sifre Deut. 32 (57f.; to 6.5); Sanhedrin 101a.

[110] On this and other stories concerning R. Eliezer's illness, see Neusner, *Eliezer* I, pp. 404–6; II, pp. 411f., 415.

[111] Büchler, *Sin and Atonement*, pp. 337–74.

effect: it leads to repentance. The point is made very clearly by an Amora: 'Raba (some say, R. Ḥisda) says: If a man sees that painful sufferings visit him, let him examine his conduct.'[112]

Understanding the relation which the Rabbis found between suffering and atonement on the one hand and suffering and punishment for transgression on the other leads us to see the second motive behind calling suffering a means of atonement: the justice of God. If God is just and if man sins, it is not possible that no payment will be exacted for transgression. Sacrifices may atone, or even a ransom paid in money,[113] but suffering is more effective and atones for more serious sins, because it is costlier. Thus the righteous are punished on earth for their sins in order to enjoy uninterrupted bliss hereafter.

Although we cannot give here a general history of the concept of the suffering of the righteous in Judaism, it is clear that the two answers to the question of why the righteous suffer had long been (1) that God cleanses those whom he loves by suffering and (2) that God is just and punishes even the righteous for their sins. Both can be seen in the Psalms of Solomon:

> Happy is the man whom the Lord remembereth with reproving,
> And whom he restraineth from the way of evil with strokes,
> That he may be cleansed from sin, that it may not be multiplied.
> He that maketh ready his back for strokes shall be cleansed,
> For the Lord is good to them that endure chastening.[114]

> Behold, now, O God, thou hast shown us thy judgment in thy righteousness;
> Our eyes have seen thy judgments, O God.
> We have justified thy name that is honoured for ever;
> For thou art the God of righteousness, judging Israel with chastening.[115]

In the Psalms of Solomon, the wicked suffered along with the righteous; in fact, the righteous, although they suffered, suffered less severely, since their sin was less.[116] A development in the concept of suffering took place during the next two hundred years, apparently caused by the intense suffering of the Jews in the two revolts against Rome and the increased emphasis on a life after death. The question of why the righteous suffer became more acute, since the wicked, instead of suffering, prospered. Marmorstein has argued that R. Akiba

[112] Berakoth 5a (ET, p. 18).

[113] R. Ishmael takes it as a sign of God's mercy that man can redeem himself with money. See Mek. Mishpatim 10 (286; III, 86f. [Nezikin 10]; to 21.30).

[114] Psalms of Solomon 10.1. Quoted from the translation by G. B. Gray in R. H. Charles, *Pseudepigrapha*, p. 643.

[115] Ibid., 8.30–2 (25–6), p. 641. On this aspect of the Psalms of Solomon, see Büchler, *Types*, pp. 128–95.

[116] Büchler, *Types*, p. 153.

was the first to emphasize the teaching that God makes the righteous pay in this world for the few 'evil deeds' which they have committed, in order to bestow upon them happiness and give them a good reward in the world to come. Just the opposite is the case with the reward and punishment of the wicked.[117]

The principal passage is a discussion between R. Akiba and R. Ishmael:[118]

Thy righteousnrss is like the mountains of God; Thy judgments are like the great deep; man and beast Thou preservest, O Lord (Ps. 36.7). R. Ishmael interpreted: To the righteous who accepted the Torah which was revealed on the mountains of God Thou showest righteousness [*tsedaqah*, charity] reaching unto the mountains of God; but as for the wicked, who did not accept the Torah which was revealed on the mountains of God, Thou dealest strictly with them, even to the great deep. R. Akiba said: He deals strictly with both, even to the great deep. He deals strictly with the righteous, calling them to account for the few wrongs which they commit in this world, in order to lavish bliss upon and give them a goodly reward in the world to come; He grants ease to the wicked and rewards them for the few good deeds which they have performed in this world in order to punish them in the future world.

In addition to the passages which we cited above[119] to the effect that the righteous suffer in this world but are rewarded in the next, we may cite others. There is an anonymous saying in Sifre Deut. which likens life to two roads, one thorny at the beginning and smooth at the end, the other smooth at the beginning and thorny at the end. If the wicked prosper at first, they suffer later, while the righteous, who suffer at the beginning, prosper later.[120] Another anonymous baraita cites Ezek. 2.10: 'It had writing on the front and on the back':[121]

'On the front' [refers to] this world and 'on the back' [refers to] the world to come. 'On the front' [refers to] the ease of the wicked and the sufferings of the righteous in this world, and 'on the back' [refers to] the gift of the reward of the righteous and the punishment of the wicked in the world to come.

Although it is likely to be the case, as Marmorstein said, that the view that the righteous suffer here *in order to be* rewarded hereafter was precisely formulated and emphasized by Akiba, the idea was not altogether new. It seems to be presupposed in a saying by R. Akiba's older contemporary, R. Eliezer. In discussing God's giving the manna to the Israelites despite their frequent disobedience, he comments, 'If God thus provided for those who provoked Him, how much the more will He in the future [*le 'atid labo'*]

---

[117] Marmorstein, *The Names and Attributes of God*, p. 186. Urbach has argued that R. Akiba dissociated suffering from punishment for transgression. On R. Akiba's position, see my 'R. Akiba's View of Suffering', *JQR* n.s. 63, 1973, pp. 332–51.

[118] Gen. Rab. 33.1. There is a parallel in Lev. Rab. 27.1.

[119] See the beginning of section 6.

[120] Sifre Deut. 53 (120f.; to 11.26).

[121] Sifre Num. 103 (102; to 12.8b); cf. ARN 25 (ET, p. 106). See further ARN 39 (ET, p. 162).

pay a good reward to the righteous!'[122] In any case, this is a relatively small development within the general idea that the suffering of the righteous is to be explained as God's just punishment for their few sins.[123] Having been punished here, they need not be punished hereafter. Thus Israel is compared to a vessel of common earthenware which, having been broken, cannot be 'punished' further. 'Thus when punishment ceases from Israel, it will not return upon them in the future.'[124]

This discussion shows again how incorrect the weighing idea is as an accurate reflection of the views of the Tannaim. It follows logically from their conception of the justice of God, and is sometimes stated. But they also thought that God had provided means of atonement which were both thoroughly efficacious and *also in accord with his justice*. If salvation be viewed as God's activity, then sufferings may be said to satisfy God's just requirement; one is not both punished *and* damned for transgression.[125] But internally, sufferings are seen by the religious man as moving him to examination and repentance. The Rabbis did not see suffering as God's just punishment for transgression and suffering as God's means of urging man to repentance as in any way in conflict. Both statements spring from deeply held religious convictions (God is just and man is liable to sin and in need of repentance) and both can be expressed by saying that suffering brings atonement.[126]

It is only a small step to saying that death atones. In addition to the statement of R. Ishmael, we have already seen Yoma 8.8, which probably reflects the view of R. Akiba. In Sifre Numbers, this view is explicitly credited to R. Akiba. Commenting on Numbers 5.8, he says that the specified guilt-offering is to be brought for a person who needs atonement, but this excludes one who is dead, since his soul (or life) has atoned for him.[127]

The logic behind the view that death atones is the same as that behind the

[122] Mek. Vayassa' 3 (165; II, 110 [ch. 4]; to 16.13).

[123] See further on this topic Büchler, *Types*, pp. 111–14 (who thinks that the general view that one suffers here *in order to* enter the world to come purified can be traced to the first century); Kadushin, *The Rabbinic Mind*, p. 218. We should note that later in the second century there was at least a partial return to the early idea (see the beginning of section 6) that the righteous prosper in this world also. Thus the sayings by R. Simeon b. Judah in the name of R. Simeon b. Yohai and by R. Simeon b. Menasya in Aboth 6.8 (cf. T. Sanhedrin 11.8): 'Beauty and strength and riches and honour and wisdom and old age and grey hairs and children are comely to the righteous and comely to the world', etc. The anonymous saying at the end of Mek. Mishpatim 18 (cited in section 8 n. 42) combines length of days with life in the world to come. And on length of days as a sign of righteousness, see the debate in Eccl. Rab. 3.2.3 (ET, pp. 76f.).

[124] Sifre Deut. 324 (375; to 32.34); Midrash Tannaim to Deut. 32.34, p. 201, top ('it does not return for ever'). For further examples of the idea that one suffers here so as to be free from punishment in the world to come, see Urbach, *Hazal*, p. 393 (ET, p. 445).

[125] God's punishment is not effective of itself, however, but should be accepted as chastisement by the righteous man. See the phrase 'accepting God's judgment' in Sifra Shemini Millu'im 23,24,28.

[126] Cf. Schechter, *Aspects*, p. 304: 'Death and suffering may be viewed either as a punishment satisfying the claims of justice or as an atonement, bringing pardon and forgiveness and reconciling man with God.'

[127] Sifre Num. 4 (7, end; to 5.8).

view that sufferings atone. The time of a man's death, if he knows that it is imminent, is a time for self-examination and repentance. (And since a man may not know when death approaches, he should repent every day.) On the other hand, death counts as paying one's account with God:[128] the man who dies repentant will not be further punished for his transgression, no matter how serious. Further, the death of martyrs (those killed 'by the hand of the nations of the world') is considered atonement.[129] Death, to be sure, must be 'accompanied' by repentance;[130] that is, it does not avail in the case of one who has denied God, thrown off the yoke of the covenant and remained defiant to the end.

The view that death as such atones for sin was developed after the destruction of the Temple. As Urbach has noted, while the Temple stood, the prescribed sacrifices atoned for transgressions against God, while the punishment of the court and the restitution required by the law atoned for offences against one's fellow.[131] Thus, as we shall see, when a man received stripes at the order of the court, he was considered to have atoned for the offence for which he was punished.[132] The view that death in general atones for sins developed from the idea that death at the hands of a court atoned for sin, provided that the one being executed repented:[133]

When [the condemned man] was about ten cubits from the place of stoning they used to say to him, 'Make thy confession', for such is the way of them that have been condemned to death to make confession, for every one that makes his confession has a share in the world to come. . . . [This is proved by quoting the story of Achan in Josh. 7.19.] Whence do we learn that his [Achan's] confession made atonement for him? It is written, *And Joshua said, Why hast thou troubled us? the Lord shall trouble thee this day* (Josh. 7.25) – *this day* thou shalt be troubled, but in the world to come thou shalt not be troubled. If he knows not how to make his confession they say to him, 'Say, May my death be an atonement for all my sins.'[134]

---

[128] In a certain sense it is true to say with Moore (*Judaism* I, pp. 474f.) that, according to the Rabbis, there is no death without sin. Thus Adam's sin was frequently thought of as the source of death, and R. Judah b. Ilai was apparently of the opinion that individuals who were sinless would not die (referring to Elijah; see Moore, ibid.). On the other hand, the general opinion in the Tannaitic period was that death belongs to the natural order, but that sins would bring an unnatural or premature death (cf. Shabbath 55a–b). Some thought that good deeds would prolong one's days; see Yebamoth 49b–50a. See further Urbach, *Ḥazal*, pp. 235–7 (ET, pp. 264–6); 'R. Akiba's View of Suffering' on the death of the righteous in the time of persecution.

[129] Sifre Deut. 333 (383; to 32.43).

[130] Yoma 8.8. For an exception, see immediately below.

[131] Urbach, *Ḥazal*, p. 382 (ET, p. 433).

[132] Below, n. 165.

[133] Sanhedrin 6.2. T. Sanhedrin 9.5 prefaces the parallel passage with the specific statement that 'those who are put to death by the court have a share in the world to come, because they confess all their sins'. Epstein (*Mebo'ot*, p. 56) argues that Sanhedrin 6.1–7.3 is basically pre-70 c.e. since the death penalty was not administered by Jewish law courts during the period beginning 'forty years before the destruction of the Temple'. (For this traditional date, see Sanhedrin 41a.)

[134] The passage continues by raising the question of whether or not a condemned man who maintained that he had been convicted by false testimony should confess. The problem was troublesome; cf. Sifre Zuṭa to Num. 5.5f. (p. 230).

The 'confession' required here is, of course, the external form of repentance. Thus the Rabbis could say that confession must be made for any transgression.[135] The model confession given in Sifra anticipates that God will cover or atone for the sins confessed; thus, confession brings atonement.[136] The following passage makes an explicit connection between confession and repentance:[137]

'But if they confess their iniquity and the iniquity of their fathers'. These words refer to repentance; for as soon as they confess their iniquities, I immediately turn and have compassion on them.

There was an opinion, however, that death would atone for all but the most serious sin even without repentance. This is seen in a comment in Sifre on Num. 15.30f.[138] The biblical passage reads: 'But the person who sins wilfully . . . is reviling the Lord. . . . Because it is the word of the Lord that he has despised, and his command that he has broken, that person must be completely cut off, his iniquity being on his own head.' The discussion, following a comment by R. Ishmael, takes the sin to which the biblical passage refers to be idolatry. R. Akiba and R. Ishmael agree that the idolater is 'cut off' both in this world and in the world to come (though their exegesis differs; cf. also Sanhedrin 64b; 90b). But then on the phrase, 'on his own head', the commentator remarks:

All who die atone by their death, but this one (the idolater) – 'his iniquity is on his own head'. . . . – [Is this the case] even if he repents? – [No, for] Scripture teaches, 'his iniquity is on his head', but not when he repents.

The parallel in Sanhedrin 90b is even more explicit: R. Akiba and R. Ishmael agree that 'he shall be cut off' does not apply if he repents; it applies only if his iniquity is 'on his head', but that is removed by repentance. The passage in Sifre is remarkable since it supposes that less serious sins than idolatry are atoned for by death even without repentance and also because it clearly shows that even the most grievous sin could be atoned for by death with repentance.[139]

We have thus seen that, as a general rule, repentance accompanies the other means of atonement, so that it is actually not a fourth means but the attitude which is always necessary for God's forgiveness.[140] The only possible

---

[135] Sifre Zuṭa to Num. 5.5f. (p. 230, near top).
[136] Sifra Aḥare parasha 2.4 (to 16.6).
[137] Sifra Beḥuqqotai pereq 8.3 (to 26.40).
[138] Sifre Num. 112 (p. 121).
[139] Urbach (*Ḥazal*, p. 383; ET, p. 435 n. 53) attributes the view that death atones without repentance to R. Judah and Rabbi. He refers to the discussion by Lieberman (*Tosefta Ki-Fshuṭah*, *Mo'ed*, p. 826) of a saying by R. Judah in T. Yom Ha-Kippurim 4(5).9.
[140] This is explicitly said in the version of R. Ishmael's four categories which appears in ARN 29, and also in p. Yoma 45b. There, when R. Mattiah b. Ḥeresh asks R. Eleazar if he has heard of R. Ishmael's four categories of atonement, R. Eleazar replies, 'I have heard, but they are three, and along with each of these there must be repentance'.

exceptions to this statement are the views that, on the one hand, the Day of Atonement or, on the other, death atones without repentance for all but the most serious sins. As we noted, however, this point seems to have been made about the Day of Atonement in order to protect the prescribed cultic acts from appearing altogether irrelevant. The Day of Atonement itself implies repentance, as do the various sacrifices prescribed in the Bible. To say that the Day of Atonement is effective apart from repentance is only to say that repentance as a separate act apart from the repentance and confession which accompany the Day of Atonement is not necessary. The distinction is a fine one. Similarly, the passage which implies that death without repentance atones for all sins but idolatry seems designed primarily to emphasize that even idolatry can be atoned for if one repents. It cannot be taken as an attempt to limit the role of repentance; it emphasizes it.

No one has better realized the meaning and significance of repentance for Judaism than Moore, and it is superfluous to try to add to what he has written.[141] There are, however, certain characteristics of repentance which it will be useful to our study to bring out. We should also give a general description of the significance of repentance in Rabbinic eyes.

Although it is quite accurate to use the English word repentance for the Hebrew word *teshubah*, we should note that the etymologies are different. Whereas repentance seems to refer to a mental act ('rethinking'), the Hebrew verb *shub* means literally 'turn' or 'return'.[142] In actual use, however, the two words are employed in the same way. English usage of the word 'repentance', of course, is greatly influenced by the biblical injunctions to turn back to God. As Moore defines repentance in Judaism, it appears no different from what would be understood by the English word:

To the Jewish definition of repentance belong the reparation of injuries done to a fellow man in his person, property, or good name, the confession of sin, prayer for forgiveness, and the genuine resolve and endeavour not to fall into sin again.[143]

Repentance and God's forgiveness, as Moore points out repeatedly, are the necessary means of salvation in a religion which emphasized obedience.[144] Thus repentance may homiletically be said to be one of the things created before the world; it was created second, just after the law itself.[145] Repentance belongs to the religious behaviour of the righteous man; it was not considered that a man would have nothing to repent for.[146] The question of

---

[141] See Moore's index, s.v. Repentance.

[142] On the meaning of *teshubah*, see Moore, *Judaism* I, p. 507; cf. Petuchowski, 'The Concept of "Teshuvah"', *Judaism* 17, 1968, pp. 180f.

[143] Moore, *Judaism* I, p. 117.

[144] Ibid., pp. 116f., 266.

[145] Ibid., pp. 266, 526.

[146] Ibid., p. 495. Note also the anonymous passage in Ex. Rab. 31.1: 'There is no creature that is not indebted to God, but being gracious and merciful He forgives (*moḥel*) all former [transgressions].' The passage continues by saying that God forgives men sin after sin, even if they do not repent.

perfect obedience to the law hardly arises in the Tannaitic literature.[147] To be sure, some Rabbis had a hard time thinking of what commandment they might have disobeyed,[148] but the fallibility of man was well known. Repentance was regarded as so efficacious that it outweighed even a life-time of sin and disobedience, as we saw in R. Simeon b. Yohai's statement in T. Kiddushin 1.15f.: even the wicked man who repents at the end of his life will be saved.[149] A similar view is represented by R. Meir: if two men suffer from the same disease and only one survives, it is because he repented.[150]

It will immediately be seen how little this comports with the view that the majority of deeds over a man's entire life is what determines his eternal destiny. The view that repentance wipes out any number of sins is brought into connection with the view that God's justice requires him to deal with a man in strict accord with his sins in this passage from Sifre:[151]

The sages say: God never reverses ('they never reverse') innocence into guilt nor guilt into innocence, but he gives the gift of the reward for [the fulfilment of] *mitsvot* and he punishes for transgressions. So why does Scripture teach, 'Let Reuben live, and not die'? Because Reuben made repentance.

The point appears to be that a strict reckoning would have had Reuben die, but repentance created a new situation, one in which his disobedience no longer counted against him. It is perhaps noteworthy that the biblical accounts do not mention his repenting (presumably for incest; see Gen. 35.22 and 49.4); the Rabbis supposed that since Deut. 33.6 said that he should live and not die, he *must* have repented. This indicates how thoroughly repentance was the Rabbinic doctrine of salvation.[152]

Repentance, like obedience, is best undertaken simply from love of God; but even repentance made from fear is better than none at all. The Rabbis do not praise it, but they do not deny its efficacy.[153]

To the mind sensitized to the question by centuries of Lutheranism, even repentance may appear as a legalistic performance to earn God's mercy. The Rabbis can in fact state the matter in such a way as to make man's initiative in repenting the absolute condition of God's mercy. That is, it will

---

[147] Büchler, *Sin and Atonement*, pp. 331ff. As R. Tarfon said, however, even though a man may not fulfil the law perfectly, he is not free to desist from trying (Aboth 2.16).

[148] Thus Mek. Mishpatim 18 (313; III, 141f. [Nezikin 18]; to 22.22[23]): when R. Simeon and R. Ishmael were going to be executed, the former could not think what sin he was being punished for. R. Ishmael suggested that he might at some time have delayed giving a judgment until he sipped his cup, tied his sandals or put on his cloak. The point is that such a sin might account for his premature death. (On the identity of this R. Simeon, see Finkelstein, *Akiba*, pp. 268, 316f.) For another instance, see Büchler, *Sin and Atonement*, p. 347. See also Büchler, *Types*, pp. 17f., where examples of near perfection are cited from Rabbinic and other literature.

[149] Cited above, section 6 n. 17; cf. n. 23.

[150] Rosh Ha-Shanah 18a (ET, pp. 70f.).

[151] Sifre Deut. 347 (404f.; to 33.6).

[152] Cf. Moore, *Judaism* I, p. 500: repentance and its other side, remission of sins, 'may properly be called the Jewish doctrine of salvation'.

[153] See Schechter, *Aspects*, pp. 318ff., on Manasseh.

sometimes appear in an individual passage as if the imperative 'repent' precedes the indicative 'and God will be merciful'. Thus, for example, one may cite this passage from Sifra:[154]

'If then their uncircumcised heart is humbled' (Lev. 26.41). – These words apply to repentance. For as soon as they humble their hearts in repentance, I immediately return and show them mercy, as is said, 'If then their uncircumcised heart is humbled and they make amends for their iniquity.'

In a sense, this impression is true. Repentance was considered to be the condition on the basis of which God forgives. God did not force one to maintain an obedient and repentant attitude against his will.[155] What is wrong with the view that repentance in Rabbinic religion is a *work* which earns 'mercy' is that it leaves out of account the fundamental basis of that religion, namely, God's election of Israel. The theme of repentance and forgiveness functions within a larger structure which is founded on the understanding that 'All Israelites have a share in the world to come'. This view, it is clear, is based on an understanding of the grace of God.

Here we must refer both to the nature of the Rabbinic material and the overall structure of Rabbinic religion. The Rabbinic religion was framed by election at one end and a share in the world to come at the other. All those who remained within the covenant partook of the covenant promises. As we have repeatedly pointed out, the Rabbis never doubted God's fidelity to the covenant. What they dealt with was how man could best be faithful. The halakic literature, by definition, deals with this question; that is, it is concerned with intra-covenantal questions. Man's faithfulness to the covenant, negatively, is not renouncing it, not treating the decrees of God as of no effect, not scorning the law and not treating his brother in such a way as to show that in fact he has no respect for the God who commanded love of the neighbour. Positively, it is doing one's best to obey the commandments and doing what is appropriate in case of failure. 'Doing what is appropriate' always involves repentance, for the unrepentant person does not take steps to redress his disobedience. 'What is appropriate' may include the bringing of a sacrifice, making restitution and other obvious acts of contrition. After the destruction of the Temple, repentance was substituted for all the sacrifices prescribed in the law, although the Day of Atonement maintained a special place in Jewish life. Ultimately, what is required is that one intends to remain in the covenant, intends to be obedient.

[154] Sifra Beḥuqqotai pereq 8.6 (to 26.41b). On the question of man or God initiating repentance, see Petuchowski, 'The Concept of "Teshuvah"', pp. 184f.
[155] The Rabbis could say that the covenantal commandments were imposed whether man liked it or not, once he had accepted the covenant. So Sifre Num. 115 (127f.; to 15.41). The intention to be religious, however, cannot be coerced: 'Everything is in the hand of heaven except the fear of heaven' (Berakoth 33b; Megillah 25a). 'Freedom of choice is given' (Aboth 3.15; ET, 3.16). Cf. Urbach, *Ḥazal*, p. 320 (ET, p. 365): in one sense the commandments are obligatory, in another they are voluntary.

Thus repentance is not a 'status-achieving' activity by which one initially courts and wins the mercy of God. It is a 'status-maintaining' or 'status-restoring' attitude which indicates that one intends to remain in the covenant. To use other language, one is already 'saved'; what is needed is the maintenance of a right attitude toward God.[156] Without it, the mercy of God is of no avail. One enters the covenant by accepting God's offer of it; one remains in it by continuing to accept it; and this implies repentance for transgressions.

We shall subsequently have occasion to inquire into the question of what light Rabbinic prayers shed on the general Rabbinic understanding of religion. As a kind of counterbalance to the passage from Sifra quoted above (n. 154), however, we may here quote one passage from a prayer which seems to imply a doctrine of prevenient grace and which clearly puts the indicative and the imperative in what even Bultmannians will concede to be the correct relationship: 'May it be thy will, Lord God, and the God of our fathers, that thou put into our hearts to do perfect repentance.'[157] The grace of God was constantly appealed to for aid in overcoming temptation.[158]

We should add that the real point of the comment in Sifra on Lev. 26.41 is that God, like the father in the parable of the prodigal son, stands ever ready to forgive. This is brought out especially clearly in a parable attributed to R. Meir.[159]

Thou wilt return to the Lord thy God (Deut. 4.30). R. Samuel Pargrita said in the name of R. Meir: This can be compared to the son of a king who took to evil ways. The king sent a tutor to him who appealed to him saying, 'Repent, my son.' The son, however, sent him back to his father [with the message], 'How can I have the effrontery to return? I am ashamed to come before you.' Thereupon his father sent back word, 'My son, is a son ever ashamed to return to his father? And is it not to your father that you will be returning?' Similarly, the Holy One, blessed be He, sent Jeremiah to Israel when they sinned, etc.

Here the repentant return is obviously a 'status-preserving' repentance, not one which earns God's favour. This is the attitude which was eventually accepted in Christianity, as may be seen in the general confession from the liturgy:

We have offended against thy holy laws. We have left undone those things which we ought to have done; and we have done those things which we ought not to have done. . . . But thou, O Lord, have mercy upon us, miserable offenders. . . . Restore them that are penitent. . . .

[156] So also Petuchowski, 'The Concept of "Teshuvah" ', pp. 178f.

[157] P. Berakoth 7d (4.2). Attributed to R. Ḥiyya b. Aba (Ḥiyyah bar Wa), who flourished at the end of the third century. But according to the subsequent comment, it was a traditional prayer. Cited from Schechter, *Aspects*, p. 279.

[158] On man's initiative and God's grace, see Schechter, *Aspects*, p. 278ff.

[159] Deut. Rab. 2.24. There is a similar passage, also attributed to R. Meir, in A. Jellinek's collection *Bet ha-Midrasch* I, pp. 21f.

Here it is assumed that one has sinned, but the penitent knows that God will forgive and *restore* the original relationship established by grace. Repentance is not a work which earns God's favour, but the means of restoring a relationship strained by transgression. The initial saving grace of God is assumed. This is also the Rabbinic attitude, and those who sin and repent are still righteous 'by the law'. Putting the imperative 'repent' before the indicative 'and God will be merciful' in such passages, whether Christian or Jewish, is not to be construed as proving the existence of a religion of 'works-righteousness'. One can make it so only by overlooking the still earlier statements of God's saving grace and by ignoring the role of repentance in restoring the relationship established by grace.

Before leaving the theme of repentance, we should consider one last point: the distinction which the Rabbis made between sins committed against God and sins committed against man; in Rabbinic terms, transgressions of commandments between man and God and those between man and his neighbour.[160] It was a fundamental Rabbinic view that sins against God were more easily forgiven than sins against one's fellow-man, since the latter require restitution.[161] God 'lifts up his face' if the sin is between man and God, but if the sin is between man and man, 'he does not lift up his face'.[162] It agrees with this that sins which the Bible indicates were to be punished by 'cutting off', *karet*, were more easily atoned for than sins which were punishable by death at the hands of a human court. *Karet* is usually translated in English as 'extinction' or 'extirpation' and refers to those biblical passages which say that 'his soul shall be utterly cut off'.[163] One might suppose that the Rabbis would have made such sins the most difficult to atone for, but their view of God's persistent mercy led them to adopt another view. If death is decreed by God's court, a man can ransom himself; there is no ransom from death decreed by a human court.[164] Or, as the Mishnah puts it, 'All they that are liable to Extirpation, if they have been scourged are no longer liable to Extirpation, for it is written, *And thy brother seem vile unto thee* (Deut. 25.3) – when he is scourged then he is thy brother.'[165] This distinction shows the fundamental moral drive of Rabbinic religion.

---

[160] For some examples, see Alon, *Meḥqarim* I, pp. 276f.

[161] God forgives transgressions between man and man only if the transgressor has appeased his fellow: Sifra Aḥare pereq 8.1f. (to 16.30); the statement has been added to Yoma 8.9. On restitution, cf. Baba Kamma 8.7. Buchanan (*Consequences of the Covenant*, p. 155) cites I Sam. 2.25 to show that sins against God were more serious than sins against man, but this was not the Rabbinic view.

[162] Sifre Zuṭa to 6.26 (p. 248), R. Jose b. Dosethai. A similar saying is attributed to R. Akiba.

[163] See the Mishnah tractate Kerithoth and Danby's notes.

[164] Mek. Mishpatim 10 (285; III, 85f. [Nezikin 10]; to 21.29, end).

[165] Makkoth 3.15; Sifre Deut. 286 (304; to 25.3). Cf. the discussion between R. Ishmael and R. Akiba in Makkoth 13a–b. And scourgings, or 'stripes', are said to atone for sins in Midrash Tannaim to Deut. 25.3 (p. 164): 'Beloved are stripes, for they atone for sins, as it is said, "in proportion to (*kedē*, Deut. 25.2) his wickedness": they are sufficient (*kedai*) to atone for wickedness' (cited by Urbach, *Ḥazal*, p. 383; ET, p. 434).

Thus for those in the covenant, repentance was the sovereign means of atonement. Except for the desire to insist on the efficacy of other means of atonement, which we have already noted, it is virtually impossible to find any exceptions to the rule that repentance atones. Urbach can cite only three examples:[166] Moses was not permitted to enter the land of Israel despite his supplications, even though God accepted repentance from the people of Israel for their many transgressions (here, however, the question is not one of salvation).[167] Manasseh was excluded from a share in the world to come by the author of Sanhedrin 10.2, even though he repented. The third example is that of Elisha b. Abuya, who despaired of repentance. On a Day of Atonement which fell on a Sabbath, he was riding his horse before the Temple, and he heard a voice coming forth from the Temple, saying, ' "Return, O faithless children", except for Elisha b. Abuya, who knew my strength and rebelled against me.'[168] As Urbach notes, this is the case of one who not only sinned but led others astray, and such are given no opportunity for repentance (Aboth 5.18). We should also note that Elisha b. Abuya is here taken as the classical case of one who 'cast off the yoke': he knowingly and wilfully persisted in transgression.

Summary

We are now in a position to see the overall pattern of Rabbinic religion as it applied to Israelites (proselytes and righteous Gentiles will be considered below). The pattern is this: God has chosen Israel and Israel has accepted the election. In his role as King, God gave Israel commandments which they are to obey as best they can. Obedience is rewarded and disobedience punished. In case of failure to obey, however, man has recourse to divinely ordained means of atonement, in all of which repentance is required. As long as he maintains his desire to stay in the covenant, he has a share in God's covenantal promises, including life in the world to come. The intention and effort to be obedient constitute the *condition for remaining in the covenant*, but they do not *earn* it.

This general understanding of religion, although not systematically developed, in fact lies behind all the Tannaitic literature. It accounts for the principal emphases in that literature, as well as for apparent contradictions on crucial points. It appears to have informed the religious thinking of the Tannaim consistently and thoroughly. Any other mode of religion doubtless would have appeared to them as unbiblical, not in accord with the revelation of God's will in the Torah. Only by overlooking this large pattern can the

---

[166] *Hazal*, pp. 410f. (ET, p. 465).
[167] Sifre Num. 136 (183; to 3.29).
[168] P. Hagigah 77b (2.1).

Rabbis be made to appear as legalists in the narrow and pejorative sense of the word. Their legalism falls within a larger context of gracious election and assured salvation. In discussing disobedience and obedience, punishment and reward, they were not dealing with how man is saved, but with how man should act and how God will act within the framework of the covenant. Within that framework, they were determined to understand and obey God's commands as best they could, but they did not think that they earned their place in the covenant by the number of *mitsvot* fulfilled. Nor did they think that the transgression of more commandments than were fulfilled would damn them. They may have made such statements, as they could also say that transgression of *one* commandment would damn, but homiletical exhortation should not be confused with basic belief. As long as a man intended to remain in the covenant, and indicated his intention by true repentance, God did not reckon the precise number of commandments fulfilled or transgressed. If God judged strictly, no man would live. Not even the patriarchs could stand God's reproof if he judged them strictly.[169]

The failure to understand the relationship between the *framework* of covenantal election and assured atonement on the one hand, and the *intra-covenantal* reliability of God to reward and punish on the other, has led to the complete misunderstanding of the essentials of Rabbinic religion. This misunderstanding has marked not only the work of scholars like Billerbeck, who could write on 'Pharisaic soteriology' without mentioning the covenant and who relegated atonement to a minor role in the effort to fulfil more commandments than one committed transgressions,[170] but also the work of a scholar like Sjöberg, who endeavoured to understand the relationship between justice and mercy in the Rabbinic view. Sjöberg noted the belief in election as represented in Sanhedrin 10.1, and he did not, as have so many, simply dismiss it.[171] He saw that it means that eternal blessedness becomes not a question of guilt or righteousness, but of belonging to Israel.[172] But how is that view to be related to the view that there is retribution according to deeds? Sjöberg solved the problem by maintaining that Sanhedrin 10.1 (and the general theory of the election) applies only to Israel as such, not to individuals within it. The governing view with regard to individuals is that they are judged according to deeds (though not so mechanically as many supposed).[173]

The significance of Sjöberg's conclusion can be seen in his section on the 'structure of the Jewish religion'. The fact that Judaism requires fulfilment

[169] R. Eliezer in a baraita, Arakin 17a, top. That the world could not endure if God judged strictly is said in Gen. Rab. 12.15 and 39.6.
[170] S.-B. IV, pp. 5f.
[171] Sjöberg, *Gott und die Sünder*, pp. 118f.
[172] Ibid., pp. 120f.
[173] Ibid., pp. 122–4; cf. pp. 106–8.

of the law leads to the conclusion that a man *makes himself* pleasing to God by obedience.[174] 'Thus the Jewish religion, as presented by the Tannaites, remains a religion in which the normal relationship with God is built on the righteousness of man and the goodwill (*Wohlgefallen*) of God which is achieved by it.'[175] Here the ideas of mercy and election, which Sjöberg saw and tried to hold in balance, have finally fallen away.

The refutation of Sjöberg's view is simple. Sanhedrin 10.1 by its very wording (literally, 'All Israel – there is for *them* a share in the world to come'; thus 'All Israelites have') indicates that it applies to individuals, not just to the continuation of the Israelite nation. The exceptions which follow further show that individuals not excluded are counted in. Most decisive, however, are the detailed efforts to work out how individuals atone for their transgressions. To repeat our frequent conclusion, the *universal* view is that *every individual Israelite* who indicates his intention to remain in the covenant by repenting, observing the Day of Atonement and the like, will be forgiven for *all* his transgressions. The passages on repenting and atoning in order to *return* to God, which are ubiquitous in the literature, *presuppose* the covenantal relationship between God and all the members of Israel. In dealing with the individual, one cannot dismiss his membership in the covenant of God with Israel.[176] The statements of reward and punishment, on the other hand, do not indicate how one earns salvation. Their opposite would not be that God is merciful and saves, but that there is no correspondence between God's rewards and man's behaviour: that God is arbitrary. If it appears that within this world God is not being just, one may rest assured that justice will be done in the world to come. The Israelite in the covenant will be punished for transgressions – by suffering, by death and even after death if necessary – but he is saved by remaining in the covenant given by God. Thus, for example, R. Akiba believed in strict punishment for deeds. Suffering reveals that one has sinned and is being punished,[177] and God will not show mercy to the righteous by refraining from punishing them for their transgressions.[178] But this describes God's behaviour within the covenant, not how one is saved. R. Akiba agreed with the statement that all Israelites have a share in the world to come, which is indicated by his glossing it by listing a few (a very few) exceptions. Further, in one sense even God's punishment of the sins of the righteous is itself mercy, since it indicates that one is being punished here in order not to be punished hereafter. Mercy and justice are not truly in conflict, nor is strict reward and punishment for deeds an alternative soteriology to election and atonement.

---

[174] Ibid., p. 188.
[175] Ibid., p. 190.
[176] So also Urbach, *Ḥazal*, pp. 454f. (ET, pp. 511f.).
[177] Mek. Baḥodesh 10 and Sifre Deut. 32, above n. 109.
[178] Gen. Rab. 33.1, above n. 118.

8. Proper religious behaviour: *zakah* and *tsadaq*

Although we have now seen the basic pattern of Tannaitic religion, it is necessary for our study to explore a few further themes. The present section will focus on the two principal words which indicate correct religious behaviour, *zakah* and *tsadaq* and their cognates.

Zakah

As we saw in section 1 above, there is a long-standing view in Christian scholarship that the Rabbis held a 'doctrine of merits'. That the Rabbis believed obedience to be meritorious and to be rewarded by God is not in question. What we shall principally be concerned to investigate is the view that merits can be compiled and *transferred at the judgment* so as to *counterbalance demerits*. This view, as we saw above, is connected with the theory that Rabbinic soteriology consists of weighing merits against transgressions (guilts). Many scholars have seen in the phrase *zekut 'abot*, 'merits of the fathers', a view analogous to the supposed Roman Catholic view of the *thesaurus meritorum*, treasury of merits, which are compiled by the works of supererogation and innocent suffering of the saints. The *zekut 'abot* can, in the traditional Christian view of Rabbinic soteriology, be transferred to others at the judgment.[1]

Moore observed that the phrase *bizekut* is frequently prepositional. He gave the analogy of the English phrase 'by virtue of', and he argued that frequently the Hebrew phrase should be translated as 'for the sake of' rather than 'because of the merit of'.[2] He saw the function of the term *zekut 'abot* to be to explain God's love for Israel: 'God's love for Israel had its origin and ground in his love for its forefathers'; 'It was natural to believe that God would show especial favor or indulgence to their descendants for the sake of the affection and esteem in which he held their fathers.'[3] Sjöberg agreed with Moore that the translation 'on account of the merits of the fathers' leads to a false comparison with the *thesaurus meritorum* from which someone could supplement his deficiencies, and he agreed that such an analogy is not correct.[4] He further agreed that Moore was generally correct in translating

[1] See the views of Weber, Charles, Bousset (there is a treasury but no means of transfer), Köberle, Billerbeck, Bultmann, Rössler (all cited in section 1 above), Barrett and Ziesler (cited immediately below). The analogy with the Roman Catholic 'treasury of merits' was denied by Moore (*Judaism* I, pp. 544f.) and Marmorstein (*Merits*, p. 31), but apparently with little effect. My colleague Dr Ben Meyer informs me that the description of the relation between works of supererogation and the treasury of merits in Catholicism which is frequently given in these discussions is itself not accurate, and that even Moore's description is in need of minor correction.
[2] Moore, *Judaism* III, p. 164 (n. 249).
[3] Moore, *Judaism* I, p. 536.
[4] Sjöberg, *Gott und die Sünder*, pp. 42f., 49, 55. The view that deficiencies can be supplemented from a treasury of merits first occurs in the Amoraic period (p. 55).

bizekut as a preposition, and he added evidence for this translation by showing parallel phrases in which an undoubted preposition (such as *bishbil* or *lema'an*) replaces *bizekut*.[5] Only in three cases whose Tannaitic origin is somewhat dubious does one see a phrase in which *zekut* has its 'full substantive meaning'.[6] *Zekut 'abot* without the preposition *b* is hardly to be found.[7] Sjöberg thought that Moore was wrong, however, in thinking that the phrase *bizekut 'abot* refers primarily to the grace of God or to his promises to the patriarchs. It does sometimes do so, but the majority of the references have in mind the actual righteousness of the fathers.[8] Further, even when the love of God and his promise to the fathers are in mind, one must note that the covenant and the promises were given to the righteous; thus the connection of the phrase with the theory of retribution (*Vergeltungsgedanken*) is maintained.[9]

Despite the work of Moore and Sjöberg, however, New Testament scholars have continued to speak of a Rabbinic doctrine of merits which can be used to supplement one's deficiencies. In addition to the examples given in section I above, we may note some others. Thus C. K. Barrett mentions that in one place Paul's 'language recalls the Rabbinic doctrine of the merit (*zakuth*) of the fathers, which forms a treasury upon which their sinful descendants can draw. . .'.[10] G. F. Moore notwithstanding, Barrett takes the 'Rabbinic doctrine' to be so well known that it requires no proof or documentation. Most recently, Ziesler has repeated the traditional view, although he recognizes that there is a more favourable reading of the Rabbinic attitude. After referring to the work of Schechter, Moore and others, he states that the doctrine of merits, 'including the transfer of merits', 'fully emerges' in Rabbinic literature[11] – a view which Moore had denied and which cannot be found in Schechter. He continues: 'If one is truly righteous, one's merit is available not only for oneself, but for others, and there are three main ways in which this happens: the merit of the Fathers. . . ; the merit of a pious contemporary. . . ; and even the merit of a pious posterity.'[12] He follows Marmorstein, however, in arguing that there was continuing opposition to the idea of the transfer of merits, and Schechter in thinking that the transfer of merits is not a commercial and externalistic transaction, but an expression of 'a fountain of grace'.[13] Thus Ziesler com-

---

[5] Ibid., pp. 49f.

[6] Sjöberg, p. 51 n. 1; citing Mek. of R. Simeon b. Yohai to Ex. 21.2; Midrash Tannaim to Deut. 34.7; ibid. to 23.5. In none of these instances, however, does *bizekut* or *bishbil zekut* have an unusual meaning. All refer to something good having happened 'on account of' or 'because of the merit of' Abraham, Moses or someone else.

[7] Sjöberg, p. 51.

[8] Ibid., pp. 44–9, 55.

[9] Ibid., pp. 49, 55.

[10] Barrett, *The Epistle to the Romans*, p. 225.

[11] J. A. Ziesler, *The Meaning of Righteousness in Paul*, p. 122.

[12] Ibid., p. 123; citing Schechter, *Aspects*, pp. 171–98.   [13] Ziesler, p. 124.

bines the traditional Christian view of the transfer of merits to offset deficiencies with a kindlier attitude toward Rabbinic Judaism: the emphasis is on grace, not commerce.

New Testament scholars have frequently based their discussions on Schechter and Marmorstein. It is Schechter who made current the neat division of the merits of the fathers, of contemporaries and of one's posterity.[14] He is frequently taken as supporting the view that the merits of these groups could be *transferred.* Actually, he granted to the merits of others 'a protective or an atoning influence', and he discussed merits within the framework of a conception of the corporate solidarity of benefit and of punishment.[15] He never mentioned the actual transfer of merits from a treasury based on works of supererogation to a deficient individual. Marmorstein, as we have seen, objected to the analogy of the Rabbinic view with the medieval Christian view, but his own incautious wording has lent much support to the Christian interpretation. Thus he always translated *zekut* as 'merit', no matter what the context or nuance, which helps give the impression of the existence of what Bultmann called a doctrine of merit 'in the proper sense of the word'. *Zekut* in Marmorstein always has its full substantive sense.[16] Further, he wrote such sentences as the following: 'they [the fathers] gathered treasures in heaven not for themselves but for others.'[17] Marmorstein's subsequent qualifications do not erase the impression made by such sentences as these on a Christian scholar who is already prepared to believe in the Rabbinic doctrine of judgment by weighing merits and demerits and of transferrable merits which offset demerits.[18] This can be seen in the widespread continuation of the view.

Recently Buchanan has made the doctrine of a treasury or ledger of merits and demerits one of the cardinal elements in the Jewish and Christian covenantal theology which he describes. His initial description is so diffuse and depends on references from so many scattered sources that it is difficult at first to know how his view was reached.[19] In his section on the Day of Atonement, however, there is a succinct discussion which indicates that he intends

---

[14] N. 12 above.   [15] Schechter, *Aspects*, pp. 170f.

[16] Similarly in his commentary on the Mekilta, Kadushin (*Conceptual Approach*, pp. 59, 61) changes Lauterbach's 'for their sake' or 'because of' as a translation of *bizekut* to 'because of their merit'. As Moore and Sjöberg showed, however, and as Lauterbach obviously thought, 'for the sake of' is often the only reasonable translation of *bizekut*.

[17] Marmorstein, *Merits*, p. 156; cf. pp. 49 ('the merits of righteous men . . . are available for others as well'), 52, 148, 160.

[18] It does not seem necessary to discuss Marmorstein's complex view in detail, since we are interested in only one point. His treatment of particular passages and his uniform translation of *zekut* will be taken up in the subsequent discussion.

[19] Buchanan, *The Consequences of the Covenant*, pp. 31–6. Here he cites some of the Rabbinic passages which explain the exodus by the phrase *bizekut* someone or something (above, section 4), without noting that they refer only to the exodus. He takes them as showing the existence of a treasury which could be drawn on. The existence of a treasury of merits is reiterated throughout the book. See, for example, pp. 156, 235, 273.

to base his view on fresh arguments. In Buchanan's view, in Judaism 'sins were understood to accumulate in a ledger both for individuals and for nations'. When one's credit was completely withdrawn, 'foreclosure proceedings followed'. He continues:

Sin was considered a debt (חוב) against a fellow Hebrew, against God, or both. A person who had committed many sins had just as much reason to be anxious as a person who had borrowed a great deal of money. The latter could know the length of time he was expected to serve, but a sinner could never be sure how much was recorded against him. . . . He believed that God was just, but the ledger sheet was not available and the offender could not know the extent of his debt. . . . God also recorded virtues, however, so it was important for Hebrews to do as many good works as possible to cancel their indebtedness.

Buchanan goes on to argue that during New Testament times Jews 'strained every nerve to build up the account of merits credited to Israel' by such activities as vows of poverty, chastity and obedience.[20]

Much of Buchanan's view rests on the legal stipulations regarding debt, foreclosure, slavery, and the jubilee and sabbatical years. Buchanan transfers the system of indebtedness, foreclosure (or forced servitude) and redemption by money or on the sabbatical or jubilee years into a system of merits and demerits in a ledger book kept by God which governs God's judgment of both individuals and nations. I must confess that I do not understand the reasoning which connects the laws governing slavery with the idea of a treasury of merits efficacious for salvation. It seems doubtful if the latter would have been concluded from the former if it were not for the continuing influence of the Christian view of 'merits' in Judaism, which rests on quite different arguments. We see, however, in Buchanan's description more or less the whole position of such writers as Weber, Billerbeck and Bousset: God weighs merits and demerits; one good deed cancels a transgression and vice versa; a man is anxious and insecure because he does not know his standing with God; and, as the one ray of light, the view that the good deeds of some can build up a treasury of merits which may be drawn on to meet the deficiencies of others.

Thus we see that many scholars, from divergent points of view, continue to find in Rabbinic literature the idea of a treasury of merits, which has always had an important position in the traditional Christian view of Rabbinic soteriology. It would be instructive for the understanding of Rabbinic religion to undertake a full study of *zakah, zekut* and *zakka'i*, but we must restrict the present study to questions of soteriology. We shall first of all note that it is misleading invariably to translate *zakah* and *zekut* as 'merit'. Secondly, we shall note *what* is merited when 'merit' is the correct translation. Finally, we shall consider the question of a treasury of merits.

[20] Ibid., pp. 223f.

1. As we remarked above, Marmorstein always translated the verb *zakah* and the noun *zekut* as 'merit'. This is often an unfortunate translation, since it seems to imply a 'doctrine of merits' where none exists. Marmorstein correctly observed that *zekut* is used as the opposite of sin, transgression and guilt.[21] But in each of these cases, he translated *zekut* (and its cognates) as 'merit'.[22] The opposite of sin or transgression is a good deed or correct action, the opposite of guilt (*ḥobah*) is innocence, and the opposite of *ḥobah* in the sense of debt is freedom from debt; and so *zakah* and *zekut* should be translated in these instances. We may take a few examples. The first is Aboth 5.18, following Danby's translation:

He that leads the many to virtue (*mezakkeh*), through him shall no sin (*ḥet'*) befall; but he that leads the many to sin (*maḥati'*), to him shall be given no means for repentance. Moses was virtuous (*zakah*) and he led the many to virtue (*zikkah*); the virtue (*zekut*) of the many depended on him. . . . Jeroboam sinned (*ḥata'*) and he led the many to sin (*heḥeti'*); the sin of the many depended on him. . . .[23]

The translation is made difficult because there is no English word which is a ready opposite of 'sin'. Danby's choice of 'lead to virtue' and 'be virtuous' for the verbs and 'virtue' for the noun is perhaps as satisfactory as any. Here, however, Marmorstein translated the *pi'el* verb as 'cause to acquire merits', while he translated the *hif'il* of *ḥata'* as 'to lead astray'.[24] In English, 'cause to acquire merits' is not a good antithesis to 'lead astray'. To speak of an acquisition of merits seems to imply a treasury of merits which can be stored up, and it is for this reason that Marmorstein's translation is misleading. The most natural translation here would be that Moses 'acted correctly' and 'led the many aright'.[25] Their 'correct behaviour' depended on him. The point is that the meaning of *zakah* is governed by its opposite, 'sin', which means to do what is wrong. This is seen clearly in two other passages. Thus T. Peah 3.8: in discussing the commandment of the forgotten sheaf, a certain pious man (*ḥasid*) tells his son: 'Can one not argue *qal vaḥomer*? If to a man who did not intend to do a good deed (*zakah*), but who did one (i.e. forgot a sheaf), God accounts it as if he did a good deed (*zakah*), how much more [will he account it good] when one intends to do a good deed and does one. . . . [And similarly] if to a man who did not intend to commit a sin (*ḥata'*), but who committed one', etc. The contrast also appears in Sifre Deut. 306 (332; to 32.1): the earth and sea were made to receive neither a gain (*sakar*) nor a loss, thus 'if they behave correctly (*zokim*) they receive no reward (*sakar*) and

---

[21] Marmorstein, *Merits*, p. 8.
[22] Ibid., pp. 6f.
[23] T. Yom Ha-Kippurim 4(5). 10f. explains why one who leads others astray is given no chance to repent: 'lest his disciples should go down to Sheol while ie inherits the world [to come]'. Cf. Lieberman, *Tosefta Ki-Fshuṭah, Mo'ed*, p. 827.
[24] *Merits*, p. 6.
[25] So also Jastrow, *Dictionary*, p. 399, who translates *mezakkeh* in Aboth 5.18 'cause to do good'.

if they do not behave correctly (*hot'im*) they do not receive punishment (*pur'anut*)', etc. It would be erroneous to follow Marmorstein's lead and render *zakah* in these cases as 'acquire merit'.

When *zekut* is opposite *hobah* Marmorstein translates the terms as 'merit' and 'guilt', although the natural translation is 'innocence' and 'guilt'. Thus he quotes the saying that God never reverses *zekut* and *hobah* to mean that 'merit and guilt are never interchanged', and he explains: 'Great merits, acquired by one, cannot lessen his burden of guilt, just as guilt does not diminish merits.'[26] This is, to be sure, a correct observation, but it does not seem to be a precise interpretation of the passage. The meaning, rather, is that God never treats innocence as if it were guilt nor guilt as if it were innocence; rather, he punishes guilt and rewards innocence.[27] We should note that the meaning of *zekut* as innocence as distinct from guilt (*hobah*) is standard in the literature.[28] An interesting instance is the comment on Lev. 7.34. The biblical passage reads: 'For the breast that is waved and the thigh that is offered I have taken from the people of Israel, out of the sacrifices of their peace offerings, and have given them to Aaron the priest and to his sons, as a perpetual due from the people of Israel.' The commentator asks why these sacrifices were taken from Israel. The answer is that they fell into guilt (*nithayyebu*). If this is the case, would Israel regain the offerings if they were innocent (*zaku*)? No, as the end of the biblical verse makes clear.[29] It would doubtless be possible to translate *zakah* here as 'if they had (sufficient) merit', but this is forcing the meaning of merit where it does not belong. The meaning is simply 'innocent'. Similarly (although Marmorstein does not give this example), *zekut* is contrasted with *hobah* when the latter means monetary debt. In this case, *zekut* means not 'merit' but 'freedom from debt'.[30]

The point in all this is not that Marmorstein is completely wrong (one who 'acts correctly' does deserve to be rewarded for it), but that the consistent translation of *zakah* and its cognates as 'merit' obscures the actual nuances of the terminology and seems to imply a consistent and thoroughgoing 'doctrine'.

2. We saw above that the Rabbis regarded it as natural to enquire, when a

---

[26] Ibid., p. 7; citing Sifre Deut. 347.

[27] Above, section 6 n. 11, and the discussion in the text there. Cf. Sifre Deut. 144 and Sanhedrin 4.1, below n. 89.

[28] See, for example, Sanhedrin 3.6 (*zakka'i*, 'innocent', in contrast to *hayyab*, 'guilty'); Sanhedrin 4.1 (*zekut*, 'innocence' or 'acquittal', in contrast to *hobah*, 'guilt'); Sanhedrin 3.7 (*mezakkeh*, 'declare innocent', in contrast to *mehayyebin*, 'declare guilty'). Similarly, I would take *kaf hoban* and *kaf zekut* to refer to the sides (of the scale) of innocence and guilt, rather than merit and guilt (as Marmorstein, p. 9).

[29] Sifra Tsav pereq 17.5 (to 7.34).

[30] Gittin 8.3. *Patar* is used as the opposite of *hub* to mean exempt from a requirement, free from an obligation or not liable under a certain law. See Bekhoroth 4.4: if he declared free of debt (*zikkah*) one who was really indebted (*hayyab*), he must make restitution. But if he was an expert, he is exempt (*patur*) from the requirement to make restitution.

man received a reward, by what merit he deserved it.[31] Now we must note that these rewards for merit are almost without exception quite concrete historical rewards and are not soteriological. That is, the conception of reward for merit does not imply that one *earns salvation* by good deeds. When New Testament scholars take exception to the Rabbinic idea of merit as indicating a legalistic works-righteousness, they seem to assume that it is precisely salvation which is being merited, but this is not the case. To recall an example already given, we saw that the tribe of Judah merited kingship since they first crossed the Sea. We may cite some other examples. Joshua's appointment as the leader of the people was 'because of his merits',[32] Aaron merited the emoluments of the priesthood and his descendants merited their continuation,[33] David merited kingship,[34] Benjamin merited that the Shekinah should dwell in his portion of the land (the location of the Temple),[35] Moses merited being made messenger between the Israelites and their Father in heaven,[36] the Israelites merited having prophets raised up among them and the early arrival of a prophet was 'because of their merit' (*bizekut*),[37] and Israel merited that they entered a land in which the houses were already full and the cisterns already hewn.[38] Similarly, it is frequently repeated that the land of Israel was given to the Israelites because of their merits.[39] One who occupies himself in the study of the Torah 'merits many things' and 'is deserving of (*kedai hu' lo* the whole world'.[40] I have noted very few instances in which the world to come is specified as the reward of merit: Abraham inherited this world and the world to come as a reward for his faith;[41] one who executes justice (to his fellow man) has his days prolonged and 'merit[s] the life in the world to come'.[42] Such sayings are analogous to those which indicate that one who fulfils *one* commandment will have a share in the world to come,[43] and they do not lead to a theory that

---

[31] Above, section 4, p. 191.   [32] Sifre Num. 139 (185; to 27.17).

[33] Sifre Num. 117 (135; to 18.8): *bizekuteka, bizekut beneka.* On the other hand, Aaron could be said to have merited (*zikkah*) for both his righteous and his wicked descendants, since the giving of the priesthood was not conditional on obedience: Sifre Num. 119 (144; to 18.20).

[34] Sifre Num. 119 (144; to 18.20).

[35] Sifre Deut. 352 (412; to 33.12); cf. Mek. Beshallah 6 (114; I, 252–3 [ch. 7]; to 14.31): the fathers merited *and* the Holy Spirit rested upon them, that is, they merited *that* it rest upon them.

[36] Sifra Behuqqotai pereq 8.12 (to 26.46).

[37] Mek. Bahodesh 9 (237; II, 271; to 20.19): God was going to raise up a prophet, but the Israelites advanced it *bizekut*. This is one of the rare instances of *bizekut* without a following noun.

[38] Sifre Deut. 38 (76; to 11.10), referring to Deut. 6.11.

[39] Sifre Deut. 156 (208; to 17.14); ibid. 170 (217; to 18.9); ibid. 57 (124; to 11.31); cf. ibid. 179 (222; to 19.1).

[40] Aboth 6.1. Chapter 6 is a later baraita. See Epstein, *Mabo' le-Nosah*, p. 978.

[41] Mek. Beshallah 6 (114; I, 253 [ch. 7]; to 14.31). The term is *besakar*, 'as a reward', in Lauterbach's edition, but *bizekut* in Horovitz's.

[42] Mek. Mishpatim 18, end (315; III, 146 [Nezikin 18]; to 22.23[24]). It is possible that here *tizku l-* should be translated 'will attain to' or 'will succeed in reaching'. Frequently the connotations of acquiring, succeeding and deserving cannot be neatly distinguished. For another possible passage in this category, see section 9 n. 31 below.

[43] Above, section 6, pp. 133f.

salvation is earned by fulfilling more commandments than one has transgressions. In general, however, the rewards for merits are concrete and specific. In most instances they refer to God's gifts in biblical history.

Occasionally the reward of meritorious action is not specified. Thus one who 'steals away from his friend and goes and studies the words of the Torah' might be called a thief, but actually he 'acquires merit for himself' (*zokeh le'atsmo*).[44] The conclusion, however, implies the sort of merit in mind: he will in the end be appointed a leader of the community and the like. Similarly, the one who repents of *piggul* and *notar* and fasts on the Day of Atonement 'benefits himself' or 'merits for himself' and his descendants (*mezakkeh lo*).[45] Here the benefit is left quite unspecified. The contrast is with Adam, who brought death to himself and his descendants by transgressing one negative commandment. The introductory sentence indicates that the argument will show 'how great the reward of the righteous in the future to come' will be. Since God is readier to give good than to punish, and since he punished one transgression so severely, one should expect a great reward for one who fulfils commandments. The Rabbi does not actually name a reward which is greater than universal death, although the logic of the argument would seem to imply that he should.[46] The thrust of the argument is that God is readier to reward than to punish, but the reward is not named. At any rate, there is no doubt that the Rabbis believed that obedience is meritorious and that God would give appropriate rewards.

3. In considering the passages which have been or can be taken to imply the notion of a treasury of merits which can be dispensed to individuals who are deficient in merit, we may employ Schechter's division of the subject by generations, which has recently been repeated by Ziesler: the merits of contemporaries, of descendants and of the fathers.

The '*merits of contemporaries*' may be easily disposed of. Statements to the effect that the world is saved from destruction by the 'merits' of the pious in each generation[47] do not mean that such merits are transferred to other individuals, particularly not at the judgment. This is simply a way of emphasizing God's mercy, for he suspends his judgment against the world for the sake of a few. This sort of homiletical statement is probably based on

---

[44] Mek. Mishpatim 13 (295f.; III, 107f. [Nezikin 13]; to 22.3, end).

[45] Sifra Hobah parasha 12.10 (to 5.17). Billerbeck (S.-B. III, p. 230) translates *mezakkeh* as *Verdienst erwirbt*, 'gains merit'. This is not, however, a good contrast with the punishment for Adam's transgression. The latter did not earn demerits for Adam's descendants; it *harmed* them by causing their death (but not their damnation). A man's good action *benefits* his descendants; it does not earn them merits.

[46] Similarly, Paul argued that, if all men died because of Adam's trespass, 'much more' will God give grace because of Jesus Christ. But it is not clear that Paul had in mind a gift which benefits *all* men 'much more' than Adam's trespass harmed them. The point of the affirmation is clear, but universal death is hard to top. See Rom. 5.17.

[47] Aboth 5.1: the righteous sustain the world; see further Ziesler, *Righteousness*, p. 123; Schechter, *Aspects*, p. 190.

such biblical passages as Gen. 18.22f. ('for the sake of ten I will not destroy [Sodom]'),[48] and implies no doctrine of, nor transfer of, merits.

Two Tannaitic passages, both connected with R. Simeon b. Yohai, have been taken to indicate the transfer of the merits of a pious contemporary. According to one, the Rabbi is said to have said, 'I am able to exempt the whole world from judgment from the day that I was born until now', etc.[49] The translator of the Soncino edition takes R. Simeon's saying to refer to his suffering, which presumably sufficed as punishment for the sins of others.[50] The saying is certainly curious and difficult, but there is nothing in it about 'merits'. The other passage is found in p. Berakoth:[51] R. Hezekiah said in the name of R. Jeremiah, 'Thus said R. Simeon ben Yohai: "If Abraham will intercede for (the people of) his generation until mine, I can intercede for (the people of) my generation until the end of all generations,"' etc. The verb is the *pi'el* of *qarab*, and 'intercede' is the only reasonable meaning.[52] Marmorstein translates it 'justify by merit',[53] and thus introduces here the 'doctrine of merits'. The passage, however, clearly refers to the intercessory prayer of a righteous man which, we know from another context, availeth much.[54] It might be possible to discuss a few other Tannaitic passages in this category, but it is pointless to do so. There is no evidence that the good deeds of one person in a generation were believed to make up for the transgressions of others by a transfer of merits.

The *'merits of descendants'* are somewhat more complicated to discuss, although here too we shall see that there is no doctrine of a transfer of merits. Schechter, who thematized the *'Zachuth* of a Pious Posterity', was aware of the shortage of early material evidencing the theme and attempted to deal with it. He refers to only one Tannaitic passage 'in favour of this doctrine', which he found in a manuscript of the Yemenite Midrash Ha-Gadol to Numbers.[55] He refers only to the folio of a manuscript in his possession, and I have been unable to find the passage in the edited text which is now avail-

---

[48] So also Schechter, ibid.

[49] Sukkah 45b; ET, p. 209; cited by Marmorstein, *Merits*, p. 52, as referring to R. Simeon's merits.

[50] Vicarious expiatory suffering is not a major theme in the Tannaitic literature, but it does occur. See Mek. Pisha 1 (4; I, 10f.; to 12.1): the patriarchs and prophets gave their lives for Israel. Cf. Moore, *Judaism* I, pp. 546–52; III, pp. 164f. (n. 250); Lohse, *Märtyrer und Gottesknecht*, p. 104; Thyen, *Sündenvergebung*, pp. 72f.

[51] P. Berakoth 13d (Krotoschin; 12d in the Venice ed.), near bottom (9.3).

[52] So also H. Freedman in the Soncino translation of the parallel in Gen. Rab. 35.2 (ET, p. 283).

[53] Marmorstein, *Merits*, p. 52.

[54] James 5.16. On intercessory prayer, see Mek. Mishpatim 18 (313f.; III, 143 [Nezikin 18]; to 22.22[23]). See further R. Le Déaut, 'Aspects de l'intercession dans la Judaïsme ancien', *JSJ* 1, 1970, pp. 35–57. We may note, however, that most of his examples of intercessory prayers by the dead for the living (p. 45 n. 1) actually refer to the prayers of the righteous at the time of judgment (so I Enoch 9.3,5, for example).

[55] Schechter, *Aspects*, p. 197 n. 2. The statement that 'children save their parents from the judgement of Gehenna', which Schechter (p. 197) also quotes from the Midrash Ha-Gadol, is not described by him as Tannaitic.

able.[56] Doubtless a sufficiently diligent search would reveal it, but for the present it is difficult to evaluate the passage which he quoted in the second half of p. 197 to prove that God suspends 'the judgement of the ancestors till their great-grandchildren are grown up, by whose righteousness they might be relieved', since he does not explicitly say that the particular passage quoted is to be attributed to a Tanna. Further, Schechter's quotations of Rabbinic material are frequently paraphrastic, which renders interpretation doubtful if the source cannot be found. He also refers, however, to the Mekilta of R. Simeon b. Yohai to Ex. 20.5, apparently intending to indicate that such a view may be found there:[57] The passage does provide a discussion of the question of the punishment of descendants for the sins of the fathers, but I find no reference to the salvation of the fathers by the merits of their descendants. The only saying which might be taken as supporting the view that the punishment of ancestors is suspended, mitigated or removed by the merit of their descendants is this: 'R. Judah says: I (God) gather their transgressions into my hand and suspend them for four generations, as in the case of Jehu ben Nimshi; for thus it says, "Your sons shall sit upon the throne of Israel to the fourth generation" (II Kings 15.12), and it happened thus.' But here the suspension is not in order to permit the father (in this case, Jehu) to be redeemed by the merits of his descendants. Rather, the punishment for Jehu's sins, which should, according to some passages in the Bible, fall on his descendants, was 'suspended' for four generations, during which time Jehu's descendants reigned in Israel. After that time the kingdom was destroyed, which is here seen as the delayed punishment for Jehu's sins. Since we do not find the 'doctrine' of the salvation of fathers by the merits of their sons here, it is perhaps permissible to remain sceptical about its existence during the Tannaitic period, especially since Midrash Ha-Gadol cannot be considered the most reliable source for Tannaitic traditions which appear nowhere else. One may hazard the guess that the author of Midrash Ha-Gadol, in the passage to which Schechter refers, has reversed a Tannaitic tradition about the suspension of punishment of children so that it becomes a suspension of punishment of fathers.

Marmorstein begins his discussion of the 'merits of the children' which benefit their parents by narrating a long and apocryphal story about a child reared by R. Akiba after the death of his wicked father.[58] Akiba taught the boy, on account of which his father was redeemed from perdition. This shows at least that such a view was current by the early medieval period. Even here, however, there may be no idea of a transfer of merits, but only of the effect of prayer for the dead. In any case, the story is not Tannaitic. The other

[56] Ed. Z. M. Rabinowitz, 1967. There is an earlier edition by Fisch.
[57] Schechter, *Aspects*, p. 197 n. 2.
[58] Marmorstein, *Merits*, pp. 156f. Marmorstein recognizes that the story is late.

principal passage cited by Marmorstein requires closer analysis and must be quoted in full. It is a comment on Eccl. 4.1:[59]

R. Judah says: It refers to the children who are buried early in life through [*b–*] the sins of their fathers in this world. In the Hereafter they will range themselves with the band of the righteous, while their fathers will be ranged with the band of the wicked. They will speak before Him: 'Lord of the universe, did we not die early only because of [*b–*] the sins of our fathers? Let our fathers come over to us through our merits' [*bezakiyotenu*]. He replies to them, 'Your fathers sinned also after your death, and their wrongdoings accuse them.' R. Judah b. R. Ilai said in the name of R. Joshua b. Levi:[60] At that time Elijah . . . will be there to suggest a defence. He will say to the children: 'Speak before Him, "Lord of the universe, which Attribute of Thine predominates, that of Grace or Punishment? Surely the Attribute of Grace is great and that of Punishment small, yet we died through the sins of our fathers. If then the Attribute of Grace exceeds the other, how much more should our fathers come over to us!"' Therefore he says to them, 'Well have you pleaded; let them come over to you'; as it is written, *And they shall live with their children, and shall return* (Zech. 10.9), which means that they returned from the descent to Gehinnom and were rescued through the merit of [*bizekut*] their children. Therefore every man is under the obligation to teach his son Torah that he may rescue him from Gehinnom.

Marmorstein concludes that 'children, when very young, die for the sins of their parents, and save them, through the study of the Torah, from the punishment of Hell'.[61] The last clause, however, is an unlikely interpretation. The conclusion about teaching one's son the Torah is obviously secondary to the passage. The children succeed in convincing God by using a *qal vaḥomer* argument: God's mercy is greater than his punishment. If his punishment is so strong that it kills children prematurely because of their parents' transgressions, all the more should God's mercy restore parents to their children. It is this successful plea, based on sound Rabbinic logic, which moves God. There is no mention of the transfer of merits. The children's first appeal, which is denied, is that the parents can 'come over to us *bezakiyotenu*'. This does not mean 'come over to us through the transfer of our merits to them', as the answer makes clear. The refusal of this appeal on the grounds that the fathers sinned after the death of the children indicates that the children's premature death was caused by the sins of the parents. Those sins, having been punished, need not be punished by having the fathers go to Gehinnom. But since the parents subsequently sinned, the appeal is denied. Thus *bezakiyotenu* does not mean 'by the transfer of our supererogatory merits', but 'on our account', or possibly, 'in consideration

[59] Eccl. Rab. 4.1 (12b); ET, p. 110; cited by Marmorstein, *Merits*, p. 158.
[60] There is a confusion here in the tradition, since R. Judah b. Ilai was a Tanna and R. Joshua b. Levi was an Amora. The commentator Ze'eb Wolf Einhorn, ad loc., suggests that the text should read simply 'R. Joshua', and that R. Joshua b. Hananiah was meant.
[61] Marmorstein, *Merits*, p. 158.

of our innocent [deaths]'. In any case, this appeal is not efficacious.

The successful plea includes the phrase '*bizekut* their children'. Here it is best to render the phrase 'on account of their children', for what is in mind is not the children's supererogatory merits but their successful argument. The parents are saved from 'the band of the wicked' by the children's appeal to the mercy of God and thus 'on account of their children'. The concluding statement about teaching one's son the Torah obviously goes back to the view expressed in the apocryphal story about R. Akiba and the son of the sinner. Such a statement supposes that a man *will be outlived* by his son, whose learning of the Torah will justify his father. Teaching the Torah counts as a good deed by the father and also permits the son to pray on his father's behalf, perhaps while the son still lives, as in the apocryphal story. But this view is at odds with the rest of Eccl. Rab. 4.1, according to which the children *die before the parents* and the plea takes place in heaven, and in which the reason for the salvation of the fathers is not the pious lives of their sons after the fathers' death, but the children's successful plea before God. There thus appears to be no clear evidence from the Tannaitic period – I am inclined to think none at all – for the view that children's merits are transferred to their ancestors.

At most we have here a view of a *transfer of punishment* from the parents to the children. The death of the children counts as punishment for the sins of the parents up until the time of the children's death. The Bible (Ex. 20.5; 34.7) states that the sins of the fathers are visited on the children. Although most Rabbis followed Ezekiel's rejection of that view (Ezek. 18) in favour of individual responsibility,[62] for some purposes the view of Ex. 20.5 could still be employed; and we see its continuance in the passage under discussion. Even here, however, the biblical view is moderated by the assumption of 'no double jeopardy'. If the sons are punished for the fathers' transgressions, the fathers themselves are not punished for those same transgressions. The entire view that descendants suffer for their ancestors' sins is, as indicated, very rare in the Tannaitic literature, but it is interesting, since it leads to something very like a view of vicarious atonement. The atonement brought by suffering, however, even vicarious suffering, does not have anything to do with a transfer of merits which are weighed in the balance. The children in the story save their parents from punishment (1) by being punished in their stead for the parents' sins until the time of the children's death, and (2) by appealing to God's mercy on behalf of their parents. No merits change hands, however.

---

[62] See Schechter, *Aspects*, pp. 185–8; Makkoth 24a (ET, p. 173); Mek. of R. Simeon to Ex. 20.5 (p. 148); Sifre Deut. 329 (380; to 32.39); Midrash Tannaim to Deut. 32.39 (p. 202); Sifra Behuqqotai pereq 8.2 (to 26.39): fathers are not judged by the deeds of their sons, nor sons by the deeds of their fathers; T. Sanhedrin 8.4: the righteous may not rely on the argument that 'we are the children of a righteous man'.

But what of the '*merits of the fathers*'? Is there not here a view of the transfer of merits? It appears not. In section 4 above, when discussing the explanations of the election, we quoted or referred to many of the passages in which the *zekut* of one of the fathers is mentioned in Tannaitic literature.[63] The dominant use of the phrase *bizekut* somebody or something is in reference to the question of why God brought Israel out of Egypt. He did so *bizekut* Abraham, *bizekut* the Israelites' observing the commandment of circumcision, *bizekut* the bones of Joseph and the like.[64] The force of the phrase in this usage is, as Moore and Sjöberg argued, prepositional or at least largely prepositional: 'for Abraham's sake' and the like. Sometimes no meritorious deed is involved. Thus in R. Eleazar b. Azariah's saying that God brought Israel out of Egypt *bizekut* Abraham, the proof text is that 'He remembered His holy word unto Abraham His servant'; that is, God brought Israel out of Egypt 'for Abraham's sake', because he had made a promise to Abraham.[65] More often, the reference is to a meritorious act. Thus R. Banaah's saying is this: 'Because of the merit of the deed which Abraham their father did' (*bizekut mitsvah*) God brought Israel out of Egypt.[66] Although *bizekut* itself may be translated as a preposition ('for the sake of the deed'), the reference is to a meritorious deed. For this reason it is not incorrect to translate *bizekut* as 'because of the merit of'.

We may give some other instances of the phrase *zekut 'abot* or *zekut* followed by the name of an individual patriarch. In Sifre Deut. the anonymous comment on Deut. 13.18(17) is that God will show the Israelites mercy and multiply them ' "as he swore to your fathers". – Everything is for the sake of your fathers' (*bizekut 'aboteka*).[67] The same comment is made on the phrase 'give you the land which he promised to give to your fathers'.[68] In these instances the reference is to God's promise, and 'for the sake of' is clearly the better translation. Individual merit is probably in mind, however, in the following passage:[69]

R. Joshua says: When Miriam died, the well was taken away, but it then came back because of the merit of Moses and Aaron [*bizekut* Moses and Aaron]. When Aaron died, the cloud of glory was taken away, but it then came back because of the merit of Moses. When Moses died, all three, the well, the cloud of glory and the manna, were taken away and returned no more.

There are two other contexts in which the merits or deeds of the fathers are referred to. One is that they can (or cannot) suspend punishment for transgression. An instance of the negative is this:

---

[63] See above, section 4, pp. 90–2.
[64] See Mek. Pisha 16 (62; I, 140f.; to 13.4); Mek. Beshallah 3 (98f.; I, 218–20 [ch. 4]; to 14.15).
[65] Lauterbach, I, 140.
[66] Lauterbach, I, 218.
[67] Sifre Deut. 96 (157; to 13.18[17]); so also ibid. 184 (225; to 19.8).
[68] Sifre Deut. 184.
[69] Mek. Vayassa' 5 (173; II, 128 [ch. 6]; to 16.35); paralleled in Sifre Deut. 305 (326; to 31.14).

R. Joshua b. Karḥa says: Great is circumcision, for no merit of Moses [*zekut le-mosheh*] could suspend the punishment for its neglect even for one hour. . . . Rabbi says: Great is circumcision, for all the merits of Moses availed him not in the time of his trouble about it. He was going to bring out Israel from Egypt and yet because for one hour he was negligent about the performance of circumcision, the angel sought to kill him, as it is said: 'And it came to pass on the way at the lodging place,' etc. (Ex. 4.24).[70]

On the other hand, the deeds of the fathers were said to be sufficient that, in consideration of them, God withholds the punishment of the world which would otherwise befall it. The comment is on Lev. 26.42 ('If they confess their iniquity . . . then I will remember my covenant with Jacob, and . . . with Isaac and . . . with Abraham. . .'.):[71]

Why are the fathers named in reverse order? Because if the deeds (Heb. singular, *ma'aseh*) of Abraham are not sufficient, the deeds of Isaac [are]; and if the deeds of Isaac are not sufficient, the deeds of Jacob [are]. [The deeds of] any one of them are sufficient that [God] will suspend [punishment] for the world on his account (*begino*).

Somewhat similarly, in seeking to reconcile the statement of Ex. 20.5 (God punishes children for the sins of their fathers) with Ezek 18.20 (he does not do so), an anonymous Rabbi comments that 'if the fathers were virtuous (*zakka'in*), God suspends [punishment] for the children, but if not, he does not suspend it for them'.[72] What is being suspended here, however, is not the punishment of the children's own sin, but that of their fathers.

The second context in which the deeds of the fathers are referred to indicates that they help subsequent generations. Thus in the Mekilta's discussion of the war with Amalek there are several references to the deeds of the fathers.[73] According to R. Eleazar of Modiim, in the battle the Israelites should rely on the deeds (*ma'aseh*) of the fathers.[74] According to the same Rabbi the passage which says that Aaron and Hur held up Moses's hands during the battle indicates that Moses 'turned to' the deeds of the fathers for strength to hold up his hands.[75] Thus the deeds of the fathers were considered beneficial, but they did not establish a treasury of transferrable merits.[76]

---

[70] Mek. Jethro Amalek I (191f.; II, 169f. [Amalek 3]; to 18.3). On the traditions about Moses's being threatened with death because he delayed circumcising his son, see Vermes, *Scripture and Tradition*, pp. 178–92.

[71] Sifra Behuqqotai pereq 8.7 (Weiss, 8.6). On the merit of one person suspending the punishment of the world, see also above, section 6, pp. 144–6. That an individual who has merit has punishment suspended is said in connection with the suspected adulteress: Sotah 3.4; Sifre Num. 8 (p. 15; to 5.15), where there is a discussion of how long punishment is suspended. R. Simeon b. Yohai argues that in this case merit does not suspend punishment.

[72] Mek. of R. Simeon b. Yohai to Ex. 20.5 (p. 148).

[73] Mek. Beshallah Amalek 1 (179f.; II, 142–5; to 17.9–12).

[74] Lauterbach, II, 142.   [75] Lauterbach, II, 145.

[76] Cf. the third-century saying by R. Gamaliel b. R. Judah ha-Nasi (Aboth 2.2): the fathers' *zekut*

There appear, then, to be several contexts in which the merit or deeds of the fathers are mentioned: (1) God performed certain deeds for Israel (e.g. parting the Sea) 'for the sake of the fathers', since he had given them promises. (2) God performed certain deeds for Israel because of the good deeds ('merit') of the fathers. (3) In view of the merit of the fathers, God does not punish the world as otherwise he would (the world being worthy of destruction). (4) The good deeds of the fathers benefit their descendants in given historical situations. *There is nowhere in Tannaitic literature a reference to a treasury of merits which can be transferred at the judgment.*

In discussing the 'doctrine of merits', Ziesler says that 'very often' the mention of the merits of the fathers is in the context of 'past or even present realities', and 'not the final Judgment'.[77] This is almost correct. In the Tannaitic literature, the context is *never* the final judgment. Merits *never* counterbalance demerits at the judgment, although, in consideration of them, God may suspend punishment.

We should here recall a point made at the beginning of section 6. It is frequently said that good deeds are rewarded by God in the world to come, rather than in this world, and in this sense one may speak of storing up treasure in heaven. Thus in T. Peah 4.18 a king who gives his earthly treasure to the poor is said to be storing up treasure in heaven or for the world to come. This means only that he will be rewarded for his charity in the world to come, and it has no more to do with a treasury of merits which cover his own or someone else's transgressions than does the 'treasure in heaven' of Matt. 6.19–21.

This is not to say that there is no sense of the solidarity of benefit in the Tannaitic literature. We should recall that it was in this sense that Schechter discussed what he called 'the doctrine of the merits of the fathers'.[78] The deeds of the fathers obviously benefit their descendants, for they cause God to remember the covenant, to do good deeds for Israel, and to suspend punishment for transgression. The existence of righteous contemporaries benefits all, for it is for their sake that God does not inflict the punishment which the world deserves. Further, a man's good deeds are of benefit to himself, since God is faithful to reward obedience. None of this, however, amounts to a transfer of merits, to a view that merits offset demerits, or, in

---

helps subsequent generations and their righteousness endures for ever. *Zekut* 'helps', but is not transferred. In Mek. Beshallah 5 (106; I, 235 [ch. 6]; to 14.22) the *zekut* of the righteous is said to help them (not others), but in very mundane ways.

[77] Ziesler, *Righteousness*, p. 123.

[78] So also Kadushin, *Conceptual Approach*, p. 47: '*Zekut 'Abot* is a sub-concept of God's justice, connoting that God rewards children for the good deeds of their fathers. Reflected in this concept is the view that fathers and sons constitute a single personality, a corporate personality. For Abraham's kindness to the angels, for example, God rewards the children measure for measure [referring to Lauterbach, I, p. 184], and yet the word *lo*, "to him" (l. 194), implies that the reward was given "to him", that is, to Abraham'.

fact, to anything which is properly called a 'doctrine of merits'. The only 'doctrine' is that God is faithful to reward and punish. We now see a further nuance, that descendants may be rewarded for their fathers' good deeds. But transgressions are atoned for or are punished, not offset; and men are rewarded for their good deeds, they do not *achieve* the world to come by piling up a 'treasury of merits', nor by drawing on one stored up by someone else. In short, the Tannaitic discussions of *zekut* do not accord it any place in 'Rabbinic soteriology'.[79]

Tsadaq

In considering *tsadaq* and its cognates, we are principally concerned to correct two misunderstandings of the significance of being called *tsaddiq*, 'righteous', in Tannaitic literature. Both depend on the traditional Christian view of Rabbinic soteriology. Ziesler has defined the 'righteous man' as 'one whose righteous deeds – and therefore merits – outweigh his evil deeds – and therefore demerits'.[80] According to Kertelge, being righteous in Rabbinic Judaism depends on obeying the law (which is correct), but this is equated with *earning* and *securing* the state of salvation, which is incorrect.[81] The study will be extended, however, to consider the principal uses of all the cognate nouns and verbs.[82] It will be useful to do this, since the terms are important for comparing Judaism and Paul and since Ziesler's recent study makes more use of Amoraic material than of Tannaitic.[83] The study is facilitated by the fact that it is relatively easy to summarize the principal uses of the various terms. We begin with the verb.

In the *qal*, the verb usually means 'to be cleared in court' and is not really distinguishable from the use of the *zakah* root to mean 'innocent'.[84] In the *pi'el*, the most common use in the Tannaitic material is in the phrase 'to

---

[79] On spontaneous good deeds beyond the letter of the law (which are not, however, works of supererogation), see Urbach, *Ḥazal*, pp. 291–3 (ET, pp. 330–3); Kadushin, *The Rabbinic Mind*, p. 80.

[80] Ziesler, *Righteousness*, p. 122.

[81] Kertelge, *'Rechtfertigung' bei Paulus*, p. 42.

[82] An exhaustive study of *tsedeq* and *tsedaqah* in Tannaitic literature has now been carried out by B. Przybylski, *The Concept of Righteousness in Matthew*, unpublished PhD thesis, McMaster University, 1975. I am indebted to Dr Przybylski for several references, as well as for critical comments on this analysis.

[83] Mach's study. *Der Zaddik*, also makes no distinction between Tannaitic and Amoraic literature.

[84] P. Sanhedrin 22b, top (4.3); cited by Jastrow, s.v. *tsadaq*. The sentence reads: 'Is it the case that if he were found innocent (*tsadaq*) in your court he will [necessarily] be found innocent (*yitsdaq*) in mine? [No, for] Scripture teaches, "I will not justify the wicked"'. The parallel in Mek. Mishpatim 20 (328; III, 171–2 [Kaspa 3]; to 23.7) reads: 'Is it the case that just as he came out from your court acquitted (*zakka'i*), he also comes out [acquitted] from mine?' (my translation). (The word *zakka'i* in the first clause is accepted by Horovitz and Lauterbach, but not by Friedmann (f. 100a); it is supported only by the Yalkut. See the apparatuses of Horovitz and Friedmann. In any case, it appears immediately before the sentence quoted.) (These passages obviously refer to a guilty man who could not be convicted in court for lack of evidence. God nevertheless regards him as guilty. They do not contradict the rule [Horayoth 1.1] that one who acts on the basis of a court's decision is innocent even if the court was in error.)

justify the sentence', i.e. to accept God's judgment as just.[85] It may also mean to make something correct, as in the phrase 'make the scales just'.[86] The *hif'il*, 'to justify', also has a forensic connotation. When the passage in Ex. 23.7 says 'I will not justify the wicked', it is clearly understood to mean 'hold innocent'.[87]

The noun *tsedeq* is fairly rare in the Tannaitic literature except in connection with its use in the Bible or in the phrase *ger tsedeq*. Sometimes its meaning cannot be specified, but sometimes it is quite clear. Difficult to determine is the understanding of *tsidqo* in Eccl. 7.15: 'there is a righteous man (*tsaddiq*) who perishes in his righteousness (*betsidqo*)'. The Rabbinic comment apparently takes the preposition *bet* to mean 'with', for the comment is this: 'the righteous man perishes but his *tsedeq* [remains] with him'.[88] It appears from the preceding story that his *tsedeq* was a good deed. Perhaps 'righteousness' is as good a translation as any. In Sifre Num. 133 (176; to 27.1) *tsedeq* refers to the righteous quality of a man who grows up in a wicked household but nevertheless acts correctly. Often, however, *tsedeq* is taken to be the same as *tsedaqah* in its meaning of 'leniency' or 'charity' (discussed immediately below):

'Justice (*tsedeq*) and only justice shalt thou pursue.' – Whence do we know that if one leaves a court [having been declared] innocent (*zakka'i*). they do not reconsider his case to declare him guilty (*le-ḥobah*)? Scripture says, '*tsedeq* and only *tsedeq* shalt thou pursue'. In the case of one who left [having been declared] guilty (*ḥayyab*), whence do we know that they do reconsider his case to declare him innocent (*le-zekut*)? It is said, '*tsedeq* and only *tsedeq* shalt thou pursue'.[89]

That *tsedeq* means leniency is also clear in the comment on Lev. 19.15: ' "In *tsedeq* shall you judge your neighbour." – Judge every man on the side of innocence (*lekaf zekut*).'[90] Similarly, the word *tsedeq* in Isa. 58.8 is under-

---

[85] Sifra Shemini Millu'im 23, 24, 28; Mek. Shirata 9 (145; II, 67; to 15.12). In the last passage the verb (צדקתם) lacks the *yod* which usually distinguishes the *pi'el*. This is probably a spelling variant, however, for the first of the three times the phrase is used in Sifra Shemini Millu'im 23, the verb also lacks the *yod*. It is doubtful that either verb is *qal*. The same phrase ('justify the sentence') appears also with the *hif'il* participle in Sifra Shemini Millu'im 23. In all these cases the verb is followed by the preposition '*al* with a pronominal ending (עליו, etc.). In Sifre Deut. 307 (346; to 32.4), the phrase with the *hif'il* participle is used without '*al*. The one who 'justifies the judgment' (*matsdiq et ha-din*) subsequently says, 'you judged me well' (יפה נידנתי).

[86] Sifra Qedoshim pereq 8.7 (to 19.36).

[87] P. Sanhedrin 22b and Mek. Mishpatim 20, n. 84 above. We should note that Ziesler (*Righteousness*, p. 113) says that the *pi'el* and *hif'il* both can mean 'treat generously' or 'be liberal', citing some of the passages cited by Jastrow (*Dictionary*, p. 1263). All the passages referred to by Jastrow, however, are attributed to third-century Palestinian Amoraim, not to Tannaim (except Num. Rab. 2.8, cited by Jastrow but not by Ziesler, which is Amoraic and anonymous), and e find no Tannaitic passages in which either form of the verb bears this meaning. This is a subject which requires closer investigation before it can be concluded, with Ziesler, that the usage may illuminate a Pauline phrase.

[88] Sifra Emor parasha 1.14 (to 21.3).

[89] Sifre Deut. 144 (199; to 16.20). Cf. Sanhedrin 4.1, where the rule is said to apply to capital cases. Non-capital cases may be reversed in either direction. On the conversion of 'justice' in the Bible to 'love' or 'charity' in Rabbinic literature, see Kadushin, *Organic Thinking*, p. 225.

[90] Sifra Qedoshim pereq 4.4 (to 19.15).

stood to refer to one's almsgiving[91] or to a deed of mercy (Moses gathered Joseph's bones).[92] When used of God, however, *tsedeq* may also refer to his strict justice. Thus *tsedeq* and *mishpaṭ* in Pss. 89.15 and 97.2 are both taken to refer to God's administration of strict justice (*din*).[93] *Tsedeq* sometimes means 'what is right': one teaches *tsedeq*;[94] or the humble character appropriate to a righteous man.[95]

In one use *tsedeq* is virtually adjectival. The *ger tsedeq* is a true proselyte. He is distinguished from the *ger toshab*, who does not make a complete conversion, although, as a resident alien, he keeps some of the Jewish laws.[96]

When used of a human action, the noun *tsedaqah*, 'righteousness', usually means alms or charity.[97] The *gabba'e tsedaqah* are the managers or collectors of charity in Jewish communities.[98] There is a classical distinction between *tsedaqah* and *gemilut ḥasadim*, 'deeds of loving-kindness':

Tsedaqah and *gemilut ḥasadim* are equal to all the *mitsvot* in the Torah, except that *tsedaqah* [can be done only] for the living, while *gemilut ḥasadim* [can be done] for the living and the dead; *tsedaqah* [can be done only] for the poor, while *gemilut ḥasadim* [can be done] for the poor and the rich; *tsedaqah* [can be done only] with money, while *gemilut ḥasadim* [can be done] with money and with one's person. (T. Peah 4.19)

Thus, although the two are equal, *gemilut ḥasadim* is of wider scope.[99] Washing the dead is one of the acts which constitutes *gemilut ḥasadim* but not *tsedaqah*.[100] Kadushin has correctly argued that the connotation of charity in Rabbinic literature is love of one's neighbour,[101] but there are only rare

---

[91] T. Peah 4.18.

[92] Sifre Num. 106 (105; to 12.15).

[93] Mek. Shabbata 1 (344; III, 2c 5; to 31.17).

[94] Sifre Deut. 144 (199; to 16.19).

[95] Sifre Deut. 334 (384; to 32.44).

[96] Sifra Behar parasha 5.1 (to 25.35); ibid. pereq 8.1 (in both cases the *ger toshab* is one who eats *nebelot*, meat of animals which were improperly slaughtered or which died a natural death); T. Arakhin 5.9; Mek. Baḥodesh 7 (230; II, 255; to 20.10); Mek. Mishpatim 18 (312; III, 141 [Nezikin 18]; to 22.20 – *ger tsedeq* contrasted with 'fearers of Heaven'); Mek. Mishpatim 20 (331; III, 178 [Kaspa 3]; to 23.12 – a *ger toshab* may do work on the Sabbath which an Israelite may do on a holy day). In the last passage a variant to *ger tsedeq* is *ger tsaddiq* (see Horovitz's apparatus), which indicates the adjectival meaning of *tsedeq* in this usage. Cf. 'just balances', etc., Sifra Qedoshim pereq 8.7 (to 19.36).

[97] Aboth 5.13; Baba Kamma 10.1; and very frequently, especially in the Tosefta.

[98] Demai 3.1; Kiddushin 4.5; and elsewhere.

[99] Lieberman (*The Tosefta* I, p. 60) comments that even though the two are equal, *gemilut ḥasadim* is preferable. He takes the word *'ella'* (translated here 'except') to indicate the preference. (*'Ella'* is missing in the parallel in p. Peah 15b-c [1.1], where there are a few other verbal differences.) In the parallel in Sukkah 49b, *gemilut ḥasadim* is said to be 'more than' *tsedaqah*, and the English translator in the Soncino edition (p. 233) takes the phrase to mean 'superior to'. In the present case, it seems more accurate to take *'ella'* to indicate simple distinction rather than preference and to understand 'more than' literally. The comment seems not to imply a value judgment, but only a definition of the scope of the terms. The passages are also cited and discussed by Mach, *Der Zaddik*, pp. 19-20.

[100] Just as God is called *tsaddiq* (see below) and has attributed to him *tsedaqah*, so he is pictured in the later literature as performing some of the deeds which qualify as *gemilut ḥasadim*, burying the dead, attending weddings and the like: Gen. Rab. 8.13; ARN 4.

[101] See M. Kadushin, *The Rabbinic Mind*, p. 110, and the further references cited there; *Conceptual Approach*, p. 11.

instances in which *tsedaqah* itself, when applied to man's action, means love or goodness in general rather than 'alms'. In T. Sanhedrin 1.3 David's *tsedaqah*, 'mercy', is contrasted with his *mishpat*, 'strict justice' (II Sam. 8.15), and in T. Sanhedrin 1.5 the judge who condemns one who is in the wrong is said to do him a 'kindness', *tsedaqah*, in punishing him for his misdeed. The only other possibility would seem to be Hillel's famous saying, 'The more *tsedaqah* the more peace' (Aboth 2.7), but here the precise meaning is not certain. In Aboth 2.2 *tsedaqah* means 'righteousness' (//*zekut*, virtue), and it may mean 'what is right' with respect to human action in Sifre Deut. 277 (295; to 24.13).

When used of God, *tsedaqah* refers to his charity or mercy towards man:[102]

'Thy *tsedaqah* is like the mountains of God' (Ps. 36.7[6]): R. Simeon b. Yohai said: Just as the mountains press down the deep, so that it does not rise up and flood the world, so *tsedaqah* presses down the quality of strict justice (*middat ha-din*) and punishing (*pur-'anut*), so that it does not come to the world.

The adjective *tsaddiq* is the general term for one who is properly religious.[103] Quite often it is simply contrasted with *rasha'*, 'wicked', with no further specification or description.[104] Other times, the word *tsaddiq* appears without even the opposite *rasha'* to help define it. It is then usually translated 'saint' or simply 'righteous'.[105] *Tsaddiq* is especially attached to the great men of Israel's past, and to Moses in particular.[106] Others called *tsaddiq* are Abraham, Isaac, Jacob, Joshua, Samuel, David and Mordecai;[107] the list is not exhaustive.[108] Further, God himself is called *tsaddiq*,[109] and men are urged to be righteous in imitation of him.[110] In Tannaitic literature,

[102] Tanhuma Noah 8 (Buber's ed., I, p. 34). See further Kadushin, *Organic Thinking*, pp. 132f., 303; 'The Rabbinic Concept of Israel', p. 89 n. 163; p. 95 n. 190.

[103] On the righteous man, see Moore, *Judaism* I, pp. 494–6; Mach, *Der Zaddik*.

[104] Negaim 12.5, end (=Sifra Metsora' parasha 5.12); Aboth 5.1; Sanhedrin 6.5; 8.5; 10.3,5; Mek. Pisha 11 (38; I, 85; to 12.22); Mek. Pisha 16 (60; I, 134–5; to 13.2); Mek. Shirata 1 (118; II, 6; to 15.1–God rejoices at the destruction of neither the wicked nor the righteous); Mek. Jethro Amalek 1 (195–6; II, 178 [Amalek 3]; to 18.12–God supplies the needs of both the righteous and the wicked; Lauterbach reads only *kesherim* instead of *kesherim* and *tsaddiqim*). In Negaim 12.5 and par. and in Mek. Pisha 11 the words are singular; in the other passages they are plural.

[105] Uktzin 3.12; Aboth 2.16; 6.8; Sifra Ahare parasha 9.7.

[106] Moses called *tsaddiq*: Nedarim 3.11; Sotah 1.9 ('Not of Moses alone have they spoken thus, but of all the righteous'); Mek. Jethro Amalek 1 (192; II, 170 [Amalek 3]; to 18.3); Mek. Shirata 9 (146; II, 69–70; to 15.13); and elsewhere.

[107] Moses, Jacob, David and Mordecai: Mek. Beshallah Amalek 2 (182; II, 149 [Amalek 2]; to 17.14); other biblical figures: Mek. Beshallah 5 (107; I, 237–8 [Beshallah 6]; to 14.24); Sifra Shemini Millu'im 23f.

[108] For a fuller list of biblical characters called 'righteous', see Mach, *Der Zaddik*, pp. 242–5.

[109] Sifra Ahare pereq 13.23 (quoting Ezra 9.15): 'Lord, God of Israel, thou art *tsaddiq*'; Mek. Pisha 16 (61; I, 138; to 13.3); cf. Ex. 9.27.

[110] In Sifre Deut. 49 (114; to 11.22), God is called both *tsaddiq* and *hasid*, and man is urged to be likewise. When God is called *tsaddiq*, it may refer to his strict justice (Mach, *Der Zaddik*, pp. 7f.) or his being fair: when Israel said that God is *tsaddiq*, God says, 'You have accepted my judgment upon you as just. . .'.; Mek. Shirata 9, cited in n. 85.

however, only one relatively recent individual was directly called *tsaddiq*: Simeon the *Tsaddiq*, one of the members of the Great Synagogue (Aboth 1.2; T. Sotah 13.7).[111]

The term *hasid*, 'pious', was apparently more readily applied to contemporaries: Jose the priest (Aboth 2.8; he was a pupil of R. Johanan b. Zakkai) and R. Jose Katnutha (Sotah 9.15, said to be the last of the *hasidim*, but his dates are uncertain). *Hasid* and *tsaddiq* are not always distinguishable, and many things which we shall say of the *tsaddiq* are said of the *hasid* in Aboth 5.10–14. On the character of the *hasid* see Büchler, *Types*; L. Jacobs, 'The Concept of Hasid'. Kadushin (*The Rabbinic Mind*, pp. 39f.) argues that a *hasid* 'is higher in the scale of virtue' than a *tsaddiq*, citing ARN 8 (Schechter's ed., p. 38), Niddah 17a and Rashi. Only Niddah 17a, however, might be Tannaitic, and it is doubtful if the distinction is early or widespread.[112] *Tsaddiqim* is more frequent in Rabbinic literature than *hasidim*, but nevertheless the Rabbis seem more reluctant to apply the term *tsaddiq* to an individual than the term *hasid*. It agrees with this that Lieberman (*Greek in Jewish Palestine*, p. 71) found that the word *tsaddiq* (or *dikaios*, the Greek equivalent) 'has not yet been found on the numerous tombstones of Beth She'arim'. *Hasid* (or the Greek *hosios*), however, was found often. Lieberman observed that 'in practical life this epithet [*tsaddiq*] was not abused in the first centuries c.e., despite its frequent appearance in Rabbinic literature'. But he did not observe that the plural is frequent, or the singular referring to an unspecified member of the group (a 'righteous man' in contrast to a 'wicked man'), while the title is directly applied to no individual who lived during the Tannaitic period.

On *qadosh* (holy) as an adjective applied to individuals, see Marmorstein, *The Names and Attributes of God*, pp. 213–17. On other titles, see Mach, *Der Zaddik*, pp. 3–8.

Although the meaning of *tsaddiq* thus often seems to be so vague and general as to defy precise definition, there are passages where greater precision of meaning appears. The righteous are not hard to complain to and their prayer is short. In the first case they are like God and in the second like Moses.[113] The righteous are opposite 'those who provoked Him'[114] and are those who have merit,[115] presumably from obeying God's commandments. A righteous man gives alms (T. Peah 4.18). The righteous are those who are to receive a reward in the future to come,[116] those who will be

---

[111] ARN 3 (ET, p. 31; Schechter's ed., p. 17) mentions a Benjamin the *Tsaddiq*, but there is no indication that the passage is Tannaitic. R. Akiba, in discussing the martyrdom of two other Rabbis, indirectly calls them *tsaddiq* by applying to their case Isa. 57.1 ('the righteous perishes'): Mek. Mishpatim 18 (313; III, 142 [Nezikin 18]; to 22.22 [23]). One Joseph b. Paksas has applied to him a similar phrase from Eccl. 7.15 (Sifra Emor parasha 1.14 [to 21.3]).

[112] Similarly Jacobs ('The Concept of Hasid', p. 151) argued that the *hasid* differs from the *tsaddiq* in going beyond the letter of the law. The contrast does not seem clear to me, however, and Jacobs's reference to Rosh Ha-Shanah 17b does not prove the point.

[113] Mek. Vayassa' 1 (155; II, 91; to 15.25).

[114] Mek. Vayassa' 3 (165; II, 110 [ch. 4]; to 16.13): 'If God thus provided for those who provoked Him, how much more will He in the future pay a good reward to the righteous.'

[115] Mek. Beshallah 5 (106; I, 235 [ch. 6]; to 14.22).

[116] Sifra Hobah parasha 12.10, above, section 5 n. 30; Mek. Vayassa' 3 (n. 114); and cf. Aboth 2.16:

treated as God's equals in the garden of Eden, i.e. the world to come.[117] In short, the righteous are those who obey God's will and fulfil their obligations:[118]

With regard to the righteous what does it say? 'When you besiege a city for a long time, making war against it, in order to take it, you should not destroy its trees by wielding an axe against them; for you may eat of them, but you shall not cut them down' (Deut. 20.19). One may argue *qal vahomer*: If to the trees, which neither see nor hear nor speak, God (*ha-Maqom*) showed consideration, because they bear fruit, that they should not be removed from the world, how much more will God show consideration to a man who does the Torah and the will of his father in heaven, that he should not be removed from the world!

The righteous mentioned in the first line are clearly those who 'do the Torah' and obey the will of God. There is a similar argument in Sifre Zuṭa to Num. 11.31: 'If thus God (*ha-Maqom*) has consideration for those who *transgress his will* in this world, how much more will he pay a good reward to *the righteous* in the world to come.' And R. Ishmael contrasts the righteous, 'who accepted the Torah', with the wicked, 'who did not accept the Torah'.[119]

Although the term 'righteous' is primarily applied to those who obey the Torah, the Rabbis knew full well that even the righteous did not obey God's law perfectly. Thus the sufferings of the righteous in this world are believed to be chastisement for their sins,[120] which indicates that they had some. There are a few instances, to be sure, of Rabbis' being surprised that they had sinned in such a way as to merit severe suffering or death,[121] but the general view was that the righteous man was not characterized by perfection – as one baraita has it, if God judged strictly, not even the patriarchs could stand his reproof[122] – but by the earnest endeavour to obey the law and by repentance and other acts of atonement in the case of transgression.[123]

'Know that the recompense of the reward of the righteous is for the time to come'; baraita Kiddushin 39b. The point of the last two passages is that the righteous receive a reward in the world to come but not in this world.

[117] Sifra Behuqqotai pereq 3.3f. (to 26.12): although God will treat the righteous as equals, and although they should not be frightened of him, they should still revere him.

[118] Sifra Qedoshim pereq 10(11).6 (to 20.16; Weiss's ed., f. 92d). Mach (*Der Zaddik*, p. 14) cites Sifre Num. 11 (17; to 5.18) as a passage which contrasts the wicked, 'who transgress his will', with the righteous, 'who do his will'. The words wicked and righteous do not appear, however. Mach does cite some Amoraic passages which explicitly term *tsaddiq* one who does the will of God, such as Tanhuma Vayyiqra' 1, attributed to R. Tanhum bar Ḥanilai (third century): 'He is *tsaddiq* who does the will of his creator. And who is this? Moses.'

[119] Gen. Rab. 33.1, beginning (ET, p. 257). On these and other passages, see Urbach, *Ḥazal*, p. 427 n. 57 (ET, p. 900 n. 80).

[120] Above, section 7, pp. 168–72; Sifre Deut. 307 (345; to 32.4): the 'completely righteousness' have 'light transgressions'.

[121] Mek. Mishpatim 18 (313; III, 141–2 [Nezikin 18]; to 22.22 [23]); Sanhedrin 101a (on R. Eliezer).

[122] Attributed to R. Eliezer, Arakhin 17a, top.

[123] So Moore, *Judaism* I, pp. 494f.

That one who sins, even grievously, but atones can be called 'righteous' is seen in a remarkable passage in Sifra. The passage is a comment on Lev. 10.1–5, which describes the death of Nadab and Abihu, the sons of Aaron, who 'offered unholy fire before the Lord, such as he had not commanded them'. As a result, 'fire came forth from the presence of the Lord and devoured them'. The passage concludes by saying that the dead men were carried in their coats out of the camp. In the comment, the anonymous Rabbi notes that God showed Nadab and Abihu consideration, since their bodies were burned and their clothes remained. If their clothes had also been burned, 'they would have been exposed and humiliated'.

And one can construct a *qal vaḥomer* argument: If, for those who offended him by bringing before him fire which was not in accord with his will, God (*ha-Maqom*) acted thus, how much more [will he do good] for the rest of the righteous![124]

The phrase 'the rest of the righteous' is especially significant, since it indicates that Nadab and Abihu were also considered 'righteous'. This is a little unusual, since the 'righteous' are generally those who actually do God's will. In this case, Nadab and Abihu were doubtless considered to have been cleansed from their sin through their suffering and death and thus to have remained in the covenant and to be worthy to be counted among the righteous.

Thus we have seen, on the one hand, that *the righteous are those who are saved*: they are those who receive their reward in the world to come and who walk in the garden of Eden with God. As another passage has it, all the righteous, like Moses, are 'gathered up' by God.[125] On the other hand, the *righteous are those who obey the Torah and atone for transgression*. Many have inferred from this a strict system of works-righteousness – those who obey the law are saved[126] – but this would not be an accurate interpretation of the Rabbinic view. The universally held view was rather this: those who accept the covenant, which carries with it God's promise of salvation, accept also the obligation to obey the commandments given by God in connection with the covenant. One who accepts the covenant and remains within it is 'righteous', and that title applies to him *both* as one who obeys God *and* as one who has a 'share in the world to come', but the former does not earn the latter. Thus R. Simeon b. Yoḥai said that one who has been righteous all his life but at the end rebels against God – which is a good deal more than simply transgressing a commandment – loses his share in the world to come. Conversely, a wicked man who repents does have a share in the world to come.[127]

---

[124] Sifra Shemini Millu'im 22–7.
[125] Sifre Num. 106 (105; to 12.15).
[126] See Kertelge, n. 81 above.
[127] T. Kiddushin 1.15f.; p. Peah 16b (1.1).

This is a very instructive saying. We see, first, that the righteous man is one who has been *faithful* to the covenant, since the opposite is *rebelling*. Being righteous does not imply perfection, but rather faithfulness. Secondly, we should note that if at the judgment the deeds of a man who was righteous all his days but who rebelled at the end were totalled, they would presumably still weigh in favour of 'merit' – if that were the way God was thought to decide a man's fate. R. Simeon's saying makes it clear that book-keeping and weighing are not in view. The man finally called 'righteous' is obviously not, as Ziesler stated, the one whose good deeds outweigh his bad,[128] but the one who is faithful to the covenant. There can be no doubt that the righteous man who rebels, though he still has a majority of good deeds, loses not only his share in the world to come but also the title 'righteous'; while the wicked man who repents, whose transgressions still outnumber his fulfilments, gains both a share in the world to come and the title 'righteous'.

R. Simeon's saying indicates not an isolated view of the righteous, but the general one. There seem to be no sayings which call those 'righteous' who simply obey oftener than they transgress. To repeat what was said before, the term applies to one who is in the covenant and loyal to it.[129] Being in the covenant both provides salvation and requires obedience: one who rebels excludes himself from God's covenantal promises, while one who repents is restored to the covenant by God's grace. It is assumed that the repentant wicked man will be obedient after his repentance.

Being righteous in the sense of obeying the law to the best of one's ability and repenting and atoning for transgression *preserves* one's place in the covenant (it is the opposite of rebelling), but it does not *earn* it. It is noteworthy that the question 'how can one *become* righteous?' is not asked. Being righteous is not the goal of a religious quest; it is the behaviour proper to one who has accepted the covenant offered at Sinai and the commandments which followed the acceptance of God's kingship. *Tsaddiq*, like *zakka'i* and its cognate words, is primarily a word indicating not an achieved, but a maintained status. Nadab and Abihu were not made righteous by being burned. They were presumably already among the righteous by virtue of being in the covenant. They transgressed within the framework of the covenant, without renouncing it, and remained righteous by their atoning suffering and death. The righteous are those in the covenant, who, on their side, obey the Torah, while God, for his part, gives them the promised inheritance, which includes a share in the world to come.

---

[128] Ziesler, *Righteousness*, p. 122.

[129] For the way in which *tsaddiq* came to mean covenant loyalty for both God and man in the Old Testament, see E. Nielsen, 'The Righteous and the Wicked in Habaqquq', *Studia Theologica* 6, 1952, pp. 54–78, esp. pp. 64–72.

9. The Gentiles

In the preceding section we have seen that the term 'righteous' usually
designates an obedient Israelite. We have further seen that, to the degree
that the Rabbis had a soteriology, it was based on membership in the
covenant. The covenantal soteriology which has been described covers both
native-born Israelites and proselytes: *accepting* the covenant both requires
and is evidenced by *obeying* the commandments. Proselytes accept the
covenant and bring sacrifices (for example) just as do native-born Israelites.[1]
It is the acceptance of the covenant which establishes one in Israel, the community of those who will have a share in the world to come, while denial of
the commandments indicates denial of the covenant and implies eternal
punishment or destruction.[2] Thus the definition of a proper proselyte is that
he is a *ger tsaddiq*, a 'righteous proselyte'; that is, like a righteous (native-
born) Israelite he obeys the Torah.[3] A man who does not intend to accept
and obey all the Torah cannot be a true proselyte (T. Demai 2.5).[4]

Precisely what the ritual was by which a man indicated his acceptance of
the covenant and thus his conversion to Judaism, and the history of the
development of the ritual, cannot be precisely recovered.[5] It is to be
assumed that males were circumcised. There are reports of questions which
were put to would-be proselytes to test their sincerity, and at some time the
custom was developed of giving proselytes a ritual bath.[6] What is important
for the present inquiry, however, is that the formal definition of a true
proselyte and a faithful native-born Israelite is the same: a man is properly in
Israel who accepts the covenant, intends to obey the commandments,
performs them to the best of his ability and the like. The native-born
Israelite, to be sure, accepts the covenant with the impetus given by the
understanding that he, his forebears and his descendants were especially
called and set aside by God. Native-born Israelites are generally considered
by the Rabbis to be 'in' unless they give evidence of being apostate (they
'break off the yoke', etc.).[7] The proselyte, on the other hand, must bear the
burden of proof to show that he accepts the covenant and intends to keep the

---

[1] Sifra Nedabah parasha 2.3; quoted above, end of section 3.

[2] On punishment and destruction, see section 7 n. 5.

[3] Above, section 8 n. 96.

[4] Also Sifra Qedoshim 8.3, above, section 6 n. 61. On intention to adhere to the Torah as the one real
condition for entering the covenant, see Bamberger, *Proselytism in the Talmudic Period*, pp. 31–7. Much
of the discussion of proselytism has focused on Rabbinic attitudes toward it. See Bamberger's 'Introduction' to the 1968 reprint of *Proselytism*, pp. xix–xxi; Urbach, *Ḥazal*, pp. 480–94 (ET, pp. 541–54).

[5] The basic texts are Yebamot 47a–b and the minor tractate Gerim. They are not in perfect agreement;
Gerim, for example, does not mention circumcision. In any case the ritual for admission which is
described may not be Tannaitic, and there is insufficient evidence to trace the history of its development.

[6] On the question of when the ritual bath was introduced, see Bamberger, *Proselytism*, pp. xxif., and
the literature cited there: the time cannot be determined.

[7] See section 7.

commandments; but the formal relationship of *accepting* and *keeping* is the same.

The question then arises, what of the Gentiles who did not become proselytes? Is the Jewish covenant like Noah's ark, outside which there is no salvation, or can Gentiles also be saved? It is here that we see clearly that Rabbinic Judaism had a soteriology in only a limited sense. There is no systematic position with regard to the fate of the Gentiles, and thus no systematic soteriology. The Rabbinic literature is addressed to members of the covenant, and from it we may deduce a kind of soteriology – and one which appears to have been universally held – for those who are in the covenant: by obeying the commandments as best they can and by atoning for transgression, they preserve their status which is given in the covenant. The Gentiles are dealt with only sporadically, however, and different Rabbis had different opinions about their destiny.[8]

We should first of all note that Gentiles as well as Israelites could be called 'righteous':

'Which he shall do' (Lev. 18.5). – R. Jeremiah used to say: You reason thus: Whence do we know that even a foreigner who does the Torah is like a high priest? Scripture teaches: 'Which a *man* shall do and live by them.' And further: it does not say, 'And this is the Torah of the Priests and Levites and Israelites,' but 'And this is the Torah of man; O Lord God' (II Sam. 7.19). And further: it does not say, 'Open the gates, that the Priests, Levites and Israelites may come in,' but 'that the righteous Gentile (*goi tsaddiq*) who keeps faith may come in' (Isa. 26.2). [The same point is made using Ps. 118.20 ('This is the gate of the Lord; the righteous shall enter through it'); 33.1 ('Rejoice in the Lord, O you righteous!'); and 125.4 ('Do good, O Lord, to those who are good').] Thus even a foreigner who does the Torah is like a high priest.[9]

Here a Gentile who does the Torah is presumably a 'God-fearer' rather than a proselyte.[10] There is some debate on whether such Gentiles should be called 'semi-proselytes'.[11] In any case, we see that R. Jeremiah would call a Gentile who does the Torah 'righteous'. A similar broad view towards the Gentiles is probably reflected in this passage: '*And He Is Become My Salvation.* Thou art the salvation of all those who come into the world, but of me especially.'[12] It is such passages as these which have led Goldin to

---

[8] See the collection of statements by the Tannaim made by E. G. Hirsch, *JE* V, p. 617; cf. Urbach, *Hazal*, pp. 482f. (ET, pp. 543f.). For differences in the Amoraic period, see Sanhedrin 59a.

[9] Sifra Ahare pereq 13.13. Some would attribute the passage to R. Meir, who is named in the parallels (Sanhedrin 59a; Baba Kamma 38a; Abodah Zarah 3a). On R. Jeremiah, a Rabbi of the school of Ishmael who is seldom mentioned, see Epstein, *Mebo'ot*, p. 572. On the passage, see Urbach, *Hazal*, p. 482 and n. 68 (ET, pp. 543f. and n. 71). See further Moore, *Judaism* I, p. 279; III, p. 87, and the passage in Bacher cited by Moore. In his edition of Sifra, Weiss (f. 86b) reads 'Gentile' where the traditional text translated here has 'foreigner'.

[10] Cf. Sifre Deut. 311 (352; to 32.8), where it is said that some Gentiles 'fear sin' and are 'worthy' (*kesherim*).

[11] Pro: Lieberman, *Greek in Jewish Palestine*, p. 75; con: Moore, *Judaism* I, pp. 326–31.

[12] Mek. Shirata 3 (126; II, 24; to 15.2).

remark that the Tannaim felt 'that God's special love for Israel co-exists with His love for all men without inconsistency'.[13] He refers also to R. Akiba's saying in Aboth 3.14(15): 'Beloved is man for he was created in the image [of God]; still greater was the love in that it was made known to him that he was created in the image of God . . .'

Other Rabbis took a more negative line, as two passages will make clear. The first is the collection of comments on Prov. 14.34 (which the Rabbis read as 'Charity exalts a nation, but the kindness of the peoples is sin'),[14] which appears in various redactions as a discussion between R. Johanan b. Zakkai and others.[15] In the various versions, the verse is taken as indicating that whatever 'kindness' (*hesed*) the Gentile nations do is counted as sin in sayings attributed to R. Eliezer, R. Joshua, R. Gamaliel, R. Eleazar b. Arak, R. Eliezer of Modiim, R. Nehunya b. ha-Kanah and R. Johanan b. Zakkai. Typical is the comment of R. Eliezer: ' "Charity exalts a nation": this refers to Israel. . . . But "the kindness of the peoples is sin": all the charity (*tsedaqah*) and kindness (*hesed*) done by the heathen is counted to them as sin, because they only do it to magnify themselves . . .' In the version in the Talmud and Yalqut Shim'oni (Ketubim 952), the penultimate exegesis is attributed to R. Nehunya b. ha-Kanah: 'Charity exalts a nation, and there is kindness for Israel and sin for the peoples.' This translation takes *hatta't* to be 'sin', which is confirmed by R. Johanan b. Zakkai's answer: 'Said R. Johanan b. Zakkai to his disciples: The answer of R. Nehuniah b. ha-Kanah is superior to my answer and to yours, because he assigns charity and kindness to Israel and sin to the heathen.'[16] R. Johanan's statement indicates that he himself had a saying on the verse, even though one has not yet been given. The redactor supplies it: 'This seems to show that he [R. Johanan] also gave an answer; what was it? – As it has been taught: R. Johanan b. Zakkai said to them: Just as the sin-offering makes atonement for Israel, so charity makes atonement for the heathen.' It is noteworthy that this baraita ('charity makes atonement for the heathen') is in direct opposition to R. Johanan's comment on R. Nehunya's statement (mercy, *tsedaqah*, and loving-kindness, *hesed*, belong to Israel, but sin to the heathen). Neusner originally explained the two statements attributed to R. Johanan b. Zakkai

[13] Goldin, *The Song at the Sea*, p. 60.

[14] The RSV reads: 'Righteousness exalts a nation, but sin is a reproach to any people.' The Rabbis took *hesed* in the more usual sense of 'kindness' rather than 'reproach', and *tsedaqah* was understood as 'charity' or 'mercy' rather than as 'righteousness'.

[15] Baba Bathra 10b. For the parallels, see Neusner, *Yohanan ben Zakkai*, pp. 135–8; rev. ed., pp. 183f., 246–9.

[16] M. Simon in the Soncino edition (p. 51) translates *hatta't* in R. Nehunya's statement as 'sin-offering', but as 'sin' in R. Johanan's reply. So also Neusner, *Yohanan ben Zakkai*, loc. cit. in n. 15. In *Development of a Legend* (p. 103) Neusner translates *hatta't* in both cases as 'sin', but erroneously attributes the translation to Simon. Another possible rendition of R. Nehunya's statement is 'kindness is for Israel and the peoples a sin-offering'; so Jastrow, *Dictionary*, p. 447, and Helfgott, *Election*, p. 47. However, the context makes this unlikely.

as representing his favourable view towards the Gentiles before the destruction of the Temple and his 'xenophobia' after the destruction.[17] Morton Smith has now more convincingly explained the anti-Gentile statement as an invention, coming from the period after 130, to make R. Johanan renounce his own irenic policy towards the Gentiles in favour of the then dominant hostility towards the Gentiles.[18] Whatever view is taken of the contradictory statements assigned to R. Johanan, the passage clearly reveals that different attitudes towards the Gentiles prevailed at different times.

The second passage is a dispute between R. Eliezer and R. Joshua:[19] The children of the wicked among the heathen shall not live (in the world to come), nor shall they be judged. But R. Eliezer holds: None of the heathen has any share in the world to come, for it is written: 'The wicked shall return to Sheol, all the heathen that forget God' (Ps. 9.17). 'The wicked shall return to Sheol' – these are the wicked in Israel. [By implication, the clause 'all the heathen that forget God' consigns all Gentiles to Sheol.][20] R. Joshua said to him: If Scripture had said: 'The wicked shall return to Sheol, all the heathen', and then said no more, I should have spoken according to thy words; but since Scripture says: 'Who forget God', behold there must be righteous men among the heathen who have a share in the world to come.

T. Sanhedrin 13.1,2,4 seems originally to have been a more or less systematic treatment of difficult groups not covered in the parallel chapter in the Mishnah, Sanhedrin 10. T. Sanhedrin 13.1 deals with the children of the wicked in Israel; 13.2 deals with the children of the wicked among the heathen; and 13.4 deals with the differing punishment meted out to transgressors of Israel and transgressors among the heathen on the one hand and to heretics, traitors and other especially damnable sinners on the other. In between, in 13.3, there is now the controversy between the school of Shammai and the school of Hillel about the three classes of Israelites.[21] It is regrettable that the anonymous statement does not explicitly deal with the righteous among the Gentiles and their children; the implication of the anonymous statement that the children of wicked Gentiles have no share in the world to come, however, may be that the righteous among the Gentiles do have a share. (Similarly, when Sanhedrin 10.2 singles out Balaam as having no share in the world to come, the implication may be that righteous Gentiles do have a share.)[22] The treatment of the children of the wicked

---

[17] *Yohanan ben Zakkai*, p. 135; rev. ed., p. 183.

[18] Morton Smith, in Neusner, *Development of a Legend*, pp. 102f.

[19] T. Sanhedrin 13.2, Danby's translation, slightly modified and emended as noted below.

[20] The mss. of the Tosefta, and Danby's translation, have here this sentence: '"All the heathen that forget God" – these are the wicked among the heathen.' But this is obviously a gloss to make R. Eliezer agree with R. Joshua, who was followed by the majority. Zuckermandel, ad loc., emends the text correctly, and the omission is supported by the parallel in Sanhedrin 105a. (In the ET, the correct reading is given in n. 3 on p. 716.)

[21] Quoted above, section 6, p. 142.

[22] Finkelstein, *The Pharisees*[3], p. cxv. According to Finkelstein, this was the old 'Hasidean' view, which was maintained by the Hillelites and supported by R. Joshua.

among the Gentiles is quite lenient; they do not live but they do not suffer. It is R. Eliezer who maintains the view that the heathen as a group are excluded from the world to come.[23] R. Joshua supports R. Johanan's view, that the righteous among the heathen do share in the world to come.

The opening statement in T. Sanhedrin 13.1, that the children of wicked Israelites have no share in the world to come, is attributed to Rabban Gamaliel; he is opposed by R. Joshua, who holds that 'The Lord preserveth the simple' (Ps. 116.6).[24] It is not unlikely that the opening statement of T. Sanhedrin 13.2 is also from R. Gamaliel.[25] One must assume that this is R. Gamaliel II, the contemporary of Joshua and Eliezer.[26] The question of the fate of the Gentiles was obviously a serious issue in the minds of those who witnessed the destruction of the Temple.

In any case, there is no one view of the situation of Gentiles which prevailed throughout the Tannaitic period. The general impression is that the Rabbis were not ungenerous except when special circumstances moved them to view Gentiles with bitterness.[27] Even those who were of the view that righteous Gentiles would have a place in the world to come do not specify what a 'righteous Gentile' is. However, the later view, that he is one who keeps the seven Noachian commandments, is probably not too far off the mark.[28] There seems to be no clear early statement to the effect that

---

[23] R. Eliezer has traditionally been seen as consistently anti-Gentile. See, for example, Bacher, *Agada der Tannaiten* I, pp. 107, 133–5, citing this passage and Gittin 45b (=Hullin 2.7): the intention of the Gentile (in slaughtering) is towards idolatry. Neusner notes that xenophobia was typical of the time (*Eliezer* II, p. 202), but he finds R. Eliezer's view of the Gentiles not to be uniform (ibid., pp. 285, 327f.), referring to the possibility that R. Eliezer may have permitted eating Samaritan bread (see ibid. I, pp. 41–3). Further, Neusner regards the reports of R. Eliezer's xenophobia to be less reliable than traditions attesting to his irenic spirit (II, p. 416). His summary statements about R. Eliezer's irenic attitude toward *Gentiles* (II, pp. 416, 421), however, do not refer to passages, and I am unable to find such passages in the material analysed by Neusner (except the ambiguous passages about Samaritan bread). T. Sanhedrin 13.2 still seems the clearest statement by R. Eliezer on the Gentiles. (I do not understand Neusner's remark 'positions reversed', II, p. 376, on the relation between Sanhedrin 10.3 and T. Sanhedrin 13.2. In the former R. Eliezer opposes R. Akiba's *exclusion* of some *Israelites*, in the latter R. Joshua's *inclusion* of some *Gentiles*.)

[24] For variants in the tradition, see Bacher, *Agada der Tannaiten* I, p. 93 n. 1. In Sanhedrin 110b, R. Gamaliel is opposed by R. Akiba.

[25] Cf. Sanhedrin 110b: 'All agree that [young children of wicked heathen] will not enter the world to come. And R. Gamaliel deduces it from [Isa. 26.14].' The editor of the Soncino edition (H. Freedman), however, notes that the Wilna Gaon deleted 'R. Gamaliel', as did Rashi (ET, p. 760 n. 10).

[26] So also Helfgott, *Election*, p. 53.

[27] For another negative opinion, see R. Ishmael's in the passage cited above, section 7 n. 17. For a positive attitude, note the possibly Tannaitic opinion in Sukkah 55b that the seventy bullocks atoned for the seventy Gentile nations. Tannaitic attitudes toward the Gentiles have been surveyed by Helfgott, *Election*. See pp. 38f., 53, 57, 61f., 68f., 97f., 109f., 118f., 132, 140f. He noted that, while some Tannaim were particularist and excluded Gentiles from the world to come, the 'preponderance of Tannaitic opinion tends to agree with R. Joshua', who took a more generous view (pp. 140f.). Kadushin (*The Rabbinic Mind*, p. 28) argues that 'the very structure of the rabbinic value-concepts necessitates the concept of "the righteous of the nations of the world" '. He also gives further references for the use of the expression.

[28] These are listed in an anonymous baraita in Sanhedrin 56a–b, with some additions by individual Rabbis. Cf. T. Abodah Zarah 8(9).4, where seven are mentioned but only six named. On the Noachian commandments, see K. Hruby, 'Le concept de Révélation', n. 17 on pp. 25–9.

Gentiles who obey the Noachian commandments will be saved, but in one passage the Gentiles are criticized for not keeping even those commandments when God offered them the law.[29] This seems to indicate what was expected of Gentiles. It was surely never contemplated that any Gentile would observe the Jewish law.[30] One who was kind and charitable and who did not transgress any of the principal prohibitions of Judaism (idolatry, robbery, eating meat cut from a living animal and the like) would presumably qualify.

We thus see that the Rabbis did not actually have a general and comprehensive soteriology. If they had been animated by the question 'who can be saved?',[31] one must presume that they would have dealt with it in their characteristically thorough and systematic fashion and that the state of the Gentiles would have been defined, distinctions among various Gentiles made, what God expected of Gentiles specified, and the like. Such discussions are notably absent from Tannaitic literature. The question which did animate the Rabbis was 'How can we obey the God who redeemed us and to whom we are committed?' We can see the Rabbis wrestling with this problem on every page of the literature. Their discussions are almost exclusively carried out within the context of the covenant.[32] They concern themselves relatively little with how one who is not born in the covenant enters it, although on this point the Rabbinic position is unambiguous: entrance requires accepting ('confirming') the covenant and committing oneself to obeying the commandments. On the question of God's attitude towards those who remain outside the covenant, there were varying opinions. It is thus not strictly accurate to speak of 'Pharisaic soteriology', as if there were one theory which covered all cases. Salvation is principally thought of as

---

[29] Sifre Deut. 343 (396; to 33.2).

[30] The Rabbis considered that Israel had special obligations which did not fall on Gentiles. Thus Sifra Aḥare parasha 6.1 (to 17.2): ' "The Sons of Israel" are obligated [to keep the commandment] about slaughtering and offering outside (the Temple). But foreigners are not obligated [to keep it]. And not only this, but foreigners are permitted to make a high place in any place and to make offerings there to Heaven.' (Apparently offerings are meant which are not to idols, but to God.) So also Sifre Deut. 345 (402; to 33.4): 'This commanding (of the Torah, which is mentioned in the text) is only for us and for our sake'.

[31] As a possible instance of such a concern, one might cite Berakoth 28b: 'Our Rabbis taught: When R. Eliezer fell ill, his disciples went in to visit him. They said to him: Master, teach us the paths of life so that we may through them win [נזכה] the life of the world to come. He said to them: Be solicitous for the honour of your colleagues, and keep your children from meditation, and set them between the knees of scholars, and when you pray know before whom you are standing and in this way you will win [תזכו] the future world.' (The word translated 'meditation' Bacher [*Agada der Tannaiten* I, p. 97 n. 5] thinks refers to reading the Bible without instruction. Marmorstein [*Essays in Anthropomorphism*, p. 145] thinks it refers to translating the Bible strictly literally.) It is clear that the answer provides no soteriology; it simply says that a man should respect his fellows, train his children and reverence God. Doing these things keeps one in the covenant as we have defined it. Their negatives might involve 'breaking off the yoke', but this is clearly addressed to those already in the covenant who wish to behave in such a way as to maintain their place.

[32] Cf. H. Loewe, 'Pharisaism', *Judaism and Christianity* I, p. 154: 'What we have on the Rabbinic side tells us how the Pharisees spoke to men who had faith already.'

promised to those who are in the covenant and who retain their status in it, but at least some Rabbis explicitly allowed for the salvation of 'righteous Gentiles'. This did not, however, lead to a fundamental re-thinking of the soteriology that applied to members of the covenant, and the Gentiles are not systematically worked into Rabbinic thought about who has a share in the world to come and on what conditions.

10. The Nature of Religious Life and Experience

We have been dealing with how Rabbinic religion 'works' (how the process of getting in and staying in was understood) and have thus said little, at least directly, about the nature of religious experience in Rabbinism, about what religion was like internally for the Rabbis, about, if we may use the phrase, religious feeling.[1] The overall study depends upon a comparison between Paul and various Jewish groups with regard to how religion was understood to function, since a comparison of the nature of religious experience in Paulinism and Judaism would prove too vague and insubstantial to be rewarding. For this reason, our discussion of the nature of Rabbinic religious experience must be brief and limited. Yet it is an important point in the present work that there is, or should be, a congruence between the pattern of religion – how it works – and the religious experience which tends to characterize the life of its adherents. If an incongruence occurs, if the traditional pattern is not responsive to new religious needs, attitudes and feelings, there is a religious crisis. This will be seen in detail when we come to IV Ezra.

It has been a common view among Christian scholars that there is such an incongruence in Judaism generally and in Rabbinic Judaism in particular. God, it has been said, became very remote in the period after the return from Babylon. He was no longer spoken of familiarly, but only by circumlocutions; and angels were necessary as intermediaries.[2] Yet Judaism possessed no means of access to the remote God save obedience to the Torah, which is manifestly insufficient and inadequate. This situation led to a religion of anxiety on the one hand (could one do enough works to earn favour with the distant God?) and smug self-reliance on the other hand (some could).[3]

This estimate of Jewish religious experience – anxiety coupled with

---

[1] In addition to the works which are discussed below, see Büchler, *Types*, pp. 69ff., on 'the religious emotions of the Jew'.

[2] A familiar statement of the view is that of R. Bultmann, *Jesus and the Word*, pp. 138f. Bultmann was aware of the strong tradition in Judaism of the presence of God (p. 140), but seems to have thought that that tradition weakened in later Judaism. Cf. also *Primitive Christianity*, p. 60: '[God] was no longer a vital factor in the present . . .'; p. 61: the idea of God's transcendence meant that 'God was no longer bound to his people'.

[3] Bultmann, *Primitive Christianity*, pp. 70f., relying on Bousset, *Religion des Judentums*, pp. 392–4.

arrogant self-righteousness – rests on three theories about Jewish theology, all wrong. They are the view that a man must do more good deeds than he commits transgressions, that God was viewed as inaccessible, and that the individual felt himself to be lost, having no access to the remote God. We have spent the bulk of the chapter thus far in an effort to show that the traditional view in Christian scholarship that Rabbinic soteriology consists of weighing deeds is wrong – it is not supported by the texts which are taken to support it and it is contradicted by another all-pervasive view. We should now point out how Bousset (and, following him, Bultmann and numerous other New Testament scholars) connected this view of Jewish soteriology with the conclusion that it led to a completely inadequate religious experience. Thus Bousset argued that despite what would appear to be the certainty of salvation implicit in Judaism, there was a deep uncertainty. Membership in the people of Israel is not of itself salvific, since there are wicked as well as pious Israelites. He continued:

One must belong to the more restricted sphere of the pious, be a member of the sect, in order to please God. But even within this sphere every individual is still thrown back upon himself and his deeds. From this labyrinth the pious can no longer find their way to simple, straightforward trust in the goodness of God. One loses oneself more and more in relativities, in an anxious recounting and weighing of individual deeds against one another. The viewpoint arises – a view which kills all true piety and all moral earnestness – that, with regard to the divine demand of righteousness, everything depends on a *numerical preponderance of good works*. Life becomes an exercise in arithmetic (*Rechenbeispiel*), an incessant reckoning of the account which the pious has with God.[4]

As one gives up Bousset's view of Jewish soteriology, one should also give up his view of the inadequacy of Jewish religious life.

The second basis of the view that there was a deep incongruity in Judaism between the religious needs and desires of the people and the theology which was current is the theory that God, in post-biblical Judaism, was considered transcendent and consequently remote and inaccessible. This is one of the aspects of Weber's view which has survived one learned refutation after another. It is my intention not to offer a full analysis of intermediaries between the supposedly remote God and his people in Jewish literature, but only to review the assertions and counter-assertions very briefly. As we observed in section 1 above, Moore considered 'Weber's original contribution to the misunderstanding of Judaism' to be the equation between God's transcendence and his inaccessibility. Weber's view was based on the existence of intermediaries in Jewish literature.[5] Bousset picked up the theme in a major way. Moore summarized his view thus:

---

[4] Bousset, *Judentum*, pp. 392f.
[5] See Moore, 'Christian Writers', p. 233.

The fundamental contrast between Jesus and Judaism, as Bousset asserts it, is the idea of God and the feeling toward him. The God of Judaism in that age was withdrawn from the world, the supramundane, transcendent. 'The prophetic preaching of the exaltation and uniqueness of Jehovah became the dogma of an abstract, transcendent monotheism.' So it is reiterated page after page.[6]

Moore's comment on reiteration is pertinent. His accusation of Bousset was that what 'he lacked in knowledge, he made up . . . in the positiveness and confidence of his opinions, and for the failure to present evidence, by an effective use of what psychologists call suggestion – unsupported assertion coming by force of sheer reiteration to appear to the reader self-evident or something he had always known'.[7] Moore considered Bousset's error in this regard to rest in part on his over-reliance on the apocalypses, from which one could 'get the picture of a God enthroned in the highest heaven, remote from the world'. Even this would be a misunderstanding, however, for that picture 'is conditioned by the visionary form'.[8]

In 1915, Wicks had already noted the tendency of Christian theologians to find in post-biblical Jewish literature a picture of God as inaccessible, as well as the fact that 'modern Jewish theologians take the gravest objection to the idea that this false notion of transcendence was ever held by their people'.[9] Wicks proceeded to show that such an idea can hardly be found in the apocalyptic and pseudepigraphic literature.[10] Abelson had previously undertaken to establish that the Rabbinic use of *shekinah* and related terms indicates the Rabbis' view that God was immanent, not remote.[11] In spite of all this, however, in *Urchristentum* (1949) Bultmann basically repeated Bousset's view: God was viewed as remote and he played no significant role in the present.[12] The connection of this view with the existence of intermediaries was repeated by H. Ringgren and described as 'well known' in his generally perceptive *The Faith of Qumran*: God's transcendence led to remoteness and required intermediaries.[13]

It is not to our purpose here to decide whether or not such terms as *shekinah* in Rabbinic literature and *memra* in the Targums represent divine

---

[6] Ibid., p. 242. Moore is here discussing Bousset's *Jesu Predigt in ihrem Gegensatz zum Judentum*, 1892. He points out, however (p. 247), that the view is repeated in *Judentum*.

[7] Moore, 'Christian Writers', p. 242.

[8] Ibid., pp. 247f.

[9] H. J. Wicks, *The Doctrine of God*, pp. 27f.

[10] See the summary, ibid., pp. 122–6.

[11] J. Abelson, *The Immanence of God in Rabbinical Literature*, 1912. His work now appears naive and simplistic. Yet he pointed in what is basically the correct direction. The work contains most of the relevant passages on the subject of God's presence. For a criticism of the use of the term 'immanent', see Kadushin, *The Rabbinic Mind*, pp. 255–7, 278f.

[12] N. 2 above.

[13] Ringgren, *The Faith of Qumran*, 1963, p. 81; cf. p. 47. On p. 47 *shekinah* is called a circumlocution, on p. 81 a hypostatic intermediary being. In either case the use of the term *shekinah* in Rabbinic literature is taken to indicate God's elevation rather than his presence, which is its real significance. Cf. Kadushin, *The Rabbinic Mind*, p. 228: '*Shekinah* is a name for God used only in statements having to do with God's nearness.'

hypostases.[14] In light of the background we have given, one will perhaps understand the sharpness of Moore's denial of any significance to such terms besides their being circumlocutions for God.[15] Even if they do represent a tendency toward hypostatization, they need not and do not lead to the conclusion that God was considered inaccessible. Box, in modifying Moore's view, agreed on that point: *memra* is a *Mittelsbegriff* – neither a hypostasis nor a circumlocution – which 'connotes a certain view of God's manifestation, a theology of immanence. . .'[16] The truth is that the terms transcendence and immanence lead to misunderstanding and are not really appropriate.[17] In particular, they do not respond to the question of God's accessibility. For the understanding of *shekinah* it is best to follow Goldberg: the term *shekinah* denotes 'eine bestimmte Weise des Daseins Gottes in der Welt als einen Teil der unermesslichen und letzlich unfasslichen Gottheit'.[18] But whatever the precise interpretation of the 'intermediaries' in Jewish literature, we may assert unequivocally that Weber's connection of intermediaries, transcendence and inaccessibility, which has often been repeated, cannot stand. The Rabbis viewed God as accessible, and this has now been shown with great clarity and thoroughness by numerous scholars,[19] most recently Peter Kuhn,[20] Goldberg[21] and Urbach.[22]

Bousset's statement that 'the essence of Jewish piety is deep discord'[23] rests, then, on the supposed clash between the legalistic system which he attributed to the Rabbis and the inner desire and longing on the part of Jews for a compassionate and merciful God. He maintained that this latter hope was denied by the remoteness and inaccessibility of God. We have seen that two of the bases of Bousset's view cannot stand: Jewish soteriology was not based on a weighing of deeds, and God was not considered remote. But there is a third aspect of Bousset's view of Jewish piety which touches more directly on the topic of this section: the Jew is characterized by the feeling of

---

[14] See the recent discussion, primarily of the views of Dürr and Ringgren, in J. T. Sanders, *The New Testament Christological Hymns*, 1971, pp. 43–57.

[15] Moore, 'Intermediaries in Jewish Theology', *HTR* 15, 1922, pp. 41–61; *Judaism* I, pp. 417–22.

[16] G. H. Box, 'The Idea of Intermediation in Jewish Theology', *JQR* 23, 1932–3, p. 118.

[17] So Moore, *Judaism* I, p. 423; Kadushin (n. 11 above); Goldberg, *Untersuchungen über die Vorstellung von der Schekhinah*, 1969, p. 535.

[18] ('A particular mode of God's existence in the world as part of the unfathomable and in the last resort incomprehensible Godhead'). Goldberg, *Schekhinah*, pp. 537f.

[19] See, for example, Marmorstein, *The Names and Attributes of God*, pp. 148–53 (using the philosophical category of omnipresence, which is no better than immanence, although the general intention is correct); Moore, *Judaism* I, pp. 369–94, 423–42 ('He who dwells in the high and holy place, dwells no less with him that is of a contrite and humble spirit', p. 442); Kadushin, *The Rabbinic Mind*, pp. 194–272.

[20] Peter Kuhn, *Gottes Selbsterniedrigung in der Theologie der Rabbinen*, 1968. His section on God's suffering with his people (pp. 82ff.) is especially important for the study of the ideas of a suffering saviour and a redeemed redeemer. See especially pp. 89f.; cf. 105f.

[21] Goldberg, *Schekhinah*.

[22] In addition to the essay cited below, n. 56, see the chapters 'The *Shekinah* – The Presence of God in the World' and 'Nearness and Distance– *Maqom* and *Shamayim*', *Ḥazal*, pp. 29–68 (ET, pp. 37–79).

[23] Bousset, *Judentum*, p. 393.

alienation and separation. He felt 'a dark and bitter seclusion' from God not only because of God's remoteness, but because of his negative estimate of humanity. He was 'unworthy to be loved'.[24] 'Human nature is so corrupt that man must change himself completely if he wants to approach God.'[25] Such a view of man's situation, if it were held by the Rabbis, would be incongruent not only with Bousset's 'system', but also with the pattern of religion which we have described. That is, if the Rabbis held man to be lost and alienated, repentance and the other means of atonement could not be effective. They are designed to *restore* man to his proper place within the covenant, not to overcome aboriginal lostness. It is noteworthy that Bousset sees repentance not as a *return* to God but as another good work by which the pious attempts to *earn* God's favour and become worthy of approaching him.[26] This is obviously a role which repentance is ill-suited to play. The pessimistic view of man's situation which Bousset finds in Judaism would require another pattern of religion than the one which we have described, one which provides means of contact with God within man's lost state. It requires, in short, a redeemer and sacraments.

Bousset, in fact, argues just that: the Jewish religious attitude should require sacraments. Since they are not provided by the 'system', Judaism must be judged to have failed. He deals in an interesting way with the point, made repeatedly in these pages, that the Rabbis were confident in God. He notes that Judaism *should* not produce anxiety about the possibility of damnation, since the Israelites are God's people and he is their God. But, he argues, since Judaism has no conception of sacraments, 'the Jewish Church has this certainty and confidence in salvation *only in general*. It has no definite security for the individual, it has developed no definite institutions and means through which individuals appropriate salvation, it possesses no sacraments.'[27] He then argues that circumcision, the cultus, the possession of the law and the like do not constitute sacraments.[28]

This argument is quite wide of the mark. It is, in effect, simply an argument that Judaism should be like Christianity. Since it is not, it is inadequate at best. Bousset appears to be thinking in Christian terms: man is damned, alienated and estranged. Salvation must be mediated to individuals by 'churchly' means, since otherwise they have no experience of God. Bousset does not see that Judaism's lack of a firm doctrine of original sin is significant,[29] nor did he reflect on why the Rabbis developed no general theoretical soteriology.[30] Bousset's view, which he states without noting statements by

[24] Ibid., p. 374.
[25] Ibid., p. 389.
[26] Ibid., pp. 389f.
[27] Ibid., p. 197.
[28] Ibid., pp. 197ff.
[29] Above, section 5 n. 48.
[30] Above, the beginning of section 9.

individual Rabbis which indicate a modest confidence in God,[31] is best answered by adducing just those statements. It may be useful, however, first to consider the problem in more general terms. We shall deal first with what the Rabbis considered the ideal religious life to be like, then with their attitude towards the nearness and remoteness of God, and finally with individual attitudes as expressed in prayer and at the time of death.

Studying and doing and the presence of God

The Rabbinic conception of the nature of the religious life may perhaps best be summarized by a saying attributed to the Tanna R. Nathan:[32] 'The Holy One, blessed be He, says: If a man occupies himself with the study of the Torah and with works of charity and prays with the congregation, I account it to him as if he had redeemed Me and My children from among the nations of the world.' We shall return to prayer, the last item in R. Nathan's list, below. The other two items may be dealt with together. For the present purpose, we should stretch the phrase 'works of charity' (*gemilut ḥasadim*, referring to acts of loving-kindness in general, not just alms) to cover 'works' in general. Although 'doing' and 'studying' appear as of equal importance in the saying of R. Nathan, their relative merits were debated among the early Tannaim. We turn first to this question to see what light it throws on the nature of religious life and experience among the Rabbis.

It is generally agreed that the Shammaites and those influenced by them preferred 'doing' to 'studying'. Thus Aboth 1.15 and 1.17:

Shammai said: Make thy [study of the] Law a fixed habit; say little and do much, and receive all men with cheerful countenance.

Simeon [b. Gamaliel] said: All my days have I grown up among the Sages and I have found naught better for a man than silence; and not the expounding [of the Law] is the chief thing but the doing [of it]; and he that multiplies words occasions sin.

Shammai's encouragement to 'say little and do much' is taken to exalt 'doing' over 'studying'.[33] On the other hand, Hillelites emphasized study over

---

[31] Confidence in God is not the same as self-righteous confidence in oneself, which Bousset is willing enough to see. The difference is put precisely by Mach, *Der Zaddik*, p. 40: 'Das Gottesvertrauen ist es, nicht das Bewusstsein der eigenen Gerechtigkeit, worauf die Heilsgewissheit des Frommen fusst.'

[32] A baraita in Berakoth 8a, ET, p. 39. R. Nathan was a contemporary of R. Meir. There are many similar sayings. See e.g. the baraita in Berakoth 5a–b on 'labouring at the Torah and *gemilut ḥasadim*'.

[33] So Finkelstein, *Akiba*, p. 49. Shammai's saying was later taken to mean 'promise little and do much', as is clear in ARN 13. One should be modest in promising hospitality and the like, but generous in providing it. See further Nedarim 21b and Baba Metzia 87a for the same meaning. Mach (*Der Zaddik*, p. 86 n. 5) understands Shammai's saying to mean what the later Rabbis take it to mean.

deed.[34] Thus Hillel said, 'the more study of the Law the more life'.[35] There is no corresponding saying in favour of 'doing', although the phrase 'the more righteousness the more peace'[36] may refer to deeds of loving-kindness. Aboth is dominated by sayings elevating the study of the Torah; being a 'Sage' is the ideal life in the view of many of the Rabbis:[37]

Jose b. Joezer of Zeredah (Aboth 1.4): 'Let thy house be a meeting-house for the sages and sit amid the dust of their feet and drink in their words with thirst.'

R. Johanan b. Zakkai (Aboth 2.8): 'If thou hast wrought much in the Law claim not merit for thyself, for to this end wast thou created.'

R. Jose (b. Halafta) (Aboth 2.12); 'Let the property of thy fellow be dear to thee as thine own; and fit thyself for the study of the Law, for [the knowledge of] it is not thine by inheritance; and let all thy deeds be done for the sake of Heaven.'

R. Tarfon (Aboth 2.16): 'If thou hast studied much in the Law much reward will be given thee.'

R. Hananiah b. Teradion (Aboth 3.2): 'If two sit together and no words of the Law [are spoken] between them, there is the seat of the scornful.' There are similar sayings by R. Simeon b. Yohai in Aboth 3.3 and R. Halafta b. Dosa in 3.6.

In the Amoraic period, the emphasis upon study was carried so far by some that one Rabbi chastised his student for leaving his study to say his prayers.[38] And it was said of Rab Judah that he prayed only once in thirty days so as to have more time for study.[39]

Our present concern, however, is not with the apparent excesses to which the emphasis on study led. The issue was formally compromised, and the formula is recorded in Sifre Deut.: 'Studying is [more] important, for it leads to doing.'[40] Something of the spirit of this compromise is seen in the saying of R. Gamaliel the son of Rabbi (Aboth 2.2): 'Excellent is study of the

[34] Finkelstein, *Akiba*, p. 49, and cf. p. 259. Finkelstein argues that the 'plebeians' held study to be more important than deed, while the 'patricians' took the opposite view. In Finkelstein's view, the plebeians were represented by such figures as Hillel and Akiba, while the patrician views were held by, among others, Shammai and Simeon b. Gamaliel, despite the fact that the latter was technically a Hillelite. See further Finkelstein's larger work, *The Pharisees*.

[35] Aboth 2.7. On the saying, see Neusner, *Yohanan ben Zakkai*, rev. ed., p. 37; cf. ibid., p. 52.

[36] Aboth 2.7.

[37] See further, Neusner, *Yohanan ben Zakkai*, rev. ed., pp. 98ff. on 'Study of Torah as a Life-Style'.

[38] Shabbath 10a.

[39] Rosh Ha-Shannah 35a. Cf. the opinion attributed to R. Simeon b. Yohai in p. Berakoth 3b, near top (1.5), that one should not stop studying even to recite the *Shema'*. There is some discussion of the point. And see Helfgott, *Election*, pp. 103f.

[40] Sifre Deut. 41 (85; to 11.13). The passage records a discussion among R. Akiba (whose saying is quoted), R. Tarfon (who says that doing is greater than studying) and R. Jose ha-Galilee (who exalts studying over doing). According to the parallel in Kiddushin 40b, all the gathered sages say that studying is greater, since it leads to doing. The question was pressing because of the proscriptions of the Hadrianic era. See Finkelstein's reconstruction, *Akiba*, pp. 258–60, where also further passages are cited. And see Sifra Behuqqotai parasha 2.3.

Law together with worldly occupation, for toil in them both puts sin out of mind. But all study of the Law without [worldly] labour comes to naught at the last and brings sin in its train.' 'Worldly occupation' is not the same as 'doing', but this saying shows both the elevation of theoretical study and the insistence on practicality.

But what did the Rabbis mean by 'doing' (*ma'aseh*)? Finkelstein has argued that the debate is about the relative merits of 'general ceremonial practice' and studying. Both the Shammaites and the Hillelites thought that 'doing' in this sense and 'studying' both preceded the Temple cultus. They only disagreed as to the relative value of studying the Torah and observing the laws of purity, tithing and the like.[41] On the other hand, Büchler has argued, with greater persuasiveness, that 'doing' refers to doing the positive precepts, those which command any action, but especially deeds of loving-kindness. He refers to R. Judah b. Ilai's saying, when he saw a funeral or bridal procession pass by the school, 'doing has precedence over studying'. Thus the Rabbi would urge the students to participate in the procession, which ranks as a deed of loving-kindness.[42] The word 'deed' or 'doing' means 'the practice of religious duties, and frequently the practice of deeds of loving-kindness'.[43] The real significance of the dispute, however, was pointed out by Ginzberg in a way which avoids giving a precise definition to 'doing':[44]

Until the time of Hillel and Shammai, the form of study was not theoretical but practical and pragmatic; that is, the accent was laid on correct action rather than pure study. . . .

Study, however, became increasingly theoretical in both schools. Still, the conservative Shammaites 'considered deed more important than thought'.[45] The question which lay between the two schools, then, was the relative merit of theory and practice, the value of act versus intention.[46] We have repeatedly seen the emphasis in the surviving Rabbinic literature on intention.[47] We now see that this may have been the result of a growing trend within Pharisaism generally, and especially within the school which became dominant, towards emphasizing theory.

Yet the Rabbis cannot be seriously accused of having neglected 'doing', however it be defined. One should study in order to do, and study was not to be used as an excuse for neglecting the commandments.[48]

---

[41] *Akiba*, p. 49. [42] P. Hagigah 76c (1.7).
[43] Büchler, *Types*, p. 87. See the discussion, ibid., pp. 84ff.
[44] L. Ginzberg, 'The Significance of the Halacha', *On Jewish Law and Lore*, p. 94.
[45] Ibid., p. 119. [46] Ibid., p. 118.
[47] See especially the beginning of section 5 above. See also the index, s.v. 'confessing'.
[48] The idea that 'studying' should lead to 'doing' was thoroughly accepted by the later Rabbis. See e.g. Lev. Rab. 35.7 and other passages cited by Mach, *Der Zaddik*, p. 15. And see also Neusner, *Yohanan ben Zakkai*, p. 145 (rev. ed., p. 191), on studying, obeying the commandments and doing acts of loving-kindness as the foundation which R. Johanan established for Judaism.

Emphasizing the theoretical and intentional side of the religious life as the foundation of actual fulfilment of concrete commandments does not, of itself, answer the frequent Protestant accusation that Jewish religious life is arid, since Judaism is a religion which is at man's disposal, a religion in which man has it within his own power to be 'saved' or not. As Billerbeck put it, Judaism is a religion of *Selbsterloesung*, self-salvation.[49] In the eyes of many, it remains so whether intent is judged more important than perform-ance or not. 'Intention' cannot be equated with the Pauline 'faith': it is still salvation by works of law. From the point of view of how Rabbinic religion worked, the obvious answer to this sort of charge is that salvation comes by God's election, not by either man's intent or actual performance. Both are required, but they are not means by which one initially earns God's favour. From the point of view of religious feeling and experience, the answer is that the Rabbis do not evidence the sort of anxiety and strain which a religion of *Selbsterloesung* would create. On the contrary, studying and doing were valued *by them* quite differently than as means to self-salvation.

If 'studying' and 'doing' are not attempts at self-salvation, why did one 'study' and 'do'? There are two answers: to obey the commandments and to be close to God. The necessity of obedience has been sufficiently discussed. The second point, however, is of direct relevance for the present section.

In a remarkable chapter, titled 'Normal Mysticism', Kadushin has shown, with great originality, clarity and insight, that Rabbinic religion cultivated the consciousness of the presence of God in a thorough, effective and methodical way.[50] Noting that prayer brings the Israelite into the presence of God[51] – a point to which we shall return – Kadushin further observes that regular and systematic prayer is prescribed by the halakah.[52] Further, the halakah attaches prayer to daily normal events (thus, 'normal mysticism'). The feeling of the presence of God is not limited to the experi-ence of the 'wholly other'. It is worth quoting Kadushin at length on this point.

Halakah gives regularity and steadiness to the drive toward concretization pos-

---

[49] S.-B. IV, p. 6.

[50] *The Rabbinic Mind*, pp. 194–272. The terminology and a brief discussion are seen in *Organic Thinking*, pp. 237–40. In what follows, I deal only with such 'normal mysticism'. It may be that ecstatic and visionary mysticism was also fairly widespread in Rabbinic Judaism. See G. Scholem, *Major Trends in Jewish Mysticism* and *Jewish Gnosticism, Merkabah Mysticism, and Talmudic Tradition*; J. Neusner, *Yohanan ben Zakkai*, pp. 97–103; rev. ed., pp. 134–41. For a positive evaluation of Scholem's work, see D. Flusser, 'Scholem's recent book on Merkabah Literature', *JJS* 11, 1960, pp. 59–68. Flusser raises the question of the relation of the mystical motifs to the more typical haggadic themes. Scholem's thesis is subjected to a searching evaluation in Urbach's essay cited in n. 56 below. My own view is that of Sandmel, *The First Christian Century*, pp. 75f.: 'It must therefore suffice to say that we face the paradox of abundant clues to the existence of first-century mystic tendencies, but their contours defy our assessment. . .' In any case, no form of Jewish mysticism has to do with achieving union with God. See Rohde's definition of mysticism in *Psyche*, p. 254, and Scholem's comment, *Major Trends*, p. 5.

[51] *The Rabbinic Mind*, pp. 207ff.

[52] Ibid., pp. 210f.

sessed by the concept of prayer, enlarges the scope of its expression, and supplies the means for its expression. The drive for concretization functions best when it is touched off by a stimulus. . . . But it is due to Halakah that instead of being haphazard the stimuli are regular and steady. It is Halakah that makes of every occasion on which a person eats or drinks a stimulus for prayer. Not only that, but Halakah sensitizes a person to stimuli for prayer otherwise barely perceptible – for example, to the different periods of the day as occasions for . . . prayer. And besides thus enlarging enormously in these and other ways the scope of prayer, Halakah supplies the individual with the *Berakot* and prayers themselves, with means of expression developed by the creative minds and spirits. At the same time, Halakah encourages spontaneous prayer and private petitions, and especially the adding of such prayers to appropriate sections of the Eighteen *Berakot*.

Is it, then, so surprising that the ordinary man and the gifted man should have had the same kind of experience of God? Through the agency of Halakah, the gifted man shared his finest achievements with the ordinary man, the spiritual leader brought the common man up to his own level.[53]

Not only is it the case that the halakah induces the feeling of the presence of God by regulating it, as it were, into the fabric of everyday life, but the study of the Torah itself causes one to feel that he is in the presence of God. Thus the Temple service, where the priest ministers before God, prayer and the study of the Torah are all called *ʿabodah*, service.[54] Wherever two speak of the Torah together, God ('the *shekinah*') is with them.[55]

So strong was the feeling that God was present when the Torah was studied that the Rabbis, in speaking of studying, employed terminology derived from the theophany on Mt Sinai, as Urbach has shown.[56] Thus it was said of one early scholar that 'when he was sitting and labouring at the Torah, every bird which flew over him was immediately burned up'.[57] The words of the Torah are like fire. The explanation is apparently to be found in Ex. 19.18: 'And Mount Sinai was wrapped in smoke, because the Lord descended upon it in fire.'[58] Urbach, after citing other passages[59] connecting studying the Torah and a blazing fire, comments:[60]

[53] Ibid., p. 211. We should note that H. Loewe, 'Pharisaism', *Judaism and Christianity* I, p. 153, had earlier remarked that Pharisaism sanctifies 'the daily round and common task'. Goldin ('The Thinking of the Rabbis', p. 11) cautions that Kadushin's view 'underestimates the dulling effects of habit'. It seems nevertheless to be the case that Kadushin has pointed out the relationship between halakah and the interior religious life *as the Rabbis perceived it*.

[54] Sifre Deut. 41 (87; to 11.13); Kadushin, p. 213. Cf. Finkelstein, *The Pharisees*, p. 279; Neusner, *Yohanan ben Zakkai*, pp. 62f.; rev. ed., p. 92.

[55] Aboth 3.2; Kadushin, p. 214. Further to the point that study of the Torah was 'at once a pneumatic and a disciplining spiritual experience', see Neusner, *Yohanan ben Zakkai*, pp. 38, 81ff. In the rev. ed., p. 64, he speaks of study as 'at once a fluid and open, but also a restraining spiritual experience'; cf. rev. ed., pp. 118ff.

[56] E. E. Urbach, 'Ha-Masorot 'al Torat ha-Sod bi-Tequfat ha-Tanna'im' ('The Traditions about Merkabah Mysticism in the Tannaitic Period'), *Studies in Mysticism and Religion*, 1967, pp. 1–28.

[57] Sukkah 28a, referring to R. Jonathan b. Uzziel, a disciple of Hillel; Urbach, 'Ha-Masorot', p. 8.

[58] Urbach, ibid.

[59] P. Hagigah 77b (2.1) and parr.; Lev. Rab. 16.4 (about Ben Azzai); Mek. of R. Simeon b. Yohai to Ex. 19.18 (p. 143, line 25): ' "In fire" – It means that the words of the Torah are compared to fire', etc.).

[60] Urbach, 'Ha-Masorot', p. 9.

The blazing fire which surrounds those who study the Torah was a kind of confirmation that the Torah which was being studied was the Torah from Sinai, the revelation of which was accompanied by flames.

He attributes the use of phrases from the theophany on Mt Sinai in describing the study of the Torah to 'the feeling of continuing revelation which was felt by those sages who, like Akiba, decided for the side of extreme freedom of exposition'.[61] Urbach does not mean, however, that only Rabbis in the school of Akiba felt the presence of God in studying the Torah. After all, in study the Rabbis were directing their minds to Heaven.[62] In any case, many of the passages connecting study with a blazing fire concern Rabbis in the generation before Akiba.[63]

Thus we see that studying and doing the Torah are connected with the feeling of the presence of God. To study the Torah is to be in the presence of the God who gave it, while the observance of the halakot inculcates the feeling of the presence of God. It thus appears that at the very heart of the Rabbis' supposed legalism is the feeling of intimate contact with God. To respond to the problem raised earlier, we should note that those who had a feeling of the presence of God in the midst of daily activities and in the one activity singled out as basic to all other religious actions, the study of the Torah, had no need for the churchly sacraments of which Bousset felt they were bereft. Their experience of God was not that he is remote, but that he is near. The study and practice of the Torah, far from being incongruent with the Rabbis' religious feelings and perceptions, are perfectly congruent. Studying and doing the Torah would be odd behaviour to be characterized as 'the ideal religious life' if God were remote and man alienated, since in that case such behaviour would only reinforce the feeling of inability, helplessness and estrangement. One could never 'study' and 'do' enough to bring down a remote God. But if a man feels that God is near, he can 'study' and 'do' with good heart. He is doing the will of his Father, and his every action reinforces the feeling of God's presence. God is repeatedly met, as it were, in the daily round.

This is a point which has been repeatedly missed by those who have known Rabbinic literature only at second hand and who have therefore not seen the religious significance which the Rabbis attached to studying and doing the law. Thus Rössler has written that in Rabbinic literature man's only relation to God is through the law, and God's only revelation is 'law and only law'.[64] Or, as he puts it elsewhere, man's relationship with God is decided

---

[61] Ibid., p. 11.

[62] So Kadushin, *The Rabbinic Mind*, p. 213, referring to Berakoth 5b (ET, p. 21). On study as piety, not just information assembling, cf. Neusner, *Understanding Rabbinic Judaism*, p. 9.

[63] The passage in p. Hagigah 77b (above, n. 59) refers to R. Eliezer and R. Joshua. On their connection with mystic experiences, see Urbach, 'Ha-Masorot', pp. 1ff.

[64] Rössler, *Gesetz und Geschichte*, p. 16.

entirely by obedience, which must be realized in each new situation.[65]
Rössler has correctly noted the important role which studying and doing the
law plays in Rabbinic literature, but his description, which makes Rabbinic
religion sound entirely legalistic, formal and cold, suffers from three grave
defects. As we noted above, Rössler incorrectly denies that the covenant and
the covenant promises had enduring value in the Rabbis' view. (Man's
relationship with God must be decided anew by each act of obedience.)[66]
Secondly, Rössler entirely overlooks the significance of prayer for the Rabbis,
a significance which will be discussed immediately below. Finally, Rössler
(like Bousset and many others) completely ignores the *significance which the
Rabbis themselves found in studying and doing the law*: they considered themselves thereby brought into the presence of God. The objections to Rabbinic
'legalism' are in part based on the inability of modern scholars to find devotional significance in obeying the law – an inability from which the Rabbis
did not suffer. There are numerous passages to the effect that God is *with* the
pious Jew when he is studying and carrying out the commandments. These
now have been collected by Goldberg,[67] and we shall quote just one:[68]

In Every Place, etc. . . . . In connection with this passage the sages said: wherever
ten persons assemble in a synagogue the Shekinah is with them . . . And how do
we know that He is also with three people holding court? It says: 'In the midst of
the judges He judgeth' (Ps. 82.1). And how do we know that He is also with two?
[Proved by Mal. 3.16] And how do we know that He is even with one? It is said:
'In every place where I cause My name to be mentioned I will come unto thee and
bless thee.'

That the Rabbis were confident of God's presence and accessibility will
become even clearer as we consider the Rabbinic attitude towards prayer.

Prayer and the time of death

The daily prayers of the Rabbis and their followers, prescribed and spontaneous, both presuppose and inculcate the feeling of God's presence. The
practice of praying throughout the day is one of the distinctive marks of
Judaism, though it has been adopted in various ways by Christianity and
Islam. The nature and texture of daily religious life may best be presented
by quoting some of the prayers of the period.

Although very few personal prayers of Tannaitic Rabbis are preserved,[69]

---

[65] Ibid., p. 32.
[66] See 'the enduring validity of the covenantal promises', section 4 above.
[67] Goldberg, *Schekhinah*, pp. 385–99.
[68] Mek. Baḥodesh 11 (243; II, 287; to 20.24).
[69] Many of those which do survive are not relevant to our present discussion. See the series of prayers
collected for the study of their formal characteristics by L. Finkelstein, 'The Development of the
Amidah', *JQR* n.s. 16, 1925–6, pp. 4ff. There is a more complete investigation in J. Heinemann,
Ha-Tefillah bi-Tequfat ha-Tanna'im ve-ha-'Amora'im, 1966.

there are many from the Amoraic period. It may be justifiable to refer to some
of them, on the supposition that there was a continuity in personal piety as
there was in the halakah. The need of even the most righteous to rely upon
God is repeatedly stated in a collection of prayers in Berakoth 16b–17a. We
may give two examples:

R. Johanan on concluding his prayer[70] added the following: May it be Thy will,
O Lord our God, to look upon our shame, and behold our evil plight, and clothe
Thyself in Thy mercies, and cover Thyself in Thy strength, and wrap Thyself in
Thy loving-kindness, and gird Thyself with Thy graciousness, and may the
attribute of Thy kindness and gentleness[71] come before Thee!

Raba[72] on concluding his prayer added the following: My God, before I was
formed I was not worthy [to be formed], and now that I have been formed I am
as if I had not been formed. I am dust in my lifetime, all the more in my death.
Behold I am before Thee like a vessel full of shame and confusion. May it be Thy
will, O Lord my God, that I sin no more, and the sins I have committed before
Thee wipe out in Thy great mercies, but not through evil chastisements and
diseases![73]

The same Raba, whose feeling of worthlessness before God is so moving,
does not betray this feeling in halakic discussions. He can rule that 'if one
constructed a side-post for an alley and raised it three handbreadths from
the ground, or removed it three handbreadths from the wall, his act is
invalid'[74] without betraying the feeling that he is 'like a vessel full of shame
and confusion'. On the contrary, one has the impression that he is in perfect
command of God's commandments and has it in his power to decide what
they are and to fulfil them. If the prayer which he repeated daily had not been
preserved, one might have supposed that he felt religiously self-sufficient,
able to do what was necessary and not in need of God's mercy. Thus we see
that the halakic material may be deceiving for understanding the full scope
and true depth of Rabbinic religion.

This change of tone should not be surprising. When someone is debating
about the definition of a commandment, he naturally talks as if religion is
under his control. But when, in prayer, he feels himself before his God, he is
impressed by his own worthlessness and recognizes his reliance on God's
grace.

---

[70] I.e. The Eighteen Benedictions. R. Johanan was a Palestinian Amora of the second generation.

[71] As opposed to the quality of strict justice.

[72] A Babylonian Amora of the fourth generation (ca. 280–352).

[73] The Talmud adds that this prayer was the confession of R. Hamnuna Zuti on the Day of Atonement. Yoma 87b attributes the prayer to R. Hamnuna (Babylonian Amora of the third and fourth centuries) and comments that Raba (the ET erroneously has 'Rab') used this confession all year and that R. Hamnuna Zuti used it on the Day of Atonement. It is still used on the Day of Atonement. Cf. *JE* VI, p. 201.

[74] Erubin 14b.

It seems likely that this same attitude is what is behind R. Johanan b. Zakkai's weeping upon his death bed. The story runs thus:[75]

When Rabban Johanan ben Zakkai fell ill, his disciples went in to visit him. When he saw them he began to weep. His disciples said to him: Lamp of Israel, pillar of the right hand, mighty hammer! Wherefore weepest thou? He replied: If I were being taken today before a human king who is here today and tomorrow in the grave, whose anger if he is angry with me does not last for ever, who if he imprisons me does not imprison me for ever and who if he puts me to death does not put me to everlasting death, and whom I can persuade with words and bribe with money, even so I would weep. Now that I am being taken before the supreme King of Kings, the Holy One, blessed be He, who lives and endures for ever and ever, whose anger, if He is angry with me, is an everlasting anger, who if He imprisons me imprisons me for ever, who if He puts me to death puts me to death for ever, and whom I cannot persuade with words or bribe with money – nay more, when there are two ways before me, one leading to Paradise and the other to Gehinnom, and I do not know by which I shall be taken, shall I not weep? They said to him: Master, bless us. He said to them: May it be [God's] will that the fear of heaven shall be upon you like the fear of flesh and blood. His disciples said to him: Is that all? He said to them: If only [you can attain this]! You can see [how important this is], for when a man wants to commit a transgression, he says, I hope no man will see me. At the moment of his departure he said to them: Remove the vessels so that they shall not become unclean, and prepare a throne for Hezekiah the king of Judah who is coming.

It is a tradition grown hoary with repetition in New Testament scholarship that this story illustrates more or less everything that is wrong with Rabbinic religion. It is taken as proof that Rabbinic soteriology, which is supposed to demand a majority of good deeds over evil deeds, produced a state of uncertain anxiety.[76] Bultmann put it this way:[77]

A further consequence of the legalistic conception of obedience was that the prospect of salvation became highly uncertain. Who could be sure he had done enough in this life to be saved? Would his observance of the Law and his good works be sufficient? For in the day of judgment all his good works could be counted up and weighed, and woe to him if the scales fell on the side of his evil deeds! When his friends visited Johanan ben Zaccai on his sick-bed, they found him weeping because he was so uncertain of his prospects before the judgement seat of God; the prospect of meeting God as their Judge awakened in the conscientious a scrupulous anxiety and morbid sense of guilt.

This same view has been enshrined in Rengstorf's section on 'Hope in Rabbinic Judaism' in the article on *elpis* in Kittel's *Dictionary*.[78] Rengstorf

---

[75] I quote the version from Berakoth 28b, according to the Soncino translation. There is a parallel in ARN 25. See also Neusner, *Yohanan ben Zakki*, pp. 172f.; rev. ed., pp. 227f.

[76] See Köberle, *Sünde und Gnade*, pp. 655f.; Windisch, *Paulus und das Judentum*, 1935, pp. 53f.; S.-B. III, pp. 218–20 (cf. IV, pp. 5, 11 (t)); Bultmann and Rengstorf, cited immediately below.

[77] Bultmann, *Primitive Christianity*, p. 70.

[78] *TDNT* II, pp. 523–9.

quotes a passing remark of Schlatter that 'Semitism has no precise parallel to *elpis*'[79] as justification for assuming that there are no words for 'hope' in Rabbinic literature. *Tiqvah*, he says, 'had as good as disappeared', citing as an exception only II Bar. 78.6.[80] Before accepting Schlatter's word on this point, he might have considered such a passage as Kiddushin 4.14: 'R. Nehorai says: . . . [The Torah] guards him from all evil while he is young, and in old age it grants him a future and a hope' (*tiqvah*). Or Rengstorf might have considered other words, such as *metuqan* ('what is prepared'), *seber* ('hope'), *sikui* ('future prospect'), or the words for trust and confidence based on *batah*,[81] not to mention such general passages as the various promises of God to save the Israelites or the statements that one may rely on God (Sotah 9.15, *lehishsha'en*). All this might have been expected in a dictionary article on hope, but such matters are outside Rengstorf's purview. He need not review terms or passages, for theology provides the conclusion to his discussion. He simply repeats the cliches about the Rabbis' uncertainty of salvation, an uncertainty which is necessitated by legalism. 'It belongs to a religion of works that its adherents cannot have assurance.'[82] As evidence of the 'lack of personal assurance of salvation', he cites the story of R. Johanan b. Zakkai, while assuring the reader in a footnote that the attitude 'is characteristic of all Rabb[inic] Judaism', a point which is proved by referring to S.-B. III, pp. 218ff.[83]

It comes as somewhat of a relief when Rössler culls other passages from Billerbeck to make the same point.[84] In one, Jacob and Moses are said to fear despite God's promises.[85] Billerbeck (and consequently Rössler) took this to indicate that even Jacob and Moses had no *Heilsgewissheit*, certainty of salvation. The passage (which is an exegesis of Gen. 32.8, 'Then Jacob was greatly afraid') makes, rather, a different point. Various Rabbis offer various possibilities as to what Jacob was afraid of, but none of them has to do with salvation. The final exegesis is that the passage shows that the righteous has no assurance in this world. Billerbeck takes this to mean 'no assurance of salvation', but the meaning is just the opposite. Even the righteous has no assurance that because of a sin (not one too many) he will not be prematurely killed in *this* world (citing Ex. 4.24). No Rabbi would

---

[79] A. Schlatter, *Der Evangelist Matthäus*, p. 402; Rengstorf, p. 523.

[80] Rengstorf, p. 523.

[81] See the passages cited below, nn. 88 and 89. On *batah*, see also above, section 4, pp. 143–6. In his discussion of hope in the Old Testament (*TDNT* II, pp. 521–3), Bultmann did discuss *batah* and its derivatives.

[82] Rengstorf, p. 527.

[83] Ibid. The passage in Billerbeck provides a small collection of passages, and two of the principal ones are discussed immediately below.

[84] Rössler, *Gesetz und Geschichte*, p. 27, citing S.-B. III, p. 208. The passages cited by Rössler reappear in S.-B. III, p. 218, the page referred to by Rengstorf.

[85] Gen. Rab. 76.1–2. On Jacob, cf. Mek. Beshallah Amalek 2 (185; II, 156f. [Amalek 2]; to 17.14).

have said 'in this world' if he had meant 'for the world to come'.[86] The second passage does indicate, on the basis of Ps. 27.13 ('I am sure to see the good reward of the Lord in the land of the living', but the Rabbis take the dots over *lule'* to indicate uncertainty; thus, 'I am not sure'), that David was sure that God would pay a good reward to the righteous in the world to come, but was not sure that he would share in it. On the basis of such passages, as we have seen, New Testament scholars have concluded that the requirement of more fulfilments than transgressions produced uncertainty.

It should be readily apparent that the meaning of such passages cannot be what has been attributed to them. Surely no Rabbis thought that Jacob, Moses and David might have transgressed oftener than they obeyed, nor can they have doubted that the patriarchs would have a share in the world to come. Citing Rabbinic statements about the patriarchs as proof of the *weighing* and *anxiety* theories should of itself lead one to doubt the theories. The entire Rabbinic attitude toward the patriarchs would stand against this construction. Concerning Moses it is explicitly said elsewhere that he trusted (*mubṭaḥ*) God that he was a son of the world to come, citing Deut. 31.16, 'And the Lord said to Moses: Behold, you are about to sleep with your fathers and rise.'[87] And before one concludes from R. Johanan b. Zakkai's death-bed story that uncertainty generally prevailed, such passages as the following should be considered:

'When you walk, they [Heb. 'it', apparently the *mitsvah* and *torah* of 6.20) will lead you' (Prov. 6.22) – in this world. 'When you lie down, they will watch over you' – at the hour of your death. 'And when you awake, they will talk with you' – in the world to come. And thus it says, 'O dwellers in the dust, awake and sing for joy,' etc. (Isa. 26.19). Lest you should say: My hope (*seber*) is destroyed, my future prospect (*sikui*) is gone, Scripture teaches, 'I am the Lord.' [It means] I am your hope and I am your future prospect and upon me [rests] your confident trust (*biṭṭeḥoneka*).[88]

On Ex. 33.29 ('Happy are you, O Israel! Who is like you, a people saved by the Lord'), Sifre Deut. comments:

All Israel gathered before Moses, and they said to him: Our Teacher Moses, tell us what good the Holy One, blessed be he, is about to give us in the future to come. He said to them: I do not know what [further] to say to you. You will be happy [in the way] that is prepared (*metuqan*) for you. . . .: 'O how abundant is thy goodness, which thou hast laid up for those who fear thee' (Ps. 31.20[19]).[89]

---

[86] Cf. Kiddushin 39b: There is no reward for precepts in *this* world (but there is in the world to come).

[87] Sifre Deut. 305 (327; to 31.14). The proof about Moses is produced by dropping the subject from 'rise' in Deut. 31.16: 'this people will rise'. On promising and trusting, see section 4, pp. 101–4. On the assurance of salvation for Moses, see also the passage cited above, section 8 n. 125.

[88] Sifra Aḥare pereq 13.11. On this section of Sifra, see Epstein, *Mebo'ot*, pp. 640f.

[89] Sifre Deut. 356 (424; to 33.29).

How, then, are the passages about R. Johanan b. Zakkai and David doubting to be understood? The passages about biblical figures doubting or fearing probably have more than one function. In large part they are simply exegetical. Faced with a passage which says that Jacob feared, the Rabbis try to imagine what he could have feared, since he had God's promises. Faced with dots over *lule'* in Ps. 27.13, a Rabbi hypothesizes that they may mean 'I am not sure'. It is exegetical abuse to turn this sort of midrashic effort into systematic theology. At another level, statements such as the one that even Jacob feared were taken as comforting subsequent Israelites in their own fears: 'If our ancestor Jacob, who had received God's assurance, was nevertheless afraid, how much the more are we [justified in feeling afraid].'[90] The point is that the world is dangerous; comfort and prosperity may be transitory. If we feel insecure in this world (*not* about the next), we may take comfort from the fact that even Jacob feared.

One should also not reason to general morbid anxiety on the basis of the story about R. Johanan b. Zakkai. While it is quite possible that, as an individual, R. Johanan was uncertain about his fate after death, it is more likely that the true significance of this is not that 'Rabbinic soteriology' was deficient, but that R. Johanan was a pious and humble man who, in the presence of God, thought of his own worthlessness and realized that, if God judged strictly, he could be condemned.[91] He knew, in other words, that he had no claim to present before God. One would think that Lutheran scholars would have found this attitude laudable. This interpretation of R. Johanan's attitude seems to be very much in accord with his saying in Aboth 2.8, 'If thou hast wrought much in the Law claim not merit for thyself, for to this end wast thou created.' This saying is itself reminiscent of Jesus' saying that, when a man has done all he can, he has only done his duty (Luke 17.7–10). This attitude, which excludes the possibility of works of supererogation, which many have found in Rabbinic thought and regarded as very objectionable, seems to be primarily what is indicated in the story of R. Johanan's death. It is very much in accord with the prayers which we have quoted from the Amoraim, and especially in accord with the prayer of Raba.

The misunderstanding of this point has played such a role in Christian attitudes towards Judaism that it may be useful to add a modern parallel. In a description of the pious Catholic, Gervase Crouchback, one of the characters in his trilogy on World War II, Evelyn Waugh writes:[92]

As a reasoning man Mr Crouchback had known that he was honourable, charitable and faithful, a man who by all the formularies of his faith should be confident of salvation; as a man of prayer he saw himself as totally unworthy of divine notice.

[90] Gen. Rab. 76.1; ET, p. 701.

[91] So Neusner, in the first edition of *Yohanan ben Zakkai*, p. 173: 'one notes in his words a profound humility'. The phrase is omitted in the rev. ed., p. 228.

[92] Evelyn Waugh, *Unconditional Surrender*, 1961, p. 78.

This seems to me to be precisely the attitude of the Rabbis. It appears that the story of R. Johanan's weeping on his death bed, rather than proving that God was perceived as remote, that a man had to obey more commandments than he committed transgressions in order to be saved, and that anxiety was the resultant religious attitude, shows rather that the Rabbi felt close to God, had a real perception of living in his sight, and was conscious of his own unworthiness. This consciousness, which is to be expected in prayer and at the time of death, when a man enters the presence of God and compares his weakness to God's strength, is not at all incompatible with a modest certainty of salvation which we have seen repeatedly in the literature, a confidence which is based on trust in God's promises, belief in the election, and reliance on God's faithfulness to forgive the sinner who repents and atones for his sin.[93]

What of the other traditional charge, that the Jews suffered not only from morbid anxiety but also from arrogance? We may cite another death-bed story:[94]

Rabbi, at the time of his passing, raised his ten fingers towards heaven and said: 'Sovereign of the Universe, it is revealed and known to you that I have laboured in the study of the Torah with my ten fingers and that I did not enjoy [any worldly] benefits even with my little finger. May it be Thy will that there be peace in my [last] resting place.' A *bath ḳol* echoed, announcing, *He shall enter into peace; they shall rest on their beds* (Isa. 57.2).

There is a similar prayer from a later period:[95]

Master of the Universe, I have examined the two hundred and forty-eight limbs which you have put in me, and I have not found that I have offended you with one of them. [If you gave me the limbs], how much more should you give me my life!

It is this sort of statement which gives apparent substance to the suspicion that the Rabbis, besides feeling insecure and uncertain, also felt boastful and self-righteous. Yet Rabbi, who showed what will be to some an offensive confidence at the time of his death, could also pray to be protected from sin by God: 'may neither our host nor we be confronted with any evil thought

[93] The result of an unreflective conflation of passages from Billerbeck on these various points is seen, for example, in Schrenk's article on the *dikai-* word group in Kittel's *Theological Dictionary*. On the one hand he writes that the Jews suffered under an 'uncertainty of the belief in justification' (*TDNT* II, p. 213). On the other hand he states that 'the basic principle' 'that all who die attain expiation by death, is firmly rooted in Jewish thinking' (ibid., p. 218). Which is it? There is a similar difficulty in J. Schmid, 'Sünde und Sühne', pp. 21-5, who sees the belief in atonement and repentance as a noble view which is contradicted by the baser view that one must increase the account of his good deeds so that they outweigh his sins, a view which results in there being no *Heilsgewissheit* in Judaism.

[94] Ketuboth 104a; ET, p. 604.

[95] P. Berakoth 8b (4.4, end). The Rabbi is apparently R. Samuel b. Naḥman, the Palestinian Amora of the third century.

or sin or transgression or iniquity from now and for all time.'[96] One who actually relies on the strength of his own virtue does not need to ask God for protection from sin. It is as mistaken to reason from such singular expressions of self-assertive confidence to a theology of self-righteousness as it is to reason from statements of humble apprehension to a theology of uncertainty and anxiety. Heinemann has now clarified the meaning of such prayers as that of Rabbi by discussing their form and *Sitz im Leben*. He notes that prayers such as those just quoted (Ketuboth 104a and P. Berakoth 8b) are completely different in tone and style from the type earlier quoted from Berakoth 16b–17a. In the type first cited, the posture is that of a servant before his master. In the second type, which is characterized by self-assertiveness and 'chutspah before God',[97] the man in prayer puts first his self-justification and then his request. This latter type is formally modelled on argumentation in the law courts; there are approximate parallels to this sort of pleading in Jeremiah[98] and Job.[99] Although we have here quoted two prayers in which the individual cites his own virtues on his own behalf, Heinemann has shown that this is not typical of Rabbinic piety. To quote from the English summary: 'The absence of this type of prayer from regular community services is self-explanatory; it could be tolerated only in times of emergency and when coming from pious men of renown, who intercede for the community.'[100] Thus it is erroneous to attribute arrogance to the Rabbis generally on the basis of such prayers as that of Rabbi. Any devout man may, at certain times, be led to boast of his security with God; while apprehension at the prospect of death is surely common in all religions. It is very difficult to reach a fair understanding of death-bed stories like that of R. Johanan b. Zakkai or that of Rabbi if one's aim is to show the superiority of Christianity to Judaism. We turn now to consider the significance of other prayers for understanding Rabbinic religious life.

There are at least two other Tannaitic traditions concerning prayer which exemplify the attitude of being close to God and dependent on him. One is the short prayer which is to be said when one 'passes through a place infested with beasts or bands of robbers'. After giving examples of short prayers said in such circumstances by R. Eliezer, R. Joshua and R. Eleazar b. R. Zadok, there follows the short prayer attributed only to 'others' but which apparently became the standard: 'The needs of Thy people Israel are many and their wit is small. May it be Thy will, O Lord our God, to give to each one his sustenance and to each body what it lacks. Blessed art Thou,

---

[96] Berakoth 46a.
[97] Heinemann, *Tefillah*, p. 128.
[98] Ibid., p. 121.
[99] Ibid., p. 130.
[100] Ibid., p. x.

O Lord, who hearkenest unto prayer.'[101] One sees here that, far from being able to claim God's gifts as a reward for merit, the Israelites appear as those who are not able even to ask properly for their needs to be fulfilled. God is appealed to to give to each what he needs.[102] The other prayer is attributed by R. Eleazar b. R. Zadok to his father, who lived in the time of the second Temple. The prayer was the short prayer on Sabbath evenings: 'From thy love, O Lord our God, with which thou loved thy people Israel, and from thy compassion, our King, which thou bestowed on the sons of thy covenant, thou hast given us, O Lord our God, this great and hallowed seventh day in love.'[103] In prayer, there is no mention of the covenant's being given as a reward for keeping the commandments; but the covenant itself and the commandments attached to it (in this case, to keep the Sabbath holy) are seen as expressions of God's love and mercy.

We have thus far been dealing only with personal prayers which were said after one of the set prayers or on some other occasion. We should also refer, however, to some of the petitions comprising the *Shemoneh 'Esreh*, the Eighteen Benedictions, also called the *'Amidah*, since the prayer is said standing. The prayers collected under this title come from different times, and the version currently in use is not necessarily the same as the one known in the Tannaitic period, if, indeed, any one form was used by all the Tannaim.[104] The Tannaim knew and referred to these prayers, but they are not actually quoted in the Tannaitic literature.[105] We may quote three of the prayers which were probably known and prayed during virtually all of the Tannaitic period in a form very like that given here. It should be remembered, however, that many of the early Rabbis seem to have exercised con-

---

[101] Berakoth 29b; ET, p. 181. According to R. Huna, 'the halaka follows the "Others"'. The passage is paralleled in T. Berakoth 3.7.

[102] Cf. the prayer which R. Hisda said in the name of Mar Ukba (Berakoth 29b): 'Even at the time when they transgress the words of the Torah may all their requirements not be overlooked by Thee.'

[103] T. Berakoth 3.7; cf. Urbach, *Hazal*, p. 492 (ET, p. 553). Lieberman (*Tosefta Ki-Fshuṭah, Zera'im*, p. 35) believes the last word, 'in love', to be an addition.

[104] Heinemann has argued against the idea of an 'original' version, from which other versions derive, and in favour of the existence of various orders of the *'Amidah*. It is likely, however, that the principal themes and the general tone represented by the selections which we shall cite below were early and widespread. See *Tefillah*, pp. 138–57; English summary, pp. x–xii. There is a very extensive literature on the origins, history and development of the *'Amidah*, and there are several attempts to reconstruct the 'original' version. A bibliography is given by Heinemann. See also the useful collection of essays in J. J. Petuchowski, ed., *Contributions to the Scientific Study of Jewish Liturgy*, 1970. Petuchowski himself is in agreement with Heinemann; see p. xxv. The tradition is that the *'Amidah* was redacted under the presidency of R. Gamaliel II. Megillah 17b gives this baraita: 'Simeon the Pakulite formulated eighteen blessings in the presence of Rabban Gamaliel in the proper order in Jabneh. R. Johanan said (others report, it was stated in a Baraitha): A hundred and twenty elders, among whom were many prophets, drew up eighteen blessings in a fixed order'. Heinemann, p. 17, gives other passages attributing the drawing up of prayers to an early period. Some have argued that some of the eighteen benedictions are from the Hasmonean period or even before. See e.g. Hirsch in *JE* XI, pp. 276f., 280f.; Finkelstein, 'The Development of the Amidah', *JQR* n.s. 16, 1925–6, pp. 1–43, 127–69.

[105] Berakoth 4.3: 'Rabban Gamaliel says: A man should pray the Eighteen [Benedictions] every day. R. Joshua says: The substance of the Eighteen. R. Akiba says: If his prayer is fluent in his mouth he should pray the Eighteen, but if not, the substance of the Eighteen.'

siderable freedom in praying even the 'fixed' prayers, adding new things each time.[106] There was some feeling against praying in a fixed form and in favour of spontaneity.[107]

Lead us back, our Father, to thy Torah, and cause us to return in perfect repentance before Thee. Blessed art thou, O Lord, who acceptest repentance.[108]

Forgive us, our Father, for we have sinned. Blessed art thou, O Lord, who multipliest forgiveness.[109]

Hear our voice, O Lord our God, and have mercy on us. Blessed art thou, O Lord, who hearest prayer.[110]

When it is remembered that prayers such as these were said daily by the Rabbis, one has a better understanding of the general religious setting in which the halakic discussions took place. All did not depend upon man's own ability, will or determination in fulfilling the commandments, important as these were; but one could turn to God for help and strength, in the confidence that God hears prayer,[111] grants man repentance, forgives sin, and will ultimately save those who trust in him. The tone of the 'Amidah, and consequently of the daily prayer life of the Rabbis, is aptly described by Heinemann:

The *shemone-'esre* as a whole is constructed according to the pattern of a plea of 'a servant before his master'. However, the 'praise' is restrained; nor is there an exaggerated stress on the lowliness of the suppliant. God is addressed unhesitatingly in the Thou-style, and the relationship between Him and man is seen both as an intimate one of mutual love as between father and son, and as one of dependence and awe.[112]

We have seen, then, that the Rabbis emphasized as strongly as possible the necessity of obeying God's commandments to the best of one's ability.

---

[106] This appears in comments in the Palestinian Talmud on Berakoth 4.4: 'R. Eliezer [the P.T. has Eleazar] says: He that makes his prayer fixed, his prayer is no supplication.' The Talmud has various comments, including the following: 'R. Aḥa said in the name of R. Jose: It is necessary to add something new to it each day.' 'R. Abbahu used to make a new benediction each day.' P. Berakoth 8a, near end (4.3; cf. ET, pp. 88f.). Zeitlin has argued that while the Temple stood there were no fixed forms or fixed times for private prayer. The fixing of both was after 70 c.e. See *Rise and Fall of the Judaean State* II, pp. 339f., and further references there.

[107] Besides Berakoth 4.4, cited in the preceding footnote, see Aboth 2.13, in the name of R. Simeon (b. Nathaniel): 'When thou prayest make not thy prayer fixed, but [a plea for] mercies and supplications before God'. Cf. Bacher, *Agada der Tannaiten* I, p. 103. Hirsch, *JE* XI, p. 227, incorrectly attributes this saying to R. Simeon b. Yohai.

[108] The fifth benediction, translated from the text given by Finkelstein, 'Amidah', p. 147. Cf. ibid., pp. 11, 13, 18. Elbogen (*Geschichte des Achtzehngebets*, 1903, p. 19) placed this prayer among the earliest.

[109] The sixth benediction; see Finkelstein, ibid., pp. 147,18. The fifth and sixth benedictions are both dated by Finkelstein to the period 10–40 c.e.

[110] The seventeenth (or sixteenth) benediction; ibid., p. 161. Finkelstein considers the prayer pre-Maccabean.

[111] On the point that God is accessible in prayer, see especially Sifre Num. 42 (45; to 6.26).

[112] Heinemann, *Tefillah*, English summary, p. xii.

But they also maintained that the door was always open for penitent sinners. Many Rabbis doubtless had confidence in their own ability to obey the law successfully. Yet they did not rely on that ability (with perhaps a few exceptions), but rather on the grace of God. This reliance on the grace of God, accompanied by a feeling of one's own worthlessness, appears especially on those occasions when the Rabbis felt themselves to be in the direct presence of God: in prayer[113] or at death.[114] While the recorded personal prayers of the Tannaim are regrettably few, the traditions which do exist, when coupled with later Amoraic prayers, afford a glimpse into the personal life of piety and devotion and self-abnegation before God which characterized at least some of the Rabbis. As valuable as this glimpse is, however, the main point that the Rabbis relied upon the grace of God does not depend upon our examination of Rabbinic prayers but upon their belief in election and atonement, a belief which is well documented from Rabbis of all schools and all periods. The examination of prayers does help us, however, to understand the nature of the material with which we have to deal and the way in which the religious 'tone' may vary with the mode of discourse.[115]

11. Conclusion

I have tried to develop two arguments at once: the negative argument that one view is wrong and the positive argument that another view is right. Negatively, I have not intended to argue that there is *another* view possible besides the view that Rabbinic religion was a religion of legalistic works-righteousness in which a man was saved by fulfilling more commandments than he committed transgressions.[1] I have argued that that view is completely wrong: it proceeds from theological presuppositions and is supported by systematically misunderstanding and misconstruing passages in Rabbinic literature. I do not find such a view in any stratum of Tannaitic literature or to be held by any Rabbi of the Tannaitic period. It has thus been my inten-

[113] On the attitude of self-abnegation in prayer, see the statement by R. Judah concerning R. Akiba (T. Berakoth 3.5): 'When R. Akiba prayed with the congregation, he kept his prayer brief for their sake; but when he prayed alone, one would leave him in one corner and find him in another, because of his kneelings and prostrations.' Parallel in Berakoth 31a (given anonymously).

[114] These are not the only occasions for the expression of reliance on God, although they are the principal ones which survive in the literature (which is not, it should be noted, a literature of personal piety). But whenever human power flags or fails, the Rabbis note that their only stay is the Father in Heaven (Sotah 9.15, repeated three times).

[115] On the nature of Rabbinic material, cf. Sandmel, *The First Christian Century*, pp. 74, 76: 'A lack of sympathy for the method of Rabbinism has misled more than one Christian scholar into a failure to recognize the content that the constrained method produced' (p. 74). The present point is that Rabbinic prayers, though relatively few, aid us in perceiving the religious depth which is partially obscured by the halakic method.

[1] Cf. the view of Longenecker, above, section 1, pp. 56f.

tion to destroy the Weberian view which has proved so persistent in New Testament scholarship, and to do so in a convincing manner: by showing that the 'evidence' on which it is based does not in fact lead to the Weberian construction.

To take two examples from earlier discussions: it has frequently been argued that the Rabbis believed in a theory of strict retribution according to works. The belief in retribution (*Vergeltungsgedanke*), which dominated the flickering hope in God's mercy, helps to establish the theory that salvation was seen as strictly in accord with one's works. On examination, we saw that the frequent assertions of reward and punishment were not actually understood *by the Rabbis* in that way. Strict justice was not exclusive of God's mercy, but the opposite of caprice. Further, the theory of retribution functioned within a larger framework of election and atonement and refers to God's intra-covenantal behaviour. It is not a theory of soteriology which undercuts the hope for mercy (see the conclusion to section 7). Secondly, we may recall the 'on condition' passages. Saying that the covenant was given on the condition of obedience might seem to imply that the Rabbis believed that disobedience would lead God to revoke the covenant promises, so that the election, in effect, had constantly to be *earned*. In fact, we found those passages never to imply such a view (which, indeed, is totally absent from Rabbinic literature), but to have quite other purposes, the most important of which was to state that a man must *confess* the commandments in order to *retain* his position in the covenant: denial of the right of God to give commandments indicates denial of the election (sections 4 and 6). The view that Judaism was a religion of works-righteousness, or that such a religion dominates Rabbinic literature, depends on providing an interpretative framework for such themes as retribution and 'on condition that'. The passages are understood not as the Rabbis meant them, but according to preconceived theological categories according to which any nomistic religion must be legalistic in the negative sense. It is this entire interpretative framework which is wrong.

It follows that the text books and reference works in which that view is found and where it is presumed to be proved – principally Bousset's *Religion des Judentums*, Billerbeck's *Kommentar*, Schürer's history and several articles in Kittel's *Wörterbuch* – are, as far as they deal with Rabbinic religion, completely untrustworthy. They cannot be corrected by new editions citing different views or by mitigating some of their harsher and more ill-founded remarks. They proceed from wrong premises, they misconstrue the material, and they are, like those Jews who cast off the yoke, beyond redemption. Billerbeck may retain some usefulness as a collection of passages on individual points, with several provisions: that the user be able to look up the passages and read them in context, that he disregard as much as possible Billerbeck's own summaries and syntheses, and that he be able to imagine how to find passages on the topic not cited by Billerbeck. There are examples ready at hand to illustrate the importance of the last point. The pages in Billerbeck on which Rengstorf relied to find passages about hope do not contain the pertinent passages which we cited in the discussion of Rengstorf's view, and consequently the passages were not available to Rengstorf. Similarly, Rössler was restricted in his study of 'promise' and 'trust' to the selection given by Billerbeck, where again one will not find the most pertinent Tannaitic passages which show that the promises of God were considered by the Rabbis to remain valid and that they were trusted in. To say that, to use Billerbeck, one must be able to find passages not given by Billerbeck, is really to say that Billerbeck's *Kommentar* should not be used by those it was designed to serve: New Testament scholars who have no ready independent access to Rabbinic material.

The positive argument, that there is another view which is all-pervasive in the literature and which reflects a broad agreement on religious principles among Rabbis of different times and different schools, has been a difficult one. It is difficult because of the lack of systematic theological analysis on the part of the Rabbis. We should recall the nature of the material and the strategy of the inquiry. The halakic material especially tends to deal with relatively minor details, with areas where there are problems. In it the Rabbis, as it were, are skirmishing on the borders of their religion. This aspect of the literature has led many to assume that minor details constituted the Rabbis' principal religious concerns; they were careful of tithing mint, dill and cummin, but neglected the weightier matters. One should rather conclude that debates on details reflect agreement on central issues. Further, and most important for the strategy of our study, the skirmishes may even reveal what the central convictions were. From debates about *why* God chose Israel we infer the centrality of the conviction *that* he chose Israel. The debates about *how* to obey reveal the *concern* to obey. Further, the concern to obey, when studied, turns out to show a reliance on God's fidelity to the covenant which contains the laws, not an anxious concern to learn how, by obedience, to win God's favour. Perhaps most telling are the debates about which means of atonement atone for which sins. Rather than revealing a concern for externalistic observance, these debates and differences of opinion reveal three things: (1) that there was a means of atonement for every transgression; (2) that the Rabbis were concerned with atonement as a living religious issue; (3) that, since atonement for individual sins *restores* the penitent sinner to the right relationship with God, he originally *had* a right relationship with God, a relationship established by God's mercy and maintained by the individual's obedience and repentance and by God's forgiveness. One could learn simply by studying the discussions about which means of atonement atone for which sins that the Rabbis believed in the *enduring validity of the covenant relationship*, that they *did not count and weigh merits against demerits* (but rather atoned for transgression), and that they *believed that God has provided for the salvation of all faithful members of Israel* – all those who maintain their place in the covenant by obedience and by employing the means of atonement provided by the covenant, especially repentance, for transgression. On the question of atonement, the debates about the means cover all periods and schools, and there are no exceptions to the general view of the significance of atonement which we just outlined. We conclude, then, that there is a generally prevalent and pervasive pattern of religion to be found in Rabbinic literature. The pattern is based on election and atonement for transgressions, it being understood that God gave commandments in connection with the election and that obedience to them, or atonement and repentance for transgression, was expected as the condition for remaining in the covenant community. The best title for this sort of religion is 'covenantal nomism'. Since this pattern, when described, explains the reason for the halakah (to determine how to obey the God who chose Israel and gave them commandments), what lies behind debates on various points (e.g. why God chose Israel and how various sins are atoned for), and also coheres with numerous explicit statements by the Rabbis themselves (all Israel will be saved, God will keep his promises to Israel, he will keep one's soul at the time of death and the like), I conclude that the pattern is not a false imposition on the material but actually reflects the view of religion which lies behind it.

We should pay special attention to the covenant conception in Rabbinic literature. The covenant, especially God's side, is more presupposed than directly discussed, but the very existence of the halakah, which discusses man's side, gives a first indication that God's side *was* presupposed, not forgotten or ignored as has often been maintained. The centrality of the covenant conception, as we have indicated above, is in part shown by the assumption which lies behind the discussions of atonement. Atonement implies the restoration to a pre-existing relationship, and that relationship is best called covenantal. The Rabbis can say that God is faithful to keep the covenant with Israel (section 4 n. 88), but they often employ other terminology. Instead of 'accept the covenant', one often finds 'confess the exodus' in passages which indicate that one who wishes to be counted among those chosen and redeemed by God will consequently accept ('confess') the covenantal commandments (above, p. 94). Often the Rabbis speak of God as King, not an oriental despot who rules without consent, but one who solicits assent by first saving and protecting the people, and who only then gives commandments (the beginning of section 4). Thus the Rabbis can remark that a man accepts the 'Kingship of Heaven' when he agrees to obey the commandments (section 5 n. 84), or that one accepts 'the yoke of the Kingdom of Heaven' before accepting the 'yoke of the commandments' (Berakoth 2.2). In slightly different terminology, the one who accepts the commandments accepts the yoke of Heaven (section 4 n. 39). The very frequent theme of accepting God's commandments as indicating that one accepts being in God's 'Kingdom' or under his 'yoke' (*not* as earning one's place in the Kingdom) well conveys the Rabbinic conception of the *covenant*, to use the most convenient single word. The conception is that God acts, that Israel accepts the action as being for them, that God gives commandments, that Israel agrees to obey the commandments, and that continuing to accept the commandments demonstrates that one is 'in', while refusing to obey indicates that one is 'out'. All this is frequently expressed without the use of the term 'covenant'.

By way of summary, we may make one further observation: Rabbinic religion, while personal and individual, was also corporate and collective. Moore especially emphasized the former aspects. Religion as a personal relation between God and man he held to be the primary characteristic of Rabbinic Judaism, and he considered that herein lies 'its most significant advance beyond the older religion of Israel'. Moore recognized, to be sure, that the personal relationship with God was maintained 'in the fellowship of the religious community'.[2] While confirming Moore's point about religion's becoming individualized and interiorized,[3] we should also note the degree to which the corporate conception was maintained. As Urbach has emphasized, the election was of all Israel; and the idea that individuals had a community responsibility to keep the commandments, as well as a direct individual responsibility to God, was not lost.[4] One can find statements to the effect that an individual's sin brings punishment on all Israel[5] as well as such statements as that one who sins by transgressing the Sabbath intentionally is 'cut off' from his people, but his people left in peace.[6] But even more than the fact that the Rabbis could speak of both collective and individual reward and punishment, the pattern of religion which we have been discussing demonstrates how individual and collective religion were combined. We note that the individual's place in God's plan was accomplished by his being a member of the group. Thus we find virtually no individual quest for salvation in Rabbinic literature. The question is whether or not one is an Israelite in good standing. On the other hand, simple heredity did not ensure

[2] Moore, *Judaism* I, p. 121.
[3] Cf. ibid., pp. 113f.; 501f.
[4] Urbach, *Hazal*, pp. 477f. (ET, pp. 538–40).
[5] Urbach, ibid., citing R. Simeon b. Yohai in Lev. Rab. 4.6 (ET, p. 55); Mek. of R. Simeon b. Yohai to 19.6 (p. 139). See also T. Sotah 7.2: one is punished for every transgression forbidden in the Torah; but in the case of one who, by making a false oath, takes the name of God in vain, both he and 'every man' are punished.
[6] Urbach, ibid., citing Mek. Shabbata 1 (342; III, 202; to 31.14).

salvation. That came to all those individual Israelites who were faithful. Further, especially after the destruction of the Temple, the group did not mediate between God and individual Israelites: a man's piety was personal, his prayers were directly to God, his forgiveness was directly from God. Rabbinic Judaism's adaptation of the traditional group-oriented covenantal religion to the spirit of individual piety characteristic of the Hellenistic period may account in large part for its strength and endurance. It is noteworthy that Christianity adopted a very similar mix of group membership and individual and personal religion.[7]

[7] See Bultmann, *Theology of the New Testament* I, p. 93.

II

THE DEAD SEA SCROLLS

1. Introduction[1]

A scarcely more than casual reading of the Dead Sea Scrolls will reveal that the themes which we discussed as the component parts of the Rabbinic structure of religion are also found in great abundance in the Qumran literature. Covenant, commandments, the punishment of the wicked, the salvation of the righteous and other common Jewish themes appear on virtually every page of the major documents and may be seen reflected in the fragments and smaller documents. Further, various studies have shown the detailed agreements between the Qumranian halakah and the Pharisaic,[2] which would incline one to think of a close and positive relationship among the various forms of Judaism of the period (despite the obvious inter-group hostilities). On the other hand, however, the argument, presented in many different forms, that the Qumran literature reveals a kind of religion which is closer to what surfaces in Christianity than is any other form of Judaism

[1] I omit here any discussion of such introductory questions as the date of the documents and the identity of the sect, as well as a description of the literature. The literature has been repeatedly described. In what follows, since the context of ideas and terms is important for our study, I rely largely on the principal Scrolls – that is, those from Cave I and the Covenant of Damascus. I accept the general scholarly opinion that the Scrolls pre-date 70 c.e. and are the literary remains of a group of Essenes. It should be noted that the Qumran material is not perfectly homogeneous. In some instances a developmental history can be traced, and the various documents – and parts of documents – represent differences of opinion on individual points as well as differences of overall intention and viewpoint. These divergences will be discussed in their appropriate places in what follows. The differences are not such, however, as to render impossible a discussion of the Qumran pattern of religion. We shall see that divergent statements on individual points not infrequently spring from the same general view of the nature of religion and the religious life. The position taken here on the use of the documents to determine the sect's basic theology, noting differences but not supposing that they represent different theologies or philosophies, is similar to that of M. Hengel, *Judaism and Hellenism* II, p. 148 n. 739 (p. 406 n. 674 in the first German edition; the second was not available to me); cf. also Maier, *Mensch und freier Wille*, p. 165. See further below, section 9.

[2] Chaim Rabin, *Qumran Studies*, 1957; S. Lieberman in *PAAJR* 20, 1951, pp. 395–404; *JBL* 71, 1952, pp. 199–206; H. Bietenhardt, 'Sabbatvorschriften von Qumrān im Lichte des rabbinischen Rechts und der Evangelien', *Qumran-Probleme* (ed. Bardtke), pp. 53–74; H. Braun, *Spätjüdisch-häretischer und frühchristlicher Radikalismus* I, pp. 117f. Rabin is of the view that the Scrolls stem from 'a die-hard Pharisee group trying to uphold "genuine" Pharisaism (as they understood it) against the more flexible ideology introduced by the Rabbis in authority' (p. 69). In a sense this is a dispute over terms, since holders of the Essene view grant that the Essenes and the Pharisees stem from common roots and are closely related.

would seem to imply that the religion of the Qumran covenanters should not easily be fitted into the same mould as other forms of Palestinian Jewish religion. The arguments that Johannine dualism,[3] or the Pauline doctrine of justification by faith,[4] or various striking concepts in Hebrews[5] are to be explained as connected with Qumranism but not other Jewish movements are, in part, arguments for the divergence of the religion of Qumran from forms of religion previously known in Judaism. The question that will confront us is this: how crucial are the points at which Essenism is unique for determining the overall type and form of the religion? Are the differences matters of detail or definition which do not alter the general structure of religion which we found in Rabbinic literature, or did the forces which drove the followers of the Teacher of Righteousness into the wilderness also compel the shaping of a basically different mode of being religious? To answer this question, we may best concentrate first on the connected themes of the covenant, the election, the identity of the elect and the wicked, and the definition of 'Israel'.

2. The covenant and the covenant people

The covenant

There are two ways of formulating God's covenant with the Essenes in the surviving literature. Both appear to amount to the same thing, although the difference in formulation may have had important theological implications within the Essene movement. One formulation, the best known and most striking, is that God had made with the community a *new* covenant (CD 6.19; 8.21; 20.12; IQpHab 2.3f.). The other formulation, which is the more frequent, is that God made a covenant with Moses (or the patriarchs) but that it contained hidden things understood only in the community, so that the community comprises the only adherents to God's covenant with Israel. Thus CD 15.5–11:

And every member of the covenant for all Israel, they shall let their sons who attain 'to pass among them that are mustered' swear with an oath of the covenant. And likewise is the ruling during the whole epoch of wickedness with regard to everyone who turns from his corrupt way: on the day that he speaks to the overseer of the Many, they shall muster him with the oath of the covenant which Moses concluded with Israel, namely the covenant to return to the Law of Moses 'with all *one's* heart and with all *one's* soul', i.e. to that which is found to be done in the

---

[3] R. E. Brown, 'The Qumran Scrolls and the Johannine Gospel and Epistles', *S&NT*, p. 195.
[4] M. Burrows, *The Dead Sea Scrolls*, p. 334.
[5] Y. Yadin, 'The Dead Sea Scrolls and the Epistle to the Hebrews', *Aspects of the Dead Sea Scrolls* (ed. Rabin and Yadin), pp. 36–55.

whole epoch of wickedness. And let no man let him know the rulings (*mishpaṭim*) until he has stood before the overseer, lest he turn out to be a fool when he examines him.

It is clear here that 'returning to the Law of Moses' is in fact equivalent to joining the 'new covenant', for we learn that a man may not learn the individual laws (*mishpaṭim*) of the covenant until he is proved to be acceptable. This is seen elsewhere when 'returning to the Law of Moses' is mentioned. Thus in IQS 5.8f., 'returning to the Law of Moses' means obeying the Law of Moses 'in accordance with all that has been revealed of it to the sons of Zadok, the Keepers of the Covenant and Seekers of His will, and to the multitude of the men of their Covenant'. The term 'their covenant' (also IQS 6.19; IQSa 1.2 = 'His covenant') is particularly telling. The antecedent of 'their' is the priestly founders of the Essene community, and *their* covenant is equated with *God's* covenant, as in IQSa 1.2f.

This is a more satisfactory formulation than calling the covenant 'new', a terminology which opens the way to difficulties (has God denied or replaced the Mosaic covenant?),[6] and which might have been totally unacceptable if it were not for the phrase in Jeremiah. That the adjective 'new' is substantially correct is, however, indicated by the necessity of claiming that the Mosaic covenant (including, for the purpose, the prophets as well as the law) contained secrets which have been only recently revealed. Thus, according to the Damascus Document, God had most of the first members of the covenant destroyed because of their disobedience. With the remnant who remained, however, he established his covenant 'by revealing to them hidden things concerning which all Israel had gone astray' (CD 3.10–14). Similarly IQS 5.11f. characterizes those who are not in the covenant as those who both went astray with regard to the 'hidden things' and insolently transgressed 'revealed things', presumably referring to the non-secret parts of the covenant, i.e. those parts common to the Essenes and other Jewish groups. According to IQpHab 7.4f. it was the Teacher of Righteousness 'to whom God made known all the mysteries of the words of His servants the Prophets'. In IQS and IQSb, however, the Zadokite priests in general are said to have established the covenant (IQSb 3.24; IQS 5.21f.; the subject of 'to establish a covenant' in IQS 8.10 is difficult to determine precisely, but may be the 'Council of the Community' in 8.5; the 'Prince of the Congregation' is apparently the subject of 'to establish a covenant' in IQSb 5.23).[7] Attributing to the Zadokite priests the establishing of the covenant, as well as the preserving of it (IQS 5.2f., 9), may indicate their role in revealing the

---

[6] On the difficulties of considering the 'new covenant' as a second, different covenant, see Jaubert, *La notion d'alliance*, p. 222.

[7] On the various ones who are said to be the recipients of the revelation, see B. Rigaux, 'Révélation des mystères et perfection à Qumran et dans le Nouveau Testament', *NTS* 4, 1957–8, pp. 243–5.

secrets of the covenant and controlling the exegesis by which the secrets are revealed, as well as their general authority to supervise God's ordinances (IQSb 3.24; IQS 5.22).

It would thus appear to be inaccurate to hold that the only reason for the establishment of a new covenant was that 'the old one had been disregarded by the majority of people',[8] for the sectarian covenant contains new revelations. It is true in one sense that the Essenes did not have the feeling of modifying the Mosaic covenant,[9] since they could reason that the new revelations were 'secret things' hidden in the Bible to be discovered. Yet it seems not quite to be the case that the only difference between the Essene covenant and the old covenant is the requirement of voluntary commitment,[10] for the sectarian covenant also supposes a new initiative on the part of God in revealing the 'hidden things' and 'mysteries' (CD 3.10–14 and IQpHab 7.4f., quoted above).

Whoever be considered the instrument by which the full and true covenant was revealed to the members of the community, and whatever the 'hidden things' and *mishpaṭim* are which differentiate the sect's covenant from the covenant otherwise accepted in Israel, it is clear that it is a prime sectarian tenet that the sectarian covenant is the only true covenant and that all who do not seek to know and accept the 'hidden things' are outside the covenant (and consequently beyond God's saving mercy). Thus the covenant which is called the 'covenant of the community' (IQS 8.16f.) or the 'covenant of the everlasting community' (3.11f.), or even '*this* covenant', that is, the one contained in or prescribed by IQS (2.13, 16), is also and more regularly called 'God's covenant' (or 'His covenant' or 'Thy covenant'). The sectarian definition of 'God's covenant' is especially clear in IQS 5.7f.: 'Whoever approaches the Council of the Community shall enter the covenant of God in the presence of all who have freely pledged themselves.' The phrase bears the same sectarian definition in CD 7.5; 20.17; 14.2. The term 'Thy covenant' is very frequent in the Hodayot, and often it is clear that clinging to 'Thy covenant' brings persecution from the rest of Judaism, as in IQH 2.21f., 28f. God's covenant and the sectarian covenant are identical.

The members of the covenant and its enemies

We may simply but accurately conclude, then, that the members of God's covenant are the members of the sect. The simple observation, however,

---

[8] So S. Holm-Nielsen, *Hodayot: Psalms from Qumran*, p. 284. Also Marx; see n. 80 below.
[9] M. Delcor, 'Le vocabulaire juridique, cultureal et mystique de l' "initiation" dans la secte de Qumrân', *Qumran-Probleme* (ed. Bardtke), pp. 112f. Similarly, Thyen (*Sündenvergebung*, p. 87 n. 4) argues that the covenant is only renewed, not new, as is proved by the sect's accepting the concept of the remnant. On the fallacy of this, see n. 35 below.
[10] Delcor, 'Le vocabulaire', pp. 110–14.

obscures a complexity which arises when we consider who is being excluded. A study of the extant literature reveals that three different groups are considered outside the covenant: Gentiles,[11] non-Essene Jews and apostate Essenes.[12] This observation has an important bearing on understanding the use of the term 'Israel' among the sectarians. We may consider each of the excluded groups in turn.

In IQH and IQS, and sometimes in IQpHab and elsewhere, the wicked, who are given a very wide variety of names and designations, are non-sectarian Israelites.

It seems unnecessary to go into great detail to list the designations of the wicked. It is perhaps worth noting that the term *resha'im* is relatively rare, although it does occur (IQS 8.7; IQH 2.24 and elsewhere). More common are more descriptive titles, such as the sons of perversity (*'avel*), the congregation of the men of perversity, the men of deceit, the men of the pit, the congregation of nought, the congregation of Belial, lying interpreters, and the famous 'seekers of smooth things' and 'sons of darkness'. Such terms and many more will be seen by casually turning through the pages of a text or translation. In IQH and IQS, the terms refer virtually without exception to non-Essene Israelites. Some of the same terms of denigration are elsewhere employed for the Gentiles, as we shall see below.

The most famous and obvious passages in which the sect's enemies are conceived as non-sectarian Jews appear in the Habbakuk commentary. For example, Hab. 2.5f. is said to concern

the Wicked Priest who was called by the name of truth when he first arose. But when he ruled over Israel his heart became proud, and he forsook God and betrayed the precepts for the sake of riches. He robbed and amassed the riches of the men of violence who rebelled against God, and he took the wealth of the peoples, heaping sinful iniquity upon himself. And he lived in the ways of abominations amidst every unclean defilement. (IQpHab 8.8–13)

This wicked priest persecuted the Teacher of Righteousness (ibid., 11.5–7) but was duly punished by God by being handed over to his enemies (9.9–12). It does not appear too fanciful to see at least this general situation being reflected when the psalmist says that 'the assembly of the wicked has raged against me' (IQH 2.12) or that 'Violent men have sought after my life'

[11] Proselytes are mentioned in CD 17.6, as being fourth in rank behind priests, Levites and (ordinary) Israelites. IQS 6.13 seems to limit membership to those born in Israel, as does 4Qflor 1.4. Different Essene groups may have followed different practices, but admitting proselytes was probably not in any case a live issue. Marx ('Prédestination', p. 165) thinks a mission to the Gentiles would have been heretical. Cf. Holm-Nielsen, *Hodayot*, p. 283.

[12] Mental and physical impediments would prevent membership in the community, or at least full membership. The point is proved not by IQSa 2.3–9, which deals with the future congregation and not the present one (a point not noted by Gärtner, *Temple and Community*, p. 6), but by CD 15.15–17 as corrected by a fragment from 4Q. See Milik, *Ten Years of Discovery*, p. 114. Milik and Gärtner both note that the exclusion of such people stems from applying to the entire community regulations which originally governed only the priesthood. Such people were probably not counted among the damned, but were excluded only from certain community functions.

(2.21).[13] The wicked and the violent in both passages are without question Israelites, and it is to the same Israelites that the psalmist refers by such titles as 'lying interpreters and . . . the congregation of those who seek smooth things' (2.31f.), 'teachers of lies and seers of falsehood' (4.9f.) and those 'who have turned aside from Thy Covenant' (4.19).[14] In IQS although the note of personal danger is missing, the wicked are just as clearly Israelites who are not in 'the covenant'. Those who enter the covenant must 'separate from the congregation of the men of falsehood and shall unite . . . under the authority of the sons of Zadok, the Priests who keep the Covenant, and of the multitude of the men of the Community who hold fast to the Covenant' (IQS 5.1–3). The 'men of falsehood' are obviously Jews who are not obedient to the Zadokite priests who preserve the covenant. Similarly, the 'men of the lot of Belial' (2.4f.) are those who are not in or entering the covenant, and the same is true of 'all the men of falsehood who walk in the way of wickedness' (5.10f.).

When the wicked are conceived as non-sectarian Israelites, the 'good' receive as rich a list of designations as the wicked.[15] They are rarely called 'the righteous', the standard term in most of Judaism (CD 11.21; IQH 1.36; the singular is slightly more common: CD 1.19, 20; 4.7; 20.20; IQH 15.15; 16.10), and never the 'pious'.[16] They are rather the sons of light, the sons of truth, the sons of righteousness, the men of the lot of God who walk perfectly in all his ways, the elect of God's pleasure and the like. They are occasionally called the 'poor', usually in opposition to the 'mighty' (IQH 2.32, 32 [using differing words]; 5.22; IQpHab 12.3, 10; 4QpPs37 2.9; 3.10; cf. IQM 11.9, 13).[17]

But now we must raise the question, of more importance for the present study, of whether or not the sect, when defining itself over against the non-sectarian Israelites, appropriated to itself the title 'Israel'. Did the sectarians, in other words, consider that the wicked Israelites, in refusing to accept the sectarian covenant, had denied God's covenant in such a way as to forfeit even the title Israel? In the first place we may note that in IQS and IQH there is no hesitancy about calling the sectarians the 'elect', usually followed by a qualifying word: the elect of God's will (IQS 8.6), the elect of man (11.16), the elect of the time (9.14), the elect of righteousness (IQH 2.13). In two of these cases a more general word such as 'sons' or 'men' could be

---

[13] IQH 2.12 is now often considered to be by the Teacher of Righteousness, while 2.21 is attributed to the community; see Appendix 1 below. In any case, the theme of persecution by enemies within Israel is apparent here, as it is in IQpHab.

[14] All three passages are attributed to the Teacher by G. Jeremias, but H. W. Kuhn attributes the first to the community. See Appendix 1 below.

[15] See the list in Jaubert, *La notion d'alliance*, pp. 141f.

[16] The term *ḥasid* in 4Qtest 14 is not a sect designation.

[17] On the 'poor' as a title, see S. Légasse, 'Les pauvres en Esprit et les "Volontaires" de Qumran', *NTS* 8, 1962, pp. 336–45.

substituted for 'elect' with no appreciable change of meaning: sons of righteousness, IQS 3.20, 22; men of (God's) will, 4QpPs37 2.24f. In IQH 14.15 'Thine elect' is parallel to 'those who know Thee'; in the commentary on Ps. 37 the congregation of His elect who do His will (4QpPs37 2.5) or simply the congregation of His elect (3.5) clearly designates the sectarian group, the 'penitents of the desert' (3.1). In the Habakkuk commentary, 'His elect' in 9.12 should probably be pointed as a singular noun, referring to the Teacher of Righteousness, although 'the elect of God' in 10.13 is most likely to refer to the community.[18] In any case, the community can be called 'the elect' or a related title such as 'those whom God chose' (IQS 11.7). Having identified their covenant as the only true covenant, and being ready to call themselves 'the elect (of God)', the community would appear to have no difficulty in appropriating the title Israel for its own exclusive use. This line of reasoning has led many scholars to say that the sectarians considered themselves to constitute the 'true Israel'.[19] Further, the community was constituted as a 'miniature Israel', complete with priests, Levites and Israelites.[20] This view is accurate in one way, since the sectarians doubtless thought of themselves as having the true covenant, and the covenant community should reasonably be 'Israel'. Yet it is important, in order to understand the sect's self-understanding, to see that it did not simply appropriate the title 'Israel'. The members seem to have been conscious of their status as sectarians, chosen from out of Israel, and as being a *forerunner of the true Israel*, which God would establish to fight the decisive war.[21] We may consider several points concerning the use of the term 'Israel'.

1. The title *shabe Yisra'el* in CD 4.2; 6.4f.; 8.16 itself points in this direction. Rabin believes that the phrase, which would be translated 'those of Israel who repent or turn back', is an abbreviation for 'they that turned (from impiety) of Israel'.[22] This appears to be supported by the phrase *shabe pesha' Ya'akob*, 'they that turned from impiety of Jacob', in CD 20.17 and such phrases as *shabe pesha'*, 'those who turn from impiety' (IQH 14.24; 2.9; IQS 10.20). One may also note the *shabe ha-midbar*, 'those who turn back (from sin) in the desert' of 4QpPs37 3.1. The phrase 'those of Israel who turn (from evil)' indicates the sect's consciousness of not being *all* Israel, but being the group which has 'repented' and joined the covenant.

2. The phrase 'elect of Israel' in CD 4.3f. is difficult, since it does not

---

[18] On the phrase, see Dupont-Sommer, ' "Élus de Dieu" ', pp. 568–72. He regards 10.12f. as clearly plural but leaves the question open for 9.9–12 and 5.3–5.

[19] Thus, for example, Vermes, *The Dead Sea Scrolls in English*, p. 35; Ringgren, *Faith of Qumran*, pp. 137, 163; Cross, *Library*, pp. 128f. (a 'counter-Israel'); Leaney, *Rule*, p. 74 (the sect 'claimed to be the true Israel'); Jaubert, *La notion d'alliance*, p. 142; Forkman, *The Limits of the Religious Community*, p. 39.

[20] Leaney, *Rule*, p. 72.

[21] So also J. Maier, according to the summary of his thesis in *TLZ* 85, 1960, cols. 705f.

[22] Rabin, *Zadokite Documents*, p. 13.

seem to mean the same as the identical phrase when it occurs in 4Qflor 1.19 or the phrase 'elect of the holy people' in IQM 12.1, which are discussed below.[23] In CD 4.2–4, the 'Sons of Zadok' are said to be the 'elect of Israel' who shall arise at the last days. Whether they are intended to be the priests of the sect, the sect as such or some other group cannot be precisely determined. In any case, the construct 'of Israel' appears to have a partitive meaning, and the 'elect' are the 'elect from among Israel'. The sectarians as such are not Israel.

3. More significant is the way in which the past history of Israel is dealt with in IQS. In IQS 1.21–5 the history of Israel's transgression and God's mercy is appropriated by the sect in the ritual for entry to the covenant:[24]

Then the Priests shall recite the favours of God manifested in His mighty deeds and shall declare all His merciful grace to Israel, and the Levites shall recite the iniquities of the children of Israel, all their guilty rebellions and sins during the dominion of Satan. And after them, all those entering the Covenant shall confess and say: 'We have strayed! We have [disobeyed!] We and our fathers before us have sinned and done wickedly . . .'

When the priests actually bless those entering the covenant, however, they bless not 'Israel' or the 'true Israel', but 'all the men of the lot of God who walk perfectly in all His ways' (2.1f.). They appropriate Israel's history with God, but they do not call themselves simply 'Israel'.

4. It has been suggested that the phrase 'majority of Israel' or 'multitude of Israel' who enter the covenant (IQS 5.22) shows that 'the true Israel is to be identified with the sectarian Community'.[25] Brownlee refers to 5.2f., where the phrase 'majority of the men of the Community' appears. He takes 'Israel' in 5.22 to equal 'men of the Community' in 5.2f. This is possible, but the meaning of 5.22 could be the majority of those Israelites who join the covenant, distinguishing them from Israelites who do not join. The latter possibility is supported by IQS 6.13f.: every man *from* Israel who volunteers to join the Council of the Community. (Joining the Council of the Community is here the same as entering the covenant; see the continuation in 6.15.) The implication here seems to be that one who is *already* an Israelite enters the covenant.

There are, to be sure, some passages in which 'Israel' is applied to the sect as such. This is likely to be the case in IQS 2.22, where 'every Israelite' seems to include the priests, the Levites and the (ordinary) people previously mentioned, all of whom are sectarians and all of whom together make up 'Israel'. When CD 12.21f. states that 'according to this ruling shall the seed

---

[23] The context is too badly destroyed to permit the meaning of the phrase 'elect of Israel' in IQS37 to be determined.

[24] On the function of this 'antecedent history' in covenant texts, see Baltzer, *The Covenant Formulary*, pp. 1–98, especially p. 91.

[25] Brownlee, *Manual of Discipline*, p. 22.

of Israel walk', it is referring to the sectarian halakic rules governing certain aspects of ritual purity. It is nevertheless not clear that 'the seed of Israel' refers to the sectarians; more likely we have here a claim that all Israel should follow the sectarian halakah. Similarly, when the sectarian covenant is called 'the covenant for all Israel' (CD 15.5), the meaning is probably that the sectarian covenant is the one in which all Israel should be, rather than that the sect is exclusively Israel; a similar claim is probably being made in CD 3.13.

In short, in spite of confident scholarly assertions that the sectarians considered themselves to be the only true Israelites, and in spite of the substantial truth in that statement – the sectarians did consider that only they knew the entirety of the covenant and that those outside their covenant were 'wicked' – they generally refrained from simply calling themselves 'Israel'.[26] They seem to have retained the consciousness of being a specially chosen part of Israel, a consciousness which must have been reinforced by the fact that one could not be a full member of the sect until adulthood (IQSa 1.8f.). Further, the sect held open the possibility that the wicked would repent and join. But these wicked were themselves Israelites. Thus those who are called such things as the 'men of the pit' in IQS and IQH are called the 'wicked of Israel' in 4QpPs37 3.12, the 'wicked of Ephraim and Manasseh' (2.17) and perhaps even the 'powerful of the covenant who are in the house of Judah' (2.13). This possibility that the term 'Israel' may include the wicked Israelites indicates that there was no clear and systematic appropriation of the title for the sect – it may be that there was no such appropriation at all, for the sect had numerous other titles. But there is a more powerful reason why the sect did not consider itself exclusively Israel, as we shall now see.

When dealing with the events of the last days, the enemies, in the view of the authors of IQM, IQSa and IQpHab, are the Gentiles, while the elect are the Israelites – apparently all of Israel which survives, not just the present sectarians. The community believed that eschatological Israel would be formed by the conversion of the rest of Israel to the way of the sect. How this is reconciled with the frequent statements that the wicked Israelites will be destroyed (which we shall consider below) we are not clearly told, although we may make a good guess. The statement of the conversion of the rest of Israel to the way of the sect is given most clearly in IQSa 1.1–6. Because of its importance, we shall quote it in full:

This is the Rule for all the congregation of Israel in the last days, when they shall join [the Community to wa]lk according to the law (*mishpaṭ*) of the sons of Zadok the Priests and of the men of their Covenant who have turned aside [from the] way of the people, the men of His Council who keep His Covenant in the midst of iniquity, offering expiation [for the Land].

[26] So also Klinzing, *Die Umdeutung des Kultus*, p. 56, and Maier (above, n. 21).

When they come, they shall summon them all, the little children and the women also, and they shall read into their [ears] the precepts of the Covenant and shall expound to them all their statutes that they may no longer stray in their [errors].

And this is the Rule for all the hosts of the congregation, for every man born in Israel.[27]

The covenant here is the same as in IQS, IQH, and elsewhere: it is the Zadokite priests' covenant, identified as God's covenant. But those who join *with* those in the covenant are called Israelites, which indicates that the community as such was not called 'Israel'. After all Israel joins the community in the last days, the document quite properly goes on to speak of the regulations for every man from Israel. Subsequently, then, the congregation is called the 'congregation of Israel' (1.20), a designation which would not previously have been appropriate and which was not used in IQS or CD. The opponents of the congregation of Israel are now seen to be 'the nations', that is, the Gentiles (1.21), not the 'men of the pit' or the 'lying interpreters'.

The same terminological difference from IQS and IQH is seen in IQM, which deals in detail with the eschatological war 'destined to vanquish the nations' which is mentioned in IQSa 1.21. In IQM the enemies are always the Gentiles. The only reference to enemies within Israel is the phrase 'offenders against the covenant' in 1.2.[28] These are said to assist the Gentile armies against whom the Sons of Light wage their first engagement. It appears that, in the 'Qumranized' version of the War Scroll,[29] the phrase 'offenders against the covenant' is a kind of circumlocution for those who are elsewhere called the 'wicked of Israel'. At the time of the eschatological war, however, these no longer receive the name 'Israel' at all. The Sons of Light now constitute the entirety of Israel, being composed of the descendants of Levi, Judah and Benjamin, the only three remaining Israelite tribes (1.2). Apart from this reference in IQM 1.2, however, the non-sectarian Israelites (who are now considered no longer Israelites at all) drop out of consideration altogether. The list of enemies in IQM 2.10–14, which is derived from Israel's biblical enemies, does not refer to them. Even more to the point, the enemies are officially termed 'Goyim' ('nations' in the sense of 'Gentiles') in IQM as in IQSa. They are called 'all nations of vanity' (IQM 4.12; 6.6) and the 'nations of wickedness' (14.7; 15.2, where the phrase is parallel to 'all [Gentile] nations'). The Gentile nations are called God's adversaries in 12.10; and in 11.8f. 'our enemies' are the same as the 'troops

---

[27] Vermes's translation, italics removed. It is remarkable that Schubert (*Dead Sea Community*, p. 82) regards the first words of this passage as indicating that the community regarded itself as the whole of Israel. The continuation clearly indicates that 'the whole congregation of Israel' *will join* the covenant; thus the present members cannot be the 'whole congregation of Israel'.

[28] See Yadin, *The Scroll of the War of the Sons of Light*, p. 26; cf. CD 20.26f.

[29] See the discussion immediately below.

of Belial' and 'the seven nations of vanity', who obviously represent all the Gentiles. The wicked of IQM do, to be sure, receive some of the customary terms of denigration: men of Belial's lot (IQM 4.2, as in IQS 2.4f.), the wicked, *resha'im* (IQM 4.4; 11.14), and the frequent 'sons of darkness' (IQM 1.1 *et passim*; cf. IQS 1.10). But just as the opponents of IQS and IQH seem always to be Israelites, so the opponents of IQM are always the Gentile nations; thus they are never called 'traitors' as they are in other Scrolls (e.g. CD 1.12; IQpHab 2.1).

It agrees with this definition of the enemies as Gentiles that in IQM the saved are Israelites. We should first note that God is called 'God of Israel' repeatedly in IQM (1.9 and very frequently), a title which occurs, as far as I have noted, elsewhere in the Scrolls only at IQS 3.24.[30] It is noteworthy that the sentence 'They do not [know that from the God] of Israel is all that is and that will be' (IQM 17.4f.) appears also in IQS 3.15 with only one difference: 'God of Israel' becomes 'God of Knowledge'. But the definition of the 'good guys' in IQM as Israel is very common. Thus in 15.1f., the 'lot of God' is parallel with 'Israel' and in contrast to the 'nations of wickedness'. The people who are 'saints of the covenant' are called the people of Israel in 10.9f. We have seen above an instance in which the first person plural pronoun is contrasted with the Gentile nations (11.8f.). The contrast implies that the 'we' of the Scroll are the Israelites, and the same point may be observed elsewhere. Thus in 11.3, after recounting God's salvation of Israel in the past (saving David from Goliath and the like), the author concludes that 'Thou didst deliver *us* many times by the hand of *our* kings'. We may thus conclude that the phrase 'elect of the holy nation' (12.1), which is a substantial equivalent to 'elect of Israel' (CD 4.3f.), does not mean 'the sect which is chosen from among Israel', but 'those Israelites chosen to fight the final battle on earth'. The 'elect of the holy nation' are the same as the elect of God in 12.4, who are mustered in companies to fight God's enemies on earth. The contrast is with the 'elect of heaven' (12.5), who appear to be the same as the 'holy ones' in heaven (12.1), who also join the fray (12.7). (Thus the lacuna in 12.2 should be supplied with 'upon earth', as Dupont-Sommer – similarly van der Ploeg, 'among the living' – rather than 'in a community', as Yadin.)

Thus we have seen in both IQSa and IQM a terminological difference from IQH and IQS. In the latter two, the sect does not employ the title Israel for itself, and its enemies are non-sectarian Israelites. In the former, the saved become 'Israel', and the enemies are Gentiles. The distinction is clearly that IQSa and IQM are addressed to the time of the eschatological

---

[30] See P. von der Osten-Sacken, *Gott und Belial*, p. 27. He takes this peculiarity to indicate that the two spirits passage in IQS 3.14–4.26 is 'at home' in the tradition behind IQM. The relative dating of IQM proposed by Osten-Sacken and others is discussed immediately below.

war. *At that time* the sect will become identical with Israel. There is, however, a difference between IQM and IQSa: in IQSa the 'rest of Israel' is converted to the sect in the last days, while in IQM it appears that at least some Israelites ally with the Gentile armies to be destroyed in the final war.[31] On the basis of present evidence, it is difficult to determine if these are different views about what would happen to non-sectarian Israelites in the last days, or if they can be harmonized by supposing that some would be converted to the sect while some would remain incorrigible.[32] It may be that IQH 6.7f. provides a clue in favour of the second possibility:

> [for] in a little while, I know,
> Thou wilt raise up survivors among Thy people
> and a remnant within Thine inheritance.

As the phrase 'in a little while' makes clear, the passage refers to the eschatological deliverance.[33] While we cannot insist too hard upon the point, it may be that the expectation of survivors and a remnant being raised up *among* (*bet*) God's people refers to the conversion of some Israelites who were not formerly sectarians.[34] We should note that the only other passages in which the sect is referred to by the term 'remnant' are also dealing with the eschatological existence of the saved, when the others have been destroyed (IQM 13.8; 14.8f.). The sect did not entitle itself 'remnant' during its historical existence.[35] The term is used in the biblical sense of those who survive the

---

[31] Other statements to the effect that wicked (non-sectarian) Israelites would be destroyed at the eschaton are cited below, p. 257.

[32] So Segal, 'Qumran War Scroll', *Aspects*, p. 141: 'There is no mention in the Scroll of Jews who were not members of the sect because no doubt the sect hoped that when the eschatological war began all Jews would either have been converted to the sect, or would have been otherwise eliminated.'

[33] This seems to be the best meaning, but for another possibility see Holm-Nielsen, *Hodayot*, ad loc., who gives a bibliography. G. Jeremias (*Lehrer der Gerechtigkeit*, p. 231) and H. W. Kuhn (*Enderwartung*, p. 188) both take the phrase as indicating the near future.

[34] It must be noted that commentators generally do take the remnant that God will raise up in IQH 6.8 to be simply identical with the sect. See the editions of Licht, Delcor, Mansoor and Carmignac. See further the next note.

[35] Apart from frequent references to the destruction of the wicked 'without remnant' (p. 257 below) and one or two occurrences which are irrelevant for the present point, the terms *she'ar* and *she'erit* appear only in CD 1.4f. in addition to the passages just cited. Many scholars (see the editions of IQH referred to in n. 34 and further references given by them; more recently, cf. Thyen, *Sündenvergebung*, p. 87 n. 4) take CD 1.4–10 to show that the sect called itself the 'remnant', and they take CD 1.4 to confirm their understanding of IQH 6.8 as equating the sect with the prophetic 'remnant'. The clear meaning of the passage in CD, however, is that the 'remnant of Israel' consisted of all the Jews who remained after the destruction of Nebuchadnezzar. This remnant is not coextensive with the sect, for some of the remnant refused to accept the Teacher of Righteousness whom God sent them (CD 1.11–21); on the contrary, some of the descendants of the survivors of Nebuchadnezzar's destruction were seen by the sect as constituting 'the congregation of the faithless' (CD 1.12). CD 1.4, in other words, uses the term 'remnant' to refer to those saved from destruction in the past. IQH 6.8; IQM 13.8; 14.8f. use the term to refer to the eschatological people of God. Nowhere is *she'ar* or *she'erit* used of the sect in its historical existence. It may be that *peletah* in CD 2.11 should be taken as referring to the sect. Here it is said that God *always* left a remnant (*peletah*), and those who constitute the remnant are contrasted with those who stray (not with the destroyed). This, however, is scant evidence on which to insist that the sect thought of itself as the remnant.

judgment[36] (thus 'survivors' is parallel to 'remnant' in IQH 6.8 and IQM 13.8). This may indicate the possibility, in agreement with IQSa, that some Israelites who were not formerly in the sect would repent and join in the last days, thus escaping destruction and being included in the remnant. The remnant, that is, may be wider than the historical sect.[37] We shall see a similar possibility in IQpHab, but now we should return to the consideration of IQM.

One of the remnant passages, IQM 14.8f., mentions that both God and the remnant have been loyal to the 'covenant with the forefathers'. This definition of the covenant is characteristic for IQM. A similar conception is seen in 13.7f. and 18.7f. (God has kept his covenant with *us* from of old). The covenant is never otherwise defined in IQM. It is not, as in IQSa, the priests' covenant which the rest of Israel is to join, nor are there any indications that there are 'hidden things' in it. This could reflect the pre-sectarian composition of the original War Scroll, but it would probably have been read by the sectarians as referring to the time after which only those Israelites who had held fast to the covenant would still be present. The covenant, that is, is not defined over against the supposed covenant of the Jerusalem community. It is simply the covenant made by God with the patriarchs, kept by him and kept by those loyal to it.

The sectarian character of IQM in its present form, while not reflected in the use of the terms 'covenant' and 'Israel', does appear in the other titles for the 'sons of light', the first of which is the term 'sons of light' itself (1.1 and frequently). Such a term as 'people of God' (1.5) is not descriptive, but the elect are also called the 'poor' (11.13; 13.14), which is known in other Scrolls as a sect designation, as well as 'the sons of His truth' (17.8; cf. IQS 4.5) and, more striking, the 'perfect of way' (14.7), a term which will be discussed below. Such designations as 'men of His lot' (1.5; cf. 15.1) and 'the lot of Thy truth' (13.12) also have a sectarian ring. In all these cases, however, the sectarian titles have been appropriated for the remnant of Israel, the 'chosen of His holy people', who will do battle in the final days.

It should be emphasized that we are dealing here with the way in which IQM would presumably have been read by the sectarians during the major period of the occupation of Qumran. It is likely that the War Scroll has an older history, and it may not have been originally a sectarian document. In comparison with the portions of text available in 4QMᵃ, IQM has been described by Hunzinger as a 'Qumranized' version of the War Scroll.[38]

---

[36] E.g. Isa. 1.8f.; Zeph. 3.11–13.

[37] Similarly Jaubert, *La notion d'alliance*, pp. 162f.: the covenanters considered themselves to be the nucleus around which would be gathered the eschatological Israel. Jaubert does not note, however, that the eschatological Israel, not the historical sect, is the remnant. She considers that the sect thought of itself as the remnant, and she takes IQH 6.7f. to be a description of the present sect (pp. 120, 138, 211).

[38] Hunzinger, 'Fragmente einer älteren Fassung des Buches Milḥamā', *ZAW* 69, 1957, p. 150.

Thus Osten-Sacken takes the terminology of IQM – in which the division is between the Gentiles and Israel – to be older than that of IQS and IQH, in which the distinction is between the members and the non-members of the covenant.[39] IQM basically derives, in his view, from the early Maccabean period, before the sect had split from the rest of the hasidic movement. It is readily conceivable that some of the terminology is to be so explained and not unlikely, on the basis of the evidence given by Hunzinger, that this is the history of the War Scroll. We may note, however, that precisely where IQM is 'Qumranized', the division is *still* between Israel on the one hand and the Gentiles on the other. This may be seen in the passage referred to above from IQM 14.8f. We find twice the phrase 'remnant of Thy people' or 'remains of the people of Israel'. In the second instance the entire phrase is missing from 4QM[a], while in the first 4QM[a] apparently had only 'Thy people'.[40] The 'Qumranizing' in IQM here consists of specifying God's people as the adherents to the sect, who will be the only Israelites available for the final war against the Gentiles. The enemies, however, are still the Gentiles (14.7, 'wicked Goyim'). The 'Qumranized' view, then, is that the sect and 'Israel' become identical at the eschaton, at the time of the war against the Gentiles, and this is also the view of IQSa 1.20f., whose sectarian nature cannot be doubted. Thus despite the fact that IQM may have a history which antedates the sectarian community, the terminology contrasting Israel (or the remnant of Israel) with the nations, rather than the sectarians with the non-sectarian Israelites, cannot be simply explained as a hold-over of an older, pre-sectarian terminology. Further, the contrast between Israel and the Gentiles is not itself proof of a pre-sectarian date.[41] The Israel/Gentile opposition is *always* seen in discussing the eschatological period, and we may see the same phenomenon not only in IQSa and IQM, but also in IQpHab, to which we now turn.

We have previously seen that the Wicked Priest plays an important role in

---

[39] Osten-Sacken, *Gott und Belial*, pp. 84–7, 239f. The view is fairly common. See, for example, L. Rost, *TLZ* 80, 1955, col. 206; Becker, *Das Heil Gottes*, pp. 74f. For different attempts at a relative dating of the Scrolls see Rabinowitz, *VT* 3, 1953, pp. 175–85; Jeremias, *Lehrer der Gerechtigkeit*, p. 176. Jeremias regards the Hodayot as older than IQS, IQM or CD.

[40] See Hunzinger's text, translation and notes, 'Fragmente', pp. 135–47.

[41] As Rost, Becker and Osten-Sacken (above, n. 39) take it to be. One may register a reservation about source criticism based on such points: Becker considers IQM 13 and 17.4–8 to be additions to IQM, since they agree with the form of dualism found in IQS 3.13ff. (*Heil Gottes*, p. 92). He had previously cited the fact that the opposition in IQM is Gentile/Israel as proof of the basic pre-Essene composition of the War Scroll (pp. 74f.). Yet this precise opposition appears in IQM 17.4–8, which he wishes to treat as an addition which agrees with IQS 3.13ff., where the opposition is rather sectarian/non-sectarian. We may also note the covenant with the forefathers (not with the sect) in IQM 13.7f. and the term 'God of Israel' in 13.13. There seem to be more agreements between these two supposed sectarian 'additions' and the rest of IQM than between them and the 'two spirits' passage in IQS. In general, it seems to me precarious to base source criticism and views of the sequence of sources on theories about a chronological sequence of ideas. With regard to the present point: there is nothing in the *idea* of an opposition between Israel and the Gentiles which must be early. The idea can 'reappear' when authors write with an eye on the eschaton.

the Habukkuk commentary, and to that extent the 'wicked' in IQpHab must be considered to be non-sectarian Israelites, as they are in IQS and IQH. They are called collectively the congregation established on a lie (10.10), a formulation which is in close agreement with those of IQS and IQH. In other passages, however, a particular passage in Habukkuk is taken to refer to the Kittim (e.g. IQpHab 3.4) or to the heathen nations who worship idols (12.12–14; 13.1f.). One passage is of prime importance for our study. I quote it according to Vermes's translation:

> Interpreted, this saying (Hab. 1.12–13a) means that God will not destroy His people by the hand of the nations; God will execute the judgement of the nations by the hand of His elect. And through their chastisement all the wicked of His people shall expiate their guilt who keep His commandments in their distress. For it is as He said, *Too pure of eyes to behold evil*: interpreted, this means that they have not lusted after their eyes during the age of wickedness. (IQpHab 5.3–6)

I believe this translation to be correct, but there are difficulties. Dupont-Sommer takes the 'their' which modifies 'chastisements' to refer back to the elect rather than forwards to the wicked and understands 'the elect' to be the subject of 'keep His commandments': 'And it is by the chastisement which the elect will dispense that all the wicked of His people will atone, because they (the elect) have kept His commandments in their distress.' Ringgren understands 'their' as does Vermes, but agrees with Dupont-Sommer in taking 'the elect' to be the subject of 'keep His commandments'. Further, he regards the verb *ye'eshmu* as 'be punished (for guilt)' rather than 'expiate guilt' or 'atone': 'through their chastisement will the wicked among His people be punished; since they (the elect) kept His commandments when they were in distress'.[42] Burrows's translation is essentially the same as Ringgren's.[43] Lohse translates the verb *büssen*, but explains that the meaning is that the elect will punish the wicked among their own people as well as the Gentiles. He too takes the subject of 'keep His commandments' to be the elect.[44] Delcor takes *ye'eshmu* to mean 'known to be guilty': when they are chastised, the wicked among his people will be known to be guilty. It is difficult to place much weight on so controverted a passage, and there are no syntactical observations which would settle the problem of translation. The relative which precedes 'keep' most naturally refers to the 'wicked' just mentioned, as Vermes has it, but the relative in the Scrolls does sometimes have a more distant antecedent. The verb most naturally means 'be guilty', but the possibility of 'expiate guilt' cannot be excluded. If Vermes's translation is correct, the passage says that even the (formerly) wicked Israelites shall

---

[42] Ringgren, *Faith of Qumran*, p. 154.
[43] Burrows, *Dead Sea Scrolls*, p. 367.
[44] So also Maier and similarly Carmignac, ad loc.: the wicked will be punished by the chastisements inflicted on them by the keepers of the commandments.

be saved, provided that, during the tribulations which accompany the end, they hold fast and do not waver. As other understandings would have it, the elect, who hold fast in the time of trial, afflict and thereby bring to repentance (and presumably salvation) the (formerly) wicked Israelites. In both these cases, 'the wicked of His people', that is, the non-sectarian Israelites, will be atoned for during the afflictions of the last days. The translations of Ringgren, Delcor and Carmignac, on the other hand, seem to exclude the wicked Israelites from eschatological atonement. If, however, we may read the present passage in the light of IQSa, it would seem likely that here is being left open the possibility that the 'wicked of His people' may join 'the elect' in the last days to form the greater and perfect Israel when the Gentiles are destroyed.

It is, at any rate, clear in the passage just quoted that at the time of the eschaton it is the Gentiles (Goyim) who will be judged and destroyed, while the wicked Israelites will only be punished, and perhaps even be redeemed. When looking forward to the eschaton, the enemies become (as in IQM and IQSa) the Gentiles, rather than the sect's historical opponents, the non-sectarian Israelites, who are otherwise mentioned so often in IQpHab. It is perhaps worth noting in this connection that Hab. 2.19f., which refers to idolatry, is interpreted in the obvious way in the commentary (13.1f.) as referring to Gentiles. The commentary immediately predicts that *at the eschaton* ('on the Day of Judgement') the idolaters will be destroyed. The connection of the Gentiles as the enemies with the eschatological period seems to have been firmly fixed.

We may finally note that the 'violent' 'or 'powerful of the Gentiles' are mentioned in 4QpPs37 2.19; 4.10. In the first case, it is said that the 'wicked of Ephraim and Manasseh' will be handed over to them for judgment, and in the second that the Wicked Priest will receive the same fate. Although the context in both cases is not so secure as one could wish, these passages seem to support the theory earlier advanced that the incorrigibly wicked among Israel would be destroyed *before* (or in the early stages of) the eschatological war with the Gentiles, while those who would, could join the covenant community and constitute the only Israel. This makes sense of IQSa, it explains why IQM (and apparently 4Qflor 1.18f.) deals almost exclusively with the Gentiles as the wicked, and it takes into account the prophecies of the destruction of the wicked Israelites.

To return to the starting point of the section: the sect did not, at least very often, think of itself as 'Israel' *during the time of its historical existence*. The members believed that they had the only true interpretation of the covenant, but there were other Israelites, the 'wicked of Israel'. At the time of the end, all Israel would join the covenant community (IQSa), except for those who were incorrigibly wicked, who would be destroyed either by the sect, or directly by God, or handed over to the Gentiles for destruction. Thus during its historical existence the sect realized that it was a sect. It was not yet the full body of Israel, although true Israel could be constituted only according to its covenant. Meanwhile the sectarians insisted on the validity of the covenant as understood by them for all Israel. Thus there is some tension in their self-conception. On the one hand, one could say that they are 'true Israel' since they have the true covenant. On the other hand, that was not their formulation. They are 'sons of God's truth' and the like, in contrast to the wicked of Israel, the 'men of the pit'; only in the last days would the 'congregation of Israel' in contrast to the Gentiles be established (IQSa 1.21).

We turn now to a different category of those who are counted outside the covenant: the backsliders from its membership. These appear primarily – it may be exclusively – in CD and IQS. The theme is announced in CD 8.1f.//19.13f.: all the members of the covenant who do not hold fast to its precepts shall be destroyed. The description which follows (8.3–12//19.15–24) does not seem especially to refer to backsliding sectarians, except for the phrase in 19.16 'they entered a covenant of repentance'. Otherwise the descriptive passage seems to refer to non-sectarian Israelites. They are called 'princes of Judah' (8.3) and they are said to be especially guilty of seeking wealth by forceful measures and of unchastity (8.5–7). Further, they shall be punished (or have been punished)[45] by 'the chief of the kings of the Greeks' (8.11). 8.3–12, in other words, as well as the parallel in 19.15–24, excluding only one phrase in 19.16, sounds like a characteristic attack on the non-sectarian Israelites and especially their leaders. Perhaps the point is to argue that apostate sectarians are to be treated like the rulers of Jerusalem, but it seems more likely that a passage on the latter has been inserted into a discussion of the former.[46] For the apostate sectarians are returned to almost immediately: 'And thus it is with all who despise the commandments of God and desert them and turn in the stubbornness of their hearts' (8.19). 'All the men who entered the new covenant in the land of Damascus and turned back and betrayed (it) and turned aside from the well of the water of life – they shall not be reckoned in the Council of the people . . .' (8.21) (my translations). If the second manuscript may be relied on for the continuation, it would seem that such a man may return when the Messiah of Aaron and Israel comes (20.1). Similarly, one who has been in the 'congregation of the men of perfect holiness' who becomes reluctant to 'carry out the commands of upright men' is also excluded from the community, but he too apparently may return (20.2–8). In 20.8–13 those who despise the covenant

---

[45] See Rabin, *Zadokite Documents*, p. 34.
[46] So also J. Murphy-O'Connor, 'The Critique of the Princes of Judah', *RB* 79, 1972, pp. 200–16: 8.3–18 has been inserted, and the section does not refer to the members of the community, but to the Jewish rulers who opposed the community at the beginning.

are said to have no share in the house of the law, and no possibility of return is specified. Reminiscent of 8.1f., with its condemnation of apostates to destruction, is 20.25–27, which says that 'all those of the members of the covenant who have broken out of the boundary of the Law' shall be 'cut off' along with the 'evildoers of Judah'. It may be that the intention of the document is to establish degrees of apostasy, some of which permit return while others involve destruction, but the degrees cannot be determined by the terminology. The word 'despise', for example, is used in 8.19 and is apparently followed by a provision for returning to the community in the days of the Messiah, while the 'despisers' of 20.8,11 are appointed no provision for return. It may be that in 2.6f. the phrase 'turn aside from the way' refers to backsliders; if so, they are condemned to destruction.[47]

Somewhat clearer are the provisions in IQS. 'Betraying (*b–g–d*) the truth' and 'walking in the stubbornness of [the] heart' results in a two-year suspension, with some privileges being granted after the first year (IQS 7.18–21). One who slanders the congregation, however, is expelled and may not return (7.16f.). A similar fate befalls one who 'murmurs against the authority of the Community' (7.17). One who has been in the Community for ten years and then betrays (*b–g–d*) it and 'departs from the Congregation to walk in the stubbornness of his heart' shall be expelled and may not return; and the same punishment applies to any accomplices after the fact (7.22–25). Earlier in IQS (2.12–18) we read a curse condemning those who enter the covenant while still intending to follow their own path to destruction without pardon.

Other references to apostate sectarians are less clear, and one cannot always be sure whether apostates or those who never entered the covenant are in view. The former may be in mind in the reference in IQS 10.21 to those who 'turn aside from the way'. The phrase *shabe beriteka* 'those who turn back from Thy covenant' might refer to apostates (IQH 14.21f.), but the psalmist has just assured us that 'none of those who approach Thee rebels against Thy command, nor do any of those who know Thee alter Thy words' (14.14f.), which seems to mean that if a man is really 'in' he will not depart. Perhaps, like modern believers in the doctrine of 'once saved always saved', the psalmist would say that those who 'turn back from the covenant' had not really known God to start with. That the psalmist knew some who were apostate seems to be supported by IQH 4.19: 'those who have withdrawn (*n–z–r*) from Thy covenant'.[48] This is not certain, however, for the preceding description in lines 13–18, as well as the titles of line 20 (men of lies, seers of error), seems to refer to the non-sectarian Israelites who are the

---

[47] Hunzinger ('Beobachtungen zur Entwicklung', p. 237) regards the possibility of return after total exclusion to reflect a later, more lenient view than the permanent exclusion prescribed in IQS.

[48] For the translation, cf. Rabin's note on CD 8.8 (*Zadokite Documents*, p. 34).

psalmist's opponents. Whether in thinking of them he has switched briefly to the traitors from his own camp, or whether he considers that those who are not with him have 'withdrawn' from him, cannot be said with certainty.[49] At any rate, in CD and IQS we see clearly that the sect knew of and provided for apostates, whether permanent or temporary.

It will by now have become clear that we are dealing with the basic soteriological conception of the sect. The distinction is between those outside the covenant – whether Gentiles, non-sectarian Israelites or apostate sectarians – *and those inside.* Thus it is said of all three groups of those outside the covenant that they will be destroyed. The heathen nations who oppose Israel in IQM will be destroyed without remnant or hope of salvation (IQM 1.6; 4.2; 11.11; 14.5,11). In IQS, the 'men of the lot of Satan' are to be destroyed without mercy or pardon (2.4–10), and there shall be no remnant (4.11–14; 5.12f.; cf. 5.19). In IQH, the 'men of lies and seers of error' will be destroyed in the judgment (4.20; cf. 14.16); the 'sons of guilt' will have no remnant (6.20–32). Similarly, the 'wicked of Israel' in 4QpPs37 3.12 will be 'cut off' (cf. 2.3f., 7). The general statements about the backsliders also predict their destruction (CD 2.6f.; 8.2; 20.25f.; IQS 2.11–18), although, as we have seen, the particular rules governing apostates seem to allow those who have not committed the most serious acts of treachery to return, at least in the days of the Messiah(s).

Conversely, those in the covenant ('the volunteers who join the elect') will be saved in the judgment (IQpMic 7–9).[50] Since the questions of atonement for transgression within the covenant and God's salvation of the elect will occupy us below, we may pass over the detailed statements here, recording only the fact that, for those outside the covenant, there is no hope for pardon, while for those inside there is pardon, forgiveness and salvation.

The crucial question, then, is that of the election: how does one gain access to the covenant, outside of which is no salvation?

3. Election and predestination

One of the most striking themes of the Qumran literature, and one which has been very often discussed, is that of predestination. Responsibility for choosing who is in the covenant, in these passages, is said to rest solely with God. Put another way, the explanation given by the elect of why they were

---

[49] The term 'traitors' in IQH 2.10 might be taken to refer to apostates, but Jeremias (*Lehrer der Gerechtigkeit*, p. 197) has soundly observed that 'seekers of deceit' takes the place of 'traitors' in the parallel in 2.33f. In both cases the reference is probably to the non-sectarians. In IQH 5.23–6 there seems to be a description of the difficulties which the author had with all his colleagues; thus the 'rebels' and 'murmurers' mentioned there were probably not apostates in the strict sense of the word.

[50] *DJD* I, p. 78.

chosen is that God has decided it so from eternity. Even though these passages are well known, it will be useful to have them before us. We may first note the principal passages in which it is said that God has assigned each man to his 'lot' or 'way':

[God] has appointed for [man] two spirits in which to walk until the time of His visitation: the spirits of truth and falsehood. Those born of truth spring from a fountain of light, but those born of falsehood spring from a source of darkness. All the children of righteousness are ruled by the Prince of Light and walk in the ways of light, but all the children of falsehood are ruled by the Angel of Darkness and walk in the ways of darkness.

The Angel of Darkness leads all the children of righteousness astray, and until his end, all their sin, iniquities, wickedness, and all their unlawful deeds are caused by his dominion in accordance with the mysteries of God. . . .

But the God of Israel and His Angel of Truth will succour all the sons of light. (IQS 3.18–25)

> I know that the inclination of every spirit [is in Thy hand];
> Thou didst establish [all] its [ways] before ever creating it,
>   and how can any man change Thy words?
> Thou alone didst [create] the just (*tsaddiq*)
>   and establish him from the womb
>   for the time of goodwill,
> that he might be preserved in[51] Thy Covenant
>   and walk in all (Thy ways),
> and that [Thou mightest show Thyself great] to him
>   in the multitude of Thy mercies,
> and enlarge his straitened soul to eternal salvation. . . .
>
> But the wicked (*resha'im*) Thou didst create
>   for [the time] of Thy [wrath],
> Thou didst vow them from the womb
>   for the Day of Massacre,
>   for they walk in the way which is not good.
> They have despised [Thy Covenant]
>   and their souls have loathed Thy [truth];
> they have taken no delight in all Thy commandments
>   and have chosen that which Thou hatest. (IQH 15.13–19; cf. 14.11f.)

Thou, [O God], didst redeem us for Thyself as an eternal people, and into the lot of light didst Thou cast us for Thy truth. Thou didst appoint from of old the Prince of Light, to assist us, [since all sons of justice are in his lot] and all spirits of truth in his dominion. And Thou wast the one who made Belial to corrupt, an angel of hatred, his [dominion] being in darkness and his counsel to render wicked and guilty. (IQM 13.9–11)

While the formulations in these three passages are not in perfect agreement, they make substantially the same point: God himself has, from the beginning,

---

[51] For 'be preserved in', Vermes has 'hearken to'. He has apparently read *shama'* for *shamar*.

determined the 'lot' of every individual. This can be put in terms of being under the dominion of one of the two spirits or the other (IQS), or in terms of having the inclination of one's own spirit established by God (IQH), or in terms of being cast into a certain 'lot'[52] (the two spirits 'helping' and 'corrupting' respectively, rather than 'ruling', IQM), but the substantial point is the same.

In close agreement with the above passages are those in which it is affirmed that God is responsible for everything: from the God of Israel (or knowledge) is all that is and that will be (IQM 17.4f.; IQS 3.15). The theme is especially prominent in the hymn material:

> All things come to pass by His knowledge;
> He establishes all things by His design
>   and without Him nothing is done. (IQS 11.11)

> For without Thee no way is perfect,
>   and without Thy will nothing is done.
>   It is Thou who hast taught all knowledge
>   and all things come to pass by Thy will. (IQS 11.17f.)

> By Thy wisdom [all things exist from] eternity,
>   and before creating them Thou knewest their works for
>   for ever and ever.
> [Nothing] is done [without Thee]
>   and nothing is known unless Thou desire it. (IQH 1.7f.)

> In the wisdom of Thy knowledge
>   Thou didst establish their destiny before ever they were.
> All things [exist] according to [Thy will]
>   and without Thee nothing is done. (IQH 1.19f.)

> Nothing is done without Thee,
>   and nothing is known without Thy will.
> Beside thee there is nothing,
>   and nothing can compare with Thee in strength;
>   in the presence of Thy glory there is nothing,
>   and Thy might is without price. (IQH 10.9f.)

These passages reinforce the idea of the direct divine determination of the fate of man not only by attributing the governance of all things to God, but also by especially emphasizing that only through the will of God is anything *known*; for knowledge is the means and sign of election. One is brought into the covenant by being given knowledge, and knowledge of God's secrets characterizes the elect. The connection of knowledge with election is sufficiently important to require a digression.

[52] Cf. being caused to inherit the lot of the Holy Ones, IQS 11.7–9.

That the gift of knowledge is the means of effecting the election is indicated in IQH 14.25f.:

> And Thou hast favoured me, Thy servant, with the Spirit of
>   Knowledge,
> [to love tr]uth [and righteousness]
> and to loathe all the ways of perversity (Dupont-Sommer).[53]

Vermes supplies the first lacuna 'that I may choose',[54] but the contrast of love and loathe is perhaps to be preferred. In any case, it is clear that the psalmist is confessing, in effect, that his being put in the right lot by God was accomplished by his being given knowledge. Frequently in IQH knowledge seems to be more or less equated with election. Thus at the beginning of many of the community hymns the psalmist gives thanks for being chosen and saved by God. He thanks God for being placed 'in the bundle of the living' (2.20); for being redeemed from the pit and raised to everlasting height (3.19f.); for not being placed in the lot of vanity (7.34); for having been dealt with wondrously and mightily (11.3); for having been given the Holy Spirit (17.26). All of these phrases seem constructively to be thanks for being elect. It is, then, noteworthy that frequently at the beginning of a hymn the author gives thanks for being given knowledge, insight or understanding: so 7.26f.; 10.14; 11.15; 14.8. In 14.12–14 this is specified as being reflective knowledge: he knows, by the understanding given by God, that he has been brought into the covenant, been given the holy spirit, and been brought near to understanding God. In other words, the knowledge is that he is elect, and being elect involves knowledge of God's will. Thus knowledge can be the means of effecting the election (one knows which path to choose); it can be more or less equated with election (one gives thanks for knowledge as for redemption and election); and it accompanies election (being elect, one knows). We shall return to knowledge within the community later.[55] Just now, the important point is that knowledge and election are intimately connected.

The reason for this view, which appears especially in the hymns, is not far to seek. As we shall see more fully below, the members of the sect were not born into the covenant. Thus they had to account for how they came to be in it. They thought of themselves, as we have seen, as predestined by God. But since those who were predestined were not marked by birth or by an external sign of the covenant such as circumcision, there had to be an

---

[53] The lacunae are filled in the same way by Habermann.
[54] So also Licht.
[55] For a more detailed analysis of the meanings of knowledge in Qumran, see W. D. Davies, *Christian Origins and Judaism*, pp. 119–44. Licht ('Doctrine', p. 98) gives a list of the subjects of knowledge, concluding that the content is 'the sectarian doctrine'. See also Nötscher, *Terminologie*, pp. 15–79; Kuhn, *Enderwartung*, pp. 139–75, especially 163–75 on the soteriological significance of knowledge.

interior way of *knowing* that they were predestined. This helps to explain the emphasis on knowledge, insight and understanding, and it helps to explain why knowledge was seen predominantly as a gracious gift from God. Now we return to the general problem of predestination.

In CD 2.2–7, it is said that the 'wicked', those who turned aside from the way and abhorred the ordinance, were *not* chosen by God from eternity (2.7). In this formulation God's choice precedes and determines the transgression, for 2.13 explicitly says that 'those whom He hated He caused to stray'. The sectarians, those who 'dug the well', on the other hand, God 'caused to hear' (6.3). Similarly the hymn in IQS says that God *caused* his elect 'to inherit the lot of the Holy Ones' (11.7f.). It seems likely that the *hif'il* verb *higgashtam* in IQH 12.23 should be translated '*caused* them to draw near' (so Dupont-Sommer; cf. Delcor and Holm-Nielsen), rather than 'admitted them' as Vermes and Mansoor have it, and God is also said to have caused the psalmist to draw near in IQH 14.13 and IQS 11.13.

God's ruling providence can be depicted not only as the decisive factor in entering the covenant, but also as preventing those within from straying: Mastema, the angel of enmity, departs from one who vows to enter the covenant, if he performs his vow (CD 16.4f.). This theme is common, however, only in the Hodayot: God has not permitted the insults of the mighty to cause the psalmist to forsake him (IQH 2.35f.; cf. 7.7f.); God will not allow those in the covenant to be led astray (4.24f.; cf. 16.15); God establishes the path of the one whom He chooses and hedges him with discernment, 'that he may not sin against Thee' (17.21f.).

Yet despite this emphasis on the eternal and irresistible grace of God as the basis for entrance into the community of the elect, the sectarians did not understand this in such a way as to exclude man's ability to choose which of two ways he would follow. The idea of God's electing grace was not formulated in opposition to man's freedom of choice, and in this sense it is anachronistic to speak of 'predestination'.[56] As we shall see, *the statements of God's determining grace answer another question than the question of whether or not man is free.* Thus we note repeatedly in the Scrolls the notion of election by God side by side with explanations of entrance into or exclusion from the covenant on the basis of the individual's choice. Thus in a passage already quoted (IQH 15.14–19), the psalmist thanks God for creating the righteous man that he might follow the right path. The wicked is also said to have been 'created' by God and vowed 'from the womb' for destruction. But then a reason is given: '*For (ki)* they walk in the way which is not good.' The psalmist continues to explain that they are outside the covenant *because* they

[56] This was correctly pointed out by Marx ('Prédestination', p. 168). He would prefer to speak simply of 'grace' (p. 181). The particular way in which God's electing and governing grace is emphasized in some passages, however, makes 'predestination' a natural term, as long as it is not understood in the technical sense of excluding free will. On Marx's view, see further n. 80 below.

despised it and loathed it. They 'have chosen' what God hates. One sees a similar alteration between God's choice and man's choice elsewhere:

> Thou hast brought me into the Council of . . .
>   . . .
> And I know there is hope
>   for those who turn from transgression
>   and for those who abandon sin
>   . . .
> Thou wilt raise up survivors among Thy people
>   and a remnant within Thine inheritance.
>   . . .
> and Thou wilt establish them in Thy Council
>   according to the uprightness of Thy truth. (IQH 6.5–10)

Here crediting God with bringing one into the Council (which is equivalent to the community of the covenant) alternates with the expression of hope for the salvation of those who 'turn from' transgression.

> I know that Thou hast marked the spirit of the just (*tsaddiq*),
>   and therefore I have chosen to keep my hands clean
>   . . .
> And I know that man is not righteous
>   except through Thee. . . . (IQH 16.10f.)

Here again God's choice alternates with man's choice 'to keep his hands clean'. Similarly in IQS those in the covenant are called both the 'chosen' (IQS 9.14) and 'those who have chosen the way' (IQS 9.17f.). The combination of human choice and God's election is seen in one phrase in IQpMic 7f.: 'those who volunteer to join the elect of God'.

In general, such terms as 'choose', 'turn' and 'despise' figure significantly in discussions of how one enters or does not enter the covenant. Those who are not in the covenant shall not be cleansed by God (and admitted) *unless* they *turn* from wickedness (IQS 5.14). The good are defined as those who *turn* from transgression, while the evil are those who *turn* aside from the way; those who are smitten (as punishment for transgression) will not be comforted *until* their way becomes perfect (IQS 10.20f.). God pardons those who turn from or repent of sin (IQH 14.24). To *join* the covenant, one must *turn* from his corrupt way (CD 15.7). We have seen above that one of the titles of the sect was apparently 'those who turn from impiety', or some such title, and such examples could be multiplied.

The fault of the 'men of perversity', those outside the covenant, on the other hand, is that 'They have neither inquired nor *sought* after Him' (IQS 5.11f.). (This is in contrast to those who keep the covenant and seek God's will, 5.9.) On the contrary, they despise the commandments of God and his covenant (IQpHab 1.11; IQH 15.18; CD 3.17; 7.9; 8.19; IQS 2.25f.; 3.5f.). The last two passages are especially striking and should be quoted:

Everyone who despises to enter [the covenant] of God (so that he may) walk in the stubbornness of his heart [shall not enter] the community of His truth.

Unclean, unclean shall he be all the days that he despises the ordinances of God – he shall not be instructed in the community of His truth (my translations).

This passage reveals another phrase which is descriptive of the non-elect: those who walk in the stubbornness of their own hearts (eight times in IQS, five times in CD, and in IQH 4.15). This phrase, like the terms 'turn', 'choose' and 'despise', indicates how far the sectarians were from denying man's freedom of choice.

This point comes out with even greater clarity when one considers the regulations for entering and being expelled from the covenant community. In IQS especially the members of the community are called 'all those who have freely devoted themselves' (1.7, Vermes) or, in Dupont-Sommer's translation, 'volunteers'. The entrance requirements correspond to the title. The entrant must humbly submit himself 'to all the precepts of God' (IQS 3.9). This means giving up the inclinations of his own stubborn heart (2.26) and following the rule of the community. Further, the entrant must be prepared to turn over his possessions to the community (6.19). We may best quote the clearest statement of how an individual is admitted to the community:

And whoever, born of Israel, volunteers to join the Council of the Community, he shall be examined on his intelligence and deeds by the man who is the overseer at the head of the Many; and if he is suited to the discipline, he will bring him into the Covenant that he may be converted to the truth and turn away from all perversity: he shall instruct him in all the ordinances of the Community. And when he later comes to present himself to the Many, they shall all consider his case, and according to whatever fate decrees, following the decision of the Many he shall either approach or depart. (IQS 6.13–16, Dupont-Sommer)

The passage continues to provide that the prospective entrant must remain on probation for a year, after which he is judged by the members again, and then, if he is approved by the priests and the majority of the other members, he may be taken into almost full membership. But a second year and a third examination and vote are required before he gains all the rights and privileges of full membership (IQS 6.16–23). There is reference to the matter being decided by the 'lot' (Dupont-Sommer, 'fate'), which presumably reflects the view that the person's admission is in accordance with God's will; but it is clear that a person's lot is in fact decided by a majority vote[57] and is

---

[57] See Leaney on IQS 5.3.

determined by his attitude (he humbly submits to the halakah of the sect), by his 'understanding' (he perceives the fact that the sect has the true covenant), and his 'deeds' (he is able to follow the rigorous requirements).

There is no indication in the entrance regulations that all these things are not within the range of human achievement. That they are is further indicated by the point already noted, that those not in the covenant and counted its enemies may turn from their wicked ways and join the community. The members themselves must all have repented and given up the ways of iniquity.[58] Just as striking is the treatment of backsliders. The severest curses of IQS are reserved for those who enter the covenant without the full *intention* to abide by its regulations. These are distinct from the 'men of the lot of Satan' (IQS 2.4f.), who are cursed by the Levites alone. The backsliders are cursed by both the priests and the Levites. They say:

Cursed be the man who enters this Covenant while walking among the idols of his heart, who sets up before himself his stumbling-block of sin so that he may backslide! Hearing the words of this Covenant, he blesses himself in his heart and says, 'Peace be with me, even though I walk in the stubbornness of my heart' (Deut. 29.18f.), whereas my spirit, parched (for lack of truth) and watered (with lies), shall be destroyed without pardon. God's wrath and His zeal for His precepts shall consume him in everlasting destruction. All the curses of the Covenant shall cling to him and God will set him apart for evil. He shall be cut off from the midst of all the sons of light, and because he has turned aside from God on account of his idols and his stumbling-block of sin, his lot shall be among those who are cursed for ever. (IQS 2.11–17)

We have already seen that for certain transgressions a man would be temporarily expelled, but could be readmitted if he corrected his way. All these passages, like the one above, suppose that membership in the covenant is subject to a man's own will, intention and success in fulfilling the commandments. In the passage just quoted we are not even told that his sin is caused by his being partially under the sway of the spirit of perversity (as in IQS 3.21–4); his sinning, on the other hand, is what puts him into the 'lot' of the cursed: it is by his own deeds rather than by the predestination of God.[59]

The conflict which we have been describing, and which has been often noted before, between the obvious supposition that membership within the elect is at one's own disposal and the repeated assertion that it depends entirely on God's will 'from the womb' was obviously not a conflict for the sectarians. Their assertion of God's governing providence did not exclude their certainty that a man could determine his own destiny. Once these are posed as two explanations of how one enters the covenant which are logically

---

[58] Cf. Carmignac, 'Souffrance', p. 373.

[59] For the point that the regulations of IQS and CD presuppose free will, see Marx, 'Prédestination', pp. 167f.

mutually exclusive, it is difficult to understand why the sectarians did not deal with the point. One scholar has suggested that the incongruence has to do with two different sources which have not been harmonized: traditional Judaism accounts for the emphasis on one's own choice, while Iranian dualism, somewhat altered, accounts for the emphasis on divine predestination.[60] Another explanation is that the two different emphases reveal the presence of different 'philosophies' within the Qumran community.[61] Other scholars have noted both points without attempting to reconcile them,[62] while some have favoured one (generally predestination) as being the dominant view, though granting that allowances for free will must have been made in practice.[63] Marx thinks that predestination is not present, but only the grace of God, and that man determines his own way.[64] Others have ascribed what we have described as a logical conflict to the lack of systematic logic typical of many religious groups.[65] Thus Holm-Nielsen has observed that predestination and individual responsibility should not be played off against each other as opposites. The former is theoretical speculation which serves to explain the existing state of affairs, while the latter is demonstrated by practical experience.[66]

The last explanation is certainly true. The Qumran sectarians, like other Palestinian Jews of the period, were not systematic theologians. Various answers to various questions would be regarded as true, without examining whether or not the various answers cohered with one another. Here we seem to have a striking instance of this situation.[67]

[60] R. E. Brown, in *S&NT*, pp. 189f. It does not seem necessary here to give an account of the detailed discussions of possible Iranian influence, which have mostly centred upon the 'dualism' of Qumran and IQS 3.14–4.26 in particular. For general comments and references to the literature, see Ringgren, *Faith of Qumran*, pp. 68–72, 78f.; Leaney, *Rule*, pp. 46–56; Burrows, *Dead Sea Scrolls*, p. 272; Huppenbauer, *Der Mensch zwischen zwei Welten*, pp. 10–13. Recently Osten-Sacken has argued that there was no Iranian influence in the light-darkness motif of IQM and elsewhere, but that Iranian influence can be seen in the conception of two spirits opposed to each other from the creation: *Gott und Belial*, pp. 81, 87, 139–41.

[61] M. Black, *The Scrolls and Christian Origins*, p. 125.

[62] Vermes, *Discovery*, pp. 111, 116.

[63] M. Burrows, *Dead Sea Scrolls*, pp. 262f.; *More Light*, pp. 281, 292f. In discussing 'the situation of man in the world', K. G. Kuhn (in *S&NT*, pp. 97–9) mentions only the aspect of 'primeval divine predestination'. He speaks of the sect's putting 'the divine predetermination in the place of the determination of man by his own choice' (p. 99). 'In tension with' might have been more accurate. Maier (*Mensch und freier Wille*, pp. 200–63) also subordinates free will to predestination: what one decides is itself predetermined (p. 221). See also n. 67 below.

[64] Marx, 'Prédestination', pp. 163–82. On pp. 163f. is found a more extensive list of ways of handling the problem than is given here.

[65] Milik, *Ten years*, p. 119; cf. Ringgren, *Faith of Qumran*, p. 111; Licht, 'Doctrine', pp. 5–7; Schubert, *Dead Sea Community*, p. 61.

[66] Holm-Nielsen, *Hodayot*, pp. 279–84; Licht, 'Nedabah', p. 81. Similarly Thyen (*Sündenvergebung*, p. 94) regards the dualistic predestinarian scheme as serving a theological anthropology.

[67] We should refer at least briefly to the detailed debate between Licht and Nötscher on predestination. See Nötscher, 'Schicksalglaube', for the fullest statement and references to earlier stages of the debate. Nötscher attempts various formulations to explain the relation between predestination and free will before granting that it cannot be captured in any one simple formula (p. 59). Some of his efforts, however, subordinate free will to grace in a coherent scheme: 'Das Mitglied der Gemeinde wählt also

Yet this explanation, while true, is not adequate to explain the remarkable emphasis on *both* God's choice of the elect and man's individual responsibility to choose; for both points are emphasized in Qumran in a way which is striking and unique. We shall now attempt to account for the very strong insistence on both these points.

The sectarians, like all other Jews, were faced with the problem of explaining the election. For the Rabbis, as we have seen, the problem was one which required explaining, and diverse explanations were given. All the explanations, however, were explanations of why God chose *Israel*. Individual Israelites did not really come into the question unless they behaved in such a way as to exclude themselves from the covenant. The sectarians, however, were faced with a much more serious problem: granted the consciousness of being the specially elect, the followers of the only true covenant, how could they account for their status? The election by definition must be by God's will; that much is obvious. But why did God now choose some Israelites and not others? This problem heightened the significance of the question of the election, and elicited two answers: God chose some but not others because he decided to do so; God chooses those who choose his way and rejects those who despise his commandments. *Both of these answers*, depending on the circumstances, could be considered to be true. Both appear, for example, in IQS, which, while it may be subject to source analysis, obviously had some kind of official status as a complete, if conflated document. The electing grace of God which chooses some and omits others would be emphasized when the author was thinking primarily of himself or of his colleagues within the sect, especially *vis à vis* God. In such a context, gratitude is the appropriate expression, coupled by wonder at being chosen, a feeling of personal unworthiness and an intense perception of God's graciousness.[68] *Vis à vis* God, no one can be worthy;[69] one's choice must be by grace. It is not surprising that this attitude is found primarily in the hymn material.[70] The hymns are in the general category of prayers or blessings,[71] and it is natural for one in the attitude of prayer to feel his unworthiness and God's

---

frei, fühlt sich aber doch als Erwählter. Wie er sich entscheidet, wie er selbst wählt, das its eben auch vorherbestimmt, ist sein ihm gnädig zugefallenes Los' (The member of the community chooses freely, but feels he has been elected. How he decided and chose was predetermined; it is the gracious lot that has fallen to him, p. 39; cf. p. 36). This seems to force, however, a connection which the members may not have seen. They appear not to have been of the view that there had to be some *relationship* between predestination and free will. Nötscher criticizes Licht for supposing that the covenanters did not perceive the problem and for thus not seeking a thorough solution (pp. 54f.), but systematizing Qumran thought on this point seems historically inaccurate.

[68] Vermes noted that the conception of an election of individuals, rather than of an entire people, led to an emphasis on God's grace and consequently on man's unworthiness: *Discovery*, pp. 111–13. Cf. Burrows, *Dead Sea Scrolls*, pp. 263f.; below p. 270 and n. 82.

[69] van der Ploeg noted that expressions of man's inability to 'direct his own steps' always refer to those who are already pious. Having chosen aright, they received further help from God: *Excavations*, p. 116.

[70] See above, p. 259.   [71] On instances in which this attitude is dropped in the hymns, see below, p. 292.

grace.[72] When considering outsiders, however, or those trying to enter the covenant, or the backsliders within the covenant, and in giving halakah to deal with these people, the sectarian authors would naturally write as if all is at man's disposal.

We have here an extreme example of a variation of religious expression which we have observed before. In prayer, the Rabbis too spoke of the grace of God and their own unworthiness, while in halakah they seemed to presuppose their own competence. The Qumran material is remarkable in part because there is so much hymn and prayer material, which gives a flavour to the total literary remains which is not found in other bodies of literature. Yet the character of the literature is not the entire answer to the problem of why, on the basic problem of the election, there is such a stark division between expressions of divine choice and statements of human choice. It must be remembered that the basic statement of the creation of the two spirits and God's establishing the design of all that is (IQS 3.15ff.) comes in the middle of what must be called the halakic section of IQS. Although the statement itself is not halakah, it is certainly not hymnic or prayer material. Although indirect Iranian influence may be observable in the formulation,[73] the impetus probably came from the sect's own need to explain the election of some Israelites over against others. Defining the sectarian covenant as the only covenant and themselves as the only elect was for the sectarians a very serious step, one which makes them members of a 'sect' as distinct from the Jerusalem parties.[74] Having taken this step, they needed to explain God's choice of them and also why the other Israelites refused to see and believe. This was such a serious matter that only God, whose workings are a mystery,[75] could be the author of it. In his grace he chose the sectarians, while assigning the other Israelites to the lot of Belial. In a similar way, the Christian church would, in taking approximately the same step, say the same of the Jews who would not be converted: God so arranged things that they could not see nor hear, lest they become converted (Mark 4.10–12). This theological position was carried to its logical extreme in neither Christianity nor Essenism: those outside could actually always be converted and come over, while those chosen could fall; in short, man's destiny was really in his own hands.[76] This does not eliminate the seriousness of the theological

---

[72] Similarly, Marx, 'Prédestination', p. 169.
[73] See n. 60 above.
[74] So Stendahl in *S&NT*, p. 7; Burrows, *Dead Sea Scrolls*, p. 251. On the sect as a sect rather than a party, see further Black, *Scrolls and Christian Origins*, pp. 6, 118f., 124. He correctly cites the importance of a variation in practice rather than belief for defining a sect, as well as the sect's exclusivism and hatred for outsiders. Cross (*Library*, p. 72 and n. 33) less convincingly attributes the sectarianism of the Qumran group to their apocalypticism, and Braun (*Radikalismus* I, p. 15) attributes it to the radical Torah observance. The real point of divergence would seem rather to be the definition of the covenant and the election, which might well have been the cause of radical Torah observance. On 'sects' and 'parties', see further the index, s.v. sect.
[75] See, for example, CD 3.18.   [76] So van der Ploeg, *Excavations*, p. 116.

position that the election and the distinction of the elect from the non-elect is by the grace of God.[77] The 'doctrine of predestination' in the Scrolls is best seen as *answering the question of why the covenanters are elect*, rather than whether or not there is free will.

The most important point for understanding the sectarian statements about election is to see their relationship with views about election in Judaism generally. It is not the case that the idea of the gracious selection of the chosen people by God – and in that sense his predestination of some to salvation – simply dropped from the Iranian sky into Qumran. All Israelites believed that God had chosen Israel before they as individuals were born. But while it is a theological problem to explain why God chose Israel and not some other nation, it is a problem of much greater severity to explain why he chose some individual Israelites but not others.[78] For the sectarians were *not* content to think of themselves simply as a faithful *remnant* which remained true to the covenant while others departed from it (though they did use such terminology on occasion).[79] If they had been so content, the problem of the election would have been much less vexing. Like the pious of the Psalms of Solomon, they could simply think that God chose Israel for whatever reason in the past and that the other Israelites 'diselected' themselves by unfaithfulness. One can see elements of such an explanation in the Scrolls (CD 3.10–14; 4.1; IQH 4.19). The sect was not content, however, with thinking of the other Israelites as simply strayed.[80] To the sect has been given

---

[77] One could make similar observations about the origin and function of dualism, which is closely related to predestination. See Huppenbauer, *Der Mensch zwischen zwei Welten*, pp. 42–4, 114.

[78] Jaubert (*La notion d'alliance*, pp. 128f., 138) contrasts the sectarian view of election, which emphasized gratuity, with the Pharisaic, which emphasized the race's *right* to the covenant based on *merit*. It is more accurate to say that both the sectarians and the Rabbis saw the covenant as the gracious gift of God, although the emphasis is stronger in the Scrolls and the election is slightly different in kind: some Israelites are chosen, rather than Israel in contrast to the Gentiles.

[79] Schubert (*Dead Sea Community*, pp. 80–4) is content with describing the sect's self-consciousness as being the elect within the framework of remnant theology. See further Becker, *Heil Gottes*, pp. 60–5; Thyen, *Sündenvergebung*, p. 87 n. 4; Jaubert, *La notion d'alliance*, pp. 120, 137f. On the term 'remnant' see above, n. 35. The term actually refers to those who survive a temporal or eschatological destruction, and so it is used in Qumran. When scholars speak of 'remnant groups', however, they frequently think of groups like that represented in the Psalms of Solomon, who see themselves as the pious faithful who hold fast while others go astray. Our contention here is that the Qumran Essenes did not think of themselves simply in these terms, whether or not this conception employs the term 'remnant'.

[80] Failure to see this point seems to be the principal cause of Marx's playing down 'predestination' somewhat too much. His point that human freedom is not negated in Qumran ('Prédestination', pp. 167f.) is certainly correct, as is his observation that in the hymns one would naturally ascribe all power to God and emphasize human weakness (p. 169), which helps explain the 'predestinarian' tone of some of the statements in the hymns. He thinks, however, that the sectarians were of the view that all Israel is elect and that they are distinguished from the rest of Israel only because the non-sectarians 'did not resist the attacks of Belial' (p. 170). The sectarians were the true observers of the law, while the others simply strayed (ibid.). He speaks of Israel as the chosen nation with whom God made a covenant. One has 'the freedom to remain in the covenant or to depart from it and suffer the consequences' (p. 171). This describes the view of the Rabbis or the Psalms of Solomon, but it is not the view of the sectarians, who speak of a new covenant established at the initiative of God with some Israelites but not with all, or of secrets of the covenant revealed by God to some but not to all. Cf. the discussion of the election above, p. 242 and nn. 8–10.

a new covenant or, alternatively, have been revealed the secrets of the covenant which were previously hidden. This is seen even in two of the passages
just cited. In CD 3.13f., 'those who hold fast to the commandments of God,
who are left over' are truly established by God only by his revealing to them
'hidden things concerning which all Israel had gone astray'. That is, the
sectarians do not just 'hold fast' to the covenant, but God takes the initiative
in revealing the 'hidden things'. Similarly, IQH 4.19 refers to 'those who
have withdrawn from Thy Covenant', apparently implying a distinction
between 'straying' and 'holding fast'. Yet the subsequent lines mention
God's *gathering* some into his covenant (4.24), which assigns to God more
initiative than would be implied by a conception of 'holding fast'. The
Qumran conception of the true covenant as being partially different in
content from the covenant of other Israelites required them to attribute
greater initiative to God than would be required or permitted by the notion
that the sectarians remained true while the others strayed. Thus it is not
surprising that God's initiative is frequently described as bestowing
knowledge, insight or understanding.[81] The sectarian view of their covenant
as one containing special revelations required them to emphasize the
initiating grace of God in deciding who would receive insight and who not,
so that the grace of God and his determination of the fate of each individual
are emphasized in the Scrolls as nowhere else in Palestinian Judaism.

The general idea of election by the grace of God, then, is by no means
peculiar to the sect. Its particular emphasis in the Scrolls seems due to the
internal theological requirements of the community as it defined itself over
against other Israelites. The emphasis on God's grace is the counterpart to
the exclusion of most Israelites from the covenant. They seem to have used,
in part at least, Iranian conceptions in formulating their views, but it seems
likely that essentially the same views would have emerged even if the conception of two spirits had not been available. There seems no justification for
regarding the sect's theology as an unharmonized marriage of Judaism and
Zoroastrianism. From the point of view of systematic harmonization, there
are real discrepancies in various statements about election and entrance into
the covenant. These come primarily from the internal stresses caused by the
sect's position *vis à vis* the rest of Israel, rather than from an unreflective
incorporation of views from different sources. Both the statement that God
determines the fate of every man and the affirmation that each man may
choose his own 'lot' are required for the sect, depending on what problem is
being addressed.

Although the Qumran community differed from other Jewish groups
only in the *degree of emphasis* which it put on the election as being the
bestowal of God's grace, there is a point at which the sectarians differed

[81] Above, p. 260.

widely from other Jewish groups in their view of the election. For understanding the self-consciousness and theology of the sect, it is important to
underline this fundamental disagreement. We have touched on the point
before, but should now spell it out more clearly: the sectarian conception of
the election is that it is an election of individuals rather than of the nation of
Israel.[82] Those outside the sect are universally considered sinners doomed to
destruction. Further, it seems that one could not be born into the sect.[83] The
covenant is not a birthright, but rather entrance requires a free act of will
on the part of an adult. As in Rabbinism, the covenant is the basic soteriological category. Unlike the Rabbis, who dealt primarily with how Israelites
should behave within the covenant and thus *remain* in it (and only occasionally with how *Gentiles* might enter), the sectarians insisted that individuals,
even though already Israelites, must consciously join their covenant.

   The act of will which is required is twofold: repentance and commitment
to the covenant. Thus the group was called, among other things, 'those who
turned from (repented of) iniquity',[84] and the covenant was a 'covenant of
repentance' (CD 19.16).[85] As the psalmist puts it, 'there is hope for those
who turn from transgression and for those who abandon sin' (IQH 6.6). A
man must give up the 'stiffness of neck' (IQS 5.5) – walking after his own
will rather than God's – which characterizes those outside the covenant.[86]
The entrant must commit himself with a binding oath to follow the law of
Moses as revealed to the community (IQS 5.8–10), and those who enter
with mental reservations are most severely condemned (IQS 2.11–18).

4. The commandments

In accord with the general understanding of the covenant in Judaism, the
sectarians considered it to contain specific commandments which should
be obeyed. Thus one notes the 'ordinances of the covenant': the sectarians
and their predecessors have sinned by walking contrary to the ordinances of
the covenant (CD 20.29); when, in the last days, all Israel joins the sectarians
before the final war against the Gentiles, they shall all be required to hear the

---

   [82] This has been decisively pointed out by Kapelrud ('Der Bund in den Qumran-Schriften', pp.
142–9); Burrows (*Dead Sea Scrolls*, p. 263); Milik (*Ten Years*, p. 114). Nötscher ('Schicksalglaube', pp.
36f.) argued that in Qumran the biblical view of Israel is not given up, but that the members thought
also of the election of the individual. In some senses this is true, but the theme of the election of Israel
in contrast to the Gentiles comes into play only when dealing with Israel's past or with the eschatological
future.
   [83] Entrants must take an oath, IQS 5.8f.; cf. the age requirements in IQSa 1.6ff. See Kapelrud, 'Der
Bund', pp. 142f.
   [84] Above, p. 245.
   [85] The phrase is missing in the parallel in CD 8.4. See Rabin, *Zadokite Documents*, p. 32.
   [86] On repentance as the requirement for entrance, cf. Braun, 'Umkehr', *Studien*, pp. 70–85, especially
p. 73. On following one's own heart and following God, see Helfmeyer, '"Gott Nachfolgen"', *RQ* 7,
1969, pp. 89–104.

'ordinances of the covenant' and to learn the statutes of the community so that they shall no longer stray (IQSa 1.5–7); those admitted to the covenant are those who volunteer to observe the ordinances of God (IQS 1.7). The particular commandments of the covenant are also indicated by such phrases as 'righteous ordinances' (CD 20.11,33), 'the rules (*mishpaṭim*) of the community' (IQS 6.15), and 'the rules of the Torah' (CD 14.8). Further, there are lists of some of the regulations in IQS and CD.

We have earlier seen that knowledge, insight and the like are connected with the election. Now we should observe that the theme of knowledge is also stressed in connection with the commandments contained in the covenant. The sectarians should study, so that they may know the content of what was commanded 'by the hand of Moses', as well as what has been subsequently revealed (IQS 8.12–16). Of the 'man of insight' (the *maskil*), it is said that 'he shall conceal the teaching of the Law from men of falsehood, but shall impart true knowledge and righteous judgement to those who have chosen the Way' (IQS 9.17f.; cf. 4.22). Here it is clear that the contents of the covenant are in part secret and are taught to the sectarians after they join the covenant, a point which is also implied in IQS 5.10–12. Thus part of the special knowledge which is emphasized in the Scrolls is knowledge of the secret contents of the covenant – the hidden things concerning which those not in the covenant go astray (IQS 5.11f.). The psalmist considers these secret things, which differ from the 'smooth things' taught by the 'teachers of lies and seers of falsehood', as a special gift engraved on his heart by God (IQH 4.9–11). It should be emphasized, however, that knowing the secret things of the covenant does not exhaust the content of the special knowledge of the sectarians. That knowledge embraces not only their election and the secret commandments, but also the mysteries to come.[87]

5. Fulfilment and transgression; the nature of sin; reward and punishment

The requirement of fulfilment

There is a very strict emphasis on the importance of actually fulfilling the commandments of the sect's covenant. When a man vows to enter the covenant ('return to the law of Moses'), the angel Mastema departs from him, *provided that* he fulfils the vow. The author emphasizes the significance of obeying without delay by citing the example of Abraham, who circumcised himself[88] on the very day when he learned that he should do so (CD 16.5f.).

[87] See Ringgren, *Faith of Qumran*, p. 62, and the literature cited above, n. 55.
[88] So Dupont-Sommer and Vermes. Rabin amends to 'was saved', but the point seems to be rather that Abraham performed what he promised without delay.

Further, if a man has taken an oath to fulfil some aspect of the Torah, he should do so even at the expense of his life. But if he has taken an oath to disobey some commandment, he should not fulfil the oath even though it cost him his life (CD 16.8–10). Those who enter the covenant are to do so in order to obey all of God's commandments (IQS 1.6f.; 1.16f.; cf. 5.20); members should transgress none of God's words (3.10f.). They are examined according to both their 'insight' and their 'deeds' (5.21; cf. 5.23f.; 6.14, 17, 18).

Destruction of the wicked

Those who are not in the covenant or who, being within it, transgress, are appropriately punished. It is a frequently repeated general statement that God (or the covenant community as God's agent) pays the 'reward' of evil: IQM 6.6; 11.13f.; 17.1;[89] CD 7.9; IQS 8.6f.,10. The Wicked Priest will receive his 'reward' when God delivers him into the hands of the powerful among the Gentiles (4QpPs37 4.9f.). In IQpHab 12.2f. the 'reward' of the Wicked Priest is said to be the same punishment which he had meted out to the sect ('the poor'). We have already seen that the 'reward' of the wicked (which may also be called their 'judgment', as in IQpHab 5.4) is destruction. This may be put in terms of destruction by the 'Wreakers of Revenge' (IQS 2.6f.), by fire (IQpHab 10.5,13; IQS 4.13), a scourge (IQpHab 9.11), or by the sword (IQM 9.5–9). It is sometimes unspecified: in IQS 5.6f. it is said that the sectarians will participate in the 'trial and judgement and condemnation of all those who transgress the precepts' (cf. IQH 4.26).[90]

Although the Scrolls do not often mention any punishment for sinners except destruction, the idea that sin brings affliction is not altogether absent. Thus in IQS 10.21 it is said that those who 'depart from the Way' are 'smitten' but not destroyed, while in IQH 15.19 those who have despised the covenant are said to have 'punishment' (*shephaṭim*) in store. In general, however, the punishment of the wicked is their destruction.

Sin as transgression

The destruction of the wicked is uniformly thought to be well deserved, a point which helps clarify the nature of sin. Even when the wicked are said to have been vowed 'from the womb' for destruction, the actual punishment is still justified by their own behaviour:[91] they despised the covenant, loathed the truth, walked in the wrong way and chose what God hates (IQH

---

[89] So Yadin and Vermes. Dupont-Sommer: 'Insure their wholeness.'

[90] On the indefiniteness of when the wicked will be punished, see Burrows, *More Light*, p. 347. On the punishment of the wicked, cf. Carmignac, 'Souffrance', pp. 365–74.

[91] Cf. Milik, *Ten Years*, p. 119.

15.17–19). That is, despite the statements indicating that man is consigned to one 'lot' or another, sin is still concretely *transgression of commandments*. The same view of sin as transgression even in the predestination passages may be seen in IQS 3.22 and IQH 14.14 ('workers of iniquity'). Thus those outside the covenant – the wicked or the sons of darkness – are simply those who transgress the covenant and refuse to follow what the sectarians considered to be God's will. The essential nature of sin is transgression and the wilfulness which accompanies it. One who prefers to follow 'the stubbornness of his heart' is said to despise 'the precepts of God' (IQS 2.26–3.7). Those who are not 'reckoned in His Covenant' are those 'who walk in the way of wickedness'. Their fault is that they have not *done* ('treated with insolence') the commandments which they knew to do ('revealed things'), while they have not sought to know, in order that they might do, the secret commandments known to the sectarians (IQS 5.10–12). They 'transgress ('*abar*) His word' and are unclean (5.14). God will destroy all those who 'despise His word'. The latter are contrasted to those who enter 'the Covenant to walk *according to all these precepts*' (5.19f.). A similar description of the wicked is given in IQH 4.14–22. They 'walk in stubbornness of heart', they receive false information about God's will from lying prophets, they do not 'give ear to Thy word', and they deny the truth of God's way. In another hymn, the fault of the wicked is that they have not followed God's commandments but have chosen what He hates (IQH 15.18f.). Those who are to be cut off at the judgment are characterized in 4.26f. as 'all those who transgress Thy word'. The same view is seen in CD very frequently. The wicked are 'those that abhor the ordinance' (2.6). The fault of the 'watchers', whose sin is paradigmatic, was that they walked 'in the stubbornness of their hearts' and did not keep 'the commandments of God' (2.19–21).

There are two points from which the view that sin is always conceived as the *avoidable disobedience of commandments* may be challenged. One is that the 'two spirits' passages (IQS 3.14–4.26; IQH 14.11–14; 15.14–19) indicate a situation in which a man is under a hostile power and commits individual transgressions only as a result of that. The other is based on the statements to the effect that sin is characteristic of man as human (flesh). The second point in particular has attracted a great deal of attention, especially in comparing Qumran with Paul, and we may turn to it first.

It will be useful to have before us at least two of the most characteristic passages. The psalmist in one of the community hymns describes himself as

> . . . a shape of clay
>   kneaded in water,
>   a ground of shame
>   and a source of pollution,
>   a melting-pot of wickedness

> and an edifice of sin,
> a straying and perverted spirit
> of no understanding . . . (IQH 1.21–3)

Such descriptions occur in other community hymns, for example IQH 3.23ff. and, more striking, IQS 11.9f.:

> As for me,
> I belong to wicked mankind,
> to the company of ungodly flesh.
> My iniquities, rebellions, and sins,
> together with the perversity of my heart,
> belong to the company of worms
> and to those who walk in darkness.

As Kuhn comments, 'In using the pronoun "I" even the believer counts himself as belonging to this "company of the flesh of evil", since he is a man, and as such, in the context of the passage, he commits sin.'[92] It does in fact seem apparent here that sin is something 'committed'; it still consists in 'iniquities, rebellions, and sins', by which transgressions of God's ordinances are clearly meant. Yet some have argued that the conception of sin in these and similar passages goes beyond that. The argument has been perhaps best made by Becker, and we may usefully consider his treatment of the theme.

Becker's argument[93] is that in the community hymns (which are distinguished from the hymns of the Teacher of Righteousness), sin is conceived as a sphere rather than as individual deeds.[94] He first notes that in IQH 4.29f. the term for 'sin' stands in the singular governed by *bet*. Such texts should be read, he argues, not as saying that a man has committed an individual transgression, 'but rather that he as a person always exists "in" sin'. He then cites IQH 11.10f.:

> For the sake of Thy glory
> Thou hast purified man of (*min*) sin (*pesha'*)
> that he may be made holy for Thee,
> with no abominable uncleanness (*niddah*)
> and no guilty wickedness . . .

---

[92] K. G. Kuhn, in *S&NT*, p. 102. See generally on the connection of flesh with sin, ibid., pp. 101–5; Davies, *Christian Origins and Judaism*, pp. 148–53; Huppenbauer, 'בשר "Fleisch" in der Texten von Qumran', *TZ* 13, 1957, pp. 298–300; Delcor, *Hymnes*, pp. 48f.; Brandenburger, *Fleisch und Geist*, pp. 86–106, especially pp. 99–102; R. E. Murphy, (BSR in the Qumran Literature', *Sacra Pagina*, especially p. 60 n. 1 for bibliography; Jaubert, *La notion d'alliance*, pp. 134f. H. Hübner ('Anthropologischer Dualismus in den Hodayoth?', *NTS* 18, 1972, pp. 268–84) has an excellent treatment of the related terms 'spirit' and 'dust'.

[93] Jürgen Becker, *Das Heil Gottes*, pp. 144–8.

[94] See Becker (ibid., pp. 51–4); Appendix 1 below. According to Becker's analysis, one of the points distinguishing the hymns of the Teacher of Righteousness from the community hymns is the conception of sin. In the former, sin is not necessarily connected with 'flesh', while in the latter it is (p. 67). One suspects that this distinction has led to the division of IQH 4.5–5.4 noted in Appendix 1, a division which

He argues that the preposition *min* before *pesha'* points to the 'spatial' aspect of sin. As further evidence for his view, he cites IQH 4.37:

> for Thou wilt pardon[95] iniquity (*'avon*),
> and through Thy righteousness
> [Thou wilt purify man] of (*min*) his sin (*'ashmah*).

One could also cite 3.21 to the same point: God is said to cleanse (*ṭ–h–r*) from (*min*) great transgression (*pesha'*). Becker concludes from this, especially from the fact that the terms for sin are in the singular, that one is not dealing with 'an individual deed', but with 'an encompassing context'.[96] We should first of all grant that in the hymns (and elsewhere, for that matter) the thought in one sense is that one moves *from* one sphere to another. The explanation for this is that righteousness and salvation exist only in the community. Everyone outside the covenant is damned and is 'in sin' in the sense that he sins. The sin *from which one who is in the community is purified* is not itself conceived as a power which holds men in bondage, however; it is always something that a man does, and of which he may repent and be forgiven. Thus the psalmist, after saying that he is 'in' iniquity and the guilt of rebellion from birth to old age (IQH 4.29f.), continues by saying that he remembered his guilty *acts* (*'ashmotai*, in the plural, 4.34; the singular appears in 4.30). When he then continues that he said 'in my transgression' (*bepish'i*) that he was forsaken by God's covenant (4.35), it is clear that 'in my transgression' means in his state of being untrusting, not in the sphere where sin reigns. Saying that he had been forsaken may be an example of one of the 'guilty acts'. He continues to say that he leans on God's grace, knowing that He will pardon him (4.37–39). The pardoning here obviously consists in forgiving the psalmist for his 'guilty acts' (and not for his being 'in [the sphere of] iniquity', as we shall shortly see).

We may first note that Becker has made too much of the singular use of some of the words for sin in the passages he quotes. Besides noting that the singular 'guilt' in 4.30 is picked up by the plural in 4.34, we may also point out that the phrase 'cleanse from transgression' (IQH 3.21; 11.10) appears as 'cleanse[97] from transgression*s*' in another community hymn (7.30). In this group of hymns, in fact (restricting ourselves here to the community hymns as defined by Becker), the terminology for sin virtually always implies evil activity in a way that cannot be misunderstood, even though the terms are sometimes grammatically singular. Thus 1.32, 'cleanse of a *multitude* of

---

is difficult to support on formal grounds. In the latter part of the hymn, which Becker calls 'secondary', sin is conceived radically. On another aspect of Becker's source analysis, see n. 41 above.

[95] On *kipper* to mean 'pardon', see pp. 298f. below.

[96] Becker, pp. 144f.: 'Ein umfassender Zusammenhang'; cf. Bröker's formulation (*TLZ* 87, 1962, col. 709): 'Ein kosmischer allgemeinsündiger Zusammenhang'.

[97] So the lacuna is universally filled. The word *ṭ–h–r* is only partially visible.

iniquity' (*rob 'avon*); 1.36, 'put away perversity' (*'avlah*) (not transfer from
it); 14.14, zeal against 'those who *work* wickedness' (*rasha'*); 14.24, 'pardoning those who repent of their transgression (*pesha'*) and visiting the iniquity
(*'avon*) of the wicked' (my translations). (I take it that a man does not 'repent'
of his spatial situation.) The singular terminology does not seem to lead to
the conclusion drawn by Becker.

In discussing these passages, Becker emphasizes God's activity in cleansing and forgiving almost to the exclusion of man's action in repenting. We
may see, however, in some of the passages quoted above, that God's cleansing is the other side of the coin from man's repenting. In the words of 14.24,
God pardons those who repent. In 1.36, one 'puts away' iniquity. The connection of repentance with cleansing is, in fact, frequently found in the
Scrolls in general. To be sure, both sides of the coin are not always mentioned
together. Thus IQH 7.26–31 speaks only of God's action in bringing near
and cleansing. As we have previously observed, God's initiative is emphasized more in the hymns, man's more in IQS and CD. Yet both appear
together sufficiently frequently to permit us to call the combination general.
Thus one may note the following lines from one of the hymns ascribed by
Becker to the Teacher of Righteousness: 'there is hope for *those who turn*
from transgression and for those who abandon sin', '*Thou wilt raise up*
survivors among Thy people and a remnant within Thine inheritance. *Thou
wilt purify* and cleanse them of their guilt' (IQH 6.6,8; Vermes has 'sin' for
the last word). Similarly, IQS 1.11f. stresses that those who 'volunteer' come
into the community to 'purify their knowledge in the truth of God's precepts', while, according to IQS 3.6f., it is by 'the spirit of true counsel
concerning the ways of man that all his sins shall be expiated that he may
contemplate the light of life. He shall be cleansed from all his sins by the
spirit of holiness uniting him to His truth. . .'

The reason for bringin out here the repentance side of the repentance/
cleansing coin is further to show that the concept of sin is not primarily
spatial, but rather refers to wrong deeds. If Becker can take the 'from' in
'cleanse from' to indicate a 'spatial' concept,[98] we must not hesitate to point
out that 'repent of' implies no spatial concept whatsoever. If, as I have argued,
one should not separate the motif of God's cleansing from man's repentance,
but should consider that they go together, the correctness of the 'spatial'
hypothesis is put further in doubt.

Now we come to a point which seems to me decisively to refute Becker's
hypothesis. In Becker's discussion, the solution to man's plight in IQH
11.10f. follows the statement of the plight in 4.29f. In 4.29f. one sees the
term '*in* iniquity'. According to 11.10, God cleanses man '*from* transgression'. Becker apparently takes it to be the case that one is *in* the damned

[98] Becker, p. 144.

state and moves *from* it to salvation. Many other scholars have been of a similar view (though not necessarily on the basis of the connection of these two passages). Thus Braun makes a logical distinction between sin as transgression and sin as 'being' (*Sündersein* and *Sündetun, Sünder in seinem Tun und in seinem Sein*).[99] He grants that the two are not actually two separate things,[100] and he observes – correctly, in my view – that both aspects of sin are opposed to obeying the Torah; thus sin 'is transgression of the Torah'.[101] He also regards both aspects of sin as part of man's 'lostness' (*Verlorenheit*)[102] and further states that salvation, which occurs when someone enters the sect, saves from 'nothingness' (equated with *Sündersein*) as well as from transgression.[103] Similarly Licht, in (correctly) emphasizing the pollution of sin, states that the psalmist considers God to have purified him from the contamination of *humanity*.[104] All three positions are that God has redeemed the covenanters from the iniquity involved in being human as such. This seems, however, not to be correct.

We may return first to Becker's passages. It appears that, contrary to his view, the 'in' statements in IQH 4.29f. are not in fact *Unheilsbegriffe*. There is no doubt that the statement of cleansing in 11.29f. refers to one who joins the covenant: he is cleansed 'that he may be one [with] the children of Thy truth'. We find in IQH 4.33–37, however, a statement of sin and restoration *within* the covenant rather than of *transfer from* the damned state to the covenantal state. Thus 4.34–36:

> When the wicked rose against Thy Covenant
> and the damned against Thy word,
> I said in my sinfulness (*bepish'i*),
> 'I am forsaken by Thy Covenant.'
> But calling to mind the might of Thy hand
> and the greatness of Thy compassion,
> I rose and stood,
> and my spirit was established
> in the face of the scourge.

The psalmist then continues by saying that he leans on God's grace and that God pardons him. It seems that the lines just quoted describe a crisis in a covenanter's life rather than a confession of God's grace for putting him in the right 'lot'. The covenant was attacked and he was afraid that he was forsaken. If this is true of 4.33–36, the same seems certainly to be true of 4.29f., which is a confession of the *sinfulness of a man in the covenant vis à vis* God.

[99] H. Braun, 'Selbstverständnis', *Studien*, pp. 113, 107.
[100] Ibid., pp. 105f.
[101] Ibid., p. 113.
[102] Ibid., pp. 109, 117.
[103] Ibid., pp. 110f. We shall return to these last points below.
[104] Licht, 'Doctrine', p. 96.

The 'in' phrases of 4.29f. state not so much a plight *from* which man is saved as a constant truth which is not altered: man, on his own, is iniquitous ('in iniquity') and full of guilty rebellion ('in guilty unfaithfulness') *'until his old age'*. He has no righteousness, nor perfection of way, for to God *alone* belong righteous deeds. Man's way is established only by God (IQH 4.29–31). The closest parallel to this is IQS 11.11f.: 'If I stagger because of the sin of flesh, my justification shall be by the righteousness of God.'[105] In both cases, the point is that man, on his own, is always a sinner. He may at any time 'stumble', which doubtless means to commit an individual transgression, not to relapse into a former sphere. This is a description of the human state from which he is *not* saved. He never, in this world, moves from the sphere in which, *vis à vis* God, his actions apart from grace are sins. The 'in iniquity' passage is a statement of human inadequacy and the constant proclivity to sin unless one's steps are established by God. *Becker's 'from' passages do not refer to being saved from the basic human condition of frailty*, in which man is unable to 'stand' or to 'establish his way' or to do any righteous deed; *they do not constitute the solution to the plight of 4.29f*. The 'from' passages refer to being cleansed from transgression and the impurity which is attached to it so that one may join the covenant. The man in 4.29, however, is already in the covenant. Yet he remains 'in iniquity' from the womb to old age. The opposite of such a man, it must be noted, is not a cleansed man, but God, to whom belong all righteous *deeds*. Man's situation 'in iniquity' is simply that he is, on his own, incapable of righteous deeds, and *this always remains the case*. The 'in iniquity' statement, in other words, is to be connected to the frequent statements in the Hodayot to the effect that man is nothing.[106] As we shall see when these passages are discussed more fully below, this is always said of man *in contrast to God*, and always *of the saved*.[107] It is not a description of man in the condition of being damned, or outside the covenant.

Thus the 'in' passages, which, in Becker's scheme, state the situation 'from' which man is saved, are not actually the counterpart to the 'from' passages. The 'in' passages refer to the inadequacy of man in comparison with God – they are equivalent to saying that man *vis à vis* God is not right-eous (so 4.29–31) – while the 'from' passages refer in the way customary in Judaism to being cleansed of (from) sin and the moral and cultic impurity

---

[105] Becker (pp. 111f.) translates 'flesh' as 'my flesh' and argues that the passage makes it clear that flesh (*basar*) is the origin of sin, the power that leads to sin. The point of the passage, however, is to contrast man ('flesh'), who is sinful, with God, who is righteous. Nothing is said about the origin of sin or its cause, but only about man's characteristic nature *vis à vis* God. Similarly Huppenbauer, '"Fleisch"', *TZ* 13, 1957, pp. 298–300: he argues, against Kuhn, that flesh stands over against God as the temporal versus the eternal, *not as the motivating power of sin* against the divine righteousness. He takes IQS 11.12 to mean: 'wenn ich in meiner Eigenschaft als Mensch zu Fall komme'. He comments: 'Als Mensch wird auch der Glaübige von Qumran immer weider schuldig.'

[106] So also Becker, p. 114.   [107] Below, p. 281 and n. 127.

which is attached to it.[108] Thus Becker's in/from scheme breaks down completely. Although there is a sphere in which sin is dominant (the sphere outside the covenant),[109] the terminology which states man's plight and the solution to it is not that he is 'in' sin and is transferred 'from' it, but that he sins and is forgiven for it and cleansed of it.[110] The plight from which one is saved by forgiveness and cleansing is not that one is 'in sin' in the Pauline sense, but that one has transgressed the covenant.

Thus we must also argue against Braun that the 'nothingness' passages are *not* statements of man's 'lostness' and that entry into the sect does *not* save from nothingness, and against Licht that the psalmist does not find cleansing from humanity within the sect.[111] During this life, man never ceases being 'nothing' *vis à vis* God, while entry into the sect cleanses from transgression, but not from being fleshly,[112] i.e. human, weak, inclined to sin and 'nothing' in comparison with God.[113]

It is important to observe, however, that in some passages it is indicated that the weakness of humanity *will* be overcome. These passages appear not to refer to this life, but to the eschaton. Thus, most clearly, IQS 4.19–22. The author writes that God has ordained an end to falsehood, and that 'at the time of His visitation' he will destroy it. This will involve abolishing the 'spirit of perversity' itself 'from his *flesh*' and cleansing him.[114] Thus the state of being 'in iniquity' will, according to IQS 4.19–22, be overcome at the eschaton.[115] The same meaning may be found in IQH 15.15–17, where

[108] See p. 116 and the literature cited there.

[109] Cf. Becker's discussion of sin in the hymns which he attributes to the Teacher of Righteousness, *Heil Gottes*, pp. 66f. Here he argues that sin is a sphere which is concretized in individual transgressions. For the 'sphere' he refers especially to the phrase 'realm of ungodliness', IQH 2.8. This 'sphere', of course, is the sphere outside the covenant, the abode of 'the assembly of the wicked' (2.12). The sphere, in other words, is the entire non-sectarian world. This world is not itself sin, but the area in which transgression of God's commandments takes place, and it may be left by repenting of those transgressions (2.9). Sin is still transgression.

[110] Similarly Hübner ('Anthropologischer Dualismus in den Hodayoth?') successfully argues against Brandenburger that the Hodayot do not contain the idea of a transfer *from* the sphere of flesh (or dust) *to* the sphere of the spirit.

[111] Above, nn. 103, 104.

[112] I omit here a discussion of the phrase 'from dust', which would lead to the same conclusion. The principal passages (IQH 3.19–23; 12.24f.; 11.10–14) have been persuasively discussed by Hübner ('Anthropologischer Dualismus in den Hodayoth?'). He shows that the phrase does not imply leaving the dust; man remains dust, insofar as he is made of it (pp. 272, 274, 277, 279). IQH 3.21, for example ('whom Thou hast shaped from dust for the everlasting Council'), does not refer either realistically or metaphorically to leaving 'the dust' during this life (cf. p. 272); it should be understood, rather, thus: 'Du hast aus Staub Wesen gebildet, deren Bestimmung die ewige Gemeinschaft ist' (p. 275). Hübner's article is a timely correction of the theses of Brandenburger and, to some extent, H. W. Kuhn.

[113] It does not seem necessary to give here a technical treatment of 'flesh' in the Scrolls. As Murphy ('BŚR', especially pp. 68, 74) has shown, the term expresses man's weakness, not the power of sin. See also Brandenburger, *Fleisch und Geist*, p. 101: 'the weakness of fleshly nature was the entrance gate of sin'.

[114] The translation of the passage is controversial, but this seems to be the best understanding. See Leaney, *Rule*, pp. 154–8; Wernberg-Møller, *Manual*, pp. 85f., for the various proposals. On the meaning of the passage, see further Licht, 'The Treatise on the Two Spirits', *Aspects*, pp. 96f.

[115] IQS 4.19–22 is also taken as referring to the salvation of the end time by Murphy, 'BŚR', p. 64, and Brandenburger, *Fleisch und Geist*, p. 96.

it is said that God gives (will give?) *eternal* salvation to the 'just' (*tsaddiq*) and that he *will* raise his 'glory' from flesh (*basar*). Here we do have a statement of salvation from (the weakness of) the flesh, but it is apparently an eschatological promise, not something that has already happened.[116] As a final example in this collection of passages concerning the future redemption from fleshly weakness, we may consider IQS 11.14f. Here the psalmist speaks of being cleansed 'of the uncleanness of man and of the sins of the children of men'. It is conceivable that this is simply equivalent to being forgiven for iniquitous deeds (*'avonot*) in the phrase just preceding the words quoted. While we can rest little weight on the 'tense' of the verbs, it seems likely that we should understand the imperfect 'will cleanse' as a future, referring to the eschatological cleansing which was promised in IQS 4.19–22.[117]

We are not discussing here the question whether or not there are any elements of present or realized eschatology in the Scrolls. H. W. Kuhn[118] devoted his thesis to the study of present eschatology in the community hymns, and the main lines of his argument are supported by Brandenburger[119] and Thyen.[120] The principal passages which Kuhn studied for this purpose are IQH 3.19–36; 11.3–14; 11.15–36; 15.[121] He took the phrase 'from dust' in 11.12, for example, to refer to being raised from the residence of worms, but not to being removed from humanity: 'With entrance into the community, death is already fundamentally overcome.'[122] He observed, however, that even where the consciousness of the presence of salvation is most pronounced, the pious of Qumran were always conscious of the 'not yet'. Each of the community hymns contains either a 'Niedrigkeitsdoxologie' or an 'Elendsbetrachtung', and these are side by side with statements of present salvation. Thus a future expectation is essential for the community hymns. The members expected a universal and completely new beginning.[123] Brandenburger similarly regarded such a passage as IQH 15.14–17 as indicating that the elevation from the realm of flesh is to be understood as a 'gegenwärtig-eschatologisches Geschehen'.[124] Although

---

[116] An alternative understanding would be this: God chooses humans ('flesh') for his community ('glory'). Cf. n. 112 above.

[117] So Leaney apparently takes it, for he simply refers the reader to IQS 4.20. Schulz ('Rechtfertigung', p. 169) takes all the verbs in the passage as past, finding more realized eschatology in the passage than I am able to do. We should note that some scholars find another 'from flesh' passage in IQH 18.14. Brandenburger (*Fleisch und Geist*, apparently following Lohse's edition) takes מבשר thus. Dupont-Sommer, Vermes and Mansoor understand the word as a *pi'el* participle 'proclaiming'. Habermann declines to point it. 'Proclaiming' seems the better reading, but the context is too uncertain to allow a firm conclusion.

[118] H. W. Kuhn, *Enderwartung und gegenwärtiges Heil*, 1966.

[119] E. Brandenburger, *Fleisch und Geist*, 1968, especially pp. 102–6.

[120] H. Thyen, *Studien zur Sündenvergebung im Neuen Testament*, 1970, especially pp. 86–92.

[121] Kuhn, pp. 44–112.

[122] Ibid., p. 88; cf. pp. 48–50; Hübner, cited above, n. 112.

[123] Kuhn, p. 177. Kuhn also notes that only salvation is both present and future, while damnation is only future (pp. 178f.).

[124] Brandenburger, pp. 105f.

one may generally agree that there is a conception of present salvation in the hymns, it seems best to understand 15.16f. as indicating God's future reward for the righteous, just as 15.19f. indicates the future punishment of the wicked. Thyen correctly emphasizes, more clearly than did Kuhn, that the covenanters' consciousness of present salvation did not extend to considering that they had already been saved from human frailty.[125] Thyen does not, however, properly formulate the significance of this constant human state; he considers the 'Elendsdoxologien' to be confessions of 'gegenwärtige Verlorenheit'.[126] We can summarize a better understanding of the community consciousness in three points: (1) Being in the community is the decisive factor in salvation, and the members were conscious of being saved (*gegenwärtiges Heil*) and of being members of the community which lived in the presence of God; (2) this salvation did not remove them from being fleshly; they have no righteousness *vis à vis* God and remain in this sense in human weakness and iniquity (*gegenwärtige Schwachheit*); (3) human weakness does not constitute 'lostness' or damnation (*keine gegenwärtige Verlorenheit*); it will be overcome at the eschaton.

In connection with the conclusion that the inadequacy ('sinfulness') of man *qua* man will be overcome only at the eschaton, we should repeat the frequent observation that the confessions of the sinfulness and nothingness of humanity apply precisely to the members of the community.[127] This state is one which being in the community does not correct. This is a most significant point for understanding the sect's conception of sin and the relationship of that conception to Paul's, and the observation has not been fully exploited for those purposes. Braun, Bröker and Becker have all argued that the most distinctive point at which Paul agrees with Qumran is the profound understanding of the sinfulness of man which is overcome by the grace of God, while he differs in seeing the grace of God as liberating one from the law, rather than as enabling one to fulfil the law.[128] The contrast is certainly correct. We must observe, however, that the point of supposed likeness – the profound conception of sin – contains an even more striking dissimilarity. It is not correct to say with Braun that for both Paul and Qumran 'lostness' lies in the flesh;[129] for in Qumran man's 'fleshly' nature *does not damn*, since it is precisely those in the community of the saved who continue to confess their human inadequacy and nothingness. One who is in the sect remains in human flesh and participates in the 'sinfulness' of humanity, but he is still among the saved. The sins *which exclude one from*

---

[125] Thyen, pp. 90f.

[126] Ibid., p. 92.

[127] Schulz, 'Rechtfertigung', p. 158; van der Ploeg, *Excavations*, p. 116; Braun, *Studien*, p. 108; Becker, *Heil Gottes*, p. 137; Huppenbauer (quoted in n. 105); Delcor, *Hymnes*, p. 48; Holm-Nielsen, *Hodayot*, pp. 274–6; Pryke, ' "Spirit" and "Flesh" ', *RQ* 5, 1965, pp. 351–4; Murphy, 'BSR', p. 66.

[128] Braun, *Studien*, pp. 115f.; Bröker, *TLZ* 87, 1962, col. 709; Becker, *Heil Gottes*, pp. 125, 143.

[129] Braun, *Studien*, p. 117; cf. Thyen's position, cited in n. 126.

the sect, and thus from the saved, are transgressions of the law which one could have, by better will or better knowledge, avoided.

Now we may turn to another possible objection to the view that sin is avoidable transgression. One could argue that, although sin is transgression in the predestination passages, it is not avoidable. If it is not avoidable, there is a sense in which sin is not itself transgression of God's commandments, for transgression implies the possibility of obedience as its reverse. We may best quote IQS 3.21–3:

The Angel of Darkness leads all the children of righteousness astray, and until his end, all their sin, iniquities, wickedness, and all their unlawful deeds are caused by his dominion in accordance with the mysteries of God.

Here, although the sins are obviously misdeeds, they are said to be caused by the Angel of Darkness, which means that their basis is not stubbornness of heart, but a power *which even being in the community cannot break*.

We have already argued that predestination and free-will should not be viewed as alternative theological positions, but as varying explanations of the community's self-consciousness. Just as, from one point of view, the members of the community are said to be the elect of God, they are, from another point of view, said to elect God or to volunteer.[30] The two statements reflect two aspects of the community self-consciousness and are not mutually exclusive. We should similarly assume here that saying that transgressions are caused by the Angel of Darkness is not intended as a denial that they are the result of man's will. The quoted statement is an attempt to explain why one in the community continues to sin. We have already seen and discussed a different explanation for this same worrisome problem: that man in comparison with God is inadequate and is 'in iniquity' (IQH 4.29). That explanation attributes man's continued sin even in the covenant to (if we may use the phrase) human nature, while the statement just quoted from IQS 3 attributes the same phenomenon to God's predestination. Presumably the phrase 'in accordance with the mysteries of God' indicates that even predestination does not seem a satisfactory solution for why one in the covenant transgresses: that God should so design things is a mystery. It is noteworthy that in giving halakah governing the punishment of those in the community who sin, IQS distinguishes only between intentional and unintentional sins (8.13–9.2).[131] Thus despite the theological theories of IQS 3.22 and IQH 4.29 as to why one in the covenant still transgresses, the practical code of the community works on the assumption that the transgressor either intentionally transgressed or did so inadvertently.

There is no doubt that, in seeking reasons for man's transgression within

---

[130] Above, pp. 257–65.
[131] 'Intentionally', *beyad ramah*, IQS 8.17, 22; 9.1; 5.12. 'Inadvertently', *bishgagah*, IQS 8.24; cf. 9.1.

the covenant which lie beyond man's will and in finding them in human frailty on the one hand and in the predestining grace of God on the other, the theologians of the community reached a more profound (or at least more pessimistic) view of human sinfulness than one finds elsewhere in Palestinian Judaism. To this degree, the Scrolls do break with the definition of sin as avoidable transgression. They say, in part, that sin is transgression, but that transgression is not altogether avoidable. On the other hand, this is a view which is not worked out. For one thing, there is no solution to the unavoidable transgressions. A man remains in them until his old age (IQH 4.29) or until the end (IQS 3.22; 4.18f.), and he can only say that the sins of the elect are to be explained by God's will which is a mystery (IQS 3.23). In other words, *these profound views of human sinfulness do not touch soteriology.* They do not state a plight to which a soteriological solution within this life is offered; that is, these statements do not appear when the transfer from the non-sectarian (damned) state to the sectarian (saved) state is being discussed, and they are not statements of human 'lostness' in the sense that those outside the covenant are lost.[132] Man needs to be cured of his nothingness, and those in the covenant will be cured; but confessions of nothingness are not confessions of 'lostness', and nothingness will not lead to the damnation of those in the sect.

It is rather the transfer from outside the sect to within the sect (a transfer which does not correct nothingness and which does not altogether eradicate the power of the Angel of Darkness) which constitutes the operative soteriology of the sect. It does seem, on the basis of such passages as IQS 3.21–3 and 4.19–22, that the sectarians hoped that they would be further purified at the end. That is, there is a kind of two-stage soteriology. One stage involves joining the group of the elect, the other the final purification of the elect. I take the former to be the operative one which governed the sect's life and thought, while the latter is a hope for the future of those already in the group of the saved. The transfer from outside the sect to within it, then, involves repentance of avoidable transgressions and 'volunteering', although the volunteers feel themselves to be the elect of God. There is, however, no outside salvific force which breaks the power which the Angel of Darkness exercises even over the elect or which makes of a frail man who cannot on his own avoid iniquity a 'new creation'.

Thus one may partially agree with Braun when he says that 'Das Heil errettet aus der *Nichtigkeit*'.[133] But this is so only proleptically, by putting one in the group which *will* be saved from nothingness.

---

[132] Thus we must confirm against Maier (*Mensch und freier Wille*, p. 324) that an efficacious conversion was possible within this life. He was so impressed with the enduring 'sinfulness' (weakness) of humanity that he wrote that 'history, the covenant, the dynamic change of disobedience and repentance are practically excluded from consideration'. On the contrary, these are all major themes in the Scrolls.

[133] Braun, *Studien*, p. 110.

Further, although man is sometimes said to be such that he cannot avoid transgression, that state itself is not equated with sin.[134] Sin remains what he does, even when his evil acts are conceived as unavoidable. Thus, although the sectarian theologians reached a profound and pessimistic view of human ability, this did not lead them to make a fundamental break with the conception of sin known elsewhere in Judaism. Sin is transgression of God's will as made known in his commandments and the sectarian interpretation of the law. Sin *which damns* is refusal to accept God's commandments in the sectarian covenant or transgressing one for which there is no repentance. There is a kind of 'sinfulness' which does not damn and which continues to characterize the elect, the sinfulness involved in man's inadequacy before God, which will not be overcome and eradicated until the end. This pessimistic and profound view does not, however, become a basic element to be overcome in the *path* to salvation, since nothing can be done about it until God destroys wickedness itself at the end. For practical purposes of the sect's life, sin remains *avoidable* transgression.

We should again emphasize that the conception of sin as transgression is in harmony with the statements that what one must do to join the covenant is to turn from transgression (*pesha'*) (IQH 6.6; 14.24; and elsewhere), *not* leave the flesh. That is, despite the statement that the wicked are under the rule of the Angel of Darkness (IQS 3.20), there is something that they can do about it: they can repent and join the covenant. This is a very significant point for understanding the relation of the Qumran view to the rest of Judaism and to Paul. In Rabbinic literature, one does not *join* the covenant by repenting of transgression, since one is born in it. The basic categories of sin as transgression[135] and of repentance as the cure for transgression, however, are the same. As we shall see, Paul agrees with the Essenes in thinking that one is not born in a covenant which is efficacious for salvation, but must join it by an act of will ('faith'). He does not, however, define sin simply as avoidable transgression of God's commandments nor prescribe repentance as the cure for man's plight.

Punishment for intra-covenantal transgression[136]

We have thus far dealt with the destruction and punishment of the wicked and the nature of sin, whether within or without the covenant. Now we

---

[134] Thus Brandenburger (*Fleisch und Geist*, p. 101) correctly observes that the connection between flesh and sin does not amount to identity.

[135] Daniélou (*Dead Sea Scrolls and Christianity*, pp. 100f.) argues that the conception of sin as 'primordial' in Qumran differs from that of Pharisaism, 'which is based on the works of the Law', and agrees with that of Paul. Although it is true that an important theme in the Scrolls is that it is only by the grace of God that sin can be overcome (below, pp. 288–91), it is nevertheless the case, as we have seen, that the definition of sin as avoidable transgression is the *same* as that of Rabbinic Judaism.

[136] There is a recent full treatment of the topic in Forkman, *The Limits of the Religious Community*, ch. 2.

should note that those who are within the covenant and transgress are also punished, but not destroyed. There are numerous regulations for the punishment of transgressors within the community in CD and IQS, and we may quote an example from each:

But everyone who goes astray so as to profane the Sabbath and the appointed time shall not be put to death, for it falls to men to guard him; and if he is healed from it, they shall guard him for a period of seven years, and afterwards he shall come into the assembly. (CD 12.4–6)

If one of them has lied deliberately in matters of property, he shall be excluded from the pure Meal of the Congregation for one year and shall do no penance with respect to one quarter of his food. (IQS 6.24f.)

The particular punishments prescribed by CD and IQS are not always in agreement, but the general character of temporary exclusion is the same. In addition, IQS regularly prescribes reduction of food as a punishment.[137] According to IQS 8.20–9.2 a select group, the 'men of perfect holiness' (presumably the same as the select fifteen of IQS 8.1–4) are judged more strictly.[138] For these, any intentional sin at all involves permanent expulsion, while an unintentional transgression results in an exclusion of two years, provided that no further inadvertent sin is committed during the trial period. According to IQS 7.22–25, those who, after being members of the 'Council of the Community' for ten years, betray (*b–g–d*) the Community and depart from it, shall not be readmitted. For others, however, 'betrayal of the truth' results in only a two-year partial exclusion (IQS 7.18–21). Thus even apostates of fewer than ten years' membership could be readmitted. There is in IQS, however, a short list of sins which require permanent exclusion: blaspheming[139] while reading the Book or praying (7.1f.); slandering the congregation (7.16f.); murmuring against the authority of the Community (7.17).[140]

---

[137] I take the 'fines' or 'punishments' of IQS 6.27; 7.2; and subsequent passages to continue to refer to the 'fine' of one quarter of one's food mentioned in 6.24f. So also Hunzinger, 'Beobachtungen zur Entwicklung', pp. 235f.

[138] Wernberg-Møller (*The Manual of Discipline*, p. 131) takes the phrase 'men of perfect holiness' to apply to the entire community. He seems not to notice that the halakah is far more rigorous than that specified for the larger community in 6.24f. Ringgren (*The Faith of Qumran*, p. 134) also takes IQS 8.22 to state a requirement applicable to the entire community. For a more detailed treatment and discussion of the views of Leaney, Guilbert, Murphy-O'Connor, Forkman and Hunzinger, see Appendix 2.

[139] Literally 'cursing', but this was probably understood as cursing God and blaspheming on the basis of Lev. 24.11–15.

[140] Hunzinger ('Beobachtungen zur Entwicklung', pp. 232–6) notes the two basic types of punishment – temporary and permanent exclusion – but attributes them to different views. He considers that, in the history of the sect, the punishments became increasingly milder. It is noteworthy that his analysis of punishments leaves out of account what the punishments are for. He speaks only of different punishments and appears to see no correlation between the severity of the punishment and the seriousness of the offence. It appears to me that there is a substantial effort to correlate the punishment with the offence in IQS. While a historical development may be observable in IQS 8–9 (I see none in chapters 6–7), the various punishments must have been taken to refer to various transgressions in the document as it now stands. See further Appendix 2.

It is noteworthy that of the list of offences for which permanent expulsion is prescribed, all but one – blasphemy – are offences against the community. That is, members are expelled for betraying the community by word or deed. Expulsion seems to be the community's ultimate sanction, and it was employed against those who had themselves rejected the community. The practicality of the sanction is noteworthy. In IQS we are told nothing about corporal or capital punishment, even though the Bible prescribes the death penalty for blasphemy. It is noteworthy that blasphemy is one of the few crimes covered by biblical law which is mentioned in the Scrolls. It may be that the entrance requirements were so strict and the community so closely knit that the more mundane crimes were not a problem.[141] At any rate, the offences against the sectarian regulations or against the sect itself were dealt with by expulsion or some variation, such as exclusion from certain communal activities, plus a reduction in the food allowance.

The various provisions for the punishment of transgression show with striking clarity the way in which the religion functioned. Commandments were given which a man was to obey. Perfect obedience was the aim, and, within the tightly ordered community structure, was not considered a totally impossible goal. Infractions were punished, and the acceptance of the punishment, together with perseverance in obedience, led to full restoration of fellowship.[142] It must be recalled, however, that the individual member thought of himself as having been appointed to the community in the first place by the grace of God.

Before leaving the theme of the punishment of the transgressions of the sectarians, we should note a group of passages in the community hymns in which the psalmist thinks of his own sins and considers his suffering to be God's chastisement for them. Thus in IQH 9.23f. the psalmist mentions his being 'rebuked' by God, but says that God's rebuke (*tokaḥat*) will become his joy while his (the psalmist's) affliction (*nega'*) will turn to healing. Similarly in 9.33 the psalmist mentions receiving God's just rebuke. IQH 17.22 mentions God's chastisement (*yissureka*) upon the one whom he has chosen. When the psalmist says (11.8f.) that 'In Thy wrath are all chastisements (*mishpeṭe nega'*), but in Thy goodness is much forgiveness', he seems to be assigning all suffering, whether that of the wicked or the righteous, to God's

---

[141] Transgression of the Sabbath is mentioned in CD 12.4–6, but the death penalty is expressly forbidden. CD 9.1 apparently prescribes the death penalty by the gentiles for 'devoting' a man to death, referring to Lev. 27.29, but the point of the ordinance is obscure. The death penalty is referred to vaguely, without mention of specific crimes, in CD 9.6, 17; 10.1. 4Q 159 apparently prescribes death for sexual offences. See on all this Forkman, *The Limits of the Religious Community*, pp. 43, 64f.

[142] Braun ('Tora-Verschärfung', pp. 349f.; cf. 'Umkehr', *Studien*, pp. 78f. and *Radikalismus* I, pp. 28f.) emphasizes the requirement to do *all* the commandments (which he sets over against Rabbinic Judaism's supposed requirement to have fulfilments simply outweigh transgressions), and concludes that a man is *lost* (*verloren*) if he does not fulfil *all*. This overlooks the actual remedies for transgressions in IQS and CD.

punishment of transgressions. Yet it is not perfectly clear in all the community hymns that suffering is considered to be punishment for sin. When in 1.33 the psalmist speaks of the 'judgment of my afflictions' (*mishpeṭe negi'e*), he seems to be referring to the afflictions executed by others against him, in the face of which God strengthened him (1.32; the context, however, is partially destroyed). It is possible, to be sure, that he saw God as both sending the chastisements and strengthening him to bear them. This seems to be what is meant in 9.10–13. The psalmist says that he chooses (God's) judgment upon himself and that he accepts afflictions willingly, since he hopes for God's loving-kindness. His hope is not disappointed, for God has upheld his spirit in the face of affliction (*nega'*, 9.12; cf. 1.32). He continues by speaking of God's comforting him in his distress and consoling him for his former transgression. Certainly the emphasis here is on God's comfort and grace in affliction rather than on affliction as punishment for sin. Yet it does seem that the latter is implied in mentioning God's judgment and his own transgression. God sends affliction for the transgression, but the affliction is not too severe (the psalmist's life is not threatened, 9.11), and God not only strengthens his servant to bear the punishment but pardons and consoles him.

It is worth remarking that, while the punishments of the righteous for their transgressions which are specified in CD and IQS are inflicted by the community, the afflictions mentioned in IQH are sent directly by God, perhaps employing the psalmist's enemies. In both cases, however, punishment is seen as being just [143] and, if accepted willingly, as having a good result. The sectarian who transgresses and is penalized will eventually be restored to full fellowship, while God's rebuke to the psalmist is seen as turning to joy and healing (9.23f.) or forgiveness and consolation (9.13).[144]

Reward, the requirement of perfection and man's nothingness

Since the theme of the punishment of transgressions has a prominent place in the Scrolls, we might also expect to find emphasized the related theme of the reward of the righteous. In fact there are only a few clear statements to the effect that God rewards the righteous for their good deeds.[145] To understand why this is, we must first consider one of the principal problems in understanding the religion of the sect: the apparent conflict between urging the members to walk perfectly, on the one hand, and saying, on the

---

[143] So Carmignac,'Souffrance', p. 379: the psalmist'sees in his sufferings the just chastisements of his transgressions'. Even when the chastisements come from the wicked, they are the execution of the will of God and are still punishment for transgressions (pp. 378f.).

[144] Carmignac (ibid., p. 383) notes the absence of the theme of the redemptive value of suffering; see further Appendix 3 below. Even if suffering is not directly described as redemptive, it still has a good result. See pp. 304f. below.

[145] Cf. Braun, *Radikalismus* I, p. 55.

other, that man is worthless and that perfection of way comes only from God. This problem, which has to do with statements about how one lives once in the covenant, is parallel to the problem created by statements about entry: entrants are, on the one hand, called 'elect', on the other, 'volunteers'. The solution is basically the same: from the point of view of the halakah, one is required to walk perfectly. From the point of view of the individual in prayer or devotional moments, he is unable to walk perfectly and must be given perfection of way by God's grace. Let us turn to the relevant passages.

One of the titles of the community members is the 'perfect of way' (*temime derek*), which is paralleled with 'upright' in IQS 4.22 and with 'the righteous' in IQH 1.36. One may compare the title 'congregation of men of perfection of holiness' (CD 20.2,5,7). The select fifteen are said to be 'perfect in all that is revealed of the Torah' in IQS 8.1, but the requirement of 'perfection' was not limited to them. The general members are also expected to walk perfectly in all that has been revealed (IQS 9.19). One does not enter the covenant unless confirmed in 'perfection of way' (IQS 8.10).[146] If he deliberately transgresses, he is not readmitted until 'all his deeds are purified and he walks in perfection of way' (8.18; cf. 10.21). Those who are members are urged to walk perfectly (CD 2.15); they enter in order that they may do so (IQS 1.8).[147] 'Walking perfectly' is clearly defined as not transgressing at all in IQS 3.9–11, to which one may compare the psalmist's oath not to transgress (IQH 14.17). CD 7.4–6 apparently promises those who walk perfectly eternal life (life for 'a thousand generations'). Yet the stipulated penalties for transgression which we discussed above show that the sectarians did in fact transgress. According to IQS 5.24, the annual review of members' actions caused some to be moved ahead in rank according to their 'perfection of way', while transgressors were reduced in rank.

On the other hand, it is repeatedly stressed in the hymns[148] that perfection of way, righteousness and any good at all are not within man's competence: they come only by the grace of God:

> But what is flesh (to be worthy) of this?
> What is a creature of clay
>   for such great marvels to be done,
>   whereas he is iniquity from the womb
>   and in guilty unfaithfulness until his old age?

[146] I take these requirements of perfection in IQS 8.10 and 9.19 to refer to all the members of the sect, not just to the select fifteen of IQS 8.1 or 'the men of perfect holiness' of 8.20. See further Appendix 2. In any case, the point that 'perfection of way' was stated as a general requirement does not rest only on this division of IQS 8–9. On the use of *tum* and cognate words, see further Rigaux, 'Perfection', *NTS* 4, 1957–8, pp. 237–62: perfection is obedience, but it is possible only because of a revelation of the mysteries by God.

[147] See Black, *The Scrolls and Christian Origins*, p. 119: the basis of perfection at Qumran is 'absolute and total obedience to the *divinely revealed tradition of the Law handed down and developed by the sect*'.

[148] For a critique of Schulz's argument on the 'nothingness' passages in the hymnic material, see Appendix 4.

> Righteousness, I know, is not of man,
>> nor is perfection of way of the son of man:
> to the Most High God belong all righteous deeds.
> The way of man is not established
>> except by the spirit which God created for him
>> to make perfect a way for the children of men,
> that all His creatures might know
>> the might of His power,
> and the abundance of his mercies
>> towards all the sons of His grace. (IQH 4.29–33)

One has no righteous deeds on which to rely, but must rely on the grace of God (IQH 7.17). Perfection of way and uprightness of one's heart are in God's hand (IQS 11.2, 10–11); without God 'no way is perfect' (11.17).

It must be carefully noted that the frequent statements to the effect that man is worthless and incapable of doing good are *always said in the context of comparing man and God*.[149] Typical is this passage from the hymn which concludes IQS:

> Who can endure Thy glory,
>> and what is the son of man
>> in the midst of Thy wonderful deeds?
> What shall one born of woman
>> be accounted before Thee?
> Kneaded from the dust,
>> his abode is the nourishment of worms. (IQS 11.20f.)

Similarly IQS 10.23 contrasts the iniquity (*ma'al*) of man with the righteous deeds of God. The psalmist's view of himself as a sinner comes from viewing himself from God's point of view: 'I will declare His judgement concerning my sins' (IQS 10.11). In the Hodayot it is repeated that righteousness is the property of God, while to men belong iniquity and deceit (IQH 1.25f.).

There are two distinguishable but closely related motifs when the psalmist compares himself (and presumably all mankind) with God. One is that man compared to God cannot be righteous or have any strength of his own. In comparison with God man appears as wicked and weak; consequently in the judgment of God man cannot stand, he cannot have his 'way' established, he cannot be 'righteous'. We have seen this motif in IQS 11.20f.; 10.23; 10.11; IQH 1.25f.; 4.29–33. It may also be seen in IQS 11.9–11; IQH 7.28f. ('Who

---

[149] Cf. Ringgren, *Faith of Qumran*, p. 101: in IQH 'man's sinfulness is a corollary of God's absolute righteousness'; similarly Bardtke, 'Considérations sur les cantiques', p. 226; Licht, 'Doctrine', p. 11; and many others. Ringgren also held, however, that since the extreme emphasis on man's nothingness in IQH is partly due to 'the radical personal experience on the part of the author', such statements should not be taken as representing the entire community (Ringgren, p. 95). Further consideration of the purpose and use of the Hodayot, as well as more recent source analysis, makes this position untenable. See Appendix 1 below. It should be noted that, of the passages discussed here, only IQH 7.17 is now attributed to the Teacher of Righteousness.

shall be righteous before Thee when he is judged?'); 10.9f.; 12.19f.; 12.24–31; 13.14–16. This does not deny that men may be righteous *vis à vis* each other or even *vis à vis* the halakah; in the spirit of prayer which pervades most of the hymns, however, mankind is seen to be unrighteous in comparison with God. The matter is put clearly in IQH 9.14–17.

> For no man can be just (*yitsdaq*) in Thy judgement
> or [righteous in] (*yizkeh*) Thy trial.
> Though one man be more just (*yitsdaq*) than another,
> . . .
>   yet is there no power to compare with Thy might.

Intimately related to the perception of one's insufficiency before God is the view that one's righteousness or perfection of way comes from the grace of God. These statements serve as a kind of theological explanatory link between the confession of man's iniquity before God and the description of the sectarians as the 'perfect of way'. The source of that perfection is the grace of God. These statements too are characteristic of the hymnic material. In addition to IQH 4.29–33; 7.17; IQS 11.2, 10f.; 11.17, cited above, one may cite such passages as IQH 16.11: 'Man is not righteous apart[150] from Thee.' In IQH 13.14–17, a statement to the effect that man is nothing in comparison with God (13.14–16) leads directly into the declaration that 'By Thy goodness alone is man righteous' (13.16f.). In IQH 10.5–10, the sequence is reversed. We find first the confession that the psalmist must be caused to 'stand' by God (10.6), which is followed by a general statement that 'Beside Thee there is nothing, and nothing can compare with Thee in strength' (10.9f.). Similarly, we read that mortals cannot 'establish their steps' (but God can) (IQH 15.13; cf. 15.21).

In the context of these statements to the effect that man's perfection of way comes only by the grace of God, we should also note the general confessions that man is saved by the grace of God. In the present, this is understood as involving not just the establishment of one's way, but the forgiveness and cleansing of sin: by his mercies (*rahamekah*) and graciousness (*hasadekah*) God has strengthened man in adversity and purified him of sins (IQH 1.31–3); God has cleansed a 'perverse spirit' (3.21); one may rely on God's grace and mercies, for he will pardon iniquity (4.37); all the sons of God's truth are brought before him in forgiveness, that he may cleanse them of their sins through his goodness (7.30); for the sake of his glory God has purified man of sin (11.10); God purifies the psalmist by his holy spirit and draws him near by his (or, in his) good will (16.12). We should quote at length on this point IQH 11.29–32:

---

[150] Vermes: 'except through'. On the translation of the preposition, see n. 220 below.

Blessed art Thou,
  O God of mercy and compassion (*rahamim* and *haninah*),
for the might of Thy [power]
  and the greatness of Thy truth,
and for the multitude of Thy favours (*hasadim*)
  in all Thy works!
Rejoice the soul of Thy servant with Thy truth
  and cleanse me by Thy righteousness (*tsedaqah*).
Even as I have hoped in Thy goodness (*tob*),
  and waited for Thy grace (*hasadim*),
so hast Thou freed me from my calamities
  in accordance with Thy forgiveness (*selihot*);
and in my distress Thou hast comforted me
  for I have leaned on Thy mercy (*rahamim*).

Further, the psalmist could look forward to the time when God would establish his people by his grace:

Thou wilt raise up survivors among Thy people
  and a remnant within Thine inheritance.
Thou wilt purify and cleanse them of their sin
  for all their deeds are in Thy truth.
Thou wilt judge them in Thy great lovingkindness (*hasadim*)
  and in the multitude of Thy mercies (*rahamim*)
  and in the abundance of Thy pardon (*selihah*),
  teaching them according to Thy word;
and Thou wilt establish them in Thy Council
  according to the uprightness of Thy truth. (IQH 6.8–10)

At first there may appear to be a significant distinction between the legal-istic works-righteousness of IQS 1–9, in which 'perfection of way' is required for membership in the community, and the theology of salvation by grace in the hymns (IQH and IQS 10–11).[151] Although these are certainly the emphases of the respective books, the distinction is not clear cut, and it seems incorrect to think that the theologies are actually different. Thus in IQH the themes of perfection and legal righteousness are not absent. After saying, in IQH 1.25f., that *man can do only the work of iniquity* and deeds of deceit, the psalmist, in the same hymn, calls on the 'righteous' (*tsaddiqim*) to put away wrong, and he *calls them the 'perfect of way'* (1.36). Thus one finds in the hymns not only the assertion that no man is righteous (16.11), but also the characterization of some as righteous (1.36). Similarly the psalmist

---

[151] Black (*Scrolls and Christian Origins*, p. 124) discusses IQS 1–9 and CD under the heading of 'legalism' and describes the religion seen there as 'a legalistic puritanism or perfectionism, with its secret code jealously guarded, and presented as a divine mystery or gnosis'. When he turns to what he calls 'the prophetic tradition of Qumran' (which he also traces to the Psalms), he says that 'perhaps we ought to allow more for different "philosophies" within Qumran itself' (p. 125). The content of the different view is established by citations from IQS 10–11 and IQH, which show the condemnation of man as 'the foil or background to the doctrine of "grace" or divine help' (p. 126).

can say that walking in the way of God's heart *leads to* being established for ever (IQH 4.21f.), which sounds as if such behaviour is at the disposal of man. The more frequent assertion, however, is that one's way is established only by God, through his mercy (4.30f.; 7.29f.; IQS 11.10). At any rate, the hymns are not totally lacking in the exhortation to walk according to God's will or the expectation that such behaviour is the way to salvation.

In a similar way, the other Scrolls are by no means without assertions of God's grace. We find that God's past deliverance of Israel was perceived to be by grace, not on account of man's deeds: 'Thou didst deliver us many times by the hand of our kings for Thy mercy's sake, *not for our deeds*, in that we have done wickedly, nor for our sinful actions' (IQM 11.3f.; cf. 18.7f.: 'for the sake of Thy name'). Similarly, in IQS 1.21–3, the priests and Levites declare God's *grace* to Israel and Israel's iniquity. The same view of the history of God's relations with Israel is found in CD 8.14–18: Israel's conquest of the nations was not due to their uprightness, but is to be attributed to God's love of the forefathers. As we have previously seen, however, the major emphasis of IQS and CD is on man's efforts to abide by the commandments and on punishment for transgression.

In part, this difference of emphasis – on legal perfection in IQS and on the grace of God in IQH – is to be explained by the difference of literary type, which influences the religious expressions of each document. The hymn-prayers naturally emphasize the inability of man and his worthlessness *before God*, while IQS 1–9 and CD emphasize what he must do to remain a member of the covenant in good standing. How significant the literary form (and the interior orientation which accompanies each literary form) is for the content and formulation of what is expressed may be seen by a striking example. Bardtke perceptively noted that the hymns do not always maintain the prayer attitude, but sometimes switch to being addresses to members of the community, in which case they are closer to wisdom literature than to psalms to God.[152] It is precisely where such a change in style takes place that the author of IQH 1 changes from describing the inability and unrighteousness of man to speaking of the 'righteous' and the 'perfect of way'. Thus 1.27, addressed as a prayer to God: 'to the sons of men is the work of iniquity and deeds of deceit'; and 1.36, addressed to the members of the community: 'O just men (*tsaddiqim*), put away iniquity! Hold fast [to the Covenant], O all you perfect of way.'

Thus there are not two different theologies, one of works and one of grace. The same people could believe on the one hand that they had no intrinsic merit to commend them to God and that they had been chosen only by his grace, while holding on the other hand that they had to walk perfectly according to God's ordinances and that they could achieve legal perfection.

---

[152] Bardtke, 'Considérations sur les cantiques', p. 228.

This is shown in part by the fact that 'legalistic' statements can appear in the hymns and that 'grace' statements appear in the other documents.

We should be permitted at this point to do a certain amount of synthesizing in order to explain the theological base from which *both* extraordinarily strict legalistic sayings and extraordinarily forceful affirmations of grace could be made. In the overall theology of the sect, the requirement of legal perfection is set within a context of gratuity. A man is purified of transgression and has his 'way' established only by the grace of God, but he is expected to maintain legal perfection. Doing so is rewarded, while transgressions within the covenant are punished. As we said above, the statements that one's perfection of way is the work of God serve to bridge the gap between the confession of man's iniquity and inability and the requirement to walk perfectly according to the commandments of the covenant.

That the requirement for legal perfection is set within a context of gratuity is made clear when one considers a group of statements concerning reward and punishment. The reward even of perfection is said to be by God's *mercy* while the wicked receive the punishment *deserved* by them. Despite the apparent double predestination of the 'doctrine of the two spirits', the Scrolls reflect the common Jewish theme that the reward of the good is by mercy, while the punishment of the wicked is by desert.[153] Thus in the blessings and cursings in IQS 2.2–8, the 'men of the lot of God who walk perfectly in all His ways' are to be blessed with good, preserved from evil, given knowledge and granted *mercy* for eternal blessedness. The 'men of the lot of Satan', on the other hand, are 'cursed *without mercy* because of the darkness of [their] deeds'. The Levites continue: 'May God not heed when you call on Him, nor pardon you by blotting out your sin.' In IQH 14.24, God is said to *pardon* those who repent but to punish the wicked *for their iniquity*. In IQH 15.15–19, the elect are appointed to walk in God's ways and receive *mercy*, while the wicked are also predestined, but are punished *for their transgression*. The hymn continues by saying that for the wicked there is no atonement for transgression (15.24). *The principal point of the punishment for deeds but reward by mercy theme is that, while man can forfeit salvation by transgression, he can never be sufficiently deserving to earn it by obedience.* This last point is clearly made in IQH 18.21f.:

> I know it is for Thyself
>   that Thou hast done these things, O God;
> for what is flesh
>   [that Thou shouldst act] marvellously [towards it]?
> It is Thy purpose to do mightily
>   and to establish all things for Thy glory.

---

[153] See 'mercy to the righteous' in the index.

It agrees with this that the psalmist, speaking as one of the elect, says that God has not judged him according to his guilt (IQH 5.6), though that is precisely the basis on which the non-elect are judged. Similarly, the psalmist is sure that at the eschaton the remnant will be 'judged' by God's kindness (*hasadim*), in the abundance of his mercy (*rahamin*) and the greatness of his pardon (*selihah*) (IQH 6.9). A similar statement concerning God's judgment of the psalmist appears in IQH 9.33f. Thus we see that the elect are expected to walk in perfection of way but are forgiven for their transgressions by God's grace, while the non-elect are punished for their transgressions without mercy.

It does not, however, seem quite correct to say, with Licht and Burrows, that 'the grace of repentance is given only to the elect'.[154] The predestinarianism of the Scrolls does not seem quite so hard as that.[155] As we have seen, those outside the covenant could repent and join. The statements which we have just cited seem to make a somewhat more general point, and one that is paralleled elsewhere in Jewish literature. The consciousness of the members of the sect was that man could never by his own merits deserve good at the hand of God; consequently, the reward of the good is given by mercy. There is a heightened sense of God's mercy, but this is probably due to the situation of the sect as a sect selected out of the rest of Israel. The wicked, on the other hand, are justly punished for their deeds.

Thus we can understand why rewards *for deeds* are seldom mentioned in the Scrolls. The members of the community are, to be sure, rewarded – they receive long life (IQM 1.9; CD 7.5f.; IQS 4.7; IQH 13.16–18), 'eternal redemption' (IQM 1.12) and apparently eternal life, characterized as 'light' (IQS 4.7f.; IQM 13.5f.; cf. CD 3.20)[156] – but the context of gratuity is so clear that the possibility of earning the reward of salvation by deeds ('works-righteousness') scarcely arises. God is considered to be a just judge who judges every man and renders to each his reward (IQS 10.18) and who brings 'forth the just judgement of [His] truth upon all the sons of man' (IQM 11.14), but these two passages seem to refer primarily to the punishment of the wicked. We have just seen that the elect are not judged strictly according to their deeds (IQH 5.6; 6.9; 9.34). There is no picture of God holding a judgment at which he weighs the deeds of each man and punishes or rewards him according to his deserts, for man's destruction or eternal reward has been determined in advance according to whether or not he is a

---

[154] Burrows, *More Light*, p. 295, following Licht, 'The Doctrine', p. 96.

[155] Ringgren (*Faith of Qumran*, p. 123) correctly observes that 'it is doubtful . . . whether the concept of predestination may be carried so far' as Licht would do. He continues, 'Forgiveness is a gift of God, it is true, but at the same time, it is inseparably connected with repenting of sin and a proper frame of mind.'

[156] On the future life, see especially the discussion by Delcor, *Hymnes*, pp. 58–61. He takes IQH 6.29–39 to be decisive in favour of a hope for resurrection.

member of the sect. How clear is the context of gratuity and how impossible self-salvation may be seen by considering briefly the passages which seem to affirm an idea of salvation by works. CD 3.14–16 mentions the ordinances established by God 'which man shall do and live thereby' (quoting Lev. 18.5). But it is clear that human obedience, although necessary, does not initially open the path to salvation, for God brings man into the right path by pardoning his transgressions and building 'a sure house in Israel' (3.18f.). Even in CD 7.5f., where life 'for a thousand generations' is promised to those who walk perfectly in the ordinances of the covenant, it is clear that what is required is the strict keeping of the covenant given by God: it is the covenant which assures its members of life, while obedience keeps one in the covenant (so also CD 14.1f.). Most characteristic is IQH 13.16–18: the righteous man receives 'everlasting peace and length of days', but he is righteous only by God's goodness.

God's grace and the requirement of performance on the part of man are both stressed so strongly in the Scrolls that it is difficult to state the precise relationship between grace and works. It will be helpful to consider the formulations of three other scholars. This is Burrows's formulation: 'The sons of light are saved by the faithful study and observance of the law, but they are able to keep the law only because they have been placed under the dominion of the spirit of light.'[157] I should prefer not to say that they are saved *by* study and observance. It appears more accurate to say that they are saved by the electing grace of God when it is responded to with repentance and commitment, and that they keep the commandments, with God's help, as a *consequence* of the election and as a *condition* for remaining in the covenant.

Schulz formulates the sect's theology by posing the question of how a member can be saved. The answer, he says, is clear: by fulfilling the law of God to the last detail. Only fulfilling the Torah can throw a bridge over the chasm which separates sinful man from the transcendent God. Yet man finds himself unable to build a bridge which will bear this weight.[158] The solution to this is the grace of God, who bestows righteousness on the members of the sect, for they cannot be righteous on their own.[159]

This does not seem to be quite an accurate formulation. It is certainly true that one is saved by grace: this point is not in dispute. But is the grace conceived as being given to men already in the community when they have failed to be sufficiently obedient, as a substitute for that obedience? It appears not. I find no suggestion that one could bridge the chasm between God and man even if one could be sufficiently obedient. Rather, one who is

---

[157] Burrows, *More Light*, p. 294.
[158] Schulz, 'Rechtfertigung', p. 163.
[159] Ibid., p. 167. On Schulz's view, see further Appendix 4 below.

elect (from God's side) and volunteers (from the side of human volition) is brought by God's grace into the community of those who are close to God. The gap is bridged in election and entrance into the sect. Thereafter one obeys the law to the most minute detail, and doing so is a condition of remaining in full fellowship. When one in the community considers himself before God, he realizes his inadequacy to have achieved his status in the community on his own, and he confesses the chasm between God and man by way of thanking God for having overcome it. Schulz presents perfection of works as an effort to reach God which failed, and the failure as being overcome by God's grace. I see no such dichotomy between grace and works. Perfection of deeds is considered to be achievable, or almost so, within the community; but it is recognized that being in the community is a result of the grace of God. Works are not a false path to salvation which is ineffective and for which God's grace must be substituted; they are the *results* of community membership and the *condition* of remaining.

One may make similar observations about Braun's formulation of the relation between grace and works. According to Braun, the doctrine of the sect is that a man is lost unless he is perfectly obedient ('Der Mensch gilt als verloren bereits dann, wenn er nicht *alles* tut').[160] Braun subsequently recognizes, however, that in fact members of the covenant sinned. He then poses the problem of how one can be at the same time sanctified and sinful.[161] He cites the passages in IQS which appeal to the grace of God for the establishment of man's way. But is reliance on God's grace thoroughly carried out and understood radically in the sect? No; for if it were, the strict requirements to obey would not be understandable.[162] Side by side with the gracious God stands the man who anxiously strives to achieve total obedience.[163] It should be clear from our discussion above that setting grace and works over against each other as alternative paths to salvation is a wrong perception of the theology of the sect. It seems to owe more to Paul and Luther than to an analysis of Jewish texts, and it fails to perceive the intimate and necessary connection between God's grace in putting one in the covenant and the requirement to obey once in the covenant.

We may pause briefly to consider the relationship of the sectarian view to that of the Rabbis. In Rabbinic literature, there is more emphasis than in the Scrolls on the even-handed distribution of punishment and reward in accordance with deeds and less emphasis on God's grace as a requirement for human righteousness. There is, however, no fundamental difference. The distribution of reward and punishment does not, in Rabbinic literature, become the basis of salvation; rather, the covenant is the main factor in

---

[160] Braun, *Radikalismus*, p. 29. Cf. n. 142 above.
[161] Ibid., p. 44.
[162] Ibid., pp. 46f.
[163] Ibid., p. 47.

salvation, while a man is punished or rewarded for his deeds within the covenant. Similarly in Qumran, one is punished for transgressions of the ordinances of the covenant and rewarded for adherence, but saved by being in the covenant itself.[164] God's grace in putting one in the covenant is emphasized more in Qumran than in Rabbinic literature. The emphasis on grace seems to have two explanations. One is that so much hymnic material has survived. If we had the Scrolls without the Hodayot and IQS 10–11, the overall impression made by the Scrolls would be much more like that made by Rabbinic literature than is now the case. More important, the Qumran covenanters doubtless did have a heightened sense of God's grace, which is to be explained by their view that they were especially elect from among Israel. The special election requires a special emphasis on the grace of God. Not only is the sense of God's grace heightened in the Scrolls, however, but so also is the requirement for obedience. The repeated admonitions to be legally perfect – even granted the provisions for correcting transgressions – far surpass in strictness anything to be found in the Tannaitic literature. It is not unlikely that the requirement of perfection also springs from the heightened self-consciousness of the Qumran community.

The heightening of both the perception of God's grace and the requirement of obedience is instructive for understanding Judaism generally, for it indicates that 'grace' and 'works' were not considered as opposed to each other in any way. I believe that it is safe to say that the notion that God's grace is in any way contradictory to human endeavour is totally foreign to Palestinian Judaism. The reason for this is that *grace and works were not considered alternative roads to salvation.* Salvation (except in IV Ezra) is always by the grace of God, embodied in the covenant. The terms of the covenant, however, require obedience. In Qumran we see with especial clarity the way in which the requirement for obedience accompanies belief in salvation by grace, since both points receive remarkable emphasis. But this is generally true of Palestinian Judaism. Thus West has accurately remarked that 'any serious study of the scrolls should bring into question those appraisals of Judaism which have interpreted the authoritative place of the Torah and the necessity of moral response of man as inconsistent with a presupposition of the priority of divine grace'.[165]

The counterpart of the heightened perception of grace in Qumran is the heightened sense of man's inadequacy. This sense is so heightened that at least one scholar can regard the point as unique. Thus Becker states that the antithesis of man's sinfulness and inadequacy, on the one side, and God's power and righteousness, on the other ('Antithese von menschlicher

---

[164] I cannot follow Delcor (*Hymnes*, p. 48) in his statement that Qumran is far removed from the Pharisaic idea of 'justification par les oeuvres de l'homme', since that seems not to be an accurate description of the Pharisaic view.

[165] West, *Justification*, p. 229.

Kreatürlichkeit und Sündenverfallenheit auf der einen Seite und göttlicher Allmacht und Gerechtigkeit auf der anderen Seite'), is not met in Judaism outside Qumran.[166] The question, rather, is one of degree. In that relatively small body of Rabbinic literature which presents man at prayer or at the moment of death – in either case 'face to face' with God – we did in fact see expressions of human inadequacy and sinfulness *vis à vis* God.[167] These passages have been taken, however, not as emphasizing God's grace – which they in fact do – but as showing the uncertainty of salvation in Rabbinic thought and as evidence of the inferiority of Rabbinic religion.[168] It will be recalled that many scholars have seen in R. Johanan b. Zakkai's apprehension before death evidence of the uncertainty caused by works-righteous legalism.[169] Presumably if he had had a firmer view of God's grace he need not have trembled at the prospect of judgment. We have previously argued that this explanation is erroneous. How erroneous it is can perhaps best be seen in the light of IQH. Few documents from Judaism or Christianity emphasize the grace of God as does IQH. Yet at least one psalmist can also say that, in contemplating the judgment, his 'heart is stricken with terror'. 'I am greatly afraid when I hear of Thy judgement of the mighty Heroes, and of Thy trial of the host of Thy Holy Ones . . .' (IQH 10.33f.). Despite the marked differences in emphasis between Rabbinic literature and the Scrolls, the basic situation appears to be much the same.

6. Atonement

We have repeatedly remarked that even the sectarians transgressed and that provisions were made for repairing the trespasses. We have seen that IQS and CD specify penalties which, if accepted with their conditions, result in a restoration of fellowship. Further, the hymnic material in particular contains many statements in which God is said to pardon the transgressions of the elect because of his mercy. We should now consider, however, the use of the term 'atonement' and the question of whether or not the usual means of atonement were considered to be efficacious.

We may note in the first place that in three of the Scrolls – CD, IQS and IQH – the verb 'atone' (*kipper*) appears with God as the subject. In all these instances, it appears that *kipper* should be translated 'pardon', for no act of atonement on man's part is implied. That is, the distinction which is seen in Leviticus between the priest's atoning and God's forgiving is not maintained.[170] The verb is used simply to mean 'forgive', and it is parallel with

[166] Becker, *Heil Gottes*, p. 167.
[167] Above, pp. 223–8.
[168] Above, ibid.
[169] Above, pp. 225f.   [170] Cf. above, pp. 16of.

other verbs used for the same purpose.[171] Thus in IQS 11.14, God is said to 'atone for' the hymnist's iniquities and to 'cleanse' him. On the other hand, God does not forgive by 'atoning for' the iniquities of the members of the lot of Satan (IQS 2.8). In IQS 3.6–8, the passive verb 'be atoned for' alternates with 'be cleansed', and the agent is said to be 'the spirit of true counsel', 'the spirit of holiness', and the 'spirit of uprightness and humility'. We may consider the subject here constructively to be God, and it is clear that no particular acts of atonement are implied. One may see further examples of 'atone' with God as subject to mean 'pardon' in IQH 4.37; 17.12; CD 2.4f.; 3.18; 4.6f.; 4.9f.; 20.34.

The attitude of the Covenanters toward the Temple sacrifices was necessarily ambiguous, since they were at present cut off by their withdrawal from Jerusalem and condemnation of those in authority, while they looked forward to their ultimate victory and emergence as the only Israelites. Looking forward to the days of the great war, after the wicked of Israel have been destroyed and only the Gentiles remain to be dealt with, the author of IQM can say without hesitation that the priests

shall stand by at the burnt-offerings and the sacrifices, to set out the incense-offering of sweet savour for the pleasure of God, to atone for all His congregation, and to bring fat sacrifices before Him perpetually on the table of glory. (IQM 2.5f.)[172]

Although the value of sacrifices for atonement is not singled out, the sacrificial system is presupposed as valid throughout CD (9.13f.; 11.17–12.2; 16.13; cf. 4.1).[173] In the present exigencies,[174] however, righteous acts and piety could substitute for the sacrifices required by the Torah. When the community is established, 'prayer rightly offered shall be as an acceptable fragance of righteousness, and perfection of way as a delectable free-will offering' (IQS 9.4f.; cf. the 'offering of the lips' mentioned in IQS 10.6). The difficult clause immediately preceding (which will be discussed immediately below) indicates that something or somebody will atone for rebellion and unfaithfulness more than (or, without) sacrifices (IQS 9.4). We need not

---

[171] See Ringgren, *Faith of Qumran*, p. 122: 'atone' is parallel with 'cleanse', and 'cleansing' is equivalent to 'forgiveness'; cf. Holm-Nielsen, *Hodayot*, pp. 282 n. 18, referring to IQH 4.37; 17.12; Jaubert, *La notion d'alliance*, p. 166.

[172] Gärtner (*Temple and Community*, pp. 8f.) thinks that this passage can refer either to the Temple services in the future or symbolically to the 'actual cultus of the community itself'. The former seems overwhelmingly the more likely. So also Yadin, *The Scroll of War*, p. 199; cf. O. Betz, 'Le ministère cultuel à Qumrân', p. 168.

[173] Delcor ('Le sacerdoce', *RHR* 144, 1953, pp. 15–41) was willing to entertain the possibility that the group responsible for CD may have had a cult site, although the Qumran group certainly did not. The issue has now been most decisively discussed by Klinzing, *Die Umdeutung des Kultus*, pp. 20–49: there was no cult outside Jerusalem during the period of the Scrolls. It is possible that the concrete laws in CD regarding sacrifices are bits of older tradition, but at the time of the composition of the document they did not refer to a temple service in use by the Essenes (p. 28).

[174] Cf. n. 194 below.

try to decide the intention of the preposition *mem*.[175] The point is that the means of atonement are at hand to the community, and that the present inability to make sacrifices at the Temple is no hindrance. As is the case in Rabbinic Judaism, good deeds do not atone because they offset or compensate for transgressions in a book-keeping way; rather they atone as substitutes for the sacrifices specified in the Bible.[176]

The last cited passage, IQS 9.4–6, leads us to a consideration of the most striking thing which is said about atonement in the Scrolls. The community itself has an atoning function.[177] We may consider a few other passages before returning to IQS 9.4, taking first IQS 5.6. The syntax and translation are difficult and controverted. Brownlee thinks that a new principal clause begins with the fourth word of 5.5, and he reads the word as EAM, which he takes to be a circumlocution for God.[178] This solves the difficulty, for God is then said to circumcise the community, to lay a foundation of truth, and to atone for the volunteers. Vermes, on the other hand, apparently reads *ki' 'im* rather than *eam* and takes the subject of 'to circumcise' to be the 'man' of 5.4: 'No man shall walk in the stubbornness of his heart . . . , but he shall circumcise in the Community . . . .'. Vermes considers the subsequent infinitives 'to lay a foundation' and 'to atone' to refer back to the men of the community, however, and supplies 'they' as the subject: 'They shall atone for all those in Aaron who have freely pledged themselves.' Burrows's translation[179] is as ambiguous as the original. Assuming that one reads *ki' 'im* at the fourth word of 5.5 rather than taking the letters which are present to be an abbreviation for God,[180] it seems apparent that Vermes's translation is generally correct. The best reading would seem to be a series of infinitives which refer back to 'the men of the community', with some parenthetical remarks in between the infinitive clauses. On the basis of this understanding of the text, the subject of 'to atone' is the 'men of the community'.[181] They atone, it appears, for themselves: for the priests and Israelites who have volunteered and for all who join them (5.6f.).[182]

---

[175] Carmignac and Milik have argued for 'by' instead of either 'more than' or 'without'. Carmignac compares IQM 2.5f. and argues that the passage in IQS refers to the eventual efficacy of sacrifices after the triumph of the sect and the establishment of a proper Temple service (*RB* 63, 1956, pp. 524–32, especially p. 531). See the discussion in Burrows, *More Light*, pp. 363–5. See further Ringgren, *Faith of Qumran*, p. 215; Betz, 'Le ministère cultuel à Qumrân', p. 168; Klinzing, *Die Umdeutung des Kultus*, pp. 38–41.

[176] Correct on Qumran is Thyen, *Sündenvergebung*, p. 79, although he attributed the theory of compensation to the Rabbis.

[177] See especially Gärtner, *Temple and Community*; Klinzing, *Die Umdeutung des Kultus*.

[178] Brownlee, *Manual of Discipline*, ad loc.

[179] *Dead Sea Scrolls*, p. 377.

[180] On this emendation, see Brownlee, *Manual of Discipline*, p. 49.

[181] Black (*Scrolls and Christian Origins*, p. 42) notes that the subject could be either the community or a group within it. Both Guilbert (in Carmignac and Guilbert's translation) and Lohse supply 'they' as the subject for 'circumcise' and have the following infinitives depend on 'they shall circumcise'.

[182] Harrison (in Black (ed.), *Scrolls and Christianity*, p. 30) takes the object of atonement to be the entire nation, but the text clearly states otherwise.

Syntactically clearer is 8.4–10. Here the 'witnesses to the truth' and the 'elect of Goodwill' are said to 'atone for the Land and pay to the wicked their reward' (8.6). Substantially the same thing is repeated in 8.10. Even though the syntax is relatively clear, there is still room for debate about the referent of the terms 'witnesses' and 'elect'. It might appear to be the twelve men and three priests who are perfect in all that has been revealed of the law, who are mentioned in 8.1. It seems more likely, however, that the subject changes near the end of 8.4, that 8.4b–10a refer to the entire community, and that the select fifteen are returned to only in 8.10b.[183] That is, 8.4ff. says that when the select fifteen are in Israel, the Council of the Community, which is an everlasting plantation, a House of Holiness for Israel and an assembly of supreme holiness for Aaron, will come into existence. I take the 'Council of the Community' here to equal the entire community, as it frequently does.[184] Thus the subject of 'to atone' in 8.6, 10 is the membership of the entire community. On the other hand, it is clear that in 8.3f. the subject of 'to atone' (*pi'el* of *ratsah*) is the group of fifteen. It is said that 'They shall preserve the faith in the Land with steadfastness and meekness and shall atone for sin by the practice of justice and by suffering the sorrows of affliction.'[185] This leads us back to IQS 9.3–5. Translated somewhat literally, these lines read as follows:

When these things come to pass in Israel according to all these rules, [it shall result in] establishing the spirit of holiness for eternal truth, atoning for the guilt of iniquity and the faithlessness of sin, and obtaining [God's] favour for the land more than (or, without) the flesh of whole burnt offerings and the fat of sacrifices.

The rendering of the lines basically follows Brownlee in translating the opening phrase 'when these things come to pass'.[186] This translation causes the subsequent infinitives (translated here as gerunds: establishing, atoning for and obtaining) to have as their subject the action of having 'these things' coming to pass. Vermes, on the other hand, translates the opening phrase 'When these become members', and he renders the infinitives as 'they shall establish', 'they shall atone' and 'that they may obtain loving kindness'. What is 'coming to pass' in 9.3 is the establishment of the 'Council of Holiness', which is composed of the 'men of perfect holiness' (8.20f.). It is clear

---

[183] For this division of the text, see Appendix 2.

[184] For example, in IQS 6.13–15, where 'join the Council of the Community' is equivalent to enter 'the Covenant'. Cf. Leaney, *Rule*, p. 211. On the ambiguity of the term '*etsah* ('Council'), see J. Worrell, *VT* 20, 1970, pp. 65–74; Ringgren, *Faith of Qumran*, p. 202. Ringgren thinks that the term in 8.4 could be understood as either the community or a sub-group (p. 203). Reicke (in *S&NT*, pp. 151f.) regards the subject of IQS 8.5–10 to be the select group mentioned in 8.1. Chamberlain (*NT* 3, 1959, p. 309), however, regards the subject to be the council in the sense of 'the entire body of full-fledged members of the sect'.

[185] On alternate understandings of IQS 8.3f., see Appendix 3.

[186] Brownlee, *Manual of Discipline*, pp. 34f. So also Gärtner, *Temple and Community*, p. 29; Lohse, ad loc. On the translation of the passage, see Gärtner, pp. 44f.

that these are not the bulk of the members of the community.[187] They may not be the same as the select fifteen of 8.1, but they are certainly a select group. At any rate, according to Vermes's translation, the 'men of perfect holiness' atone for sin, while according to Brownlee's their existence establishes a situation in which sin is atoned for. It is perhaps not necessary to make the distinction too rigid. In any case, we have already seen in 8.3 that the select fifteen 'atone'.

There is one last passage to be considered, IQS 1.3.[188] Here it is said that 'the men of His Council who keep His Covenant in the midst of iniquity' atone for 'the Land'. Thus it is clear that the members in general 'atone' and that the select fifteen 'atone'. It may also be that the establishment of the community is considered to 'atone'. But what do these passages mean? In what sense do the members, whether in whole or part, atone?

The passage which is clearest is IQS 8.3f. The select fifteen atone through practising righteousness and suffering. It appears here that righteousness and suffering in effect take the place of sacrifices, which is also more or less suggested by 9.4f., where 'perfection of way' is considered as a substitute for sacrifice (though suffering is not mentioned). We are not told for whom the fifteen atone, whether for themselves alone, or also for the other members, or for the Land.[189] It is not unlikely that all three, or at least the first two, are meant. If this is the case, the fifteen are seen as having a priestly function, atoning on behalf of others. It is noteworthy that this involves suffering, which implies a notion of suffering for the atonement of others.[190]

The priestly function of the community (or of the 'men of perfect holiness') is also seen in IQS 9.3–5. Prayer and perfection of way take the place of sacrifices. It is apparently such things which atone 'more than' or 'without' the offering of sacrifices. In either case the atonement is clearly one in which deeds and piety replace the sacrificial system. It is probably in mind that the existence of the community, with the 'men of perfect holiness' in their midst, constitutes a substitute for the entire sacrificial system. The particular phrase 'flesh of whole burnt offerings and the fat of sacrifices' might seem best to refer to the daily whole burnt offerings. The phrase does not, for example,

[187] Appendix 2.

[188] A detailed and admirable exegesis of the most pertinent passages is given by Klinzing, *Die Umdeutung des Kultus*, pp. 60–88. In addition to those discussed here, he deals with CD 3.18–4.10; 4Qfl 1.1–7; IQpHab 12.3f.

[189] Somewhat curiously, Black (*Scrolls and Christian Origins*, p. 129) takes the object of atonement in IQS 8.3f. to be Israel as contrasted with the Gentiles. I see no support for this in the text, and it is intrinsically highly improbable. Cf. n. 182 above, n. 193 below.

[190] For the suggestion that the vicarious nature of atonement is modelled on the Servant of the Lord, see Ringgren, *Faith of Qumran*, p. 197 and the literature cited there. Klinzing has argued that Deutero-Isaiah has not influenced the atonement passages which we have been considering (*Die Umdeutung des Kultus*, pp. 57–9). This seems generally correct. He makes the view vanish from IQS 8.1–4, however, only by separating 8.1 from 8.2–4 (Appendix 3 below). His argument that 8.2–4 originally referred to the entire community may well be correct, in which case the clear implication of vicarious suffering as atoning in IQS 8.1–4 *as it now stands* would have come about only through textual conflation.

call to mind the sacrifice of the scape-goat on the Day of Atonement. Yet the scope of the atonement mentioned in IQS ('the guilt of iniquity and the faithlessness of sin, and obtaining [God's] favour for the Land' [my translation]) is greater than what could be assigned to the whole burnt offering.[191] The scope of the atonement implies the inclusion of the Day of Atonement, while private sacrifices (free-will offerings) are mentioned in the next clause. Thus 9.3–5 must constructively refer to the entire sacrificial system. There is a kind of universalism implied in the passage under consideration; for all Israelites would be guilty, to some degree or other, of iniquity and faithlessness. Yet we know that the existence of the community was not really considered to atone for the sins of Israelites outside the sect, for they are clearly condemned to destruction. Thus the existence of the community, while substituting for the atoning sacrifices of the Temple, is not effective in and of itself. As we have already seen, and as we shall see again below, there is no atonement for those outside the covenant. What clearly *is* atoned for is 'the Land'. In IQS 8.6,10 and IQSa 1.3, the Land is also said to be atoned for by the community, and in all three cases only the Land is mentioned.[192] We are nowhere told precisely what it means to atone for the Land, but we may hazard a guess: the Land, like the Temple, was at present being defiled by its occupation and use by non-sectarians. God himself would build a pure Temple in the last days (see the beginning of 4Qflor), but presumably the Land itself would remain. The Land of Israel must be atoned for; else it would have to be destroyed, for defilement as well as transgression requires atonement. The existence of the community provided constant atonement for the defilement of the Land, in order to preserve it for its future occupation by the sect after the destruction of the wicked.[193]

To summarize: the community, with the good deeds and pious prayers of its members, and especially those of the most pious and righteous men, constituted a substitute for the Temple sacrifices (IQS 8.3f.). As such, the community itself atoned for the sins of its members (IQS 5.6; perhaps also 9.4), but more particularly for the defilement of the Land, to preserve it for future occupation and use (IQS 8.6, 10; 9.4; IQSa 1.3).[194]

[191] See Moore, *Judaism* I, p. 497.

[192] Black (*Scrolls and Christian Origins*, p. 42), following Wernberg-Møller, emends *ratson* to the *pi'el* of *ratsah* in 9.3 (thus conforming it to 8.3) and translates 'redeem the Land' rather than 'obtain favour for the Land'. This would yield a fourth instance of the phrase, 'atone for the Land'.

[193] Burrows (*More Light*, p. 369), referring to 8.4–10, speaks of atonement 'for the sins of Israel', apparently taking 'the Land' to include its inhabitants. The sectarian view of non-sectarians, however, renders this unlikely. Cf. Klinzing, *Die Umdeutung des Kultus*, p. 57; Jaubert, *La notion d'alliance*, pp. 171f. We should note that Jub. 6.2 mentions that after leaving the ark Noah offered a sacrifice to atone for the guilt of the earth. Here it is clear that the atonement is not for the inhabitants (for they have been destroyed), but to render the land fit for habitation by those saved in the ark.

[194] Klinzing has argued that the view which has most concerned us – that the community constitutes a substitute for the Temple – is later than and in opposition to the view that a new (or renewed) Temple would exist in the future. He notes that the former view is absent from IQH, IQM and 4QpPs37. The

That good deeds substitute for sacrifices as acts of atonement[195] is seen further when one considers the use of the noun *kippurim*, '[acts of] atonement'. The one who walks perfectly in the ways commanded by God, transgressing not a single commandment, procures pardon from God 'through pleasing acts of atonement' (*kippurim*, IQS 3.10f.). On the other hand, the man who prefers to follow the stubbornness of his heart rather than to submit to the commandments of the covenant will not be purified by lustrations; for him there are no acts of atonement (IQS 2.26–3.4). As we have repeatedly noted, those who do not join and submit to the covenant find no forgiveness. The same point is made in IQH 15.24: there is no atoning indemnity (*kopher*) for works of wickedness. Obedience is the condition *sine qua non* of salvation.

We now turn to the question of whether or not suffering atones. Suffering as atoning clearly does not have the significance in the Scrolls that it has in Rabbinic literature; yet it must be remembered that it was only after the destruction of the Temple that the view that suffering atones came to full and systematic expression.[196] There are a few indications in the Scrolls that suffering could be considered atoning.[197] We have already seen the most interesting passage, IQS 8.3f., in which the sufferings of the select fifteen join their 'practice of justice' to atone for sin. As we noted, here the suffering is vicarious. We have also already discussed IQpHab 5.3–6, which, according to some translations, may refer to atonement being made for the sins of Israelites through chastisement.[198] In addition to these two passages, I have noted only IQpHab 8.1f. According to the interpretation there given, Hab. 2.4b ('the righteous shall live by his faith') refers to 'all those who observe the Law in the House of Judah, whom God will deliver from the House of Judgement because of their suffering (more literally, 'trouble') and because of their faith in the Teacher of Righteousness'. Although the word 'atone' does not actually appear here, God's deliverance is partially motivated by the suffering of the elect. In one sense, all the punishments for transgressions which are specified in IQS and CD indicate that atonement is achieved by suffering, in which case 'suffering' means accepting the pre-

---

expectation of a future Temple would have been especially preserved by the priests within the sect. See *Die Umdeutung des Kultus*, pp. 89–93. Thus Klinzing rejects the view that the community uniformly understood itself as a substitution for the Temple cultus during the interim. Some expected a future Temple, while others regarded the community as a permanent substitute for the Temple. Klinzing's suggestion is possible, but the contrast may be too sharp. I am not persuaded, for example, that those responsible for the community as Temple passages in IQS would have denied that the sacrificial system would be reinstated.

[195] There is a brilliant discussion of the substitution of good deeds, prayer, etc. for sacrifices in Klinzing, *Die Umdeutung des Kultus*, pp. 93–106; cf. also 143–52. He correctly observes that no rejection of the value of sacrifices is implied.

[196] Above, pp. 168–72.

[197] On Carmignac's view to the contrary, see n. 144 above and Appendix 3.

[198] Above, pp. 253f.

scribed penalty. The idea of suffering as atoning, however, is not thematized.[199]

Likewise not thematized as a means of atonement is repentance. We have seen above that 'repenting' or 'turning back' is one of the important terms used in discussing those who *enter* the sect, and it appears that 'those who return from (or, repent of) transgression' is one of the titles for the sectarians.[200] Yet the term *shub* seems not to be used for the correction of intra-covenantal transgression. Even when we read in IQH 14.24 that God pardons 'those who repent of their sins', while punishing the 'wicked', the phrase 'those who repent' may be a name for the sectarians, who are here set in opposition to the 'wicked' (*resha'im*). That is, one might as easily say that God pardons the elect. Yet this term does give a certain character to the elect. It is obvious that their continuing life in the community as well as at the time of their entrance is to be characterized by repentance. Accepting the discipline of the community which is necessary for full restoration after a transgression implies repentance, and thus a repentant attitude was necessary for remaining in the sect.

7. The righteousness of God and the righteousness of man[201]

We have previously dealt in passing with the themes of the righteousness of God and the righteousness of man. It will be useful now, however, to separate these themes for discussion. This is especially important because of the significance which has been attached to the theme of 'righteousness' for comparing Paul and Qumran. Thus, for example, Burrows cites IQH 4.30f. ('Righteousness, I know, is not of man, nor is perfection of way of the son of man: to the Most High God belong all righteous deeds') as parallel to Rom. 3.20 and Gal. 2.16 (denials that man is 'justified' by works). Burrows grants that the general idea that only God is righteous appears in the Old Testament. But he finds Paul's idea of 'justification by the righteousness of God' in IQS 11.12 ('my justification shall be by the righteousness of God') and IQS 11.14 ('In his faithful righteousness he has judged me'). He concludes, 'The point of prime importance here is that while man has no righteousness of his own, there is a righteousness which God, in his own righteousness, freely confers. The meaning of the righteousness of God in Romans 3.21–26 is thus illustrated and shown to be rooted in pre-Christian Judaism.'[202]

---

[199] I do not take the 'crucible' passages other than IQS 8.3f. (e.g. IQS 1.17; CD 20.26f.; IQM 17.9) to refer to atonement by suffering, but to the destruction of the wicked (thereby purifying the elect group), or to a test to be withstood.

[200] Above, p. 245.

[201] See now B. Przybylski, *The Concept of Righteousness in the Gospel of Matthew*, ch. 2, '*Tsedeq, Tsedaqah* and *Tsaddiq* in the Dead Sea Scrolls'.

[202] Burrows, *Dead Sea Scrolls*, p. 334.

Black basically agrees with Burrows's analysis, though modifying it by noting that the 'religious sentiments' of the Scrolls on this point are not only a *praeparatio evangelica*, but also a continuation of the piety of the Psalms and Prophets. He notes that Jeremiah 10.23 ('It is not in man to direct his steps') supplies the basic doctrine of the Qumran statements.[203] Stendahl's formulation is close to that of Burrows and Black.[204] Schulz has analysed at length the doctrine of justification in Paul and Qumran and concluded that Paul's view of justification *sola gratia* is derived from Qumran.[205]

Other scholars have voiced hesitations about the parallel,[206] but it seems necessary here to engage in a brief analysis of the Qumran statements. Our aim will not be a complete catalogue of everything said about righteousness or justification in the Scrolls, but rather we shall concentrate on the principal statements about the righteousness of God and man's righteousness or lack of it.

One of the most striking usages of the term *ts–d–q* in relation to God is found in the comparisons of man with God. We have repeatedly had occasion to observe the importance of these passages, and now we may investigate part of their terminology. In IQS 1.21–2.4, the priests are said to recite the *tsidqot* of God, while the Levites recite the iniquities of the Israelites. Since the priests recite not only the *tsidqot* ('righteous deeds') of God, but also his merciful grace (1.22), Vermes here translates *tsidqot* 'favours'. It seems better, with Leaney, to put the emphasis on the contrast between God's righteous deeds and man's unrighteous deeds, but it is likely that God's righteous deeds are understood as being merciful.[207]

The contrast of God's righteousness and man's wickedness is clearer in the hymnic material. Thus IQS 10.23 contrasts the *tsidqot* of God with the faithlessness (*ma'al*) of men. In IQH 1.26, the psalmist asks what a man can say concerning his sin and iniquities, and how he shall reply to 'righteous judgment' (*mishpat ha-tsedeq*). He continues by saying, with a characteristic formula of ascription (*lekah 'atah*, 'thine, thine'),[208] that to God belong all deeds of righteousness (*ma'ase ha-tsedaqah*), while to men belong the work of iniquity and deeds of deceit. (We may note that in IQH 4.21 the psalmist says that in God's design there is no 'deceit'.) Similarly, in IQH 4.29–31 God, to whom belongs deeds of righteousness (*ma'ase tsedaqah*), is contrasted with man, who has no *tsedaqah* or perfection of way (*tum derek*). In IQH

---

[203] Black, *Scrolls and Christian Origins*, p. 128.
[204] Stendahl, *S&NT*, pp. 8–10.
[205] S. Schulz, 'Zur Rechtfertigung aus Gnaden', p. 184.
[206] Becker, *Das Heil Gottes*, p. 125, on IQS 10.9–11.22: one can speak of *sola gratia*, but this applies only to the sect and it does not free members from the law. While the law does not bring *tsedaqah*, it is still constitutive of the way to salvation. Cf. p. 143. For the contrast of salvation *for* with salvation *from* the law, see also Braun, 'Selbstverständnis', *Studien*, pp. 113, 116; Bröker, in *TLZ* 87, 1962, cols. 709f.
[207] Cf. Huppenbauer, *Der Mensch zwischen zwei Welten*, p. 21.
[208] See below, pp. 309f.

12.30f., man's inadequacy before God is put in terms of his not being able to answer God's rebuke (cf. 1.26), for God is righteous (*tsadaqtah*) and none can oppose him. The verb here seems to bear the same meaning as does the noun in the other passages cited. In either case the primary sense is 'in the right' and 'perfect of way'. The real point of the sayings lies in the contrast with man. God is perfect, but man is sinful and inadequate.

The second principal usage which we may note appears in a collection of passages, entirely in the hymnic material, which deal with cleansing, judging and judgment or vindication. In each case, as we shall see, the term *tsedaqah* can be paralleled with a term meaning 'mercy'.

In IQS 11.3, it is said that God will wipe out the psalmist's transgression through *tsidqot*. In 11.14, God will cleanse the psalmist through *tsedaqah*. In IQH 4.36f., the psalmist says that he leans on God's grace (*hasadim*) and on the multitude of his mercies (*rahamim*), for God will pardon iniquity and cleanse man of guilt through his *tsedaqah*. In IQH 11.29f., the psalmist blesses God for his mercy and compassion. He then pleads that his soul may be rejoiced with God's truth and that he might be cleansed through (*bet*) God's *tsedaqah*. He continues,

> Even as I have hoped in Thy goodness,
>   and waited for Thy grace,
> so hast Thou freed me from my calamities
>   in accordance with Thy forgiveness;
> and in my distress Thou hast comforted me
>   for I have leaned on Thy mercy. (IQH 11.31f.)

Thus we see, especially in the two passages from IQH, that being *cleansed* by God's *tsedaqah* is set in a context of thanks for and trust in God's grace, mercy and loving-kindness. Further, in the hymns it is directly said that one is *cleansed* through God's *mercy*. Thus IQH 1.31f.: 'By Thy mercies (*rahamim*) and by Thy great goodness (*hasadim*), Thou hast strengthened' man and cleansed him. Similarly, in IQH 7.29–31 the psalmist says that God cleanses man through his goodness (*tob*). When the psalmist mentions being cleansed by the holy spirit,[209] the line is parallel to being 'drawn near' by God's loving-kindness (*hasadim*).

In IQS 11.14 we read that God will *judge* (*sh–p–t*) the psalmist in or by (*bet*) *tsedaqah*. In the Hodayot, however, God's *judgment* of the members of the sect is said to be by *mercy* or loving-kindness. Thus IQH 9.34: there is abundance of mercy (*rahamim*) when you judge me; 6.9: God will judge the remnant in or by his *hasadim*, and the psalmist continues by speaking of God's mercy and pardon. In connection with the idea that one who is in the community is judged by grace, we may compare IQH 5.6, where the

---

[209] IQH 16.11f.; cf. IQS 3.7; 4.21. The spirit is a 'manifestation of God's grace' (Ringgren, *Faith of Qumran*, p. 89).

psalmist says that God has not judged him according to his guilt, and 9.14f.: the psalmist hopes in God's loving-kindness, for no man can be righteous in God's judgment.

We come now to the phrase which has, more than any other, led to comparisons with Paul: the statements in IQS 11.5, 12 that *mishpat* is by *tsedaqah*. If *mishpat* is translated 'justification' and *tsedaqah* 'righteousness', the phrase is that justification is by God's righteousness. Burrows obviously understood *mishpat*, which he translated 'justification', to be constructively equivalent to righteousness, for it is on the basis of this statement that he concludes that man's righteousness is derived from God's righteousness.[210] We shall refrain from a discussion of the relation of Paul's thought to the thought of Qumran on this point, reserving that discussion for the conclusion. It may be worth noting now, however, that, apart from the passage at hand, it is clear in the Scrolls that man's way can be perfected only by the grace of God.[211] To suppose that this is substantially the same as Paul's conception of man's righteousness being derived from God's, one would have to suppose that human righteousness in Paul means the same as perfection of way in Qumran and that God's righteousness in Paul is equivalent to God's grace in Qumran. Neither point seems very likely, but this can be considered further below.

With regard to the statements that one's *mishpat* is by *tsedaqah*, we must first note that in IQS 11.13f. it is said that one's *mishpat* is by God's loving-kindness (*hasadim*). We should also note the full context of the statement in IQS 11.12:

> As for me,
>   if I stumble, the mercies of God (*hasdē 'el*)
>   shall be my eternal salvation.
> If I stagger because of the sin of flesh,
>   my justification (*mishpat*) shall be
>   by the righteousness of God (*tsidqat 'el*) which endures
>   for ever.

It is hard to resist the conclusion that these lines are in synonymous parallelism.[212] Note especially 'if I stumble ... If I stagger'. If this is the case, then *mishpat* is the parallel to *yeshu'a* (salvation), while *tsidqat 'el* is the parallel to *hasdē 'el*. This seems likely, since we have repeatedly seen that, when prefaced by *bet* (by, through or in), *tsedaqah* is frequently parallel to or set in sequence with the terms for mercy, loving-kindness and goodness (IQS 11.13f.; IQH 4.36f.; 11.29–32). It seems fair to conclude that in the three contexts which we have just been considering (cleansing by *tsedaqah*, being judged (*sh–p–t*)

---

[210] Above, n. 202.
[211] Above, p. 290.
[212] So also Kertelge, '*Rechtfertigung*' *bei Paulus*, p. 29.

by *tsedaqah* and *mishpaṭ* by *tsedaqah*), the primary meaning of *tsedaqah* is 'mercy'. This is perhaps seen best in IQS 11.13f., the key terms of which are these:

draw near	by *rahamim*
mishpaṭ (vindication, justification)	by *hasadim*
being judged (*sh–p–ṭ*)	by *tsedaqah*
pardon ('atone')	by *ṭob*
cleanse	by *tsedaqah*

It would be simplistic to suppose that the terms in each column are synonymous, for each one carries its own meaning and connotation. On the other hand, there are substantial positive relationships among the words of each column. Being drawn near, being cleansed and being pardoned ('atoned for') are frequently placed in parallel,[213] while *rahamim*, *hasadim* and *ṭob* appear to be interchangeable. It appears inescapable that *tsedaqah* in this context means primarily the same as *rahamim* and the other terms.[214] Unless this is what Paul meant by the righteousness of God, the proposed parallel begins to break down. We should also note that IQS 11.12 says that *mishpaṭ* comes by *tsedaqah*, while in 11.13f. *mishpaṭ* comes by God's *hasadim* (loving-kindness) and one is *judged* (*sh–p–ṭ*) by *tsedaqah*. It seems eccentric to find in this rich context, in which words are freely interchanged, *one* phrase (*mishpaṭ* by *tsedaqah*) which establishes the background of Paul's thought. I do not see any difference between saying that one's justification (in the sense of aquitting judgment, *mishpaṭ*) is by *tsedaqah* and saying that it is by mercy (*rahamim* or *hasadim*), or between the former expression and the statement that one is judged (the verb of *sh–p–ṭ*) by *tsedaqah* or by *hasadim*.

There are other passages in which *tsedaqah*, *tsidqot* or (once) *tsedeq* may connote, in part at least, mercy, although that is not so clearly or decisively the meaning as in the passages just considered. When the psalmist says, 'Thine, thine is righteousness, for it is Thou who hast done all [these things]!', what God has done is to have 'graced me with Thy spirit of mercy' (IQH 16.9).[215] When the psalmist says again, 'Thine, thine is righteousness', he continues by saying that according to God's righteousness (*tsedaqah*) he has redeemed him (17.20). The reference to redemption may also imply mercy, for in the preceding lines (17.17f.) he had cited God's *tsidqot* and gone on to speak of pardoning the sins of the forefathers and to beg God's mercy for his own sin. Here *tsidqot* is connected with God's 'long-suffering' (17.17). (The same connection appears, using the verb *tsadaqtah*, in IQH

---

[213] Above, pp. 298f.

[214] Cf. especially Becker, *Heil Gottes*, pp. 121f. On 'righteousness' as grace, cf. Ringgren, *Faith of Qumran*, pp. 66f.; Nötscher, *Terminologie*, pp. 183–5; Kertelge, '*Rechtfertigung*' *bei Paulus*, pp. 28–33.

[215] When the line, 'Thine, thine is *tsedaqah*, O Lord, for it is Thou who hast done all this' appears in 4QBt3 6.3f., what God has done is removed 'our transgressions' and cleansed 'our sin for Thine own sake'.

1.6.) When, however, the psalmist says 'Thine is righteousness' (*lekah ha-tsedeq*) in IQH 11.18, *tsedeq* apparently covers both God's mercy towards the psalmist and the destruction visited on those outside the covenant. Here, that is, the meaning of *tsedeq* is tending closer to distributive justice.[216] God is righteous in that he (correctly) destroys the wicked and shows mercy to the elect. *Tsedaqah* is probably closer to grace or mercy in IQH 7.19f.: in God's *tsedaqah* he has placed the psalmist in the covenant.

In the 'thine, thine' passages there is probably another connotation besides that of mercy. The repetition of the phrase is probably intended to assert that *tsedaqah* is *God's and not man's*, which would put this usage in close connection with the first discussed. When the formula without the repeated 'thine' occurs in IQM 11.2 (*lekah ha-milḥamah*, 'Thine is the battle') and 18.12 (*lekah ha-geburah*, 'Thine is the might'), the meaning is that the battle and the might are God's and not man's, and the same connotation is likely in the *lekah 'atah ha-tsedaqah* phrases.

The two most striking and characteristic usages of *ts–d–q* in connection with God, then, are the assertions of his righteousness in contrast to man's sinfulness and inadequacy and the statements of God's righteousness as approximately equivalent to his grace. One can, to be sure, find other usages. When the psalmist says that God is truth (*'emet*) and that all his deeds are *tsedeq*, he probably means that they are correct (IQH 4.40). Similarly his judgments are *'emet* and *tsedeq* (CD 20.29f.). The counsel of his *tsedeq* is his right counsel (IQS 1.13), just as *mishpaṭe tsedeq* are right laws (IQS 3.1; cf. 9.17). The word is occasionally clearly used of distributive justice. God will do true judgment (*lehatsdiq*) to all the sons of men (IQM 11.14). When the psalmist declares God's judgment to be right (*'atsdiq*, IQH 9.9), he is declaring that God is a just judge. This may also be the meaning of declaring God to be *tsaddiq*: he blots out wickedness and reveals his righteousness (*tsedaqah*, IQH 14.15).[217] The psalmist speaks of God's just rebuke ('the rebuke of Thy righteousness', *tsedeq*, IQH 9.33), which is presumably the punishment inflicted by God in his function as the one who does righteous judgment (*mishpaṭ ha-tsedeq*, IQH 1.26).

We turn now to examine the righteousness of man. We have previously noted that the members of the sect are occasionally called 'righteous', although this is not one of the more characteristic titles. Thus the psalmist addresses them as 'wise men' (*ḥakamim*), 'righteous men' (*tsaddiqim*) and 'men perfect of way' (*temime derek*) (IQH 1.35f.). Similarly, the author of

---

[216] Kuhn (*Enderwartung*, p. 36) takes the term here to refer only to the *Heilshandeln Gottes*.

[217] Licht ('Doctrine', pp. 8f.) takes IQH 14.15 to refer to God's distributive justice, and he cites IQS 10.18 as a parallel. Similarly Carmignac ('Souffrance', p. 372), who points out that the statement that God's *tsedaqah* is revealed is probably derived from Ps. 98.2. Kuhn (*Enderwartung*, pp. 36f.), however, understands *tsedaqah* in IQH 14.15f. to refer only to God's *Gemeinschaftstreue* (= 'das endzeitliche Heil für die Deinen').

IQH 7.12 says that God distinguishes through him between the righteous (*tsaddiq*) and the wicked (*rasha'*). Apparently one who follows the way of the psalmist and enters the sect is a *tsaddiq*.[218]

On the other hand, it is a characteristic assertion of the Hodayot that no one can be righteous (*yitsdaq*) in God's judgment (IQH 9.14f.). Although the immediate context is destroyed, this is also apparently the meaning of IQH 12.19: 'There is no righteous man before you' (*'en tsaddiq 'imkah*). The statement is put less categorically in IQS 3.3f.: a man is not righteous (*yitsdaq*) when he follows[219] the stubbornness of his heart; he is not reckoned with the perfect. But in the hymns it is man *qua* man who cannot be righteous before God. 'Who,' asks the psalmist, 'can be righteous before you when he is judged' (*mi yitsdaq lefanekah*)? The answer is clearly 'no one' (IQH 7.28). The categorical 'no one' statement also appears in IQH 4.30f. using the noun: man has no *tsedaqah*, and the son of man no perfection of way (*tum derek*).

The passages cited from IQS 3.3 and IQH 4.30f. make clear what human righteousness would be: 'perfection of way', that is, obedience without fault. In God's sight, when man is judged (IQH 7.28; 9.14f.), or simply in comparison with God (IQH 12.19), no one is righteous; all have sinned. How is it, then, that some are called righteous? God, in his mercy, forgives the sons of his truth and cleanses them of their transgressions (IQH 7.30). Although man on his own has no *tsedaqah*, since to God belong all deeds of *tsedaqah*, nevertheless God can establish the way of man and make perfect a way for him (IQH 4.31f.). As IQH 13.16f. has it, man is righteous (*yitsdaq*) only by God's goodness (*tob*). He himself has no righteous deeds (*tsidqot*) to deliver him, but he must rely on God's grace (IQH 7.17f.). Since man is not righteous (*yitsdaq*) apart from [220] God, the psalmist pleads that God will draw him near by his grace (16.11f.). Similarly, no way is made perfect without God (IQS 11.17), although presumably some ways are made perfect by God. It is in this sense that the author of IQS 10.11 can call God his 'righteousness' (*tsedeq*). The grace of God which enables one to be righteous is connected with predestination in two of the hymns: God has *created* some to be *tsaddiq* (IQH 4.38; 15.14f.). This may also be the meaning of IQH 16.10: God has marked the spirit of the *tsaddiq*.

Two related but still distinguishable elements of the sectarian self-consciousness are reflected in these statements. On the one hand, there is the

---

[218] In a similar context in IQH 2.8f. (which like 7.12 is often attributed to the 'Teacher'), those who follow the psalmist are called 'all who turn from transgression'.

[219] The verb has proved difficult for translators, but is convincingly explained as an Aramaizing form of *tur* by Licht (*Rule Scroll*, p. 78). The phrase is based on Num. 15.39.

[220] Dupont-Sommer and Mansoor translate 'beside Thee', Vermes 'except through Thee'. In IQH 10.9; IQS 11.17, however, all the principal translations are 'without Thee' or 'apart from Thee', and it seems better to maintain this translation in IQH 16.11. In II Sam. 22.32, the preposition means 'except', but this cannot be the meaning in the Scrolls.

sense of human inadequacy before God which we have often noted; no one can be righteous or perfect before God; no one, on his own, has 'righteous deeds'. On the other hand, there is the consciousness of being elect; thus some are righteous (*tsaddiq, yitsdaq*), but only by the grace of God.

There is a striking 'Pauline' ring to the statements that 'no one is righteous'. As Becker has noted, righteousness does not come by works of law.[221] Yet human righteousness *is* works of law, being equivalent to perfection of way (cf. IQS 11.17) and the opposite of transgressions (IQH 7.28–31). A man is elect by God's predestining grace and thus classed as *tsaddiq*. The only way to remain *tsaddiq* or perfect of way, however, is to do the commandments of God as specified by the sect's covenant and not to sin. As we have said above, the members of the sect were obviously more conscious of the context of gratuity than were the Rabbis, but in both cases, being *tsaddiq* involves doing the law, while salvation comes by God's election. That is, doing the law is the *condition of remaining elect*. The sect differs from the Rabbis in insisting on a far stricter standard of obedience for its members to remain in the covenant.[222]

8. The religious life

We have thus far said little about the interior religious life of the covenanters. There are various lists of virtues and vices which describe the religious ideals of the community. Most of these are not remarkable. The good should possess humility (IQS 4.3; 11.1); that is, they should not be stiff-necked and arrogant (5.4f.). They should not acquire wealth unrighteously (CD 6.15f.). They should seek God (CD 1.10) and keep his commandments (CD 3.12,20). They should pursue the truth rather than falsehood (IQS 6.15). They should love their brothers (CD 6.21) and exercise charity toward their fellow members of the covenant (IQS 4.5). It goes without saying that the wicked are characterized by the absence of these virtues.

There are two points, however, which are especially characteristic of the sectarian exhortations: the members should be *separate* and they should *know*. Thus they are urged to keep apart from the children of the pit (CD 6.15; IQS 5.1f.; 8.13). This admonition to physical separation from evil has only one exception: the purchase of goods (IQS 5.14–20). Basically, however, no mingling should take place, for *all* the deeds of those who are not in

---

[221] Becker, *Heil Gottes*, p. 125.

[222] On the root *ts-d-q* in the Scrolls, see further Becker, *Heil Gottes*, pp. 115–22; 155–60; Huppenbauer, *Der Mensch zwischen zwei Welten*, pp. 19–22; Ziesler, *Meaning of Righteousness*, pp. 85–103. We should note that the usage in the Scrolls does not support Ziesler's general hypothesis that the verb is forensic and the adjective and nouns ethical; for verb, noun and adjective are used to make precisely parallel statements.

the covenant are 'defilement' and *all* their possessions are unclean (ibid.).

The emphasis on separation for the sake of purity – to avoid 'defilement' (*niddah*, impurity, IQS 5.19) – seems to have two sources. One is that the sectarians apparently applied to themselves the rules of ritual purity which the Bible prescribes for the priests.[223] Since the ritual observances of non-sectarians were wrong, it would follow that ritual purity for the sectarians could be achieved only by separation. Defilement was not conceived of only in ritual terms, however; in fact it was not conceived of primarily as ritual contamination. Just as one is 'cleansed' from transgression (e.g. IQH 11.10), so 'uncleanness' is involved in transgression. 'All who transgress his word are unclean' (IQS 5.14). The man who cannot be 'purified' by acts of atonement, nor 'cleansed' by water, nor 'washed clean' by ablutions is precisely the man who follows the desires of his own heart and who 'despises the precepts of God' (IQS 3.3–6). It is for this reason that even when he is purified with water, he is really made clean 'by the humble submission of his soul to all the precepts of God' (IQS 3.8f.). Similarly the psalmist parallels uncleanness (*niddah*) with faithless guilt (IQH 11.11). He keeps his hands 'clean' by avoiding 'every work of iniquity' (IQH 16.10f.). The equation of uncleanness with transgression is further indicated in IQM 13.2,5, where God's 'deeds of truth' are contrasted with the 'work of unclean defilement' done by the spirits of Belial's lot. Thus it seems likely that the emphasis on separation springs more from the desire to avoid the corruption and defilement of transgression than from a concern for ritual purity *per se*.[224]

Coupled with the emphasis on physical separation is the emphasis on knowledge, understanding or insight. One of the main faults of those from whom the members of the community must remain separate is that they have not sought God so as to *know* the hidden things of the covenant (IQS 5.11f.). The characteristic of the members of the community, however, is that they have been taught the statutes, have the insight of understanding, have heard the voice of glory, have seen the angels of holiness, are open of ear and hear deep things (IQM 10.10). One of the principal points of thanksgiving in the hymns is for enlightenment:

I thank thee, Lord, because, by thy loving-kindness to an evil man and the greatness of thy mercy to a perverted heart, thou hast given me insight into thy truth, and in thy wondrous mysteries hast thou given me knowledge. (IQH 7.26f.)[225]

The virtue list of IQS 4.2–6 includes no fewer than four terms indicating the

[223] Gärtner, *Temple and Community*, p. 5; O. Betz, 'Le ministère cultuel à Qumrân', p. 167, who refers especially to the influence of Ezek. 43.18–44.26. On the priestly influence on the sect, see Klinzing, *Umdeutung*, pp. 106–43; Jaubert, *La notion d'alliance*, pp. 145–52.

[224] Cf. the discussion of Cross, *Library*, p. 76.

[225] The translation is that of Sanders, *RQ* 6, 1968, p. 430.

special knowledge of the members of the community: insight (*sekel*), understanding (*binah*), great wisdom (*hokmah*) and a spirit of knowledge (*da'at*). The emphasis on knowledge is seen especially clearly in the paraphrase of the blessing in Num. 6.24–26. In the following quotation, the words added to the biblical text are italicized:[226]

> May he bless you *with all goodness*,
> and keep you *from all evil*.
> And may he enlighten *your heart with the insight of life*;
> and may he be gracious to you *with eternal knowledge*.
> May he lift up his *merciful* face upon you for *eternal* peace.
>
> (IQS 2.2–4, my translation)

Particularly instructive is the third line of the blessing, where 'the Lord make his face to shine upon you' becomes 'may he enlighten your heart with life-giving insight'.

Both of these special emphases – the emphasis on separation and the emphasis on special knowledge or insight – obviously bear witness to the sectarian character of the community. Physically separated, but secure in the confidence that only they knew the truth, they cultivated hostility towards outsiders[227] but reliance on and commitment toward one another. The sectarian consciousness must have been complete. It could lead not only to a feeling of close community with the insiders, however, but also to suspicion and intolerance; for one had to stay separate from all sin, and consequently members were at least partially excluded from the fellowship for any transgression.

The sectarians, perhaps as the counterpart of physical separation from the rest of Israel and in agreement with their feeling of being especially chosen by God, seem to have felt intensely that they were living in the presence of God.[228] This is expressed especially clearly in the hymnic material,[229] as one might expect, but is not missing from the other documents. Thus IQM 13.8 mentions the sectarians' remembrance of God's presence, and the passage goes on to discuss the superiority of God's direct help to that of any other being, presumably with an eye on the eschatological war (13.12–14). Ringgren couples the feeling of the presence of God with the lack of hypostases or intermediate figures. He shares here the common mistake of thinking that the 'hypostases' (wisdom, 'the word') and angels in other Jewish literature reflect the conception that God was distant.[230] Their

---

[226] Cf. Burrows, *Dead Sea Scrolls*, p. 248.

[227] See the analysis of hatred of the wicked outsiders as an *imitatio Dei* in Jaubert, *La notion d'alliance*, pp. 186–9.

[228] Cf. Barthélemy, 'La sainteté selon la communauté', pp. 204–11; on the tension between the 'already' and the 'not yet', see Jaubert, *La notion d'alliance*, pp. 237, 245.

[229] See especially H. W. Kuhn, *Enderwartung und gegenwärtiges Heil*.

[230] Ringgren, *Faith of Qumran*, p. 81. For a criticism of this view as it touches Rabbinic literature, see above, pp. 213–15.

absence or relative scantiness in Qumran he takes as being linked with the sectarians' intense feeling of the presence of God. Yet in IQSa 2.8f. it is the presence of the angels, not of God, which is given as the reason for maintaining very strict ritual purity in the eschatological community.[231] In any case, the sectarians' consciousness of the presence of God is not in question.

We have noted before the word 'draw near' as a term indicating the act of being brought into the covenant and one which is used in connection with forgiveness and cleansing.[232] We should now note that one is brought near *to God* (IQH 16.12; cf. IQS 11.13f.; IQH 12.22f.; 14.13). Using a different verb, the psalmist says, 'Thou bringest all the sons of Thy truth in forgiveness *before Thee*' (IQH 7.29f.). Similarly, the sectarians are said to stand (or to be caused to stand) before God: IQH 4.21; 7.31; 11.13. It is conceivable that standing before God could refer only to the future life and not to life in the community. In IQH 4.21 and 7.31 'before Thee' is followed by 'for ever', while in 11.13 it is followed by 'with the everlasting host and with [Thy] spirits [of holiness], to be renewed . . .', apparently referring to the renewal which comes at the eschaton. Yet it is likely that although standing before God was thought of as a state which would continue 'for ever', it was also thought of as a state which began on entry to the sect. The 'bring near' and 'bring' passages cited above clearly refer to joining the sect or to being brought nearer to God within the sect.

It is probable that this same attitude – of entering the presence of God on entry into the sect and of continuing in God's presence for ever – also lies behind IQH 3.20–3:

> I walk on limitless level ground,
> and I know there is hope for him
>   whom Thou hast shaped from dust
>   for the everlasting Council.
> Thou hast cleansed a perverse spirit of great sin
>   that it may stand with the host of the Holy Ones,
> and that it may enter into community
>   with the congregation of the Sons of Heaven.
> Thou hast allotted to man an everlasting destiny
>   amidst the spirits of knowledge,
> that he may praise Thy Name in a common rejoicing
>   and recount Thy marvels before all Thy works.

It seems likely that the members of the community were thought to enter into community with the 'Sons of Heaven' when they joined the sect. In IQH 6.12f. they are said to 'share a common lot with the Angels of the Face'.[233] At any rate, entering the community is called 'being united to

---

[231] Cf. Sifre Num. 1, pp. 81f. above.   [232] Above, p. 309: IQS 11.13f.
[233] On community with the angels, see Kuhn, *Enderwartung*, pp. 66–73; Jaubert, *La notion d'alliance*, pp. 189–98.

God's council'[234] and involves walking 'before Him' (IQS 1.8).[235]

The depth of personal piety that could obtain in the community can best be seen in the Hodayot. The hymns are so well known, and have been so much quoted in the course of the discussion so far, that no special quotations are required to prove the point. The author or authors of the hymns are aware of human sinfulness and frailty and deeply conscious of the grace of God; and through the hymns these two points were given thematic and regular expression in the life of the community.[236] The confession of those who enter the covenant, according to IQS 1.24–2.1, covered precisely these two points. The entrants confess their sin, and that of their fathers, and thank God for his mercy. The priests, in blessing them, emphasize the grace of God (2.2–4).

We should recall that 'repentance' is not a category of religious behaviour which is singled out for separate description when discussing life within the sect.[237] The idea of repentance is evident, however, in the confession just cited. Further, the psalmist at least twice depicts himself as praying about sin (IQH 16.6; 17.17f.). Even though the context in each case cannot be precisely reconstructed, the general intent is clear: he is describing prayers of repentance. More frequently God is thanked for his mercy and forgiveness without separate mention of human repentance, but the tone of the prayers is such that the repentance of the sinner is obvious. It seems evident that the confession formalized in IQS 1.24ff. is more than a formal confession of human transgression and God's mercy; it reflects a real and substantial part of the pious life of those who left the habitations of the wicked, received insight into God's mysteries and lived in his presence.

9. Conclusion

It may properly be asked whether or not the soteriological pattern which we have described actually underlies the various Qumran documents. It is certainly true that, in Qumran literature as in other Jewish literature, the stages leading from election to atonement which we have described are not

---

[234] I take the 'council of God' here to be the community; so Licht, Dupont-Sommer, Wernberg-Møller and Lohse. It is possible to translate 'be united in God's counsel'; so Leaney, Vermes, Brownlee and Burrows. For the parallel phrases, see Licht, *Rule Scroll*, p. 60.

[235] Gärtner (*Temple and Community*, pp. 32f.) takes the presence of God theme to be a Temple motif, since it was believed that one who entered the Temple came into the presence of God or his angels. On the widespread expectation that a new Temple would come down whole out of heaven at the eschaton, see David Flusser, 'Two Notes on the Midrash on 2 Sam. vii', *IEJ* 9, 1959, pp. 99–104. For a discussion of the community as the heavenly Jerusalem, see G. Jeremias, *Der Lehrer der Gerechtigkeit*, pp. 245–9. Further bibliography on salvation as present in the community is given above, pp. 280f. See especially H. W. Kuhn's analysis of IQH 3.21–3, *Enderwartung*, pp. 48–50.

[236] See n. 149 above and Appendix 1 below.

[237] Above, p. 305.

spelled out in precisely that sequence. This is not surprising, since we do not possess a theological treatise which gives the stages of the way to salvation. Further, it is no disproof of the general hypothesis, since one need not suppose that these stages were consciously perceived as the stages in a sequence. The question is whether or not the soteriological pattern which we have described gives an adequate account of what is found in the literature.

We may best pose the question by asking if there is another pattern. Bardtke has suggested that IQH 11.3–14 contains a description of the 'way of salvation' in an almost catechetical form.[238] It is not clear that he thinks that the elements which he finds in IQH 11.3–14 are actually exhaustive of the Qumranian way of salvation, since he subsequently speaks of 'the catechetical presentation of the doctrine of the sect in all the psalms of Qumran'.[239] By 'catechetical' he seems to mean presented in a manner appropriate for inculcating the ideas of the sect in its members,[240] rather than a statement of all the essential elements in the sect's 'way of salvation'. At any rate, Bardtke's six steps of the 'way of salvation' were picked up by Ringgren and made the basis for his discussion of the 'way of salvation' in Qumran,[241] so that this view of the essential parts of Qumran soteriology has been given very wide circulation. The six components are these:

1. Knowledge of God's truth
2. Insight into his marvellous mysteries
3. Cleansing from sin
4. Sanctification by separation from abomination and infidelity
5. Association with the sons of truth (membership in the sect)
6. Participation in the lot of the holy people (a more precise description of what entrance and the quality of membership signify):
    (*a*) he is as a dead man raised from dust
    (*b*) he is delivered from the perverse spirit
    (*c*) he has a place before God
    (*d*) he has communion with the angels
    (*e*) he belongs to the community of jubilation.

It is not in dispute that all of these are important elements in the Qumran literature. The question is whether or not they constitute a 'pattern', a 'way of salvation' which provides a truer explanation of the thought of Qumran than does the pattern which I previously outlined. We may note several points.

I have not given knowledge and insight a separate role in the soteriological pattern. The theme of knowledge seems to have two special functions in the Qumran scrolls, one connected with the election and one connected with the

---

[238] Bardtke, 'Considérations', p. 229.
[239] Ibid., p. 230.
[240] Ibid., pp. 230f.
[241] Ringgren, *Faith of Qumran*, pp. 112–32.

commandments. Thus one must have a certain knowledge, which would be perceived as a gift of God to the elect, to volunteer – to dedicate himself – to follow God's precepts. 'How shall I seek Thee unless Thou uncover my heart?' (IQH 12.34f.). This is the knowledge which, as we observed before, is virtually tantamount to election. This view is especially clear in IQH 7.26f., in which the psalmist thanks God for enlightening him. Parallel to this note at the beginning of a hymn is the thanks for not placing the psalmist's lot 'in the congregation of Vanity' (IQH 7.34) or for placing his soul 'in the bundle of the living' (IQH 2.20). Knowledge here is double-pronged: one knows, by God's grace, that salvation is to be found in the community; and one knows, in retrospect, that it is precisely the gift of knowledge that is essential to effect election (IQH 14.12f.). That is, God's making the member of the sect 'know' is the way in which the member is able to appropriate the election.

The knowledge that one is elect, and that one's election has been given effect by knowledge that he is elect, does not, however, exhaust 'knowledge'. After he enters the community his knowledge must still be purified (IQS 1.12). One of the main points of the priestly blessing on entrants is that God will give them wisdom and eternal knowledge (IQS 2.3). The members receive further knowledge concerning the bifurcation of mankind into the elect and the non-elect after they enter (IQS 3.13f.). Further, it is clear that some elements of essential knowledge can be gained only after entry into the sect (IQS 5.11f.; 6.16; CD 15.5–11). Thus there is no quarrel with placing knowledge first in the 'way of salvation', as long as it is understood that the knowledge thus referred to is that connected with the election of the sectarians. That one must be given knowledge in order to be counted among the elect helps explain, as we have noted, why some in Israel are elect and some not.

We have previously noted that members are purified on entry. One of the most basic views of the Qumran community was that all outside the sect were damned. Since one cannot be born into the Qumran covenant, it follows that there must be purification at the time of admission. We may note, again, that purification is repeatedly referred to by the psalmist in terms that indicate that it is connected to election and entry into the sect. This is the case, in fact, in the hymn cited by Bardtke, where the purification is for the purpose of making man holy for God and so that he may join the community (IQH 11.10–12). On the other hand, purification does not stop there. The member after entry may still sin, and this requires repeated purification, and it is apparently for this that the psalmist prays in IQH 16.11f.

This brings us to the only substantial difference between Bardtke's 'way of salvation' and the soteriological pattern which I have described: Bardtke gives no place (as IQH 11.3–14 does not) to the role of the commandments and atonement for transgression of them after entry. The 'way' moves directly from purification from sin to participation in the holy community. We do not hear about the intermediate steps of learning the commandments, being on probation, being punished for transgression of commandments and the like. Although such matters as these play little role in the hymns, it can hardly be doubted that this is the way the religion actually worked. IQS must be taken as representing the views and practice of the community on these points. While it is typical of the hymns not to dwell on law, legal obligations, punishment for transgression and the like – emphasizing rather thanksgiving for being among the elect and the consciousness of being unworthy – one can see even in IQH that the content of the new covenant, its particular obligations, are taken for granted. Thus the psalmist excoriates the 'teachers of lies' for scheming in an effort to make him 'exchange the Law' taught him by God for their 'smooth things' (IQH 4.9f.). Similarly, the psalmist vows to 'hold fast to the truth of [God's] covenant' (IQH 16.7). The theme of punishment for transgression by those within the covenant is even directly referred to in the hymnic material in IQS: '[I] will have no pity on all who depart from the Way. I will offer no comfort to the smitten until their way becomes perfect' (IQS 10.20f.). Thus the tendency of the psalmist to move from election to cleansing to participation in the 'congregation of the Sons of Heaven' (IQH 3.21f.) should not be taken as indicating the existence of an alternative 'pattern', one in which the giving of commandments and punishment for transgression have no part. Such passages simply indicate that the psalmist's view is fixed on God's grace and its ultimate result, rather than on the stages which lie between. Thus I take the 'way of salvation' outlined by Bardtke on the basis of IQH 11.3–14 not to offer a soteriological scheme which is different from the one outlined in this chapter on the basis of the principal Scrolls considered together.

Indeed, I see no evidence of different soteriological patterns anywhere in the Scrolls. Scholars such as Hunzinger have frequently emphasized that the Scrolls cannot be taken as uniformly representing the same view. Historical changes and differences of viewpoint can be traced.[242] This is certainly the case with regard to individual points. Thus Hunzinger has in mind the different statements on exclusion for transgression: in some sections of IQS, for example, total exclusion is always permanent, while in CD there seems to be the opportunity for those totally excluded to return.[243] This seems to be an accurate observation. The general character of the religion is not, however, affected by differences on such halakic points. We

---

[242] Hunzinger, 'Beobachtungen zur Entwicklung', p. 231, and further references cited there. The difficulties involved in considering all the Scrolls together have recently been stated by Przybylski, *The Concept of Righteousness in the Gospel of Matthew*, pp. 14–25. He points especially to the distinctiveness of CD.

[243] Above, n. 140.

find no layer in the Qumran material in which obedience to the law is not required or in which transgression is not punished. Further, the place of obedience in the overall scheme is always the same: it is the *consequence* of being in the covenant and the *requirement for remaining* in the covenant. Even if there are variations as to what constitutes perfect obedience and as to what are appropriate penalties for transgressions, the soteriological pattern is unaltered. In the preceding analysis of the Scrolls, I have tried to give due attention to divergencies on individual points, but I have seen no reason to suspect the existence of more than one soteriological pattern. We earlier saw that the suggestion that there are two basic theologies which appear in the material – one of salvation by works and the other of salvation by grace – cannot be maintained.[244]

Thus the general pattern of religion which we found earlier in Rabbinic literature is also present in Qumran, although there are striking differences and special emphases with regard to individual points. One is elect by God's grace. God's predestining election was not perceived as excluding human choice, but the emphasis on it rather reflects the sectarians' acute self-consciousness of being chosen, not as a nation, but as individuals. While from the point of view of human worthlessness and as an explanation of why some but not others are in the covenant community the predestining grace of God was emphasized, human commitment was emphasized from the stand-point of what one should do. The emphases on God's choice *and* on human commitment ('volunteering') *both* reflect the *crucial significance of election and membership in the covenant for salvation*. Once in the covenant, members took upon themselves to *obey its regulations*. Although individual rewards for individual fulfilments are mentioned very rarely (although members are advanced in accordance with their degree of perfection), the general notion of *reward for obedience and punishment for transgression* was held. It is reflected especially clearly in the detailed lists of punishments for transgressions. *Obedience to the commandments* was not thought of as earning salvation, which came rather by God's grace, but was nevertheless required as a *condition of remaining in the covenant*; and not obeying the commandments would damn. Although all humans are sinful and are seen as such in comparison with God, the explicit *sinfulness* which would either keep one out of the community or remove one from it was conceived as *transgression of commandments*. The deeper human sinfulness which is found in all men, including the elect, would be eradicated only at the eschaton. For most transgressions within the covenant, *means of atonement were available*, although some transgressions could not be forgiven (at least according to 1QS). For those outside the covenant, there would be no mercy and forgiveness, but strict requital for their deeds.

[244] Above, pp. 291–3; cf. p. 239 n. 1; Appendix 4 on Schulz's view.

We shall now consider whether or not the same basic pattern of religion is to be found in representative books of the apocrypha and pseudepigrapha.

Appendix 1

The Authorship and *Sitz im Leben* of the Hodayot

The related questions of the authorship of the Hodayot and their use (private, cultic etc.) are large ones which have attracted a great deal of scholarly activity which has not yet led to definitive results, although real progress has been made. We do not need to come to decisions on most of the questions raised in the discussion, and the present appendix will aim only at describing in very brief terms the state of the question and at indicating the line taken in the present work.

On the basis of the view that one man wrote all the hymns (which was assumed by many and vigorously argued by Licht),[1] the principal question was the meaning of the 'I'. Were the religious sentiments those of an individual who could not be taken as representative of the community,[2] or was the 'I' collective and representative?[3] Bardtke ('Considérations') sought a solution by proposing that the hymns were used privately (rather than in public worship services), but were intentionally didactic, designed to inculcate the sect's theology in the members.

The line of discussion was fundamentally changed by a series of theses written under the supervision of K. G. Kuhn. Gert Jeremias (*Lehrer der Gerechtigkeit*, 1963) proposed a strict source division. In *one group* of hymns the 'I' is a distinct individual, whom Jeremias identified as the Teacher of Righteousness: 2.1–19; 2.31–39; 3.1–18; 4.5–5.4; 5.5–19; 5.20–7.5; 7.6–25; 8.4–40 (p. 171). Bardtke erred in not distinguishing the use of 'I' in the different groups of hymns (pp. 174f.).

In *Das Heil Gottes* (1964), Jürgen Becker proposed a slight modification of Jeremias's list. Becker proposed as the hymns most certainly to be attributed to the Teacher the following: 2.1–19; 2.31–39; 3.37–4.4; 4.5–5.4 (although 4.29–5.4 is 'secondary'); 5.20–39. Probably also to be included are 2.20–30; 3.1–18; 5.5–19; 6.1–36; 7.6–25; 8.4–40 (Becker, pp. 51–4). One of the points distinguishing the hymns of the Teacher of Righteousness from the rest ('community hymns') is the conception of sin. In the former,

---

[1] Licht, 'Doctrine', p. 2; *Thanksgiving Scroll*, pp. 22–4.
[2] Ringgren, *Faith of Qumran*, p. 95.
[3] For a sound presentation of this view, see Holm-Nielsen, *Hodayot*, pp. 316–48; ' "Ich" in den Hodajoth'.

sin is not necessarily connected with 'flesh', while in the latter it is (p. 67).

H. W. Kuhn (*Enderwartung und gegenwärtiges Heil*, 1966) turned his attention to the community hymns. He also proposed, however, a further modification to Jeremias's list. Further, he hesitated to call the author of the more individualistic hymns the Teacher of Righteousness. For convenience, he did call some hymns 'Lehrerlieder' to distinguish them from 'Gemeindelieder', but the full title of the former is 'berichtende Loblieder des Offenbarungsmittlers' (p. 23). The list of the 'Lehrerlieder' is as follows: 2.1–19; 4.5–5.4 (except for 4.29b–5.4, which is a 'secondary addition'); 5.5–19; 5.20–6.36; 7.6–25; 8.4–40 (Kuhn, pp. 23f.). The community hymns were primarily used cultically in connection with the admission of new members to the community or with the yearly observation of the renewal of the covenant (p. 31). By extension, they may have been used in daily prayers, since these could be considered as occasions for 'entering' the covenant (as in IQS 10.10) (pp. 32f.). The 'I' in the community hymns is not biographical, but refers to the pious of Qumran (p. 25).

It is perhaps too early to determine whether or not the division proposed by Jeremias, with modifications, will prevail in critical work on the literature. Thyen, for example, supports the G. Jeremias/H. W. Kuhn division of the Hodayot and even calls Jeremias's hymns 'Lehrerlieder'. He so defines these, however, that Jeremias's position is completely reversed. The 'Lehrerlieder' are not the composition of the Teacher, but rather they are hymns which evidence the *community's reflection* about the significance of the Teacher (Thyen, *Sündenvergebung*, 1970, pp. 81–3). In his usage, the term 'Lehrer' is 'nur Chiffre für die qumranische "Lehre"' (p. 85).

For the purpose of the present study, the only view which would have to be seriously controverted is the one expressed by Ringgren: that all or a large part of the hymns are individualistic and do not represent the community.[4] A contrary position has been taken, though from quite different perspectives, by such scholars as Bardtke, Holm-Nielsen and H. W. Kuhn. As it happens, most of the passages from the Hodayot used in the present study are from those identified by Jeremias and Kuhn as community hymns. Even if the other hymns were written by the Teacher of Righteousness and not intended for public use, I would not suppose that they represent a totally unique theology and religious viewpoint. At any rate, the present use of the hymnic material, especially the community psalms in IQH and the final two columns of IQS, as representing a way of thinking widespread in the community, seems well-grounded.

With regard to the particular source analysis proposed by Jeremias and his successors, one may express general sympathy but not total satisfaction. IQH 2.1–19 and 8.4–40, for example, do seem distinct from many of the

[4] Above, n. 2.

other Hodayot by being so individualistic. On the other hand, the phrase 'Violent men have sought after my life' (2.21, a community hymn) is difficult to distinguish from 'the assembly of the wicked has raged against me' (2.12, a *Lehrerlied*). There are other criteria than that of personalistic expression, to be sure, but the similarities between the two groups are often striking. Questions about the division are raised especially by the problematic passage IQH 4.29–33. Although Jeremias (pp. 204–17) attributed it to the Teacher, both Becker (pp. 54f.) and Kuhn (p. 23 n. 3) regard it as a secondary (community) addition to one of the *Lehrerlieder*, despite the fact that there are no formal grounds for the division. Since the passage contains just the doctrine of sin that Becker denies to the *Lehrerlieder* (see above, n. 94), one cannot help suspecting that source criticism is being bent somewhat to suit a particular theory of theological development. Despite these and other possible caveats, it must be agreed that Jeremias's division has proved very fruitful. The primary gain is in freeing the bulk of IQH from being thought to be individualistic and private prayers which do not represent the thought of the community.

Appendix 2

IQS 8.1–9.2

As noted above (nn. 138, 146), I take some parts of this section of IQS to refer to the general community, but other parts to refer to a select group which was subject to more rigorous standards. While this position is not essential to the overall discussion of the Dead Sea Scrolls, it may be useful to sketch the rationale behind it and to consider some alternative positions.

IQS 8.1 clearly refers to a select group of fifteen, twelve laymen and three priests. Leaney, in his commentary ad loc., takes the entire passage 8.1–9.26 to deal with this group, which he conceives of as the 'pioneer community', that is, an early group of settlers rather than a select number within a larger group (so also Sutcliffe, *JSS* 4, 1959, pp. 134–8). It seems, however, that the discussion changes from the select fifteen at 8.4b ('When these things come to pass in Israel') and returns to a more select group only at 8.20, although 8.10b–12a may also refer to the select group. The ground for the distinction is this: in 8.16–19 the punishment for a *deliberate* transgression is *temporary exclusion* until the offender's behaviour is corrected, while in 8.22f. and 9.1 the punishment for a *deliberate* or deceitful transgression is *permanent expulsion*; the punishment for an inadvertent transgression is temporary exclusion for a minimum of two years. The rigour of the punishment in 8.22–

9.2 in comparison with 8.16–19 seems to require a different group.

P. Guilbert ('Le Plan') has argued that IQS in its entirety is a composition which displays 'a rigorous logic' and a unity of style which withstands source analysis (p. 323). He regards 8.1–9.11 as forming a coherent section which refers to the part of the entire community which is established in the desert. He notes that the penal code for this group is stricter and that the terms are slightly different from those met elsewhere in IQS (pp. 333–6). When he notes the strictness of the penal code in relation to that of columns 6 and 7, however, he cites only 8.20–9.2 (p. 335), apparently overlooking the fact that the preceding lines, 8.16b–19, contain a penalty in disagreement with 8.20–9.2 but in agreement with the code which begins at 6.24.

The most sustained efforts to give a source analysis of IQS are those of J. Murphy-O'Connor, 'La genèse littéraire' and C.-H. Hunzinger, 'Beobachtungen zur Entwicklung'. Murphy-O'Connor's basic hypothesis is that IQS was built up over a period of years, with each addition reflecting a certain stage in the community's life. He puts 8.16b–19 and 8.20–9.2 in the same stage of development, but he does note that the 'penal legislation is not homogeneous' (p. 533). He takes account of the different halakot in the two sections which deal with how deliberate transgressions are punished by suggesting that one section, probably 8.16b–19, the more lenient, is older. The more severe legislation (permanent exclusion for any deliberate or deceitful transgression) of 8.22f. he regards as more casuistic and presumably more developed. (The relatively lenient rule of 6.24f. on punishment of deliberate lying with regard to property is put still later, however; see p. 534.)

Hunzinger also takes the different penal sections in IQS to represent different stages in the sect's history (pp. 242–5). He dismisses the possibility that the contradiction between 8.18f. and 8.20–24 is to be explained by having 8.20–24 refer to a smaller group with stricter ordinances. He takes 8.20ff. rather to be an element of an older, because more severe, tradition (p. 243). He compares the view that decisions are made by the priests (9.7, regarded as an older element) with the view that decisions should be made by a majority of members (5.2, a more lenient and newer element). He makes the important observation that in 4QS^e 8.15–9.11 is missing. In Hunzinger's view, the shorter form is not the earlier; rather, one sees here the complete dropping of the strict section in favour of the milder view which subsequently prevailed (pp. 244f. Cf. Forkman, *The Limits of the Religious Community*, p. 62.)

It is certainly reasonable to think that IQS does reflect different stages of the community's development and to account for divergences in terms of temporal development. Of the two theories of chronological development (Murphy-O'Connor: the stricter is later because more casuistic; Hunzinger: the stricter is earlier because the tendency was to soften the requirements),

I somewhat prefer Hunzinger's. Both of these analyses, however (as well as those of Wernberg-Møller, Sutcliffe and Leaney), fail to explain how IQS, in its present form, could ever have been an effective legislative document. If in its present form it was used as a 'Rule', which seems intrinsically likely, then the relatively lenient rule regarding deliberate transgression in 8.16b–19 (cf. also 6.24f.) and the strict rule in 8.22f. and 9.1–2 must have been applied to different groups. It is impossible for *both* rules to apply to the same group *at the same time*, even if a historical development accounts for the divergence. If, that is, a member sinned deliberately, he would either be suspended temporarily or excluded permanently, but not both. For both halakot to make sense, they *must* have been taken to refer to different categories of members. Theological disparities can be accommodated, but the halakah on a given point cannot be two different things at once. Thus I take it that, in IQS as it stands at present, 8.20–9.2 governs a different group from that governed by 8.16b–19.

It seems likely (though it cannot be proved conclusively) that, from this standpoint, the select fifteen, 'perfect in all that is revealed of the Law' (8.1f.; not 'perfectly versed', as Vermes), would have been understood to be the same as the 'men of perfect holiness' governed by 8.20–9.2. It may also be that the men confirmed for two years 'in perfection of way' who are 'set apart as holy within the Council of the men of the Community' (8.10f.) would be taken by the readers of the document in the form in which we have it to be the same men. The rest of 8.4b–19, however, seems to refer to ordinary members of the community.[1]

The key to this analysis, it must be emphasized, is the assumption that IQS must have made sense as a document which governed behaviour and penalties for transgression. I do not suppose that the readers of the document could have distinguished divergent halakot as belonging to different historical periods. They would have had to be rationalized in some other way. Forkman (*The Limits of the Religious Community*, pp. 59–61) has fully realized the need to make sense of the two levels of requirement in the passage under discussion. He proposes that the phrase 'every member in the Covenant' in 8.16b refers to the novices attached to the sect who were not yet full members, while the 'men of perfect holiness' of 8.20 are the ordinary members of the sect. This seems a less likely understanding of the titles of the two groups than the one proposed here, and it also overlooks the connection between the select fifteen of 8.1 and the men of perfect holiness of 8.20 as the Scroll now reads (even if 8.20 was not originally written with 8.1 in mind).

---

[1] Klinzing's analysis is similar (*Umdeutung des Kultus*, pp. 51f.): 8.1–9.11 is composed of several smaller units. 8.4–10 is a separate unit, and 8.10ff. returns to the special group mentioned in 8.1. On his further separation of 8.2–4 from 8.1, see Appendix 3.

Appendix 3

IQS 8.3f.

These lines are usually taken to say that the fifteen men mentioned in 8.1 'shall atone for sin by the practice of justice and by suffering the sorrows of affliction'. This gives Vermes's translation, but the general sense is the same in most other translations and commentaries. Three objections, all of which merit serious consideration, have been raised to this understanding.

Chamberlain ('Toward a Qumran Soteriology', *NT* 3, 1959, pp. 305–13) takes 8.1–4 to state the preconditions for the corporate atonement which is mentioned in 8.5–10. The task of the select fifteen of 8.1–4, he argues, is to establish the community. It is only the community which will atone. In 8.3–4, instead of 'atone for sin by practising justice and suffering . . .', he translates, 'expiate the sins of the Community by judging and punishing sinners'. He sees the select fifteen to have a juridical role. *Ratsah* in 8.3 he understands not as 'to atone', but as 'to cause justice to be practised and to refine offenders out of their evil' (p. 311). We should note, however, that *ratsah* in the *pi'el* can equal *kipper* in Rabbinic usage: see Sifre Deut. 32 (Finkelstein, p. 57); Sifra Vayyiqra Nedabah pereq 4.8, end (to Lev. 1.4). (Licht, in his commentary, explains the verb here by using *mekapper*.) Further, I fail to see how Chamberlain finds 'punishing sinners' in *tsarat matsrēp*, which best refers to afflictions endured. (On *matsrēp*, see Wernberg-Møller, *Manual*, p. 49, on 1.17.)

Carmignac ('Souffrance') takes as his general point of departure the observation that, with the possible exception of IQS 8.2–4, suffering in the Scrolls is not seen as redemptive (p. 383). The crucial phrase he translates 'à faire *grâcier la perversion* par ceux qui pratiquent le droit et (subissent) l'angoisse de la fournaise' (p. 384, his emphasis). The translation of *ratsah* as 'pardon' is based on the comparison with Isa. 40.2, 'her iniquity is pardoned', *nirtsah*. By taking the act of pardon to be *for those who* suffer, rather than *by* suffering, Carmignac eliminates the reference to redemptive suffering. The passage, he says, is based on Gen. 18.17–33. The meaning is that God's grace will be bestowed on all the land in order not to punish the few righteous men in it (p. 384). Thus the passage is not connected with the suffering servant passages of Second Isaiah (p. 385). On this point there is an appreciable variation between the thought of Qumran and that of 'orthodox Judaism', where suffering, including vicarious suffering, is commonly thought to be redemptive (p. 385). It seems more likely, however, that we should follow Carmignac's own reference to Isa. 40.2 and find here a reminiscence of the suffering servant motif (so Black, *Scrolls and Christian Origins*, p. 128). Admittedly, this is not a major theme in the Scrolls, but the clear sense of 8.3–4 is that atonement is by righteous deeds and suffering.

Klinzing has argued with considerable persuasiveness that all the principal passages in which the community is said to atone (e.g. IQS 8.4–8; 8.8–10; 9.3–6; 5.4–7) go back to a basic formulation (*Die Umdeutung des Kultus*, p. 72). He takes the atoning group in every case to be the entire community. He further considers IQS 8.2–4 to have been originally separate from IQS 8.1, and he thus considers the subject of 'to atone', 'to practise righteousness' and 'to suffer affliction' to be the entire community, not the select fifteen of 8.1. Consequently, the only suffering referred to here is the suffering of exile, and the meaning of the passage is analogous to Ps. Sol. 13.10, in which God cleanses the righteous by suffering (*Umdeutung*, pp. 51f., 102–4). It is certainly possible that Klinzing's analysis of the origin of 8.1–4 is correct. His argument, however, shows the weakness of discussing the meaning of passages exclusively on the basis of a reconstructed original. In IQS 8 as it stands at present, the subject of 'to atone' and 'to suffer' can be read only as the select fifteen. Unless we suppose that the readers of IQS performed the same source analysis as has Klinzing, they must have regarded the text as saying that the fifteen atone for sin, and presumably for the sin of others, not just their own. Thus Klinzing's denial of the idea of representative atonement would seem to refer only to possible sources behind IQS, not to the document as we have it.

Appendix 4

The Nothingness of Man and *Gattungsgeschichte*

Schulz ('Rechtfertigung', p. 167) notes that the themes of the nothingness of man and his salvation (*Rechtfertigung*) by God's grace are almost exclusively found in the hymnic literature. Following Morawe's analysis of the *Gattungen* in the Hodayot,[1] he further notes that these themes occur most often in 'Stücke im Lehrstil' and in 'Reflexionen' (p. 169). These two *Gattungen* he considers to go back to the catechetical material of the community, its 'didache' (p. 171). Further, this catechetical material is limited to IQS and IQH, which fall temporally between the early IQM and the relatively late CD and IQpHab. Thus the themes of nothingness and salvation *sola gratia* represent one view (*eine Schicht*) within the Qumran literature, a view which was current at a certain point in the sect's history (p. 173). The didactic material containing these themes was probably used at the initiation rites (p. 174). Although he separates this theme chronologically from others, he

---

[1] G. Morawe, *Aufbau und Abgrenzung der Loblieder von Qumrân* (ca. 1961). Morawe's analysis was discussed and modified by G. Jeremias (*Lehrer der Gerechtigkeit*, p. 170) and H. W. Kuhn (*Enderwartung*, pp. 21–6).

does note that the members of the sect did not perceive the contradiction between salvation by grace and the demand to fulfil the law which characterizes other stages of the sect's life (p. 175).

The principal fault of this analysis is that it requires removing the 'didactic' themes from their actual setting in the context of prayers to God. We may take, for example, the first four 'Stücke im Lehrstil' cited by Schulz. The query, 'What shall a man say concerning his sin' is clearly in a prayer addressed to God: 'For Thine . . . are all righteous deeds' (IQH 1.25–7). Similarly the statement that man 'is in iniquity from the womb' (4.29f.; the passage as defined by Schulz is 4.29b–33a) follows immediately the confession to God that 'Thou hast done wonders before the Congregation for the sake of Thy glory' (4.28). The next passage, 7.32b f. ('And what is a man of Naught and Vanity') immediately follows the statement that 'Thou art an eternal God; . . . and there is none other beside Thee.' IQH 10.3b–4a ('What then is man that is earth') is in the context of the question to God, 'what can I devise unless Thou wish it' (10.5). One could go on, but the point is clear. All of these 'nothingness' passages are in the context of comparing God and man and in the setting of prayer to God. This is what is distinctive about the passages and what gives them their character. It may certainly have been the case that these prayers were used 'catechetically' in the sense indicated by Bardtke, as inculcating this theology in the hearts and minds of the members. There is no reason for us to suppose, however, that this theology was characteristic of the sect at a given period. *It always occurs in the attitude of prayer* and, as we have shown, it disappears when that attitude is changed to actual exhortation (as in IQH 1.35f.; is this not didache?) or in halakah (e.g. IQS 1–9). Schulz's suggestion would be more nearly persuasive if he could find some prayer material from which the theme of the nothingness of man and the mightiness and grace of God is missing.

As for the failure to perceive the contradiction between salvation by grace and by rigorous obedience: there is no contradiction, since these were not alternative ways to salvation.[2] Salvation was always by grace (unmerited election) and always required perfection (even in IQH; see, for example, 17.21f.; 14.17: 'with an oath I have undertaken never to sin against Thee, nor do anything evil in Thine eyes. And thus do I bring into community all the men of my Council.').

---

[2] See above, pp. 295f. Thyen (*Sündenvergebung*, pp. 94–8) has correctly argued against Schulz that, despite the way in which grace is emphasized in the Scrolls, it is incorrect to see there the Pauline contrast of grace versus works. For Paul, sin rules in observing the law; for the covenanters, in transgressing it (p. 97).

III

APOCRYPHA AND PSEUDEPIGRAPHA

1. Ben Sirach[1]

The election and the covenant

A large proportion of the 'Wisdom of Jesus Ben Sirach' is devoted to the kind of admonition and advice to individuals which was generally characteristic in the Near Eastern wisdom schools.[2] Thus Ben Sirach advises his reader on disciplining his son (30.1–13), watching over his daughter (42.9–11), keeping silent and speaking at the right moment (20.1–8), and selecting his friends carefully (11.29–34), among many other things. He discourses on such matters as the characteristics of a wise magistrate (10.1–5) and on how to behave when confronted with a formidable adversary (8.1–19). Despite the universal tone of such passages and the use of various widespread wisdom motifs, the election and the covenant with Israel are never far from the author's mind. Thus chapter 17, which starts out as if it deals with mankind, in fact is written with the biblical history in mind, as is seen when the author explicitly passes to the discussion of Israel, the Torah and the covenant, beginning with v. 11. 'He established with them an eternal covenant' (17.12). The section concludes, 'He appointed a ruler for every nation, but Israel is

---

[1] The translation, except where otherwise noted, is that of the RSV. I have also consulted the translations of the NEB, the Jerusalem Bible, and of Box and Oesterley in Charles, *Apocrypha*, as well as the translations and notes of selected Hebrew portions in Schechter and Taylor, *The Wisdom of Ben Sira*. The Hebrew text is that of Segal, and I have also made some use of his retroversion into Hebrew where Hebrew manuscripts are lacking. I have checked Segal's text with the Hebrew text edited by Israel Lévi and with Yadin's edition of the Matsada fragments (covering 39.27–43.30). For the Greek text I have used the editions of Rahlfs and Swete. These translators and editors are cited simply by name in the notes and text. Where no page number is given, the reader should see the appropriate passage in the translation or edition.

General references and quotations in which Greek and Hebrew terms are not specifically cited are according to the enumeration system of the RSV. Where Hebrew terms are being discussed, Segal's Hebrew enumeration is indicated in brackets if it differs from that of the RSV. Lévi's sometimes differing enumeration is not cited. When the Greek text is directly referred to, and the Greek enumeration differs from the English, that enumeration is given in brackets prefaced by the term 'Greek'.

For a discussion of the history of research on Ben Sirah, especially as regards his religiousness, see J. Haspecker, *Gottesfurcht bei Jesus Sirach*, 1967, pp. 6–41. The reliability of the text is discussed on pp. 39–41. See further J. Marböck, *Weisheit im Wandel*, 1971, pp. 1–5. A recent discussion of the date of the book (between 175 and 190 b.c.e.) is in G. Maier, *Mensch und freier Wille*, pp. 24f.

[2] For an indication of how much of Ben Sirach's book consists of the repetition and development of traditional themes, see G. von Rad, 'The Wisdom of Jesus Sirach', *Wisdom in Israel*, pp. 240–62.

the Lord's own portion' (17.17). Similarly, 10.19 passes from mentioning the 'human race' to specifying that it is the faithful among Israel who are 'worthy of honour':

> What race is worthy of honour? The human race. [Greek and Heb., 'seed']
> What race is worthy of honour? Those who fear the Lord.
> What race is unworthy of honour? The human race.
> What race is unworthy of honour? Those who transgress the commandments.

Here the distinction is apparently between those Israelites who transgress the commandments of the covenant and those who obey them ('fear the Lord').[3]

The specification of Israel as the elect is seen clearly in chapter 24, the praise of Wisdom which Ben Sirach has Wisdom speak in the first person. Thus the Lord told Wisdom ' "Make your dwelling in Jacob, and in Israel receive your inheritance" ' (24.8).[4] After Wisdom 'takes root' in Israel (24.12), she produces sweet fruit, the eating and drinking of which causes men to hunger and thirst for more (24.19–21). Ben Sirach comments, apparently referring to the produce:

> All this is the book of the covenant of the Most High God,
>   the law which Moses commanded us
>   as an inheritance for the congregations of Jacob.
> It fills men with wisdom, like the Pishon,
>   and like the Tigris at the time of the first fruits. (24.23–5)

It is thus clear that Ben Sirach recognized that the law was given especially to Israel. He also sometimes explicitly connects his admonitions, which are usually couched in very general terms, with obeying the commandments or keeping the covenant.

> Remember the commandments,
>   and do not be angry with your neighbour;
> remember the covenant of the Most High, and overlook ignorance. (28.7)
> Help a poor man for the commandment's sake,
>   and because of his need do not send him away empty. (29.9)

We may conclude, then, that Ben Sirach, like the Rabbis after him, presupposed the biblical view of the election of Israel and wrote within the

---

[3] I cannot follow Burkill ('Theological antinomies: Ben Sira and St Mark', *New Light on the Earliest Gospel*, p. 143; *IDB* II, p. 21) in regarding 10.19 as an example of Ben Sirach's 'universalism': 'the conception of race can be construed entirely in terms of piety and morals'. It is not general piety and morals which are meant, but the commandments of the covenant. I take 'those who fear the Lord' and 'those who transgress the commandments' to be the righteous and the wicked within Israel.

[4] Ben Sirach's connection of wisdom with the election of Israel was also observed by Marböck, *Weisheit im Wandel*, pp. 130f.; cf. p. 71. He notes that the use of wisdom to express the election of Israel had not been previously observed (p. 131). If so, this is curious, since the connection of wisdom and election seems strikingly obvious.

context of the doctrine of the covenant. We should note that 'the covenant' seems to be basically a unitary conception in Ben Sirach, and it is defined primarily as being embodied in the Mosaic Torah (so 24.23, quoted just above). In other terms, however, Ben Sirach can speak of a succession of covenants with the patriarchs (for example 44.20,22,23),[5] but these do not represent different covenants from the Mosaic which are currently available.

For the general understanding of the book, it is important to note the point of connecting the admonitions of wisdom literature ('help a poor man') with the Mosaic covenant ('for the commandment's sake', 29.9). The variation between admonitions of a very general tone and explicit mention of obeying the commandments given by Moses is to be explained by the fact that Ben Sirach was intentionally defining the values of the well-established wisdom tradition in terms of the Mosaic covenant: that wisdom which is universally sought is in fact truly represented by and particularized in the Torah given by God through Moses (see especially 24.23); further, that system of prudential behaviour which wisdom teachers of all nations extol is identified as obedience to the commandments of the Jewish covenant (wisdom is the 'fear of the Lord' and involves obeying the commandments, 19.20; cf. 19.24). Thus Ben Sirach's conception of the election of Israel is clearer than might at first appear to be the case from the general nature of much of the material.[6]

Ben Sirach does not deal much with the Gentiles, except in one section of a strikingly nationalistic and traditionally Jewish character (36.1–17). Here he calls upon God to hasten the day when he will destroy the Gentile nations, gather again *all* the tribes of Jacob, and establish the Israelite theocracy throughout the earth. Thus it is clear that Ben Sirach had a firm view of the election of Israel and of the ultimate fulfilment of God's covenant to establish the chosen people ('let thy prophets be true', 36.16).[7]

Chapter 36 alone should have given pause to those who wish to argue that Ben Sirach gave approximately equal weight to 'universalism' and 'particularism'.[8] As Marböck has shown, the connection of wisdom with the entire creation provides a universalistic motif in the book (see e.g. 1.10; 24.3–6).[9] The point of these statements, however, is to lead up to an argument. The wisdom which dwells with all flesh (1.10) is *really* acquired through 'fear of

[5] Cf. Jaubert, *La notion d'alliance*, pp. 32, 36, 39.

[6] G. von Rad ('The Wisdom of Jesus Sirach', pp. 244f.) has objected to the equation of wisdom and nomism, observing that 'the didactic material presented by Sirach arises solely . . . from didactic wisdom tradition and not from the Torah' (p. 244). The point of Ben Sirach's pronounced identification of wisdom and Torah, however, has not to do with the *content* of the instruction, but with the idea of *election*: only Israel really has wisdom.

[7] The translation is that of Schechter and Taylor from the Hebrew.

[8] Thus for example Burkill; see n. 5 above.

[9] *Weisheit im Wandel*, pp. 34, 61f., 63, 131.

the Lord' (= obeying the Jewish law, 1.20). The wisdom which has a possession among every nation (24.6) *truly and fully* resides in Israel (24.12) and is the equivalent of 'the law which Moses commanded us' (24.23). 'Universalism' and 'particularism' are not equal concerns with Ben Sirach; in fact, he does not even frame the theological discussion in those terms. There has been some discussion of what the main theme of the book is. Haspecker, for example, has argued that the pious relationship with God (for which 'fear of God' is the most common term)[10] is the *Gesamtthema* of the book.[11] He correctly notes, for example, that in 1.1–2.18 the theme of wisdom drops away 'as soon as it has fulfilled its role of illustrating the significance of the fear of God'.[12] One cannot quarrel with the argument that the importance of a pious relationship with God was a principal concern of the author; but the *argument* of the book, and in that sense its *theme*, seems to lie in the dialectic between wisdom and law. Ben Sirach argues that if a man wants wisdom (which everyone does), he should not seek it from secular teachers, but rather observe the covenant with Moses. One may compare the argumentation of the Gospel of John: the universally agreed upon desires and values of the surrounding culture (truth, light and the like) are in fact actualized in Jesus Christ. Thus 'universalism' and 'particularism' are not really balanced or held in tension.[13] In Ben Sirach's answering theology (to use Tillach's phrase), the universal quest for wisdom (the value of which is affirmed) is really answered in the Mosaic covenant.[14] It is neither the case that Torah overwhelms wisdom,[15] nor that the Torah is simply legitimatized and interpreted 'from the realm of understanding characteristic of wisdom'.[16] The relationship is dialectical, and neither subordinates the other. Wisdom is good and is to be sought; it is embodied in the Torah; one will be wise who fears God and obeys the Mosaic commandments; the content of

---

[10] *Gottesfurcht bei Jesus Sirach*, pp. 4, 45.

[11] Ibid., especially, pp. 88–105.

[12] Ibid., p. 98.

[13] As Marböck maintains. See n. 9 above.

[14] This formulation is closer to that of Marböck, who sees Ben Sirach as a theologian responding to the questions of the time (*Weisheit im Wandel*, p. 9), than to that of Haspecker. Haspecker, however, has correctly defined and analysed the content of Ben Sirach's concern for individual piety. We should also note that an 'answering theology' which affirms some of the values of the surrounding culture cannot be called a declaration of war against Hellenism (against Hengel, *Judaism and Hellenism* I, p. 138; Hengel is citing Smend; followed by Maier, *Mensch und freier Wille*, pp. 45–7, 58); so also Marböck, pp. 171f.

[15] Maier (*Mensch und freier Wille*, p. 46) points to 19.23f. (a God-fearer without intelligence is better than a wise transgressor) as evidence that Ben Sirach prefers Torah obedience to Hellenistic wisdom. This is too simplistic; it overlooks the great mass of traditional wisdom material which forms much of the content of the book and which has convinced von Rad that wisdom overwhelms Torah. See nn. 6 and 16.

[16] This is the formulation of von Rad, 'The Wisdom of Jesus Sirach', p. 245. Cf. p. 247: Ben Sirach knows about the Torah, but it is primarily of importance 'only in so far as it is to be understood on the basis of, or as it is otherwise connected with, the great complex of wisdom teachings'. Von Rad misses what is new about Sirach and what is important in his references to the Torah: the connection of wisdom and election.

proper behaviour is closely allied to the common wisdom tradition, but specified as being in agreement with and embodied in the Torah. Ben Sirach seeks a fruitful theological harmonization which maintains the value of the wisdom tradition but which sets it within the framework of the election of Israel and the divine law given to Israel through Moses.

The fate of the individual Israelite; reward and punishment

What Ben Sirach has to say about the fate of the individual is not thematically connected with his traditional picture of the salvation of Israel at the time of the Lord's coming. That is, individual soteriology (such as it is) is not discussed in terms of being 'in' or 'out' of the group of the saved on the day of the Lord. 36.11 simply supposes that God will, on that day, save all the tribes of Jacob. The question of whether or not any individual Israelites will be excluded from the tribes of Jacob on that day is not focused upon. It would appear that Ben Sirach's eschatological hope was not for an imminent confrontation of God with Israel's enemies and that the question of being a traitor to Israel was not one that arose in his time.

Thus, except for the ultimate hope of salvation for Israel, the question of the election has no soteriological consequences. What Ben Sirach has to say about the fate of the individual, whether happy or dolorous, does not depend on whether or not the individual is elect – presumably only Jews are addressed in the book – but on whether or not he is counted among the wicked or the righteous; that is, on whether or not he more or less satisfactorily keeps the commandments of the covenant. The author's view of the strict justice of reward and punishment in this life (which will be described below) prevents the question of the election from being sharply focused as regards the individual. Just as Ben Sirach does not probe the question of the fate or the standing of righteous Gentiles, so he does not explicitly raise the problem of whether or not an Israelite could sin in such a way as to remove himself from the covenant. Thus the question of a 'true Israel', of those who are *really* among the elect, does not arise. The distinction between the wicked (probably *rasha'*; Greek and ET: sinner) and the righteous (probably *tsaddiq*; Greek *eusebēs*; ET godly) (23.8,12) does not lead to a re-examination of the question of the election.

We shall return to the question of the wicked and the righteous below. First we should note, however, that the term 'soteriology' is being used in a very limited sense. Being 'saved' does not lead to eternal bliss, while being 'damned' does not lead to eternal perdition. If there is a shadowy existence in Hades (14.16), it does not provide an opportunity for reward and punishment. 'Whether life is for ten or a hundred or a thousand years, there is no inquiry about it in Hades' (41.4). 'Who will sing praises to the Most High in Hades, as do those who are alive and give thanks?' (17.27). Such passages as 7.17 ('the punishment of the ungodly is fire and worms') and 21.9 (the end of the wicked 'is a flame of fire') might seem to indicate that there will be punishment for the wicked after death. But 7.17 in Hebrew reads 'for the hope of man is worms', a reading which is supported by its being quoted in Aboth 4.4. The same idea is clearly stated in 10.11, and in 18.12 it is said that the end of all men will be evil. 21.9 thus seems not to refer to a post-mortem punishment. The imagery of burning tow probably reflects such passages as Isa. 1.31 and Mal. 4.1 (Heb., 3.19; 'the arrogant and evildoers will be stubble; the day that comes shall burn them up'). Ben Sirach 34.13 ('The spirit of those who fear the Lord will live') is likewise not to be taken as a prophecy of a resurrection of the just. His spirit will not remain sorrowful, but will revive to new life because of his hope in God.[17]

Such passages as 7.17 and 18.12 do not, however, imply that there is no distinction between the fate of the wicked and the fate of the righteous.[18] On the contrary, the heart of Ben Sirach's religion may be described as confidence in God's justice tempered by confidence in his mercy: pragmatic nomism modified by the assurance of compassion.[19] Thus one's obligation is to obey the law, to do what God commanded.

> Those who fear the Lord will not disobey his words,
>   and those who love him will keep his ways.
> Those who fear the Lord will seek his approval,
>   and those who love him will be filled with the law. (2.15–16)

> All wisdom is the fear of the Lord,
>   and in all wisdom there is the fulfilment of the law. (19.20)

Those who obey are appropriately rewarded, while those who disobey are punished. God's punishment of sin is the result of his *wrath*; his doing good to the obedient is the result of his *mercy*:

> Even if there is only one stiff-necked person,
>   it will be a wonder if he remains unpunished.
> For mercy (*raḥamim, eleos*) and wrath (*'aph, orgē*) are with the
>   Lord;

[17] See Segal, p. 218.

[18] My colleague Dr A. Baumgarten has suggested to me that Ben Sirach was written as a refutation to Qoheleth. This seems a fruitful suggestion for exploring the *Sitz im Leben* and motivation of the book. We have here one of the principal points: Qoheleth, in teaching that all is vanity, effectively denied the basic Jewish doctrine of a just God who rewards and punishes. Ben Sirach vigorously insisted on a distinction in the fate of the righteous and the wicked, as we shall see. We should also note Ben Sirach's concern (above, p. 331) to define wisdom as the Mosaic Torah, which can be taken as a counter to the more universalistic posture of Qoheleth. Cf. now Crenshaw, 'The Problem of Theodicy in Sirach', *JBL* 94, 1975: Ben Sirach is polemical against 'a vocal group bent on attacking divine justice' (p. 47). Sirach 'tenaciously held on to the traditional dogma of retribution in spite of Job and Qoheleth' (p. 59).

[19] On the *attitude* which is appropriate to the righteous man, and which is in one sense 'the heart of Ben Sirach's religion', see below, pp. 345f.

he is mighty to forgive, and he pours out wrath.
As great as his mercy, so great is also his reproof;
 he judges a man according to his deeds.
The sinner (*'avval*, wrongdoer) will not escape with his plunder,
 and the patience of the godly (*tsaddiq*) will not be
  frustrated.
He will make room for every act of mercy; [Heb.: Everyone who
 does righteousness (*tsedaqah*, perhaps 'acts
 charitably') has his reward (*sakar*)];
 every one will receive in accordance with his deeds. (16.11–14)

Consider the ancient generations and see:
 who ever trusted in the Lord and was put to shame?
Or who ever persevered in the fear of the Lord and was forsaken?
Or who ever called upon him and was overlooked?
For the Lord is compassionate and merciful;
 he forgives sin and saves in time of affliction. (2.10–11)

In the last passage it appears especially clear that God's mercy and compassion consist in his saving those who trust in him and obey him.[20]

 God's doing good to man is generally conceived, however, as his just payment for man's own good deeds. Thus if one does good to a righteous man, one will be repaid, if not by the man, by God (12.2). In addition to the blessings bestowed on a righteous man during his life (39.22–7) and on his descendants (44.10f.), there are two principal rewards mentioned by Ben Sirach for those who obey the commandments: long life and an absence of suffering at death.

To fear the Lord is the root of wisdom,
 and her branches are long life. (1.20; cf. 1.12)

With him who fears the Lord it will go well at the end;
 on the day of his death he will be blessed. (1.13)

The day of death, in fact, looms large in Ben Sirach's view as the time when accounts are settled.[21] According to his optimistic but – as it now appears – naive legalism, those who do the will of God are never let down by him (2.10, above; cf. 7.1f.), nor does good ever come 'to the man who persists in evil' or who does not give alms (12.3). This view obviously leaves unexplained why the wicked flourish and the righteous do not. Ben Sirach's answer is that all will be put right on the day of death: 'call no one happy before his death'. The righteous will pass peacefully away, while the wicked will die in torment:

---

[20] Cf. 18.14, p. 337 below.
[21] Cf. Crenshaw, 'The Problem of Theodicy', who would add sleep and fantasy to death as occasions for divine retribution (p. 60).

²¹Do not wonder at the works of a sinner,
> but trust in the Lord and keep at your toil;
> for it is easy in the sight of the Lord to enrich a poor man
>   quickly and suddenly.
²²The blessing of the Lord is the reward of the godly (*tsaddiq*),
> and quickly God causes his blessing to flourish.
²³Do not say, 'What do I need,
> and what prosperity could be mine in the future?'
²⁴Do not say, 'I have enough,
> and what calamity could happen to me in the future?'
²⁵In the day of prosperity, adversity is forgotten,
> and in the day of adversity, prosperity is not remembered.
²⁶For it is easy in the sight of the Lord
> to reward a man on the day of death according to his conduct.
²⁷The misery of an hour makes one forget luxury,
> and at the close of a man's life his deeds will be revealed.
²⁸Call no one happy before his death;
> for it is by his end that a man will be known. (11.21–8 [26–35])[22]

Although the crucial verse 26 has dropped out of the Hebrew text which remains (see Segal's note to v. 31 in his enumeration), the intent of the passage is nevertheless clear. Lacking a view of an after-life in which reward and punishment would be meted out, Ben Sirach relied on the final hours of a man's life to prove that God's justice was, after all, maintained. For Ben Sirach's view obviously rests on a firm belief in the unwavering justice of God – God is *ha-tsaddiq*, the righteous one (18.2).

It is natural, then, that the author appeals to the possibility of a real distinction between the righteous and sinners on the day of death to support his parenesis. 'In all you do, remember the end of your life, and then you will never sin' (7.36; cf. 18.24; 28.6). The point of the exhortation is not that a man should not sin in view of the fact that he will some day die, but that he should not sin so that he may avoid great suffering at the time of death.

Just as God rewards the righteous, he punishes sinners. In part, this is couched in 'measure for measure' terms: 'Whoever loves danger will perish by it' (3.26); 'Do no evil, and evil will never befall you. Stay away from wrong, and it will turn away from you' (7.1).[23] Generally, however, sin is seen as being directly punished by God.

> Do not commit a sin twice;
> even for one you will not go unpunished. (7.8)

---

[22] The last line is from the Jerusalem Bible, translating the Hebrew. So also the NEB. The RSV, following the Greek, reads: 'a man will be known through his children'.

[23] Conversely, the reward sometimes fits the deed. If a man is like a father to orphans, God will be like a father to him (4.10).

> And the Lord will not delay,
>   neither will he be patient with them,
> till he crushes the loins of the unmerciful
>   and repays vengeance on the nations;
> till he takes away the multitude of the insolent,
>   and breaks the sceptres of the unrighteous (*adikoi*);
> till he repays man according to his deeds,
>   and the works of men according to their devices; . . .
>   (35.18–19; Greek 35.19–22)

We have already seen that the wicked may expect to suffer at the time of death. Ben Sirach also regarded other afflictions in life to be the result of sin; see 10.13 and 12.6, where the wicked are said to be afflicted and punished. He is confident, however, that the righteous, on the other hand, escape affliction:

> Blessed is the man who does not blunder with his lips
>   and need not suffer grief for sin. (14.1)

> No evil will befall the man who fears the Lord,
>   but in trial he will deliver him again and again. (33.1)

Although the Lord will not delay avenging the righteous when they pray and is then not patient with the wicked (35.18, immediately above; God's haste is in response to the prayer of the humble), he is generally long-suffering with man. His slowness to anger may mislead the wicked into thinking that their sins will go unpunished (5.4). Although, as we saw above, God's mercy is thought of as being shown to those who obey him, he is mindful of man's evil plight and therefore inclined to be patient:

> What is man, and of what use is he?
>   What is his good and what is his evil?
> The number of a man's days is great if he reaches a hundred years.
> . . . .
> Therefore the Lord is patient with them
>   and pours out his mercy upon them.
> He sees and recognizes that their end will be evil;
>   therefore he grants them forgiveness in abundance.
> The compassion of man is for his neighbour,
>   but the compassion of the Lord is for all living beings.
> He rebukes and trains and teaches them,
>   and turns them back, as a shepherd his flock.
> He has compassion on those who accept his discipline
>   and who are eager for his judgments. (18.8–9, 11–14)

His patience and forbearance, however, will not prevent his punishing the sinner strictly for his transgressions.

Atonement

But what of atonement? Is the sinner irrevocably doomed to suffering in life and torment at the time of death? Apparently not, since Ben Sirach shared the general belief that atonement is possible. Among good deeds, two are singled out which atone for transgression. They are honouring one's father and giving alms.

> Whoever honours his father atones for sins. (3.3)

> For kindness (*tsedaqah*) to a father will not be forgotten,
>   and as a substitute for sins it shall be firmly planted;[24]
> in the day of your affliction it will be remembered in your
>   favour;
>   as frost in fair weather, your sins will melt away.
> Whoever forsakes his father is like a blasphemer,
>   and whoever angers his mother is cursed by the Lord. (3.14–16 [13–15])

> Water extinguishes a blazing fire:
>   so almsgiving (*tsedaqah*) atones for sin. (3.30 [28]; cf. also 7.32)

> Store up almsgiving (probably *tsedaqah*) in your treasury,
>   and it will rescue you from all affliction. (29.12)

> He who returns a kindness offers fine flour,
>   and he who gives alms sacrifices a thank offering. (35.2)

The precise significance attached by the author to the sacrificial system for obtaining atonement is difficult to estimate. Aaron, he says, was chosen 'to offer sacrifice to the Lord . . . to make atonement for the people' (45.16). It seems likely that Ben Sirach accepted the efficacy of the Temple sacrifices for

---

[24] This line is from the translation of Box and Oesterley in Charles, *Apocrypha*, ad loc. Similarly Schechter and Taylor: 'But it shall be planted instead of sin.' The RSV reads 'and against your sins it will be credited to you'. This inaccurate and tendentious translation requires explanation. The Greek verb is *prosanoikodomeomai*, which Liddell and Scott translate 'to be added for edification', citing only this passage. The Hebrew is תנתע, which makes no sense in this connection: it is apparently the verb translated as 'break' in Job 4.10, where, however, according to Brown, Driver and Briggs, it may be an Aramaic form or a mistake. Box and Oesterley would translate the Greek 'it shall be added to build thee up'. The NEB translates 'put to credit against your sins', and the Jerusalem Bible 'will serve as reparation for your sins'. Following the Syriac of the present passage, Segal suggests תנטע (Schechter had previously made the same emendation). Segal comments: 'The intention is that the kindness will be planted and bring forth good fruit in place of sin' (Segal, p. 16). If the Greek reflects a different original, it would probably be תבנה, 'built', or perhaps 'established' (see Segal, ibid.). In any case the RSV 'credited' and the NEB 'put to credit' imply too legalistic a conception. The *tsedaqah*, kindness, shown to one's father is not 'credited against' one's sins, but *established* or *planted instead of* them (RSV 'against'; Greek, *anti*; but Hebrew, *temur*, instead of). The 'credited against' translation corresponds neither to the Greek nor to any imaginable Hebrew but is an invention, the result of which is to make the passage agree with supposed Jewish ideas of credit and debit. Cf. Büchler's comment in discussing 3.3–5 ('Ben Sira's Conception of Sin and Atonement', *JQR* n.s. 13, 1922–3, p. 471) that, although Christian commentators have found there 'the favorite idea of the balance of sin and merit', he has 'not succeeded in discovering it'.

atonement. There are several passages which mention the Temple service
with obvious appreciation (50.11–21, a description of Simon the High
Priest; 7.29–31, an admonition to honour the priests and present sacrifices).
As Büchler has pointed out, however, Ben Sirach never mentions a private
offering of atonement (a sin- or guilt-offering). (We may also note that he
does not mention the Day of Atonement.) While he accepts the atoning
efficacy of the high priest's daily offering for the people, the private sacrifices
which he recommends are all voluntary offerings. Only 34.19 implies that
individuals bring offerings for atonement, and there the author is concerned
to deny that the offerings of the wicked are efficacious and that a multitude of
such offerings will atone for one who does not correct his behaviour.[25]
It would be a mistake, however, to conclude from his neglect of private
sacrifices of atonement and the Day of Atonement that Ben Sirach would
have denied their efficacy. They are commanded in the Bible, and he
respects the law too much to deny what it commands. It seems more likely
that Ben Sirach presupposes the regular observance of the entire Temple
cultus. Since it is not in danger of being neglected, he need not spend much
time emphasizing its observance. His concern is rather to denounce abuses
of the Temple service, to contest any possible view that it might be efficacious
automatically, and to connect the sacrificial system with the moral life. Thus
a man should not take the efficaciousness of the sacrificial system for granted,
deliberately repeating a sin and supposing that his sacrifices will atone for it:

> [8]Do not commit a sin twice;
>   even for one you will not go unpunished.
> [9]Do not say, 'He will consider the multitude of my gifts,
>   and when I make an offering to the Most High God he
>   will accept it'. (7.8–9)[26]

On the contrary, God will not accept sacrifices bought with ill-gotten goods:

> If one sacrifices from what has been wrongfully obtained,
>   the offering is blemished [Heb., *'olat 'avel*, an
>   offering of iniquity];
>   the gifts of the lawless (*rasha'*) are not acceptable.
> The Most High is not pleased with the offerings of the ungodly
>   (*resha'im*);
>   and he is not propitiated for sins by a multitude of
>   sacrifices [Heb.: and iniquity is not atoned
>   for by a multitude of offerings].
> Like one who kills a son before his father's eyes
>   is the man who offers a sacrifice from the property of the
>   poor. (34.18–20; Heb., 34.19–20)

[25] A. Büchler, 'Ben Sira's Conception of Sin and Atonement', *JQR* n.s. 14, 1923–4, p. 61 n. 124 on
pp. 62f.; cf. pp. 66, 74f., 78.-
[26] V. 9 is missing from the Hebrew because of homoioarchon; Segal, p. 45.

It is only the sacrifice of a righteous man which 'anoints the altar' and which is pleasing to God (35.6f.).

One should, however, make sacrifices, since they are commanded by God (35.1,5). Further, they should be given generously (14.11); a man should spend on them all that he can afford in the confidence that God will repay him sevenfold (35.10f.). When ill, one should not only pray, but present a generous sacrifice (and secure the services of a physician) (38.9–15).

If a man transgresses, he should not only sacrifice, he should repent. As Ben Sirach puts it, he should not be ashamed to turn (*shub*) from iniquity (4.26[27]; RSV: 'to confess your sins', following the Greek). God's forgiveness is extended to those who repent:

> Yet to those who repent he grants a return,
>   and he encourages those whose endurance is failing.
> Turn to the Lord and forsake your sins;
>   pray in his presence and lessen your offences.
> Return to the Most High and turn away from iniquity,
>   and hate abominations intensely.
>   . . . .
> How great is the mercy of the Lord,
>   and his forgiveness for those who turn to him! (17.24–26, 29)

It is clear that Ben Sirach is more interested in having the reader turn away from sin in the sense of avoiding it (so also 35.3) than in encouraging subsequent mental regret. When a man is 'on the point of sinning', he should turn back (18.21). The author does, however, recognize the value of interior reflection. Thus he urges his reader to examine himself before judgment, so that in the hour of visitation he may find forgiveness (18.20), and we read that one who fears the Lord will repent 'in his heart' (21.6). The self-examination presumably gives occasion for the resolution to correct one's conduct.

Just as a man should not presume that he may sin and that his offerings will atone, he should not presume upon God's grace in granting forgiveness and delay turning from iniquity and to the Lord:

> Do not be so confident of forgiveness (RSV: atonement, following the Greek)
>   that you add sin to sin.
> Do not say, 'His mercy is great,
>   He will forgive the multitude of my sins,'
> for both mercy and wrath are with him,
>   and his anger rests on sinners (*resha'im*).
> Do not delay to turn (*shub*) to the Lord,
>   nor postpone it from day to day; . . . (5.5–7a)

What we should call repentance is presumably in mind when Ben Sirach urges that a man should 'pray about' his sins (21.1). If a man forgives his neighbour's wronging him, his own iniquities will be forgiven when he prays (28.2). And prayer will avail to deliver one from the hands of the wicked and from affliction (35.17; 51.8–12). Supplication to the Lord for forgiveness may also involve fasting:

> So if a man fasts for his sins,
>   and goes again and does the same things,
> who will listen to his prayer?
>   And what has he gained by humbling himself? (34.26; Heb., 34.27f.)

But it is clear that the main thing is avoiding transgression and doing what is right.

Covenant, commandments, sin and atonement in Ben Sirach and Rabbinic literature

In many ways Ben Sirach remains closer to the Old Testament, and particularly Deuteronomy, than he is to the Rabbis. He does not believe in the resurrection; he believes that a man is rewarded in this life strictly according to his merits; he thinks that God causes the descendants of a righteous man to flourish, while the children of the wicked are wicked (41.5). The prophets have also set their stamp on his thought, which is seen especially in his emphasis on righteousness in discussing the sacrificial system and on 'turning away' from sin. Yet all these elements – and others – are combined and neatly balanced in a way very like the Rabbinic. He is not far from the view that sacrifices atone *with* repentance (understood as turning away from sin and to the Lord), although the precise formulation is not yet made. Although almost all of Ben Sirach's admonitions concern the treatment of one's fellow and the sins which he excoriates are all transgressions against man and only thereby against God, and not against God alone (as would be the case in transgression of the Sabbath),[27] his demands for private and social justice are not based, as in the case of the prophets, on an appeal to an immediate 'word of the Lord', but on an appeal to 'the commandments', as is the case with the Rabbis. Man will do what is right if he does what God has already commanded, since God's law is eternal (cf. 24.9, on the eternality of wisdom). Charity is elevated as it will also be in Rabbinism. But the main similarity is that one sees here – in the form of 'wisdom' rather than halakah – a neat 'system' which regulates one's relations with God and man. The commandments are given by God and must be obeyed. Transgressions are punished and obedience is rewarded. Yet the transgressor who will can repent, supplicate the Lord, forsake his wrong-doing and escape the punishment of his transgression.

---

[27] Cf. Büchler, *JQR* 14, p. 83; *JQR* 13, p. 472. Haspecker (*Gottesfurcht bei Jesus Sirach*, p. 5) correctly observes that concentration on the relationships between man and man is typical of wisdom literature.

The wicked and the righteous

Büchler argued that there is a distinction in Ben Sirach between the 'transgressions of the habitual sinner' and the 'occasional lapses of the average, observant Jew'.[28] Although, as he noted, it is difficult to define 'the extent of the failure of [habitual] sinners to carry out commandments',[29] the distinction seems to be correct. In Hebrew, the sinners were apparently usually called the 'wicked' (*resha'im*), which was usually translated 'sinner' (*hamartōlos*) or 'ungodly' (*asebēs*) in Greek (and consequently in the RSV).

It is not possible to give a complete or completely accurate account of Ben Sirach's vocabulary for the righteous and the wicked, not only because there is no Hebrew text for about a third of the book, but also because of the disagreements between the Greek and the Hebrew and the general uncertainty as to whether the surviving Hebrew manuscripts and fragments are descendants of the original Hebrew, or whether they may be, at least in part, retranslations from Greek (and/or Syriac).[30] It seems safe enough, however, to indicate the principal terms.

The most frequent Greek word for the wicked in Ben Sirach is *hamartōlos*, sinner. It usually stands where *rasha'* stands in Hebrew (e.g. 5.6; 8.10; 9.11; 13.17; and frequently), although it sometimes represents *ra'* (12.4, 6) or *zed* (זד, insolent) (11.9); cf. 9.11, where *'ish rasha'* is parallel to *zadon*, insolence. *Rasha'* is also translated into Greek (in order of frequency of occurrence) by *asebēs*, 'ungodly' (12.6; 41.5; 41.7; 42.2), *anomos*, 'lawless' (40.10), and *adikos*, 'unrighteous' (35.18[21]). *Rasha'* is clearly the principal Hebrew word for the wicked. A wicked man is also called *'avval*, 'unjust man', 'wrongdoer' (16.13; Greek, *hamartōlos*), just as the author also speaks of 'injustice' or 'wrong' (*'avlah*, 16.1). Another parallel term is 'insolent man', *zed* (12.5[7]; cf. *zadon*, 'insolence), 16.3; 13.24[28]).

The principal term for the good man is in Greek *eusebēs*, in Hebrew *tsaddiq*: 11.17(21); 11.22(28); 12.2; 13.17(19); 16.13. *Eusebēs* also translates 'good', *tob* (12.4[7]; 39.27[37]) and 'good man', *'ish tob* (33.14[17]). It does not, as far as I have noted, translate 'pious', *ḥasid*. (Segal supplies *ḥasidim* in 43.33, but the Hebrew fragment is defective; he also supplies *ḥasid* in 27.29, where there is no Hebrew text.) Once *eusebēs* translates 'fearer' (37.12). *Dikaios* is occasionally used for *tsaddiq*: 9.16 (*andres dikaioi* for *'anshe tsedeq*); 44.17.[31]

All the terms for the wicked apply to the same group, just as the terms for the righteous do. Thus *ra'* is parallel to *rasha'* (41.5), *'ish rasha'* is parallel to *zadon*

---

[28] Büchler, *JQR* 13, p. 304.   [29] Ibid., p. 311.

[30] For the debate, see A. A. Di Lella, *The Hebrew Text of Sirach*, 1966. Di Lella argues that the Cairo Genizah mss. basically represent the original Hebrew. In the case of some doublets, one member of which is 'classical' and close to the Greek while the other is Mishnaic, he explains the latter as a retroversion from Syriac. The Cairo mss. had as their *Vorlage* a ms. or mss. found in a cave near Jerusalem, probably at Qumran, near the end of the eighth century. Fragments recently found at Qumran generally agree with the Cairo mss. (p. 92). The Matsada fragment agrees with 'style B' of the Genizah version (pp. 80f.). Di Lella's theory about retroversions from Syriac has been contested by Rüger, supported by Marböck. See *Weisheit im Wandel*, pp. 4f. The general reliability of the Genizah manuscripts is not however, in dispute.

[31] Cf. Ziesler, *The Meaning of Righteousness in Paul*, p. 73. He does not note the translation in 9.16 of *'anshe tsedeq* by *andres dikaioi*, which is substantially equivalent to translating *tsaddiqim* by *dikaioi*.

(9.11f.; *zadon* here and in 13.24[28] seems to be used to mean 'the insolent', not 'insolence'), *rasha'* is parallel to 'tribe of insolence' (*zadon*, 35.18[21]), and *rasha'*, *zed* and *ra'* are all parallel in 12.4–6(6f.). In the same passage, they are opposite *tob* and *makh*, 'humble'. *Rasha'* is opposite *tsaddiq* in 13.17(19). The *'anshe tsedeq* (9.16) are doubtless the opposites of the *'anshe rasha'* (41.8[11]).[32] Similarly, *'avval* is opposite *tsaddiq* (16.13).

The distinction between the wicked and occasional sinners may be seen in chapter 21, which begins with a gentle admonition to the reader, presumably the 'average, observant Jew':

> Have you sinned, my son? Do so no more,
> but pray about your former sins. (21.1)

Later the author speaks of another group in the third person:

> An assembly of the wicked is like tow gathered together,
> and their end is a flame of fire.
> The way of sinners is smoothly paved with stones,
> but at its end is the pit of Hades. (21.9f.)

Similarly, it is the wicked (those who will later be called the 'completely wicked') who are in mind in 41.5–10 (8–13):

> The children of sinners (*ra'im*)[33] are abominable children,
> and they frequent the haunts of the ungodly (*rasha'*).
> The inheritance of the children of sinners will perish,
> and on their posterity will be a perpetual reproach.
> Children will blame an ungodly (*rasha'*) father,
> for they suffer reproach because of him.
> Woe to you, ungodly men (*'anshe rasha'*),
> who have forsaken the law of the Most High God!
> When you are born, you are born to a curse;
> and when you die, a curse is your lot.
> Whatever is from the dust returns to dust;
> so the ungodly go from curse to destruction.

After this harsh word to the wicked, Ben Sirach turns to his 'children' (41.14), gently urging them to be ashamed of immorality, of lying, of transgressing, of iniquity, of unjust dealing and of theft (41.17–19). These individual sins, while they are to be avoided and should be atoned for, clearly do not put the transgressor in the category of the 'wicked'. Presumably one could commit even such sins and still be one of the *tsaddiqim*. He would not, of course, be called *tsaddiq* when his transgression was in mind, but if all

---

[32] *Rasha'* is restored by Segal, but *'avval* by Lévi. The Hebrew ms. has a lacuna.

[33] The Matsada ms. has *toldot ra'im* for the curious *dabar ra'im* of the Cairo Genizah ms. If *toldot* is understood as 'generations' in the sense of 'descendants', the Greek *tekna* is seen to be substantially correct. For an effort to derive the right meaning from *dabar*, see G. R. Driver, 'Hebrew Notes on the "Wisdom of Jesus Ben Sirach"', *JBL* 53, 1934, pp. 282f.

Israel is divided into the *tsaddiqim* and the *resha'im*, as it appears to be in Ben Sirach (see below), individual transgressions do not serve to make one a *rasha'*. The *tsaddiqim* will not, however, be guilty of the most heinous sins, such as blasphemy, which bring death (23.12).

Besides the general charge of having *forsaken God's law* (41.8), the sin which is singled out as characterizing the wicked is *exploitation of and unjust behaviour towards others*. They build their houses with the money of others (21.8), offer their sacrifices with money derived from the poor (34.20), and deprive the poor and their own employees (34.21f.). But what underlies this unjust behaviour is arrogance and pride towards both man and God. Pride and false confidence, on the other hand, are generated by sin and the thought that one is 'getting away with it'. 'Arrogance is hateful before the Lord and before men' (10.7), but arrogance is bred when one departs from the Lord (10.12). The sinner should not say ' "I sinned, and what happened to me?" ' (5.4). That attitude, which leads one arrogantly to postpone repentance (5.5–7), epitomizes the attitude of the wicked. Thus a man should not suppose that he can sin and later buy God off with gifts (7.9; 35.12), nor that God does not see him when he sins (23.18f.), nor that he is secure in his unrighteous prosperity (11.23f.). Such a person persists in evil (12.3; cf. 23.10), and this persistence is one of the defining characteristics of the wicked. Their behaviour is thus characterized as 'insolent' (35.18[21]; 9.12; 13.24; the last two are translated 'ungodly' in Greek), and they are proud and stubborn (3.26–28). If even these repent, however, God 'grants a return' (17.24; this is also apparently the point of the exhortation to the wicked in 5.4ff. to return).[34]

Ben Sirach appropriately observed that just as good is the opposite of evil, the wicked (*rasha'*; Greek: 'sinner') is the opposite of the good man ('*ish tob*; Greek: 'godly') (33.14[17]). As he puts the alternative elsewhere:

> What fellowship has a wolf with a lamb?
> No more has a sinner (*rasha'*) with a godly man (*tsaddiq*). (13.17[19])

The righteous man is frequently considered one who fears the Lord. The meaning of the phrase can best be understood by quoting a passage about one who does not fear the Lord:

> A man who breaks his marriage vows
>   says to himself, 'Who sees me?
> Darkness surrounds me, and the walls hide me,
>   and no one sees me. Why should I fear?
> The Most High will not take notice of my sins.'
> His fear is confined to the eyes of men,
>   and he does not realize that the eyes of the Lord
>   are ten thousand times brighter than the sun;

[34] So also Büchler, *JQR* 13, p. 314.

> they look upon all the ways of men,
>> and perceive even the hidden places. (23.18f.)

Just as the attitude of the wicked man is arrogance and the false confidence that he can 'get away with' his sin, the attitude of the righteous is humility and respect for the Lord. Thus the humble of 35.17 are opposed to the insolent and the wicked of 35.18. It is the attitude of humility which Ben Sirach calls 'fearing the Lord' (2.17: 'those who fear the Lord ... will humble themselves before him'), and this is the precise opposite of the insolent attitude of the wicked man who fears only man but not God (23.18f., quoted immediately above). The righteous man humbly accepts God's discipline and his judgments (18.24), while the wicked think that they are immune. It is evident that Ben Sirach's nomism, which is based on confidence in God's justice and mercy, is not to be equated with works-righteous legalism in the pejorative sense, in which a man arrogantly thinks that his good deeds establish a claim on God. Arrogance is precisely what Ben Sirach excoriates. The righteous man is humble and trusts in God's mercy.

The attitude of humility and respect leads to obeying the Lord's commandments, and 'fearing the Lord' cannot be separated from obeying: 'nothing is better than the fear of the Lord, and nothing sweeter than to heed the commandments of the Lord' (23.27). Similarly, the one who fears the Lord is paralleled with the one who keeps the law in 15.1, while in 10.19 and 19.24 fearing the Lord is the opposite of transgressing his commandments. In 19.20 the author says that fear of the Lord is wisdom, while in wisdom there is fulfilment of the law.

Fear of the Lord, however, is not a negative kind of fear which leads to obedience as the easiest means of avoiding punishment. It can be described in much more positive terms than that:

> The fear of the Lord is glory and exultation,
>> and gladness and a crown of rejoicing.
> The fear of the Lord delights the heart,
>> and gives gladness and joy and long life.
> With him who fears the Lord it will go well at the end;
>> on the day of his death he will be blessed. (1.11–13)

Further, it is equated with loving the Lord:

> Those who fear the Lord will not disobey his words,
>> and those who love him will keep his ways.
> Those who fear the Lord will seek his approval,
>> and those who love him will be filled with the law.
> Those who fear the Lord will prepare their hearts,
>> and will humble themselves before him. (2.15–17; so also 34.15–17)[35]

[35] For a fuller description of 'fear of God' as a term for true piety, see Haspecker, *Gottesfurcht bei Jesus Sirach*, especially pp. 205–335.

It is evident, however, that even one who 'fears the Lord' does not obey his commandments perfectly. The bulk of the book seems to be addressed to people who are basically righteous but in need of admonition and correction (at least in the author's opinion).[36] It appears that one who respects and loves the Lord, though he may transgress, does not do so arrogantly, does not suppose that he is beyond God's reach, does not delay repentance or rely on abundant sacrificing at some later date, but hastens to repent and does not repeat the transgression. The many admonitions against depriving one's fellow may seem to imply that compensation for wrong-doing would also be expected, although this is not explicitly stated. (Compensation is, of course, required by the Old Testament.) The person who thus repents and does whatever else is appropriate, it would appear, retains the adjective 'righteous', is not classed with the wicked, and continues to be one who 'fears the Lord' and who will therefore enjoy long life, an easy death and righteous children. We should recall our earlier observation that Ben Sirach does not bring the distinction between the righteous and the wicked into connection with the election of Israel. The unrepentant wicked are not explicitly said to forfeit their place among the elect, although this may be implied in saying that they have forsaken the Torah (41.8). Their fate is primarily formulated individualistically. In distinction to the righteous, they have a short life or, failing that, a painful death, and their children are 'abominable' (41.5).

2. I Enoch[1]

Introduction

I Enoch offers difficulties of two different kinds for our study. First are the standard introductory problems, which are unusually complex. The book is universally recognized as composite, and there is even widespread agreement on the major divisions.[2] The date of each section is, however, uncertain, as is the date of the final redaction;[3] and one can by no means safely assume

---

[36] So also Büchler, *JQR* 13, pp. 311f.

[1] Quotations are from Charles's translation in *Pseudepigrapha*. For the fragments of the Greek text I have used Bonner's edition of chs. 97–107 and those of Lods and Charles (in *I Enoch*) for the fragments of chs. 1–32. I have also consulted the Greek fragments in Black's recent edition. Aramaic fragments have been found at Qumran, and an edition has been announced by Milik and Black. See J. T. Milik, 'Problèmes de la Littérature Hénochique à la Lumière des Fragments Araméens de Qumrân', *HTR* 64, 1971, p. 333.
[2] See Charles's analysis in *I Enoch*, pp. xlvi–lvi, as well as his introductions to each section in his commentary. The same views are found in shorter form in *Pseudepigrapha*, pp. 168–71. Charles's basic divisions are generally accepted. See e.g. Rowley, *The Relevance of Apocalyptic*,[3] pp. 57–64 (citing also further literature); Black, *Apocalypsis Henochi Graece*, p. 5; Dupont-Sommer, *The Essene Writings from Qumran*, p. 299 (the major divisions are supported by the Qumran fragments).
[3] See Rowley, *Apocalyptic*, pp. 93–8.

that each major division is itself integral.[4] In what follows, I have generally followed Charles's division of the book. I have not followed him, however, in thinking that some of the sections are pre-Maccabean.[5] Each of the parts seems to fit well into a context in the Maccabean period, and I have made no effort to date the material more precisely. A very precise dating of the component parts could be little more than conjecture.

The knottiest and most important problem among the standard introductory questions is the date of the Similitudes. chs. 37–71. The question is whether they are pre-Christian or post-Christian. The possibility of post-Christian origin was pressed by Milik, against the prevailing consensus, on the ground that no fragments from this section were found at Qumran, although fragments of all the other sections were found.[6] Scholars seem generally to have been unpersuaded by this argument, holding the absence of fragments to be accidental.[7] Milik has now given a more detailed and more convincing argument.[8] To summarize a lengthy treatment very briefly: Milik has argued that the division of the book into five sections is early, the divisions being modelled on the Pentateuch. The second book, however, was originally the Book of the Giants, which is evidenced by its having been used by Mani (Milik, p. 373). A Christian redactor of I Enoch substituted the Similitudes as the second book (p. 375). I Enoch 56.6f. refers to the invasions of the Byzantine Empire during the third century c.e. and in particular to the victories of Sapor I which culminated in the imprisonment of Valerian in September 260 (p. 377). Further victories of the Parthians followed, and these are what are in mind in the Similitudes (p. 377). The references to the blood of the just (47.1–4) are to the persecution of Christians in 249–51 and 257–8; the book was written *ca.* 270 (p. 377).

Another setting has been given the Similitudes by J. C. Hindley.[9] He notes the absence of fragments from Qumran (Hindley, p. 553) and, more important, the paucity of even possible references to the Similitudes in the New Testament and the early fathers (p. 564), but the main argument concerns the reference to the Parthians in 56.5–7 and the connection between the Parthians and the return of the exiles in chs. 56–57. Hindley makes an unusually cogent argument that these passages are best explained by dating the Similitudes between 115 and 117 c.e.

It would be premature to accept any one reconstruction for the date of the Similitudes, but it now seems the better part of wisdom to regard the section

---

[4] See Charles, above, n. 2.
[5] See Rowley's discussion, *Apocalyptic*, pp. 93–8.
[6] Milik, *Ten Years of Discovery*, p. 33.
[7] Thus Dupont-Sommer, *The Essene Writings from Qumran*, pp. 299f.
[8] Milik, 'Problèmes de la Littérature Hénochique', *HTR* 64, 1971, pp. 333–78.
[9] Hindley, 'Towards a Date for the Similitudes of Enoch', *NTS* 14, 1968, pp. 551–65.

as probably post-Christian in origin. Milik's negative argument, that the Similitudes have displaced a former Book II in the collection, while still speculative, seems at least as likely as not. The possibility of finding other historical contexts which are at least as fitting as the Maccabean period robs the argument for pre-Christian origin on the basis of historical congruence of its force. The Christian ring of the passages about the Son of Man sitting on the throne of his glory (e.g. 62.5) seems easier to explain on the hypothesis of a post-Christian date than not. The alternative that Christianity took over the figure and the characteristics of the otherwise unattested Son of Man and attributed them to Jesus cannot be conclusively disproved, but the remarkable role played by the Son of Man seems to favour a post-Christian origin. Accordingly, chs. 37–71 are omitted in the following discussion.[10]

I Enoch is also difficult for our present purposes because of the character of the work. In typical apocalyptic fashion, the work deals with generations more than individuals. As we shall see, the righteous and the wicked are constantly discussed, but one gains very little idea of how, in the view of the various authors, an individual lived a righteous life, what happened if he sinned, and where the line between the righteous and the wicked is. The principal problem of the book as a whole, as it touches our investigation, is the identity of the righteous and elect. The necessity to obey and punishment for disobedience and reward for obedience are constant themes, and they need not be singled out for special comment. But the questions which are difficult to answer are these: who are the elect, what does one obey, and how obedient does he have to be to be considered among the righteous? We shall deal with these themes section by section.

The Book of Noah

Charles identified the Book of Noah as being found in chs. 6–11; 54.7–55.2; 60; 65–69.25; 106–7.[11] It is perhaps more common now to connect chs. 6–11 with 12–36, to consider chs. 106–7 to constitute the Noah appendix, and to consider all the material of chs. 37–71 to be integral to that section.[12] In the present discussion I shall follow Charles in connecting chs. 6–11 with 106–7 and treating 12–36 separately, but the sections attributed to the Book of Noah which are now in the Similitudes will be disregarded.

The primordial sin in the Book of Noah – as in other parts of I Enoch and

[10] Similarly E. Schweizer, *Jesus*, ET, p. 18: the Similitudes cannot be dated.

[11] Charles (I Enoch, p. xlvii and elsewhere) lists the second fragment as beginning with 54.1 rather than 54.7. It is evident from his edition, however, that he considered the fragment to begin at 54.7. On the separate identity of the Book of Noah, see Dupont-Sommer, op. cit., p. 299.

[12] Thus, for example, Rowley, *Apocalyptic*, p. 57; Black, *Apocalypsis Henochi Graece*, p. 5. Black notes that section I is not homogeneous, but he does not connect 6–11 to 106–7. Charles's reconstruction is closely followed by Rost, *Einleitung in die alttestamentlichen Apokryphen und Pseudepigraphen*, p. 103.

in Jubilees – is the union of the 'sons of God' with the daughters of men (Gen. 6.3).[13] The sons of God are considered to be fallen and evil angels (I Enoch 6.1ff. and passim). The nature of the sin is not sharply defined. The angels are doubtless considered to have transgressed the ordained order and thereby the will of God (106.14: they commit sin and transgress the law in uniting themselves with women). They are also guilty of unlawful fornication (the offspring are bastards, 10.9), and they may have been thought to have copulated with women during the menstrual period, which is against Jewish law. Thus in 10.11 they are said to have 'defiled themselves with [women] in all their uncleanness', where 'their uncleanness' may refer to the menstrual impurity of women. This possibility gains some support from 15.4 (presumably from another source), where the watcher angels are said to have defiled themselves with the blood of women. In any case, the fallen angels not only transgressed themselves, but passed on secrets to men which led them to transgress and consequently share the angels' punishment (9.6–9; cf. 65.6f., where the secrets are specified). Magic and sorcery, as well as astrology, are also mentioned as having come from the fallen angels in chs. 7 and 8. Men will continue in transgression until the generation of righteousness, when transgression is destroyed and sin passes away (107.1).

A little help for understanding what is counted as sin comes from the list of terms in 10.20: 'And cleanse thou,' God says to Michael, 'the earth from all oppression, and from all unrighteousness, and from all sin, and from all godlessness: and all the uncleanness that is wrought upon the earth destroy from off the earth. And all the children of men shall become righteous,[14] and all nations shall offer adoration and praise Me, and all shall worship Me. And the earth shall be cleansed from all defilement, and from all sin, and from all punishment, and from all torment, and I will never again send (them) upon it from generation to generation and for ever.' The terms in Greek are these: cleanse the earth from all *akatharsia* and from all *adikia* and from all *hamartia* and *asebeia*; and eradicate all the *akatharsia*. While there is no reason to suppose that the author followed a strict definition of terms, it is likely that 'uncleanness' refers both to transgression of purity laws and to the moral defilement which comes from certain other transgressions and that 'oppression' (*adikia*) refers to wrongs against one's neighbour, while 'sin' and 'godlessness' are probably translations of 'sin' and 'wickedness' in Hebrew or Aramaic and refer generally to transgression of biblical commandments. While what it is wrong to do is persistently left vague, it seems that the author of the Book of Noah had no unique definition. The

---

[13] For the history of the myth, see Julian Morgenstern, 'The Mythological Background of Psalm 82', *HUCA* 14, 1939, pp. 29–126; the myth of the union is discussed on pp. 76–114.
[14] This phrase is not in the Gizeh Greek fragment.

sinners are those who transgress the will of God. We should note that a transgressor is 'guilty' or a 'debtor' (6.3, Greek: *opheiletēs*), which is probably a translation of a derivative of *ḥub*.

With regard to the definition and characteristics of the righteous we are told very little in these fragments. The righteous will escape destruction on the day of judgment when the wicked are destroyed (10.17), but one is left to infer who they are only from the definition of the wicked. The most general way of putting it is that the righteous must be those who obey the will of God, just as the unrighteous disobey. They presumably avoid sin, wickedness and uncleanness.

I Enoch 12–36

In chs. 12–13, as in the Book of Noah, the fallen angels are condemned because of having shown men godlessness (*asebeia*), unrighteousness (*adikēmata, adikia*) and sin (*hamartia*) (13.2). They find no forgiveness (*aphesis*, 12.5), despite the fact that they prevail upon Enoch to present a petition for forgiveness on their behalf. Even the stars which did not 'come forth at their appointed times' are considered to have 'transgressed the commandment of the Lord'. They provoked God's anger (*orgisthē*) and are punished (18.15).[15] In 19.2 the angels are said not only to have defiled mankind, but to have led them astray 'into sacrificing to demons'. Otherwise their sin is not specified.

In 22.9–13, all men are divided into three groups. One division is that of the righteous (22.9, *dikaioi*) or pious (22.13, *hosioi*). They are put in Sheol into a 'hollow place' 'in which there is a spring of bright water'. Sinners who were not punished in their lifetime are segregated from those who were. The latter 'shall not be punished in the day of judgement nor shall they be raised from thence' (22.13). The righteous are apparently raised and rewarded, while the unpunished sinners are raised and punished.

It appears not only from 22.9,13, but also from 25.5 that 'righteous' and 'pious' (Charles, 'holy') are used synonymously. If the Greek fragment here accurately represents the Hebrew or Aramaic, the term *dikaioi* probably translates *tsaddiqim*, while *hosioi* translates *ḥasidim* (or the Aramaic equivalents). In 25.5 the righteous and pious are equated with the elect. The righteous, pious and elect, after God visits 'the earth with goodness' (25.3), will enter 'the holy place' where there is a fragrant tree, and there they shall live a long and untroubled life (25.3–7). It is especially noteworthy that God's 'true judgement' condemns the 'accursed', while the righteous bless God 'for the mercy in accordance with which He has assigned them (their

---

[15] Cf. also 21.6. The stars which transgress are not the same as the fallen angels, despite Charles's heading to ch. 21: 'Punishment of the fallen Angels (stars).' The seer goes from the place where the stars are punished (21.6) to 'another place' (21.7) where the angels are punished (21.10).

lot)' (27.3f.). We shall repeatedly see that whereas God pays the wicked their just deserts, he is considered to show mercy to the righteous. Their very 'allotment' as righteous and elect is due to the mercy of God.

I Enoch 83–90

The section of the 'dream-visions' opens with a grim warning: 'upon the earth there will be great destruction' (83.9) because of sin. Enoch is urged to pray to God, since he is a believer, that a remnant may remain and that all the earth will not be destroyed (83.8). In his prayer, he acknowledges that God's wrath abides on mankind until the great judgment (84.4) and prays that God will 'destroy from the earth the flesh which has aroused [his] wrath', while establishing 'the flesh of righteousness and uprightness' (84.6).

Although Israel, which is compared to a flock of sheep, had been pastured and fed by the Lord (89.28), not all remained faithful to him. 'Sometimes their eyes were opened, and sometimes blinded' (89.41). Finally they 'erred and went many ways, and forsook that their house' (the Temple, 89.51). In return, God forsook the Temple and handed the sheep over to the lions, rejoicing in their destruction (89.56–58). The sheep that were left were given to seventy shepherds, who were commanded to destroy some of the sheep but keep others alive (89.59f.). The shepherds, however, went beyond their instructions and destroyed sheep which were to be kept alive (89.61,69), for which they are punished at the judgment (90.25). This is evidently an explanation for the death of righteous Israelites, as well as wicked, at the hands of their enemies.[16]

At the judgment, some of the sheep – the blinded ones – are 'judged and found guilty and cast into [the] fiery abyss' (90.26). The remnant of the sheep that remain are all good (90.30,33). 'And the eyes of them all were opened, and they saw the good, and there was not one among them that did not see' (90.35).

This section is remarkable because it concentrates on the wicked within Israel rather than Israel's enemies. We are not told precisely what distinguishes a blind sheep which deserves destruction from one which does not, but the issue seems to have been one of basic loyalty to Judaism. The blind sheep forsook the Temple (89.51). Although, in the chronology of the section, this reference may be to the period before the first destruction of the Temple, it is very likely to indicate the issue alive in the author's day. Those who are loyal will be saved at the judgment, while apostates will be destroyed.

[16] So also Charles, commenting on 89.59. 'Had they [the Shepherds] only fulfilled their commission, the Gentiles could not have made havoc of Israel and apostate Jews only could have been cut off' (*I Enoch*, p. 200).

I Enoch 91–104

This section is especially interesting for our study, since we are told a great deal about the unrighteous.

> Woe unto you, ye sinners, for your riches make you appear like
>   the righteous ... (96.4)

> Woe to you who work unrighteousness
> And deceit and blasphemy:
> It shall be a memorial against you for evil.
> Woe to you, ye mighty,
> Who with might oppress the righteous;
> For the day of your destruction is coming.
> In those days many and good days shall come to the righteous –
>   in the day of your judgement. (96.7f.)

> And unrighteousness shall again be consummated on the earth,
> And all the deeds of unrighteousness and of violence
> And transgression shall prevail in a twofold degree.
> And when sin and unrighteousness and blasphemy
> And violence in all kinds of deeds increase,
> And apostasy and transgression and uncleanness increase,
> A great chastisement shall come from heaven upon all these,
> And the holy Lord will come forth with wrath and chastisement
> To execute judgement on earth.
> In those days violence shall be cut off from its roots,
> And the roots of unrighteousness together with deceit,
> And they shall be destroyed from under heaven.
> And all the idols of the heathen shall be abandoned,
> And the temples burned with fire,
> And they shall remove them from the whole earth,
> And they (i.e. the heathen) shall be cast into the judgement of fire,
> And shall perish in wrath and in grievous judgement for ever.
> And the righteous shall arise from their sleep,
> And wisdom shall arise and be given unto them. (91.6–10)

The sinners are repeatedly condemned for being rich (cf. also 94.8; 100.6; 104.6), doubtless because their gold and silver has been acquired 'in unrighteousness' (97.8), which apparently involves not just dishonest dealings (they 'build their houses with sin' and acquire gold and silver in judgment, 94.7), but plundering the righteous (104.3). They have behaved violently (91.6; 104.6; cf. 92.18). Those who plunder the righteous do so with the support of the rulers (104.3). They are the 'mighty' (96.8). They persecute the righteous (95.7), rejoice in their tribulation (98.13), and behave unrighteously towards them, or oppress them. 'Oppression' is mentioned in Charles's translation in 94.6; 96.8; 98.6; 98.8; 99.15 (the list is not necessarily exhaustive). For 94.6 and 96.8 there is no Greek fragment extant. In 98.6, 'oppression' is in Greek *adikon*, which is parallel to *ta ponēra*, 'evil deeds'. In 98.8 the Greek word is *adikēmata*; in 99.15 it is apparently *adikia*; only *adi–* is left. The Greek could just as well imply other kinds of unrighteousness than 'oppression'. Yet it is clear in any case that the wicked did oppress the righteous. We have already seen that they are violent. They are also said to slay their neighbours (99.15), to 'afflict the righteous and burn them with fire' (100.7), and to 'execute judgement on the righteous' (100.10).

It is difficult to determine whether those who so treat the righteous are Gentiles, unrighteous Jews or both. Charles thought that the righteous were the Pharisees and the wicked an alliance of 'the Sadducees, sinners, apostates, and paganizers'. This strange alliance was, in his view, maintained in a period when the Sadducees and the ruling Maccabees acted in concert.[17] Charles's general method for dating the Enoch material (and also other pseudepigrapha) was to identify the works as Pharisaic and to date them according to Josephus's account of the fortunes of the Pharisees. Since, however, it is very unlikely that I Enoch, either in whole or in part, is Pharisaic, Charles's explanation collapses. The strangeness of the alliance which must have been in effect on Charles's view (Sadducees and paganizers) should in any case warn against the precise identification of the righteous as Pharisees and the sinners as Sadducees and their allies.

The wicked do appear, in part at least, to have been Israelites. They are accused of perverting 'the words of uprightness' and transgressing 'the eternal law' (99.2; cf. 104.10, the sinners 'will alter and pervert the words of righteousness [Greek, 'truth'] in many ways'). While the heathen could be accused of transgressing the law, it seems more likely that the wicked are here apostate Jews who appeal to an erroneous (from the point of view of the author) interpretation of the law. The accusation that the wicked blaspheme (above, 91.7; 96.7; also 94.9) seems also to refer to apostates, although, again, Gentiles cannot be completely excluded. The rich and mighty do not seem to be identical with the rulers, but supported by them. Thus 104.3 reads (in Charles's translation of the Ethiopic): 'For all your tribulation shall be visited on the rulers, and on all who helped those who plundered you.' The Greek fragment does not mention rulers, but refers only vaguely to those who helped and partook in the oppression of the righteous. If the Ethiopic is followed, it is still not perfectly clear whether the rulers plundered and were helped by others or whether they were among those who helped the plunderers, although the latter seems more likely. This is supported by the accusation against the rulers that they fail to redress the wrongs suffered by the righteous (103.14) and help the plunderers (103.15). Otherwise, however, the rulers are not the object of direct attack

[17] Charles, *Pseudepigrapha* and *I Enoch*, commenting on 103.14f. See further *I Enoch*, pp. 221–2.

by the author. They seem to be the distant authorities – whether Syrian, Maccabean or Roman – with whom the apostate Israelites collaborate in their active persecution and despoliation of the righteous.

The phrase which caused Charles to add 'paganizers' to the list of the allies against the righteous was doubtless 99.7: 'And they who worship stones, and grave images of gold and silver and wood [and stone] and clay, and those who worship impure spirits and demons, and all kinds of idols not according to knowledge, shall get no manner of help from them' (cf. also 99.9). Those in mind here are neither apostate Jews nor 'paganizers' in the sense of those who built a gymnasium in Jerusalem. Unless 99.7 is an interpolation (for which there is no evidence), it indicates that the wicked included Gentiles. This is supported by the reference in 91.9 to the coming destruction of heathen idols and temples. Thus it seems that the wicked are both the apostate and traitorous Israelites who collaborate with the rulers, thus gaining the right to become rich at the expense of loyal Jews, and the 'carpet-bagging' Gentiles who are in league with them. The author, it would appear, saw no real difference between the foreign wicked and the natives who betrayed their people for their own interest. The section, it would seem, comes from a period when Palestine was under foreign influence, if not direct rule.

The attitude of the sinners is false confidence in their own security and the assumption that there is no retribution after death:

> Woe to you who acquire silver and gold in unrighteousness and say:
> 'We have become rich with riches and have possessions;
> And have acquired everything we have desired.
> And now let us do what we purposed:
> For we have gathered silver,
> And many are the husbandmen in our houses.'
> And our granaries are (brim) full as with water,
> Yea and like water your lies shall flow away. . . . (97.8f.)

> And yet when ye [the righteous] die the sinners speak over you:
> 'As we die, so die the righteous,
> And what benefit do they reap for their deeds?
> Behold, even as we, so do they die in grief and darkness,
> And what have they more than we?
> From henceforth we are equal.
> And what will they receive and what will they see for ever?
> Behold, they too have died,
> And henceforth for ever shall they see no light.'[18] (102.6–8)

---

[18] Charles not unreasonably took the passage to represent the Sadducean view (see his comments ad loc.). It could just as well, however, represent the view of the heathen, idolaters and apostates. The nearest parallel is Wisd. Sol. 2.1–5, 21–24; 5.4 ('We thought . . . that his [the righteous man's] end was without honour'), which does *not* represent the Pharisee/Sadducee argument. It is simplistic to suppose that all who believed in the resurrection were Pharisees and all who denied it Sadducees.

And, although ye sinners say: 'All our sins shall not be searched out and be written down,' nevertheless they shall write down all your sins every day. (104.7; cf. 98.7 on the recording of sins.)

In a word, the sinners of this section of I Enoch, like those of Ben Sirach, 'fear not the Most High' (101.9; cf. 101.7). The falseness of their self-confidence will be manifest at the judgment, when the rich see that their wealth does not save them (100.6).

The righteous, on the other hand, 'fear' God (101.1; Greek: fear to do evil before him). Unlike the sinners, they obey the law. They

> . . . accept the words of wisdom, and understand them,
> And observe the paths of the Most High, and walk in the path of
>   His righteousness (*dikaiosyne*),
> And became not godless with the godless;
> For they shall be saved. (99.10)

The righteous, of course, are the opposite of those who do violence (91.18f.; 94.1f.) and those who walk in the paths of wickedness and death (94.3). They suffer here, but are promised that in the hereafter they shall find rest and peace:

> Wherefore fear not, ye that have suffered;
> For healing shall be your portion,
> And a bright light shall enlighten you,
> And the voice of rest ye shall hear from heaven. (96.3; cf. also 102.4f.)[19]

Those who are righteous (*dikaioi*) and pious (*hosioi*) are urged not to complain of their troubles and persecutions, nor even of the fact that the rulers who should have defended them 'helped those who robbed us' (103.9-15). In this long passage the author adroitly states in full the complaint of the righteous, while also urging that the righteous should not complain. The last lines of the complaint (103.14f.) demonstrate beyond doubt that the oppressors are in collaboration with and have the support of the rulers. The righteous are assured, however, that even though their plight goes unheeded here, the angels remember them before God (104.1), and they shall be vindicated and 'shine as the lights of heaven' (104.2; cf. 103.3), while their tribulation shall be visited on the rulers and those that plundered them (104.3).

Just as sin is voluntary (98.4: 'sin has not been sent upon the earth, but man of himself has created it'), the righteous are able to 'choose for [themselves] righteousness and an elect life' (94.4). It is especially striking that 'election' can be chosen (a phenomenon which we saw also in the Dead Sea

---

[19] 102.4 reads in Charles's translation: 'Fear ye not, ye souls of the righteous, And be hopeful ye that have died in righteousness.' In Greek it is 'Be of good courage, the souls of the righteous (*dikaioi*) that are dead, the righteous (*dikaioi*) and pious (*eusebeis*).'

Scrolls). This exhortation corresponds to the constant exhortations not to walk 'in the paths of wickedness' (94.3).

The wicked are consistently said to be paid according to their deeds:

> Woe to you who requite your neighbour with evil;
> For you shall be requited according to your works. (95.5)

> Woe to you, sinners [Greek: 'unrighteous'], on the day of
>   strong anguish,
> Ye who afflict the righteous and burn them with fire:
> Ye shall be requited according to your works. (100.7)[20]

While the righteous are also said to be recompensed in the final judgment for their labours (103.3),[21] the author characteristically thinks that the reward of the righteous in the resurrection will not be earned by works, but be given by the mercy of God; even the righteous man's continuing uprightness in the new life will be by grace:

> He [God] will be gracious to the righteous and give him eternal
>   uprightness,
> And He will give him power so that he shall be (endowed) with
>   goodness and righteousness,
> And he shall walk in eternal light.
> And sin shall perish in darkness for ever,
> And shall no more be seen from that day for evermore. (92.4f.)

On the other hand the wicked, being paid strictly according to their works, will receive no mercy, nor is there atonement ('ransom') for them:

And for your fall there shall be no compassion,
And your Creator will rejoice at your destruction. (94.10)

Woe to you who fulminate anathemas which cannot be reversed:
Healing shall therefore be far from you because of your sins. (95.4)

Woe to you, ye fools, for through your folly shall ye perish: and ye transgress against the wise, and so good hap shall not be your portion. And now, know ye that ye are prepared for the day of destruction: wherefore do not hope to live [Greek: 'be saved'],[22] ye sinners, but ye shall depart and die; for ye know no ransom; for ye are prepared for the day of the great judgement, for the day of tribulation and great shame for your spirits. (98.9f.; so also 98.12, 14)

Despite this hard view, the author apparently thinks it possible for the sinners to turn and repent, although the word is not used. Thus he addresses to them this appeal:

---

[20] According to 98.5, a 'measure for measure' punishment is sometimes meted out on earth: a woman who dies childless does so because of her own sins.

[21] Cf. also 104.13: all the righteous who learn the paths of uprightness from 'the books' will be recompensed.

[22] Bonner (*The Last Chapters of Enoch in Greek*, p. 39) notes that the Ethiopic translator regularly used 'live' and 'life' for *sōdzesthai* and *sōtēria*.

And now I show unto you that light and darkness, day and night, see all your sins. Be not godless in your hearts, and lie not and alter not the words of uprightness, nor charge with lying the words of the Holy Great One, nor take account of your idols. . . . (104.8–9)[23]

Yet in keeping with the general apocalyptic view, we are not told how an individual might *transfer* from the group of the unrighteous to the righteous. The lines are drawn without taking account of individual transgression and atonement; the author's concern is to promise the righteous a reward and the wicked punishment, and the individual transgressions of the righteous are even less in mind than the possibility of the conversion of the un- righteous.

From the Greek fragments of this section, it appears that the author used indiffer- ently the terms 'righteous' (*tsaddiqim*), 'holy' (*qedoshim*) and 'pious' (*ḥasidim*) (or the Aramaic equivalents). In 100.5a he speaks of the righteous and holy (*dikaioi* and *hagioi*), and they are apparently the same as the pious or godly of 100.5d (*eusebeis*). Here *eusebeis* (which, as we have seen, translates *tsaddiqim* in Ben Sirach) apparently translates *ḥasidim*. This is also probably the case in 102.4, which reads in Greek, 'Be of good courage, souls of the righteous (*dikaioi* = *tsaddiqim*) that are dead, the righteous and pious (*dikaioi* = *tsaddiqim*; *eusebeis*, probably = *ḥasidim*).' *Eusebeis* also occurs in 102.6 and 103.3 (Greek: 'souls of the dead *eusebeis*' for Charles's 'spirits of those who have died in righteousness'). In 103.9, where the *dikaioi* and *hosioi* are mentioned (Charles: 'righteous and good'), *hosioi* probably represents *ḥasidim*. This is also probably the case in 104.12: *dikaioi* = *tsaddiqim*; *hosioi* = *ḥasidim*; *phronimoi* = *ḥakamim*. (Cf. 'piety', *hosiotēs*, 102.5; Charles, 'goodness'.)

There appear to be two views in this section on how and when the righteous will be rewarded and the wicked punished. On the one hand, a cataclysmic event on earth is depicted, perhaps a war, during which the righteous themselves will wreak vengeance on the wicked, repaying them for their persecution in kind:

Fear not the sinners, ye righteous;
For again will the Lord deliver them into your hands,
That ye may execute judgement upon them according to your desires.
(95.3; similarly 96.1)

Woe to you who love the deeds of unrighteousness (*adikia*): wherefore do ye hope for good hap unto yourselves? Know that ye shall be delivered into the hands of the righteous, and they shall cut off your necks and slay you, and have no mercy upon you. (98.12)

[23] 101.3 would be relevant here if we could be sure of the reading. Charles's translation of the Ethio- pic: 'If he sends his anger upon you . . . , ye cannot petition him; for ye spake proud and insolent words against His righteousness.' The Greek (Bonner's translation, p. 92) is: 'If he sends his anger . . . , will you not be entreating him? Why do you utter with your mouths', etc. If the Greek is original, as Bonner thinks (p. 55), repentance of the unrighteous is obviously possible.

On the other hand, the righteous are depicted as praying to God for vindication,[24] as a result of which the wicked shall have all their words of unrighteousness 'read out before the Great Holy One', who shall himself
inflict punishment (97.3–6).

> In those days the angels shall descend into the secret places
> And gather together into one place all those who brought down sin,
> And the Most High will arise on that day of judgement
> To execute great judgement amongst sinners. (100.4)

A slight variant on this theme is the statement that the sinners who were not
punished in their life shall *at death* 'descend into Sheol' where 'they shall
be wretched in their great tribulation' (103.6f.).

> And into darkness and chains and a burning flame where there is
>   grievous judgement shall your spirits enter;
> And the great judgement shall be for all the generations of the
>   world.
> Woe to you, for ye shall have no peace. (103.8)

> At the time of judgement, the righteous shall be protected:
> And over all the righteous (*dikaioi*) and holy (*hagioi*) He will
>   appoint guardians from amongst the holy angels
> To guard them as the apple of an eye,
> Until He makes an end of all wickedness and all sin,
> And though the righteous (*eusebeis*) sleep a long sleep, they have
>   nought to fear. (100.5)

The righteous are told: 'Ye shall not have to hide on the day of the great
judgement and ye shall not be found as sinners, and the eternal judgement
shall be far from you for all the generations of the world' (104.5). On the
contrary, in the judgment the righteous will be saved (99.10).

To sum up: the wicked are primarily powerful native Israelites, now
considered disloyal and apostate, and the heathen in league with them,
both supported in their wickedness by the 'rulers'. They violently plunder
the righteous and, prospering, think themselves secure. They transgress
the law and blaspheme against God; some (probably the Gentiles) are
accused of idolatry. The righteous obey the law and remain loyal to their
God, despite their suffering and persecution. They thus show themselves
to be the true elect; the wicked thus appear as apostates. There will be a
judgment, at which the wicked shall be justly punished while the righteous
will be blessed according to God's mercy.

---

[24] With the prayer of the righteous in 97.5 ('the prayer of the righteous shall reach unto the Lord'),
compare Ben Sirach 35.17 ('The prayer of the humble pierces the clouds, and he will not be consoled
until it reaches the Lord'). In both cases God speedily vindicates the righteous suppliant.

I Enoch 1–5; 81; 108; 93.1–10; 91.12–17

There are a few sections not yet treated, and they may be very briefly dealt with. In the 'Apocalypse of Weeks' (93.1–10; 91.12–17), the 'children of righteousness' are apparently the same as 'the elect' and 'the plant of uprightness' (93.1). The seventh 'week' is that of 'an apostate generation', which will be succeeded, in the eighth week, by the election of 'the elect righteous of the eternal plant of righteousness' (93.9f.). It thus appears that in this section, as in others, the righteous and the elect are identical, and are the opposite of the apostates (or, as elsewhere, foreign oppressors). We may also note that the righteous avenge themselves on 'the oppressors' (91.12).

Chapter 108 is obviously a special source added from a different Enoch tradition: thus it begins, 'Another book which Enoch wrote'. It is not in the Greek fragment of the last chapters of Enoch.[25] It is noteworthy for being a (presumably) early martyrology. The sinners are opposite the humble, who are the same as or closely related to 'those who have afflicted their bodies' and 'those who have been put to shame by wicked men' (vv. 7f.). They were persecuted, but since they 'loved heaven more than their life in the world', God rewards them (v. 10; cf. v. 12: those who loved God's name are brought forth in shining light). Verse 11 is somewhat enigmatic:

And now I will summon the spirits of the good who belong to the generation of light, and I will transform those who were born in darkness, who in the flesh were not recompensed with such honour as their faithfulness deserved.

The ones born in darkness are mentioned also in v. 14: 'And they [the faithful] shall see those who were born in darkness led into darkness, while the righteous shall be resplendent. And the sinners shall cry aloud . . .' Charles's explanation is that those 'born in darkness' are Gentiles. Some of them are 'faithful' and are rewarded (v. 12), while the rest remain 'in darkness', missing the blessing of salvation, which is here considered light (vv. 11,14). This seems the best explanation. If it is correct, it is one of a small handful of explicit references to the possibility of salvation for Gentiles in Palestinian Jewish literature before the Rabbinic period.[26] The 'sinners' of v. 15 are then presumably sinners among the Israelites, who are amazed and astounded to see the righteous revealed as resplendent. If they are the opposite of the 'humble', they are those who 'put to shame' the humble and loved gold and silver (v. 8) and the life of this world more than God (v. 10). That is, they were apostates and traitors, turning against their own people for material gain.

[25] Bonner, op. cit., p. 4. Ch. 105 is also missing from the Greek.
[26] Note the reference to 'the whole world' in 91.14. 90.33, where the 'beasts' and 'birds' gather with the 'sheep', may also refer to the salvation of those Gentiles who did 'homage to those sheep' (90.30).

In chapters 1–5, which Charles thinks may have come from the final redactor,[27] the elect are again the righteous and the opposite of the wicked (1.1). There will be a judgment of all flesh (1.7, 9), but the righteous elect will be protected by God's mercy (1.8). They are forgiven for their sins and receive mercy, peace, forbearance and salvation (5.6).[28] After the judgment the elect receive wisdom from God and never again transgress (5.8f.). As a consequence, they live out their lives, without their being shortened by sin, in peace and gladness (5.9). The wicked, on the other hand, find no mercy nor salvation (5.5,6). The accusation against them is this:

> But ye – ye who have not been steadfast, nor done the commandments of
>   the Lord,
> But ye have turned away and spoken proud and hard words
> With your impure mouths against His greatness.
> Oh, ye hard-hearted, ye shall find no peace. (5.4)

It is not just the transgression of commandments which makes the sinners 'sinners' – the righteous elect also transgress (it is a change when after the judgment they transgress no more). It is rather that the sinners have 'turned away' and spoken against God. Their turning away, like their hard-heartedness (in contrast to the humble, 5.8), may well indicate a refusal to turn to God, that is, to repent. Those who reject God remove themselves from the sphere of his mercy, and consequently find no forgiveness. Their damnation is that they shall be cursed for ever (5.5f.).

In 81[29] we may note that one 'who dies in righteousness and goodness' is not judged and has no 'book of unrighteousness' written about him (v. 4). The sinners are clearly designated apostates (v. 8). It is worth noting that, unlike 5.9, death is not the normal lot of all men. The righteous die because of the deeds of the godless (v. 9); that is, they die indirectly because of sin. Presumably if there were no sin there would be no death.

We have thus far left out of account the rest of chapters 72–82, the 'Book of the Heavenly Luminaries', as Charles titles the section. This section has nothing of interest for the present study, but we may note that, as always, those who walk in the way of righteousness are the righteous, who are opposite the sinners (82.4). In this case, sin consists of following the wrong calendar and thus observing the holy days on the wrong days.

---

[27] *I Enoch*, p. 2: 'It is difficult to say anything definite regarding [these chapters]. They look like an introduction to the entire book written by the final editor.' He therefore dates them in the first century b.c.e.

[28] I take the subject of 5.6d to be the righteous. The text is corrupt. For the possible interpretations, see Charles, *I Enoch*, ad loc., and Black's apparatus. But despite the corruption of the text, clearly the righteous are meant.

[29] On ch. 81 as an insertion into 72–82, see Charles, *I Enoch*, pp. 148f.; *Pseudepigrapha*, p. 245 (it 'came probably from the editor of the complete Enoch').

Summary

In spite of the divergencies, there are many points in common in the various sections of I Enoch. The most striking point is this: the righteous are always the loyal and obedient; their opponents are either Gentiles hostile to them or apostate Jews or both. The terms 'sinners', 'wicked', 'godless' and the like never refer to those who commit individual transgressions, but to the kind of transgression which puts the sinners in fundamental opposition to God and his chosen people. That is, we have here the conception of a 'true Israel', called 'the righteous', 'the righteous and elect', 'the holy', 'the pious' and the like, and their opponents are condemned apostates and/or heathens. The individual transgressions of members of 'the righteous' hardly come into view (5.8 is an exception). Only rarely are any others mentioned besides the wicked and the righteous. When they are referred to, however, it is not in an ungenerous way. The few references to the Gentiles (other than the oppressors) all hold out the possibility that at least some will be saved.

David Hill correctly observed that in I Enoch and the Dead Sea Scrolls *dikaioi* (= *tsaddiqim*) is 'a quasi-technical term'.[30] In his view, it refers 'to a special or sectarian group in Israel' in I Enoch.[31] It is more likely that the righteous of the various parts of I Enoch did not see themselves as members of a sect *within* Israel, but as the *only true* Israelites. It seems that in I Enoch the righteous *are* the elect and that all others are apostates or heathen.

We are now in a position to see more clearly the force of Finkelstein's argument that Sanhedrin 10.1 ('all Israel has a share in the world to come') is pre-Maccabean and explicitly designed to exclude apostates and paganizers from 'Israel'.[32] Still without attempting to decide whether or not the occasion to which Finkelstein attributes Sanhedrin 10.1 is correct, we may unreservedly agree with the general point. Sanhedrin 10.1 promises salvation to all those who are truly in Israel. The question then becomes how the elect are defined. The Rabbis, as we have seen, generally took a broad view. Those who deny the covenant or who sin in such a way as to deny the God who gave the commandments are not elect, but other Israelites are. The questions of how one shows oneself to be elect, of what one must do to forfeit the election, and of why some are elect and others not, are not worked out in I Enoch in detail in the way that they are in Rabbinic literature. The emphasis on a 'for us or against us' choice, however, is similar. The righteous are loyal to God and the traditions (in this sense they 'choose' election, 94.4), the wicked apostates are not.[33] They deny God and destroy his people.

---

[30] D. Hill, 'Δίκαιοι as a Quasi-Technical Term', *NTS* 11, 1965, pp. 296–302, especially pp. 300–2.
[31] Ibid., p. 300.
[32] Above, pp. 148f.
[33] Ziesler's definition of the righteous (*The Meaning of Righteousness*, pp. 81f.; cf. p. 79) in this literature as primarily those who are loyal to the covenant is thus seen to be correct. This analysis is also in agreement with Rössler's view of apocalyptic literature (*Gesetz und Geschichte*, pp. 78f.; 87f.).

It thus appears that, within the framework of apocalyptic, we find much the same pattern of religion as we found in the Rabbis. Some of the parts (individual transgression and atonement) are missing because of the nature of the literature and the scale on which the problem of loyalty and disloyalty is seen. But we still find that salvation depends on election and that what is necessary to *maintain* the elect state – to be righteous – is to maintain loyalty and obedience to God and his covenant.

3. Jubilees[1]

The election

One of the main concerns of the author of Jubilees was to establish the basic distinction between the faithful, covenant-keeping Israelites on the one hand and the apostates and Gentiles on the other. His use of Genesis gave the author frequent opportunity to appeal to the election and the covenant:

And I will build My sanctuary in their midst, and I will dwell with them, and I will be their God and they shall be My people in truth and righteousness. And I will not forsake them nor fail them; for I am the Lord their God. (1.17f.)

The phrase 'elect of Israel' (1.29) probably does not refer to a sect within Israel, the members of which are the only elect; it perhaps should be understood as 'the elect, Israel',[2] for it is clear that *all* Israel is elect:

And they shall be called children of the living God, and every angel and every spirit shall know, yea, they shall know that these are My children, and that I am their Father in uprightness and righteousness, and that I love them. (1.25)

I cannot agree, however, with his argument from silence that the failure to mention explicit commandments indicates an important distinction from the Rabbinic view of the law. Against this, cf. Thyen, *Sündenvergebung*, p. 55 and n. 2.

---

[1] Jubilees is usually dated before 100 b.c.e., and there seems to be no reason to object to this view. See Charles, *Pseudepigrapha*, p. 1; Testuz, *Les idées religieuses du Livre des Jubilés*, pp. 34–9; Milik, *Ten Years of Discovery*, p. 36; Jaubert, *La notion d'alliance*, pp. 473–6; Rowley, *The Relevance of Apocalyptic*, pp. 99–105, where there is a discussion of other views. For a discussion of the integrity of the book and its proposed Essene authorship, see Appendices 1 and 2 below.

The translation used here is that of Charles in *Pseudepigrapha*. Small fragments of Jubilees have been found at Qumran, but they thus far do little more than confirm the existence of the work in Hebrew. See Denis, *Introduction aux Pseudépigraphes grecs*, pp. 157f.

[2] M. Testuz (*Les idées religieuses*, pp. 33f., 180) takes the phrase to mean 'the elect from among Israel'. This depends on his identifying the author as an early Essene and on his view that the covenant promises are understood to apply only to the author's separate community. On this, see Appendix 1. We may note two points here, however. (1) In 1.29 the phrase is used in the context of the blessings of the renewal of the earth; they shall come on 'the elect of Israel'. Elsewhere in Jubilees the future blessings are intended for all Israel: 1.28 ('Father of all the children of Jacob'); 50.5 (Israel will be cleansed by God). Thus the phrase appears not to refer to an existing sect as it does in Qumran. (Cf. Jaubert, *La notion d'alliance*, p. 94.) (2) The phrase which is opposite 'the elect of Israel' is 'the sinners of the Gentiles' (23.23), who are also called 'the sinners, the Gentiles' (23.24). On the phrase 'elect of Israel' in CD 4.4 and similar phrases in the Dead Sea Scrolls, see the index, s.v. elect.

Similarly, in 1.28, God says that he is 'God of Israel and the Father of all the children of Jacob'. Jacob is the key figure in the covenant, and descent from him puts one among the elect.[3]

. . . from the sons of Isaac one [viz, Jacob] should become a holy seed, and should not be reckoned among the Gentiles. For he should become the portion of the Most High, and all his seed had fallen into the possession of God, that it should be unto the Lord a people for (His) possession above all other nations and that it should become a kingdom and priests and a holy nation. (16.17f.)

Similarly, in 19.18 God is said to choose Jacob 'to be a people for possession unto Himself, above all peoples that are upon the face of the earth'. There are numerous blessings of Jacob, usually attributed to Abraham. Thus 22.11ff.:

> Blessed be my son Jacob
> And all the sons of God Most High, unto all the ages:
> May God give unto thee a seed of righteousness;
> And some of thy sons may He sanctify in the midst of the
>   whole earth;
> May nations serve thee,
> And all the nations bow themselves before thy seed.
> Be strong in the presence of men,
> And exercise authority over all the seed of Seth.
> Then thy ways and the ways of thy sons will be justified,
> So that they shall become a holy nation. (22.11f.)

We should not take the phrase 'some of thy sons' to indicate that only a portion of Jacob's descendants is elect. This is negated by the prayer that 'thy sons' should become 'a holy nation' in the same passage and by the reference to 'all his seed' in 16.18, as well as by other references to the descendants of Jacob without qualification. The seed of Jacob, that is, all his descendants, as such is holy (22.27; 25.3; cf. 33.20, 'Israel is a holy nation') and sacred (22.13). Israel is a 'plant of righteousness' (16.26; 21.24; 36.6), a 'seed of righteousness' (22.11), and a 'righteous nation' (24.29); Jacob's children will be a 'righteous generation' (25.3).

That God of his own will chose Israel is the predominant theme in Jubilees, but the author can also say that Abraham chose God and his dominion (12.19). As always in Judaism, the divine choice does not eliminate freedom of action.

The special status of Israel as God's elect is a theme of which the author never tires.[4] They are separated unto God by the Sabbath (2.19) and are a 'peculiar people above all peoples' (2.21). Israel alone was sanctified to keep

---

[3] Cf. Testuz, *Les idées religieuses*, pp. 72f.; Charles, *Jubilees* and *Pseudepigrapha*, on 1.24; Jaubert, *La notion d'alliance*, p. 99.
[4] Cf. Charles, *Jubilees*, pp. li–lviii.

the Sabbath (2.31). They are God's own people, 'above all peoples that are on the face of the earth' (19.18). Israel is holy unto the Lord, 'and a nation of inheritance, and a priestly and royal nation and for (His own) possession'. Consequently, all uncleanness should be kept from it (33.20; cf. 33.11). In this case the uncleanness refers to the moral pollution of sexual transgression, but the author also uses the same reasoning to prove that Israel should remain separate from the Gentiles. Since Israel is holy, it should not be defiled by intermarriage (30.8), and Abraham is depicted as urging Jacob,

Separate thyself from the nations,
And eat not with them:
And do not according to their works,
And become not their associate;
For their works are unclean,
And all their ways are a pollution and an abomination and uncleanness. (22.16)

The commandments

Israel's role in the covenant relation is to keep the commandments. As a result of accepting the covenant, Abraham is to see that every male is circumcised (15.11). In another passage, God promises that, after the Israelites confess their sin, he will 'circumcise the foreskin of their heart', create in them a holy spirit, and cleanse them so that they will no longer stray. As a result, 'Their souls will cleave to Me and to all My commandments, and they will fulfil My commandments, and I will be their Father and they shall be My children' (1.23f.). Similarly, Israel is urged to 'love the God of heaven' and to 'cleave to all His commandments' (20.7).

It is noteworthy that most of the commandments specified in Jubilees are those which the Rabbis categorized as 'commandments between man and God'. The commandments which govern man's behaviour towards man seem to be presupposed and are doubtless to be kept. Thus Jacob is instructed to honour his father and brother (35.1; cf. 7.20: honour father and mother, love the neighbour), and the prohibition of and punishment for murder are specified in 4.32. Nevertheless, the commandments which govern man's behaviour to God are those which are emphasized, almost to the exclusion of others. We include in the 'man and God' category the sexual sins prohibited by the author, since those specified – certain forms of incest and nakedness – do not involve the abuse of another person, but are more in the nature of taboos. This emphasis fits the author's concern to distinguish the Israelites from the Gentiles, for it is these commandments which serve to set Israel apart. Thus they are to keep the Sabbath (2.18), cover their nakedness (3.31, so as not to be like the Gentiles; not an explicit biblical commandment); observe a period of uncleanness after childbirth (3.8–11), refrain from eating meat with the blood in it (6.10; 21.18 and elsewhere), observe the Feast of Weeks (6.17),[5] tithe (13.24), circumcise their sons (15.25ff.), observe the Feast of Tabernacles (16.29), not to give the younger daughter in marriage before the elder (28.6, a halakah unknown elsewhere), not to intermarry (30.7), not to commit incest (33.10)[6] and to observe the Passover (49.8). The only 'commandment between man and his fellow' which is especially emphasized as are the preceding commandments between man and God is the commandment to love one's brother (36.8–11). In the context of Jubilees' narration of the biblical history, the commandment is given to Esau and Jacob by Isaac, but it is apparently meant to refer to the Israelites' love for one another.[7]

Negatively put, the members of the covenant are not to behave like the Gentiles, particularly by avoiding idolatry, but also by avoiding the 'uncleanness' of the Gentiles, which refers not only to idolatry, but also to other transgressions, especially sexual ones.[8] Thus idolatry is warned against or forbidden: 1.9 (the uncleanness, shame and idolatry of the Gentiles); 11.4 (the transgression and uncleanness of idolatry); 11.16 ('went astray after graven images and after uncleanness'); 12.2; 20.7 ('walk not after their idols, and after their uncleannesses'); 22.22; 36.5. Sexual sins are frequently warned against without being specified: 16.4–6 (the Sodomites and others 'defile themselves and commit fornication in their flesh, and work uncleanness on the earth'); 20.3–5 (Israelites should refrain 'from all fornication and uncleanness'); 25.7 (Jacob says that 'with regard to lust and fornication, Abraham, my father, gave me many commandments'); 50.5 (Israel will eventually be cleansed 'from all guilt of fornication, and uncleanness, and pollution, and sin, and error'). While we cannot always be sure just where the fault of 'fornication' lies (except in the case of incest), the author's repeated emphasis on avoiding it may be based on his desire for Israel not to mingle with the Gentiles. That is, 'fornication' in Jubilees may refer to any unlawful union, but especially to intercourse with Gentiles. Thus Esau, all of whose ways are 'unrighteousness' (35.13), is condemned because he went 'after his (Gentile) wives and after their uncleanness and after their error' (35.14). Union with Gentiles leads to forsaking the God of Abraham (ibid.) and to uncleanness (perhaps here of idolatry), and thus is itself repeatedly linked with 'uncleanness'. The principal concern, however, was idolatry and

---

[5] On the Feast of Weeks as the time of an annual renewal of the covenant, see Jaubert, *La notion d'alliance*, pp. 100–4; Leaney, *Rule*, p. 101.

[6] The only degrees of relationship for which sexual intercourse is specifically forbidden are one's mother or step-mother (33.10, 'a man should not lie with his father's wife'), one's daughter-in-law and one's mother-in-law (41.25). As we shall see, sexual transgressions are frequently warned against in general terms.

[7] On the 'horizontal' aspects of the covenant, see further Jaubert, *La notion d'alliance*, pp. 108–11.

[8] Cf. Jaubert, *La notion d'alliance*, p. 95: the author's primary concern was the preservation of Israel's 'holiness'. On impurity as idolatry and fornication, cf. p. 97.

forsaking the other characteristics of Judaism. Thus Moses prays to God to keep Israel from foreign dominion, 'lest they should rule over them and cause them to sin against Thee' (1.19). The sin in mind might be covering circumcision (cf. 15.34: 'treated their members like the Gentiles') or idolatry. Similarly, the warning not to 'walk according to the feasts of the Gentiles' (6.35) might refer either to participating in actual Gentile feasts (which would involve idolatry) or observing their own feasts according to the Gentile calendar, which would be just as clear a case of forsaking the peculiar covenant between God and Israel.

Reward and punishment

The author of Jubilees holds the traditional view that there is reward for obedience and punishment for transgression. Both are meted out here and 'eternally'. Thus those who profane the Sabbath will die eternally, while the children of Israel, who keep it, will 'not be rooted out of the land' (2.27). Similarly, those who eat meat with blood in it and their descendants 'shall be rooted out of the land'; while of the Israelites, who observe the commandment, it is said that 'their names and their seed may be before the Lord our God continually' (6.12f.; cf. 21.23f.). According to 5.10, there will be a 'day of the great condemnation, when judgment is executed on all those who have corrupted their ways and their works before the Lord'. On the other hand, sin is also punished in this life. Thus the flood came as a result of sin (7.21). Retribution is sometimes in kind; as Cain killed Abel with a stone, he was himself killed by a stone (4.31). The righteous are also rewarded in this life. If the Israelites are righteous, their nation will spread 'over the face of the whole earth' (7.34), and all that they plant shall prosper (7.37).

The image of book-keeping in heaven (5.13; 28.6; 30.19; 30.22; 36.10; 39.6; cf. 4.23, where Enoch keeps the books) might seem to imply that salvation is according to the majority of one's deeds. This seems especially implied when the author says of one who marries his younger daughter before the elder that 'they set down guilty against him in heaven' (28.6), or when he says of Levi that his slaughtering the Shechemites is inscribed 'as a testimony in his favour on the heavenly tablets' (30.19). But the books are not actually account ledgers with debits and credits beside each name. They are the 'book of life' (30.22; 36.10) and the 'book of those who will be destroyed' (30.22).[9] All names go into one book or the other, on what basis we shall shortly see. But it is clear that when 'they set down guilt against him in heaven' (28.6), it is worse than entering a debit on an account card

[9] With the 'book of life', which contains the names of those who will be saved, not an account of transgressions and good deeds, one may compare 1QM 12.2: '[. . . and the enumer]ation of the names of all their host is with Thee in Thy holy abode . . .' (transl. Yadin).

which can be cancelled by a subsequent credit, for 'none is righteous' who gives the younger daughter in marriage before the elder (ibid.).

We should also note that the author maintains the old view of the collective punishment of the entire people because of the unatoned or unpunished sin of an individual. 'The whole nation together [will] be judged for all the uncleanness and profanation of this man' (30.15).[10] This view appears also in 41.26:

And do thou command the children of Israel that there be no uncleanness amongst them, for every one who lies with his daughter-in-law or with his mother-in-law hath wrought uncleanness; with fire let them burn the man who has lain with her, and likewise the woman, and He will turn away wrath and punishment from Israel.

Here we see that punishment of the individual for his transgression will avert the punishment which would otherwise fall on the entire people.

The basis of salvation; the 'true Israel'

It is repeatedly emphasized that the basis of salvation is membership in the covenant and loyalty to it:

And every one that is born, the flesh of whose foreskin is not circumcised on the eighth day, belongs not to the children of the covenant which the Lord made with Abraham, but to the children of destruction; nor is there, moreover, any sign on him that he is the Lord's, but (he is destined) to be destroyed and slain from the earth, and to be rooted out of the earth, for he has broken the covenant of the Lord our God. For all the angels of sanctification have been so created from the day of their creation, and before the angels of the presence and the angels of sanctification He hath sanctified Israel, that they should be with Him and with His holy angels. And do thou command the children of Israel and let them observe the sign of this covenant for their generations as an eternal ordinance, and they will not be rooted out of the land. (15.26–8)

Salvation here appears to be both eternal (with God and his angels) and temporal (in possession of the land), but in any case we see that whatever salvation is, it is Israel's. Even though Israel transgresses, God does not forsake them (1.5; cf. 1.18); he ultimately will cleanse them of all sin, and evil will be eradicated, so that Israel may dwell 'with confidence in all the land' (50.5). The same prediction of the salvation of Israel is found elsewhere in Jubilees. Thus God commands the angel of the presence: ' "Write for Moses from the beginning of creation till My sanctuary has been built among them for all eternity. And the Lord will appear to the eyes of all, and all shall know that I am the God of Israel and the Father of all the children of Jacob, and King on Mount Zion for all eternity" ' (1.27f.). Similarly,

---

[10] Following Charles in reading 'of this man', with the Latin. The Ethiopic is 'this profanation'.

chapter 23 predicts the salvation of 'Israel' and 'Jacob' (23.23) from 'the hand of the sinners, the Gentiles' (23.24).[11] The Mishnah's statement that 'all Israel has a share in the world to come' (Sanhedrin 10.1) is no clearer than these repeated predictions of Israel's salvation.

Despite this view and the emphasis on physical descent from Jacob, the author is of the view that some Israelites will be damned. *Physical descent is the basis of the election, and the election is the basis of salvation, but physical descent from Jacob is not the sole condition of salvation.* We may best quote at length again from chapter 15:

But over Israel He did not appoint any angel or spirit, for He alone is their ruler, and He will preserve them and require them at the hand of His angels and His spirits, and at the hand of all His powers in order that He may preserve them and bless them, and that they may be His and He may be theirs from henceforth for ever.

And now I announce unto thee that the children of Israel will not keep true to this ordinance, and they will not circumcise their sons according to all this law; for in the flesh of their circumcision they will omit this circumcision of their sons, and all of them, sons of Beliar, will leave their sons uncircumcised as they were born. And there will be great wrath from the Lord against the children of Israel, because they have forsaken His covenant and turned aside from His word, and provoked and blasphemed, inasmuch as they do not observe the ordinance of this law; for they have treated their members like the Gentiles; so that they may be removed and rooted out of the land. And there will no more be pardon or forgiveness unto them . . . for all the sin of this eternal error. (15.32–4)

Here we see that 'Israel', which will be preserved and blessed by God for ever, is distinguished from (some of) the 'children of Israel', who become apostate and are damned without hope of pardon. One who does not observe the commandment to circumcise has not just disobeyed, he has 'broken the covenant' (15.26) or 'forsaken His covenant' (15.34).

Thus we come to one of the most interesting features of Jubilees – the list of commandments which are 'eternal', transgression of which is a 'sin unto death' without atonement. Rejection of any one of these commandments, like transgression of the commandment to circumcise, was regarded by the author as forsaking the covenant and thus forfeiting one's status as a member of Israel and one destined for eternal salvation. Of the commandments singled out by the author (listed above, pp. 364–6), several are called 'eternal' or ones which are written 'on the heavenly tablets', but atonement for transgression is not explicitly excluded. These are the provision for a period of uncleanness after childbirth (3.8–11), the prohibition of nakedness

---

[11] In ch. 23 the sequence of thought is difficult, and the chapter has figured largely in source hypotheses. See, for example, Davenport, *The Eschatology of Jubilees*, p. 45. The conclusion of the chapter as it now stands, however, is unquestionably intended to predict ultimate salvation for Israel after a time of trouble and destruction.

(3.31), the Feast of Weeks (6.17), tithing (13.25f.), the Feast of Tabernacles (16.29f.) and the commandment not to give one's younger daughter first in marriage (28.6). That the one who, like Cain, strikes his brother treacherously is cursed (4.5) is also 'written on the heavenly tablets', and the author obviously believed in the death penalty for murder (4.31f.). But even murder does not cause one to be expelled from Israel.[12] Transgression of the others implies forsaking the covenant, and there is no atonement. Thus the commandment to keep the Sabbath is 'a law for ever' (2.33) which was kept in heaven (2.30), and he who profanes it will die eternally (2.27). If a man eats meat with the blood in it, 'he and his seed shall be rooted out of the land' (6.12). One who gives his daughter or sister in marriage to a Gentile shall be stoned and the woman burned, 'and she shall be rooted out of Israel' (30.7). 'And to this law there is no limit of days, and no remission nor any atonement: but the man who has defiled his daughter shall be rooted out in the midst of all Israel' (30.10). God will not accept the offerings of such a man (30.16). In the case of one who has intercourse with his father's wife,[13] 'there is no atonement for ever'; 'he is to be put to death and slain, and stoned with stones, and rooted out from the midst of the people of our God' (33.13). The case of Reuben, who had intercourse with his father's concubine, does not provide a precedent to the contrary, for the law had not been completely revealed in his day (33.15f.). But now the law is established eternally, and there is no atonement for transgression (33.16f.). In this connection Moses is urged to write the commandment down for Israel, so that they may observe it and 'not commit a sin unto death' (33.18), which is obviously a sin for which there is no atonement.[14] Similarly, the Passover is an eternal ordinance, and one who is able to keep it (that is, who is ritually clean and who is close enough to come to Jerusalem) must observe it or be 'cut off' (49.8f.).[15] Finally, one who, instead of loving his brother, 'devises evil against' him 'shall be rooted out of the land', his descendants will be destroyed, he will be written in the book of destruction rather than of life, and he will 'depart into eternal execration' (36.8–11).

Thus we see that all Israel will be saved. Excluded from Israel are those

---

[12] Unless murder is included under 'devising evil against his brother', listed below. The latter, however, seems to be more treachery to Israel than a crime of passion.

[13] It may be that intercourse with one's daughter-in-law or mother-in-law should also fall in this category as a form of incest for which there is no atonement. See 41.23–28. The author does not explicitly say that there is no atonement, but his explaining why Judah's seed was 'not rooted out' because of his intercourse with Tamar (v. 27) seems to suppose that ordinarily this would be the case. See further below, pp. 376f.

[14] The phrase 'sin unto death' occurs in 21.22 and 26.34 without the sin being specified.

[15] The author does not provide for a second Passover for those who were unclean at the time of the regular Passover celebration, and his saying that it must be observed 'once a year, on its day' and that it cannot be adjourned 'from day to day, or from month to month' (49.7) may be directed against the practice. Testuz (*Les idées religieuses*, p. 146) takes the phrase 'once a year' to be directed against a supposed practice of celebrating Passover twice, once according to the calendar of Jubilees and once according to the official calendar. But this seems a less likely explanation.

who transgress a commandment which is, in the author's view, tantamount to denying the covenant (not circumcising, not keeping the Sabbath, intermarrying or permitting intermarriage with Gentiles, not keeping the Passover, devising evil against fellow Israelites) or those who blatantly commit a heinous transgression which is, by inference, a denial of the God who gave the commandment (eating blood, having intercourse with one's father's wife and perhaps with one's mother-in-law or daughter-in-law). We should consider why the author attached so much importance to the last two transgressions. It seems likely that he saw the commandment not to eat meat with blood in it to be a distinguishing feature of Israel *vis à vis* the Gentiles, just as are the commandments to observe the Sabbath, to circumcise and the like. This is supported by 21.5f., where the prohibition of eating blood directly follows an exhortation to avoid idolatry. That not eating meat with blood in it was a distinguishing mark of Jews is also indicated by Acts 15.29, which lists this as one of the minimum commandments which Gentile Christians must keep in order to satisfy the Jerusalem church. They must 'abstain from what has been sacrificed to idols and from blood and from what is strangled and from unchastity'. The reference to 'unchastity' here may help explain why the author stresses sexual transgressions so much. He may consider Gentiles to be especially prone to sexual transgression, so that Israelites should distinguish themselves by the opposite behaviour. This does not explain, however, why intercourse with one's father's wife is a sin for which there is no atonement. It is not a characteristic sin of Gentiles, as I Cor. 5.1 makes clear. This seems to be the only one in the list which is not tantamount to rejection of Israel and following the way of the Gentiles. It may be that the sheer heinousness of the crime makes it one which results in the transgressor's being 'rooted out of Israel'. At any rate, it is a fundamental commandment, along with the commandments to circumcise, keep the Sabbath and the like. Those who observe these commandments are true Israelites, while those who transgress are apostates; they are 'cut off' and 'rooted out of the land'.

It should be noted that all the commandments which, if transgressed, lead to expulsion from Israel are biblical commandments. This is true even of the prohibition of intermarriage, where the biblical view is not quite so clear. It appears from 20.4 that the author understood Deut. 7.3 to forbid all intermarriage with Gentiles (not just with the seven nations mentioned),[16] and his reading of Lev. 18.21 supported the same view.[17]

We conclude, then, that the soteriology of the book of Jubilees is that which we have found to be so widespread in Palestinian Judaism: salvation

---

[16] Deut 7.3 is not quoted in Jub. 20.4, but it seems to be alluded to. Cf. the Rabbinic discussions of the meaning of the verse in Abodah Zarah 36b and Kiddushin 68b.
[17] See Charles's note and the reference to the Targum to Lev. 18.21.

is given graciously by God in his establishing the covenant with the fathers, a covenant which he will not forsake (1.18); individuals may, however, be excluded from Israel if they sin in such a way as to spurn the covenant itself. Those who are faithful and do not sin in such a way and (as we shall see) who confess and repent for their transgressions constitute a kind of 'true Israel', although the term is not employed. To be sure, Jubilees differs from other depictions of Judaism in important ways: Jacob, rather than Abraham, is the primary patriarch; some transgressions cannot be atoned for; some of the individual halakot are otherwise unknown. The basic pattern, however, is thus far the same. We should now consider two scholarly views which are opposed to this conclusion.

We may first note that Becker has argued that, in order to understand the soteriology of Jubilees, one must start with the heavenly tablets. These contain God's law, not as a gift of life, but simply as information about what one should do. On them are also recorded the deeds of men. The tablets are decisive at the judgment, for there the commandments are *compared* with man's deeds. The result of this comparison determines the final judgment.[18] It thus appears to be Becker's opinion that salvation and damnation, in the view of the author of Jubilees, are equally according to works. If a man obeys the commandments he is saved, while if he transgresses them he is damned. It is difficult to see, however, how such a view can be maintained. Becker appears to have overlooked Jubilees' statements to the effect that God will not forsake his people *despite* their transgressions (1.5,18). It is clear in such statements that salvation is not earned by obedience, although it may be forfeited by disobedience. Obedience, as is generally the case in Judaism, is the *condition* of salvation (when it is coupled with repentance for transgression), but not its cause. This is further clear from the way in which the threat of eternal death is stated. Thus, for example, the author warns that those who profane the Sabbath will die eternally (2.27). There is no statement to the effect that those who keep it will live: the assumption is that Israel will be saved (1.22–25; 50.5), and only those who transgress in certain ways are excluded from Israel (e.g. 6.12; 30.7). The commandments written on the heavenly tablets do not exhaust the covenant, which also includes God's promise of fidelity. Thus the tablets of commandments do not contain the gift of life, as Becker notes; but it is also true that observing the commandments on the tablets is not, of itself, action which *brings* salvation. It would be more accurate to say that obedience *preserves* salvation. The commandments do not have the soteriological function which Becker attributes to them.

It is perhaps also worth noting that there is no hint in Jubilees of judgment

---

18 Becker, *Das Heil Gottes*, p. 22.

of individuals on the basis of how their behaviour compares with the commandments. The comparison of individual behaviour with the commandments on the tablets appears to be a view which Becker has introduced into the book of Jubilees; I cannot find it. The eschatological passages deal with the cleansing and perfection of Israel (presumably excluding those who have sinned in such a way as to be extirpated), not with the judgment of individuals. We do not have in Jubilees the picture of the judgment which is known from Matt. 25, in which individuals are called before God and judged according to their individual good deeds and transgressions.

Testuz is of the opinion that the author of Jubilees thought that God had established a new covenant with some among Israel and that all those outside this new covenant are apostate.[19] 'The blessings of the covenant are actually restricted to a small group of faithful Israelites, to those who compose the community of Jubilees.'[20] This community he identifies as an early Essene community.[21] Those who do not observe the peculiar halakot of the Essene sect are not faithful Israelites and, like Gentiles, are condemned to destruction.[22]

This view does not, however, seem to be correct. In the first place, Testuz has not paid sufficient attention to the character of the 'life and death' commandments. The author of Jubilees differs from 'official', or at least from Rabbinic, Judaism in denying the possibility of atonement for certain commandments; but his view is not greatly different from that of the Rabbis. They too would say that one who transgresses in such a way as to deny the covenant forfeits the covenant promises, although they would allow repentance and atonement for any sin. But what is noteworthy is that the list of transgressions which, in Jubilees, constitutes denial of the covenant is no more Essene than it is Pharisaic. They are commandments which should be kept by all Israelites, and they are in no way sectarian.[23] There is nothing Essene about saying that everyone who is not circumcised is not a child of the covenant but a child of destruction (15.26). The implication is that those who are circumcised *are* children of the covenant. Similarly, the commandment to keep the Sabbath is for all Israel and excludes the *Gentiles*, not other Israelites (2.31: 'he did not sanctify all peoples and nations' to keep the Sabbath, but only Israel). The fact that intercourse with one's wife is forbidden on the Sabbath (50.8), which is not true in the Rabbinic period, also does not argue that the author is an Essene or a member of any other

---

[19] Testuz, *Les idées religieuses*, pp. 74, 174.
[20] Ibid., p. 74. The primary text on which he bases this view is 23.19–21, a passage which he elsewhere (pp. 39–42) classifies as added by a redactor between 65 and 38 b.c.e., but which he here takes as indicating the view of the principal author. (See Appendix 2.)
[21] Ibid., pp. 33, 197.
[22] Ibid., p. 74.
[23] So also Jaubert, *La notion d'alliance*, p. 94.

identifiable sect. This view may have been relatively widespread in his day.[24] In short, the author differs from Pharisaism, at least from what we know of it, in denying atonement for some transgressions and in some of his individual halakot. The points for which atonement is denied and the halakot which are peculiar to Jubilees are not characteristic of the Qumran community nor of any other particular group of Jews known to us. There is no evidence that the author restricted the concept of Israel to those who were members of a sect. He did restrict it to those descendants of Jacob who did not commit one of the unforgivable transgressions; but these are limited in number, not sectarian in character (Sabbath, circumcision, love of the neighbour, etc.) and almost all of the type which, if committed, imply denial of Israel and God's covenant.

Secondly we must note, as Testuz himself confesses, that there is no mention in Jubilees of a new covenant.[25] Thirdly, the repeated stress on physical descent from Jacob as the primary qualification for sharing in the covenant promises and the constant distinction of Israel from the Gentiles (not from other Jews who are given an opprobrious title such as 'seekers of smooth things') militate against Testuz's view.[26] It seems to be rather the case that the author thought that all Israel would be saved, save those who break the commandment to circumcise, do not keep the Sabbath, do not keep the Passover, intermarry or permit intermarriage with Gentiles, eat blood, have intercourse with their father's wife (or with their daughter-in-law or mother-in-law) and devise evil against their brothers. Other passages make it clear that idolatry also involves removing oneself from Israel and consequently from the blessings of the covenant (22.22f.). Thus there is a concept of a true Israel, but it is not so limited as Testuz maintains. The author condemns other transgressions without saying that the transgressors are cut off from Israel, and the distinction is important. There is no indication that he restricted the blessings of the covenant to his own 'community' and several indications to the contrary. There is no discussion of a new covenant, but the expectation, as we shall see, of the fulfilment of the old by the elimination of transgression. Testuz, having identified the author as an early Essene, appears to have read back into Jubilees several of the characteristics of the Dead Sea Scrolls. It is better, with Jaubert, to see the author of Jubilees as speaking for a *confrérie* rather than a *secte*. She correctly notes that some of

[24] See Charles's note in *Jubilees* and *Pseudepigrapha* ad loc. He cites Niddah 38a–b, according to which 'the pious men of old' had intercourse only from Wednesday on so that their wives would not go into labour on the Sabbath. This is not the same as the regulation in Jubilees, but it indicates the practice of such restrictions. Finkelstein ('The Book of Jubilees and the Rabbinic Halakah', p. 48 n. 30), however, thinks that the discussion in Kethuboth 3b, which concerns the days on which a marriage may take place, may originally have referred 'to the prohibition of marital relations on the sabbath'.
[25] Testuz, p. 74.
[26] Jubilees 1.28 and other passages quoted above. On receiving the covenant promises, see below, p. 37.

the views expressed in Jubilees tend toward separatism, but the schismatic rupture described so well in the Qumran scrolls has not yet taken place. Jubilees is still adressed to all Israel.[27] Davenport's view is also similar to the one taken here: in many respects Jubilees continues the Old Testament faith. The author emphasizes 'God's love for Israel and his faithfulness to them, his demand for obedience, his power to do what he promises to do, and his willingness to forgive the repentant.'[28]

The Gentiles

It goes almost without saying that Gentiles are condemned. We have already seen that unrighteousness is to live like the Gentiles. Thus Israel when attacked by 'the sinners of the Gentiles' will pray to be saved from 'the sinners, the Gentiles' (23.23f.). It may be that 'of Gentiles' was originally a genitive of specification and that the first phrase means the same as the second. That the Gentiles are 'sinners' in such a way as to be condemned to destruction is explicitly stated in a passage in which Israel is warned against intermarriage:

> Be thou ware, my son Jacob, of taking a wife from any
>   seed of the daughters of Canaan;
> For all his seed is to be rooted out of the earth.
> For, owing to the transgression of Ham, Canaan erred,
> And all his seed shall be destroyed from off the
>   earth and all the residue thereof,
> And none springing from him shall be saved on the
>   day of judgment. (22.20f.)

The constant urgings to avoid mingling with the Gentiles (22.16) and to avoid intermarriage as something that defiles Israel (30.7,16) are clear indications that Gentiles as such are sinners. They have no portion in the future world, for Israel 'shall judge all the nations [i.e. the Gentiles] according to their desires, and after that they shall get possession of the whole earth and inherit it for ever' (32.19). The author thus takes a much harder line toward the Gentiles than was taken by the authors of the various sections of I Enoch who refer to Gentiles, or by the majority of the later Rabbis. Like R. Eliezer, he excluded Gentiles from the possibility of being saved. It is probably for this reason that he emphasizes that the law was given only to Israel and is to be kept only by Israel. The Feast of Tabernacles is 'ordained on the heavenly tablets concerning Israel, that they shall celebrate' it (16.29). Similarly, the author stresses that God 'did not sanctify all peoples and nations to keep [the] Sabbath . . . , but Israel alone' (2.31). The command-

---

[27] Jaubert, *La notion d'alliance*, p. 115.
[28] Davenport, *The Eschatology of the Book of Jubilees*, p. 79.

ment not to appear in public naked touches 'all those who know the judgment of the law', that they should not act like the Gentiles, who uncover themselves (3.31).

God's mercy; man's repentance and atonement

As in Ben Sirach and I Enoch, God's punishment of transgression is depicted as his paying sinners their just deserts and is thus a function of his being righteous[29] (21.4: God is righteous and judges transgression), while the righteous and obedient are considered to receive mercy. 'It is the Lord who executes judgment, and shows mercy to hundreds and thousands and to all that love Him' (23.31). Similarly, when Jacob tells Isaac how he has prospered, 'Isaac blessed the God of his father Abraham, who had not withdrawn his mercy and his righteousness from the sons of his servant Isaac' (31.25; 'righteousness' here may mean 'benevolence'). And Jacob tells Joseph near the end of his life that God has 'not withheld His mercy and His grace from His servant Jacob' (45.3).

We see, in fact, that in spite of what appears to be the very strict legalism of Jubilees, the mercy and grace of God are constantly appealed to, and the author thought of God as being always merciful and gracious towards his people. We saw above that the Rabbis, whose extant literature deals primarily with how to fulfil the law, perceived God's goodness to be the result of his mercy rather than of their legal perfection, and that this perception could be seen in the prayers which remain. One may see a similar situation in Jubilees. On the one hand, it is said of Noah that 'his heart was righteous in all his ways, according as it was commanded regarding him, and he had not departed from aught that was ordained for him' (5.19). This perfection led not only to his own salvation from the flood, but to that of his sons. Noah was accepted 'on behalf of his sons', whom God saved 'on his account' (ibid.; apparently an early use of the conception of 'the merits of the patriarchs'; cf. 30.20; 24.11,22). Yet Noah, according to the author, perceived the situation as one of God's mercy. Thus when he is told that his sons are being led into sin after the flood, he prays:

> God of the spirits of all flesh, who hast shown mercy unto me,
> And hast saved me and my sons from the waters of the flood,
> And hast not caused me to perish as Thou didst the sons of
>   perdition;
> For thy grace has been great towards me,
> And great has been Thy mercy to my soul;
> Let Thy grace be lifted up upon my sons,
> And let not wicked spirits rule over them
> Lest they should destroy them from the earth. (10.3)

[29] On God's righteousness, cf. Becker, *Das Heil Gottes*, p. 24.

Although the harsh tone of the halakah seems to suppose that man's religious behaviour is entirely within his own power, God is constantly appealed to to prevent him from sinning. Thus in the introduction Moses prays to God that he will create in the Israelites an upright spirit and prevent their being governed by the spirit of Beliar, who will lead them from the paths of righteousness and into destruction (1.20). Abraham prays that he may be delivered 'from the hands of evil spirits' and that they may not be allowed to lead him astray (12.20), and he similarly prays to God to strengthen Jacob 'to do righteousness, and His will before Him' (22.10). The prayer continues to request that God will remove Jacob from the uncleanness and error of the Gentiles (22.19), that he will preserve him from destruction and that he will keep him from the paths of error (22.23).

It is not surprising that an author who so values the mercy and grace of God would emphasize the repentance of man. As in Ben Sirach, what we should now call repentance is turning away from sin and to God. Thus Abraham admonishes Isaac:

> Turn away from all their deeds and all their uncleanness,
> And observe the ordinance of the Most High God,
> And do His will and be upright in all things. (21.23)

The author looks forward to a time when

> . . . the children shall begin to study the laws,
> And to seek the commandments,
> And to return to the path of righteousness. (23.26)

It is interesting to note what happens when the author's belief in repentance comes into conflict with his belief that there is no atonement for some transgressions. We have already noted that Reuben's continuing to live after having intercourse with his father's concubine, a crime for which there is no atonement, is explained by the fact that the law had not been fully revealed. The author's treatment of Judah, who had intercourse with his daughter-in-law, is interesting for the present question.

And Judah acknowledged that the deed which he had done was evil . . . and he acknowledged that he had transgressed and gone astray . . . , and he began to lament and to supplicate before the Lord because of his transgression. And we told him in a dream that it was forgiven him because he supplicated earnestly, and lamented, and did not again commit it. And he received forgiveness because he turned from his sin . . . ; and every one that acts thus, every one who lies with his mother-in-law, let them burn him with fire. . . . And do thou command the children of Israel that there be no uncleanness amongst them, for every one who lies with his daughter-in-law or with his mother-in-law hath wrought uncleanness; with fire let them burn the man who has lain with her, and likewise the woman. . . . And unto Judah we said that his two sons had not lain with her, and for this reason his seed was established for a second generation, and would not be rooted out. (41.23–27)

It is possible that we have here the work of a somewhat clumsy redactor, who introduces intercourse with one's mother-in-law into a discussion of Judah's transgression with his daughter-in-law. In any case, as the passage now stands, two reasons are adduced for Judah's being treated leniently. His earnest repentance apparently suffices for his forgiveness; thus he is not executed. The fact that there was a mitigating factor in his transgression – his second and third sons had not consummated a relationship with Tamar – seems to have prevented his 'seed' from being 'rooted out'.

It is doubtful, however, if the author would agree that forgiveness could be given to a repentant contemporary transgressor of one of the commandments for which there is no atonement. In the case of Judah, he was faced with the fact that Judah had not been burned and his descendants not immediately destroyed, and, like the Rabbis later, the author attributed Judah's being forgiven to his repentance.[30] In a lengthy passage in chapter 1 we see another instance in which repentance was considered to have secured forgiveness for Israel in the past, although the author was well aware that the Israelites had transgressed the eternal ordinances and forsaken God's commandments. God, addressing Moses, prophesies that Israel 'will forget all My commandments'. They will 'walk after the Gentiles . . . , and will serve their gods' (1.9). Although God will send them witnesses, they will slay them (1.12), 'and they will abrogate and change everything so as to work evil before My eyes' (ibid.). Consequently God will turn them over as prey to the Gentiles (1.13); and, being scattered among the Gentiles, 'they will forget all My law and all My commandments and all My judgments, and will go astray as to new moons, and sabbaths, and festivals, and ordinances' (1.14).

And after this they will turn to Me from amongst the Gentiles with all their heart and with all their soul and with all their strength, and I will gather them from amongst all the Gentiles, and they will seek me, so that I shall be found of them, when they seek me with all their heart and with all their soul. (1.15)

The passage continues by having God promise that he will dwell with his people and 'not forsake them nor fail them' (1.17f.). After a prayer by Moses that God should keep the people from evil, God says:

I know their contrariness and their thoughts and their stiff-neckedness, and they will not be obedient till they confess their own sin and the sin of their fathers. And after this they will turn to Me in all uprightness and with all (their) heart and with all (their) soul, and I will circumcise the foreskin of their heart and the foreskin

[30] Above, p. 176.

of the heart of their seed, and I will create in them a holy spirit, and I will cleanse them so that they shall not turn away from Me from that day unto eternity. (1.22f.)

It is noteworthy that repentance passes from being the explanation for the historical continuation of Israel, despite their past transgressions which should have brought destruction (1.15), to being the condition on the basis of which God can, in the future, create an Israel which is so cleansed of sin that they remain perfectly obedient (1.22f.).[31] That this is the author's view of the future is confirmed by 50.5, which prophesies a time at which Israel will be 'cleansed' and will dwell 'with confidence in all the land, and there shall be no more a Satan or any evil one, and the land shall be clean from that time for evermore'.

It thus appears that the author's view that there is no atonement for forsaking the covenant, when it conflicts with the *historical reality of the continuation of Israel* and with his *conviction that Israel is elect and will ultimately be cleansed and saved*, yields. It must be confessed that we cannot achieve complete clarity on the matter. In 15.32–34, quoted above, he seems to distinguish between a 'true Israel', which remains loyal to the covenant, and the rest, who forsake the covenant (and do not observe the command- ment to circumcise). Yet in chapter 1 he seems to grant that all Israel has at some time forsaken God. They were gathered again after the exile because of repentance and will ultimately be saved by God's cleansing, the presupposi- tion of which is repentance. It may be that these two views are not really in direct conflict.[32] The 'true Israel' conception of chapter 15 functions to separate the true Israelites from the apostates in the author's generation, while the idea that all Israel forsook God and returned serves to explain historically the continuation of Israel despite the most serious transgressions. The theme of repentance and perfect cleansing[33] looks forward to the final judgment and does not take direct account of the apostates of the author's day, although they presumably will no longer be part of Israel, and thus not able to participate in the final cleansing.

Put another way, repentance atoned in the past and will atone in the future, but the crisis of the author's time is so acute that certain transgres- sions permit no atonement. In his day, the line is sharply drawn. One will either be loyal or not, and there is no time for a second chance.

In speaking of sin and atonement, we should note that the author pays

---

[31] Jaubert (*La notion d'alliance*, pp. 106f.) has argued well that the passages on the confession of sins in 1.6 and 1.22–25 reflect a ritual of confession repeated annually by the community of Jubilees. The confession is part of the renewal of the covenant which was connected with the Feast of Weeks.

[32] Davenport's redactional hypothesis would explain any discrepancy here by source criticism. See Appendix 2 below.

[33] 1.22f.; 23.26ff.; 50.5. We thus see that ch. 1 confirms our view, against Testuz, that all Israel sins but is restored if they return to God. There is no indication that those who sin and need to repent are only the non-Essenes.

attention only to serious and intentional sins. Others are scarcely mentioned one way or another, although the author's attitude is made fairly clear when he has Abraham pray that Jacob may be forgiven for sins which he committed ignorantly (22.14). Apparently such sins were atoned for by a general prayer of repentance. We thus see that when the author says – or appears to say – that any transgression at all removes one from the covenant, that is not what is intended. Thus he writes about the 'evil generation' which forsakes the covenant, according to which they had agreed that 'they should observe and do all His commandments and His ordinances and all His laws, without departing either to the right hand or the left' (23.16). It might appear here that any departure from the commandments is a forsaking of the covenant. This may be correct in the way meant by the Rabbis, according to whom any intentional and high-handed sin, if not repented of, would indicate that the covenant had been spurned. But the provision of prayer, repentance and (as we shall see) sacrifices as means of atonement shows that a transgression as such would not remove one from the covenant. Similarly when the author writes that if the Israelites 'transgress and work uncleanness in every way, they will be recorded in the book of those who will be destroyed' (30.22), he either means *every* way literally (not *any* way), or he means those who sin in such a way as to remove themselves from the covenant. As we have seen, those ways are specified in other passages. This warning appears in the context of a warning against intermarriage. Despite these general warnings against all transgressions, which are intended to encourage obedience to all God's laws, the author seems to have been almost exclusively interested in preventing what appeared to him as the worst sins, especially those which indicate basic disloyalty to God.

Again like Ben Sirach, the author mentions the daily sacrifice (*Tamid*) as atoning. If the commandment to eat no blood is observed, Israel will be preserved, 'so that they (presumably the priests) may continue supplicating on your behalf with blood before the altar: every day and at the time of morning and evening they shall seek forgiveness on your behalf perpetually before the Lord that they may keep it and not be rooted out' (6.14). When it is said that the sacrifices of one who gives his daughter in marriage to a Gentile will not be accepted (30.16), the implication is that the sacrifices, if accepted, would atone. The Sabbath may also be violated for the purposes of maintaining the sacrifices, which 'atone for Israel' (50.11). We should also note that the Day of Atonement atones:

They should make atonement for themselves thereon with a young goat on the tenth of the seventh month, once a year, for their sins. . . . And this day has been ordained that they should grieve thereon for their sins, and for all their transgressions and for all their errors, so that they might cleanse themselves on that day once a year. (34.18f.)

It is clear here that the Day of Atonement implies repentance.

The author has an opportunity to discuss individual sacrifices when he mentions Abram's burnt sacrifice to the Lord (13.3f.,9), but he does not employ it to initiate a discussion of the value of private sacrifices. Abram's sacrifice is not one of atonement, but is made so that God 'should be with him and not forsake him all the days of his life' (13.9). There is a discussion of how a peace-offering should be sacrificed in 21.7–15, but still no mention of a private offering of atonement. This neglect may be attributed to the author's view that unwitting sins are atoned for by prayer alone – sin- and guilt-offerings are in any case not brought for intentional sin.[34] We cannot infer, however, that the author would not have accepted the efficacy of private sin- and guilt-offerings. He presumably accepted the entire sacrificial system, even though he does not describe very much of it; else he would have stated his disagreement. As is generally the case, a great deal is either presupposed or simply not mentioned, and we should suppose that the private religious lives of individuals should go on, in the author's view, as usual, even though the list of things not covered by the author's halakah is very extensive. Besides private offerings of atonement, one could mention oaths and vows and dietary regulations. The author, for example, does not mention the prohibition of eating pork, but he doubtless accepted it. The implication should similarly be that he accepted the entire sacrificial system and its atoning function.

The righteous

We may turn now to the question of who is 'righteous' in the author's view. We have already noted that Noah is called righteous (5.19, 'his heart was righteous in all his ways'), and this is because 'he had not departed from aught that was ordained for him' (ibid.). Similarly, it is said of Noah in 10.17 that 'he excelled the children of men save Enoch because of the righteousness, wherein he was perfect'. Of Abraham it is said that he 'was perfect in all his deeds with the Lord, and well-pleasing in righteousness all the days of his life' (23.10). (Abraham had earlier been admonished by God to be perfect, 15.3.). In 23.10, 'well-pleasing in righteousness' presumably means that he was righteous, which seems to be the same as 'perfect in all his deeds'. Elsewhere it is emphasized that Abraham was 'faithful', a term which covers both his fidelity to the commandments of God (17.15) and his fidelity to God in affliction (17.16). In 18.16 Abraham's faithfulness again implies his obedience to all that God commanded, while in 19.18 his being 'faithful' is being 'patient in spirit' in affliction.

Jacob is said to be 'on the upright path' and 'a perfect man' as well as

[34] Kerithoth 7a; Shebuoth 13a; Sifra Emor pereq 14.1–2 (on Lev. 23.27).

'faithful' (27.17). The adjectives 'perfect' and 'upright' are applied to him again in 35.12. His wife Leah was also 'perfect and upright in all her ways'; 'she was gentle and peaceable and upright and honourable' (36.23). Joseph 'walked in uprightness, for he was without pride and arrogance, and he had no respect of persons, and did not accept gifts, but he judged in uprightness all the people of the land' (40.8).

It is evident from this brief survey of the patriarchs (and one matriarch) that 'righteous' does not have in Jubilees quite the status which it has in other Jewish literature as the principal word used for those who are properly religious. The adjective is apparently replaced in part by 'upright',[35] and when the two nouns appear together (36.3, 'practise righteousness and up-righteousness on the earth') the difference in meaning is not evident. Just as being righteous is to do God's will, so is walking 'in uprightness' (25.9). Proper religious behaviour, whether defined by the adjective 'righteous' or not, is obedience to the law. Perfect obedience is specified, but we have already seen the author's recognition that people do in fact transgress and his provision for atonement. This meaning of being righteous is also evident in a prophecy of the new creation. The time will come when God will make[36] 'for all his works a new and righteous nature, so that they should not sin in their whole nature for ever, but should be all righteous each in his kind always' (5.12). Being 'righteous' here includes the rest of creation as well as man, and each creature is righteous 'in his own way'.[37] Living in accord with God's intention (not sinning) is clearly in mind. Thus also one who gives his younger daughter in marriage first is not righteous (28.6), for he has trans-gressed one of the ordinances 'ordained and written in the heavenly tablets' (ibid.), while one who observes the commandment of the year of release is called righteous (7.37).

We have previously seen that sin was regarded as polluting or rendering unclean. We should expect, then, that to be righteous and obedient is to be clean. Rebecca promises Jacob that his descendants shall be righteous and holy (25.3; cf. 25.18, 'blessed and holy'), and Israel is a 'righteous nation' (24.29) or a 'plant of righteousness' (36.6 and frequently). This is apparently the same as being a 'holy nation' in which there will be no uncleanness (33.20; cf. 33.11). And in the time to come, Israel will be 'cleansed' and without sin (50.5), which parallels the prophecy of 5.12 that Israel would be 'righteous'.

Just as the adjectives 'righteous', 'perfect' and 'upright' apply to the patriarchs, then, all Israel will in the future be 'righteous', 'holy' and 'clean'. There is a sense in which being righteous is an eschatological hope which

---

[35] To observe the commandment regarding sacrifices is to be 'upright', 21.15.

[36] Charles points out that the mss. read 'and he made', but that a corruption of tense must have occurred. The new creation plainly requires a future tense. See *Jubilees* and *Pseudepigrapha* on 5.12.

[37] Thus in 7.21 the 'watcher angels' are said to have gone 'against the law of their ordinances'. Cf. Testuz, *Les idées religieuses*, p. 93: 'everything that God made received a rule of conduct'.

will come with the new creation at the hand of God.[38] (To paraphrase Ephesians, righteousness is by grace, although it is postponed until the future new creation.) On the other hand, Israel, having been sanctified by God, is now a holy nation (33.20). The indicative is followed by an impera- tive, 'there shall be no such uncleanness appear in the midst of the holy nation', and clearly has an exhortative purpose. If we may systematize what the author says, it appears to be this: Israel has been set apart by God and therefore is a holy and righteous nation; therefore the people should avoid the uncleanness of transgression and act righteously. Ultimately they will be made perfectly clean and righteous, thus fulfilling the promise of the election.

The noun 'righteousness' is used in the expected ways. To do righteous- ness is to do God's will (22.10). If a man 'observes the way of the Lord', he will 'work righteousness' and love his neighbour and 'do judgment and righteousness' (20.2f.). If the Israelites 'work judgment and righteousness', they will be 'planted in righteousness over the face of the whole earth' (7.34). Here 'righteousness' is primarily 'what is right', though the emphasis in the first instance, where it is connected with loving the neighbour, may be on righteousness as benevolence. That one who observes the way of the Lord does righteousness is noteworthy, for it implies the imitation of God. This is also evident in 16.26, where the 'plant of righteousness' and the 'holy seed' will 'become like Him who had made all things'. Similarly those who, with God and the angels (7.30), keep the Sabbath will 'be holy and blessed' like them (2.28). Just as God is righteous (5.15f.; 21.4), so also should Israel be. In 7.20 'to observe righteousness' is to observe the commandment not to appear naked, to bless God, honour father and mother, love the neighbour and 'guard their souls from fornication and uncleanness and all iniquity'. It is obviously the same as being 'righteous'. The same meaning is implied in 35.13f.: Esau has 'no righteousness in him, for all his ways are unrighteousness and violence', and he has forsaken God. One who observes the way of God is also said to follow 'the path of righteousness' (25.15). Those whose deeds are 'uncleanness and an abomi- nation and a pollution' have no righteousness in them. But if a man turns from their deeds and does God's will and is upright, he will raise up from him a 'plant of righteousness' (21.21–24), which is obviously a nation which obeys the will of God.

Righteousness as perfect or nearly perfect obedience is not, however, the 'soteriology' of the author. The author emphasizes more than most the will of God in electing Israel and God's initiative in cleansing them of sin. The

---

[38] In 23.30f. the righteous are apparently the dead Israelites, those of former generations (cf. Volz, *Eschatologie*, p. 29). There is some tendency to use the term for the good men of former generations and for the future Israel, rather than for the author's contemporaries.

'soteriology' is thus election and the final purification, both initiated by God, the latter dependent on repentance. As we have now come to expect, the emphasis on God's mercy is coupled with a strict demand to be obedient. But Israel should be 'clean' because God has sanctified the nation. Despite a strict legalism of one sort, the author's view is not the kind of legalism which is summed up in the phrase 'works righteousness', for salvation depends on the grace of God.

Appendix 1

Jubilees and the Essenes

Similarities between Jubilees and the Dead Sea Scrolls have been noted for some time. Thus Brownlee early published an article entitled 'Light on the Manual of Discipline from the Book of Jubilees' (*BASOR* 132, October 1951, pp. 30–2), in which he discussed instances of the influence of Jubilees on IQS, and Milik suggested that Jubilees was an Essene book on the basis of the Calendar (*Ten Years of Discovery*, p. 32). Milik's view was opposed by Rabin (*Qumran Studies*, pp. 79f.). The question of Essene or proto-Essene authorship has now been raised again by Testuz (*Les idées religieuses du Livre des Jubilés*) and Davenport (*The Eschatology of the Book of Jubilees*). Their views will be briefly described and commented on.

Testuz argues that Jubilees emanates from an early stage of the Essene sect. The principal connection which he sees between Jubilees and the Dead Sea Scrolls is that both come from a community which has withdrawn from the rest of Israel and which considers its members to be the only true Israelites. Thus in comparing Jubilees with CD, he points out that in the latter 'the group has separated from Israel and Judah' (Testuz, p. 179, referring to CD 4.2f.). After listing some other points, he writes (p. 180), 'in all these points, the Damascus Document seems to have been inspired by Jubilees'. There is no doubt that CD was inspired by Jubilees, but that does not prove that they originate from the same sect. It is apparent that the group from which CD comes did separate itself from the rest of Israel: they 'went out from the land of Judah' (CD 4.3). Whether the 'going out' is physical or metaphorical, the separation is explicit. But there is no indication in Jubilees of a separation from Israel. The only phrase which Testuz can cite is the phrase 'elect of Israel' (Jub. 1.29), which he thinks must imply separation. But this is by no means the case. We have already noted (above, n. 2) the parallel phrase is 'sinners of the Gentiles', which means 'the sinners, the Gentiles'. In any case, it is precarious to build so much on one phrase, especially in a remote translation, when there is no other evidence of separation in the document.

Testuz, to be sure, does see other evidence. Thus he writes: 'By the repeated unfaithfulness of the Israelites, one reads in the first chapter of Jubilees, the covenant concluded between God and his people on Sinai is broken. But a new covenant has been made between God and a group of faithful [Israelites] . . .' (p. 183). Unfortunately for Testuz's theory, there is no hint of this in chapter 1 of Jubilees. On the contrary, the idea that the old covenant is broken and a new covenant made seems to be explicitly excluded. Thus God prophesies to Moses that Israel will break the commandments which he is about to give, but he wants Moses to write down the covenant, so that subsequent generations 'may see how I have not forsaken them for all the evil which they have wrought in transgressing the covenant which I establish between Me and thee for their generations this day on Mount Sinai' (1.5). This is the clearest possible statement that the covenant between God and the *people of Israel at Sinai* will *not be considered broken* by God despite subsequent transgression. Similarly, God predicts that the Israelites will forsake God but return to him. Then he will build his sanctuary in their midst and dwell with them (1.9–17). He concludes: 'I will be their God and they shall be My people in truth and righteousness. And I will not forsake them nor fail them; for I am the Lord their God' (1.17f.). The author could easily have said that it would be a select group within Israel with whom God would keep the covenant promises if that had been his intention, and a member of a sect with a theory of a new covenant would certainly have done so and have mentioned the new covenant. (Cf., for example, CD 3.10–14.) There is no such reference here. What we find is God's promise to be faithful to the covenant despite Israel's transgression. When they turn and repent, he will be found to be ready to accept them.

Davenport has proposed a much less far-reaching connection between Jubilees and the Essenes than that suggested by Testuz. He grants that, with regard to the angelic discourse (which constitutes the bulk of the book according to his source hypothesis) and the first redactor (see the next appendix), very little can be said about the provenance of composition. Such evidence as there is, however,

suggests a close connection between the circles in which Jubilees was produced and those from which the Qumran community developed. The citation of the angelic discourse in the Damascus Document [CD 16.3f.], the use of the Jubilees calendar at Qumran, the similarity of attitude toward the faithful nation as the instrument of God in the great eschatological battle, and the likelihood that R_2 [the second redactor] resided at Qumran point to a close kinship between the milieus (p. 17).

Thus there is a 'close connection', but only the second redactor (who is responsible for 1.27f.; part of 1.29; 4.26; 23.21; and 31.14) resided at Qumran. The argument concerning the second redactor is this:

The conjunction of the use of the Jubilees calendar there [Qumran], the hostility of the Qumran community toward the Temple hierarchy, and the similarity of views in the Temple scroll and Jubilees as to the future Temple . . . make [Qumran] a highly probable location (p. 16).

The only point which goes beyond *similarity* of viewpoint and which lends itself to being used to prove an identity of sectarian commitment between the Qumran sect and the author or one of the redactors of Jubilees is the calendar. Here we run into an extraordinarily murky issue which cannot possibly be clarified in an appendix – if at all. Briefly, we may say this: *if* the Qumran calendar is identical with the calendar of Jubilees and *if* both calendars represent actual practice which differed from the Temple observances, *then* there is a good case for continuity of sectarian commitment between Jubilees and Qumran. I am not competent to judge whether or not the calendars are identical or only similar, and it is not clear that enough evidence exists to allow the decision to be made.[1] Even if uniformity could be proved, one would still have to reckon with the possibility that the calendar in Jubilees is theoretical more than practical.[2] In this case, the influence of Jubilees on Qumran would be that of theory on practice. This does not seem to me unlikely. I have argued throughout that the tone of the halakah of Jubilees indicates that it is addressed to all Israel. The author's opinions may not have been commonly accepted, but he is still arguing that they should be. One does not have the impression that he is ruling for the governance of a special group obedient to his halakah, as is the case, for example, with IQS. Thus, with regard to the calendar, he argues that those who follow another calendar 'go wrong' (6.36), but he does not say that there is no forgiveness, nor that they will be 'cut off', nor that they and their descendants will be 'rooted out'. Thus the author of Jubilees seems not yet to have made the decisive step toward sectarianism by arguing that those who do not accept his halakah are not really in Israel. The influence of Jubilees on Qumran is beyond dispute, but I cannot find in Jubilees as a whole or in any of its parts identity with the Qumran community in terms of sectarian commitment.[3]

---

[1] Note that Jaubert, who is an expert in calendar matters, speaks of a 'similar' calendar (*La notion d'alliance*, p. 90; she responds directly to Testuz, ibid., n. 5). Also cautious on the identity of the calendars are J. Obermann (*JBL* 75, 1956, pp. 295–7); Morgenstern (*VT* 5, 1955, p. 65); David Hill (*NTS* 11, 1965, p. 300). In favour of identity are S. Talmon ('The Calendar Reckoning of the Sect from the Judaean Desert', *Scripta Hierosolymitana* IV, ed. Rabin and Yadin, pp. 177–9, though Talmon recognizes that the evidence is not complete; the point of identity is the exclusive reliance on a solar year of 364 days) and Leaney (*Rule*, pp. 68, 94).

[2] So Morgenstern, *VT* 5, 1955, p. 64.

[3] Compare the position of Jaubert (*La notion d'alliance*): Jubilees is pre-Qumranian; the author was a member of a distinct movement, but the separation had not reached the point of actual rupture from the sacrificial services of the Temple (pp. 90f.), although the views of Jubilees would eventually lead to a rupture (p. 96).

Appendix 2
The Integrity of Jubilees

Both Testuz and Davenport have presented redactional hypotheses. Testuz argues that three passages have been added by a later redactor, whom he identifies as a member of the same sect who worked between 65 and 38. The passages given by Testuz as redactional are these: 1.7–25, 28; 23.11–32; 24.28b–30. We may make the following comments:

1. Testuz himself uses the redactional passages as if they represent the principal author's view. Thus in his section on the 'renewed covenant', he writes that 'for our author, there are no true servants of God except in the community to which he belongs' (p. 69). The passages cited to prove the point are 1.7,10,13,25,28; 2.20. All but the last are from the 'later redactor'. Similarly, when he argues that outside the covenant with the sect represented by Jubilees there is no salvation, Testuz bases the discussion exclusively on the 'redactional' passage 23.11–32 (p. 74). In discussing the eschaton (pp. 165–72) he notes that the views in chapters 23 and 1 have probably been modified by a later redactor (p. 165), but in the subsequent discussion he intersperses references to these sections with references to others without distinction and as if they all could be equally used to determine the view of Jubilees.[1]

2. Apart from this internal inconsistency, Testuz's observations about the passages are not always compelling. Thus he states that the added sections express an 'ardent hate' of the Gentiles, while in the rest of the work they are more scorned and ignored than hated (p. 40). The distinction is dubious. The malediction against the Gentiles in 22.22f. is at least as fierce as anything in the passages selected by Testuz. On this point, as well as with respect to the view of the future blessings of Israel, the sections picked out by Testuz seem to agree with the rest of the work (see e.g. 50.5).[2]

Davenport has recently argued that Jubilees consists of an original angelic discourse with a brief introduction (1.1–4a; 2.1–50.4) which has undergone two subsequent redactions. The first redactor (R_1) modified the work by adding 1.4b–26 and 1.29 in an earlier form, as well as 50.5. He probably also added 23.14–31 (pp. 14f.). The second, 'sanctuary-oriented', redactor (R_2) added 1.27f.; part of 1.29; 4.26; 23.21; and 31.14 (pp. 15f.). This division explains certain inconsistencies in the book. Davenport admits, however, that neither redactor 'saw any significant contradictions between his work and that of his predecessor' (p. 17) and that, with regard to eschatology, their views were generally the same (pp. 72–5). The first redactor was concerned to emphasize the national hope. The original prob-

---

[1] The inconsistency has been noted by Jaubert, *La notion d'alliance*, p. 93 n. 11.
[2] Similarly Jaubert, loc. cit.

ably dates from the late third or early second century b.c.e. (p. 14), while the first redactor worked in the time of the Maccabean wars, around 166–60 b.c.e. (p. 15). The second redactor added the dimension of a cosmic expectation (a renewal of creation) and a concern with the Temple. He is dated around the time of Simon and John Hyrcanus and may have worked at Qumran (p. 16).

It may be that Davenport has found some seams in Jubilees. Thus he observes that in 1.4 God tells Moses to write the discourse, while in 1.27 God tells the angel to write it for Moses. Nevertheless, I am not fully persuaded by Davenport's stratification. Attributing all the Temple and renewal passages to a second redactor seems to me to be arbitrary. The renewal of the earth (1.29; 4.26) and the perpetual establishment of the sanctuary (1.27; 4.26) may not be precisely the same as the cleansing of Israel and the land for all time (50.5), but the grounds for thinking that they represent two different authors' views on the national hope seem to me slight. Similarly, in suggesting that 50.6–13 (which mentions the Temple sacrifices, the Sabbath laws and the writing of the instructions by the angel) may have been added by the 'sanctuary-oriented' redactor, Davenport has to grant that the addition of Sabbath laws after 50.5 is not surprising, since 50.1–5 dealt with the Sabbaths of years and of the land (p. 68 n. 2). Further, we may note that interest in the Temple is not limited to the passages which Davenport attributes to the second redactor (see 6.14). When one grants an overall compatibility of viewpoint and argues for redactional work which was seen and may still be seen as complementing and supplementing the original document, the distinctions made by Davenport are not very significant for our present purpose. Even if they are there, the work as it stands shows greater harmony of viewpoint than one usually finds in ancient documents. One can always find discrepancies in ancient (or modern) literature if one looks hard enough, and there are some in Jubilees. The author doubtless used sources, and there may well have been later revision. On the whole, however, it seems best to take the entire work as integral. Arguments to the contrary appear riskier than the assumption of unity of composition.[3]

4. The Psalms of Solomon

Introduction

The introductory questions concerning the Psalms of Solomon are answered relatively easily.[1] They were written in Hebrew in the middle of the first

---

[3] Cf. Jaubert, op. cit., p. 90: 'L' unité de cette composition provient surtout de la chronologie rigoureuse qui charpente le livre . . .'.

[1] See G. B. Gray in *Pseudepigrapha*, pp. 625–30; P. Winter, 'Psalms of Solomon' in *IDB* III, pp. 958–60; Denis, *Introduction*, pp. 63f.; Stein in Kahana, *Ha-Sepherim ha-Hetsonim* I.2, pp. 431–6;

century b.c.e. They are probably not all by one author, but the general outlook is very consistent. We may note a few discrepancies in our discussion. As outside dates, Denis's suggestion[2] of 80 and 40 b.c.e. seems safe enough, although some would prefer a slightly narrower range. Thus Stein suggested 70–45.[3] It has been almost universally thought that the Psalms of Solomon are Pharisaic,[4] but this has now been challenged.[5] It seems best to follow O'Dell and others in seeing the Psalms of Solomon as coming from a broad religious movement which cannot be precisely identified with Pharisaism. In any case, the question of party identity need not be settled for our immediate purpose.

The pattern of religion in Ps. Sol. 9

The view of the way in which religion 'works' is so similar in the Psalms of Solomon to what we have seen in other literature, especially the Rabbinic, that at first it seems unnecessary to do more than quote one or two of the Psalms. There are, however, special points which require detailed analysis. We may begin by tracing the argument of Ps. 9 and then proceed by studying the relevant themes.

The Psalm opens by describing, like the first chapter of Jubilees, the past defection of all Israel from God. They 'fell away from the Lord who redeemed them' and consequently were 'cast away from the inheritance' (9.1f. [2]). God punished them and thereby demonstrated his righteousness; for sin is by man's own volition, and God is a just judge (vv. 2–8 [2–4]).

Ryle and James, *Pss. Sol.*, pp. xxxvii–xliv, lviii–lx, lxxvii–lxxxvii; Maier, *Mensch und freier Wille*, pp. 264–81.

The Greek text used is the one printed by Rahlfs, which is a reprint of the text established by O. Gebhardt, *TU* XIII 2, 1895. For estimating the probable Hebrew, I have used both Frankenberg's retroversion (*Die Datierung der Psalmen Salomos*, 1896) and the Hebrew translation by Stein. Quotations are from the translation by G. B. Gray.

The editions and translations by Gray, Stein, Ryle and James, Harris and Mingana, Gebhardt and Frankenberg are hereafter cited by the name of the author only.

[2] Loc. cit. in n. 1.

[3] Stein, pp. 432f.

[4] See e.g. H. Braun, 'Vom Erbarmen Gottes über den Gerechten', *Gesammelte Studien*, p. 9. He accepts the view and traces it back to Wellhausen. Recently see also Wayne Rollins, 'The New Testament and Apocalyptic', *NTS* 17, 1971, p. 464: Pss. Sol. 'is a patently Pharisaic document'. Rollins's definition of 'Pharisaism' is very broad: it is also represented by the Babylonian Talmud. Maier (*Mensch und freier Wille*, pp. 283–94) has discussed the matter at length and concluded in favour of Pharisaic origin. The only positive evidence, however, is the supposed belief in the resurrection (Maier, p. 294, cites 3.11; 15.10, 12f.). Maier did not note Büchler's argument (*Piety*, pp. 153–5; n. 11 below) that the resurrection is not in mind in these passages. We should also repeat our observation that belief in the resurrection need not have been exclusively Pharisaic.

[5] See J. O'Dell, 'The Religious Background of the Psalms of Solomon', *RQ* 3, 1961–62, pp. 241–57, and the earlier literature cited by him (pp. 252–4). O'Dell's opinion: the Psalms of Solomon come from the general circle of eschatologically-minded and devout groups and individuals – usually called the *Hasidim* – but not specifically from the Pharisaic party. Similarly Jaubert, *La notion d'alliance*, p. 254; Holm-Nielsen, 'Erwägungen zu dem Verhältnis zwischen den Hodajot und den Psalmen Salomos', in *Bibel und Qumran* (ed. S. Wagner), pp. 118f.

God, that is, pays each man according to his works (vv. 9f. [5]). He shows mercy to those who call on him, and he forgives transgression (vv. 11–13 [6]). Those who repent are the righteous, who receive God's goodness (vv. 14f. [7]). There then follows an appeal to God to be merciful to the chosen ones, who are called 'the seed of Abraham' and 'us' (vv. 16–19 [8–10]). The Psalm concludes with the formula, 'The mercy of the Lord be upon the house of Israel for ever and ever.'

We see in this Psalm all the elements of the pattern of religion which characterizes not only Rabbinic literature but also other Palestinian Jewish literature. The election is explicitly appealed to ('Thou didst choose the seed of Abraham before all the nations',[6] v. 17 [9]). It is not explicitly stated that God gave commandments as a consequence of the election, but it is clearly implied that God had given commandments, for Israel's fault was his 'transgression' (v. 3 [2]). God punishes disobedience and rewards obedience, which is in accord with his being a just God. Yet there is provision for repentance and forgiveness. The 'righteous' are not the perfect, for they have sins to confess. 'And to whom doth He forgive sins, except to them that have sinned? Thou blessest the righteous . . . when they repent (vv. 14f. [7]).

The election

The principal problem in our study of the Psalms of Solomon is the definition of the righteous and the elect in the author's generation. We shall reserve this question for the present. It is clear, however, that there is no conception of a special covenant, for all Israel was chosen by God:

> And now, Thou art our God, and we the people whom Thou hast loved:
> Behold and show pity, O God of Israel, for we are Thine;
> And remove not Thy mercy from us, lest they assail us.
> For thou didst choose the seed of Abraham before all the nations,
> And didst set Thy name upon us, O Lord,
> And Thou wilt not reject[7] (us) for ever.
> Thou madest a covenant with our fathers concerning us;
> And we hope in Thee, when our soul turneth (unto Thee).
> The mercy of the Lord be upon the house of Israel for ever
> and ever. (9.16–19 [8–10])

Similarly, the psalmist elsewhere says that

---

[6] The Greek for 'before' is *para* with the accusative. The probable Hebrew preposition is *mem*, 'from'. Cf. Jub. 2.21, 'above all peoples', which may rest on a similar translation of *mem*.

[7] 'Reject' is the conjecture of Gebhardt, followed by Frankenberg (*tiznaḥ*), probably because of the parallel in 7.8. Stein translates *tereph* ('forsake'), here, on the basis of biblical Ps. 138.8, but *tiznaḥ* in 7.8. Ryle and James suggest 'Thou wilt abide *among us* for ever'. Harris and Mingana have 'thou wilt not remove for ever'. The Greek is literally 'will not cease for ever'.

... Thou wilt pity the seed of Israel for ever
And Thou wilt not reject (them). (7.8)

The commandments; chastisement; reward and punishment

Although it is sufficiently clear that Israel is to obey God's commandments, as we shall see when we discuss the 'righteous', it is a peculiarity of the Psalms of Solomon that God is seldom depicted as giving commandments (an exception is 14.1 [2]), particular commandments are almost never specified, and particular transgressions are only infrequently itemized (2.3; 2.14f. [13], see below). The psalmist(s), that is, had very little halakic interest, and in this respect the Psalms of Solomon differ widely from Jubilees and Rabbinic literature but are closer to the various sections of I Enoch. While keeping the commandments is implied, though not emphasized as the special activity of the covenant people, the author primarily defines the particular situation of the elect in another way, and one which is both unique and striking. The terms of the covenant are that God will be faithful and will not desert his people, and the people are under God's yoke and 'the rod of [His] chastening' (7.8 [9]). That it is the special role of God's people to be chastened and suffer is repeatedly emphasized. God's 'chastisement is upon us as (upon) a first-born, only-begotten son, to turn back the obedient soul from folly (that is wrought) in ignorance' (18.4f. [4]; cf. 8.32 [26]; 8.35 [29]; 10.2f.).

This is especially striking in the light of the traditional view that the righteous prosper in this life, which was still dominant in Ben Sirach and which appears in some layers of the Rabbinic literature.[8] It is in some way maintained in the Psalms of Solomon, at least to the degree that the righteous do not suffer so much as do the wicked. They are chastised but not destroyed (13.1–7 [1–8]).[9] The author of Ps. 1, however, takes rather ironic note of the traditional view. He had counted himself righteous because of his prosperity, so that when war threatened he thought that God would protect him (1.2f.). But he has to grant that the prosperity of his enemies (probably the Romans, though possibly the Hasmoneans) exceeded anything he had imagined: 'Their wealth spread to the whole earth, and their glory unto the end of the earth' (1.4). If prosperity is a test of righteousness, the Romans (or Hasmoneans) must have been really righteous! But they became insolent; their sins were in secret (1.6f.) – that is, they were not punished for them and still appeared prosperous and consequently righteous. In this situation the view

---

[8] See above, p. 125.

[9] In 13.7 (8), Gray suggests either 'secretly' or 'sparingly' for *en peristolē* as describing the way in which the righteous are chastened. Stein has 'a little' and Frankenberg leaves a lacuna. Ryle and James translate 'secretly' but were tempted by 'a little'. In any case the difference between the destruction of the wicked and the chastisement of the righteous is clear.

seems to have developed that it is the special characteristic of the pious to be chastened. This combines the old view with the new situation. The sign of righteousness is to be chastened for one's sins rather than to be prosperous, for the wicked may be prosperous; but not to be destroyed, for the wicked will ultimately be destroyed.

The final salvation of the righteous after their chastening and the destruction of the wicked are repeated themes. 'Destruction' here seems to mean both death and eternal death or torment.[10] Thus the wicked are said to 'perish for ever' (15.13b [12]), to inherit 'Sheol and darkness and destruction' (14.6 [9]), and to be pursued into Sheol by their iniquities (15.11 [10]). The precise view of the situation of sinners after death is not clear, but it is evident that the sinners will be punished both here and eternally. The pious, on the other hand, are rewarded with 'life' and are preserved from the destruction of the sinners, even though they do suffer from God's chastisements. Using a phrase reminiscent of the promise in Jubilees that Israel would be a 'plant of righteousness' which would 'not be rooted out' (Jub. 36.6), the psalmist writes:

> The Paradise of the Lord, the trees of life, are His pious ones.
> Their planting is rooted for ever;
> They shall not be plucked up all the days of heaven. (14.2f. [5, 4])

As the sinners inherit destruction, the pious 'inherit life in gladness' (14.7 [10]). Further, God protects the pious. 'The flame of fire and the wrath against the unrighteous shall not touch' the one who calls on God (15.6 [4]). God has marked the righteous so that they may be saved from his wrath (15.8 [6]). The destruction of the sinner does not touch the righteous (13.5 [6]); although he is chastened, his chastening is not like the 'overthrow of the sinners' (13.5 [7]).[11] The best summary statement of the salvation of the righteous and the punishment of the wicked on the basis of behaviour is 9.9f. (5):

> He that doeth righteousness layeth up life for himself with the Lord;
> And he that doeth wrongly forfeits his life to destruction;
> For the judgements of the Lord are (given) in righteousness
> to (every) man and (his) house.

[10] See Winter in *IDB* III, p. 959: some passages suggest that sinners have no part in the world to come (13.10 [11]; 3.13f. [10f.]; 9.9 [5]), while others indicate suffering for them after death (14.6 [9]; 15.11 [10]; 15.15b [13]; the last passage does not, however, seem to be put in the appropriate category). This is one of the minor inconsistencies which may be attributed to different authors, although it is not impossible that the same author could say both things.

[11] We need not establish here whether or not an after-life is envisaged for the righteous. While granting that the pious of the period did believe in the resurrection of the body, Büchler has strongly argued that such passages as 14.7 (10); 15.13–15 (11–13); 9.9 (5) do not refer to it, but only to the salvation of the righteous at the time of the physical destruction of the wicked (*Piety*, pp. 150–5). Braun, on the other hand, with many others, considers that a passage such as 15.15 (13) shows that life after death is the reward expected by the pious ('Erbarmen Gottes', p. 15). Büchler's seems the better understanding of the texts.

God's justice and mercy

In apparent contradiction to this view of the strict justice of God in dispensing reward and punishment on the basis of deeds is the more frequent assertion that sinners are dealt with according to strict justice, while the righteous or pious receive mercy.[12] Thus in the verses immediately following those last quoted, the righteous are said *not* to be reproved for the sins which they commit when they repent; and God is described as good and merciful to Israel, to those who call on him and to 'us' (9.11–18 [6–9]). The distinction in the treatment of the sinners and the righteous is frequently stated:

> Bless God, ye that fear the Lord with wisdom,
>> For the mercy of the Lord will be upon them that fear Him,
>>> in the Judgement;[13]
> So that He will distinguish between the righteous and the sinner,
>> (And) recompense the sinners for ever according to their deeds;
> And have mercy on the righteous, (delivering him) from the affliction
>> of the sinner,
>> And recompensing the sinner for what he hath done to the
>>> righteous.
> For the Lord is good to them that call upon Him in patience,
>> Doing according to His mercy to His pious ones,
>> Establishing (them) at all times before Him in strength. (2.37–40 [33–36])

> Let God destroy them that insolently work all unrighteousness,
>> For a great and mighty judge is the Lord our God in
>>> righteousness.
> Let Thy mercy, O Lord, be upon all them that love Thee. (4.28f. [24,28])

> For the life of the righteous shall be for ever;
>> But sinners shall be taken away into destruction,
>> And their memorial shall be found no more.
> But upon the pious is the mercy of the Lord,
>> And upon them that fear Him His mercy. (13.9b–11 [11f.])

The tension between rewarding the righteous according to their deeds and according to God's mercy is pointed up by noting the use of the phrase 'live by'. In Psalm 14 the pious are said to live 'by the law':

> Faithful is the Lord to them that love Him in truth,
>> To them that endure His chastening,
>> To them that walk in the righteousness of His commandments,

---

[12] Cf. Büchler, *Piety*, p. 180.
[13] Greek: *meta krimatos*, which probably translates *bemishpat*, 'in judgment'. Ryle and James: 'for the mercy of the Lord is with judgement upon them that fear him'. Harris and Mingana: 'mercies . . . on them that fear Him with judgement'.

> In the law which He commanded us that we might live.
> The pious of the Lord shall live by it[14] for ever. . . . (14.1f. [1–3])

On the other hand, the pious who fear God are said to live by his mercy:

> And sinners shall perish for ever in the day of the Lord's judgement,
> When God visiteth the earth with His judgement.
> But they that fear the Lord shall find mercy therein,
> And shall live by the compassion of their God;
> But sinners shall perish for ever. (15.13b–15 [12f.])

In both cases the Greek for 'live by' is *zēsontai en*, and the Hebrew was presumably *yiḥyu b-* (so both Stein and Frankenberg). We are dealing with a point which is very important for understanding the religious perception of the psalmist(s). The righteous on the one hand do obey the law (Ps. 14) and God is faithful to reward obedience, just as he punishes disobedience. On the other hand, the salvation of the righteous is due not to their own merits, but purely to the mercy of God, who chose them and who forgives them.[15]

The themes of strict judgment according to their deeds for the sinners and mercy for the pious are very common in the Psalms of Solomon. In addition to the passages already noted, we may cite 2.7–9 (God treats sinners as they deserve and shows no pity); 2.17 (16) ('For Thou hast rendered to the sinners according to their deeds'); 8.14f. (13f.) (the sinners 'left no sin undone. . . . Therefore God mingled for them a spirit of wandering'); and, most striking, 17.10–12 (8–10):

> According to their sins didst Thou recompense them, O God;
> So that it befell them according to their deeds.
> God showed them no pity;
> He sought out their seed and let no one of them go free.
> Faithful is the Lord in all His judgements
> Which He doeth upon the earth.

On the other hand, God is merciful to the poor (5.2; 10.7 [6]; 15.2 [1]); he has mercy on the house of Israel (9.19 [10]; 18.1); he pities the seed of Israel (7.8; 11.2 [1]) and shows mercy to the house of Jacob (7.9 [10]). The righteous obtain mercy (14.6 [9]; 16.15), and God is merciful to those who truly love him (6.9 [6]). The psalmist prays that God will have mercy on 'us', who are identified as 'the dispersed of Israel' (8.33f. [27f.]), and

---

[14] The Greek *en autō* could be either 'by it' (the law) or 'in him' (God), for both *kyrios* and *nomos* are masculine. Both the Hebrew translators use the feminine pronoun, referring to Torah, law.

[15] Similarly Büchler (*Piety*, p. 130), in discussing Ps. Sol. 6.6–9 (4–6), in which the righteous man confidently expects God to heed his prayer, points out that 'such certainty he did not derive from the great number of "works" . . . , nor did he present those to God as a bill of claims, nor accompany it by an insistent demand for the equivalent reward; but all he expected in his firm reliance was that God would show "mercy" to those who love Him sincerely'.

similarly he gives thanks for God's unmerited mercy toward himself. The psalmist was 'nigh unto the gates of Sheol with the sinner' and would have been destroyed 'Had not the Lord helped me with His everlasting mercy' (16.1–3). God's mercy is in part shown in his heeding prayer (5.7 [5]; 5.14 [12]; 6.8 [5]). Even though sinners in the day of judgment will receive no mercy, the psalmist can even say that God's mercy is upon all the earth (5.17 [15]; 18.1,3).

Several of the points which we have just been discussing have been singled out by Braun, although his understanding of them is different from that just presented. The difference may be instructive. Braun first notes the passages in which God's mercy is attributed to his own will and is presented as 'groundless', i.e. independent of actions on the part of the recipients. Here Braun discusses the numerous passages in which God is said to deal mercifully with *Israel*,[16] since Israel is the covenant people.[17] In contrast to this he sets the statements in which God's mercy is said to be given to the *righteous*,[18] judgment being the lot of the wicked but not the righteous.[19]

In Braun's discussion, it is clear that he regards as determinative for understanding the Psalms of Solomon the theme of God's mercy to the righteous, which he regards as being in contrast with God's mercy to Israel. The theme of God's mercy to the righteous he takes in the following way: human righteousness is a *presupposition* for God's mercy.[20] Thus all the pious acts – the fear and love of God, prayer and praise, willingness to suffer and readiness to confess transgression – are to be understood as 'presuppositions for the attainment of the divine mercy, therefore as an achievement which man accomplishes . . .'.[21] Even prayer for mercy is to be understood as a 'work' which produces God's grace.[22] The love of God itself is consequently a 'camouflaged self-love'.[23]

On the basis of this analysis Braun can conclude that one should not be deceived by the constant statements of confidence in salvation (*Heilsgewissheit*).[24] Although there are no statements indicating uncertainty about salvation, his analysis is nevertheless able to show that behind all the obvious statements of *Heilsgewissheit* stands a final uncertainty of salvation (*Heilsunsicherheit*).[25] The reasoning is this: the very swing of the pendulum from statements of the free mercy of God to earned mercy is a clear symptom of uncertainty.[26]

[16] Braun, 'Erbarmen Gottes', pp. 18–24.
[17] Ibid., p. 21.
[18] Ibid., pp. 25–9.
[19] Ibid., pp. 35–46.
[20] Ibid., p. 29.
[21] Ibid.
[22] Ibid., p. 30.
[23] Ibid., p. 33.
[24] Ibid., p. 46.
[25] Ibid., p. 47.   [26] Ibid.

Thus Braun has conformed the Psalms of Solomon to the picture of Pharisaic Judaism which is usual in Christian, and especially Lutheran scholarship, and which is usually supported by quotations from Rabbinic literature: it is a religion of works-righteousness in which the occasional statements of God's free mercy are submerged under the statements of self-righteousness, of salvation attained by works. Such a religion, however, leads to uncertainty, since a man can never know whether or not he has been sufficiently righteous. We have shown that this view, when referring to Rabbinic literature, is based on systematic misunderstanding of the material and the religious convictions behind it. The same point can be made about Braun's analysis of the Psalms of Solomon.[27]

The fundamental error is in considering the statements of God's mercy to Israel to be in conflict with the statements that God shows mercy to the righteous. Braun seems to have misunderstood the last theme completely. He regards it as 'very astonishing' that the righteous do not receive judgment, but rather mercy, while the wicked are judged.[28] One should not be surprised. We have seen this theme or will see it in virtually all the literature being surveyed here, and it is one of the more common themes of Palestinian Jewish literature. Braun misunderstands the theme by not understanding what it is opposite: he takes it to be a statement of earned 'mercy', opposite to statements of gratuitous mercy. The statement that God shows *mercy* to the righteous is actually opposite to statements to the effect that God rewards the righteous *for their merits*. One can find in the Psalms of Solomon a statement to the effect that God evenly distributes punishments and rewards on the basis of deeds (9.4 [2]), just as one can find such statements in Rabbinic literature, the Dead Sea Scrolls and Paul, among other places.[29] Basically, however, the righteous did not wish to claim good from God on the basis of merit, and so said that God is *merciful* to the righteous. When speaking *of God*, one can say that he is a just judge who rewards and punishes in accord with fulfilment and transgression. When speaking of one's own treatment by God, however, *particularly in the form of prayer to God*, one would hesitate to attribute good treatment by God to one's own merit. Before God, man can best hope for mercy.

There is another way in which it may be seen that Braun has misunderstood the themes of God's mercy to Israel and to the righteous. When he contrasts God's free grace with grace which is 'earned' ('Das Dilemma zwischen einer dem Menschen frei und umsonst zugewandten bnu einer vom frommen Menschen verdienten Barmherzigkeit Gottes'),[30] Braun is

---

[27] It is noteworthy that Braun does not once cite Büchler's definitive work on the Psalms of Solomon (*Piety*), in which the religious convictions of the author(s) are clearly set out.

[28] Braun, pp. 46f.

[29] Sifre Deut. 307; IQS 10.17–21; II Cor. 5.10.

[30] Braun, p. 35.

contrasting two things which are not in fact in competition with each other. The 'free grace' passages (God's mercy to Israel) have to do with the *election and preservation of Israel*. They show, as we have pointed out, that all Israel is elect and as such is 'saved'. The passages dealing with *God's mercy to the righteous* have to do with their *relative protection from temporal harm*. The wicked are considered to be those who have transgressed the covenant so severely that they are treated as Gentiles; i.e. they have forfeited their place in the free, unmerited grace bestowed by God in electing and preserving Israel, and consequently are destroyed. That original electing grace is not earned by the righteous. Rather, by being righteous they keep their place in the covenant established by grace, the preservation of which is guaranteed by God. In the view of the author of the Psalms of Solomon, God would have forfeited his unmerited covenant promises *to Israel* if he had not shown mercy to *the righteous* by preventing the destruction of those who kept the covenant. This is clearly seen in 9.11–19 (6–10), where God's mercy to the righteous is *based on* his having chosen the seed of Abraham, which involved the commitment not to reject Israel. The hope of *the righteous* for mercy springs from the covenant with *Israel*. Thus the reward is that established by God's grace. The good deeds of the righteous do not merit it, and that expression, which Braun wishes to read into the text, is precisely one which is avoided. The deeds of the righteous consist in remaining true to the covenant when others desert it and thus *remaining the chosen people* who receive God's *unmerited* grace.[31] The righteous who receive God's mercy constitute Israel. Mercy to the righteous cannot be played off against mercy to Israel.[32]

Braun seems to understand the two sorts of statements – which he depicts as statements of free and merited mercy – as options which are not only mutually exclusive logically, but which speak unequally to the basic condition of man. Thus he observes that the statements of mercy as earned by works do not 'apply to the fundamental lostness of man', but to concrete situations which place one in danger.[33] Here one sees clearly the theological presuppositions which Braun brings to the text and which

---

[31] It is instructive to note Wellhausen's discussion of grace and reward in the Psalms of Solomon. He was of the view that the hope of the pious was for *reward*, but reward was conceived as *mercy* (*Pharisäer und Sadducäer*, pp. 118f.). The view is not actually one of simple works-righteousness, since the deeds of individuals do not come to the fore: God's wrath is against the godless as a group and his mercy is on all the pious (pp. 116–18). He regarded this as a less objectionable view than that which he found elsewhere in 'Pharisaism', where simple works-righteousness is the rule. He did note, however, that in practice everything still probably depended on individual deeds of righteousness (p. 119). He offered several explanations for the superiority of the formulation of the Psalms of Solomon: in prayer individual self-achievement naturally yields to the feeling of dependence on God; the difficult times did not lend themselves to the 'Pedantismus des geistlichen Virtuosenthums' ; it is likely that the Pharisees ossified with age (p. 119).

[32] The identity of the 'righteous' and 'Israel' is demonstrated in the sub-section on the righteous and the wicked.

[33] Braun, p. 45.

have led him to misconstrue it. The author(s) of the Psalms of Solomon, like other Jews of the period, *have no* view of man's fundamental lostness. (We have already seen that even the Qumranian view of man's essential inadequacy and sinfulness is not a view of fundamental lostness, since those characteristics are maintained by those who are not 'lost'.) It is useless to criticize the statements of God's grace to the righteous for not correcting a situation which was not perceived to exist. If there was any fundamental lostness, it was eradicated by the election, which is often given thanks for and recalled. Thus the pious of the Psalms of Solomon stand within the covenant of salvation given by God's grace. They maintain their place in the covenant of the saved by remaining faithful to the commandments. Their fidelity is 'rewarded' by God by their being preserved from temporal destruction, although they do not speak of God's rewarding them, but rather of God's mercy to the pious, which is contrasted with his payment of their just deserts to the wicked (and which is not contrasted with the free grace shown in the election of Israel).

Repentance and atonement

The only means of atonement mentioned in the Psalms of Solomon are connected with God's chastening and man's repentance. We have already quoted 9.12–15 (6f.), which indicates that God forgives repentant sinners. The righteous man atones for his unwitting sins by 'fasting and afflicting his soul', and consequently God counts him guiltless (3.8–10 [7f.]); when the righteous repent, God does not reprove them for their sins (9.15 [7]). That is, repentance atones so that punishment is not necessary. God may use his chastening, however, to lead the righteous man who has sinned to repent: 'If I sin, Thou chastenest me that I may return (unto Thee)' (16.11). God's chastisement makes the ways of the righteous straight (10.3); that is, it causes him to correct his behaviour, and he is restrained 'from the way of evil with strokes' (10.1). Again, the psalmist writes that God's chastisement is for the purpose of turning back 'the obedient soul' from transgressions of ignorance (18.5 [4]). On the other hand, God's chastening punishment may count as sufficient penalty for the unwitting sins of the righteous.

> For the Lord spareth His pious ones,
>   And blotteth out their errors by His chastening. (13.9 [10])

God's forgiveness is described as his *cleansing* the repentant transgressor (9.12 [6]), and similarly God's chastisements are said to cleanse one from sin (10.1f.). The psalmist looks forward to the time when Israel will be cleansed (18.6 [5]; cf. 17.36 [32]).

The only sins which are specified as being atoned for when one repents or is chastened are the unwitting sins of the pious (3.8f. [7f.]; 13.5 [7]; 13.9 [10]). The general promise that God forgives those who repent in Psalm 9 does not specify what sin has been committed, but it is possible that the unwitting sins of the righteous are in mind. The only definite indication that those who have sinned more grievously can also return to God is Psalm 16, to which we have already referred. It is a first person singular prayer by one who was 'far from God', whose soul 'had been well-nigh poured out into death', who had been 'nigh unto the gates of Sheol with the sinner', and whose soul had 'departed from the Lord God of Israel'. In his mercy, God 'pricked' the psalmist, 'as a horse is pricked', that he might serve Him (16.1–4). This apparently indicates that God chastised the wanderer and thus moved him to return to the path of righteousness (cf. 16.11). What is significant for the present point is that the psalmist had apparently not been securely within the fold of the 'pious' all his life. It thus appears that even serious departure from God can be forgiven.

The failure to mention the sacrificial system as atoning is probably due to the nature of the Psalms and their immediate concerns. As we shall see when we discuss the character of the sinners, one of the sins was the pollution of the Temple, which indicates that the pious of the Psalms held the Temple and its sacrifices as sacred.[34]

The identification of the righteous and the wicked

We should now turn to the most pressing question: the identity and character of the righteous and the sinners and the attitude of the righteous toward the rest of the Israelites. It will already have become clear that a number of terms are used interchangeably to indicate the righteous. Perhaps the most characteristic term is 'pious' (*hosioi*, which probably reflects the Hebrew *ḥasidim*): 2.40 (36); 3.10 (8); 8.40 (34); 9.6 (3) (the pious do righteous deeds, *dikaiosynai*);[35] 13.11 (12); 14.2 (5); 14.6f. (9f.). In the last passage, the pious are paralleled with the righteous: the righteous will obtain mercy at the judgment; the pious shall inherit life. The term 'righteous' (*dikaioi*,

---

[34] On the attitude toward the Temple cult, see further Büchler, *Piety*, pp. 170–4. He argued that there were two schools of the *ḥasidim*, one favouring sacrifices as a means of atonement, and one finding them unnecessary (pp. 193f.). This may be too much to conclude from the fact that the Psalms of Solomon do not expressly mention atonement by sacrifice.

[35] Büchler (*Piety*, pp. 155–64) correctly criticized Ryle and James for taking *dikaiosynai* to refer especially to ceremonial observances and works of mercy (charity). The term refers to the actions of the righteous in general (ibid., p. 160). Büchler, however, relying on the use of terms in Josephus and Philo, also argued that *pious* refers to one's fear and love toward God, while *righteous* refers to one's justice and love toward his fellows (pp. 160–4). That this is the case in Philo and Josephus, and elsewhere in Hellenistic Jewish literature, cannot be contested. It is possible that the distinction is also in mind in the Psalms of Solomon, although it is not clearly marked. 'Righteous' and 'pious' seem more likely to be undifferentiated synonyms, and the 'righteous deeds' of the pious in 9.6 (3) may refer to their actions toward both God and man.

tsaddiqim) occurs almost as often: we have already seen numerous examples, and they are listed by Gray. The pious or righteous are also called the 'poor' (5.2; 15.2 [1]; cf. 16.14),[36] the humble (5.14 [12]), those who fear the Lord (2.37 [33]; 3.16 [12]; 4.26 [23]; 5.21 [18]; 6.8 [5]; 13.11 [12]), and those who love God (6.9 [6]; 10.4; 14.1).[37] The righteous are also indicated by the second person plural pronoun: 'we' or 'us': 4.27 (23); 5.9 (7); 7.8f. (9f.); 9.16 (8). Most striking, the righteous are also called 'Israel' and other equivalent phrases: 5.21 (18); 11.2 (1); 12.7 (6); 10.6 (5); 14.3 (5).

It is evident that all these terms refer to the same group. Many of them occur in one psalm, Psalm 14. God is faithful to *those who love him*, who endure his chastening and who walk in his commandments, that is, in the law which he commanded *us*. The *pious* live by the law and are the 'Paradise of the Lord'. They shall never be uprooted, since *Israel* is God's portion. Their opposites are the *sinners* and *transgressors* (14.4 [6]), who shall be destroyed. But the *righteous* shall obtain mercy and the *pious* inherit life. Parallelism of the terms in numerous other passages indicates their basic synonymity. Thus the pious are parallel with those who fear God in 13.11 (12); the righteous, the pious, those who call upon God and those who fear him are all parallel in 2.37–40 (32–6); Israel, the pious and the poor are parallel in 10.6–8 (5–7); Israel is parallel with the pious in 12.7 (6); Israel is parallel with those who fear God in 5.21 (18); Israel is parallel to 'we' or 'us' in 7.8 (8–9), and the house of Jacob is parallel to 'us' in the next verse; the equation of 'us' with Israel is also seen in 9.14–19 (7–10) (v. 17 [9]: 'Thou didst choose the seed of Abraham . . . And didst set Thy name upon us . . .') and in 8.33f. (27f.). Those who fear the Lord are parallel to 'us' in 4.26f. (23). These interlocking parallelisms, and others which might be cited, show beyond question that the terms all refer to the same group.[38]

The characteristics of the righteous or the pious are readily described. They obey the law (14.1 [2]) and are scrupulous to avoid even sins of ignorance (3.8 [7]); they do not pile sin on sin (3.7 [6]), but are steadfast (ibid.), although they may stumble (3.5). They always give thanks to God, even when they suffer, for they see in suffering God's chastening (3.4; 10.1f.; 14.1). No matter what their plight, they always declare God to be right (3.3,5; 2.16 [15] and elsewhere). They remember the Lord and patiently call upon him (3.3; 2.40 [36]; 6.1f.). Despite their scrupulousness in avoiding sin, they may still sin, in which case they atone and repent (3.9 [8]; 9.11–15 [6f.]). Some of their characteristics are evident from what they

[36] On the history of the term 'poor' as a designation for the properly religious, see Gélin, *Les Pauvres*. He traces the identification of the remnant as 'poor' to Zeph. 3.11–13; 2.3 (pp. 33f.).

[37] For a list of occurrences of each term which is sometimes more complete than that offered here, see Gray, *Pseudepigrapha*, p. 628. He did not note, however, that the pious are also called 'us' and 'Israel'. So also Ryle and James, p. xlviii.

[38] This is generally accepted. See Gray, p. 628; Winter, p. 959.

are called. They fear God (doubtless in the sense of Ben Sirach, as we shall see when we deal with those who do not fear him) and love him. They are poor and they suffer at the hand of sinners (2.39 [35]); thus they are also called the 'humble' (5.14 [12]).

The sinners are, in part, foreign aggressors, at least in Psalm 2:

> When the sinner waxed proud, with a battering-ram he cast
> down fortified walls,
> And Thou didst not restrain (him).
> Alien nations ascended Thine altar,
> They trampled (it) proudly with their sandals. (2.1f.)

The sinners here are obviously the Roman soldiers under Pompey.[39] It may also be these sinners who 'assailed' and caused the psalmist to cry unto the Lord in Psalm 1.1. The psalmist laments that 'Their transgressions (went) beyond those of the heathen before them; they utterly polluted[40] the holy things of the Lord' (1.8). Here the phrase 'heathen before them' probably refers to *other* heathen, and the sinners of Psalm 1 are also probably the Romans.[41] In 17.26 (23) the 'sinners' who will be 'thrust out by God' are probably the 'nations' who trample Israel down.[42]

The sinners principally in mind in the Psalms, however, are fellow Jews. The Roman invasion, in fact, was a punishment for the sins of Israel. They profaned the Temple 'because the sons of Jerusalem' had already 'defiled the holy things of the Lord, had profaned with iniquities the offerings of God' (2.3). This view is probably also in mind in 8.15f. (14f.). The same logic appears in 17.6 (5), where the psalmist says that the sinful Jews who oppress the pious have arisen because of the sins of the pious themselves. The nature of the sinfulness of the Jewish sinners is most fully described in Psalm 8, which may be quoted at length.

> In secret places underground their iniquities (were committed)
> to provoke (Him) to anger;

---

[39] See the reference to Josephus in Gray, ad loc.

[40] 'Polluted' is in Greek *ebebēlōsan*; the probable Hebrew is *hillēl*. 'Profane' is better than 'pollute', which seems to refer to ritual impurity rather than profanation. In 2.3, however, 'render unclean' (*miainō, tama'*) is parallel with 'profane' (*bebēloō, halal*).

[41] Gray, p. 628, equates the sin of 1.8 with that of 2.3a, and thus implies that the sinners of 1.8 are, like those of 2.3a, Israelites. Winter, p. 959, also takes 1.8 to refer to Israelites who are worse than heathen, not to Romans who were worse than other Gentiles. So also Büchler, *Piety*, p. 140; Ryle and James, p. xlvii. This is certainly a possible interpretation, but I incline toward the view that the sinners of Psalm 1 are Romans. Certainly their sin is similar in kind to that of the sinful Jews (insolence, profanation), but that is one of the author's points. The reference to defiling Jerusalem in 8.26 (22) seems even more clearly to refer to the Romans rather than to Jewish sinners, whom the Romans have already destroyed and led away (8.20–24 [18–21]). Following that 'defilement', God is said to judge 'the nations' (8.27 [23]). Gray, however, also takes the defilement of 8.26 (22) to be that of the Jewish sinners (p. 628). So also Winter, p. 959; Ryle and James, p. xlvii.

[42] This is also not certain, since the parallelism could be progressive: he purges Jerusalem of the Gentiles and also casts out (native) sinners.

> They wrought confusion, son with mother and father with
>   daughter;
> They committed adultery, every man with his neighbour's
>   wife.
> They concluded covenants with one another with an oath touching
>   these things;
> They plundered the sanctuary of God, as though there was
>   no avenger.
> They trod the altar of the Lord, (coming straight) from all
>   manner of uncleanness,
> And with menstrual blood they defiled the sacrifices, as
>   (though these were) common flesh.
> They left no sin undone, wherein they surpassed not the heathen.
>   (8.9–14 [9–13])

The psalmist continues that God punished them by bringing war against Jerusalem, as we have already noted. The sinners even collaborated in bringing the invaders into Jerusalem. Pompey turned on them, however, and destroyed the leaders and 'led away their sons and daughters, whom they had begotten in defilement' (8.15–24 [14–21]).

It is noteworthy that the Jewish sinners are considered by the pious to have sinned in the same way that heathen sin, and in fact to have been worse (8.14 [13]; cf. 2.11 [9]). The only two types of transgression singled out are sexual transgressions and sins against the sanctity of the Temple. The Jewish sinners committed both incest and adultery. It is not clear what 'oaths' they took 'concerning these things', unless they are being accused of having formed a secret wife-swapping society. Sexual sins are also mentioned in 2.15 (13): the daughters of Jerusalem 'defiled themselves with unnatural intercourse', and the 'profane man' is accused of being sexually promiscuous (4.4–6). Transgression against the sanctity of the Temple and the Temple service is also indicated in 2.3, which we have already quoted. The way in which the sinful Israelites were worse than the heathen seems especially to be in 'profaning' the offerings and in 'defiling' the 'holy things of the Lord', which probably refers to the Temple and its contents; for this is the kind of transgression which the Israelite sinners share with the Gentiles. The Gentiles 'profane' the holy things of the Lord (1.8) and 'defile Jerusalem and the things that had been hallowed to the name of God' (8.26 [22]).[43] It would not be correct to call transgressions against the sanctity of the Temple 'ceremonial' sins. As Büchler has correctly pointed out, the contraction of levitical impurity itself is not a sin.[44] The sin in part is in the plunder of the sanctuary (8.12 [11]), but the real heinousness of the crime is in the sinners' attitude. They behave as if there is no avenger (ibid.)

[43] See n. 41 above.
[44] Büchler, *Piety*, p. 143.

and wilfully disobey the commandments of God regarding the Temple service. It is not ceremonial fault itself which is condemned, but the attitude that is indicated when the priests wilfully treat the sacrifices as if they were 'common flesh'.

Other specific sins of the sinners are harder to itemize. The sinful man is a hypocrite and a 'man pleaser' (4.1–8 [7]). He lies even when he swears an oath (4.4). When the psalmist says that he scatters families and lays waste houses by deceit (4.13,23 [10f., 20]), it is not clear whether the crime is oppression or moral seduction. The latter seems to be indicated by the comparison with the Serpent (4.11 [9]) and by the statement that with deceit the sinners 'beguiled the souls of the flawless' (*akakoi, tamimim*) (4.25 [22]).

The attitude of the sinner is spelled out clearly, however, in Psalms 3 and 4; it is remarkably like the attitude of the sinner in Ben Sirach. Whereas the righteous man stumbles and declares God righteous (3.5), the sinner stumbles and curses his life, his birth and his mother's labour (3.11 [9]). The righteous man seeks out sin to atone for it (3.8 [7]), while the sinner adds sins to sins (3.12 [10]). We have seen that he is hypocritical, a man pleaser and governed by sexual lust. The reason for his actions is his attitude toward God. Unlike the righteous man, who remembers God (3.3) and fears him, the sinners do not remember nor fear God (4.24 [21]). The sinner thinks that 'there is none that seeth, or judgeth' (4.14 [11]). He is, in short, insolent in his unrighteousness (4.28 [24]), and is thus in this way too like the Roman aggressors (1.4–6).

The most common term in Greek is 'sinners', which, despite Gray, probably does not translate a Hebrew word *hatta'im*, but *resha'im*, 'wicked'.[45] It is not unlikely that the Greek 'unrighteous' (*adikoi*) translates the same word, or possibly *ra'im* (12.6 [5];[46] 15.6 [4]).[47] They are also called 'transgressors' (14.4 [6]; 4.21 [19]; 12.1, 4), which is *paranomoi* in Greek and which could be *pesha'im* in Hebrew, although the Hebrew translations by Stein and Frankenberg use either *resha'im* or *ra'im* for *paranomoi*.

The general scholarly view is that the pious are the Pharisees and the sinners the Sadducees.[48] The harsh indictment of the sinners is thus taken to indicate a party dispute. As Gray puts it, 'it must of course be remembered,

---

[45] See Gray, p. 628, where a list of occurrences is given. The improbability of *hatta'im* is shown by the Hebrew translations. Thus both Frankenberg and Stein have *rasha'* for *hamartōlos* in 2.38 (34) and frequently. They do occasionally use *hatta'* for *hamartōlos*, apparently for the sake of variety. Thus in 15.9–13 (8–12), Frankenberg translates *hamartōlos* with *rasha'* three times and with *hatta'* once; Stein uses each word twice, but he does not use *hatta'* where Frankenberg does. The Greek may well have translated the same Hebrew in all four cases, however, and the most probable word is *rasha'*. *Ra'* is more likely than *hatta'* as an original alternative to *rasha'*.

[46] Stein *ra'im*, Frankenberg, *'oshqim*.

[47] Stein *ra'ah*, Frankenberg *ra'*.

[48] Gray, p. 630; Winter, p. 959; Ryle and James, pp. xliv–lii; Rengstorf, *TDNT* I, p. 324; note 4 above.

and allowed for, that we are dealing with a strongly partisan work. Neither
the righteousness of the righteous, nor the sinfulness of the sinful, must be
accepted too literally.'[49] There is some truth to Gray's observation, although it should be modified. In the first place, there is nothing to indicate
that the sinners are the Sadducees as such. It is far more likely that they are
the Hasmonean High Priests and their supporters, especially those who
collaborated in allowing Pompey into the city. The two characteristic
differences between the Pharisees and the Sadducees – the questions of
the oral law and the resurrection – are not mentioned.

That the enemies of the pious are the Hasmoneans[50] and their supporters
seems clearly indicated in 17.6–8, in which a representative of the pious
laments that they are dominated by sinners who rule Israel:

> But, for our sins, sinners rose up against us;
>   They assailed us and thrust us out;
>   What Thou hadst not promised to them, they took away
>   (from us) with violence.
> They in no wise glorified Thy honourable name;
>   They set a (worldly) monarchy in place of (that which was)
>   their excellency;
> They laid waste the throne of David in tumultuous
>   arrogance. (17.6–8 [5f.])

The psalmist continues by saying that now God has punished these sinners
by means of 'a man that was alien to our race', probably Pompey. Their
seed is removed from the earth. God sought them all out 'and let not one
of them go free' (17.8b–12 [7–10]). The Sadducees were not destroyed by
Pompey or by Herod. The Hasmoneans, however, lost their power, and
in that sense were destroyed, when Pompey took Jerusalem. It remained
for Herod to complete the destruction of the Hasmoneans, but the present
reference seems to be to Pompey's conquest rather than Herod's systematic
murder of the Hasmoneans.[51] In any case, there is no support in the description of God's destruction of the enemies of the pious for the view that they
were Sadducees. Their identification as Sadducees seems to rest in part on a
simplifying equation of the Hasmoneans and the Sadducees. Thus Gray,
after saying that the 'sinners' are the Sadducees, correctly points out that
it is opposition to the non-Davidic monarchy which characterizes the Psalms
of Solomon.[52] The second point is intended to support the first. He ap-

---

[49] Gray, p. 628.

[50] Büchler (*Piety*, pp. 171–3) argues persuasively that the Hasmoneans were criticized for usurping
the kingship and for despoiling the Temple and holding the sanctity of the Temple and the sacrifices
lightly. Their priesthood as such is not challenged, only their performance of it and their usurping
the kingly title.

[51] 17.14 (he sent the sinners away to the west) seems to refer to Pompey rather than Herod. So Gray,
ad loc.; Ryle and James, ad loc.; Büchler, *Piety*, p. 172.

[52] Gray, p. 630; cf. Ryle and James, pp. xlv–xlvii.

parently thinks of the Sadducees as representing the non-Davidic monarchy. Similarly Winter says that the complaints against the priests are against 'the priestly Sadducean aristocracy'.[53] But the Hasmoneans were the High Priests, and they cannot be simply identified with the Sadducees.[54]

Apart from the question of party identification, the religious criticism of the sinners is clear: those are sinners who, in the view of the 'pious', have sinned *in such a way as to break the covenant between God and Israel.* They either robbed and profaned the Temple and its services, and were thus like Gentiles, or they actually cooperated in betraying Israel to the Gentiles. The accusations of sexual immorality may, as Winter suggests, be 'conventional'.[55] On the other hand, the charge that the Hasmonean priests served in the Temple while in a state of ritual impurity may be factual rather than simply conventional. If they did so, they were, in the view of any observant Jew who believed the Bible, wilfully flouting the express will of God. The particular charge that the priests served in the Temple after intercourse with their wives when the latter had not purified themselves after the menstrual period, to be sure, would be hard to substantiate in detail (8.13 [12]: 'And with menstrual blood they defiled the sacrifices'), and doubtless represents a general halakic dispute rather than particular knowledge of individual cases.[56]

In any case, *the sins of the sinners were considered so heinous as to cause those who committed them to forfeit their place in the covenant.* They are no longer called 'Israel'; but, as we should again point out, the title 'Israel' is applied to the righteous, the pious, those who fear and love God. Thus in 12.7 (6), the psalmist prays that the Lord's salvation may 'be upon Israel His servant for ever'. He continues by praying that the sinners may perish, while the pious inherit the covenant promises. Similarly in 7.8 (8f.) the psalmist states his assurance that God will 'pity the seed of Israel for ever' and not reject them; on the contrary, 'we' shall be under God's yoke for ever. In 18.4 (3f.) the psalmist says that God loves 'the seed of Abraham, the children of Israel', and consequently chastises 'us'. The identification is equally clear

---

[53] Winter, p. 959.

[54] The question of the relation between the Sadducees and the Hasmoneans is complex and cannot be fully treated here. They were not, however, identical. The Sadducean priesthood was probably replaced by the Hasmoneans, and the Sadducees continued as an important party after the Hasmoneans were destroyed. Further, it is unlikely that the Hasmonean priest-kings thought of themselves as belonging to one of the 'parties' (despite Ryle and James, pp. xlvf.). On the other hand, the Hasmoneans and the Sadducees probably had similar interests and views, dictated by their wealth and position. It is also noteworthy that the 'daughters of the Sadducees' are not regarded as observing the Pharisaic rules concerning purification after the menstrual period (Niddah 4.2). Cf. the accusation of the Hasmonean priesthood in Ps. Sol. 8.13 (12). Doubtless many of the supporters of the Hasmoneans were Sadducees. Nevertheless, it is stretching the similarity to describe the Psalms of Solomon as representing the party dispute between the Pharisees and the Sadducees.

[55] Winter, p. 959.

[56] See Niddah 4.2, n. 54 above.

in 9.17 (9), quoted above, and in 10.6–8 (5–7). There are two sides to this identification. One is the exclusion of those who sin in certain ways – by deliberately profaning the Temple and its sacrifices, by aiding and abetting the enemy, and by insolently being immoral and not repenting. On the other hand, the remaining 'pious' do not appear to be only a small party within Israel which arrogates to itself the titles 'Israel', 'seed of Jacob', 'seed of Abraham' and the like. The titles themselves and the constant concluding prayers that the mercy or salvation of God be upon the house of Israel (see the concluding lines of Psalms 7, 8, 9, 10 and 11) indicate that the psalmist or psalmists knew that the covenant promises include all Israel and that only those who sin in such a way as to exclude themselves are cut off from Israel. That is, if we actually had a narrowly partisan view here, the party spirit would be more evident than it is. We might expect references to those who call themselves Israelites but are not or to a special covenant concluded between God and the members of the party. But the sinners among the Jews who forfeit the name 'Israel', are only those who sin worse than the Gentiles. There is no reason to think that this charge was lightly levelled against all those in a party which disagreed with the Pharisees on the interpretation of the law. The pious are, in one respect, a limited group of the specially scrupulous. On the other hand, all those who fear and love God and who do not commit one of the three types of sin listed above can be counted among the pious and are in Israel. That is, while the concept of 'Israel' is limited, it is not limited to the members of a neatly defined party, but to those who fear and love God and do not insolently and heinously transgress his will.

This point may be seen most clearly in Psalm 17, which contains a prophecy of the new age to be inaugurated by God by means of a 'son of David' (17.23 [21]). The psalmist prays that the coming king will be strengthened,

> . . . that he may shatter unrighteous rulers,
> And that he may purge Jerusalem from nations that trample
> (her) down to destruction.
> Wisely, righteously he shall thrust out sinners from (the)
> inheritance,
> He shall destroy the pride of the sinner as a potter's
> vessel.
> With a rod of iron he shall break in pieces all their substance,
> He shall destroy the godless nations with the word of his
> mouth;
> At his rebuke nations shall flee before him,
> And he shall reprove sinners for the thoughts of their heart. (17.24–7 [22–5])

The question here is whether the 'sinners' are the same as the 'nations'. The parallelism appears to be progressive rather than synonymous, and it seems that the prophecy is that the king will both purge Israel of foreigners (cf.

also 17.31 [38]) and cast out domestic sinners. After this purging, a 'true Israel' will remain, which is called 'a holy people'; and all are 'sons of God' (vv. 28, 30 [26f.]; cf. 36 [32]). The author can speak of the 'tribes of the people that has been sanctified by the Lord', so that it appears that a full nation will remain, not just a handful of the ultra-pious (v. 28 [26]). As in the apocalyptic hope in Jubilees, Israel will then be sinless (vv. 29 [27]; 36 [32]; 46 [41]), and the ruler himself will be 'pure from sin' (v. 41 [36]). In those days Israel will be served by the Gentiles (v. 32 [30]), although their subjugation will be accomplished not by force of arms, but by God himself, and in part will be the result of the Gentiles' awe at the glory of Israel and the king (vv. 34–39 [30–35]). The psalm concludes:

> Blessed be they that shall be in those days,
>> In that they shall see the good fortune of Israel which God
>> shall bring to pass in the gathering together of
>> the tribes.
> May the Lord hasten His mercy upon Israel!
>> May He deliver us from the uncleanness of unholy enemies!
> The Lord Himself is our king for ever and ever. (17.50f. [43])

Here we see again the identification of 'us' with Israel, but again no indication that 'Israel' is restricted to a small party. On the contrary, the 'gathering together of the tribes' seems to imply that a goodly number of Jews, perhaps many currently dispersed, will not be counted as sinners and cast out, but will be included in 'Israel' when the nation is sanctified. The expansion of 'us' to include all Israel except the worst sinners seems also to be indicated in 7.9 (10): 'Thou wilt establish us . . . showing mercy on the house of Jacob.'

It is noteworthy that in Psalm 17, again as in Jubilees, the promise of the purging of Israel from sinners and the gathering of a holy people follows the statement that *all* Israel has gone astray:

For there was none among them that wrought righteousness and justice;
From the chief of them to the least (of them)[57] all were sinful;
The king was a transgressor, and the judge disobedient, and the people
sinful. (17.21f. [19f.])

The new, glorious, and sinless Israel which will arise will be created by God, through the king, out of a sinful people. The eschatological deliverance will result in more than the deliverance of the 'pious'. Apparently all Israel, including many who have sinned, will be gathered together, with only the 'wicked', who have sinned in such a way as to renounce the covenant, excluded.

[57] On the reading, see Gray, ad loc. A similar emendation is made by Stein; so also Ryle and James.

The righteousness of God

We may now turn briefly to the concept of the 'righteousness of God', which is one of the most frequent themes in the Psalms of Solomon.[58] When the psalmist says that God is righteous, he asserts that God's judgment is righteous; God is a righteous judge. Thus 2.36 (32); 4.28 (24); 8.8; 8.27–32 (23–6); 9.3–10 (2–5). God's justice makes him the avenger of sin (8.12 [11]). Just as all his judgments are just (righteous, *dikaios*), they are good (8.38 [32]). God's reliability in being the just judge also justifies the title 'faithful': he is 'faithful in all His judgements' (17.12 [10]), just as he is faithful to save those who love him and who patiently endure his chastening (14.1ff.). In his justice he punishes both sinful Israelites (2.12 [10]) and Gentiles. If his judgment against the latter sometimes seems delayed (2.29 [25]), it is nevertheless sure (2.30–6 [26–32]).

One of the most striking elements is the constant assertion that God is righteous or (using the verb) is justified, which is apparently made in the face of events which would seem to call his justice into question.[59] Thus 2.14ff. (12ff.): in spite of the open transgression of some in Israel, yet the psalmist will 'justify' God (*dikaiōsō se*), that is, declare him to be just. He continues:

> For in Thy judgements is Thy righteousness (displayed), O God.
> For Thou hast rendered to the sinners according to their deeds,
> Yea according to their sins, which were very wicked.
> Thou hast uncovered their sins, that Thy judgement might be manifest;
> Thou hast wiped out their memorial from the earth.
> God is a righteous judge,
> And he is no respecter of persons. (2.16–19 [15–18])

The righteousness of God (his *dikaiosyne*, *tsedaqah*) is thus not his charity or leniency, but his fairness; he does not respect persons. As far as I have noted, *dikaiosyne* = *tsedaqah* never refers in the Psalms of Solomon to leniency or charity.

It is a characteristic of the righteous to perceive and declare God's justice despite his observation that the pious are suffering: 3.3; cf. 8.31 (26). When all of God's dealings with men are reviewed, the psalmist can justify God (*edikaiōsa*, Gray, 'I held God righteous') (8.7). The psalmist grants the correctness of the dispersion of Israel, which was just punishment for Israel's sins and which was done so that God might 'be justified' in his righteousness (9.3 [2]). In Psalm 4, which may be one of the earliest in the collection,[60] the psalmist prays that God may remove 'those that live in hypocrisy in the company of the pious' (v. 7 [6]), so that then 'the pious may

---

[58] Cf. Becker, *Das Heil Gottes*, pp. 29–32. Becker's analysis is not followed here.
[59] See further Büchler, *Piety*, pp. 167–9.
[60] Cf. Ryle and James, p. xliv.

count righteous (*dikaiōsaisan*) the judgement of their God' (4.9 [8]). In Psalm 2, which was quoted above, however, the psalmist says that God has in fact made his judgment, and consequently his righteousness, manifest by punishing sinners. This assertion is repeated in Psalm 8:

> God laid bare their sins in the full light of day;
> All the earth came to know the righteous judgements of God. (8.8)

> God hath shown Himself righteous (*edikaiōthe*) in His judgements
>   upon the nations of the earth;
> And the pious (servants) of God are like innocent lambs in
>   their midst.
> Worthy to be praised is the Lord that judgeth the whole earth in
>   His righteousness. (8.27–9 [23f.])

This emphasis on the manifestation of the righteousness of God, which is evidenced in the destruction of sinners, serves not only to 'justify' God, but also the views of the pious, who were not totally destroyed and thus could hold themselves to have been chastised, but spared, by God.

To conclude: we see in the Psalms of Solomon the same general view of religion which we have seen elsewhere in Palestinian Judaism. As Jaubert puts it: 'Thus the principal classical categories of the covenant are represented: the covenant with the fathers and perpetual pardon by God; faithfulness to the laws.'[61] God's covenant is the basis of salvation, and the elect remain in the covenant unless they sin in such a way as to be removed. There is some lack of clarity about who is and who is not in the covenant. Definitely excluded are the rulers, the Hasmoneans, their immediate supporters, and those who betrayed Jerusalem to Pompey. I see no definite evidence to indicate that all those who were not members of a certain party were excluded, and certainly none to indicate that the Sadducees as such were excluded. The latter would have been excluded to the degree that they were among the aristocracy which supported the Hasmoneans. The 'pious' of the Psalms can, on the one hand, identify themselves with Israel, which would seem to limit Israel to the members of the 'pious' party. On the other hand, the mention of the gathering of the tribes and the general description of the coming king who would rule over a purified Israel as a great king over a great nation seem to indicate that the vision of who would ultimately be counted in 'Israel' went beyond the members of a certain sect and included all who were not branded as 'sinners' and traitors. The pious, in other words, think that they are the *true Israel in the sense that they live as Israelites should* (note that they consider that they commit only inadvertent sins, 3.8f. [7f.]; 13.5 [7]). On the other hand, they hope that all Israel will one day be 'pious', which indicates that the rest have not been definitely excluded from the

---

[61] Jaubert, *La notion d'alliance*, p. 256.

covenant. In political terms, the pious of the Psalms of Solomon are still within the framework of the greater society and are struggling to have their view prevail. They have not given up hope on the rest of Israel, except the worst sinners, nor have they concluded that they have the exclusive right to be called the covenant people.

5. IV Ezra[1]

IV Ezra in recent scholarship: the problem posed by the book

The treatment of IV Ezra will be somewhat different from the treatment of the preceding works, and we shall not analyse one by one the various themes traditional in a covenantal type of religion; for there is only one question to be determined: whether or not the covenant maintains its traditional efficacy in the view of the author of IV Ezra. To anticipate the conclusion: the view argued for here is that it does not, that in IV Ezra one sees how Judaism works when it actually does become a religion of individual self-righteousness. In IV Ezra, in short, we see an instance in which covenantal nomism has collapsed. All that is left is legalistic perfectionism.

It must immediately be noted that this view is contrary to the generally prevailing view. We may conveniently set out the issues by considering the views of three recent interpreters.[2]

Rössler saw IV Ezra as one of the three representatives of apocalyptic Judaism (the other two are II Baruch and I Enoch), which together present a uniform view of the relation between law, covenant and history.[3] It will be recalled that in apocalyptic Judaism, according to Rössler's analysis, salvation was seen as being given in the election of God, while the requirement of the election was loyalty, not necessarily minute observation of particular laws.[4] This view was contrasted by Rössler with the supposed view of Rabbinic Judaism, in which the covenant and election play virtually no role

[1] For recent views on introductory questions, see Rost, *Einleitung in die Apokryphen*, pp. 91–4; Breech, 'These Fragments I Have Shored against My Ruins: The Form and Function of 4 Ezra', *JBL* 92, 1973, pp. 267f. (on source hypotheses). The translation used here is that of Box in Charles, *Pseudepigrapha*.
The only important introductory question for this study is that of the book's integrity and coherence. This will not be decided in advance, but will be returned to at the end of the section. I do presuppose, however, that IV Ezra can be studied independently of II Baruch, since it seems more likely that II Baruch is dependent on IV Ezra than vice versa. For bibliography on the question, see P. Bogaert, *Apocalypse de Baruch*, 1969, vol. I, p. 26.
[2] We shall not here consider the history of research, but it may be noted that the question of IV Ezra's stance on soteriology has previously divided interpreters. In favour of the more pessimistic interpretation, which is the one argued for here, one may cite from the older literature Köberle, *Sünde und Gnade*, pp. 651–60. The contrary view was argued by Box, *The Ezra Apocalypse*, pp. xxxix–xliii; cf. pp. 129f.
[3] D. Rössler, *Gesetz und Geschichte*.
[4] Rössler's view was anticipated by Box: 'In the theology of S [the Salathiel-Apocalypse] it is the acceptance of the law that is the standard by which men must be judged at the last, not the observance of it' (p. xxxix, emphasis removed).

and salvation depends on the compilation of numerous individual acts of obedience. Thus with regard to IV Ezra, Rössler cited 3.13ff.; 5.27; 6.55, 59; 7.119 to prove that election determines salvation (Rössler, pp. 63, 70, 75). Despite sin, Israel is still saved (p. 74). Obedience is the condition of salvation (pp. 76f.) but does not directly earn it. On the contrary, keeping the law implies that the pious *already* belong to the *Heilsgemeinde*, and obedience determines only whether or not one remains in the *Heilsgemeinde* (pp. 101f.). Rössler cites 7.89 as exemplifying his point that 'keeping' the law means a 'fundamental "yes" to the law and not a formally understood fulfilment of commandments' (p. 86). Similarly 7.94 indicates that 'it is beyond question that a formal fulfilment of the commandments is not meant, but that attitude (*Haltung*) whose opposite is characterized as "despising"' (p. 86). In an excursus (pp. 106–9), Rössler notes the more pessimistic view of the human condition which appears in IV Ezra (3.21; 7.118; 7.68). He regards this as *Rabbinic*. Fundamentally, however, IV Ezra is regarded as differing from the Rabbis in confirming that the *Heilsgemeinde* chosen by election endures despite sin.

It will readily be observed that Rössler's view of religion in IV Ezra is very close to the description of Rabbinic religion given in this work, though Rössler held the Rabbis' view to be opposite to that of IV Ezra. Here the contrast will be maintained, but the positions more or less reversed. Just as I have argued that the description of IV Ezra given by Rössler actually fits the Rabbis, so I shall also try to show that his description of the Rabbis more or less fits IV Ezra (at least with regard to the question of the efficacy of the covenant). We shall save our own analysis, however, until the studies of Harnisch and Breech have been described.

Harnisch has carried out a remarkably penetrating and incisive analysis of IV Ezra and II Baruch,[5] and he has produced a work which relieves us of the necessity of dealing with many of the problems of IV Ezra in detail here. I find myself compelled to disagree with Harnisch on only one significant point, but even here the difference may be seen as a modification of his work rather than a direct contradiction. Whether modification or contradiction, however, the point must be insisted on, since it is crucial to the present study. It will be useful first to give a general review of Harnisch's conclusions about IV Ezra. We shall then consider Breech's recent article, which can be seen as developing the position taken by Harnisch, and finally describe the view taken here and give the evidence for it.

In Harnisch's view, the problem posed by the seer ('Ezra') in IV Ezra is that of the reliability of God (pp. 19–42). It arises from the discrepancy between the divine promises to Israel and concrete historical reality: Israel is trampled underfoot by the Gentile nations (p. 20). The problem is

---

[5] W. Harnisch, *Verhängnis und Verheissung der Geschichte*, 1969.

sharpened by the universality of sin as represented by the evil impulse which dominates the heart of man (pp. 42–58).[6] God gave the law to save, but it is prevented from bearing fruit by the evil impulse (pp. 48f.). This posing of the problem by the seer, however, does not represent the view of the author of the apocalypse (pp. 60–7). Following a suggestion by Mundle[7] which was further worked out by Brandenburger,[8] Harnisch argues that the view of the seer is a sceptical view current in the period which the book as a whole polemicizes against (p. 67). The debate between the seer and the angel in the dialogues does not represent an internal debate in the heart and mind of the author, but is rather the debate between one point of view and another. The view of the author of the apocalypse is seen in the angelic replies to the seer, in which the extreme scepticism is denied (pp. 64f.; cf. p. 323).

The answer to the problem posed by 'Ezra' is really given in the apocalypse's 'two-aeon theory' (pp. 89–247). From the point of view of the eschaton and of the fate of the world beginning with the sin of Adam, the historical period is seen as a whole as one in which sin and fate reign (pp. 106–42, especially pp. 124, 128, 131). In contrast to the historical period, the end-time offers promise of salvation (pp. 125f., referring to 7.113f. and 8.53f.), which corresponds to God's intention in creation, an intention which was perverted by transgression (p. 136). The historical period thus has the character of an interim. Notwithstanding the universality of sin and the dominance of fate during this age, the individual is held responsible for his actions (pp. 142–240). It *is* possible to obey the law (p. 152). Further, one's actions in the present determine whether or not he participates in the coming salvation (p. 149). Only the righteous will be saved (p. 177).

The concluding *Geschichtsapokalypsen* serve to assure the righteous that salvation will come, and will come within a short time (pp. 248–67); but the author wished to discourage excessive apocalyptic enthusiasm by insisting on the predetermination of the time (pp. 268–321).

Breech's view,[9] which is in fundamental agreement with that of Harnisch, is based on the insight that there is a relationship between form and meaning. He sees IV Ezra as a 'literary whole which moves perpetually from distress to consolation' (p. 270). It is this sequence which determines the meaning of the work. The early part of the book is dominated by statements of distress, and this 'distress is fully overcome only after [Ezra] has received the dream visions of the eagle and the man from the sea (13.57–58)'. Breech continues:

---

[6] These pages contain a penetrating analysis of the relationship between the fate of Israel and the power of sin which dominates all mankind. The dominating concern, Harnisch correctly notes, is the fate of Israel (pp. 57f.).

[7] W. Mundle, 'Das religiöse Problem des IV. Esrabuches', *ZAW* 47, 1929, pp. 222–49; Harnisch, pp. 60–3.

[8] E. Brandenburger, *Adam und Christus*, 1962; Harnisch, pp. 63–5.

[9] Art. cit. in n. 1 above.

'If one focuses on the motif of consolation, instead of on the contents of the several sections, then one notices that the work moves from Ezra's distress, through his efforts to console a bereaved mother, to his own consolation and subsequent speech of comfort to his community (14:27–36)' (p. 270). About the dialogues between Ezra and the angel from 3.1 to 9.22, in which the angel adamantly insists that only those who obey the law perfectly will be saved and that these will be very few, Breech comments that 'it is important to notice that these dialogues are inconclusive'. Ezra is not content and continues to ask about the end (ibid.).

The dream visions which conclude the book serve to 'reaffirm that the Most High is the true source of life and death for the community, revindicate his power, and dispel the prophet's confusion' (p. 272). 'The visions console Ezra by reassuring him that the Most High "governs the times and whatever comes to pass in their seasons" (13.58). Neither the dream visions nor the interpretations actually answer Ezra's initial questions. The religious confusion that is dispelled by the climactic section is not primarily intellectual' (pp. 273f.).

The view which is common to these three recent investigators – which is also the point at which I disagree – is the view that, according to IV Ezra, Israel will ultimately be saved. Against Rössler's position, it can be observed that the passages cited by him in favour of the election as saving (3.13–19; 5.27; 6.55, 59; 7.119) are all in the repeated pleas of the seer, who does not represent the author's viewpoint. Against Harnisch's position it must be argued that the seer not only represents the sceptical charge against God that the election and the law are of no avail, but also vainly pleads that God will overlook transgression, will exercise compassion instead of strict justice and will save sinners. The appeals are systematically denied by the angel, who (as Harnisch correctly observed) represents the author's view. Harnisch discusses these passages and notes that the appeal is denied by the angel: God will save only those who do not sin.[10] But he does not bring the seer's plea for compassion into connection with his scepticism about the value of the election. The 'Ezra' who hopefully pleads for God's compassion does not seem to represent the same party as the one who concludes that God has forfeited his promises to Israel. We see, rather, various propositions being put to the angel and confirmed or denied. While agreeing that the angel represents the author's point of view, one may doubt that 'Ezra' represents any one particular party.[11] What is consistent is the angel's position. The seer first laments Israel's situation and charges that the law and the election

---

[10] See Harnisch, pp. 235–40, on the plea in 8.20–36 and the reply. Some (e.g. Schweitzer, *Mysticism*, p. 216; Bornkamm, *Paul*, p. 139; Longenecker, *Paul: Apostle of Liberty*, p. 42) have taken the plea for compassion as representing the author's view. That view is better found in the angel's rejection. The ironic technique of the rejection is described by Harnisch, pp. 237f.

[11] Cf. Breech, pp. 271f.

are in vain. The angel replies that man himself is to blame for transgressing the law. The seer then supplicates God for mercy, saying that judgment by works will prove fatal. The angel ironically 'agrees', indicating that God has no concern for sinners but will save only the righteous, who are perfect like Ezra.[12]

Against Breech's position, it may be said that his analysis of the form, while full of insight, errs by requiring the reader to pay no heed to the content of what is actually said in chapters 1–9, but to note only that they register 'distress'. This is surely to allow form to determine meaning too exclusively. The assumption should be that what the angel actually says is important and that the content of what is said was meant to be taken seriously. Further, Breech's case is weakened by the fact, which he himself notes, that the final visions do not actually answer 'Ezra's' complaints. But even more important, *they do not reply to the angel's answers* to 'Ezra's' complaints, and it is precisely in these answers that the negative thrust of the work is carried.

We should turn from this brief commentaty on the positions of Rössler, Harnisch and Breech to an analysis of the text of IV Ezra. For the present purpose only two points will be investigated: what Ezra appeals for and the angel's response, and how the final visions do or do not give a solution to the problem posed by the dialogues.

The dialogues

It is not intended here to analyse every element of the dialogues, but only to capture the thrust of the questions and answers, so that the position of the author will become clear. The first dialogue is inconclusive. 'Ezra' charges that God, in allowing Israel to be punished, is not just; for if the deeds of Israel and the Gentiles were balanced against each other, Israel's would prove better (3.34). The angel replies that the ways of God are beyond human comprehension (4.1–21). The seer presses the question: he did not intend to ask about heavenly matters, but about the fate of Israel: 'Why is Israel to the heathen given over to reproach?' (4.23). The answer is simply that the age is hastening to the end (4.26–32). Although signs are discussed subsequently, that is the essence of the reply. We are not told that the end will bring Israel's vindication, nor that it will not.

In the second dialogue the question is the same: why 'have they who denied thy promises been allowed to tread under foot those that have believed thy covenants?' (5.29). The answer is again enigmatic, but somewhat more reassuring. God really loves Israel (5.33), but how that love is given effect is beyond 'Ezra's' comprehension (5.40). After a description of the end, the angel does give some assurance. Whoever survives the end-time tribulations

---

[12] These dialogues are analysed below.

will see salvation (6.25). It is still not known who these are. Evil will be blotted out (6.27), but the question is, who will the individuals be who will profit from it. After the problem of Israel has been put by the seer one more time (6.38–59), the gap between present reality and God's intention in creation (the world was created for Israel's sake, 6.55) and in the election of Israel is finally responded to by the angel. The world was, to be sure, created for Israel. But unfortunately Adam sinned, so that the world is difficult. The future world provides salvation, but only for those individuals who can make it through the difficulties of this world (7.11–14). 'Ezra' seizes the point immediately: it is the righteous who will have the comfort of the coming world, while the wicked will perish (7.17f.). The angel agrees:

Yea, rather, let the many that now are perish than that the law of God which is set before them be despised! For God did surely command them that came (into the world), when they came, what they should do to live, and what they should observe to avoid punishment. Nevertheless they were disobedient, and spake against him. . . . (7.20–22)

This is the rigorous position which the angel will maintain throughout.

Ezra launches several appeals. It is all very well to say that those who keep the commandments will live, but mankind is afflicted with an evil heart and is estranged from God. Mankind as it is walks the path of death, and that applies to 'well nigh all that have been created' (7.45–48). The angel agrees: 'I will rejoice over the few that shall be saved', 'and I will not grieve over the multitude of them that perish' (7.60f.). The seer reiterates the evil plight of man, which is so bad that not being born would be better (7.62–69), and again the angel agrees. God *has been* long-suffering, but now the time for justice has come, and sinners will be dealt with as they deserve (7.70–74). The angel favours 'Ezra' with a description of the fate of the souls of the wicked and the righteous, but the operative definition of the latter is that they 'painfully served the Most High, and were in jeopardy every hour, that they might observe the Law of the lawgiver perfectly' (7.89).

Perhaps, proposes the seer, the righteous can intercede for the ungodly at the judgment (7.102). The angel replies, in short, no. Only individual righteousness will count (7.104–15). The plight of man is returned to by the seer: *what is the point of the promise of salvation for obedience when everyone in fact sins?* (7.116–26). The angel again *agrees* with the seer's pessimistic appraisal of man's situation, adding the exhortation that those who are victorious (and obey the law) can receive the promised salvation (7.127–31).

'Ezra' then launches his most moving appeal, based as it is on the entire Jewish conception of the mercy of God and his steadfastness toward his chosen people. God is called 'compassionate' and 'gracious' (he accepts the repentant); he is 'long-suffering', 'since he is ready to bestow favour rather than exact'. He is 'of great mercy', 'good' and, most important, 'forgiving, for if he did not pardon those that were created by his word, and blot out the multitude of their iniquities, there would, perchance, be very few left of an innumerable multitude' (7.132–40). Here are all the traditional Jewish terms for God, used in an appeal for mercy. But the angel picks up only the last words: 'This age the Most High has made for many, but the age to come for few'; 'many have been created, but few shall be saved!' (8.1–3). God's character as compassionate, gracious, forgiving and the like is effectively denied; or at least the seer's argument on the basis of those characteristics is denied: say what he will about how God should prove himself compassionate, the seer's appeal for the restoration of sinners is refused. The same appeal is repeated but again denied. God will be called gracious if he will have compassion on those without works of righteousness; the good, after all, can stand on their own. The trouble is that 'there is none of the earthborn who has not dealt wickedly'. Thus God's compassion is desperately needed (8.31–36). But the angel is adamant.

Some things thou hast spoken aright, and according to thy words so shall it come to pass. For indeed I will not concern myself about the creation of those who have sinned, or their death, judgement, or perdition; but I will rejoice (rather) over the creation of the righteous, (over) their pilgrimage also and their salvation and their recompense. (8.37–39)

The one difference between 'Ezra's' most pessimistic statement of the case (all sin and all therefore die) and the angel's reply is that there are a few righteous. Ezra himself is named among them, and he will be saved (8.47–54). But 'Ezra' is admonished to 'ask no more concerning the multitude of them that perish' (8.55). It would seem that the martyrs are also counted among the few righteous (8.57; cf. 7.89). Thus we see that the comfort given in the promise that the end will soon come applies to very few, to those who are more or less perfect and who remain completely obedient even though they suffer persecution and death.

There is nothing in the dialogues which contradicts this rigorous view. The possibility of repentance is briefly mentioned by the angel (9.12; cf. 7.82), but the point is that transgressors have not repented. The angel continues by reiterating how few will be saved. They compare to the wicked who are doomed as a drop to the flood, as a grape to a cluster, as a plant to a forest. 'Perish then, the multitude which has been born in vain; but let my grape be preserved, and my plant, which with much labour I have perfected' (9.13–22).

Nor is there any indication that the few are Israel and the multitude the Gentiles. In the course of the dialogues the emphasis shifts from the plight of the nation of Israel to the plight of the individuals who are given the law but who *transgress* it. These last are presumably themselves Israelites, and *they* are condemned. In any case the angel's position that only perfect (or nearly perfect) obedience suffices is consistently maintained. The requirement of perfection is seen not only in the angel's definition of the righteous (7.89), but it is clearly implied in 'Ezra's' laments and appeals. The point of the seer's saying that the plight of man is that all (or 'well nigh' all, 7.48) are *evildoers* (7.138–40) who did not keep the *precepts* (7.72), but have committed *iniquities* (7.138–40; 7.68, 72) and done *works* and *deeds* which bring damnation (8.33; 7.120) is precisely that *transgression* is inescapable. They are blessed who *keep the commandments* (7.45), but who can do so adequately? Despite the characterization of the multitude of the wicked as those who *despise, deny* and *scorn* God and his law (7.24; 8.55f.) and the failure to itemize instances of disobedience, the requirement of God is not only that of basic loyalty, as Box and Rössler have argued, but of actual obedience (7.22). *Loyalty* is not impossible for well nigh all, but perfect obedience is. Man's plight is demonstrated by God's attitude. His *love* for Israel (5.40) is shown in his maintaining his *requirements*: obey or be damned. It is better for transgressors to perish than for the glory of the law to be besmirched by having mercy on them. This appears to be the view of the author of the dialogues, and on this basis we must disagree with Rössler's position that the election as such saves, and also with Harnisch's that it is primarily the seer's scepticism which is answered by the angel. The seer's pessimism is *confirmed*, while his appeals for mercy upon transgressors are denied.

The visions

We must now consider the proposal, made by Harnisch but taken further by Breech, that the concluding visions provide an answer to the problem posed by the dialogues. We should first note that, while 9.22 marks the end of the visions in which the seer holds dialogue with the angel, the angelic position of 3.1–9.22 is immediately confirmed in the succeeding section, only now presented as having been accepted by 'Ezra'. The point of 9.29–37 is summarized in the final two verses: 'We who have received the Law and sinned must perish, together with our heart, which has taken it in: the Law, however, perishes not but abides in its glory.' Here God's power and the righteousness of his law are affirmed, but this does nothing for the individual who transgresses. He remains just as doomed as in 3.1–9.22. The vision which immediately follows, that of the disconsolate woman, does nothing to dispel this view. Most of those who are born go to destruction (10.11). The eternal glory of Zion is revealed (10.50), but nothing is said about the salvation of Israelites who transgress. The law and Zion are good and glorious *in and of themselves*; they do not, however, bring salvation. The picture of the glory of Zion in 10.50 seems simply to confirm the prose statement about the glory of the law in 9.36f.: those who sin perish but the law remains glorious.

The eagle vision, which follows, responds less directly, or perhaps not at all, to the problem of the damnation of the many. If 12.34 is authentic and not an interpolation as Box thought, we learn that those who survive (the final war with Rome?) will be delivered. We cannot determine, however, whether or not those who survive will be only those very few (a drop compared to a flood, cf. 9.16) who succeeded in obeying the law perfectly. If it is those who are meant, there is then some consolation for them. If Israel is meant, however, then this vision is in simple contradiction to the view of the earlier part of the book in a way that cannot be overlooked, harmonized or made to disappear. I am generally of the view, however, that the promised ultimate victory of Israel over Rome which is the burden of the eagle vision is simply not responsive to the earlier problem of sin and damnation and thus reveals that the original *Sitz im Leben* of the eagle vision is divergent from that of the earlier chapters.

It is only in the vision of the man from the sea that the earlier pessimistic view may be directly countered. We read, to be sure, that those who survive will be those who 'have works and faith towards' God (13.23). The subsequent interpretation, however, seems to presuppose that there will be a *lot* of such people. When the man stands on Mount Zion, all the nations will come to fight against him, but he will destroy them (13.33–38). These are obviously the Gentile nations, for there is another multitude gathered, consisting of the reassembled ten tribes (who managed to keep the statutes in exile by migrating to an unknown land) and the resident Jews of Palestine (if 13.48 is not an interpolation). This reassembled and united Israel the man defends by destroying the (Gentile) nations (13.39–51).

This last vision, by appealing to the traditional images of the reassembling of Israel and the destruction of the Gentiles, simply presupposes that Israelites keep the law and will be ultimately saved by God. The final redactor may have seen such a vision as a 'saving' conclusion to IV Ezra, one which would make it palatable and bring it into conformity with the prevailing Jewish hope. By implication the angelic view of the earlier chapters is denied, but the author does not engage in the probing analysis on the question of transgression and damnation which consumed the author of the Ezra-angel dialogues. One can confirm Breech's hypothesis if one has in mind the view of the final redactor who added this vision (and possibly the others) to the dialogues. But one cannot appeal to the man from the sea vision to deny (as Breech seems to do: the dialogues are inconclusive) that the author of the dialogues meant precisely what he had the angel say: that perfect obedience to the law is required for salvation; that transgressors, whether Gentile or Jewish, are destroyed; and that hardly anyone, judged by this strict criterion, will be saved.

Thus the answer to the meaning of the book is, in part, determined by the answer one gives to the question of authorship. If it is considered that the work is unitary and that its real meaning is given in the final vision, one must agree with the position of Breech and Harnisch. It is hard to see, however, how one can hold this view so firmly as to overlook the reiterated negative replies which the angel gives to the hopes and pleas of the seer in 3.1–9.22. One would have to suppose that the author who so carefully constructed the dialogues and who dealt there with the most pressing questions of human existence – whether there is hope for man since he habitually sins, whether it would have been better not to have been born – decided, with the final section, to dismiss those questions from mind and to depict a traditional (and comparatively naive) victory of Israel over the Gentiles. It seems to me more likely that the final vision (and chapter 14) constitute a 'saving' appendix to make IV Ezra more palatable in Jewish circles. It thus appears best to consider the *view of the main author* of the book – a view which is not contradicted by the visions which immediately follow the dialogues – *to be that of the angel* in the dialogues. It is the 'angelic' position that, in effect, the covenant as such does not bring the benefits of God's protection from torment and even destruction (contrast the Psalms of Solomon: chastened but not destroyed), but that only the perfectly righteous, who are few, will be saved by God, and that only after suffering and pain. One has here the closest approach to legalistic works-righteousness which can be found in the Jewish literature of the period; for only here are the traditional characteristics of God – he freely forgives and restores sinners and maintains the covenant promises despite transgression – denied. Put another way, IV Ezra differs from other literature which we have studied by viewing sin as a virtually inescapable power (see 3.20), while still considering it to be transgression of the law which must be punished accordingly. We noted that in Qumran men, even the elect, were considered to be 'in sin' in the sense of being participants in human frailty, but that human frailty as such did not condemn. Means were provided for the atonement of most transgressions, and the elect were not 'lost' despite being 'in sin'. In IV Ezra, however, the human inability to avoid sin is considered to lead to damnation. It is this pessimistic view of the human plight which distinguishes the author from the rest of Judaism as it is revealed in the surviving literature.

IV

PALESTINIAN JUDAISM 200 b.c.e.–200 c.e.

Conclusion

Covenant and law

One of the principal issues in understanding the Judaism of the period studied is the relationship between law and covenant. In Christian scholarship there has generally been the conviction – all but universally held – that there was a degeneration of the biblical view in post-biblical Judaism.[1] The once noble idea of the covenant as offered by God's grace and of obedience as the consequence of that gracious gift degenerated into the idea of petty legalism, according to which one had to earn the mercy of God by minute observance of irrelevant ordinances. This thesis has been pushed to its utmost limits with regard to Rabbinic literature by Rössler, but he by no means originated it. The view is common in biblical scholarship. One may mention, for example, the generally admirable essay on the covenant published by H. A. A. Kennedy in 1915. Describing the relation between covenant and law in the Old Testament, he wrote:

it must not be forgotten that the conception of the revealed legal system presupposed the existence of the Covenant. It is given to the community as standing *within* the Covenant. And that relationship in turn presupposed what we can only call faith in the mercy and goodness of God. So that all that is done by the worshipping people in the later ritual is not for the purpose of reaching fellowship with God: its aim is to maintain the fellowship unbroken.[2]

However, the balance shifted in the later period:

But for this period, the crowning proof of Israel's election is its possession of the Law. Obedience to the Law, therefore, is the chief token of its acknowledgement

---

[1] In addition to the introduction to Chapter I above, see the ample documentation given by Koch, *The Rediscovery of Apocalyptic*, pp. 37, 46f. Limbeck (*Die Ordnung des Heils*) has also discussed the widespread view that post-biblical Judaism represents an ossification of the religion of Israel. He shows how the view (which he traces to Wellhausen) entered not only New Testament scholarship (he discusses Bousset, Bultmann, Bornkamm and Conzelmann; pp. 13, 18f.), but also Old Testament scholarship (Noth and von Rad; p. 16). He attributes the slight influence of Moore and Bonsirven to the dominating position of Billerbeck (pp. 19f. n. 30). His own construction, however, does not include Rabbinic literature.

[2] Kennedy, 'The Covenant Conception', p. 389.

of the Divine grace. But as this obedience came to involve the observance of minute regulations, the notion of merit was bound to insinuate itself, and so the rigid contract-conception overshadowed that of the Covenant, which rested on the mercy of God.[3]

I have maintained, and I hope demonstrated, that this rests on a misreading of the later Jewish material and that the *first* description of the covenant conception given by Kennedy was maintained in Israel, not excluding the Rabbis, who supposedly are the best representatives of a petty legalism which supplants the idea of the covenant by God's grace and Torah obedience as man's proper response within the covenant.

This relation between covenant and law we found to be almost universal in the material surveyed. The one exception is Ben Sirach, who does not bring the question of obedience to the law into connection with the question of election. This is doubtless to be explained by two facts: 1. he addressed only Israelites (despite the general character of many of his admonitions), and the question of the elect versus the non-elect scarcely arose (he does present a traditional picture of the redemption of Israel in chapter 36); 2. he had no conception of punishment and reward in the world to come; thus he dealt with only the relative degrees of prosperity and suffering experienced within this life. He could treat the fate of the righteous and the wicked in this world by use of the general doctrine of retribution, and the question of whether or not an individual was truly 'in' and would thus be 'saved' did not arise. Otherwise, however, in all the literature surveyed, *obedience maintains one's position in the covenant, but it does not earn God's grace as such.* It simply keeps an individual in the group which is the recipient of God's grace. This is true also of IV Ezra. Even the pessimistic position of the dialogues does not actually reverse this relationship between covenant and obedience. The difference is that obedience must be perfect, so that transgression leads to damnation. Thus salvation in the dialogues of IV Ezra is constructively by works – one must be perfectly obedient to be saved; but the formal relationship between covenant and law is maintained – obedience keeps one in the covenant.

It has frequently been urged as evidence against the primacy of the covenantal conception in 'late Judaism' that the word 'covenant' does not often appear. Thus van Unnik, agreeing with Bousset that the covenantal idea receded in Judaism, notes that Bousset correctly did not place 'covenant' in his index.[4] Word studies are not always deceptive, but they can be, and this one is. On the basis of the analysis of the Rabbinic conception of the covenant and election in Chapter I above, I would venture to say that it is the

---

[3] Ibid., p. 392.

[4] W. C. van Unnik, 'La conception paulinienne de la nouvelle alliance', *Littérature et théologie pauliniennes*, by A. Descamps and others, p. 113. Similarly Roetzel, *Judgement in the Community*, pp. 55f.

fundamental nature of the covenant conception which largely accounts for the relative scarcity of appearances of the term 'covenant' in Rabbinic literature.[5] The covenant was presupposed, and the Rabbinic discussions were largely directed toward the question of *how* to fulfil the covenantal obligations. The very arguments and the way in which the questions are worded show the conviction that the covenant was in force – that God was being true to his covenantal promises. The question was precisely how Jews should be true to their covenantal obligations. Similar observations could be made about most of the rest of the literature. The covenant is directly mentioned in the Dead Sea Scrolls relatively frequently because the very existence of the sect was based on the sectarians' conviction that they had the true covenant (or the true interpretation of it) and because of the need to define special requirements for being admitted to and staying in the covenant. Generally, however, the word does not much appear in the literature of the period, even though covenantal ideas are absolutely common. Further, obedience is universally held to be the behaviour appropriate to being in the covenant, not the means of earning God's grace.

The uniformity of Judaism on this point, as well as the unique position of IV Ezra among the literature which remains, can be seen by considering the theme of God's *mercy*. This is a theme which, in all the literature surveyed except IV Ezra, sits side by side with the theme of strict retribution – to each according to his deeds. There are two different formulations concerning mercy and justice. One is that of Rabbinic literature: God's mercy is greater than his justice. In the other literature, the usual formulation is that God punishes the wicked *for their deeds*, while bestowing *mercy on the righteous*. The theme of mercy to the righteous is worked out especially elaborately in the Dead Sea Scrolls and the Psalms of Solomon, and it appears also in Ben Sirach, Jubilees and I Enoch.[6] The themes of *mercy* and *retribution* or *justice* are not actually in competition, but serve different functions. Statements to the effect that God pays each man his just due serve to assert the justness of God and to assure both sinners and the righteous that what they do matters. God is not capricious. He will neither punish for obedience nor reward transgression. The theme of mercy – whether put in terms of God's mercy in electing Israel, God's mercy in accepting repentant sinners (repentance does not earn a reward, but is responded to by God in mercy), or God's 'rewarding' the righteous because of his mercy – serves to assure that election

---

[5] A second reason would be the use of other terms, such as 'Kingdom of Heaven' and 'yoke of Heaven'. See Chapter I, sections 4 and 11. One may here compare Heinemann's conclusion, on the basis of a study of *diathēkē*, that Philo did not know the covenant conception. Heinemann overlooked other terms, such as 'commonwealth'. See 'The Covenant as a Soteriological Category and the Nature of Salvation in Palestinian and Hellenistic Judaism', *Jews, Greeks and Christians (Festschrift W. D. Davies)*, ed. Hamerton-Kelly and Scroggs, 1976, n. 55.

[6] See 'mercy to the righteous' in the index. From Rabbinic sources, see also the prayers cited above, pp. 224f.

and ultimately salvation cannot be earned, but depend on God's grace. One can never be righteous enough to be worthy in God's sight of the ultimate gifts, which depend only on his mercy. The theme of God's mercy as being the final reliance even of the righteous appears in all the literature surveyed except IV Ezra: there God's compassion is denied by the angel, and judgment *is* strictly according to deeds. The presence of the theme of God's mercy in the rest of the literature and its absence in IV Ezra help to show that salvation was not generally held to be earned by merit. It is in IV Ezra that it is clearly said that the righteous *merit* redemption and do not require mercy (IV Ezra 8.33),[7] and there is certainly no mercy for the wicked. In IV Ezra there appears to be no room for one who is basically loyal (in Rabbinic terms, one who 'confesses') but who disobeys. The question is, how perfect must obedience be to prove basic loyalty? In IV Ezra the requirement is extreme. Those who 'believe' also obey, while those who transgress are considered to 'deny'.[8] Thus the theme of God's mercy to the basically righteous but not always obedient members of Israel (that is, virtually all Israelites) does not appear. This is why so few are counted among the saved. Put another way, IV Ezra differs from the other literature surveyed by not specifying that only *certain* transgressions amount to denying God and the covenant. This, too, is a theme generally found in the literature but absent in IV Ezra.[9] There it is transgression as such, not just the most deliberate or heinous transgressions, which amounts to a denial of God.

The common pattern of religion: covenantal nomism

The distinctiveness of IV Ezra helps point up the degree to which the type of religion best called 'covenantal nomism' is common to Judaism as it appears in the literature considered here. The 'pattern' or 'structure' of covenantal nomism is this: (1) God has chosen Israel and (2) given the law. The law implies both (3) God's promise to maintain the election and (4) the requirement to obey. (5) God rewards obedience and punishes transgression. (6) The law provides for means of atonement, and atonement results in (7) maintenance or re-establishment of the covenantal relationship. (8) All those who are maintained in the covenant by obedience, atonement and God's mercy belong to the group which will be saved. An important interpretation of the first and last points is that election and ultimately salvation are considered to be by God's mercy rather than human achievement.

---

[7] 8.33 is spoken by 'Ezra', but it is one of the things which the angel considers him to have 'spoken aright' (8.37).
[8] Rössler, Harnisch and others define disobedience in IV Ezra as being *only* basic disloyalty. It seems better to define disloyalty as *any* disobedience.
[9] See 'denial of God (the covenant)' in the index.

Not every single document studied contains every one of the motifs just listed. I Enoch, for example, is notably 'defective'. I believe that even in the various parts of I Enoch one can see enough to justify the assumption that the elements which are not mentioned are presupposed. Thus one can note the requirement of obedience and infer that something must have been given to be obeyed, even though the giving of the law is not rehearsed. Similarly, we may note the existence of the theme that the righteous receive mercy while the wicked are punished strictly for their deeds. This again seems to imply the view that election and salvation as such are not by works of law, although obedience is the condition of remaining righteous.

It is certainly not the case that there is uniformity of systematic theology among the material studied, and this is not implied by arguing for a basic consistency in the underlying pattern of religion. The Qumran definition of the covenant and the commandments 'given by the hand of Moses' certainly differs from the Rabbinic; but there is agreement on the primacy of the covenant and its significance and on the need to obey the commandments. The means of atonement are not precisely identical, but there is agreement on the place of atonement within the total framework. That differences within a common pattern can cut very deep is shown by the existence of the Qumran community as a separate sect, but the differences should not prevent us from seeing what was common.[10] Thus to the frequent assertion that there were numerous *Judaisms* in the Palestine of the period studied, one can reply yes or no, depending on just what is meant. There were obviously different groups and different theologies on numerous points. But there appears to have been more in common than just the name 'Jew'.[11]

Apocalypticism and legalism

This study lends no support to those who have urged that apocalypticism and legalism constitute substantially different religious types or streams in the Judaism of the period.[12] The existence in Qumran of a strongly nomistic group with a pronounced expectation of an imminent end should be a major caution against accepting this simple dissection. The Dead Sea Scrolls indicate that a heightened expectation of an imminent end is not itself constitutive of a distinct religious type or even sect. The general type of religion found in Qumran is not exceptional, although there are noteworthy

---

[10] So also Sandmel, *The First Christian Century*, pp. 23f., 83.

[11] The material studied here is all of Palestinian provenance, and thus the conclusion about what was common must be limited to Palestinian Jewish literature. I have elsewhere argued that 'covenantal nomism' is also characteristic of much of Hellenistic Judaism, although one finds important emphases in Hellenistic Jewish theology which are not extant in any Palestinian literature. See 'The Covenant as a Soteriological Category and the Nature of Salvation in Palestinian and Hellenistic Judaism'.

[12] The problem is discussed, for example, by Koch (*The Rediscovery of Apocalyptic*, p. 53) and Russell (*The Method and Message of Jewish Apocalyptic*, pp. 23–8).

and unique aspects. Further, the apocalypticism of the sect is not what makes it a sect. It is a sect because of a different definition of the *election* and of membership in the covenant. There is no reason to think that everyone who expected the end to come shortly redefined the covenant and the election.

I am unpersuaded by the view that the conception of *obedience* is distinctive in the apocalyptic literature. The fact that no particular commandments are specified in I Enoch and IV Ezra does not seem to imply that concrete obedience to the biblical commandments was not expected. On the contrary, as we noted in our discussion of IV Ezra, it is the *precepts* and *commandments* which are to be obeyed. Obedience demonstrates basic loyalty, but this is also true of Rabbinic literature, as our discussion of the theme of confessing and denying demonstrated. Jubilees is also instructive here. While not principally a work of apocalyptic expectation,[13] it has a definite futurist orientation, especially in chapters 23 and 50. Yet few works are more 'legalistic' in the sense of specifying commandments to be obeyed.

I should not wish to deny that some Jews were more concerned with apocalyptic expectation and speculation than others; I simply doubt that this matter is constitutive of a distinct type of religion. On the contrary, we see the same underlying pattern in works of greater and less apocalyptic orientation. It should be remarked that in all of the literature surveyed except Ben Sirach there is some future expectation. In Rabbinic literature, for example, we noted the change in the understanding of the promise of 'the land' in Kiddushin 1.10. It was at first presumably a literal promise of the land of Israel, while it was later taken to mean the world to come. This shift, however, does not affect the basic question of how one gets 'in' and stays 'in'. Our question was principally how one gets and stays in the community of the saved, not when the decisive salvation will occur and what it will be like. Speculative differences on the time and nature of the end are not, to repeat, constitutive of different types or patterns of religion. This becomes clear once one focuses on the pattern of getting in (election) and staying in (obedience).

Thus I should not wish to subordinate apocalyptic literature to Rabbinic literature (so Moore), nor so to elevate the difference that the two represent basically different religions (so Rössler). We have been concerned with the question of whether or not there is a basic common ground to be found in the various bodies of literature, and the answer is affirmative. This does not settle the historical issues of whether or not apocalyptic and Rabbinic literature emanate from mutually exclusive groups, how many Rabbis held strong apocalyptic expectations and the like. We simply find that in the various literary remains there is a common 'pattern of religion'.

---

[13] Cf. Russell, *Method and Message*, p. 54.

Sects and parties

By focusing on the questions of getting and staying 'in', we also gain a viewpoint for discussing Jewish sects and parties. It is commonly thought, more or less following Josephus, that the various groups in Judaism were equally 'sects' or 'parties', and the two terms can be used interchangeably.[14] It seems useful, rather, to make a distinction on the basis of what we may call soteriological exclusivism. A group may deny salvation to all but the members of the group, or it may simply say that all in the larger community *should* agree with the party tenets. One may readily give a modern analogy. As long as the Conservatives argue that they should be governing Canada and that Canada would be better off if they were, they are a *party*. If the present Tory leadership (or any other group) moved to northern Manitoba, established a parliament and courts and proclaimed that all who did not obey their laws were not true Canadians, but traitors to Canada, they would be a *sect*. In this sense, the only definitely sectarian literature is the Dead Sea Scrolls.[15] Even there, there was reluctance simply to apply the title 'Israel' to the group, but non-sectarians were called traitors, and *the* covenant was defined as the *sect's* covenant. Jubilees revealed some tendency toward sectarianism because of the question of the calendar, but a definitely sectarian viewpoint seems not to be present. The Rabbinic literature, with its implicit (and occasionally explicit) inclusion of the *'amme ha-'arets* in 'Israel', is definitely not sectarian in the sense in which the term is being used here. If all the Rabbis were *ḥaberim* (a point about which there is some question), there would be a practical exclusivism in terms of social intercourse. But as long as the *'amme ha-'arets* were not excluded from 'Israel', the outlook is that of a party rather than a sect.

It seems less important to give a name to all the parties and sects. There has been considerable effort expended in the attempt to attribute the surviving literature to one of the parties mentioned by Josephus. This may be rather like the desire to attribute each book of the New Testament to a person mentioned elsewhere in the New Testament. The older tendency was to note the distinction between the Sadducees and the Pharisees on the resurrection, and accordingly to attribute most of the surviving literature to the Pharisees, since the resurrection is usually confirmed or at least implied. Thus Charles considered Jubilees Pharisaic,[16] although the calendar should

[14] Thus, for example, Neusner, *From Politics to Piety*, p. 4; *Understanding Rabbinic Judaism*, p. 12; Buchanan, *Consequences of the Covenant*, pp. 80, 238 ('various sects . . . believed themselves the only true remnant of Israel'); J. A. Sanders, 'The Old Testament in 11Q Melchizedek', p. 373 (the 'Jewish denominations' with 'their several claims to be the true Israel'). Cf. Chapter I, section 7 n. 52.

[15] Russell (*Method and Message*, p. 22) opposes the use of 'sect' because there was no orthodoxy from which 'sectarians' could separate. The Dead Sea Scrolls nevertheless show that a group could withdraw from the larger community and condemn those outside the group to destruction. This justifies the term 'sect'.

[16] See *Pseudepigrapha*, p. 1.

have prevented the identification. The Psalms of Solomon are still some-times classified as Pharisaic on the grounds that they are not Sadducean, Essene or Zelotian.[17] I am by no means convinced that all the literature has to be assigned to one party or another.[18] If Josephus is to be followed, then surely one should also regard the numbers which he assigns to the Pharisees, which he calls the leading party.[19] If there were 6,000 Pharisees, it follows that most Jews did not belong to a party. Thus our discussion of 'party' and 'sect' is not intended to match the literature with named parties and sects, but to point out the 'party' or 'sectarian' character of each book or body of literature.

Judaism in the time of Jesus and Paul

Our study has not been designed to answer the question of what Judaism was like in Palestine before 70 c.e. We have not discussed the Pharisees and Sadducees as such, for example, but only the surviving literature. It seems to me quite possible that we not only have no Sadducean literature, but also virtually no Pharisaic literature, apart from fragments embedded in the Rabbinic material. Thus I know a good deal less about Pharisaism than has been 'known' by many investigators. There are, however, some things about Judaism before 70 that can be said on the basis of the present study.

Because of the consistency with which covenantal nomism is maintained from early in the second century b.c.e. to late in the second century c.e., it must be hypothesized that covenantal nomism was *pervasive* in Palestine before 70. It was thus the basic *type* of religion known by Jesus and presumably by Paul. (One knows very little about distinctive characteristics of Judaism in Asia Minor.) The possibility cannot be completely excluded that there were Jews accurately hit by the polemic of Matt. 23, who attended only to trivia and neglected the weightier matters. Human nature being what it is, one supposes that there were some such. One must say, however, that the surviving Jewish literature does not reveal them. It should be remembered that the surviving Jewish literature was not all preserved by Jews. The Apocrypha and Pseudepigrapha were preserved by Christians, while the Dead Sea Scrolls were found by accident. Thus in all this literature con-sidered together one has Judaism as it spoke for itself during the period, not just Judaism as subsequent generations wanted it remembered (which is the case with Christianity). On the assumption that a religion should be understood on the basis of its own self-presentations, as long as these are not manifestly bowdlerized, and not on the basis of polemical attacks, we must

---

[17] Maier, *Mensch und freier Wille*, pp. 283–93.

[18] So also Sandmel, *The First Christian Century*, p. 24; Reicke, 'Official and Pietistic Elements of Jewish Apocalypticism', *JBL* 74, 1960, pp. 137–50.

[19] Josephus, *War* II.162; *Antiquities* XVIII.12.

say that the Judaism of before 70 kept grace and works in the right perspective, did not trivialize the commandments of God and was not especially marked by hypocrisy. The frequent Christian charge against Judaism, it must be recalled, is not that some individual Jews misunderstood, misapplied and abused their religion, but that *Judaism necessarily tends* towards petty legalism, self-serving and self-deceiving casuistry, and a mixture of arrogance and lack of confidence in God. But the surviving Jewish literature is as free of these characteristics as any I have ever read. By consistently maintaining the basic framework of *covenantal nomism*, the gift and demand of God were kept in a healthy relationship with each other, the minutiae of the law were observed on the basis of the large principles of religion and because of commitment to God, and humility before the God who chose and would ultimately redeem Israel was encouraged.

We further see that IV Ezra is not a particularly good representative of Judaism. It is a venerable tradition in Christian scholarship that IV Ezra accurately represents Pharisaism or the Judaism known by Paul. Köberle argued the case systematically: 'On the whole . . . the author of IV Ezra without doubt gives us a correct presentation of the repercussion of the belief in the future judgment on the religious expressions of individual Jewish piety. *All the many expressions of belief in God's grace and mercy appear to be denied.*'[20] The position that IV Ezra is representative has been frequently maintained. Thus Dodd considered IV Ezra best to represent 'Paul's pre-Christian position',[21] Longenecker considered IV Ezra to be one of the principal sources for 'early Pharisaism',[22] and Bornkamm stated that Jewish apocalypticism finds its inevitable end in IV Ezra.[23] We should first remark, with regard to the use of IV Ezra as representative of Judaism *before* 70, that no work is more profoundly marked by the fall of Jerusalem. Its very *raison d'être* is the physical oppression of Israel by Rome. It is if anything less representative of Judaism before 70 than Rabbinic literature, since it may be doubted if its viewpoint could have been held *at all* had it not been for the difficult situation of Israel after the war. One must even doubt its usefulness as a representative of very much of Judaism *after* 70. The pessimism of the dialogues was corrected (on the view of the work taken here) by the depiction of Israel's triumph in the concluding vision. II Baruch used a large amount of the work, but reversed the general viewpoint; for II Baruch returns to the view that sinners can be restored and Israel redeemed, despite transgression.[24] (I assume that II Baruch used IV Ezra.) The pessimism of the dialogues, where the doctrine of salvation by works is expressed, seems not

[20] Köberle, *Sünde und Gnade*, p. 657.
[21] C. H. Dodd, 'The Mind of Paul II', *New Testament Studies*, p. 118.
[22] Longenecker, *Paul: Apostle of Liberty*, p. 8.
[23] Bornkamm, *Paul*, p. 147.
[24] See 'The Covenant as a Soteriological Category' (n. 5 above).

to have been compatible with the view generally held in the Jewish community. If Pharisaism was continued by the Rabbis, one can best see the 'Pharisaic' view in the pleas of the seer of the dialogues, pleas which are denied. The book of IV Ezra can hardly represent Pharisaism. In the entire body of surviving Jewish literature, the view that transgression necessarily leads to destruction and the equation of loyalty with absolute obedience are unparalleled. Thus IV Ezra has to be bracketed as representing a minority view, and a view which does not seem to have existed at all before the destruction. (If one accepts the interpretation of IV Ezra given by Box, Rössler, Harnisch and Breech, the conclusion would be that the view which I have described as unique to IV Ezra is completely unattested in Jewish literature.)

Thus, while we cannot on the basis of this study draw conclusions about the historical relationship of the parties and sects, the relative dominance of Pharisaism and the like, we can justifiably draw conclusions about the *character* of Judaism before the destruction. Even if the different themes and motifs of covenantal nomism were not worked out precisely as they were subsequently in Rabbinic literature, covenantal nomism must have been the general type of religion prevalent in Palestine before the destruction of the Temple.

PART TWO

PAUL

V

PAUL

1. Introduction

Sources

The principal purpose of this brief sub-section is to outline some of the critical judgments which underlie this treatment of Paul's thought, without attempting to defend them or prove them: not that they cannot be defended. The world is simply not in need of further introductions to Pauline literature. I take the sources for studying Paul to be the seven letters whose authenticity is unquestioned: Romans, I and II Corinthians, Galatians, Philippians, I Thessalonians and Philemon. Since there is little of religious or theological substance in Philemon, we are effectively limited to six letters. There is still a considerable body of scholarly opinion which regards Colossians and II Thessalonians as authentic,[1] and many maintain the authenticity of Ephesians and even the Pastorals.[2] The case in favour of Colossians is the closest to being a 'draw' in scholarly opinion, but I believe that it can be shown with a high degree of probability that Paul did not write the principal 'theological' part of Colossians, if he wrote any of it at all.[3] Some would maintain that the two principal deutero-Pauline letters, Colossians and Ephesians, should be used as sources for Paul even if he did not write them.[4] They are unquestionably substantially influenced by Paul's thought, to the point of quoting his letters extensively;[5] but using them as sources for Paul seems to lead to confusion and inaccuracies, to imprecisions which should

---

[1] See Conzelmann, *An Outline of the Theology of the New Testament*, p. 155; see Kümmel's treatment of each book in his *Introduction to the New Testament*, where both are held to be genuine.

[2] Lists of scholars who have supported or denied the Pauline authorship of these works are given in Kümmel, op. cit.

[3] 'Literary Dependence in Colossians', *JBL* 85, 1966, pp. 28–45. See also P. N. Harrison, *Paulines and Pastorals*, 1964, pp. 65–78. A similar position on Colossians was adopted by G. W. MacRae in 'The Colossian Heresy and Modern Gnostic Scholarship', a paper read at the 1972 *SNTS* meeting (Colossians is too Pauline to be Pauline!)

[4] Thus, for example, M. Zerwick, *The Epistle to the Ephesians*, 1969, p. viii.

[5] On Colossians, see n. 3. On Ephesians, see E. J. Goodspeed, *The Meaning of Ephesians*, 1933; C. L. Mitton, *The Epistle to the Ephesians*, 1951.

be avoided if they can be.[6] The soundest approach is to deal with the letters which Paul can be reliably supposed to have written.

It is perhaps unnecessary to say that the speeches in Acts which are attributed to Paul cannot be used as a source for his thought. My own position on the use of Acts for the general study of the career of Paul is that of John Knox.[7] Since we shall not go into any aspects of Paul's career, except his conviction that he was called to be the apostle to the Gentiles, the book of Acts will drop virtually out of view.

There is one important aspect of Paul's letters which should be remarked. Romans, I and II Corinthians and Galatians were all written within a very short period of time. I Thessalonians seems to be from several years earlier, and Philippians is somewhat difficult to date.[8] Since most discussions of Paul inevitably focus on the letters first mentioned, it must be recalled that they present Paul at a crucial moment in his history – with difficulties in his previously evangelized churches breaking out just as he was hoping to complete the collection for Jerusalem and press on to the west – and these circumstances forced him into a critical examination of 'his gospel' and the restatement of it *vis à vis* seriously competing views. I do not see any signs of major theological 'development' in Paul's thought, but there are certainly alterations in the way in which he expressed himself, and these prove the severest test of the exegete at the same time that they offer the greatest opportunity for understanding.[9]

---

[6] See, for example, section 3 nn. 9, 11, 12 below. Whiteley (*The Theology of St Paul*, p. xiii) argues against conflating Ephesians with the authentic letters to make a coherent theology, but he himself uses Colossians in this way, as may be seen in his discussion of the *church* as the *body* of Christ (ibid., pp. 190–9).

[7] J. Knox, *Chapters in a Life of Paul*, 1950.

[8] Knox, op. cit., pp. 86–8: I Thessalonians not long after 40; Galatians between 51 and 54; I and II Corinthians 51–3; Romans 53–4; Philippians probably 47–50. Bornkamm, *Paul*, pp. 241f.: I Thessalonians 50; Galatians 54; most of Corinthians 54–5; Philippians 54–5; Romans 55–6. Philippians is complicated because of hypotheses about partition. See Bornkamm, ibid., pp. 246f.; Bornkamm, 'Der Philipperbrief als paulinische Briefsammlung', *Geschichte und Glaube* II, pp. 195–205. In favour of the integrity of Philippians are V. P. Furnish ('The Place and Purpose of Philippians iii', *NTS* 10, 1963, pp. 80–5); T. E. Pollard ('The Integrity of Philippians', *NTS* 13, 1966, pp. 57–66); and R. Jewett ('The Epistolary Thanksgiving and the Integrity of Philippians', *NT* 12, 1970, pp. 40–53).

[9] The major development which is most often thought of is a revision of the future eschatological expectation, often with II Cor. 5 and Phil. 1.22–4 in mind. For theories of evolution, see C. H. Dodd's two essays on 'The Mind of Paul' in his *New Testament Studies*; Schweitzer, *Mysticism*, pp. 135f.; Cerfaux's trilogy on Paul; D. M. Stanley, *Christ's Resurrection in Pauline Soteriology*, ch. 3; J. C. Hurd, *The Origin of First Corinthians*; Buck and Taylor, *Saint Paul, a Study of the Development of his Thought*. For a less elaborate theory of change, see W. D. Davies, *The Gospel and the Land*, pp. 208–30. R. Jewett has paid attention to the possibility of chronological change in Paul's anthropological terms (*Paul's Anthropological Terms*). It should be remarked that the views of Dodd, Cerfaux and Stanley depend on accepting Colossians and Ephesians as authentic, which aids hypotheses about a development considerably. For the state of the question, see Kümmel's report on the *SNTS* seminar, *NTS* 18, 1972, pp. 457f. With regard to the special problems of II Cor. 5 and the two apparently different eschatologies, see C. F. D. Moule, 'St Paul and Dualism: The Pauline Conception of Resurrection', *NTS* 12, 1966, pp. 106–23. Moule argues for basic consistency behind varying formulations, a view which seems to me to be fundamentally correct. Hanhart ('Paul's Hope in the Face of Death', *JBL* 88, 1969, pp. 445–57) argued that Paul had no specific future expectation, but rather 'a radiant hope of life eternal "with

This provides a way of answering the standard question of whether or not Paul's religion was his theology,[10] or the similar (though more naive) question of whether or not he was a 'theologian'.[11] To give a brief answer, which the entire chapter will have to serve to substantiate, one may say that Paul *was* a theologian in that he reflected on his gospel, but that he was not a *systematic* theologian, not even when he wrote Romans. His theology is not his religion, but his own effort to express it in the circumstances which the various letters reflect. Further, I view Paul as a *coherent* thinker, despite the unsystematic nature of his thought and the variations in formulation.[12]

Method of proceeding

What needs to be accomplished in this chapter is a presentation of Paul's 'pattern of religion' which can be compared with those which were presented in Part I. Following the usual procedure, we shall attempt to determine the basic coherent structure of Paul's thought (assuming for the moment that there is one). In the case of Paul, it is easier than it was in the case of Judaism to describe the pattern of religion simply as 'soteriology'; for Paul had a pronounced soteriology. Since soteriology is not an independent theme, however, but is intimately connected with other themes (especially Christ-ology, eschatology and anthropology, to give the themes the usual titles), it is still best to call this description one of Paul's pattern of religion, rather than simply of his soteriology.

In Part I, it was best in virtually every case to begin our analysis with the question of the election and the covenant, for those conceptions can always be seen as the starting point for analysing Judaism. In the case of Paul, however, the matter is more difficult. The related questions of the starting point for seeing Paul's religious thought accurately and of the centre of his thinking are among the most difficult in Pauline studies. As we shall see, the

---

Christ"' (p. 445). Kümmel (*Theology*, pp. 237–43) has succinctly pointed out that the expectation of II Cor. 5 and Phil. 1.22–24 cannot be a development away from the expectation of a future resurrection, since the latter view also appears in Romans, which is later than II Corinthians and Philippians. The two views must be understood in terms of Paul's basic interest: 'Paul obviously is interested only in the fact that the Christian always remains in fellowship with his heavenly Lord' (p. 242).

My own view is that chronological change would be interesting and important if it could be definitely established. There are some changes which are obvious: thus the discussion of the law in Romans is more developed and more nuanced than the discussion in Galatians (a point which I owe to W. D. Davies). It does not necessarily follow that Paul changed what he *thought*, although he may have done so. It seems safest to take such changes as developments in *presentation* and *argument*. I do not know of any decisive evidence that Paul changed what he thought during the period of the surviving correspondence, although the possibility that he did so cannot be excluded; and the variations in argument in the letters will always provide grounds for speculations on this score.

[10] W. Wrede, *Paulus*, pp. 47f.; cf. Conzelmann, *Theology*, p. 157.

[11] Munck, *Paul*, pp. 65–7. Munck is primarily concerned, however, to deny that Paul is 'a theologian in the modern sense' (p. 66). 'His theology arises from his work as apostle and directly serves that work' (p. 67).

[12] See further section 7 below.

choice of the starting point is usually decisive in determining the adequacy of the description, and for this reason it is important to choose the starting point with care and to begin where Paul began.

The question of the centre and the beginning point

It was Albert Schweitzer who, with his usual critical acumen, put his finger on this question as decisive for understanding Paul. As long as one studies Paul under the *loci* of systematic theology, relegating eschatology to the last place in one's discussion, understanding of Paul is hindered if not completely obscured.[13] Further, as long as one takes the central theme in Paul's gospel to be 'righteousness by faith alone', one misses the significance of the realism with which Paul thought of incorporation in the body of Christ, and consequently the heart of his theology.[14] Many aspects of Schweitzer's presentation of Paul's thought have rightly proved unacceptable to New Testament scholars. One may mention, for example, his over-emphasis of the importance of predestination in Paul's thought,[15] his view of baptism as *ex opere operato*[16] and his theory of two resurrections;[17] but it is somewhat surprising that the two aspects of his view which we first mentioned have not found wider favour. Munck did, to be sure, agree that one must begin with eschatology. Despite the many useful insights of his book, however, one must note that he ends without giving anything like a satisfactory account of Paul's soteriology, although it is abundantly clear that soteriology was one of Paul's chief concerns.[18] Schweitzer has been ignored in much of German Protestant scholarship, which constitutes the most influential single body of scholarship on Paul. His term 'mysticism' has been rejected by scholars such as Bornkamm and Conzelmann on the basis of definitions which Schweitzer himself would not have accepted,[19] and other parts of his view

---

[13] See Schweitzer, *Paul and his Interpreters*, pp. 33f., 36, 53f., 57f., 102f.

[14] Schweitzer, *Mysticism*, pp. 220–6.

[15] E.g. *Paul and his Interpreters*, p. 215 ('Those who are "called" inevitably receive salvation; those who are not can never in any way obtain it'); *Mysticism*, p. 9; and frequently. Contrast Bultmann, *Theology* I, pp. 329f.

[16] *Paul and his Interpreters*, pp. 225f. ('in the moment when he receives baptism, the dying and rising again of Christ takes place in him without any co-operation, or exercise of will or thought, on his part'); *Mysticism*, pp. 116 ('inclusion . . . is not effected in the moment of believing, and not by faith as such. It is first by Baptism . . .'), 128. Contrast Bultmann, *Theology* I, pp. 311–13; Davies, *Paul and Rabbinic Judaism*, pp. 98f.; Tannehill, *Dying and Rising with Christ*, p. 41.

[17] Schweitzer, *Mysticism*, pp. 90–5; so also Schoeps, *Paul*, p. 104. See Davies's convincing critique, *Paul and Rabbinic Judaism*, pp. 288–98.

[18] Munck's *Heilsgeschichte* theory does give an implicit soteriology, but precisely how it works never becomes clear.

[19] Bornkamm, *Paul*, p. 155: 'These and similar expressions have little in common with mysticism . . . For an essential element in mysticism is the blurring of the boundary between God and man'; Conzelmann, *Theology*, p. 184: the theme of hope prevents misunderstanding Pauline thought as mysticism, which is defined as 'unhistorical pneumatism and sacramentalism'. Such definitions are rejected by Schweitzer, *Mysticism*, ch. 1. The term did enjoy a vogue and is still used by some scholars. See for example Schneider, *Die Passionsmystik des Paulus*, 1929, and Schneider's bibliography; Alfred Wiken-

treated lightly or not at all. Bornkamm's attempt to take account of the
pervasive importance of eschatology in his discussion at the *end* of his
section on Paul's thought does not really meet Schweitzer's point.[20]
Bultmann's decision to start with anthropology and to consider first man
without faith has been decisive for Bornkamm and Conzelmann also, and
this starting point coheres with understanding 'righteousness by faith'
as the central theological theme and with focusing the discussion on the
individual rather than on the eschatological, cosmic and participationist
features of Paul's thought.[21]

It would be instructive to give a Schweitzer-like review of scholarly work
on Paul since Schweitzer, and the field of Pauline studies could profit from
such an analysis and sifting of the material.[22] The task is beyond the scope
of the present study, however, and we shall note, in our attempt to locate a
beginning point for the study of Paul, only the one scholarly debate which
is most revealing: Käsemann's 'war on two fronts', against Bultmann,
Bornkamm and Conzelmann on the one hand and against Stendahl and
others on the other.[23] In Käsemann's thesis and in his early essays on Paul,
the themes most prominent were the reality of Paul's conception of participation in the body of Christ[24] and the cosmic aspects of Christ's lordship.[25]

hauser, *Pauline Mysticism*, ET, 1960; M. Bouttier, *Christianity According to Paul*, ET, 1966, p. 32 (the
term has difficulties but should be retained). 'Mysticism' has generated so much misunderstanding,
however, that perhaps it is better to drop it than to hedge it by repeated definitions. For arguments
against the term, see Schoeps, *Paul*, p. 46 n. 1; Tannehill, *Dying and Rising*, n. 7 on pp. 3f.
[20] See Bornkamm, *Paul*, pp. 197f.
[21] Whiteley (*Theology of Paul*, p. xiv) accurately notes that Paul's thought could be worked out from
any one of a number of motifs. He mentions Christ, the cross, the church and eschatology. He actually
proceeds according to the traditional theological *loci*: creation, fall and the like. Along the way he pays
considerable attention to the question of how Paul did or did not agree with the propositions of later
theology, such as the Trinity and the person and the work of the Second Person of the Trinity. This
attention and this arrangement may be helpful for answering certain sorts of questions (how much of
the creed is supported by Paul), but it seems to me to distract from seeing Paul's thought on its own
terms. Cf. the review by E. E. Ellis, *JBL* 84, 1965, pp. 454f.
[22] The appendix to this section by Manfred Brauch deals with one of the principal themes of recent
scholarly discussion, and I am grateful to Dr Brauch for allowing it to be included. It will have to stand
in place of the usual review of scholarly opinions, which have so proliferated that an adequate analysis
would itself require a substantial book. For reviews of research, see for example the following: J. Coppens, *L'état présent des études pauliniennes*, 1956; E. E. Ellis, *Paul and His Recent Interpreters*, 1961;
B. Rigaux, 'L' interprétation du paulinisme dans l'exégèse récente', *Littérature et théologie pauliniennes*,
by A. Descamps and others, 1960; H. Conzelmann, 'Current Problems in Pauline Research', *Interpretation* 22, 1968, pp. 171–86; Schoeps, *Paul*, ch. 1.
[23] See Käsemann's reference to his position between two fronts in 'Justification and Salvation History',
Perspectives on Paul, p. 76 n. 27.
[24] See for example *Leib und Leib Christi*, 1933, p. 183 ('Der Mittelpunkt paulinischer Verkündigung
ist das "im Christus"'); 'The Pauline Doctrine of the Lord's Supper' (which originally appeared in
1947–48), *Essays on New Testament Themes*, ET, pp. 109, 111, 118, 132; 'Ministry and Community in
the New Testament' (1949), ibid., p. 70.
[25] 'The Lord's Supper', *Essays*, pp. 117, 132, 135 (Christ as Cosmocrator); 'Ministry', *Essays*, pp. 68,
72 (Cosmocrator). From slightly later, cf. 'On the Subject of Primitive Christian Apocalyptic' (1962),
New Testament Questions of Today, pp. 133–6. It is surprising that Gibbs (*Creation and Redemption*),
who wishes to emphasize the lordship of Christ as the main theme of Paul's theology, did not make
greater use of Käsemann's contribution on this point. In response to Gibbs's view, I would say that,

Käsemann subsequently added apocalyptic as a, perhaps the, major motif in Paul and early Christianity in general.[26] The negative thrust of his position was against Bultmann's anthropocentricism: 'the righteousness of God does not, in Paul's understanding, refer primarily to the individual and is not to be understood exclusively in the context of the doctrine of man'.[27] Bultmann replied with vigour,[28] and both Bornkamm and Conzelmann maintained that, in fact, Paul's doctrine of righteousness does apply primarily to the individual.[29] Bornkamm further accused Käsemann of emphasizing God's righteousness as power to such an extent that 'the co-ordinate relation of God's righteousness and faith recedes curiously into the background' in Käsemann's essays.[30] With regard to the first criticism, Käsemann maintained his position: righteousness by faith *is* the centre of the Pauline gospel, but it is *not* primarily concerned with the individual.[31] On the second charge, Käsemann replied with an essay on faith in which he tried to correct what he saw as a misunderstanding of his position.[32] It is noteworthy that here he remarked that 'as the acceptance of the divine address, faith in Paul remains primarily a decision of the individual person, and its importance must not therefore be shifted away from anthropology to ecclesiology'.[33]

The negation 'not . . . to ecclesiology' indicates the other front on which Käsemann is compelled to fight. In a penetrating essay Stendahl had argued (1) that the usual (Lutheran) interpretation of Paul's view of righteousness by faith is historically erroneous, since it understands the doctrine as freeing one from the guilt of an 'introspective conscience', while Paul had not suffered from such a dilemma;[34] (2) that in any case the centre of Pauline

---

while Christ's lordship is a *central Pauline conviction*, in itself it does not give the key to Paul's soteriology, since it does not explain how believers *participate* in Christ's death to sin and consequently will participate in his reign.

[26] See 'The Beginnings of Christian Theology' (1960), *Questions*, pp. 82–107; 'Primitive Christian Apocalyptic' (1962), *Questions*, pp. 108–37.

[27] The quotation is from '"The Righteousness of God" in Paul' (1961), *Questions*, p. 150. Cf. earlier: Paul's view of the *charismata* 'makes it unmistakably clear that a purely individualistic interpretation of justification cannot legitimately be constructed from the Apostle's own teaching', 'Ministry', *Essays*, p. 76. Cf. 'On Paul's Anthropology' (1965), *Perspectives on Paul*, ET, p. 10.

[28] 'Δικαιοσύνη θεοῦ', *JBL* 83, 1964, pp. 12–16.

[29] Bornkamm, *Paul*, pp. 146f.; Conzelmann, *Theology*, p. 172 ('The result is a radical individualization: the message encounters the individual and isolates him'). On righteousness by faith as individualistic and uncosmic, cf. Schweitzer, *Mysticism*, p. 219.

[30] Quoting Käsemann, 'Justification and Salvation History', *Perspectives*, p. 78 n. 28. The reference is to Bornkamm, *Paul*, p. 147.

[31] 'Justification and Salvation History', *Perspectives*, p. 74. Cf. earlier, 'Ministry', *Essays*, pp. 75f. On justification interpreted as a universal and social act of God, see also M. Barth, 'The Kerygma of Galatians', *Interpretation* 21, 1967, pp. 141–3.

[32] 'The Faith of Abraham in Romans 4', *Perspectives*, pp. 79–101.   [33] Ibid., p. 83.

[34] Stendahl's observation on this point was preceded by Cerfaux's (*The Christian in the Theology of St Paul*, n. 1 on pp. 375f.): Christ's appearance to Paul 'was destined not to resolve a crisis of the soul, but to call him to a great mission. . . . Introspection was not much practised in this era. Augustine had not passed into history.'

theology is not righteousness by faith but the history of salvation described especially in Romans 9–11.[35] Käsemann responded, pointing out that similar views had been held by Wrede, Schweitzer and others, and arguing that righteousness by faith is the central theme of Paul's theology.[36] The theme should not be understood as an individualistic one, however, but rather righteousness by faith and the history of salvation belong together.

Yet Stendahl and his friends are right in protesting against the individualist curtailment of the Christian message. . . . The Pauline doctrine of justification never took its bearings from the individual, although hardly anyone now realizes this.[37]

Since 'hardly anyone' realizes the history-of-salvation and cosmic dimensions of the doctrine of righteousness by faith, and since Käsemann had protested long and vigorously against Bultmann's individualism; since, further, both Bornkamm and Conzelmann protest against Käsemann that righteousness by faith concerns the individual, and even Käsemann acknowledges (as we saw above) that faith is primarily an individual decision, it is somewhat surprising to read that it is 'in the English-speaking world' that 'the key-words of law and justification are associated almost inevitably with a legalistic construction. The existentialist interpretation of faith rouses uneasiness because it seems to end in individualism.'[38] Käsemann is clearly in a difficult position in his two-front war. He wants to maintain the centrality of righteousness by faith, deny too much individualism to it, and insist that faith is an individual decision. In denying an over-emphasis on individualism, he must himself attack his teacher, Bultmann, and yet also pass off the fear that Bultmann's existentialist position is too individualistic as a misunderstanding characteristic of the English-speaking world, where the influence of the Reformation has faded.

It is important to note that Käsemann's defence of the centrality of righteousness by faith and his fear of its being subordinated to salvation history do not entirely spring from disinterested exegesis, and he makes this abundantly clear. Among German theologians of his generation, the rediscovery of the Reformation doctrine of righteousness by faith, says Käsemann,

---

[35] K. Stendahl, 'The Apostle Paul and the Introspective Conscience of the West', *HTR* 56, 1963, pp. 199–215. The summary is given by Käsemann, 'Justification and Salvation History', *Perspectives*, pp. 6of. Käsemann stresses salvation history somewhat more than Stendahl did, who was principally concerned to argue that the problem of Jews and Gentiles, not that of a guilty conscience, accounts for most of Romans. Chapters 9–11 are not an appendix, but the climax of chs. 1–8 (p. 205). Stendahl agreed with Schweitzer on the limited role of righteousness by faith in Paul (p. 204 n. 10). Stendahl's position has been accepted, for example, by J. A. Fitzmyer, 'Saint Paul and the Law', *The Jurist* 27, 1967, p. 19.
[36] 'Justification and Salvation History', *Perspectives*, pp. 6of., 73f.
[37] Ibid., p. 74.
[38] Ibid., p. 64.

immunized us deeply against a conception of salvation history which broke in on us in secularized and political form with the Third Reich and its ideology. It will be understandable that as burnt children we are unwilling to add fuel to the fire which at the present day, for the third time in a century, is awakening such general enthusiasm.[39]

Further, Käsemann suspects that the attractiveness of salvation history is not entirely without its support in modern religious aspirations. He sees it as being agreeable to the ecumenical movement, which tends 'to stress what binds rather than what divides, and looks for the same disposition in the New Testament'.[40] Käsemann does not consider his own view to be based on modern theological considerations, but they clearly impart an urgency to the question and to its right solution as he sees it.

What is instructive about this debate is this: both Käsemann and his critics are right, although in different ways. Käsemann, Stendahl and others are correct that the heart of Paul's theology cannot be centred on the individual, while Bultmann, Bornkamm and Conzelmann are correct in maintaining that the particular formulation 'righteousness by faith' does primarily concern the individual.[41] What this means is that the catch-word 'righteousness by faith' must be given up as the clue to Paul's thought. To some extent, it is a dispute about terms, as we shall see; for Paul can in certain circumstances summarize his own position by that very phrase. Yet that phrase, if taken as the centre or starting point of Paul's theology, leads one to miss its basic thrust. *How* we are to understand 'righteousness by faith' we shall discuss in a subsequent section. We shall here only summarize the reasons for which it is inadequate as a *term* to indicate the centre of Paul's theology.

The reasons which tell against the phraseology 'righteousness by faith' as central to Pauline thought were briefly and persuasively put by Schweitzer, and we may quote his summary:

In the Epistle to the Galatians, where it [righteousness by faith] lies before us in its simplest and most original form, the doctrine of the righteousness by faith is

---

[39] Ibid. On the sometimes confusing overlapping of Käsemann's current theological battles and his exegesis of Paul, see G. A. Lewandowski, 'An Introduction to Ernst Käsemann's Theology', *Encounter* 35, 1974, pp. 236–8. Cf. also H. Hübner, 'Existentiale Interpretation der paulinischen "Gerechtigkeit Gottes"', *NTS* 21, 1975, p. 464.

[40] 'Justification and Salvation History', p. 64.

[41] In 'Justification and Salvation History', Käsemann does not make it clear *how* righteousness by faith can be cosmic and not individualistic. It may be that a clue to his thought in this regard is given in the essay 'The Spirit and the Letter', *Perspectives*, p. 165: 'Pauline soteriology simply means the presence and lordship of Christ and therefore the justification of the ungodly.' Käsemann takes 'the justification of the ungodly' to be the core of 'righteousness by faith'. He then defines 'the justification of the ungodly' as being given in the presence and lordship of Christ – and these are cosmic. I find myself essentially in agreement that Paul's participationist and cosmic language should define the righteousness by faith terminology (pp. 502–8 below), and not vice versa – if this is what Käsemann means. But then one wonders why the phrase 'righteousness by faith' is taken to indicate the key concept in Paul's soteriology. Is it any more than agreement with Lutheran tradition?

not yet independent, but is worked out with the aid of conceptions drawn from the eschatological doctrine of the being-in-Christ.

Always, whether in Galatians or Romans, it only appears where the controversy over the Law has to be dealt with, and – very significantly – even then only where a Scriptural argument is to be based on the as yet uncircumcised Abraham. Only when it can find a point of attachment on this Scriptural argument does it come into prominence.

Another point . . . is that Paul does not bring into connection with it [righteousness by faith] the other blessings of redemption, the possession of the spirit, and the resurrection. Once Paul has left behind the discussion necessitated by his Scriptural argument, about faith-righteousness and Law-righteousness, it is of no more service to him. Neither in seeking a basis for ethics, nor in the doctrines of baptism and the Lord's Supper, does he have recourse to it in any way.[42]

Many of these points are worked out in much greater detail elsewhere in Schweitzer's work. Thus, for example, with regard to ethics' not being derived from righteousness by faith, but from what Schweitzer called the mystical doctrine of being-in-Christ, Schweitzer argued that, to derive ethics from the doctrine of righteousness,

it would have been necessary to show how the man who previously was inherently incapable of producing good works received through the act of justification the capacity to do so. That capacity can only be bestowed upon him through Christ; but according to the doctrine of faith-righteousness, all that Christ does to believers is to cause them to be justified.[43]

Paul, however, never made an argument which would bridge the gap between being justified and ethics. Ethics, rather, are derived from 'the mystical doctrine of the dying and rising again with Christ', a doctrine which, Schweitzer then observed, used to be called precisely Paul's ethical doctrine rather than his mystical doctrine.[44] The force of Schweitzer's argument will immediately be seen by anyone who will work through the letters of Paul trying to find instances in which righteousness by faith serves as the source for ethics[45] (or is used to explain the sacraments, and the like). Without pausing here to note in detail how Bultmann and others have attempted to derive ethics from the conception of righteousness by faith, we may cite one sentence: 'Therefore, the *imperative*, "walk according to the Spirit", not only does not contradict the *indicative* of justification (the believer is rightwised) but results from it . . .'[46] This is absolutely correct, except for one thing. In Paul's own terminology the *indicative* which cor-

---

[42] Schweitzer, *Mysticism*, pp. 220f.

[43] Ibid., p. 295.

[44] Ibid. On the connection of Paul's ethical exhortation with the theme of dying and rising, see also Tannehill, *Dying and Rising*, pp. 77–83.

[45] See the list of passages in which the imperative follows the indicative given by Bornkamm, *Paul*, p. 202.

[46] Bultmann, *Theology* I, p. 332.

responds to the imperative 'walk by the Spirit' is not *righteousness*, but *living in the Spirit* (Gal. 5.16–25; Rom. 8.1–17; cf. I Thess. 4.1–8).[47]

This is not to say that Schweitzer's position is completely correct. It is oversimplified in one minor way and in one major way. It is possible, for one thing, to find some passages in which 'faith', if not 'righteousness by faith', is related to ethics,[48] although one must note that Paul generally works out his ethical statements on the basis of the believers' life in the Spirit. But more important – and this is basically what is wrong with Schweitzer's theory as a whole – Schweitzer did not see the *internal connection* between the righteousness by faith terminology and the terminology about life in the Spirit, being in Christ and the like (terminology which here will be called 'participationist',[49] which seems better than the controversial term 'mystical'), a connection which exists in Paul's own letters. Thus Schweitzer did not note that besides saying that one becomes one body with the Lord in the sacraments (I Cor. 10.17; 12.13), Paul *also* wrote that the Spirit is received through faith (Gal. 3.1–5).[50]

Nevertheless, despite over-simplifications and errors in detail, Schweitzer's arguments against considering the terminology of righteousness by faith to be the central theme of Paul's theology, and consequently the key to his thought, are, considered cumulatively, convincing; and they have never been effectively countered. Thus Bornkamm noted and agreed with Schweitzer's point that 'other important subjects and ideas in the Pauline theology are not directly derivable' from righteousness by faith,[51] but for

[47] It is instructive that Furnish, in order to relate ethics to justification, has to define justification by the categories of *participation* and *belonging*: 'Those who belong to him [*sc.*, Jesus Christ] are thus brought under the dominion of God's power. This is their "justification", by which they are freed from the "worldly powers". . . .'; '. . . the believer, who on the basis of his faith has been rightwised, thereby belongs to a new realm. He stands under the aegis and hegemony of a new sovereign. He has been given not just the *possibility* of a new life, but an actually and totally new existence' (Furnish, *Theology and Ethics*, pp. 224f.). Furnish follows Bultmann in considering righteousness a forensic-eschatological concept (Furnish, p. 147), and it is not clear how a forensic declaration frees one from hostile powers, puts one under a new lordship and gives one a totally new life. Paul's ethics are here actually connected with participation and belonging, and rightly so, but participation and belonging are titled 'justification'.

[48] See Gal. 5.6 and perhaps Rom. 14.23. In discussing Gal. 5.6 ('faith working through love') and 5.22–24 (the fruits of the Spirit), Bornkamm (*Paul*, p. 153) comments that 'justification is [the] precondition' for the fruits of the Spirit. This, however, is just what Paul does not say, and it is precisely in Gal. 5.5 that righteousness or justification is said to be expected in the *future*. Thus Gal. 5.6 does not lead to the conclusion that ethics are connected with the terminology 'righteousness by faith' as such. In Rom. 14.23 ('whatever does not proceed from faith is sin'), the meaning of 'faith' is probably simply 'conviction' (see the NEB and Whiteley, *Theology of St Paul*, p. 59; cf. the Jerusalem Bible: 'done in bad faith'), so that again ethics are not based on being justified by faith.

[49] Käsemann argued that 'participation' is too weak, since it does not sufficiently describe the power of Christ's lordship which seizes believers: 'The Lord's Supper', *Essays*, p. 124. It nevertheless seems the best general term. So also Whiteley, *Theology of St Paul*, e.g. pp. 130, 152, 154 ('the main consistent set of symbolism expresses participation'). Note also Tannehill's terms: 'corporate patterns of thought' (*Dying and Rising*, p. 24), 'inclusive patterns of thought' (p. 24).

[50] Thus Schweitzer (*Mysticism*, p. 221) was incorrect in asserting that the possession of the Spirit is never connected with righteousness by faith. It is at least connected with faith.

[51] Bornkamm, *Paul*, p. 116.

some reason did not see this to be problematic. The fact that righteousness is so prominent in Romans assures him that 'the basic theme in his theology with which he began remained the same to the end'. Further, it was on the basis of his conception of righteousness by faith that Paul broke with the Jewish law[52] (an argument which, we shall subsequently show, is not precisely correct). But neither argument is an effective response to Schweitzer's argument that a theme cannot be central which does not explain anything else. Similarly Conzelmann, in pointing to the frequent distinction of a juridical and a mystical answer to the question of how one is saved (righteousness by faith and being in Christ, respectively), simply asserts that the mystical interpretation cannot stand, since the phrase 'in Christ' 'appears in the very passages where "reconciliation" is spoken of in juridical, objective terms' (as in II Cor. 5.18–21). He further remarks that faith and 'in Christ' are connected.[53] These observations do help to make it clear that there is no neat division in Paul's thought between 'mystical' and 'juridical', but they in no way counter the force of Schweitzer's argument against the centrality of the *terminology* of righteousness by faith, nor do they lead to the conclusion that the latter is the central doctrine in Paul. The limited applicability of the righteousness by faith terminology cannot be overcome by appeal to the widespread and very varied use of *pistis* and *pisteuō* in Paul, nor does the observation that apparently juridical terms intermingle with apparently 'mystical' terms necessarily show that Paul's 'true' view is best represented by the juridical terminology. The simple fact is, as Schweitzer said, that righteousness by faith can be derived from and understood on the basis of other aspects of Paul's thought such as possession of the Spirit and living in the Spirit, but not vice versa. It is for this reason that beginning with the assumption that the opening argument of Galatians and Romans gives the clue to all of Paul's theology is ultimately misleading. To show this in further detail would involve writing the rest of this chapter in summary here, and thus we must appeal to the argument of the following pages for proof of what has just been said.

How then, shall we begin? There appear to me to be two readily identifiable and primary convictions which governed Paul's Christian life: (1) that Jesus Christ is Lord, that in him God has provided for the salvation of all who believe (in the general sense of 'be converted'),[54] and that he will

---

[52] Ibid.   [53] Conzelmann, *Theology*, pp. 208f.

[54] *Pistis* and *pisteuō* are very common in Paul, and the terms often have a very general meaning which is not especially charged with the connotation of 'righteousness by faith and not by works of law'. The plural participle 'believers' is perhaps the most common term for 'Christians' (as distinct from both Jews and pagans [e.g. I Thess. 1.7–9 'all believers', 'you turned to God from idols'; I Cor. 1.21–3 'those who believe' contrasted with Jews and pagans]). For 'believe' as 'convert', cf. also I Cor. 3.5; Rom. 13.11. For 'believers' (Christians) contrasted with 'non-believers', *apistoi* (non-Christians), see I Cor. 14.22–24; II Cor. 6.15; and, by inference, I Cor. 6.1, 6; 7.12–14; II Cor. 4.4. See Bultmann's admirable summary, *TDNT* VI, pp. 203–19.

soon return to bring all things to an end;[55] (2) that he, Paul, was called to be
the apostle to the Gentiles. The two convictions, as Munck has especially
pointed out, go hand in hand.[56] Paul's role as apostle to the Gentiles is
connected to the conviction that salvation is for all who believe, whether
Jew or Gentile, and also to the nearness of the end of the age. In view of the
approaching end, he was under compulsion, as apostle to the Gentiles, to
preach the gospel as quickly as possible to the whole world. It is on the
basis of these two *convictions* that we can explain Paul's *theology*, his complicated and often obscure reflections on the significance of the salvific events
and his role in them.

2. The solution as preceding the problem

In saying that one of Paul's principal convictions is that God has provided
for salvation in Christ, I intend to exclude one of the traditional ways of
setting up the discussion of Paul's theology: by describing first the plight
of man to which Paul saw Christ as offering a solution. This is the way
chosen by Bultmann, Conzelmann and Bornkamm,[1] for example; and
Bultmann in particular justified it by observing that Romans is structured
with the discussion of sin preceding the solution to it.[2] He seems to argue
that only by proceeding in this way will one come to a correct understanding
of Paul's message:

> . . . in Romans, where Paul is connectedly presenting the main issues of his mes-
> sage to a hitherto unknown congregation in order to legitimate himself as a genuine
> apostle, he – unlike the Hermetic tractates with their initial cosmological teachings
> – does not first present the salvation occurrence, the credibility of which would
> first have to be acknowledged. Instead he begins by exposing the plight of man-
> kind, so that then the proclamation of God's salvation-deed becomes a decision-
> question. In keeping with this is the train of thought in Rom. 7.7–8.11: after
> man-under-the-Law has been made to see his situation under it as that of the
> 'miserable wretch' groaning for deliverance from the 'body of death', he can then
> see the salvation-occurrence as salvation-bringing.[3]

---

[55] In favour of starting with Christ's lordship is W. Thüsing, *Per Christum in Deum*, ch. 1. In favour
of starting with Christ or with Paul's eschatological expectation, rather than with man's pre-Christian
plight are, for example, Fitzmyer, *Pauline Theology* (Paul thinks from the fulfilment backwards); Giblin,
In Hope of God's Glory; Amiot, *The Key Concepts of St Paul*. Both Kümmel (*Theology*, p. 142) and
Furnish (*Theology and Ethics*) favour starting with the future expectation, while still regarding justification as the central concept. This seems to indicate only a partial rethinking of the standard Lutheran
position.
[56] Munck, *Paul*, pp. 41, 66f.

---

[1] Bornkamm describes the content of Paul's gospel as I do (see n. 7 below), and he also recognizes
that Paul's 'drastic verdict' on the state of man was 'attainable only on the basis of the Christian salvation'
(*Paul*, p. 120). He nevertheless begins with man's lostness; and, having begun where Paul did not, he is
not able to utilize fully his own insight.
[2] See Bultmann, *Theology* I, pp. 190, 227.   [3] Ibid., p. 301.

In addition to the argument from the structure of Romans, one could make the obvious and necessary observation that *plight* and *solution* should correspond. This being the case, it seems logical to begin with the discussion of man's plight as perceived by Paul. It seems likely, however, that Paul's thought did not run from plight to solution, but rather from solution to plight. The attempts to argue that Romans 7 shows the frustration which Paul felt during his life as a practising Jew have now mostly been given up, and one may rightly and safely maintain that the chapter cannot be understood in this way. The chapter describes, rather, the pre-Christian or non-Christian life as seen from the perspective of faith. It may be further observed on the basis of Phil. 3 that Paul did not, while 'under the law', perceive himself to have a 'plight' from which he needed salvation.[4] If he were so zealous as to persecute the church, he may well have thought that those who were not properly Jewish would be damned, but the solution to such a plight would be simply to become properly Jewish. It appears that the conclusion that all the world – both Jew and Greek – equally stands in need of a saviour *springs from* the prior conviction that God had provided such a saviour. If he did so, it follows that such a saviour *must* have been needed, and then only consequently that all other possible ways of salvation are wrong. The point is made explicitly in Gal. 2.21: if righteousness could come through the law, Christ died in vain. The reasoning apparently is that Christ did not die in vain; he died and lived again 'that he might be Lord both of the dead and the living' (Rom. 14.9) and so that 'whether we wake or sleep we might live with him' (I Thess. 5.10). If his death was *necessary* for man's salvation, it follows that salvation cannot come in any other way and consequently that all were, prior to the death and resurrection, in need of a saviour. There is no reason to think that Paul felt the need of a universal saviour prior to his conviction that Jesus was such.[5]

---

[4] The fundamental demonstration was that of W. G. Kümmel, *Römer 7 und die Bekehrung des Paulus*, 1929. The view was confirmed and developed by Bultmann, 'Romans 7 and the Anthropology of Paul', *Existence and Faith*, pp. 147–57 (first published 1932). For further references see Conzelmann, *Theology*, p. 181 n. 1. There is a recent treatment in Luz, *Das Geschichtsverständnis des Paulus*, pp. 158–68; bibliography is given on p. 160. The most recent article accepting this view of Rom. 7 and Phil. 3 which I have noted is that of J. Dupont, 'La conversion de Paul', *Foi et Salut selon S. Paul* (by M. Barth and others), p. 75. Some dissenting scholars are cited below, section 4 n. 23. Dissent from this view is usually based on the judgment that Rom. 7, with its deeply moving phrases, gives Paul's view of his own history, while Phil. 3 is hyperbolic. The following points seem to me decisive in favour of the position followed here: (1) Gal. 3.11f., by repudiating the law on the grounds of Christology and soteriology, rather than because of its supposed unfulfillability, supports the view of Phil. 3 that Paul had no trouble fulfilling the law satisfactorily. It is most important that Paul's argument concerning the law does not in fact rest on man's inability to fulfil it (below, pp. 478f. and n. 23; 483–5). (2) The entire argument of Rom. 6–8, in which Paul contrasts life in Christ with life under the law, indicates that Rom. 7 should be read in the same light. The fact that Paul can express the pathos of life under the law as seen through Christian eyes does not mean that he had himself experienced frustration with the law before his own conversion.

[5] Professor Sandmel has reasonably suggested to me that, although it may be the case that no preconversion plight may be evidenced from the letters, Paul may have had an 'underground' plight – a difficulty with the law as adequate to human need – which he does not describe. This may well have been the case; but Paul's description in Phil. 3 and also such passages as II Cor. 3.10 ('what once had

This means that the way the problem is posed in Romans may not reflect Paul's actual missionary preaching. It seems unlikely that he followed the modern fundamentalist tactic of first convincing people that they were sinners and in need of salvation.[6] Paul's own references in his letters to what he preached are not sufficiently clear to allow us to come to a firm decision on this question, but they do give some indication that he did not *start* from man's need, but from God's deed.[7] The content of his preaching he calls the 'gospel of God' (I Thess. 2.8f.; II Cor. 11.7) or 'of Christ' (I Thess. 3.2; II Cor. 2.12; Rom. 15.9) or simply 'the gospel' (Gal. 1.11; 2.2; I Cor. 9.14) or 'Christ' (Phil. 1.18). Or he may call his message the 'word of God' (Phil. 1.14), the 'word of the cross' (I Cor. 1.18) or the 'word of reconciliation' (II Cor. 5.19). These last two phrases in particular seem to point to the fact that Paul considered his message to be what God had done in Christ. This is even clearer in I Cor. 1.23 ('we preach Christ crucified') and, most especially, in I Cor. 15.1–15. Here Paul defines his preaching (which he considers identical with the common message of Christianity) as being that Christ died, was buried, and was raised. He continues, 'If it is preached of Christ that he was raised from the dead, how can some of you say that there is no resurrection of the dead?. . . . If Christ was not raised, our preaching is empty and your faith is empty, and we are found to be false witnesses concerning God, because we testified concerning God that he raised Christ' (I Cor. 15.12–15). Here the content of the *preaching* and the *faith*, what was preached and believed, is the resurrection. Similarly Paul subsequently writes to the Corinthians that what he preached among them was Jesus Christ as Lord (II Cor. 4.15). These summaries ('the word of the cross', Jesus Christ crucified, that Christ was raised from the dead, that Christ is Lord) are not to be taken as exhaustive of what Paul preached. But it is noteworthy that he never specifies the plight of man as what is preached. It is always the action of God in Christ.

Support for this observation comes from considering further what it is that, according to Paul, Christians *believed*. As we saw in I Cor. 15, the common content of the Christian message, which converts believed, was the death and resurrection of Christ. And so it frequently appears in Paul. Thus I Thess. 4.14: 'For since we believe that Jesus died and rose again, even so, through Jesus, God will bring with him those who have fallen

---

splendour has come to have no splendour at all, because of the splendour that surpasses it') seems to indicate that he saw nothing wrong with the law before the revelation of Christ to him.

[6] So also Bornkamm, *Paul*, p. 121. Bornkamm's formulation here seems intentionally to counter that of Bultmann cited in n. 3 above.

[7] Cf. Bornkamm, op. cit., p. 109: 'Jesus Christ himself and the salvation based on and made available through his death on the cross, his resurrection, and his exaltation as Lord form the subject of Paul's proclamation.' On the difficulty of precisely identifying Paul's missionary preaching, see Munck, *Paul*, p. 91 and further references there.

asleep.' Belief in Jesus' death and resurrection is also implied in Rom. 6.8 ('But if we have died with Christ, we believe that we shall also live with him') and explicitly stated in the common confession cited in Rom. 10.9: 'if you confess with your lips that Jesus is Lord and believe in your heart that God raised him from the dead, you will be saved.' Bultmann has accurately pointed out that phrases such as 'believe in Jesus Christ' (Gal. 2.16) are equivalent to 'believe that he died and was raised' (I Thess. 4.14).[8] Wherever Paul mentions 'those who believe' or 'faith' absolutely (I Thess. 1.7,8; 2.10,13; Phil. 1.29; Gal. 1.23; I Cor. 1.21; 14.22-4; 15.17; II Cor. 13.5; Rom. 1.8,16), it is presumably this faith which is in mind, which *implies also hope in one's own salvation* by being raised to be with Christ (II Cor. 4.13f.). Thus 'believers' is the word for 'Christians' (which was not yet coined), and both Jews and pagans are called 'unbelievers' (*apistoi*).[9]

There are further implications of saying that the content of Paul's preaching and his hearers' faith was the death and resurrection of Christ. First, resurrection implies Christ's *lordship*, his *return*, the *judgment* and the *salvation of those who believe*. The well-known passage concerning the events of the end in I Cor. 15.20-28 is by no means unique. We should note, for example, Phil. 3.18-21:

For many, of whom I have often told you and now tell you even with tears, live as enemies of the cross of Christ. Their end is destruction, their god is the belly, and they glory in their shame, with minds set on earthly things. But our commonwealth is in heaven, and from it we await a Saviour, the Lord Jesus Christ, who will change our lowly body to be like his glorious body, by the power which enables him even to subject all things to himself.

The subjection of 'all things' is especially reminiscent of I Cor. 15.27f. Similar is I Thess. 4.15-17:

For this we declare to you by the word of the Lord, that we who are alive, who are left until the coming of the Lord, shall not precede those who have fallen asleep. For the Lord himself will descend from heaven with a cry of command, with the archangel's call, and with the sound of the trumpet of God. And the dead in Christ will rise first; then we who are alive, who are left, shall be caught up together with them in the clouds to meet the Lord in the air; and so we shall always be with the Lord.

All of this gives a good idea of what the 'gospel of Christ' or 'gospel of God' which Paul preached was: that Christ had died and that God had raised

---

[8] *TDNT* VI, p. 203.

[9] Above, section I n. 54. Bultmann correctly noted that 'in Christ' often does not refer to Paul's ecclesiological formulation of entering the body of Christ, but simply means 'Christian': *Theology* I, p. 311. The same observation applies, *mutatis mutandis*, to 'faith' and 'believe'.

I cannot follow Ford's view that *apistoi* means 'untrustworthy' (= non-*ḥaberim*) rather than 'unbeliever' ("'Hast thou tithed thy Meal" and "Is thy child Kosher"', *JTS* n.s. 17, 1966, pp. 74f.), despite the soundness of several of her observations.

him, that Christ is Lord, that the Lord will return, that the *apistoi* will be destroyed (II Cor. 4.3f.), that the believers would be saved – if alive by having their bodies transformed and if dead by being raised in a 'spiritual body' (I Cor. 15.44).[10] Paul doubtless preached many other items, but this is his gospel. Thus he did not begin with the sin and transgression of man, but with the opportunity for salvation offered by God (from which sin could exclude one). Put another way, Paul did not preach about men, but about God. It is true that, in the press of explaining the implications of his gospel, he comes closer to working out what can be called an 'anthropology' than any other New Testament author,[11] but that is *only the implication of his theology, Christology and soteriology*. It is not worked out for its own sake, for man's plight does not seem to be primarily what Paul preached *about*.

A second implication of the observation that the above outline comprises the main elements of the Pauline message is that, while the message is not about man and does not describe him, it is intended to elicit 'faith', and faith can only be individual. *What God is doing is of cosmic significance and affects 'all things', and it is this that Paul preaches about; but individuals will be affected differently, depending on whether or not they believe.* It is true that Paul can describe God's saving action virtually without reference to the believing response of man. Thus Rom. 8.28–30,33:

We know that in everything God works for good with those who love him, who are called according to his purpose. For those whom he foreknew he also predestined to be conformed to the image of his Son, in order that he might be the first-born among many brethren. And those whom he predestined he also called; and those whom he called he also justified; and those whom he justified he also glorified. . . . Who shall bring any charge against God's elect?

Schweitzer viewed the predestination of the elect as a main aspect of Paul's thought, regarding individuals as having only the right of refusal.[12] Bultmann, on the other hand, paid scant attention to predestination, emphasizing the necessity of individual decision.[13] Although the individual's ability to decide and commit himself to a way or a Lord seems to us to exclude predestinarian statements, we should recall that the two generally go together in Judaism. Just as the Qumran covenanters are called both the elect and those who choose God, so Paul has no difficulty in thinking of those who *accept* the gospel as being the *elect* of God (cf. also I Thess.

---

[10] On the question of the coherence and uniformity of Paul's future expectation, see above, section 1 n. 9 and the beginning of section 3 below.

[11] See further the end of section 4 below.

[12] Schweitzer, *Mysticism*, pp. 101–18, esp. p. 117; 128–30; above, section 1 n. 15.

[13] See *Theology* I, pp. 228f., 232, 240, 256, 270 (all to the effect that man's choice or decision determines everything), 329f. (predestination cannot be understood literally, since that would destroy the character of faith as decision and obedience).

1.4; I Cor. 1.24,26; Rom. 9.11f; 11.7). Precisely how we should formulate the balance between predestination and decision in Paul is difficult to say. One may compare with Rom. 8.28–30 (predestine, call, justify) Rom. 10.13–17. Commenting on Joel 3.5 ('every one who calls upon the name of the Lord will be saved', 2.32 in the ET), Paul asks, 'but how are men to call upon him in whom they have not believed? And how are they to believe in him of whom they have never heard?' And he concludes, 'So faith comes from what is heard, and what is heard comes by the preaching of Christ.' Here the sequence preaching, hearing, faith leaves out of account the very predestination which was insisted on two chapters earlier. The lists could be harmonized: God chooses who shall hear and believe the message and, on the basis of faith, he justifies and glorifies them. It is noteworthy that Paul did not feel compelled to make the harmonization. When he has in mind the assurance of salvation, God's action in giving it to men and God's grace in so doing, he can employ predestination terminology.[14] When he has in mind the human need for decision for Christ's lordship, the terminology is that of 'faith'. Statements of the latter type predominate in Paul's letters, but the predestination and grace statements prevent them from being understood as offering the possibility that one may be saved by his own efforts.[15]

To summarize: the main theme of Paul's gospel was the saving action of God in Jesus Christ and how his hearers could participate in that action. We have briefly indicated that the principal word for that participation is 'faith' or 'believing', a term which Paul doubtless took over from the earlier Christian missionaries. We have now to consider in greater detail how Paul understood and formulated human participation in God's saving action, and it is this discussion that will bring us into the heart of Paul's soteriology.

3. Pauline soteriology

The future expectation and its present guarantee

No two elements of Paul's thought are more certain, or more consistently expressed, than his conviction that the full salvation of believers and the destruction of unbelievers lay in the near future and his related conviction that Christians possessed the Spirit as the present guarantee of future salvation. We have cited above the most detailed passages which express the future hope (I Cor. 15, esp. vv. 23–28; I Thess. 4.15–17; Phil. 3.18–21). Schweitzer was of the view that Paul's future expectation was detailed and

---

[14] So Whiteley, *Theology of St Paul*, p. 93: Rom. 8.29f. deals with the assurance of salvation, not predestination.
[15] Similarly Conzelmann, *Theology*, pp. 173, 252–4.

explicit and that one could give a 'calendar' of events of the last time.[1] Subsequent scholars have pointed to the lack of uniformity in Paul's future expectation, taking the lack of uniformity to indicate a general but vague conception.[2] This is a question which we do not need to decide in detail, although we may observe that the fact that Paul does not always describe 'the end' in precisely the same terms does not mean that he held no unified conception of it.[3] The various passages just listed answer different questions, but they seem to be generally coherent: Christ will come, believers will be saved, unbelievers destroyed and all things put into subjection to God.[4] It is true that I Cor. 15 does not provide for the general resurrection and judgment[5] (and thus not for the destruction of unbelievers), but this need not lead either to Schweitzer's theory of two resurrections[6] and two judgments[7] (Christ's at the beginning of the Messianic kingdom and God's at the general resurrection), nor to the conclusion that Paul had no coherent view. In I Cor. 15 Paul is concerned to prove that the resurrection is in fact to come, just as in I Thessalonians he is concerned to answer the question of what happens to those who die before the end. The different problems lead to different statements, but the overall conception seems coherent.

The expectation of the coming of the Lord is very frequent in Paul's letters, and it is this general point which we are concerned to establish here.[8] Thus Paul writes that the faith of the Thessalonians is well known, how they turned from idols to serve the true and living God, 'and to wait for his Son from heaven, whom he raised from the dead, Jesus who delivers us from the wrath to come' (I Thess. 1.9f.). That the Lord is at hand (Phil. 4.5) and the time near (I Cor. 7.29,31; 10.11; Rom. 13.11) and the Day of the Lord expected suddenly (I Thess. 5.2; cf. Phil. 1.6; I Cor. 5.5) are often repeated. Christians are to be faultless, holy and blameless on the Day of the Lord (I Thess. 3.13; 5.23; Phil. 1.10; I Cor. 1.7f.). The future hope in Christ (I Thess. 1.3) may be specified either as the hope of salvation (I Thess. 5.8) or as the hope of righteousness (Gal. 5.5). It is of special interest to Paul that on the Day of the Lord his own work will be vindicated. Those

---

[1] Schweitzer, *Mysticism*, pp. 63–8.

[2] Bornkamm, *Paul*, pp. 219f.; Conzelmann, *Theology*, pp. 185f. ('Of course, apocalyptic imagery is there'; 'the picture of the parousia does not become an independent theme and . . . the ideas about the parousia are not a unity'). Conzelmann in particular thus reduces the significance of one of Paul's paramount convictions and concerns: the nearness of the Day of the Lord.

[3] On the general question of the coherence of Paul's future expectation, see W. D. Davies, *Paul and Rabbinic Judaism*, pp. 311–18. On the traditional and thorny problem of how to relate I Cor. 15 and II Cor. 5, see section 1 n. 9 above.

[4] Cf. Davies, op. cit., p. 297.

[5] Schweitzer, *Mysticism*, pp. 67f.

[6] Ibid., p. 93.   [7] Ibid., pp. 66f.

[8] On the appropriateness of the term 'apocalyptic' to describe the imminent expectation of the parousia, see Käsemann, 'On the Subject of Primitive Christian Apocalyptic', *Questions*, p. 109 n. 1. Bornkamm opposes the term on the grounds that Paul focused on the individual, not the cosmos (*Paul*, p. 147). Cf. Conzelmann's reservation, *Theology*, p. 256.

who are saved by hearing his gospel and who are found blameless at the Day will show that he is a true apostle (I Thess. 2.19: 'For what is our hope or joy or crown of boasting before our Lord Jesus at his coming? Is it not you?'; Phil. 2.14–16: '. . . that you may be blameless and innocent . . . , so that in the day of Christ I may be proud that I did not run in vain or labour in vain'; cf. II Cor. 1.14). Further, his work as an apostle, as well as that of others, will be tested (I Cor. 3.10–15; 4.5).

It is further to be observed that the verb 'save' in Paul is generally future or present, but only once past (aorist) tense. Even here, however, Paul writes that 'we were saved in *hope*' (Rom. 8.24).[9] More characteristic are such passages as 'we shall be saved through him from the wrath' (Rom. 5.9); 'if you confess . . . and believe . . . you shall be saved' (Rom. 10.9); 'in order that his spirit may be saved on the Day of the Lord' (I Cor. 5.5; effectively future); 'in order that in all ways I may save some' (I Cor. 9.22; cf. Rom. 11.14). Especially striking is the use of the present passive participles 'being saved' and 'being destroyed' in I Cor. 1.18 (the word of the cross is folly to those being destroyed but the power of God to those being saved) and II Cor. 2.15 ('For we are the aroma of Christ to God among those who are being saved and among those who are perishing'). That the work of salvation is already under way will concern us later; here we may also note the present tenses in I Cor. 7.31, 'the form of this world is passing away', II Cor. 3.18, 'we . . . are being changed into his likeness from one degree of glory to another', and II Cor. 4.16, 'our inner nature is being renewed every day' (contrast the future in Phil. 3.21, 'who will change our lowly body to be like his glorious body').[10] In any case, the consummation is still in the future.

We may finally note that the resurrection is future. This distinction is maintained by Paul even when the discussion of participation in Christ's death might seem to lead to the conclusion that Christians *have* participated in his resurrection. But Paul seems to take care to say that 'we *shall* . . . be united with him in a resurrection like his' (Rom. 6.5) and that 'we shall also live with him' (6.8), even though in a certain sense the Christian already 'lives' to God (6.11). The resurrection is also clearly described as future in I Cor. 6.14; 15.22 ('will be made alive'); Phil. 3.11.[11] Similarly, the

---

[9] The perfect tense of Eph. 2.5, 8 thus represents a distinct theological development.

[10] On the present beginning of the transformation, see especially Bouttier, *Christianity According to Paul*, pp. 22–8.

[11] It is said that the Christians *have been* raised in Col. 3.1, and accepting this as Pauline leads Davies to stress too much the realization of the eternal order: *Paul and Rabbinic Judaism*, p. 318. Cf. also Bouttier, *Christianity According to Paul*, p. 40, where the view of Colossians is regarded as complementary to that of the *Hauptbriefe*. Tannehill regards Col. 2.11–13 ('you were also raised') as more primitive than Rom. 6.4f., where the resurrection is future. It seems better to view Col. 2.11–13 as a theological development. The formulation seems to depend on the literary conflation of several passages in Romans. See 'Literary Dependence in Colossians', *JBL* 85, 1966, pp. 40–2.

kingdom of God (a term that does not often appear in Paul) will be inherited in the future (I Cor. 6.9f.).[12]

While the Christians are waiting for God's son from heaven (I Thess. 1.9f.), they have the Spirit. While there may be some ambiguity in Paul as to whether *life* is present or future, there is no ambiguity about the Spirit. It is the present possession of the Christians and their guarantee of salvation. Further, it is manifest in spiritual gifts. We may first note that Paul reminds his readers that he brought his gospel not only with the word but also with manifestations of the Spirit. Thus I Thess. 1.5 ('for our gospel came to you not only in word, but also in power and in the Holy Spirit'); I Cor. 2.4 ('my speech and my message were not in plausible words of wisdom, but in demonstration of the Spirit and power'); II Cor. 12.12 ('the signs of a true apostle were performed among you in all patience, with signs and wonders and mighty works'); Rom. 15.18f. ('by word and deed, by the power of signs and wonders, by the power of the Holy Spirit'). Paul bases his advice to his churches on the fact that he has the Spirit (I Cor. 7.40), and he hopes on his visit to Rome to impart 'some spiritual gift' (Rom. 1.11). Secondly, Paul repeatedly says that Christians 'have the Spirit': I Cor. 2.12; 3.16 ('you are God's temple and . . . God's Spirit dwells in you'); 6.19 ('your body is a temple of the Holy Spirit'); II Cor. 1.22 ('he has put his seal upon us and given us his Spirit in our hearts as a guarantee'); 4.13; 5.5 (God 'has given us the Spirit as a guarantee'); Gal. 3.2,5; 4.6; Rom. 5.5; 8.9 ('you are in the Spirit, if the Spirit of God really dwells in you'); 8.11,23 ('we ourselves, who have the first fruits of the Spirit').[13] Paul can also say that 'Christ lives in me' (Gal. 2.20) or that God lives in Christians (II Cor. 6.16, based on his paraphrase of several Old Testament passages, 'I will live in them'), but the possession of the Spirit is the dominant form of expression.[14]

It agrees with this that Paul expects all Christians to have spiritual gifts, *charismata* or *pneumatika*: I Thess. 5.19f. ('Do not quench the Spirit, do not despise prophesying'); I Cor. 1.7 ('you are not lacking in any spiritual gift [*charisma*], as you wait for the revealing of our Lord Jesus Christ'); 7.7 ('each has his own special gift [*charisma*] from God, one of one kind and one of another'); 12.1,4,11; 14.1 ('Make love your aim, and earnestly desire the spiritual gifts [*pneumatika*], especially that you may prophesy'); Rom. 12.6 ('Having gifts [*charismata*] that differ according to the grace given to us, let us use them: if prophecy, in proportion to our faith').

In their present life the Christians have been *sanctified* in the sense of

---

[12] Col. 1.13 again takes the transfer to 'the kingdom of his beloved Son' to have taken place. See Davies, *Paul and Rabbinic Judaism*, p. 296.

[13] On the gift of the Spirit to all Christians, see also Whiteley, *Theology of St Paul*, p. 125.

[14] Cf. Käsemann, 'Ministry', *Essays*, p. 65: 'The Spirit is our present participation in eternal life, but we can possess him and participate in his gift only as he possesses us.'

cleansed (I Cor. 1.2), and Paul urges them to remain *pure and blameless* until the Day of the Lord. Thus Paul writes to the Corinthians:

Do you not know that the unrighteous will not inherit the kingdom of God? Do not be deceived; neither the immoral, nor idolaters, nor adulterers, nor homosexuals, nor thieves, nor the greedy, nor drunkards, nor revilers, nor robbers will inherit the kingdom of God. And such were some of you. But you were washed, you were sanctified, you were justified in the name of the Lord Jesus Christ and in the Spirit of our God (I Cor. 6.9–11).[15]

It is Paul's earnest hope that his Gentile converts will remain thus purified 'so that the offering of the Gentiles may be acceptable, sanctified by the Holy Spirit' (Rom. 15.16). Similarly he prays concerning the Thessalonians that the Lord will 'establish [their] hearts unblamable in holiness before our God and Father, at the coming of our Lord Jesus with all his saints' (I Thess. 3.13), and he hopes that the Thessalonians may be kept 'sound and blameless at the coming of our Lord Jesus Christ' (I Thess. 5.23). To the Corinthians he writes that the Lord Jesus Christ 'will sustain you to the end, guiltless in the day of our Lord Jesus Christ' (I Cor. 1.8). He considers it right that one should be anxious 'about the affairs of the Lord, how to be holy in body and spirit' (I Cor. 7.34). He frequently urges his converts to 'stand steadfast in the faith', unwavering though tempted; i.e. neither losing their confidence that they will be saved in the day of the Lord nor relapsing into idolatry, sexual immorality and the like: I Thess. 3.5 ('I sent that I might know your faith, for fear that somehow the tempter had tempted you and that our labour would be in vain'); Phil. 2.15f. ('be blameless and innocent, children of God without blemish in the midst of a crooked and perverse generation, among whom you shine as lights in the world, holding fast the word of life, so that in the day of Christ I may be proud that I did not run in vain or labour in vain'); I Cor. 15.1f. ('. . . the gospel, which you received, in which you stand, by which you are saved, if you hold it fast – unless you believed in vain'); 15.58 ('be steadfast, immovable, always abounding in the work of the Lord, knowing that in the Lord your labour is not in vain'); 16.13 ('stand firm in your faith'); II Cor. 4.16f. (we do not lose heart in momentary affliction); 11.3 ('I am afraid that . . . your thoughts will be led astray from a sincere and pure devotion to Christ'); Gal. 6.9 ('And let us not grow weary in well-doing, for in due season we shall reap, if we do not lose heart'); Phil. 1.27f. (stand firm and do not be frightened); 4.1 (stand firm); Rom. 11.20 ('you stand fast only through faith'); 12.11 ('Never flag in zeal'); Phil. 1.9–11 ('And it is my prayer that your love may abound. . . . so that you may approve what is excellent, and may be pure and blameless for the day of Christ, filled with the fruits of righteousness'); I Thess.

---

[15] On idolatry and sexual immortality, cf. I Cor. 10.7f.

4.3–8 ('For this is the will of God, your sanctification: that you abstain from immorality. . . . For God has not called us for uncleanness, but in holiness'). While Paul's principal view thus seems to be that Christians *have been cleansed* and *established in the faith*, and that they should *remain so*, so as to be found blameless on the day of the Lord, he can also urge them to cleanse themselves: 'Since we have these promises, beloved, let us cleanse ourselves from every defilement of body and spirit, and make holiness perfect in the fear of God' (II Cor. 7.1). Faced with a lapse into obvious sexual immorality in Corinth, Paul writes that he fears that when he comes there again 'I may have to mourn over many of these who sinned before and have not repented of the impurity, immorality, and licentiousness which they have practised' (II Cor. 12.21). Thus Paul is aware that not everyone consistently remains in the cleansed state, and, at least on this one occasion, he sees repentance as the way to re-establish it.[16]

It agrees with his view that the Christians have been sanctified (*hēgias-menois*, I Cor. 1.2) that his other principal word for them, besides 'believers', is 'saints' (*hagioi*): thus Rom. 1.7; 8.27; I Cor. 1.2 and very frequently. Although Christians are also said to have been 'justified' (I Cor. 6.9–11; Rom. 8.30), he does not call them 'the righteous', *dikaioi*; the plural adjective appears only in Rom. 5.19 and 2.13, and it does not seem to be a title in either place. Paul's emphasis on cleansing and 'sanctification' may be connected with his being the apostle to the Gentiles, who obviously (from his point of view) were tainted with moral impurity.

Thus far we have described a soteriology of cleansing, awaiting the coming salvation in a pure state, possession of the Spirit as the guarantee of future salvation and the provision of repentance for the repair of relapses. (The last point is made only once, while the other themes are very frequent.) We have seen that participants in this soteriological situation are called 'saints' and 'believers' in contrast to 'the wicked' (I Cor. 6.1) and 'unbelievers' (I Cor. 6.6); thus the characteristic act of the Christian is 'faith', and Christians are characteristically 'blameless'. It is likely that we should connect baptism and the death of Christ with the cleansing which Christians receive, although, as we shall see, participation in Christ's death through baptism has another application. There is every reason to believe that the soteriology which we have just described was common in Christianity. It is well known, however, that Paul was not content merely to say that Christians, while waiting for the coming of the Lord, had spiritual gifts and should remain clean. Pressed by opponents on various sides, he expounded the significance of the present state of the Christian life in such a way that the simple theology of future expectation and present possession of spiritual gifts was greatly deepened. We could do no better than guess by what chain of reasoning

---

[16] On repentance, see further below, pp. 500f.

or under what history-of-religions influence Paul deepened the idea of the *possession* of the Spirit as a *guarantee* so that it became *participation* in one Spirit, or the idea of Christ's death as *cleansing* former trespasses so that it became the means by which one *participated* in Christ's death to the *power* of sin, but it is clear that he did so, and that herein lies the heart of his soteriology and Christology.[17] It is also clear that this 'deepening' did not appear to Paul as unusual, surprising or unique. He expected his readers to understand and agree with him. Whether such ideas were actually common in Christianity is hard to determine;[18] but, as we shall see, when he expresses them Paul does not consider himself as an innovator, but only to be reminding his readers of the implications of their own Christian experience.

One body, one spirit

It is possible that modern scholars have been too strongly struck by Paul's view of *participation and union* to give it precise justice. The 'discoverers' of the view, such as Deissmann and Schweitzer, may justly be accused of giving it too much prominence as a unique, creative and ultimately (to modern man) incomprehensible view. In reaction, there has been some tendency to de-emphasize the view, almost to the point of eliminating it from Paul's thought. Thus Bultmann not only divided up and parcelled out the various 'participatory' passages in Paul in such a way that he did not have to discuss the theme as such – *en Christō* is treated under ecclesiology,[19] the idea of being a member of Christ's body is derived from gnosticism,[20] participation in his death is a conception derived from the mystery religions[21] – but he also insisted that these various conceptions which Paul picked up from contemporary soteriological schemes must be interpreted in terms of Paul's 'real' view: there is 'no magical or mysterious transformation of man'; rather, 'a new understanding of one's self takes the place of

---

[17] Schweitzer (*Mysticism*, p. 75) argued that Paul was not content with future expectation because of the problems posed by eschatology itself. But this depends on accepting his highly schematized view of the necessary logic of eschatology; see e.g. ibid., p. 79.

[18] Käsemann, for example, has argued that the idea that the eucharist was considered to provide participation in the body and blood of Christ was common in pre-Pauline Christianity: 'The Lord's Supper', *Essays*, pp. 109f. Cf. Bornkamm, *Paul*, p. 191.

[19] Bultmann, *Theology* I, p. 311. Bultmann's observation that the phrase is ecclesiological and eschatological – not a formula of personal mysticism – is, in part at least, correct; but one must note that being in Christ (as a member of the body of Christ, the eschatological community) is also *soteriology* – one is thereby saved –; and Bultmann did not discuss the phrase under soteriology, nor did he bring it into connection with the 'righteousness by faith' terminology. Bultmann does connect the phrase with ethics, ibid., pp. 327f. For a denial that 'in Christ' is an ecclesiological formula, see Käsemann, 'The Faith of Abraham', *Perspectives*, p. 101. Better is Davies's formulation (*Paul and Rabbinic Judaism*, pp. 86–8): it is ecclesiological, but it implies a personal relationship; 'in Christ' must be interpreted in light of the passages about dying with Christ.

[20] Bultmann, *Theology* I, p. 310.

[21] Ibid., pp. 311f.

the old'.[22] Bultmann, Conzelmann[23] and, to a lesser degree, Bornkamm,[24] have been so concerned to deny that Paul held a view which implies more than a change in self-understanding – put another way, that his language implies a view which cannot be made readily applicable to modern Christianity by existentialist demythologizing – that both the force of what Paul wrote and the *naturalness* of his own conception have been obscured. To see how easily Paul's mind moved into the categories of *participation* and *unity*, we may best consider two passages from I Corinthians. The first should be quoted at length:

The body is not meant for immorality, but for the Lord, and the Lord for the body. And God raised the Lord and will also raise us up by his power. Do you not know that your bodies are members of Christ? Shall I therefore take the members of Christ and make them members of a prostitute? Never! Do you not know that he who joins himself to a prostitute becomes one body with her? For as it is written, 'The two shall become one.' But he who is united to the Lord becomes one spirit with him. Shun immorality. (I Cor. 6.13b–18a)

Here Paul is not explaining some 'mystery' of the Christian faith known only to him, nor describing a unique 'experience', nor even, for that matter, a situation found only among Christians. The argument is that one participatory union can destroy another, even though the two are not on precisely the same level. The RSV omits from the quotation of Gen. 2.24 the word 'flesh', but Paul indicates that a union of 'flesh' can destroy a union of spirit. That Paul did not actually think in terms of humans as divided into flesh, spirit and soul is well known, and it is seen clearly here.[25] A *person* cannot participate in two mutually exclusive unions.[26] The argument is introduced to clinch the point that Christians should not engage in sexual immorality. And here we see the ease with which Paul moves to a conception which strikes modern men as quite remarkable. The argument about sexual

[22] Ibid., pp. 268f. See further section 7 below.

[23] Conzelmann, *Theology* I, pp. 208–10 (*en Christō*); 260–3 (the body of Christ treated under ecclesiology, and a connection with soteriology denied; even saying that 'we enter the body of Christ by obtaining a share in the death of Christ' (p. 264) does not lead Conzelmann to attribute any soteriological significance to the concept; but Conzelmann does not derive the concept from gnosticism); 268–74 ('incorporation in the church through the sacraments'; but the theme is dealt with under 'revelation in the present', not under 'the saving event'). Thus the various themes of participation are parcelled out. All are interpreted in terms of righteousness by faith, and they are not allowed to assert their own meaning.

[24] Bornkamm (*Paul*, p. 155) lists most of the participatory phrases together, instead of distributing them to different theological *loci*. Their force, however, is denied: 'in Christ' 'only expresses membership in the church. Obviously, no profound theological, let alone "mystical" meaning should be wrested from such turns of phrase' (pp. 154f.) – as if being in the church were not of profound salvific significance! Cf. also pp. 151f. and section 7 below.

[25] Bultmann, *Theology* I, pp. 192–210. Although Bultmann's analysis of Paul's anthropological terminology may be subject to correction in detail, it remains the best general treatment available and a testimony to his remarkable exegetical powers. On this point cf. Käsemann, 'On Paul's Anthropology', p. 7.

[26] Cf. Schweitzer, *Mysticism*, p. 128.

immorality is based on facts about participatory union which Paul supposes his readers will immediately understand and agree with: 'Do you not know?' Everyone agrees so readily with Paul's conclusion (Christians should not commit sexual immorality) that it is easy to miss how strange the logic behind it is for us and how natural to Paul. We might expect an argument that a Christian should not behave in such and such a way, since immorality is not appropriate to being Christian, since it is forbidden in the Bible or since such a transgression will result in punishment from God; but to say that one should not fornicate because fornication produces a union which excludes one from a union which is salvific is to employ a rationale which today is not readily understood. Against the view that Paul's real meaning involves only a new understanding of one's self, we must note that although there is a problem of *understanding* on the part of the Corinthians involved (one who reflects on the significance of what Paul says will amend his actions, and the commission of the actions indicates that such reflection has not taken place), the problem is not one *of* self-understanding. The facts that a union with a prostitute threatens to sever one from Christ, and that Christians are members of Christ's body and one Spirit with him, should be *reflected* in the way one understands himself and God, but they do not consist of that understanding. The participatory union is not a figure of speech for something else; it is, as many scholars have insisted, real.[27]

The second passage, I Cor. 10, is closely related to the one just quoted. The thrust of the argument is that the participation in Christ which is given in the Lord's Supper does not establish the sort of salvific union which cannot be destroyed. In I Corinthians Paul is repeatedly concerned about two of the traditional Gentile sins – idolatry and sexual immorality – and here he deals with idolatry. He first argues, on the basis of the Old Testament, that the Jews who were 'baptized into Moses' and who ate the supernatural food and drank the supernatural drink (which came from the Rock, Christ), were nevertheless destroyed when they committed idolatry (I Cor. 10.1–7).[28] The point of the Old Testament narrative, Paul writes, is to instruct Christians that their participation (*koinōnia*) in the body and blood of Christ will not save them if they commit idolatry. Again, idolatry involves a participatory union which excludes one from union with Christ (10.14–22). Here Paul does not argue *that* one participates in the body and blood of Christ in the Lord's Supper; rather that *since* one does so, one may not participate in food and drink in which demons share. Thus it is not simply that a *transgression* removes one from union with Christ; rather, union with Christ and union with demons are mutually exclusive. Paul had a wealth of

---

[27] Cf. Schweitzer, *Mysticism*, pp. 128f.; Käsemann, 'The Lord's Supper', *Essays*, pp. 109, 118, 132; especially J. A. T. Robinson, *The Body*, 1952, pp. 47, 50–3.
[28] On the passage, cf. Käsemann, 'The Lord's Supper', *Essays*, pp. 116–18.

Old Testament passages on which to draw to show that idolatry was wrong. He brought forward none of the obvious passages, however, that would prove that idolatry was wrong *because it is a transgression* against the commandment and will of God. The argument, rather, is that it establishes a union which excludes one from participation in the body of Christ. The Old Testament passage simply shows that even baptism and eating and drinking can be nullified by unions of idolatry and immorality (10.8). Eating sacrificial food makes one a participant (*koinōnos*) in the altar of the god to whom the sacrifice is made (cf. 10.18).

Further passages could be cited to show how easily Paul could appeal to Christians' participation in Christ to prove other points. Perhaps the main thing to observe is precisely that he does appeal to it to prove other points, not as something which itself requires proof, and for that reason the general theme of participation is evident in both *controversy* and moral *exhortation*. It agrees with this that Paul does not have one fixed terminology for participation. Attempts to decide which is the key phrase (e.g. being in the body of Christ, the short phrase 'in Christ', and the like)[29] do not seem decisive or even essential for understanding the centrality of the general theme of participation. The centrality appears in what was just mentioned: *it is the theme, above all, to which Paul appeals both in parenesis and polemic.* Further, the very diversity of the terminology helps to show how the general conception of participation permeated his thought.[30]

We have already encountered several of Paul's terms, and we should now review them all, for each adds some dimension to the overall conception.[31]

1. Members of Christ's body, the body of Christ. We have already seen I Cor. 6.15 ('your bodies are members of Christ') and 10.16 (participation, *koinōnia*, in the blood and body of Christ). In the latter passage, Paul continues, 'Because there is one loaf, we who are many are one body, for we all partake of the same loaf' (10.17). The same conception appears in connection with both baptism and the Lord's Supper in I Cor. 12:

For just as the body is one and has many members, and all the members of the body, though many, are one body, so it is with Christ. For by one Spirit we were all baptized into one body – Jews or Greeks, slaves or free – and all were made to drink of one Spirit. (12.12f.)
. . . .

[29] See Schweitzer's reasonable explanation, *Mysticism*, pp. 122–7; see further Conzelmann, *Theology*, p. 210 n. 1; Davies, *Paul and Rabbinic Judaism*, pp. 85–9; Käsemann, 'The Theological Problem Presented by the Motif of the Body of Christ', *Perspectives*, p. 106: the question of which is prior, 'in Christ' or 'the body of Christ', is not important (against Brandenburger, *Fleisch und Geist*, p. 49); Conzelmann, *Theology*, p. 265: the two concepts overlap but do not coincide.

[30] Cf. J. A. T. Robinson (*The Body*, pp. 46f.) on the common denominator meaning of the diverse participatory phrases.

[31] For discussions of Paul's participationist terminology, see J. Dupont, ΣΥΝ ΧΡΙΣΤΩΙ. *L'union avec le Christ suivant saint Paul*, 1952; M. Bouttier, *En Christ*, 1962; Bouttier, *Christianity According to Paul*; W. Thüsing, *Per Christum in Deum*, 1965.

Now you are the body of Christ and individually members of it. (12.27)

The argument of the passage as a whole is that the Christians at Corinth who have the most spectacular *charismata* should not boast of them. There are many gifts but one Spirit (12.4). As in the human body each member is indispensable, especially the 'weaker' ones, so in the body of Christ (12.14–26). The conclusion of saying that 'you are the body of Christ' is that there are different functions served by various Christians: some are apostles, some prophets and the like (12.28–31). Thus we see the use of the terminology 'members' and 'body' in parenetic instruction.

A formulation similar to that of I Cor. 12.12f. is Gal. 3.25–29:

But now that faith has come, we are no longer under a custodian; for in Christ Jesus you are all sons of God, through faith. For as many of you as were baptized into Christ have put on Christ. There is neither Jew nor Greek, there is neither slave nor free, there is neither male nor female; for you are all one in Christ Jesus. And if you are Christ's, then you are Abraham's offspring, heirs according to promise.

It is a difficult exegetical problem to describe the precise line of argumentation in Gal. 3–4, and in the verses just quoted Paul is drawing several threads together. This may be seen in part by the compactness of the passage and the diversity of the terminology: 'faith', 'sons', 'baptized into Christ', 'put on Christ', 'one [person] in Christ Jesus', 'Christ's', and 'heirs'. The passage falls under the current heading because of the phrase 'you are all one [person] in Christ Jesus'. Here the terms 'members' and 'body' do not appear, but 'one person' (*heis*) seems to imply the same conception. Without attempting a detailed exegesis of the passage, we may say that the general argument is *polemical* against the possibility that Paul's Galatian Christians might observe the Jewish law. It is one of Paul's main themes, as we shall see when we consider the law, that Jews and Greeks must have equal access to salvation. We have already seen, in I Cor. 12.12f., how this point ('one body', 'Jews or Greeks') can be inserted into a discussion of idolatry, and here we see the fuller force of the 'Jews or Greeks' theme. The basis of the lack of distinction between Jews and Greeks with regard to salvation, and consequently the basis for Paul's view that the law should not be obeyed by Gentiles, is that 'all are one [person]'.

We may finally cite Rom. 12.4–6, in which the argument is basically the same as in I Cor. 12, although the controversial thrust is not present:

For as in one body we have many members, and all the members do not have the same function, so we, though many, are one body in Christ, and individually members one of another. Having gifts [*charismata*] that differ according to the grace given to us, let us use them: if prophecy, in proportion to our faith. . . .

2. One Spirit. We have already quoted the one passage in which Paul says

that Christians are 'one Spirit' with the Lord: I Cor. 6.17. The phrase appears as a verbal contrast to 'one flesh' with a prostitute, and there is no reason to think that being one Spirit with the Lord is in any way different from being the members of the body of Christ. In I Cor. 12.13 Paul writes that Christians are baptized into one *body* by one Spirit and that all drink of one Spirit. Just as Paul can speak of participation in or the fellowship of the body and blood of Christ (I Cor. 10.16), he can also speak of participation in or the fellowship of the Holy Spirit (II Cor. 13.13, *koinōnia c. gen.*). More frequently, however, Paul speaks in terms of one's *having* the Spirit or of the Spirit's dwelling in the Christian (as the Temple), as we have seen above, and, conversely, of one's dwelling in the Spirit (Rom. 8.9–11).

The Spirit, as is well known, plays a major role in providing the grounds of Paul's *parenesis*. Since a man has the Spirit in him and is in the Spirit, he should *walk* by the Spirit, be *led* by the Spirit or produce the fruits of the Spirit (Rom. 8.9–14; I Cor. 6.19; Gal. 5.16–25). That Christians received the Spirit by faith rather than by works of law is a substantial part of Paul's *polemical* argument against Judaizing (Gal. 3.1–5), and Paul can say that his faith and message are based on his having the Spirit (II Cor. 4.13).

3. In Christ. This phrase has attracted more attention than any of the other participatory phrases,[32] principally because of Deissmann's theory which was built around it[33] and subsequent denials that it bears a 'mystical' meaning.[34] Schweitzer, it may be recalled, regarded the phrase 'in Christ' as 'merely a brachyology for being partakers in the Mystical Body of Christ'. Schweitzer's observations are worth being quoted more fully:

Since 'in Christ' is the more frequent expression, it has been held to be the most original, and the attempt has been made to take it as the starting-point in investigating Paul's mysticism. But that path led into a *cul-de-sac*. The phrase which is regarded as the most original is really a derivative one, from which the real nature of the conception cannot be apprehended. The very fact that alongside of the 'in Christ' there [occur] these other phrases, such as 'with Christ', ought to have suggested the idea that possibly there should be sought behind the 'in Christ' a more general conception, the *common denominator* for these various forms of expression. . . . Since [the expression 'in Christ'] did not contain in itself the implication that the individual has his part in the Body of Christ along with the multitude of the Elect, it led investigators astray. It misled them into trying to explain as an *individual* and *subjective* experience that which according to Paul happens to believers as a *collective* and *objective* event.

'Being in Christ' is therefore the commonest, but not the most appropriate, expression for union with Christ. It becomes the most usual, not only because of its shortness but because of the facility which it offers for forming antitheses with

---

[32] For a history of the discussion, see M. Bouttier, *En Christ*, ch. 1.

[33] The *en* is local. Most conveniently, see Deissmann, *Paul*, Harper Torchbook, p. 297.

[34] Bultmann, *Theology* I, p. 311; Bornkamm, *Paul*, p. 155; Conzelmann, *Theology* p. 184. Cf. n. 19 above.

the analogous expressions 'in the body', 'in the flesh', 'in sin', and 'in the spirit', and thus providing the mystical theory with a series of neat equations.[35]

The main points of Schweitzer's analysis seem to me to be precisely correct.[36] We shall therefore simply cite the principal passages where 'in Christ' and related phrases appear and then note in what contexts they appear.

Therefore, if any one is in Christ, he is a new creation; the old has passed away, behold the new has come. (II Cor. 5.17)

For our sake he made him to be sin who knew no sin, so that in him we might become the righteousness of God. (II Cor. 5.21)

. . . for in Christ Jesus you are all sons of God, through faith. (Gal. 3.26)

. . . in order that I may gain Christ and be found in him, not having a righteousness of my own. . . . (Phil. 3.8f.)

There is therefore now no condemnation for those who are in Christ Jesus. (Rom 8.1)

As Schweitzer noted,[37] and as was true of the Spirit, Paul may make the converse statement, 'Christ in you': Rom. 8.10; II Cor. 13.5. Again, just as Paul could mention the *koinōnia*, participation in or fellowship with, the blood and body of Christ (I Cor. 10.16) and the Spirit (II Cor. 13.13), so he can mention the *koinōnia* of God's son, Jesus Christ our Lord (I Cor. 1.9). We have already noted the phrases 'baptized into Christ' and 'put on Christ' (Gal. 3.27).

We should first note that 'in Christ' and related phrases cannot be quite so neatly parcelled out to parenetic and polemical contexts as 'in the Spirit', 'one body' and related phrases. II Cor. 13.5 is parenetic in quite the same way as are many of the 'Spirit' passages: 'Examine yourselves, to see whether you are holding to your faith. Test yourselves. Do you not realize that Jesus Christ is in you? – unless indeed you fail to meet the test!' We have already observed that the general context of Gal. 3.26 is a pulling together of several threads in a polemical argument against the Galatian Christians' observing the law. There is a sense in which Rom. 8.1,10 ('if Christ is in you') are the same. Rom. 7 deals with the question of the function of the law in such a way as to answer negatively the question of whether salvation comes by the law. Rom. 8.1 then gives the solution: there is no condemnation for those in Christ, as there is for those who are under law. The term 'con-

---

[35] Schweitzer, *Mysticism*, pp. 122f., my emphasis. Schweitzer is sometimes understood as having thought that the *in Christ* motif as such is the central element in Paul's thought. Thus C. Roetzel, *Judgement in the Community*, p. 10.
[36] Apart from the question of which phrase came first, which we need not decide; above, n. 29.
[37] Ibid., p. 125.

demnation' seems to refer back also to the discussion in 5.16–21, where the argument is that in Adam there is condemnation, though not for those in Christ (although here the 'in' phrases do not occur). In more general terms, however, Rom. 8 is not simply polemical against the law; it is an argument that Christians are 'alive' and will be saved at the end. It is in terms of the *assurance of salvation* that Paul says that those in Christ are not condemned (8.1), that those in the Spirit please God (8.8), that for those in whom Christ is, the Spirit means life (8.10), and that God will raise those in whom the Spirit dwells (8.11). Thus we see here that having the Spirit as *guarantee* and salvation by *participation* in the Spirit or in Christ (or participation with the Spirit or Christ by having them in one) are not separate themes. The force of the guarantee, in other words, goes beyond having *charismata* which demonstrate the presence of the Spirit. Having the Spirit results in (or is) real participation in the Spirit and the resurrected Lord, which participation provides the best guarantee of all: Christians *are* sons of God (Rom. 8.16; Gal. 4.7).

It is even more difficult to give a definite setting for II Cor. 5.17. The general context is Paul's relieved apologia for himself as an apostle and reflection on his work and his gospel. He had been afraid that either he would be rejected or that he would have to take very harsh (though unspecified) action in Corinth (II Cor. 10.1–4; 12.21; 13.1–4), but even when he learns that the Corinthians are obedient to him (II Cor. 7.6f.) he cannot abandon his defence of himself: 'Are we beginning to commend ourselves again?' (II Cor. 3.1); 'Therefore, having this ministry by the mercy of God, we do not lose heart' (4.1); 'But we have this treasure in earthen vessels, to show that the transcendent power belongs to God and not to us' (4.7); 'So we do not lose heart. Though our outer nature is wasting away, our inner nature is being renewed every day. For this slight momentary affliction is preparing for us an eternal weight of glory beyond all comparison' (4.16f.); 'So we are always of good courage; we know that while we are at home in the body we are away from the Lord. . . . We would rather be away from the body and at home with the Lord' (5.6–8); 'Therefore, knowing the fear of the Lord, we persuade men; but what we are is known to God, and I hope it is known also to your conscience. We are not commending ourselves to you again . . .' (5.11f.). It is in this context of relieved reflection upon and justification of his own ministry that Paul writes an (not *the*) epitome of his message and his own role in God's plan: Christ died for all; therefore all have died (5.14); one who is in Christ is a new creation (5.17); the message of reconciliation was given to Paul (and presumably the other apostles) (5.20). We may observe here a point which will have to be fully explored later: in this passage, as in others, there is a mixture of supposedly 'mystical' terminology ('in Christ') and 'juridical' terminology ('reconciliation').

Phil. 3.3–16, like II Cor. 5, also does not have a parenetic or polemical setting.[38] Here again Paul is reflecting on his own situation and the gospel which he has preached. We shall return to the significance of this passage when we discuss 'transfer terminology' below.

4. Christ's, Servants of the Lord. Paul repeatedly, especially in parenesis, turns from talking about participation in the Spirit or in the body of Christ to saying that Christians are Christ's, that they belong to him, or that they should consider themselves his servants. Thus in I Cor. 6.12–20, in which Paul discusses the significance of fornication with a prostitute for those who are Christ's members and who are one Spirit with him, he concludes: 'You are not your own; you were bought with a price. So glorify God in your body.' Similarly, after discussing the fruits of the Spirit as contrasted with the fruits of the flesh in Gal. 5.16–23, Paul concludes that 'those who belong to Christ Jesus have crucified the flesh with its passions and desires'. In Rom. 6, after discussing dying with Christ (which takes place so that one may no longer be enslaved to sin, 6.6), there appears the principal parenetic section in which the relation to Christ is conceived as being a 'slave'. The Christians were once 'slaves of sin' (6.17), but are now slaves of obedience which leads to righteousness (6.16) or simply 'slaves of righteousness' (6.18). Paul hastens to add here that he is speaking 'in human terms' because of the limitations of his readers (6.19). Presumably the term which might lead to misunderstanding is 'slaves'. It may be noted that for us today the terminology of slavery and service, with its consequence, obedience, is more readily comprehended than such phrases as being members of the body of Christ or being one Spirit with Christ, terminology which Paul did not feel compelled to explain or apologize for.

The terminology of being Christ's or belonging to him (as a slave to a master, although the analogy is not always drawn) is fairly frequent. Thus Rom. 14.8f.:

If we live, we live to the Lord, and if we die, we die to the Lord; so then, whether we live or whether we die, we are the Lord's. For to this end Christ died and lived again, that he might be Lord both of the dead and of the living. (Rom. 14.8f.)

. . . and you are Christ's; and Christ is God's. (I Cor. 3.23)

For he who was called in the Lord as a slave is a freedman of the Lord. Likewise he who was free when called is a slave of Christ. You were bought with a price; do not become slaves of men. (I Cor. 7.22f.)

We destroy arguments and every proud obstacle to the knowledge of God, and take every thought captive to obey Christ, being ready to punish every disobedience,

---

[38] The passage is in part polemical against the law (3.1f.), but this does not fully account for it. Paul is reflecting on his own situation and hopes.

when your obedience is complete. Look at what is before your eyes. If any one is confident that he is Christ's, let him remind himself that as he is Christ's, so are we. (II Cor. 10.5–7)

But each in his own order: Christ the first fruits, then at his coming those who belong to Christ. (I Cor. 15.23)

It is obvious that the terminology of being Christ's, of being his servants and of belonging to him, is less 'participationist' than the language of being members of his body and the like. That Christ is Lord and that Christians should serve and obey him is obviously a prime tenet of Paul's message. What the generic relation is between this way of putting the relationship and the ones that are more participationist cannot, in all probability, be decided. What is important to note is that Paul did not consider *belonging* to Christ to be different from being *in* him. Thus, for example, Rom. 8.9: 'But you are not in the flesh, you are in the Spirit, if the Spirit of God really dwells in you. Anyone who does not have the Spirit of Christ does not belong to him.' Verse 10 continues: 'But if Christ is in you, then although the body is dead on account of sin, the Spirit is life on account of righteousness.'[39] The difficulties of the translation of v. 10 need not be unravelled here.[40] The point is that Paul passes from saying 'you are *in* the Spirit', to the qualification 'if the Spirit of God dwells *in* you', to mentioning 'the Spirit of Christ' as being *in* one, to a statement of *belonging to* Christ, and then back to Christ's being *in* the Christian. To belong to Christ is not different from being 'in' him. I would take the argument to be that having the Spirit of Christ makes one Christ's, which will lead to life at his coming. But in any case we see the close connection between belonging, indwelling and being indwelt.

We earlier noted the possibility of a simple eschatological soteriology based on the expectation of future salvation, which is guaranteed by possession of the Spirit, which in turn is manifested by *charismata*. We must now repeat that having the Spirit as guarantee of the future salvation is not different from dwelling in the Spirit and having the Spirit dwell in one. Not only should we recall that the function of the sequence just cited from Rom. 8.9f. is to *guarantee* that the Christian *will* have life (v. 11), but we may also cite II Cor. 5. Just before saying that one *in* Christ *is* a new creation (II Cor. 5.17), Paul has mentioned the possession of the Spirit as a *guarantee* (5.5). Thus we nowhere have in Paul a simple soteriology of eschatological expectation divorced from the present reality of participation in Christ or in the Spirit. Rather, the two go together. Thus Schweitzer was completely

---

[39] My translation. RSV: '. . . although your bodies are dead because of sin, your spirits are alive . . .'
[40] Bultmann's solution (*Theology* I, pp. 208f.) seems satisfactory: the difficulty is due to the 'pointed, rhetorical formulation'. 'Hence, we have here a rhetorical paraphrase of the simple thought: "If Christ dwells in you, then the life-giving Spirit also dwells in you" (*cf.* v. 11).'

correct in emphasizing that the 'mystical' and the eschatological conceptions are intimately related, even if his explanation of the logic by which they came to be related is not completely convincing.

Drawing together the various strands of the discussion thus far, we could put Paul's view this way: God has appointed Christ as Lord and saviour of the world. All who believe in him have the Spirit as the guarantee of future full salvation and are at present considered to participate in Christ's body, to be one Spirit with him. As such, they are to act in accordance with the Spirit, which is also to serve Christ as the Lord to whom they belong.

Transfer terminology

We saw above that Paul considered his Gentile Christian converts to have been *cleansed* of their former sins: washed, sanctified, justified (I Cor. 1.2; 6.9–11; cf. II Cor. 12.21). Despite the prominence of the cleansing terminology in I Corinthians, however, where Paul has, among other things, the traditional Gentile sins to deal with, it is not the most characteristic terminology for expressing the *transfer* to being Christian. The most used and the most general term is 'believe', which often means 'be converted'. Christians are believers and others are unbelievers, *apistoi*. As we have seen, the content of faith in this case is the saving death and resurrection of Jesus Christ: in general terms, God's salvific action in Christ.[41] Before attempting to penetrate further into Paul's conception of faith, however, it will be well to consider some of the other terminology indicating the transfer to being in the group (the elect, the believers or the saints) who will be saved.

1. Participation in the death of Christ.[42] Just as Paul describes the state of the Christian as being in Christ, in the body of Christ, in the Spirit and the like, so he describes the means of entering that situation as dying with Christ. Just as we observed that Paul does not regard his participationist language as remarkable or as asserting strange or incomprehensible facts, so we must note that he does not consider it remarkable to say that Christians have died with Christ.

It is well known that Paul inherited the view that Christ died for trespasses. The general Christian view was presumably that by his death he achieved *atonement* for the trespasses of others, so that they would not be reckoned to those who accepted his death as being for them. This is a view which Paul repeats without hesitation.

---

[41] Above, section 1 n. 54; section 2 nn. 8, 9.

[42] See especially Tannehill, *Dying and Rising*. Despite his intention to do so (p. 1), Tannehill did not succeed in bringing the dying and rising theme into an illuminating connection with other main themes, such as justification by faith. His work does, however, provide a valuable analysis of the principal passages connected with dying and rising with Christ.

For there is no distinction; since all have sinned and fall short of the glory of God, they are justified by his grace as a gift, through the redemption which is in Christ Jesus, whom God put forward as an expiation by his blood, to be received by faith. (Rom. 3.22b–25)[43]

[Righteousness] will be reckoned to us who believe in him that raised from the dead Jesus our Lord, who was put to death for our trespasses and raised for our justification. (Rom. 4.24bf.)

For I delivered to you as of first importance what I also received, that Christ died for our sins in accordance with the scriptures. . . . (I Cor. 15.3)[44]

While we were yet helpless, at the right time Christ died for the ungodly. Why, one will hardly die for a righteous man – though perhaps for a good man one will dare even to die. But God shows his love for us in that while we were yet sinners Christ died for us. Since, therefore, we are now justified by his blood, much more shall we be saved by him from the wrath of God. (Rom. 5.6–9)[45]

It is not clear, however, that all the references to Christ's dying 'for us' should be taken as referring to his *sacrificial death for past transgressions*, as is usually the case.[46] On the contrary, Paul often gives quite a different significance to the death of Christ. Thus II Cor. 5.14f.:

For the love of Christ controls us, because we are convinced that one has died for all; therefore all have died. And he died for all, that those who live might live no longer for themselves but for him who for their sake died and was raised.

Here the significance of Christ's death 'for all', *hyper pantōn*, is not primarily that it is expiatory. We note here the ease with which Paul uses categories of participation to explain his meaning: 'therefore all have died', not 'therefore all have had their sins expiated'. It is true that in 5.19 Paul

---

[43] For the problems, details and history of exegesis of this much discussed passage, see Lohse, *Märtyrer und Gottesknecht*, pp. 147–54; Davies, *Paul and Rabbinic Judaism*, pp. 237–42; Whiteley, *Theology of St Paul*, pp. 145f.; W. G. Kümmel, 'Πάρεσις and ἔνδειξις. A Contribution to the Understanding of the Pauline Doctrine of Justification', *Journal for Theology and the Church* 3, 1967, pp. 1–13 (= *ZTK* 49, 1952, pp. 154–67); J. Reumann, 'The Gospel of the Righteousness of God', *Interpretation* 20, 1966, pp. 432–52; C. H. Talbert, 'A Non-Pauline Fragment at Romans 3.24–26?', *JBL* 85, 1966, pp. 287–96; George Howard, 'Romans 3.21–31 and the Inclusion of the Gentiles', *HTR* 63, 1970, pp. 223–33. Whatever the precise meaning of *hilastērion*, and whatever decision one makes on the difficult syntax, I take the passage to refer to *atonement for the past transgressions of all* by Christ's death and the shedding of blood. This agrees with Howard's conclusion (p. 233): 'The intricate details of the inner workings of the atonement remain obscure in this passage. Paul does not explain himself. However, the thrust of the passage as well as Paul's *use* of the atonement section is clear. The entirety of the context argues for the inclusion of the Gentiles into the kingdom of God.' This view supposes that, even if Paul is using a traditional formulation, he is *using* it.

[44] Lohse (*Märtyrer und Gottesknecht*, pp. 147–9) takes I Cor. 15.3 and Rom. 4.25 to be the principal passages in which Paul quotes traditional formulas on the death of Christ. On formulas and Paul's use of them cf. also Käsemann, 'The Saving Significance of the Death of Jesus in Paul', *Perspectives*, pp. 39f.

[45] Cf. Davies, *Paul and Rabbinic Judaism*, p. 234: in Rom. 5.8–10 the death and blood of Christ have a backward look.

[46] Bultmann, *Theology* I, p. 296. Bultmann gives a list of the passages containing traditional formulations.

says that God did not count former trespasses, but it is equally true that the meaning of 5.14 cannot be restricted simply to this 'overlooking' of former trespasses. Rather, in Christ, one dies to the *power* of sin, and does not just have trespasses atoned for.[47] It is probable that we should read Gal. 1.4 in the same way. When Paul writes that the Lord Jesus Christ 'gave himself for our sins to deliver us from the present evil age', we note the implication that not only are past transgressions remitted, but that Christians are delivered from the evil aeon. Thus the *purpose* of Christ's death was not simply to provide expiation, but that he might become Lord and thus save those who belong to him and are 'in' him. This is put even more clearly in Rom. 14.8f.:

If we live, we live to the Lord, and if we die, we die to the Lord; so then, whether we live or whether we die, we are the Lord's. *For to this end Christ died* and lived again, that he might be Lord both of the dead and of the living.

I should also be inclined to read I Thess. 5.10 in the same light: Christ's death 'for us' assures us that 'whether we wake or sleep we might live with him'. We cannot exclude the possibility that Paul's thought is that Christ's death, by atoning for previous sins, assures those who hold fast that they will receive future salvation. But the emphasis unquestionably falls elsewhere: not backwards towards the expiation of past transgressions, but forwards, towards the assurance of life with Christ whether one is alive or dead at his coming.[48] This, says Paul, is the *purpose* of Christ's death.

I shall not attempt here a full review of scholarly views on the death of Christ in Paul, although some comments should be made. I differ from Bultmann (*Theology* I, p. 296) in not agreeing that all the passages which say that Christ died 'for our sins' are propitiatory (or expiatory). In such a passage as II Cor. 5.14, for example, which Bultmann classifies under this head, the idea of 'for all' is immediately given: therefore all have died. The terminology 'for all' doubtless comes from the tradition, but the explicit meaning of the passage is more participatory than propitiatory or expiatory. Nor do I find it worthwhile to try to distinguish precisely among the sacrificial ideas of propitiation, expiation and substitution (or vicarious death) (cf. Bultmann, op. cit., pp. 295–7), preferring to speak of all the sacrificial passages as referring simply to atonement for past transgressions. Expiation, propitiation and substitution may be theoretically distinguished, but it is not clear that such distinctions were made in the first century or are relevant for Paul. I agree completely with Bultmann and most other scholars that what is distinctive in Paul is not the repetition of the traditional sacrificial view (ibid., pp. 297f.). Thus also Davies, *Paul and Rabbinic Judaism*, p. 242: 'although in labouring to do justice to the significance of the Death of Jesus he uses sacrificial terms, Paul does not develop these but leaves them inchoate'. Cf. Käsemann, 'The

[47] Similarly Stanley, *Christ's Resurrection in Pauline Soteriology*, pp. 139f. So also Tannehill, *Dying and Rising*, pp. 66–9: the abrupt shift from 'one died' to 'therefore all died' is to be explained on the basis of the view that Christians die with Christ.
[48] Similarly Tannehill, *Dying and Rising*, pp. 133f.

Saving Significance of the Death of Jesus', *Perspectives*, p. 41: Rom. 3.25 refers to 'forgiveness of previously committed trespasses'. 'But for Paul, salvation does not primarily mean the end of past disaster and the forgiving cancellation of former guilt. It is, according to Rom. 5.9f.; 8.2, freedom from the power of sin, death and the divine wrath; that is to say, it is the possibility of a new life.' I would differ only in classifying Rom. 5.9f. with Rom. 3.25.[49]

This interpretation goes completely against the view of Schoeps and Buchanan, both of whom see atonement for transgressions as the principal meaning of Christ's death for Paul. Schoeps's view (*Paul*, ch. 4) is that Paul's soteriology is centred in the atoning death of Christ and that Paul developed the significance of the atoning death on the analogy of the binding of Isaac, only substituting Jesus for Isaac and God for Abraham. This not only misconstrues the significance of the death as atoning in Paul, but gives to the motif of the binding of Isaac a significance in Jewish thought which it cannot bear (cf. above, pp. 28f.).

Buchanan (*Consequences of the Covenant*) sees the significance of Christ's death for Paul against the background of the supposedly dominating motif of covenantal theology: the doctrine of merits (cf. above, Chapter I, section 8). Buchanan argues that 'sins were classified as debts' (p. 228) and that 'God would not let the kingdom come until the account had been corrected' (p. 229). Paul regarded Christ as the 'sin offering that God made on our behalf' which cancels our debts (p. 230). Paul shared the Jewish view that atonement for transgression was needed and that it requires three things: repentance, reconciliation with one another and sin and guilt offerings (p. 230). God provides the latter in the death of Jesus. 'That which was left for Christians was the business of reconciliation. They had to repent of their sins so that the atonement could be completed' (p. 230; citing Rom. 5.6–11; it is worth noting that the following citations are all from Colossians). This view suffers from defects which are similar to the ones we remarked with regard to Schoeps: it takes what is minor in Paul as being determinative and makes an analogy with Judaism which is not supported by Jewish literature itself.

My own view is much closer to that of Whiteley (*Theology of St Paul*). Discussing what he calls the *modus operandi* of salvation, Whiteley prefers the term 'salvation through participation' (p. 130) and even argues that the sacrificial statements regarding Christ's death should not be understood in terms of a theory of substitution (pp. 130–51). He does accept that not all of Paul's statements about the death of Christ are participatory. Some are expressed in 'the religious language of Judaism' (p. 134). But even the foundation stones of the substitution theory – Rom. 8.3f.; II Cor. 5.21; Gal. 3.16 – do not really convey the doctrine of redemption by substitution. They are primarily participationist (pp. 134–7).

That Paul, in thinking of the significance of Christ's death, was thinking more in terms of a *change of lordship* which guarantees future salvation than in terms of the expiation of past transgression, is readily seen by reviewing the passages concerning the Christian's *death with Christ. It is these passages which reveal the true significance of Christ's death in Paul's thought.* The

---

[49] I Cor. 11.24 is also frequently taken as referring to Christ's sacrificial death (so Bultmann, *Theology* I, p. 296), but it need not do so. As Daube has pointed out (*Wine in the Bible*, pp. 15f.), the phrase 'is for you' should not be pressed to mean 'given' or 'broken for you'. It may be more general: 'which is for your good'.

entirety of Rom. 6.3–11 is concerned with this theme, and it may be quoted in full, together with other relevant passages:

Do you not know that all of us who have been baptized into Christ Jesus were baptized into his death? We were buried therefore with him by baptism into death, so that as Christ was raised from the dead by the glory of the Father, we too might walk in newness of life.

For if we have been united with him in a death like his, we shall certainly be united with him in a resurrection like his. We know that our old self was crucified with him so that the sinful body might be destroyed, and we might no longer be enslaved to sin. For he who has died is freed from sin. But if we have died with Christ, we believe that we shall also live with him. For we know that Christ being raised from the dead will never die again; death no longer has dominion over him. The death he died he died to sin, once for all, but the life he lives he lives to God. So you also must consider yourselves dead to sin and alive to God in Christ Jesus. (Rom. 6.3–11)

Likewise, my brethren, you have died to the law through the body of Christ, so that you may belong to another, to him who has been raised from the dead in order that we may bear fruit for God. (Rom. 7.4)

For I through the law died to the law, that I might live to God. I have been crucified with Christ; it is no longer I who live, but Christ who lives in me; and the life I now live in the flesh I live by faith in the Son of God, who loved me and gave himself for me. (Gal. 2.19f.)

And those who belong to Christ Jesus have crucified the flesh with its passions and desires. (Gal. 5.24)

But far be it from me to glory except in the cross of our Lord Jesus Christ, by which the world has been crucified to me, and I to the world. (Gal. 6.14)

. . . that I may know him and the power of his resurrection, and may share his sufferings, becoming like him in his death, that if possible I may attain the resurrection from the dead. (Phil. 3.10f.)

The reference in the last passage to suffering with Christ is to be connected with other passages in which Paul says that Christians share Christ's sufferings so as to share his life: Rom. 8.17 ('. . . fellow heirs with Christ, provided we suffer with him in order that we may also be glorified with him'); II Cor. 4.10 ('. . . always carrying in the body the death of Jesus, so that the life of Jesus may also be manifested in our bodies'). This can also be put in terms of 'imitating' Christ's sufferings: I Thess. 1.6.

Thus we see in all these passages that the prime significance which the death of Christ has for Paul is not that it provides atonement for past transgressions (although he holds the common Christian view that it does so), but that, by *sharing* in Christ's death, one dies to the *power* of sin or to the old aeon, with the result that one *belongs to God*. The *transfer* is not only from the uncleanness of idolatry and sexual immorality to cleanness and holiness, but from one lordship to another. The transfer takes place by *participation* in Christ's death. We should repeat here what we said above: the resurrection itself remains future for Paul. One dies with Christ and lives to God, but will be raised only in the future.

2. Freedom. It agrees with the view that the death of Christ provides for a transfer of lordship that Paul can express the transfer in terms of liberation or freedom from bondage. One is free from the power of sin (or the law) and free to live for God. Thus, just as Paul could describe Christians as having been sanctified from heathen transgression*s* (I Cor. 6.9–11), he can also say that they have been 'set free from sin' in the *singular* (Rom. 6.18,22) or 'set free from the law of sin and death' (Rom. 8.2). In Galatians, the contrast is between the freedom for which Christ has set the Christians free (5.1) and the slavery of the law or the fundamental spirits of the universe (4.1–9).[50] His hope for the world is that it 'will be set free from its bondage to decay' (Rom. 8.21).

3. Transformation, new creation. We briefly referred above to the use of terms for changing or being transformed in the present and future tenses.[51] We should recall these expressions here, since they also count among Paul's 'transfer terminology'. Thus II Cor. 4.16: 'So we do not lose heart. Though our outer nature is wasting away, our inner nature is being renewed every day.' The full transformation, and hence the complete transfer from the old creation or old aeon to the new, still lies in the future, as II Cor. 5.1–5 makes clear; but Paul sees the renewal as being already at work. That presumably means that when in II Cor. 5.17 Paul writes that one in Christ is a new creation (or, if one is in Christ there is a new creation), the new creation is considered present either proleptically or at least incompletely. The brief reference to a new creation in Gal. 6.15 should presumably be understood the same way. The language of change in progress, but not complete, appears also in II Cor. 3.18: 'And we all, with unveiled face, beholding the glory of the Lord, are being changed into his likeness from one degree of glory to another . . .'

It is a standard observation that Paul can use the same transfer terms both in the indicative and the imperative, or in a conditional clause which has the effect of an imperative. Thus he can write that those who belong to Christ Jesus *have* crucified the flesh with its passions and desires (Gal.

[50] I take it that in Gal. 4.1–9 Paul equates the bondage of the law with the bondage of the *stoicheia tou kosmou*. I cannot agree with Whiteley (*Theology of St Paul*, p. 25) that the passage is to be explained on the grounds that some Jews practised astrology. Rather, being under the astral powers and being under the law are materially equivalent: both are bondage. See the detailed discussion in Bo Reicke, 'The Law and this World According to Paul', *JBL* 70, 1951, pp. 259–76.

[51] On the ongoing nature of the transformation, see especially Robinson, *The Body*, pp. 8of.

5.24) and also that *if* one puts to death the deeds of the body he will live (Rom. 8.13); he can write both that Christians *have* become slaves of righteousness (Rom. 6.18) and that they *should* yield themselves to God and their members to God as instruments of righteousness (Rom. 6.13); those who live by the Spirit should also walk by the Spirit (Gal. 5.25), and in I Cor. 3 he can imply that those Christians who have the Spirit may not be really 'spiritual' after all (I Cor. 3.1–3). In the same way he can urge Christians who are presumably in the process of being transformed and renewed (II Cor. 3.18; 4.16) to *be* transformed 'by the renewal of your mind' (Rom. 12.2). We should also mention here Gal. 4.19, 'My little children, with whom I am again in travail until Christ be formed in you!', where Paul apparently means that the possibility that the Galatians will accept the law means that Christ is not really 'in' them and that the transformation to the new creation (Gal. 6.15) or the transfer from slavery to sonship (Gal. 4.1–7) is threatened with cancellation.

4. Reconciliation.[52] The noun *katallagē* and the verb *katallassō* are peculiar to Paul in the New Testament, appearing principally in two passages, Rom. 5.10f. and II Cor. 5.18–20. The noun also occurs in Rom. 11.15 and the verb in I Cor. 7.11, with regard to the reconciliation of husband and wife. We may quote the passages:

For if while we were enemies we were reconciled to God by the death of his Son, much more, now that we are reconciled, shall we be saved by his life. Not only so, but we also rejoice in God through our Lord Jesus Christ, through whom we have now received our reconciliation. (Rom. 5.10f.)

For if their [the Jews'] rejection means the reconciliation of the world, what will their acceptance mean but life from the dead? (Rom. 11.15)

Therefore, if any one is in Christ, he is a new creation; the old has passed away, behold, the new has come. All this is from God, who through Christ reconciled us to himself and gave us the ministry of reconciliation; that is, God was in Christ reconciling the world to himself, not counting their trespasses against them, and entrusting to us the message of reconciliation. So we are ambassadors for Christ, God making his appeal through us. We beseech you on behalf of Christ, be reconciled to God. For our sake he made him to be sin who knew no sin, so that in him we might become the righteousness of God. (II Cor. 5.17–21)

There are several things to be observed about these passages. In the first place, we note that reconciliation is consistently in the past. The reference in II Corinthians to God's reconciling the world 'in Christ' is probably to be understood in light of the reference in Romans to reconciliation by the death of Christ. The death of Christ accomplished the 'reconciliation' of 'the

[52] See the study by J. Dupont, *La réconciliation dans la théologie de saint Paul*, 1953. Dupont, however, includes Colossians and Ephesians.

world': in this case, referring to mankind. The reference in II Corinthians to God's not counting trespasses is reminiscent of the argument in Rom. 3.24f.: righteousness has been given through the expiatory death of Christ, when received with faith. 'This was to show God's righteousness, because in his divine forbearance he had passed over former sins.' Secondly, we may note that reconciliation, unlike the other 'transfer' terms previously discussed, refers to sin as *human transgression* rather than to sin as power. Reconciliation is only preparatory to being given life. By itself, it is not a term which is capable of showing how one obtains life by participation in Christ, or how the transformation from the power of sin and of the present evil age to sonship and freedom from sin is even now taking place. It speaks only to the overcoming of enmity by God's not counting trespasses, a 'not counting' which has to do in some way with the death of Christ. Thus the reconciliation theme is 'juristic', but we must note how limited the language which surrounds it is. There is no discussion of men *repenting* in order to obtain the reconciliation for past offences, nor even to their *accepting* reconciliation: they only *receive* it (Rom. 5.11). All Paul says, characteristically after saying that the world has been reconciled, is 'be reconciled to God'. He does not even say, 'repent and believe the gospel of reconciliation' as one might expect. The reason for this will become apparent only after our discussion of justification and justification by faith.

5. Justification and righteousness. We should begin by reminding readers of the difficulties of translating *dikaioō* and *dikaiosynē* into English.[53] The noun is best translated 'righteousness', but English has no cognate verb. Thus it is customary to translate the verb 'justify', which leads to the occasional translation of the noun with the cognate 'justification'. The words 'justify' and 'justification' are usually thought to be inappropriate to Paul's meaning, however, so that there are endless difficulties about how to translate what he wrote. Grobel, in translating Bultmann's *Theology of the New Testament*, sought to overcome the difficulty by translating the verb 'rightwise'.[54] This is a solution which has some merit, although it suffers from the defect of employing a word which is not otherwise used in contemporary English. The translation of the verb as 'make righteous' is objected to on the ground that it implies that one is made to *be* righteous, whereas it actually refers to the establishment of a right relationship.[55] There is no perfect solution to this problem, and so we shall have to be content with describing

---

[53] Cf. J. Reumann, 'The Gospel of the Righteousness of God', p. 444.

[54] Bultmann, *Theology* I, p. 253.

[55] Cf. Whiteley, *Theology of St Paul*, pp. 141, 156–61. Goodspeed vigorously defended his translation 'make upright or righteous', however, against Metzger's criticism (see E. J. Goodspeed, 'Some Greek Notes: III Justification', *JBL* 73, 1954, pp. 86–91). Goodspeed's defence was against the view that the verb means 'declare upright though one is not actually so', i.e. that it refers to imputed righteousness. He actually thought that Paul's view of a new creation went well beyond the meaning 'make upright' (ibid., p. 88).

the way we shall deal with it, recognizing that any translation at all can be objected to. It seems to me that in fact the verb does not always bear precisely the same meaning in Paul, being sometimes parallel to 'reconcile' and 'sanctify', in which case 'justify' is a perfectly good translation, and sometimes being equivalent to having, attaining or being given *dikaiosynē*, righteousness (cf. Phil. 3.9, 'having righteousness'), in which case 'make righteous' or 'become righteous' is a more or less adequate translation. It is hoped that one can learn to read 'make righteous' in a neutral sense, as a translation of the verb which conforms it to the translation of the noun as 'righteousness', a translation which seems necessary in such a passage as Gal. 2.15–21.

The verb principally appears in Gal. 2–3 and Rom. 2–5, especially ch. 3, the chapters in which Paul discusses 'righteousness by faith' and 'being made righteous by faith', the theme which so many take to be the heart of his theology. It may be useful to note first the other uses of the verb. Clearest is I Cor. 6.9–11, which we have quoted in another context but which bears repetition:

Do you not know that the unrighteous [*adikoi*] will not inherit the kingdom of God? Do not be deceived; neither the immoral, nor idolaters, nor adulterers, nor homosexuals, nor thieves, nor the greedy, nor drunkards, nor revilers, nor robbers will inherit the kingdom of God. And such were some of you. But you were washed, you were sanctified, you were justified in the name of the Lord Jesus Christ and in the Spirit of our God.

The point of all the verbs here, including 'justified', is that the Christians were *cleansed* of the sins just enumerated. A similar meaning is seen in Rom. 5.9:

While we were yet helpless, at the right time Christ died for the ungodly. Why, one will hardly die for a righteous man – though perhaps for a good man one will dare even to die. But God shows his love for us in that while we were yet sinners Christ died for us. Since, therefore, we are now justified by his blood, much more shall we be saved by him from the wrath of God. (Rom. 5.6–9)

The passage continues by speaking of being reconciled, and here the meaning of 'justified' is the same as 'reconciled': past transgressions have been overlooked or atoned for.[56] It is likely that the meaning in Rom. 8.30 is the same: 'And those whom he predestined he also called; and those whom he called he also justified; and those whom he justified he also glorified.' In all these cases being justified refers to being cleansed of or forgiven for past transgressions and is an intermediate step between the former state of being

---

[56] This interpretation of 'justified' in Rom. 5.9 is supported by the use of the word 'sinners' in 5.8. While by the word 'sin' Paul usually means sin as a power, he does not use 'sinner' to refer to the fact that men are under that power, but to their actually sinning, i.e. transgressing. Thus Rom. 5.19 (cf. 'trespass' in 5.20) and Gal. 2.15 ('Gentile sinners').

an enemy of God and a transgressor and the future state of being glorified. The meaning is equivalent to 'reconciled'. In one case the verb is equivalent to 'set free': 'For he who has died is freed (*dedikaiotai*) from sin' (in the singular) (Rom. 6.7), which is equivalent to Rom. 6.18, 'having been set free (*eleutherothentes*) from sin'.[57] Thus far it appears, then, that 'justify' as a 'transfer' term can be paralleled either with 'sanctify' and 'reconcile' (referring to past transgressions), or with 'set free' (referring to sin as an enslaving power).

We have repeatedly observed the existence in Paul of the language of cleansing from trespasses and liberation from the power of sin, noting also that this distinction, like the one between 'mystical' or 'participatory' and 'juristic' conceptions, was not presented by Paul as a distinction; the two repeatedly appear together. We now, however, encounter a problem of presentation which arises from Paul's integrated way of thinking. Before we can completely sort out the relationship between the participatory and the juristic terminology and come to a fair understanding of 'righteousness by faith' in Romans and Galatians, we shall have to give some consideration to Paul's conception of man's plight – which itself can only be understood on the basis of his exclusivist soteriology of salvation by Jesus Christ. We began the discussion where it appears Paul began, with the conviction that Christ is Lord and Saviour. We have now discussed the principal terms for being among the group of the saved ('one body' and the like) and for 'transferring' from the group which will be destroyed to the group which will be saved ('dying with Christ' and the like). The interrelations of the various terms can best be understood, however, after the analysis of Paul's attitude toward the law and of his conception of man's plight. We must thus proceed in a circle. But before taking up the law and man's plight and completing the circle of interpretation, we should consider one last point of Paul's soteriology, the question of the object of salvation: who is saved?

Salvation of mankind and the world

The question of universal and cosmic salvation in Paul's thought is potentially very complicated, but I wish to deal with it briefly. One could conclude

---

[57] R. Scroggs ('Romans vi. 7', *NTS* 10, 1963, pp. 104–8) proposed quite a different explanation: 6.7 refers to the martyr's death of Jesus, which atones for others. This seems to leave out of account the simplest explanation of the syntax of the sentence, according to which the verb is passive and could not mean 'he who dies justifies . . .'. Nor is it easy to have *ho apothanōn* refer both to the death of Jesus and that of the believer with him ('he who dies [with Christ] is justified [by his atoning death]'). I agree with Scroggs that the Rabbinic notion that one's death atones for transgressions is not present here (for references, see Scroggs's article and Käsemann, *An die Römer*, p. 162). Cranfield (*Romans*, p. 311) curiously argues that 'freed from' cannot be meant here, since Paul did not believe that one is free from sin in this life. This overlooks the two verses which determine the meaning: 6.6, 'no longer enslaved to sin', to which 6.7 is the positive counterpart; and 6.17f., 'once slaves to sin', followed by another phrase giving the positive counterpart, '*eleutherothentes* from sin'.

on the basis of the Adam/Christ passages that all men will be saved:

Then as one man's trespass led to condemnation for all men, so one man's act of righteousness leads to acquittal and life for all men. (Rom. 5.18)

For as in Adam all die, so also in Christ shall all be made alive. (I Cor. 15.22)

Some have argued that, in principle at least, Paul meant precisely what he wrote,[58] and in support of such a view can be cited the passages on the reconciliation of 'the world', where 'the world' refers to humanity (Rom. 11.15; II Cor. 5.19).[59] There is, however, a fatal objection to this view: Paul too often mentions those who are perishing or those who will be destroyed on the Day of the Lord (I Cor. 1.18; II Cor. 2.15; 4.3; Phil. 3.19; cf. Rom. 2.12; I Cor. 8.11; 6.9; and the general warning of destruction in I Cor. 10.6–12).[60] I do not think that we should change what Paul wrote in I Cor. 15.22 to read 'all who are in Christ will be made alive',[61] even though that is effectively what he meant. He seems rather to have been carried away by the force of his analogy and argued more than he intended. This can be seen especially clearly in Rom. 5.19. After saying 'condemnation for all men' and 'life for all men' in v. 18, he immediately modifies to 'many': 'as by one man's disobedience many were made sinners, so by one man's obedience many will be made righteous'. I do not understand this as a semitizing use of 'many' to mean 'all'.[62] What he actually thought is abundantly clear in passage after passage: apart from Christ, everyone will be destroyed; those who believe and participate in the body of Christ will be saved. Thus he means really neither 'all . . . all' nor 'many . . . many', but 'all . . . many'. The Adam/Christ analogy does not permit this last formulation, however, and Paul has allowed the form and force of his argument to lead him into a confusing statement. The real force of the analogy is given in Rom. 5.17: if one man's trespass led to death, *all the more* will those who accept it receive life through Jesus Christ.[63]

It is a different matter with regard to the non-human cosmos. There is the hint of Christ's role in the creation of the cosmos in I Cor. 8.6, and the explicit statement that 'the creation itself will be set free from its bondage to decay and obtain the glorious liberty of the children of God' in Rom. 8.21.

---

[58] E.g. Gibbs, *Creation and Redemption*, pp. 48–58. Gibbs, however, does not argue that the second 'all' is to be taken quite literally: the term is 'corporate rather than exhaustive in connotation' (pp. 52f.).

[59] On 'the world' as humanity, cf. Bultmann, *Theology* I, p. 255.

[60] Whiteley (*Theology of St Paul*, pp. 97f., 271–3) holds the view that Paul did not think that all would be saved, but he curiously states that Paul 'simply has not told us what will happen to those who are not Christians' (p. 272). This seems to overlook the destruction passages just cited.

[61] So Whiteley, op. cit., p. 271.

[62] See H. Müller, 'Der rabbinische Qal-Wachomer-Schluss in paulinischer Typologie', *ZNW* 58, 1967, p. 82 n. 49; Jeremias in *TDNT* VI, pp. 540f.

[63] I thus agree with Conzelmann (*Theology*, pp. 187f.): 'at the decisive point the analogy does not work: left to itself it does not take faith into account.' For the form of the argument, compare Sifra Hobah parasha 12.10, listed in the index.

I Cor. 15.27f. seems to support the view of the ultimate redemption of the creation,[64] and there are no statements to the contrary. Once Colossians is excluded from consideration, the cosmos is seen to play a smaller role in Paul's thought than it appears to in the descriptions of scholars who take Colossians to be authentic,[65] but one must allow that here Colossians is building on a genuine Pauline view: the cosmos will be redeemed. Paul's general focus, however, is on the world of men.

4. The law, the human plight and the relationship of the solutions to it

The most important observation to make in order to understand the situation of the non-Christian in Paul's view is the one which has already been made: that, for Paul, the conviction of a universal solution preceded the conviction of a universal plight. It is perhaps the principal fault in Bultmann's treatment of Paul that he proceeded from plight to solution and supposed that Paul proceeded in the same way. On page after page of Bultmann's discussion of Paul's conception of 'man prior to faith' I have marked 'backwards'. This is so important a matter that we may consider some examples. Thus Bultmann wrote that 'the view that all men are sinners, which he develops at length in Rom. 1.18–3.20, is a basic one for his doctrine of salvation'.[1] I should have said that his doctrine of salvation led to the necessary conclusion that all men required salvation, with the result that his description of the human plight varies, remaining constant only in the assertion of its universality.[2]

---

[64] See Davies, *Paul and Rabbinic Judaism*, p. 58 and n. 4.

[65] Cf. Davies, op. cit., p. 177: 'Had it not been for the heresy at Colossae. . .' See also Ralph Martin's review of Gibbs's *Creation and Redemption*, *JBL* 91, 1972, pp. 429–31.

---

[1] *Theology* I, p. 227. There is here a difficulty in understanding Bultmann's view which should be noted, although we shall not attempt a full exegesis of his view. He argues at length that Paul's soteriology and his attitude towards the law, for example, are *based on* his view of man's plight (see further below, pp. 481f.). It is this argument which is under criticism here. On the other hand, Bultmann did not view Rom. 7 as an autobiographical statement of how one moves from unfaith to faith, and thus would presumably have agreed with the view which is argued for here, that Paul saw man's plight from the point of view of one who is in Christ. (On Rom. 7 see above, section 2 n. 4.) It is not clear precisely how he would hold together the view that Paul's conception of man's plight depended on the Christ-event and the view that his conception of soteriology and his attitude toward the law depended on his analysis of man's plight. I shall try to show, in any case, that the second view is wrong. I am indebted to Dr Gerd Lüdemann for critical remarks on my presentation of Bultmann on this score.

The view that the universality of sin is the *basis* of Paul's soteriology is very common. Cf. Davies, *Paul and Rabbinic Judaism*, p. 58: 'The universality of sin he knew, apart from any proofs that Scripture might supply, through the knowledge of his own heart and of the ways of men, both Jewish and Gentile; the universality of forgiveness and reconciliation burst upon him with the light of the knowledge of the glory of God in the face of Jesus Christ.'

[2] E.g.: all men sinned, Rom. 3.23; 5.12; all die in Adam, Rom. 5.18; I Cor. 15.22; men are slaves of the *stoicheia tou kosmou*, Gal. 4.3. Cf. Conzelmann, *Theology*, pp. 196–8: Rom. 4.15 (that there is no sin without law) cannot be consistently maintained by Paul. Rom. 5.13f. does not solve the problem. Rom. 1–3 argues the case for the universality of sin 'without recourse to the events of Old Testament history'.

Bultmann noted that sin 'forces all men without exception into slavery', and he then raised the question of the *reason* for Paul's holding his view:

And is there a necessity that natural human 'life in the flesh' must without exception become 'life in the flesh' in the negatively qualified sense – i.e. must it become 'life according to the flesh'?

That is evidently Paul's opinion. In man – because his substance is flesh – sin slumbers from the beginning. Must it necessarily awaken? Yes, because man encounters the Torah with its commandment: 'you shall not desire' (Rom. 7.7ff.).[3]

It is certainly true that Bultmann is pointing to an *explanation* in Paul of how it is that every man sins and is under the power of sin, but it should be equally clear that it was not *from* the analysis of the weakness of the flesh and the challenge of the commandment that Paul actually came to the conclusion that all men are enslaved to sin. This is a view which springs from the conviction that God has provided for universal salvation in Christ; thus it follows that all men must need salvation, and Rom. 7 is a somewhat tortured explanation of the law and its purpose in the light of this.

Paul's logic seems to run like this: in Christ God has acted to save the world; therefore the world is in need of salvation; but God also gave the law; if Christ is given for salvation, it must follow that the law could not have been; is the law then against the purpose of God which has been revealed in Christ? No, it has the function of consigning everyone to sin *so that* everyone could be saved by God's grace in Christ. It seems to me completely impossible to make the argument run the other way, beginning with an anthropological analysis which shows in advance that humans are bound over to sin because of the desire to save themselves. One must grant that Bultmann has made such argument as plausibly as it can be made, and with great exegetical penetration; but finally the analysis of the human plight as boasting in one's own strength, which leads one farther and farther from God, fails as the *starting point* for Paul's theology. Although it would be expected in advance that the conception of the plight should precede the conception of the solution, Paul's thought seems to have run the other way.

The law; righteousness by faith

The strongest confirmation that Paul's thought ran from solution to plight comes from an analysis of one of the most discussed problems of his thought:

Only in Rom. 7 can Paul satisfactorily handle the problem of the universality of sin (p. 197). Whiteley (*Theology of St Paul*) regards Rom. 5.12 as presenting Paul's 'fundamental teaching' on the fall (p. 50) and Rom. 1.18–32 as giving 'almost a parallel version of the fall, a presentation of the same realities by means of different symbols' (p. 51). But Whiteley does not explain the difference. The only coherence seems to be in the conclusion: everybody is under the power of sin. On the incongruence of Paul's different explanations of sin, see also Cerfaux, *The Christian in the Theology of St Paul*, pp. 412–17. The problem is returned to below, pp. 497–9.
[3] Bultmann, *Theology* I, p. 249.

his attitude towards the law. Understanding Paul's attitude towards the law will also aid us in understanding *how* he conceived man's plight and consequently how the solutions to it, which were briefly sketched in section 3, should be understood. The question of the law will also lead us into an initial consideration of 'righteousness by faith'. The question of Paul's attitude towards the law may be most sharply formulated in this way: why did Paul think that those who accepted the law were excluded from being saved by Christ? We shall begin our discussion by considering first the views of Albert Schweitzer and Rudolf Bultmann, who may be seen here, as on many other points, as representing different and important schools of thought.

Schweitzer viewed Paul's problematic and the solution to it as in general the same as that seen in IV Ezra and II Baruch, although Paul obviously gave the solution a dramatic change by insisting that the beginning of the end was already realized in the resurrection of Jesus, that the death of Jesus had atoning power, that the end-time was already beginning in the resurrection of Jesus, and that there was the possibility of a 'mystical' participation in Jesus' death and resurrection.[4] The question of whether or not the *problem* for Paul was really different from that faced by the Jewish apocalypticists did not, however, receive very careful scrutiny. Schweitzer seems to have taken it for granted that the problem was the same. He summarized the Jewish view thus:

In general, the view of Jewish eschatology is that the evil of the world comes from the demons, and that angelic beings have, with God's permission, established themselves between Him and mankind. In its simplest form the conception of redemption is that the Messianic Kingdom puts an end to this condition.[5]

This is also, according to Schweitzer, Paul's general view, although, as we noted, his solution is more complicated.[6] What role does Paul's view of the law play?

Into this eschatological conception of the dominion of the Angels and the termination of it by the Messiah, Paul strangely imports a view peculiar to himself, namely, that the Law was given by Angels who desired thereby to make men subservient to themselves, and that by the death of Jesus their power has already been so shaken that the Law has now no more force.

This assertion is inspired by his desire to conceive of the future redemption as already in large measure present. That the Law comes to an end when the Messianic reign begins is for Jewish thought self-evident. But Paul represents it as already invalidated by Jesus' death.[7]

---

[4] Schweitzer, *Mysticism*, pp. 54–68.
[5] Ibid., p. 55.
[6] Ibid., pp. 63–8.
[7] Ibid., pp. 68f.

Schweitzer returns to the question of Paul's attitude toward the law in his chapter on 'Mysticism and the Law'.[8] Paul's admittedly complicated view can satisfactorily be kept straight, he says, if one will consistently distinguish two questions: (1) 'In what sense and to what extent is the Law no longer valid?' (2) 'What is the right attitude of believers towards the Law, in so far as it is no longer valid?'[9] The answer to the first question, says Schweitzer, is easy: 'The Law belongs to that natural world which lies under the dominion of the Angels. In so far as this world, since the death and resurrection of Jesus, exists or does not exist, in so far is the Law in force or not in force.' 'The Law is no longer valid for those who are in-Christ-Jesus.'[10] Actually, according to Schweitzer, the law and eschatology were always incompatible, because of 'the intrinsic impulse of eschatology towards an immediate and absolute ethic' and because of 'the supramundane character of the Messianic mode of being, to which the Law, established for the natural world, is not appropriate'.[11] The Jewish view that the law leads to attainment of the Messianic kingdom will not actually work. In attempting this combination of eschatology and the law, late Judaism had built 'a bridge which looks quite well, but has no adequate carrying capacity'.[12] The impossibility of the attempt to make the law and a transcendental, immediate eschatology compatible was *de facto* admitted by the apocalypticists of late Judaism.

It is true that the Late-Jewish Apocalpyses never go so far as to affirm in principle that the Law will cease to have significance in the future Kingdom. But practically they are influenced by it, and take up a corresponding attitude. Surprising as it may appear, they never assert that the Law will be in force in the Messianic Kingdom, and they never picture the life of the Coming Kingdom as a life of perfect Law-keeping, but always as a life in a new and blissful condition which is enfranchised from all earthly limitations. How would it be possible for the Book of Enoch, according to which the Saints 'become angels in heaven' (Enoch li.4, lxi.12), to carry through the idea that they live according to the Law?[13]

Schweitzer continues by arguing that in the Psalms of Solomon, IV Ezra and II Baruch the Messianic kingdom is not pictured as the kingdom in which the law is kept. The law, rather, serves to attain the kingdom, but once in it 'a man walks according to God's will by natural impulse, in virtue of the new condition'.[14] Applied to Paul, the argument runs thus: 'In Paul's conception of an ethic inspired by the spirit of the resurrection the immediacy of this ethic combines with the supernatural character of the Messianic mode of existence in opposition to the Law.'[15] This leaves one factor unaccounted

---

[8] Ibid., pp. 177–204.
[9] Ibid., p. 187.
[10] Ibid., p. 188.
[11] Ibid., p. 189.
[12] Ibid.
[13] Ibid., p. 191.
[14] Ibid.
[15] Ibid., p. 192.

for. Why is it that Jewish Christians, in Paul's view, may observe the law but 'Gentile converts were forbidden to do so on pain of jeopardising their salvation'?[16] The answer, says Schweitzer, is Paul's theory of the *status quo*: 'In the state in which each was called, therein shall he continue' (I Cor. 7.20; cf. 7.17).[17] This was not a lightly held precept. 'Paul's preaching of freedom from the Law is thus by no means conceived in a spirit of free-thinking. He compels Jews and non-Jews alike to remain in the state in which they first became believers.'[18]

The question of the law comes up in still a third context in Schweitzer's book, the discussion of righteousness by faith. Here Schweitzer argues that Paul himself had felt the impossibility of attaining righteousness by the law (referring to Rom. 7), that he considered this impossibility to be generally applicable, and that in fact the feeling of impossibility is also reflected in IV Ezra and II Baruch.[19] Paul agrees with IV Ezra and II Baruch, over against the self-righteousness of the Psalms of Solomon, in asserting that reliance on the grace of God is necessary. Schweitzer must then attempt to explain why the natural Jewish view of repentance and forgiveness is completely missing in Galatians.[20]

There are actually, then, three different explanations of Paul's attitude toward the law in Schweitzer: (1) that the law becomes inoperative with the beginning of the Messianic kingdom, which was inaugurated by the resurrection of Jesus; (2) that a man should not change the state in which he was called; (3) that Paul had experienced the impossibility of righteousness by the law and knew that one must rely on God, and that in this conviction he agreed with 'at least certain circles among the Scribes of his time'.[21] Although it may be possible to harmonize all three explanations in accounting for Paul's view, they do not seem immediately and naturally to cohere. Number 2 is regarded by Schweitzer as complementary to number 1, but number 3 seems quite independent. Many subsequent scholars have fastened on either number 1 or number 3 without necessarily agreeing with the other.[22] In fact, however, neither of these arguments will stand. The third argument has been so decisively refuted by convincing evidence that Rom. 7 is not autobiographical that I do not propose to discuss it here. This is one of the instances in which New Testament exegesis seems to me to have made decisive and irrefutable progress, despite the fact that many scholars have

[16] Ibid., p. 193.
[17] Ibid., p. 194.
[18] Ibid., p. 196.
[19] Ibid., pp. 213f.
[20] Ibid., pp. 214–17.
[21] Ibid., p. 217.
[22] In favour of Schweitzer's view that the Torah was considered in Judaism to be abrogated in the Messianic period are Schoeps, *Paul*, p. 171, and Fitzmyer, 'Saint Paul and the Law', *The Jurist* 27, 1967, pp. 21f. Those favouring Schweitzer's third explanation of Paul's view of the law are cited in the next note.

continued to see Paul's own frustration with the law as one of his reasons for denouncing its validity as a way to salvation. It seems clear, rather, that Rom. 7 is not autobiographical and that Paul did not reach his view of the law through despair.[23] We thus turn briefly to Schweitzer's first explanation.

I do not wish to enter here into a lengthy discussion of whether or not the view that the law would cease with the coming of the Messiah was widespread or even existent in the Judaism of Paul's day. I shall allow myself the comment that Schweitzer's argument from the silence of the Apocalypses does not seem persuasive[24] (in fact, his reliance on IV Ezra and II Baruch as representing a 'circle of scribes' of Paul's day is completely unconvincing: no works more clearly depend on the destruction of Jerusalem for their outlook), and any attempt to establish the view on the basis of Rabbinic literature could not stand investigation.[25] Schweitzer actually argued the case on the basis of what appeared to him logically necessary: the more transcendent the kingdom, the less useful the law which applies to this world; the more immediate the kingdom, the less useful the law as a basis of ethics. Whether or not any first-century Jews would have followed the same logic is difficult to say, and I know of no texts which show that any did. Schweitzer's view is at best an unproven (and unlikely) possibility. This need not long delay us, however, for it seems certain in any case that Paul did not base his view on such reasoning. *He never appeals to the fact that the*

---

[23] Against Rom. 7 as autobiographical, see section 2, n. 4 above. Some do still take Rom. 7 as autobiographical and explain Paul's attitude towards the law on that basis. Thus Buchanan, *Consequences*, p. 183: the 'I' passages are autobiographical and relate progressively to the time before the bar mitsvah, etc. Similarly Davies, *Paul and Rabbinic Judaism*, pp. 24, 30. Cf. Sandmel's position (*The Genius of Paul*, pp. 24, 28, 32f., 48): the observance of the law was problematic for Paul before his conversion – not in the sense of inconvenience, but as a way to solve the human dilemma, since one could not obey it sufficiently. Sandmel takes Rom. 7 as autobiographical and leaves Phil. 3 ('as to the law, blameless') out of account. Cf. also John Knox, *Chapters in a Life of Paul*, pp. 153–6; Schoeps, *Paul*, p. 184; Via, 'Justification and Deliverance', *SR* 1, 1971, p. 209. It is better to take Phil. 3 as autobiographical and interpret Rom. 7 in another way. M. Goguel ('Remarques sur un aspect de la conversion de Paul', *JBL* 53, 1934, pp. 257–67) took both Phil. 3 and Rom. 7 as autobiographical and reconciled them by attributing the former to Paul the Jew and the latter to Paul the Christian. His article has the merit of taking Phil. 3 seriously as showing that Paul's 'problem' was not frustration over his inability to fulfil the law.

[24] Without noting his agreement with Schweitzer, Wilckens argued that there must be a *religions-geschichtliche* explanation of Paul's attitude toward the law, and he found it in apocalyptic literature. He followed Rössler's distinction of Rabbinic and apocalyptic (see the index, s.v. Rössler) with regard to the understanding of the law, and his theory must fall with Rössler's view. See 'Die Bekehrung des Paulus', *Rechtfertigung als Freiheit*, pp. 19–21. Wilckens's view of apocalyptic literature as the source for Paul's attitude toward the law was correctly denied in advance by E. Bammel, ' Νόμος Χριστοῦ', *TU* 88, p.122.

[25] See the decisive refutation of the view that the Rabbis expected the law to be abrogated in the Messianic period by Sandmel, *The Genius of Paul*, pp. 40f. Sandmel denies the interpretation of Sanhedrin 97a and other passages on which such scholars as Schoeps and Fitzmyer (above, n. 22) have based their view. Against finding the proposed view in Rabbinic literature, see also Bammel (cited in the preceding note). Davies (*Torah in the Messianic Age and/or the Age to Come*, 1952, pp. 78–83) found scant evidence to support the view of Baeck and Silver that the law was expected to be abrogated in the Messianic age. Cf. J. Jervell, 'Die offenbarte und die verborgene Tora. Zur Vorstellung über die neue Tora im Rabbinismuc', *Studia Theologia* 25, 1971, pp. 90–108. The argument that there would be a *new* Torah in the Messianic Age (see Davies's monograph just cited and *Paul and Rabbinic Judaism*, pp. 72f.) is a different one. This also, however, cannot explain Paul's attitude to the Mosaic law, as the subsequent discussion will show.

Messiah has come as a reason for holding the law invalid.[26] He has many opportunities to do so, for he discusses the law at great length, and there are several treatments of its place in God's overall plan.[27] Nothing would have been easier than to say in such a context as Rom. 7 or 9–11 that the law is inoperative because the Messiah has come and, as everybody knows, the law ceases with the coming of the Messiah. If such reasoning governed his view, he kept it completely to himself. Schweitzer here has gone too far in trying to explain Paul on the basis of Jewish apocalyptic. Schweitzer first argues (without much evidence) that this was the view of Jewish apocalypticism and then proceeds to assume that Paul must have shared it. But why did Paul not state it? What Paul says is that a law has not been given which can make alive; therefore righteousness cannot come by the law (Gal. 3.21); that righteousness by definition cannot come by the law, since Scripture says it comes by faith (Gal. 3.11f.; Rom. 4.2f.; 10.5,11); that the law served the function of making sin be sinful indeed and thus holding the whole world under condemnation until *faith* should come (Gal. 3.22f.; cf. Rom. 5.20). Even if this means the same as saying that the purpose of the law was fulfilled with the coming of the *Messiah*, this does not constitute evidence that Paul regarded the law as abrogated because of a pre-existing Jewish view. He may have *come* to the view that the coming of 'faith' (or the Messiah) abrogates the law, but he seems to have come to it after the fact.[28] The argument in Gal. 3.21–25 has to do with the law's inability to give *life*, which comes only by *faith* in Christ (who, to be sure, is the Messiah). But the *fact* that Jesus is the Messiah is not the proof that the law must be abrogated.[29]

Schweitzer's second explanation falls with the first. It is brought in to explain a subsidiary point: granted an initial bias against the law common to Jewish apocalypticism when dealing with the Messianic age, why is it all right for some but not others to obey the law? Because the *status quo* should be maintained. But this point does not explain the ferocity of Paul's attack against those in Galatia who would accept circumcision, on the one hand, and his placidity with regard to whether or not Peter kept the law, on the other. He appears not to have considered Peter's keeping of the dietary laws in itself to have been wrong, only wrong because it cut him off from Gentile Christians. That is, left to himself Peter either could or could not accept the law. But in a Gentile church he must *not* follow those parts of the law

---

[26] Similarly Bammel (cited in n. 24).

[27] Gal. 3.19–26; II Cor. 3.7–11; Rom. 5.20; Rom. 7.7–25; Rom. 10.4–13.

[28] I am indebted for these comments on Gal. 3.22f. to a remark by Professor Wayne Meeks.

[29] I leave aside here detailed discussion of Cranfield's position that 'for Paul the Law is not abolished by Christ' (C. E. B. Cranfield, 'St Paul and the Law', *SJT* 17, 1964, pp. 43–68, quotation from p. 54). One may agree with Cranfield's desire to retain ethics and to do justice to Paul's positive statements about the law, but this statement can hardly stand as an exegetical interpretation of Paul's view. The problem raised by Cranfield is dealt with more penetratingly by S. Lyonnet, 'St Paul: Liberty and Law', *The Bridge*, ed. J. M. Oesterreicher, pp. 229–51.

which cut him off from other members of the body of Christ (Gal. 2.11–14). If Schweitzer's theory of the *status quo* were correct, Paul should have insisted that Gentile Christians never keep the law but that Jewish Christians always keep it; but the second half of that insistence is lacking. It is a major fault in Schweitzer's work that he cannot, on the basis of his theory, adequately explain Paul's attitude toward the law, an attitude which played such a major role in Paul's controversies.

Bultmann's explanation of Paul's attitude towards the law seems much more to the point of what Paul actually said, and considering it will lead to an analysis of the most relevant passages. Bultmann first notes that the law is not faulty because it requires the wrong thing: the will of God as expressed in the law is the same as that revealed to the Christian.

The reason why man's situation under the Law is so desperate is not that the Law as an inferior revelation mediates a limited or even false knowledge of God. What makes his situation so desperate is the simple fact that prior to faith *there is no true fulfilment of the Law*.[30]

Man's problem with the law is that 'he cannot exhibit "the works of the Law" in their entirety'. Further, says Bultmann, Paul thought not only that one *could* not fulfil the requirement of the law, but that one was not *intended* to do so. 'Paul thinks in this manner in consequence of his concept of God, according to which whatever factually is or happens, is or happens according to divine plan.'[31] But why did Paul regard 'the way of works of the Law and the way of grace and faith' as 'mutually exclusive opposites'? Here we come to the heart of Bultmann's position and must quote at length:

Because *man's effort to achieve his salvation by keeping the Law* only leads him into sin, indeed this effort itself in the end *is already sin*. It is the insight which Paul has achieved into the nature of sin that determines his teaching on the Law. This embraces two insights. One is the insight that sin is man's self-powered striving to undergird his own existence in forgetfulness of his creaturely existence, to procure his salvation by his own strength . . . , that striving which finds its extreme expression in 'boasting' and 'trusting in the "flesh"' . . . . The other is the insight that man is always already a sinner, that, fallen into the power of sin, he is always already involved in a falsely oriented understanding of his existence. . . . The reason, then, that man shall not, must not, be 'rightwised' by works of the Law is that he must not be allowed to imagine that he is able to procure his salvation by his own strength; for he can find his salvation only when he understands himself in his dependence upon God the Creator.[32]

Penetrating as this is, and persuasively as it is put, I should say that it is wrong by being backwards. It is not Paul's analysis of the nature of sin which

---

[30] Bultmann, *Theology* I, pp. 262f.
[31] Ibid., p. 263.
[32] Ibid., p. 264.

determines his view, but his analysis of the way to salvation; not his anthropology, but his Christology and soteriology. Paul's own reason for maintaining that 'man shall not, must not, be "rightwised" by works of the Law' is
not that man must not think of procuring his own salvation, but that if the
law could save, Christ died in vain (Gal. 2.21); and man does not find
salvation by understanding 'himself in his dependence upon God the
Creator', but by participating in the death of Christ, which assures his
resurrection with Christ (Rom. 6.5). The contrast, in other words, is not
between self-reliance and reliance on God – two kinds of self-understanding
– but between belonging to Christ and not belonging to Christ. The conviction that only belonging to Christ brings salvation precedes the analysis of
one's position before God and the change in one's self-understanding.
Bultmann held that Paul's view was that works of the law could not justify
because one must not have anything to boast of before God.[33] But it seems
more likely that Paul's view that attempting to do the law is itself sin is not
the *cause* of his view that keeping the law and being Christian are incompatible; it is the *consequence* of it.[34] *Since* salvation is only in Christ, *therefore* all
other ways toward salvation are wrong, and attempting to follow them has
results which are the reverse of what is desired. What is wrong with following
the law is not the effort itself, but the fact that the observer of the law is not
seeking the righteousness which is given by God through the coming of
Christ (Rom. 10.2–4). Effort itself is not the sin; the sin is aiming towards
any goal but being found 'in Christ' (Phil. 3.9). We should now show that
Paul thought in this way.

We must first note that in Galatians, the reason for not keeping the law
which Bultmann adduces (that keeping it is itself sinning, because it leads
to sin: boasting before God) is notably not in evidence. Paul clinches his
argument that righteousness comes by faith, not by works of law, with the
statement that 'if righteousness were through the law, then Christ died to no
purpose' (Gal. 2.21). He then proceeds to prove his point by appealing to
the Galatians' having the Spirit not by works of law, but by *akoēs pisteōs*
(3.2,5). It is difficult to know precisely how to translate the phrase. A strict
contrast with 'works of law' would produce 'hearing of faith', which might
mean either 'faithful hearing' (in contrast to legalistic works) or 'hearing
about faith' (in contrast to doing the law). I am somewhat inclined to take
the phrase, however, to mean 'believing what was heard', i.e. believing the
gospel (so the NEB and the Jerusalem Bible).[35] This would follow the

---

[33] Ibid., p. 283.
[34] Cf. Pfleiderer (*Paulinism*, vol. I, pp. 3–6), who argues in approximately the same way (with some
psychologizing explanations) and who also cites Gal. 2.21 as the key text for understanding the grounds
on which Paul rejected the law. So also van Dülmen, *Die Theologie des Gesetzes bei Paulus*, pp. 26f.
[35] Burton (*Galatians*, ICC, p. 147) translates 'a hearing of faith', but he interprets the phrase to mean 'a
hearing (of the gospel) accompanied by faith'.

common Pauline (and general Christian) view that those who 'believe', i.e. who accept the gospel concerning the death and resurrection of Jesus and the significance of those events, receive the Spirit as a guarantee. But whatever the precise meaning of the phrase *akoēs pisteōs*, it is clear that the Galatians will have to assent immediately that they received the Spirit on the basis of hearing the gospel and faith and not by obeying the law. As we said above, there is nothing clearer in Paul than that all Christians believed and received the Spirit.

From this argument, which would appear already to be conclusive, Paul proceeds to his two main proof-texts of the proposition that righteousness is by faith: Gen. 15.16, Abraham 'believed God, and it was reckoned to him as righteousness', and Hab. 2.4, 'he who through faith is righteous shall live' (Gal. 3.6,11).[36] After citing the first he concludes that those who have faith will be blessed with Abraham who had faith (3.9), while after the second he drives home the point: 'but the law does not rest on faith, for "He who does them shall live by them"' (3.12, citing Lev. 18.5). In between the two proof-texts lies another designed to discourage Gentiles from accepting circumcision. In 3.10 Paul argues, citing Deut. 27.26, that one who accepts the law must keep all the laws and that failure to keep them all brings a curse. It is clear, however, that the weight of the argument is not borne by the curse on those incapable of fulfilling the whole law. It lies, rather, on the other two proof-texts, and especially on Hab. 2.4; for here, by quoting Lev. 18.5, Paul states what is wrong with the law: it does not rest on faith, and only those who are righteous through faith will live.[37]

There follows still a further argument from the Bible, that the promises to Abraham preceded the giving of the law and that they were intended for Abraham's heir, Christ, and obviously not for Moses's followers (3.15–18). Does the law then have a purpose at all? Yes, a temporary one. But the purpose was not to give life: 'if a law had been given which could make alive, then righteousness would indeed be by the law' (3.21). Paul then repeats the theme of the temporary purpose of the law, to consign all things to sin so that those who believe in Jesus Christ might inherit the promises (3.22),

---

[36] There are other proof-texts in favour of faith *versus* the law, such as Isa. 28.16 (Rom. 9.33; 10.11), but these two connect *righteousness* with faith.

[37] Similarly Rom. 10.5–13, where Lev. 18.5 is refuted by a series of passages and a credal formula to show that only faith brings salvation. In neither case does Paul agree with Lev. 18.5, that those who keep the law will live, as some exegetes have taken to be the case. Thus, for example, Fitzmyer, 'Saint Paul and the Law', p. 23. The arguments show what is wrong with the law: it rests on works, but salvation can *only* be by faith. Correctly Whiteley, *Theology of St Paul*, p. 81: it is not *possible* to be saved by the law, citing Gal. 3.21. On p. 82, however, he curiously states that the question of whether or not it would be theoretically possible to be saved by works of the law is never raised by Paul. Paul seems to me explicitly to raise the possibility and deny it in Gal. 3.11f. and to deny it dogmatically throughout Galatians. Gal. 3.11f. in particular seems to militate against Wilckens's view that works of law cannot justify because man is in fact a sinner. See '"Aus Werken des Gesetzes wird kein Mensch gerecht"', *Rechtfertigung als Freiheit*, p. 104. I would emphasize more the dogmatic character of Paul's view: the law could not justify (= give life, Gal. 3.21) in any case, since it rests on works, and only faith gives life.

and he concludes by arguing that those baptized in Christ have become Christ's and consequently Abraham's heirs (3.26–29).

Paul's discussion of sonship and slavery continues, but we have reviewed the argument sufficiently for our purpose. Throughout, the argument is *dogmatic*; there is *no* analysis of the human situation which results in the conclusion that doing the law leads to boasting and estrangement from God. Gal. 2.21 and 3.21 seem to be substantially the same and to give the main thrust of Paul's thought: if one could be righteous by the law Christ need not have died; if the law could make alive, one could be righteous by the law. The inference which the reader must draw from the last passage is that no law was given which could make alive and that righteousness must come another way. He has already said how it comes: by the death of Christ and by faith. The quotations of Gen. 15.6 and Hab. 2.4 have the same dogmatic thrust. Righteousness *cannot* be by law, *since it is by faith*, not since doing the law leads to boasting. It is true that faith excludes boasting (Rom. 3.27), but that is not the argument here. The argument is that what the Galatians hope to achieve by the law *can* come *only* another way, by the death of Christ and by believing. Gal. 3.1–5 seems especially telling for seeing how Paul thought: the Spirit is the guarantee of salvation; the Spirit came by faith; therefore it cannot come any other way. This is what is meant by saying that the solution precedes the predicament. Paul does not start from or reason from the nature of man's sinful state. He starts rather from the death and resurrection of Christ and receiving the Spirit. If the death and resurrection of Christ provide salvation and receiving the Spirit is the guarantee of salvation, *all other means are excluded by definition*. This explains the dogmatic character of 3.11f. Since *only* the one who is righteous by faith shall live (which is how Paul reads Hab. 2.4),[38] one *cannot* 'live' by the law, since those who perform the commandments live by them. The two propositions are mutually exclusive dogmatically, and Paul uses them to prove that, since only by faith comes life and since the law does not rest on faith, *life* or *righteousness* cannot be by the law. Having denied the law a salvific role, Paul then assigns it another role in the history of salvation, assigning all to sin so that all could be saved by faith. But this is only a corollary of his main theme.

Similarly, in II Cor. 3.7–18, where Paul contrasts the 'dispensation of death, carved in letters on stone' with 'the dispensation of the Spirit', there is no analysis of the human predicament. What is wrong with the old dispensation is not that it prescribes what cannot be fulfilled, nor even that

---

[38] For the contrary view, that Hab. 2.4 in Gal. 3.11 and Rom. 1.17 should be read 'the righteous shall live by faith' (connecting 'by faith' to 'live' rather than 'righteous'), see D. M. Smith, 'Ο ΔΕ ΔΙΚΑΙΟΣ ΕΚ ΠΙΣΤΕΩΣ ΖΗΣΕΤΑΙ', *Festschrift Kenneth Clark*, ed. Daniels and Suggs, pp. 13–25; J. Cambier, 'Justice de Dieu, salut de tous les hommes et foi', *RB* 71, 1964, pp. 569f. Rom. 1.17 does not seem so clear as Gal. 3.11, where the contrast between being *righteous by law* ('no man is justified before God by [*en*] the law') and being *righteous by faith* ('he who through [*ek*] faith is righteous shall live') seems decisive.

fulfilling it leads to boasting and estrangement from God. Rather, 'what once had splendour has come to have no splendour at all, because of the splendour that surpasses it' (3.10). We can see the same way of thinking in Phil. 3. As to righteousness under the law, says Paul, he was blameless; and he was zealous for Judaism. Zeal and righteousness are not themselves bad (cf. also Rom. 10.2), and no human plight is depicted. Paul puts his view of his former life in Judaism thus: 'But whatever gain I had, I counted as loss for the sake of Christ. Indeed I count everything as loss because of the surpassing worth of knowing Christ Jesus my Lord' (Phil. 3.6–8). This logic – that God's action in Christ alone provides salvation and makes everything else seem, in fact actually *be* worthless – seems to dominate Paul's view of the law. This way of stating Paul's position modifies Bornkamm's view that on the basis of justification by faith Paul broke with the Jewish law.[39] Precisely put, it was on the basis of salvation only through Christ. Only if one identifies Paul's soteriology as being exhaustively defined by 'righteousness by faith' can Bornkamm's view be maintained.

How, then, shall we understand Rom. 1–5; 7, the chapters on which Bultmann explicitly based his view and in which many New Testament exegetes understand Paul to be working out his fundamental line of thought? For here it is clearly said that (1) all those under the law have sinned and been condemned for it; (2) God *then* provided for men's salvation apart from the law; (3) faith is the opposite of boasting; (4) what is wrong with the law is that it is deceitful; it promises life but gives death to the man who seeks life by it. We cannot solve all the problems which confront one in reading Romans, but it will be necessary to give a sketch of the argument and to understand the place of Paul's discussion of the law in it. We shall then be in a position to consider precisely what Paul's view of man's plight was.

Schweitzer, in concluding his argument that the theme of righteousness by faith is not a whole doctrine in Paul, but can be understood only in light of Paul's eschatological Christ-mysticism, noted the difference between Galatians and Romans. In Galatians, there is no attempt to make the doctrine of righteousness by faith independent of the doctrine of being in the body of Christ, but in Romans there is. The attempt, however, is not completely successful:

In the Epistle to the Romans an amazing thing happens, that, after the new righteousness has been presented at length as coming from faith in Christ's atoning sacrifice (Rom. iii.1–v.21), it is explained a second time, without any reference whatever to the previous exposition, as founded on the mystical dying and rising again with Christ (Rom. vi.1–viii.1). To the presence of these two independent expositions of the same question is due the confusing impression which the Epistle to the Romans always makes upon the reader.[40]

[39] Cited above, section 1 n. 52.
[40] Schweitzer, *Mysticism*, pp. 225f.

Thus Schweitzer regarded chapters 6–8 as repeating 1–5, and he took the fact that the repetition was required to prove that 'the doctrine of righteousness by faith is something incomplete and unfitted to stand alone'.[41] We have already seen that Schweitzer regarded the account of the law in Romans 7 as autobiographical.

Bultmann gave another analysis of the structure of Romans:

After the section 1.18–3.20 has demonstrated that before the revealing of 'God's righteousness' both Gentiles and Jews stood under the 'wrath of God', the thesis of righteousness now established by the occurrence of salvation in Christ is presented in 3.21–31 and the Scripture proof of it is offered in 4.1–25. For the Jew, with whom Paul is debating in all these arguments, the assertion of the present reality of eschatological righteousness could only appear absurd; for where, he could ask, are the blessings that were to be given along with righteousness? Where is 'life'? Are not death and sin still present realities?

Paul replies in chapters 5–8. In chapter 5 he endeavours to demonstrate that eschatological life, though a matter of hope, is, nevertheless, in a certain manner already a present reality. Further, he shows in 6.1–7.6 that even sin has lost its domination for the rightwised. Then, after a digression (7.7–25) has discussed the significance of the Law in the history of salvation, chapter 8 is the conclusion; it deals once more with freedom from sin (8.1–11) and from death (8.12–39), pointing out again the peculiar double character of salvation: future and yet already present.[42]

There are numerous other attempts to analyse the argument of the first eight chapters of Romans,[43] but we see here the principal problems: either 5 goes primarily with 1–4 (Schweitzer) or primarily with 6–8 (Bultmann); the second set of chapters, however defined, constitutes either a repetition of the argument of the first in different terms or a continuation of it which presupposes the argument of the first and deals with the life of the one who has been made righteous. There is something to be said for each of these positions, and in particular it should be emphasized that there is more to be said for Schweitzer's view than seems generally recognized. One could observe, for example, that sin in Rom. 1–3 is conceived of as consisting of man's transgressions, while, in chapter 6, sin suddenly becomes exclusively singular and is conceived more in terms of a power which controls man (or does not control those who die with Christ).[44] The solution to sin offered

---

[41] Ibid., p. 226.

[42] Bultmann, *Theology* I, p. 279.

[43] See, for example, Conzelmann, *Theology*, p. 239: the divisions are chs. 1–4, 5–8, 9–11; Lyonnet, 'Pauline Soteriology', *Introduction to the New Testament*, ed. by Robert and Feuillet, p. 840: Rom. 1–4 deal with justification, Rom. 5–8 with the salvation which depends on it; E. Dinkler, 'Prädestination bei Paulus'.

[44] Cf. Conzelmann, *Theology*, p. 194: 'In Paul the concept [of sin] no longer describes the individual failure against the individual commandment, but a trans-subjective power. Paul therefore uses the word predominantly in the singular. The plural is used only when he borrows from the tradition.' Similarly Bornkamm, *Paul*, p. 133. This is oversimplified, since it overlooks the use of the verb, especially in Rom. 2.12; 3.23; 5.12–16. Here the dominant conception is of sin as transgression: it is what one does.

in chapter 3 is righteousness as a gift, through Christ's expiatory death, if appropriated with faith, while in chapter 6 it is being set free from the power of sin and in chapter 8 dwelling in the Spirit and having the Spirit in one (or being in Christ and having Christ in one). It is tempting to see the second formulation (death to sin as a power and life in Christ Jesus) as Paul's 'real' view and the first formulation (expiation for sin as transgressions) as a traditional view which Paul repeats. It could then be observed that the death of Christ plays two different roles: an expiatory sacrifice in chapter 3 and as offering the opportunity for participation in death to sin and death in chapter 6.

I think that there is a certain amount of truth to this analysis. There are, however, things to be said against it. It leaves out of account Paul's obvious attempt to make the argument flow. Thus chapter 5 is clearly a linking chapter, picking up the theme of righteousness by faith as providing the grounds for the Christian's status (5.1), repeating the view of Christ's death as leading to acquittal (5.18), and concluding with the statement that grace reigns 'through righteousness to eternal life', thus distinctly tying righteousness to the life theme which follows. Further, 8.1 returns to the theme of 5.16–18. In the latter, Christ's death leads to acquittal and life instead of *condemnation*, while in 8.1 being 'in Christ' is said to result in one's not being condemned.[45] The juridical and participatory statements are not in fact kept in water-tight compartments, as we have seen also to be the case in such passages as Phil. 3.8–11 and Gal. 3.24–29.

Two observations made by Bornkamm about Romans may help us to unravel the problems which confront us. One is that Romans repeats a remarkable number of the themes which appear in Galatians, Philippians and Corinthians.[46] We shall not give here all of Bornkamm's list, but we may quickly note the discussion of righteousness by faith in Galatians and Romans, in which even the same biblical proof-texts are used, and the contrast of Christ and Adam, which appears also in I Cor. 15. The significance of the point is that the controversies in mind when Paul wrote Romans were those *behind* him, not *before* him in Rome. That is why Romans reflects so much of the previous correspondence. The second observation is that the *Sitz im Leben* of Romans is *not* some imagined situation in the Roman church, but Paul's own thinking on the question of the Jews and the law in light of his impending visit to Jerusalem. Romans, says Bornkamm, revolves around 'the questions connected with the apostle's theology and its aims, which he was

---

The whole argument of Rom. 1–3 is that men commit transgression*s*, even though the noun *hamartia* does appear in the singular in 3.9.

[45] On the interconnections between Rom. 5–8 and 3–4, see J. Reumann, 'The Gospel of the Righteousness of God', *Interpretation* 20, 1966, p. 434.

[46] Bornkamm, *Paul*, pp. 93f.; 'Der Römerbrief als Testament des Paulus', *Geschichte und Glaube* II, pp. 130–3.

shortly to have to justify and stand up for in Jerusalem, and which were also to continue as the basis of his coming mission to the Gentiles. . .'.[47] Thus the 'opponent' in Romans is not 'this or that section in a particular church, but the Jews and their understanding of salvation, which was still extremely influential in the early Jewish-Christian church, particularly in Jerusalem'.[48]

The purpose and occasion of Romans have been very vigorously debated in recent years. For a discussion of recent literature, see Bornkamm's article 'Der Römerbrief als Testament des Paulus', *Geschichte und Glaube* II, pp. 120–39 (discussion of the literature, pp. 120–9); U. Wilckens, 'Über Abfassungszweck und Aufbau des Römerbriefes', *Rechtfertigung als Freiheit*, pp. 110–70 (discussion of the literature, pp. 110–26); K. P. Donfried, 'False Presuppositions in the Study of Romans', *CBQ* 36, 1974, pp. 332–55; R. J. Karris, 'The Occasion of Romans: A Response to Professor Donfried', *CBQ* ibid., pp. 356–8. Wilckens is close to Bornkamm: Paul's purpose was to argue out what he planned to say in Jerusalem and to seek the Romans' recognition and support of it (p. 139; cf. p. 167). The last clause represents Wilckens's primary innovation. I find myself in general agreement with Karris in the Karris/Donfried debate: Romans had a specific occasion, but the occasion was not a debate within Rome. I would say, in agreement with Bornkamm and others, that the occasion was the impending trip to Jerusalem and then to the West and Paul's worry about the Jewish-Gentile problem, informed by his recent difficulties. The letter to Rome, while recapitulating many themes from other correspondence, is really concerned with the Jewish-Gentile problem and is not a summary of Paul's theology in the sense of a tract. Bornkamm's phrase 'Paul's testament' is, however, unfortunate, since it too much suggests an intentional summary at the end of his career.

With regard to Donfried's argument, I should further note that his first assumption is not convincing. He argued that since all the other Pauline letters were written in response to a concrete situation in the church addressed, so was Romans (p. 333). Romans is unique in being addressed to a church not founded by Paul in a city not visited by Paul, and I see no force to an argument based on the occasion of the other letters.

The wisdom of Bornkamm's observations can immediately be verified in the first four chapters of Romans, for it is clear that one of Paul's major concerns is to assert that salvation is for both Jews and Gentiles and that it must be *based on the same ground*.[49] That ground cannot be the law and must therefore be faith. Thus Paul opens the letter by mentioning his appointment as apostle to bring to faith the Gentiles (1.5), a theme which is reiterated in 1.13f. The gospel, says Paul, is for 'the Jew first and also . . . the Greek' (1.16; cf. 2.10). The thrust of this is not to claim superiority for the Jew: that is virtually presupposed. Paul is, in effect, arguing for the equality of the

---

[47] *Paul*, p. 93.

[48] Ibid., p. 95; 'Testament', p. 135. On the setting of Romans, cf. Munck, *Paul*, pp. 196–200, relying on T. W. Manson.

[49] Similarly Stendahl, *HTR* 56, 1963, p. 205: the principal problem in Romans is that of Jews and Gentiles; so also Wilckens, 'Abfassungszweck und Aufbau', p. 167.

Gentile. The argument that the Jews are not in a privileged position becomes explicit in 2.14–16 ('When Gentiles who have not the law do by nature what the law requires . . .') and 2.27 ('Then those who are physically uncircumcised but keep the law will condemn you who have the written code and circumcision but break the law'). The entire theme of 2.12–29 is enunciated in 2.11: 'God shows no partiality.' Paul must then ask what advantage the Jew has (3.1), a question to which he will recur (Rom. 9.4f.; 11.29f.)' The answer as regards soteriology is clear, however: none. Thus 3.9: 'What then? Are we Jews any better off? No, not at all; for I have already charged that all men, both Jews and Greeks, are under the power of sin . . .'. The clinching point with regard to the law as being in any way efficacious for salvation is 3.20: 'For no human being will be justified [made righteous] in his sight by works of the law since through the law comes knowledge of sin.' After maintaining that salvation is possible for all who believe, *without distinction*, through Christ (3.21–26), Paul reiterates the point of the equality of Jews and Gentiles:

Or is God the God of Jews only? Is he not the God of Gentiles also? Yes, of Gentiles also, since God is one; and he will justify the circumcised on the ground of their faith and the uncircumcised because of their faith. (3.29)

Here we see clearly the thrust that there must be *one ground* of salvation in order that Jews and Gentiles may equally have access to salvation.[50] This is, in effect, an argument against the law as being in any way necessary for salvation.

The argument continues in chapter 4. The blessing of Abraham, which was given before Abraham was circumcised, must apply to the uncircumcised as well as to the circumcised (4.9). Abraham is thus the father of all who believe, whether circumcised or not (4.11f.). The point is then turned explicitly against the requirement to keep the law:

The promise to Abraham and his descendants, that they should inherit the world, did not come through the law but through the righteousness of faith. If it is the adherents of the law who are to be the heirs, faith is null and the promise void. (4.13)

Paul's reasoning is put as clearly as possible in v. 16: 'That is why it depends on faith, in order that the promise may rest on grace and be guaranteed to all his descendants – not only to the adherents of the law but also to those who share the faith of Abraham, for he is the father of us all . . .'

There are actually two reasons given by Paul why salvation ('the promise', 'righteousness') comes by faith and not by law. (1) The promise *cannot* be inherited on the basis of keeping the law, because that would exclude

[50] We may here recall Paul's argument *for* equal standing and *against* the law in Gal. 3.25–29 on the basis of both Jews and Greeks becoming one person in Christ Jesus.

Gentiles. But Gentiles *cannot* be excluded, for God has appointed Christ as Lord of the whole world and as saviour of all who believe, and has especially called and appointed Paul as apostle to the Gentiles. 2. If it is necessary and sufficient to keep the law in order to inherit the promises of God, Christ died in vain and faith is in vain. The two arguments – the inclusion of the Gentiles and the death of Christ – stand together, as we see in Rom. 3.21–26. But it is clearly for these reasons, rather than for any others, that Paul rejects the requirement to keep the law. This means that he did not reject the necessity to keep the law because of a preconceived theory that the law would cease to be valid when the Messiah came (Schweitzer), nor did he reject it because the effort to keep it leads man away from his true self (Bultmann). Both these solutions require Paul's view of the law to be determined by other factors than his conviction that salvation is attained *only through Christ*. The first requires Paul simply to be following the putative view of Jewish apocalypticism, the second requires him to be following his analysis of man's existential situation. While Paul may have been influenced on many points by apocalypticism, and while he did put forward a penetrating analysis of man's situation, neither of these things seems to have *led* to his view of the law. The first he never mentions at all in this connection, while the second is the result of his soteriology, not one of the analyses which went toward producing it.

That Paul's argument in Rom. 1–4 is *against the necessity of keeping the law* can be confirmed by noting the changing meaning of the noun 'faith' or the verb 'believe'.[51] In Rom. 3.25, for example ('whom God put forward as an expiation by his blood, to be received by faith'), 'faith' means accepting the gratuity of salvation. In Rom 4.16–23, however, the 'faith' terminology means 'trust that God will do what he promises'. Thus Abraham in hope 'believed against hope' (4.18), and 'he did not weaken in faith when he considered his own body'. Abraham's faith is contrasted with 'distrust', as the RSV correctly translates *apistia* in Rom. 4.20. Faith as accepting the gift and faith as trusting God to act as he promised are not incompatible, but they are also not precisely the same. Thus Rom. 3.27–4.25, which would seem at first to be the passage which most decisively supports Bultmann's interpretation of faith as 'obedience' (the surrender of one's previous self-understanding, an understanding which involved an effort towards self-salvation) and as the opposite of boasting,[52] turns out not to be so decisive; for in it the definition of faith shifts from being the opposite of boasting (3.27) to being the opposite of distrust (4.20) – a meaning which Bultmann himself notes as being atypical in Paul.[53] This means that the argument

---

[51] Cf. J. J. O'Rourke, '*Pistis* in Romans', *CBQ* 35, 1973, pp. 188–94.

[52] Bultmann, *Theology* I, pp. 314f. Against the view that faith is primarily obedience, cf. Whiteley, *Theology of St Paul*, p. 162.

[53] Bultmann, *TDNT* VI, p. 218.

about 'faith' in Rom. 1–4 is not *for* some one definite definition of faith, but primarily *against* the requirement of salvation by the law. The positive argument of Rom. 1–4 is that Jews and Gentiles stand on an equal footing (1.16; 2.6–11,12; 3.9, 22, 29; 4.9, 11–12,16), and this requires the negative argument against the law, which is contrasted with faith. But no one positive definition of faith emerges from the argument. Faith, to be sure, is always faith in God, and especially it has as its content the fact that he raised Jesus the Lord from the dead (cf. Rom. 4.24), but it represents a more general theological conception than is generally realized: Christianity versus Judaism. Faith excludes boasting, but it is not defined simply as the opposite of boasting; faith involves trust, but it is not precisely trust;[54] faith involves accepting salvation as a gift, but it is not just that either. Faith represents man's entire response to the salvation offered in Jesus Christ, *apart from law*; and *the argument for faith is really an argument against the law*.[55] Without denying the qualities of trust and obedience to Paul's understanding of faith, we should conclude that the actual *argument* in Rom. 4 is formal and terminological. Paul wishes to counter the claim of the law. He does so with the term 'faith', using different arguments and Old Testament passages, in the course of which the meaning of 'faith' shifts.

It agrees with this that, in these chapters, 'righteousness' does not have any one fixed meaning. The righteousness of God is the *power* and *action* of God which are manifest in both wrath and grace (1.16–18; 3.21), as it is also his *rightness* and *fidelity* to what he promised and intended (3.1–7, where God's *dikaiosynē* is parallel to his *pistis* and *alētheia* and opposed to man's *adikia*). These definitions are no more incompatible than the different definitions of faith, but it seems unnecessary to beat them all into one meaning.[56] The righteousness of man is his uprightness before God with regard to his *works* (2.13) or the right relationship to God which is received by faith and *not* by law (4.11). Being 'justified' or 'made righteous' *is the acquittal* achieved by Christ's death (5.9f., 18), or the possibility of salvation achieved by Christ's resurrection *in contrast to the acquittal* of trespasses achieved by his death (4.25). It agrees with this that in general 'righteousness'

[54] Davies (*The Gospel and the Land*, pp. 174f.) understands Paul's use of the Abraham story in Rom. 4 to indicate a material agreement between Paul's understanding of faith and that attributed to Abraham: faith is trust. 'Paul recognizes in Abraham's trust in the promise the same quality of faith that he knew himself.' This view, like Bultmann's (faith is obedience), is based on some aspect of Paul's argument.

[55] G. Taylor correctly observes with regard to *pistis*: 'its usefulness to [Paul] lies in the answer it provides to the problem of the law'. 'It is when he must refute the claim that the Mosaic law is the source of δικαιοσύνη that Paul uses this LXX correlation [of *pistis* with the *dik*-root] to show that the real source of that commodity is πίστις.' G. Taylor, 'The Function of ΠΙΣΤΙΣ ΧΡΙΣΤΟΥ in Galatians', *JBL* 85, 1966, pp. 6of. I do not, however, agree that, since *nomos* is a juridical term and since *pistis* is contrasted with it, *pistis* must itself be juridical. This pushes logic too far. On the negative meaning of faith, cf. also Cerfaux, *The Christian in the Theology of St Paul*, pp. 377–84.

[56] For attempts to find one meaning in the term righteousness, see Dr Brauch's appendix below.

is sometimes the forensic[57] status of being justified (sanctified) from trans-gression *so that* one may *then* have life (Rom. 5.1,9) and sometimes simply the *equivalent* of life.[58] In other terms, righteousness may be either past (Rom. 5.1,9) or future (Rom. 2.13; Gal. 5.5). 'Righteousness by faith', in other words, is not any *one* doctrine.[59] It is the heuristic category employed by Paul against the notion that obedience to the law is necessary. We should repeat here the observation that 'righteousness by faith' receives very little *positive* working out by Paul. It does not lead to ethics, it is not employed in explaining the significance of the sacraments, it does not explain the gift of the Spirit, and it does not account for the participatory soteriology which we have already discussed. 'Faith' alone, in a way, *is* a prerequisite, since it signifies conversion and being Christian: the Spirit is received by believing the gospel message. But all this can be and is discussed without reference to a supposed doctrine of 'righteousness by faith'. The latter remains primarily a negative category, directed against the view that obedience to the law is either the necessary or sufficient condition of salvation.

These two points – that righteousness by faith is not any one doctrine and that it serves primarily as a negative argument against keeping the law as sufficient or necessary for salvation – may also be seen by returning briefly to the argument of Galatians. We have already observed (above, pp. 482–4) that in Galatians the argument against the law is dogmatic and is not based on an analysis of how self-estrangement is the result of keeping the law. We may now observe that, as in the case of Romans, the argument of Galatians is *terminological* and *negative*: a positive definition of what it means to be 'righteous' by faith is not precisely given (although it may be inferred from the terms which are parallel to 'righteousness'), and the principal thrust of

---

[57] The term 'forensic' is somewhat ambiguous, since it can refer to God's declaring one to be righteous (though he is not), a meaning conveyed by the term 'imputation' and the catch-phrase *simul justus et peccator*. This meaning arises from Luther's theology (see, for example, his *Commentary on Galatians*, ET, pp. 22f., 26, 137f., 223–9), and it is a meaning which I do not find in Paul. Paul does use the term forensically in the sense of the acquittal of past transgressions (= forgiveness), and this is the sense referred to here. Jeremias ('Justification by Faith', *The Central Message of the New Testament*, pp. 51–70) argues that righteousness by faith is 'soteriological' rather than 'forensic' (p. 54), but he proceeds to define 'soteriological' as meaning free pardon, and that alone (pp. 60, 64, 66). Thus he means by 'forensic' 'imputation'. Jeremias's definition is followed by Hunter, *The Gospel According to St Paul*, p. 21.

The *locus classicus* for arguing that 'justify' means 'impute righteousness where it does not exist' is Rom. 4.5, 'who justifies the ungodly'. It has been supposed that the meaning here is 'impute righteousness to those who are not actually righteous', with an implied contrast to Judaism, where people stand or fall strictly on their merits. The imputation theory is supported by the following verb, 'reckoned', which is quoted from Gen. 15.6. It is better to understand 'justify' here as 'forgive' (so Ziesler, *Righteousness*, p. 195). In this case the only contrast with Judaism is the use of the verb to mean 'forgive' rather than 'declare to be right on the basis of the facts'. There is no material contrast, for Judaism fully believed in forgiveness. Cranfield (*Romans*, p. 232 n. 1) correctly counters the view that here Paul describes 'God as doing what the Old Testament forbids'.

[58] See the excursus immediately below.

[59] Cf. Styler, 'The basis of obligation in Paul's christology and ethics', *Christ and Spirit in the New Testament*, ed. B. Lindars and S. Smalley, p. 176.

the argument is against 'works of law'. The following list will make this evident:

righteousness	by faith	not by works of law (Gal. 2.16)
('justified')		
Spirit	by faith	not by works of law (3.1–5)
sons of Abraham	by faith	(3.7)
blessing of Abraham	by faith	(3.9)
[contrast: cursed		by works of law (3.10)]
righteousness	by faith	not by works of law (3.11)
promise of the Spirit	through faith	(3.14)
inheritance	by promise	not by law (3.18)
life and righteousness		not by law (3.21)
(verb and adjective)		
promise	by faith	(3.22)
sons of God	through faith	(3.26)

In the argument of Gal. 2–3, even where the negative 'not by works of law' does not appear, it is implied (so, 3.7, 9 and elsewhere). 'Not by works of law' is the persistent and reiterated point of the argument, and the primary thrust is thus negative. We see again that 'faith' is the *term* which is played off against 'by works of law', although just what faith is (obedience, trust or something else) is not said. The argument in favour of faith and against works of law is grounded either in scriptural proof-texts (Gal. 3.6, 11) or Christian experience (Gal. 3.1–5). *What* is received by faith and not by works of law, however, varies, depending primarily on which scriptural proof-text is in mind. The only terms which Paul introduces which are not backed up by a scriptural quotation are the Spirit (Gal. 3.1–5, 14), life (indicated by the verb 'make alive', 3.21), and sons of God (3.26). 'Righteousness by faith' is thus not a set doctrine – it is only one formulation among many – and it serves a primarily negative purpose. The argument is that *whatever* is religiously good – righteousness, the promise of Abraham, the Spirit, life and the like – does not come by works of law and must come another way: by faith. Further, righteousness, the Spirit and the like are thus available to all, whether Jew or Gentile, without distinction and on the same basis (Gal. 3.7, 28f.).

In 'Patterns of Religion in Paul and Rabbinic Judaism', *HTR* 66, 1973, pp. 470f., 477f. (the latter pages in criticism of Ziesler's *The Meaning of Righteousness in Paul*, 1972), I argued that the 'real' meaning of righteousness (whether indicated by the verb, adjective or noun) is *life*, disagreeing with Bultmann's view that righteousness is primarily an eschatological/forensic term and Ziesler's view that the noun righteousness and the adjective righteous are ethical, while the verb ('justify') is forensic (referring to acquittal, not imputation; see n. 57). Dr Ziesler has now indicated to me that he does not disagree with the position that righteousness is *more than* ethical uprightness. He had been concerned to emphasize that it meant at least uprightness against the view that it refers to imputed 'fictional' righteousness. The key passages in which 'righteousness' means 'life' (and is not simply forensic or ethical) are Rom. 6.16; Gal. 3.21; and possibly II Cor. 3.8f. In fact, the forensic sense (acquittal) seems almost totally missing in Galatians, and I would take Gal. 2.15–21 to be constructively an argument that *salvation* is by faith and not by works of law, not that one is forensically declared righteous or forgiven or ethically made righteous. I should now note, with regard to the history of the terminology, several points: (1) Ziesler's precise view, while generally correct, is not supported by the usage in Qumran (above, Chapter II, section 7 n. 222). (2) There is nevertheless enough evidence in support of Ziesler's view to justify the attempt to work out Paul's usage as he does. (3) Bultmann's view that in Judaism righteousness is a forensic/eschatological term has very little to be said for it. The view is that one does not know whether or not he is righteous until the judgment, at which time God will assess his deeds and declare him righteous or not (Bultmann, *Theology* I, pp. 270–4). As such, righteousness is held to be the *precondition* of life. Schweitzer was of a similar view: righteousness 'belongs, strictly speaking, to the future. To be righteous means to acquire by keeping the commandments a claim to be pronounced righteous at the coming Judgment, and consequently to become a partaker in the Messianic glory' (*Mysticism*, p. 205). But where in Jewish literature is the righteousness terminology used in this way? As we saw throughout Part I, in much of Palestinian Judaism the term 'righteous' was applied to those who were proper members of the covenant – those who obeyed the commandments and atoned for transgression. They do not wait to be declared righteous; the righteous are alive and well. Thus Bultmann's description, which is widely shared (see e.g. Furnish, *Theology and Ethics*, p. 147), sets the problem up wrong. The history of the righteous and righteousness terminology is incorrectly given. 4. Similarly incorrect is the Käsemann/Stuhlmacher position that 'the righteousness of God' was a fixed technical term in Judaism and that it bears the same meaning in Paul (see Dr Brauch's appendix below). I find no instance of it as a technical term for God's saving *power* in Hebrew literature (see the index for my discussion of one of the main passages cited by Käsemann, IQS 11.12). One may also refer to Thyen's telling critique of Stuhlmacher: *Sündenvergebung*, pp. 56ff.; similarly Conzelmann, *Theology*, p. 218.

With regard to Paul's usage, I would argue as follows: (1) Bultmann's view that the formal meaning of righteousness is the same for Paul and Judaism (forensic/eschatological) is wrong (*Theology* I, p. 273). Bultmann, followed by many others (e.g. Thyen, *Sündenvergebung*, p. 60), supposed that the term basically meant the same thing to both parties, the only question being how one *obtains* righteousness. As we shall show later in this section, in connection with Phil. 3.4–12, *the goal which is being sought is itself different*. Thus Paul does *not* differ from Judaism in saying that one is *already* righteous (Bultmann follows the Lutheran distinction: righteousness is already *imputed*, *Theology* I, p. 274), since in Judaism the adjective righteous was applied to living Jews. Rather, Paul differs as to the meaning of *true* righteousness. (2) Against Bornkamm (*Paul*, p. 153), Conzelmann (*Theology*, p. 273), Buchanan (*Consequences of the Covenant*, p. 233) and many others, I would argue that Paul did not systematically think of righteousness as what has been achieved in the present which serves as the precondition for life. That is, to be sure, the meaning in Rom. 5.1 and elsewhere, but righteousness is sometimes future (Gal. 5.5) or the equivalent of 'life' (Gal. 3.21). (3) I would therefore have to modify my former view about Paul's 'real meaning'. He does not use the righteousness terminology with *any one* meaning. It may be used as the equivalent of salvation and life; or it may refer to acquittal in the present for past transgressions, or to future vindication in the judgment (Rom. 2.13). (4) This also means that the Käsemann/Stuhlmacher attempt uniformly to derive the meaning of righteousness in Paul from the supposed technical term 'righteousness of God' as God's saving power cannot stand, although, to be sure, the phrase 'righteousness of God' in Rom. 1 does bear the meaning which Käsemann assigns to it.

Finally, we must observe that 'righteousness by faith' is sometimes *limited* to the forensic category of acquittal for past transgressions and sometimes *explained* by the participatory language which describes how one in Christ dies to the power of sin in order to live a new life to God. When it has the former function, it does not correspond to Paul's main 'transfer' terms; when it is explained by other terms, the 'righteousness' terminology is clearly less appropriate than the participatory language. Before the question of the 'more appropriate' language can be fully settled, however, we should summarize the argument thus far, conclude the discussion on the law and consider Paul's conception of man's plight.

We began by rehearsing the theories of Schweitzer and Bultmann on Paul's attitude toward the law. Schweitzer's various explanations were seen not to be correct. Bultmann's explanation led us to a consideration of the argument of Galatians, short passages in Corinthians and Philippians and the argument of Romans. The last discussion required a consideration of the meaning of faith and righteousness (a topic not yet exhausted; the positive meanings of the terms have yet to be considered, and they can be fully considered only after we pause to consider man's plight in Paul's view). By way of summary of the argument here concerning Paul's attitude toward the law, it will be useful to refer to W. D. Davies's most recent description. In a chapter on Paul and Judaism which is to appear in the forthcoming *Cambridge History of Judaism*, Davies gives his most persuasive treatment of Paul's view of the law. He first describes how Paul's statements concerning the law differ from letter to letter, and he takes the sharp polemic of Galatians more fully into account than he had previously done.

In Romans [Paul] presents a more positive estimate of the Law even while he still strikes against it. A more restrained and subtle Paul emerges. In Galatians he had treated the Law with a clinical, almost impersonal detachment difficult to reconcile with his Pharisaic past. In Romans he is no less critical, but more circumspect and sensitive. The subtle variations in his discussion of the Law militate against any simplistic dismissal of his criticisms of it.

Davies then explains the criticisms:

It was not that as a Diaspora Jew he had an attenuated understanding of the Law as simply ethical and divorced from the rich matrix of the covenant; nor that he had mistaken the Law to be a means to justification and salvation (rather than a sign of the possession of these as it was in Pharisaism) which could be opposed to faith; nor that as an Apocalyptic extremist who regarded the Law as a simple monolithic totality, he could easily dismiss it *in toto* – it was not from any of these positions that Paul criticized the Law. The one essential clue to his criticism of the Law was that the Messiah had come in a crucified Jesus who had died under the curse of the Law. The confirmation of the Messiahship of that Jesus Paul saw in his power to draw those outside the Law, even Gentiles, to Himself. In Him the people of God could be constituted and that not in terms of Torah.

I agree with this analysis entirely, *except for the emphasis on the fact of Jesus' messiahship*. Davies's first two negatives should be especially emphasized, since they both respond to proposals that Paul's view of the law rests on a misunderstanding of Judaism. The first view (that Paul's view of the law resulted from his being a diaspora Jew) is especially associated with the name of Montefiore,[60] and the second view (that Paul took the law to be a means to salvation rather than a sign of it) with the name of Schoeps.[61] It is my own view that Paul did not so much misunderstand the role of the law in Judaism as gain a new perspective which led him to declare the law abolished. I take the position, that is, that Paul was not disillusioned with the law in advance of his conversion and call to be the apostle to the Gentiles, as he would have been if he had misunderstood it. Nor can we find a background to Paul's view in Judaism, despite the numerous attempts to do so.[62] There is no body of Jewish literature which expects the abolition of the law with the advent of the Messiah, nor do we know of any other Christian groups or theologians which drew Paul's conclusion about the law, as would be the case if the view were predetermined by his background. What is distinctive about Paul's view of the law – and in fact about his theology – was correctly pointed to in the statement quoted from Davies: Christ saves Gentiles as well as Jews. This was not only a theological view, but it was bound up with Paul's most profound conviction about himself, a conviction on which he staked his career and his life: he was the apostle to the Gentiles. The salvation of the Gentiles is essential to Paul's preaching; and with it falls the law; for, as Paul says simply, Gentiles cannot live by the law (Gal. 2.14). Further, it was a matter of common Christian experience that the Spirit and faith come by hearing the gospel, not by obeying the law (Gal.

[60] C. G. Montefiore, *Judaism and St Paul*, pp. 92–112.

[61] See Schoeps, *Paul*, pp. 200; 213–18; 260: Paul misunderstood the relation of law and covenant and thus missed Judaism's emphasis on grace and *reciprocal* commitment. Like Montefiore, Schoeps attributed the misunderstanding to Hellenistic Judaism.

[62] Against Wilckens, n. 24 above.

3.1–5). More important, they come *only* this way. *It is the Gentile question and the exclusivism of Paul's soteriology which dethrone the law, not a misunderstanding of it or a view predetermined by his background.*

The central Pauline soteriological conviction is not well denominated as a conviction *that* Jesus was the Messiah. What is essential is that Jesus Christ came to save *all*, both Jew and Gentile.[63] It is on this point that I disagree with Davies's emphasis. It would seem to push Jewish expectations about the Messiah too far to say that Paul's view is simply a radicalizing of the expectation that Gentiles would be brought in at the eschaton. That view has to do with obeisance to the Jewish law and the worship of the one true God on Mount Zion, not the universalizing of the way of access to salvation (being in Christ rather than a member of the covenant); and it certainly does not imply the abolition of the law.

Having declared the law abolished with regard to salvation, Paul must then answer the question of why God gave the law. The answer is that it was to condemn: since all the world can be saved only through Christ, all the world must have stood condemned, and it was the law's role to condemn. It is for this reason that Paul can link the law with sin, 'the flesh' and death and equate being under the law with being enslaved by the fundamental spirits of the universe (Rom. 6.15–20; 7.4–6; Gal. 4.1–11). Apart from this, however, Paul has only good things to say about the law. Its requirement is just, in itself it aims aright. But the requirement is fulfilled only in Christ (Rom. 8.4), and the aim, life, is accomplished only in Christ (Rom. 7.10; 8.1–4).

Man's plight

Man's plight is basically to be understood as the antithesis to the solution to it as Paul understood that solution. We have noted above two sets of 'transfer' terms in Paul, one participationist and one juristic. In contrast to saying that one dies with Christ to sin and consequently belongs to Christ, man's plight without Christ is described as being enslaved by sin or being ruled by sin (Rom. 6.20). In contrast to being in the Spirit or in Christ stands primarily the term being 'in the flesh' (Rom. 7.5; 8.9). Being under sin can be equated with being under the law (Rom. 6.15–20), just as also being in the flesh can be equated with being under the law (Rom. 7.4–6). The dominant conception here is the transfer from one *lordship* to another. One could say, from one *sphere* to another (from being in the flesh to being in the Spirit), as long as 'sphere' is not understood to imply that the complete change has taken place.[64] As we have often noted, Paul always becomes reserved on this point.

---

[63] So also Wilckens, 'Die Bekehrung des Paulus', *Rechtfertigung als Freiheit*, p. 18.

[64] For the 'sphere' terminology, see Käsemann, 'Primitive Christian Apocalyptic', *Questions*, p. 136; Conzelmann, *Theology*, p. 194.

The present form of the world is passing away, the aeons are changing and Christians are being transformed; but the resurrection and the full transformation of the Christians who do not die before the end always lie in the future.

It has been much debated whether or not, when Paul speaks in terms of Sin in the singular as a power, of 'the flesh', of the rulers of this world or of the fundamental spirits of the universe, he actually has in mind spiritual beings which are more or less the opposite numbers to Christ. It appears, especially from Gal. 4, that he does, although it may be that the 'beings that by nature are no gods' (4.8) do not have quite the same reality in his own mind as Christ, who frees believers from them. It thus seems more likely that I Cor. 2.6–8 refers to spiritual powers than to earthly rulers (so also, among others, Kümmel, *Theology*, pp. 188f.; Furnish, *Theology and Ethics*, p. 116; the contrary view is held by Gene Miller, 'ΑΡΧΟΝΤΩΝ ΤΟΥ ΑΙΩΝΟΣ ΤΟΥΤΟΥ – A New Look at I Corinthians 2:6–8', *JBL* 91, 1972, pp. 522–8). For reference to the enemy powers, see also I Cor. 15.24; Rom. 8.38. On the other hand, by accepting the authenticity of Colossians and Ephesians, Jung Young gives the spiritual powers more significance than they have in the authentic letters ('Interpreting the Demonic Powers in Pauline Thought', *NT* 12, 1970, pp. 54–69). This means that sin should not be simply identified with boasting (Bultmann, *Theology* I, pp. 239–43; followed by Furnish, *Theology and Ethics*, p. 137) or self-regard (Moule, ' "Justification" in its relation to the condition ματὰ πνεῦμα (Rom. 8: 1–11)', *Battesimo E Giustizia in Rom 6 e 8*, ed. Lorenzo de Lorenzi, p. 183; 'Obligation in the Ethic of Paul', *Christian History and Interpretation*, ed. W. R. Farmer and others, p. 393), although those terms do indicate the personal and existential manifestation of being under the power of sin. Sin itself, however, is the enemy power which governs men who are not in Christ.

Although the dominant conception is the change of lordships, Paul frequently writes of the transfer as being cleansing of past *transgressions* in a way that does not call to mind the 'participationist' view of dying *with* Christ to the power of sin (but of Christ dying *for* transgressions). The clearest single passage is I Cor. 6.9–11, where Christians are said to have been washed, justified and sanctified of the blatant Gentile transgressions (idolatry and sexual immorality head the list). The reconciliation passages are also to be understood as referring to the overcoming of past transgression, and the definition of man's plight in Rom. 2–3 is that he has transgressed.[65] In Rom. 5 Paul binds the two by indicating that man became a slave of sin by sinning. It is only in Rom. 6, however, that the term 'sin' consistently appears in the singular as a power which enslaves, without reference to transgression. Thus, again, there are two different ways of construing Romans. Either chapter 6 repeats the earlier chapters, but puts man's plight in Paul's own terms – in contrast to the traditional terminology of everybody

---

[65] Stendahl (*HTR* 56, 1963, p. 200) does not take Rom. 2–3 to refer to individual transgressions as such: 'The actual transgressions in Israel – as a people, not in each and every individual – show that the Jews are not better than the Gentiles. . .'

sinning and falling short of the opening chapters – or else Rom. 6 builds on Rom. 1–5: everybody transgresses, transgression puts one under the power of sin, Christ's death both provides for expiation of past transgression (Rom. 3.21–6) and for death to the power of sin (6.1–11). Our answer is that neither is precisely correct. Paul actually came to the view that all men are under the lordship of sin as a reflex of his soteriology: Christ came to provide a new lordship for those who participate in his death and resurrection. Having come to this conclusion about the power of sin, Paul could then *argue* from the common observation that everybody transgresses – an observation which would not be in dispute[66] – to *prove* that everyone is under the lordship of sin. But this is only *an argument to prove a point*, not the way he actually reached his assessment of the plight of man.

Although most speculations about what Paul thought before his conversion and call should be avoided, it seems inescapable that he could not, before the revelation of Christ, have thought that all men, Jew and Gentile alike, were enslaved to sin. Had he thought so, there would have been no reason for him to have been zealous for Judaism, for zeal will not break bondage. It was only the revelation of Christ as the saviour of all that convinced him that all men, both Jew and Gentile, were enslaved to sin. Before then, he must have distinguished between Jews, who were righteous (despite occasional transgressions), and 'Gentile sinners' (Gal. 2.15). But once he came to the conclusion that all men were enslaved to sin and could be saved only by Christ, he could then readily relate the transgressions which he must previously have supposed were atoned for by the means provided by Judaism to the all-encompassing power of sin, and in fact use the former to prove the latter. We are, then, finally in a position to understand why repentance and forgiveness and, indeed, the whole expiatory system of Judaism – about which he could not conceivably have been ignorant – play virtually no role in his thought. *They do not respond to the real plight of man.* It is true that all men sin; it is true that Gentiles especially must be cleansed of their heinous transgressions (and, by analogy, Jewish transgressors must be justified by the blood of Christ); but Paul did not come to his understanding of man's plight by analysing man's transgressions, and consequently he did not offer as the solution of man's plight the obvious solution for transgression: repentance and forgiveness. He has the opportunity to speak of man turning to God in repentance and being forgiven, but he twice – almost explicitly, it seems – rejects it. In Rom. 3.25 he writes that God 'passed over former sins' – without mentioning repentance or any of the prescribed means of atonement; and in II Cor. 5.19 he speaks of God's 'not counting their trespasses against them',

---

[66] We have frequently remarked on the ubiquity of the view that everybody sins; see the index, s.v. 'sin'. Paul's statements to this effect in Rom. 1–3 would have been readily agreed with in any Palestinian or Hellenistic synagogue.

this time on the basis of God's work in Christ. There is still no reference to man's repentance. The reason for this is that the characteristic act of Christians was to believe the gospel message that God had raised Christ and would raise those who believe, and thereafter to receive the Spirit and participate in the Spirit. All of this can take place without reference to Christians' becoming convinced of their transgressions, repenting of them and being forgiven for them. To repeat the point, Paul did accept the common Christian view that Christ's death was expiatory, just as he accepted the common Christian (and Jewish) view that everybody transgressed. But the main conviction was that the real transfer was from death to life, from the lordship of sin to the lordship of Christ. The real plight of man, as Paul learned it not from experience, nor from observation, nor from an analysis of the result of human effort, but from the conviction that Christ came to be lord of all, was that men were under a different lordship. Repentance, no matter how fervent, will not result in a change of lordships. Men's transgressions do have to be accounted for; God must overlook them or Christ must die to expiate them; but they do not *constitute* the problem. Man's problem is not being under Christ's lordship. Since this is the real problematic, the traditional language of repentance and forgiveness is almost entirely missing, the language of cleansing appears primarily in hortatory passages (I Cor. 6.9–11), and the discussion of transgression is used only rhetorically to lead to the conclusion that everybody needs Christ (Rom. 1–3).

The significance of Paul's 'omission' of repentance and forgiveness for a comparison with Judaism was discussed in section 1 of the Introduction and will be returned to in the Conclusion. The absence has been variously explained, and it is not possible to reply directly to all the explanations. One of the most probing and at the same time provocative treatments is that of John Knox in *Chapters in a Life of Paul*, pp. 141–59. Knox argued that Paul's use of justification instead of forgiveness led to his dealing inadequately with sin as transgression and consequently to his not offering a solution to guilt. Knox viewed the two conceptions of sin (as transgression and as power) as being of equal significance, but he held that the former was inadequately met in Paul's solution. A discussion made it clear that Knox had in mind Christian, not pre-Christian, sins. To the Christian who sins, God does not say 'repent and be forgiven', but 'the law is of no effect, there is no one to condemn, the case is dismissed': thus Knox understands the use of justification in Paul. Knox reasonably sees that sort of response to transgression as not meeting the real problem of human sin. I agree completely that Paul has an inadequate treatment of Christian sins – but not for the reason mentioned by Knox. There is one passage on repentance dealing with Christian sins (II Cor. 12.21), but otherwise his response to post-conversion transgression is to tell his readers not to do it, but to live according to the Spirit. He contents himself, that is, with reminding them of the significance of being in Christ. As Knox said, sin is not wrong because it is transgression of the law; it is wrong because it is inappropriate for one who is in Christ. Thus he really does *not* deal with sin as *guilt*. I do not, however, agree that the justification terminology is at fault here. The important thing to note is that 'righteousness' is primarily a *transfer term* in Paul. One who becomes a Christian is 'justified' from sins (I Cor. 6.9–11) or from the power of sin (Rom. 6.7). Paul hardly if ever applies it to the continuing life of the Christian; nor, as we have said repeatedly, does he derive ethics from it. Perhaps one should say that the theory of life in Christ does not allow Paul to account adequately for sin as guilt. Secondly, I should respond to Knox's position that the two conceptions of sin (transgression leading to guilt and power which enslaves) do not seem to me to be equipollent in Paul's thought. I have argued just above that Rom. 1–3, where sin is transgression, is a rhetorical formulation which does not fundamentally describe *what* is wrong with man: its intention is only to prove *that* man is in need of a saviour. That does not mean that Paul would deny the conception of sin as transgression; on the contrary, he employs it. But it does not seem of equal significance to him with the conception of sin as power. This helps explain why he does not have what we may regard as an adequate response to the guilt of sinful transgression.

In response to Knox's position on the absence of repentance and forgiveness in Paul, see also the contributions to the Knox *Festschrift*, *Christian History and Interpretation*, ed. W. R. Farmer and others, by P. Schubert ('Paul and the New Testament Ethic in the Thought of John Knox') and C. F. D. Moule ('Obligation in the Ethic of Paul').

Similar to the view taken here is that of Bultmann (*Theology* I, p. 287) and Bornkamm (*Paul*, p. 151): forgiveness is not used because of Paul's conception of sin as a power. Similarly on Sin as more important than sins, Whiteley, *Theology of St Paul*, p. 53. See further Stendahl, *HTR* 56, 1963, p. 202 n. 5 and the references there. Note also Mary E. Andrews, 'Paul and Repentance', *JBL* 54, 1934, p. 125: the absence of repentance, which is the foundation stone in Judaism, is not accidental. 'When he made possession of the Spirit the *sine qua non* of salvation as well as of a worthy ethical life, repentance was excluded by the simple expedient of being replaced by something more effective.' I would say not only more effective, but something which responds more to the plight of man as Paul perceived it: bondage.

Paul did not have a bifurcated mind, in one part of which he thought in terms of transgression and expiation, while in the other part thinking of sin as dominion and freedom as participation with Christ; nor did he reason to sin's dominion on the basis of an analysis of human transgression (as the reading of Rom. 1–6 might understandably suggest). He reasoned to sin's dominion as the reverse of his soteriology and Christology, and he was then easily able to work 'sinning' in – either as the *cause* of the dominion for argumentative purposes (as in Romans) *or* as the *result* of being in the flesh (Gal. 5.19–21). This very variation in considering transgression as cause or result of bondage to sin indicates that it was not his starting point.

That Paul could readily hold together the 'juristic' and the 'participatory' (or lordship) categories, and consequently the two conceptions of man's plight, is seen elsewhere than in Romans. The best known passage is II Cor. 5.14–21:

For the love of Christ controls us, because we are convinced that one has died for all; therefore all have died. And he died for all, that those who live might live no longer for themselves but for him who for their sake died and was raised.

From now on, therefore, we regard no one from a human point of view. . . . Therefore, if any one is in Christ, he is a new creation; the old has passed away, behold, the new has come. All this is from God, who through Christ reconciled us to himself and gave us the ministry of reconciliation; that is, God was in Christ reconciling the world to himself, not counting their trespasses against them, and entrusting to us the message of reconciliation. . . . For our sake he made him to be sin who knew no sin, so that in him we might become the righteousness of God.

The passage is interesting from several points of view. We see, for example, the way in which 'righteousness' does not always have the same meaning. Elsewhere Christ is called the Christians' righteousness (I Cor. 1.30), and we have already seen the variation in the term between meaning what is provisional to life and being equivalent with life. Of central interest, however, is the double meaning of the death of Christ. At the beginning of the passage just quoted, the foremost thought is participation in the death of Christ. The importance of his death is that Christians die *with* him. But this happens only because he died *for* all. The same sequence of *for* and *with* occurs in the last verse, although those prepositions are not used. In saying that God made Christ to be 'sin' or a 'sin-offering', Paul clearly has in mind Christ's death *for* us. Yet this takes place *so that in Christ* Christians might become 'the righteousness of God', whatever the precise meaning of 'righteousness' is here. Further, participation in Christ and the transfer to the new creation in v. 17 stand cheek by jowl with the discussion of reconciling and overlooking trespasses in v. 19. Thus Paul did not see any contradiction between Christ's death for transgressions and his death as providing the means by which believers could participate in a death to the power of sin, and he saw no contradiction between the reconciliation provided by God's overlooking past transgressions and the new creation provided by being 'in Christ'. It is conceivable that there is in fact here a merger of two historically different conceptions of man's plight and of the effect of Christ's death, but they did not present themselves to Paul as conceptually different.

Righteousness and participation

There should, however, be no doubt as to where the heart of Paul's theology lies. He is not primarily concerned with the juristic categories, although he works with them. The real bite of his theology lies in the participatory categories, *even though he himself did not distinguish them this way*. This can be seen by several considerations: (1) Despite the repetition of the formulas of Christ's death for us, and the fact that Paul can make non-formulaic statements to the same effect (I take the statements in II Cor. 5 to be non-formulaic), references to Christ's death as providing the occasion for participation in a death to sin and life to God are more frequent and typical, and they also appear in Paul's discussion of the sacraments and in his parenesis. (2) Paul's juristic language is 'defective', lacking a discussion of repentance and forgiveness (except for II Cor. 12.21, where repentance is indicated as the correction of transgression and forgiveness is implied; but here the terminology refers not to *soteriology*, but to maintenance of status within the body of Christ). The lack of the terminology of repentance and forgiveness has been often noted, but we should now add to this observation the lack of terminology for *guilt* in Paul. The adjective 'guilty', *enochos*, appears only in I Cor. 11.27 ('guilty of the body and blood of the Lord'), and this reinforces the point that Paul did not characteristically think in terms of sin as transgression which incurs guilt, which is removed by repentance and forgiveness. It is noteworthy that even in Rom. 1–3, where what is wrong with man is described as transgression, the conclusion is not that everybody is guilty before God, but that all are 'under sin' (3.9). It corresponds with this that the solution to man's problem is not that God forgives transgression and removes guilt, although he is said to have passed over former sins (Rom. 3.25). (3) Although Paul can say that those who transgress in certain ways will not inherit the kingdom of God (Gal. 5.21; cf. I Cor. 6.9), and although it appears at the beginning of I Cor. 6.12–20 and 10.6–14 that he is going to argue that those who *transgress* by committing sexual immorality or idolatry are excluded from the kingdom, the actual development of the argument in both cases is different. It is not the transgressions *qua* transgressions which exclude one (as a punishment for them), but the fact that they *establish unions* which are not compatible with union with Christ. (4) Paul's 'juristic' language is sometimes pressed into the service of 'participationist' categories, but never vice versa. Thus we have already noted that the verb *dikaiomai*, which in I Cor. 6.11 means 'acquitted' (parallel to 'washed' and 'sanctified'), is used in Rom. 6.7 as a parallel to 'set free' in the context of a discussion of death *with* Christ as setting one free from the power of sin. In Rom. 6 the general context of participation in Christ's death so that one may participate in life determines the meaning of *dikaoumai*. It *cannot* mean 'justified' in the sense of I Cor. 6.9–11, where one is justified from sin*s*. Thus the usually juristic *dikaoumai* does not determine the meaning of Rom. 6.7, but is rather pressed into the service of another conception. Paul says both that one 'dies to' sin (Rom. 6.11) and 'is justified' from sin (6.7). There is no doubt in Rom. 6 that the 'dies to' terminology better expresses his real meaning. In a similar way we have noted that *dikaiosynē*, which often means the righteousness which *leads to* life, can become simply the equivalent of 'life' (e.g. Gal. 3.21). Here again *dikaiosynē* does not determine the meaning of such passages, but is determined by them.

The normally juristic, forensic or ethical language of righteousness is forced to bear the meaning of 'life by participation in the body of Christ'. But this reversal of meaning never works the other way around.

It will be profitable here to consider two lengthy quotations in which the terminology is mixed – or at least appears mixed once we make the distinction:

Though I myself have reason for confidence in the flesh also. If any other man thinks he has reason for confidence in the flesh, I have more: . . . as to righteousness under the law blameless. But whatever gain I had, I counted as loss for the sake of Christ. Indeed I count everything as loss because of the surpassing worth of knowing Christ Jesus my Lord. For his sake I have suffered the loss of all things, and count them as refuse, in order that I may gain Christ and be found in him, not having a righteousness of my own, based on law, but that which is through faith in Christ, the righteousness from God that depends on faith; that I may know him and the power of his resurrection, and may share his sufferings, becoming like him in his death, that if possible I may attain the resurrection from the dead.

Not that I have already obtained this or am already perfect; but I press on to make it my own, because Christ Jesus has made me his own. (Phil. 3.4–12)

But now that faith has come, we are no longer under a custodian; for in Christ Jesus you are all sons of God, through faith. For as many of you as were baptized into Christ have put on Christ. There is neither slave nor free, there is neither male nor female; for you are all one in Christ Jesus. And if you are Christ's then you are Abraham's offspring, heirs according to promise. (Gal. 3.25–29)

There are several things to be observed about these passages, and we shall resort to enumeration:

1. The verses in Galatians are in some sense the conclusion to the argument about whether *righteousness* comes by law or by faith (although the discussion of slavery and sonship continues into chapter 4). But in this clinching, concluding argument, the term righteousness drops out. What is received by faith is 'sonship', and sonship 'in Christ Jesus'. The language immediately becomes completely 'participationist': baptized into, put on, all one person, Christ's. In a similar way in Gal. 2 Paul had clinched the argument about righteousness by faith with participationist language: 'I have been crucified with Christ; it is no longer I who live, but Christ who lives in me . . .' (2.20).

2. In the Philippians passage we do have the righteousness/faith correspondence which many feel is the heart of Paul's theology, but here that correspondence hardly determines the meaning of the passage. The Christian righteousness (i.e. that which comes by faith, not by works of law) is given to one who is 'found in him' (Christ). It does not appear in this passage, as it does in the sequence of chapters in Romans, that righteousness is a preliminary status having to do with the overcoming of past transgressions, a

status which *leads to* or *makes possible* 'life in Christ Jesus'. Rather, the two terms, being found in him and having the righteousness which is based on faith, simply stand together. Further, in standing together, it is evidently the participationist terms of being found in Christ, sharing his sufferings and death (and consequently sharing eventually in his resurrection) and belonging to Christ which determine the whole thrust and point of the passage. The concern is not with 'righteousness' as a goal in itself, nor is righteousness treated as a necessary preliminary to being in Christ. The righteousness terminology enters because of the discussion of the attacks of Jews and their apparent charge that they and not the Christians are 'the true circumcision' (Phil 3.3). The soteriology of the passage – being found in Christ, suffering and dying with him and attaining the resurrection – could have been written without the term 'righteousness' at all. But it is inconceivable that the reverse could be true – that we would have any true conception of Paul's soteriology had he limited his discussion to righteousness and not described how one attains the resurrection: by dying and rising with Christ.

3. We further see in the Philippians passage, and this is the only point at which this does become clear, that *Paul himself was aware of his own shift in the meaning of the term righteousness.* There *is a* righteousness which is based on works of law. Here Paul does not, as he does in Galatians and Romans, simply deny that there is any such thing. In Philippians, rather, he argues, in effect, that the righteousness based on works of law is not *true* righteousness or the right kind of righteousness. Just as circumcision of the foreskin of the penis does not, in Paul's definition, constitute true circumcision – since only Christians are the true circumcision – so also righteousness based on law is *not the right kind*. The only proper righteousness is Christian righteousness, which must be based on something else. Since the characteristic act of the Christian is belief in the God who raised Christ and made him Lord, the true or Christian righteousness is based on faith. I believe that it is in this light that we should consider all those passages in Galatians and Romans to the effect that righteousness cannot come by works of law: it is the right kind of righteousness that cannot come by works of law, and the reason for this is that it comes only by faith in Christ. The *definition* of this righteousness, as we have seen, varies. It may be presented as preliminary to life or as equivalent to life. The point is that *any true religious goal*, in Paul's view, can come only through Christ. He is rather unparticular about terminology. If the Corinthians want wisdom, he asserts that Christ is the wisdom of God and that only Christians can attain true wisdom (I Cor. 1–2). If the Jews and Judaizers want righteousness, he asserts that true righteousness comes only through Christ. It would be as erroneous to define Paul's own soteriological goal by the term 'righteous-

ness', which he employs in debates with Jews and Judaizers, as it would be to define it by the term 'wisdom'. He finds neither terminology difficult or alien, but research into the history of these and other terms will not reveal how Paul defined the goal of religion. He tells us that over and over again: the goal of religion is 'to be found in Christ' and to attain, by suffering and dying with him, the resurrection.

This means, as we said above, that we must give up the view that 'right-eousness' in Paul has strictly the same 'forensic-eschatological' meaning which it is supposed to have in Judaism.[67] The righteous man in Judaism is actually the man who is properly religious, who obeys the law and repents of transgression. Paul accepts only the heuristic definition: it is a term which can be employed for being 'properly religious'. When he denies that righteousness – i.e. *true* righteousness – can come by the law, he cannot be denying that *Jewish* righteousness comes by the law; for that righteousness is *defined* as being Torah obedience, as Paul knows perfectly well (Phil. 3.9). He is rather denying that the *true goal of religion* comes by the law. And the reason for this is, to make the point again, that it comes only through Christ. Paul does not know this on the basis of his analysis of human exist-ence, but on the basis of his experience of the power of Christ's resurrection.

This means, further, that righteousness by faith and participation in Christ ultimately amount to the same thing.[68] Paul sometimes speaks of righteous-ness as the preliminary juristic status which leads to life in Christ. Had Paul been a systematic theologian, compelled to work both sets of terminology into a coherent and logical whole, he might well have chosen this solution. Scholars have understandably concluded on the basis of Romans that he did choose it.[69] But there are weighty arguments against seeing righteous-ness as the gateway to life: (1) The very fact that the verb *dikaioumai* appears in Rom. 6.7 as the equivalent of 'set free' from the power of sin by participa-tion in Christ's death should caution against such a conclusion. (2) In Paul's other letters, righteousness by faith, the Spirit by faith or sonship by faith mix indiscriminately with participationist language in such a way as to

[67] Bultmann, *Theology* I, pp. 270–3; Conzelmann, *Theology*, pp. 216–18.

[68] Similarly E. Schweizer, 'Dying and Rising with Christ', *NTS* 14, 1967, pp. 1–14; Pfleiderer, *Primitive Christianity* I, pp. 347–51: faith results in being in Christ (not just in acquittal, uprightness or imputed righteousness).

Recently to the contrary is the argument by Via ('Justification and Deliverance', *SR* 1, 1971, pp. 204–12). Via sees that the two soteriological terms overlap, but he insists that Paul's 'dominant tendency' was to distinguish justification (which he understands to mean simply acquittal) from deliverance (freedom from the power of sin). The difference between his view and that taken here is principally the result of a different evaluation of two passages. Via understands Rom. 5.1 as giving Paul's systematic thought and Gal. 3.24–27 as being an instance in which Paul 'uses language inexactly and simply juxtaposes the two in an unclear way' (p. 205). I regard Gal. 3.24–27 (for example) as reflecting better the way Paul thought and Rom. 5.1 as being an unusually schematic presentation which he does not systematically maintain.

[69] See, for example, Bornkamm, *Paul*, p. 153; Conzelmann, *Theology*, p. 273; Lyonnet, 'Pauline Soteriology', p. 840; Via (preceding note).

exclude the possibility of a systematic working out of righteousness as the forensic preliminary to life in Christ Jesus. (3) We should reiterate that righteousness is sometimes future rather than past (Rom. 2.13; Gal. 5.5). (4) Paul's thought does not seem actually to have run from transgression to justification (= acquittal) to life (despite the organization of Rom. 1-6), but from Christ as Lord to human bondage under another lord, sin, to individual trangressions as proof of that bondage. Thus the *first* thing is the transfer of lordships, which *involves* acquittal for transgressions. The latter is not preliminary to the former. (5) There is a final proof against the view that righteousness is preliminary: Paul speaks of Christ's death both as expiating sins and as providing for participation in the death to the power of sin. If the juristic status of being justified *preceded* the life in the Spirit described in Rom. 8, one would have to suppose that Christ's death, as it were, applied twice: once as the expiatory sacrifice which achieves for the believer acquittal for past transgressions and the preliminary status of righteousness, and once as the event by participating in which the believer receives life in the Spirit. This is a clearly impossible supposition, and means that the view that Paul systematically related righteousness to life in the Spirit as the forensic doorway to the full Christian life breaks down.

We cannot, on the other hand, think that Paul was conscious of any bifurcation in his own thinking. Christ's death was for acquittal and to provide participation in his death to the power of sin, and these are conceived not as two different things, but as one. Once we make the distinction between juristic and participationist categories, however, there is no doubt that the latter tell us more about the way Paul 'really' thought. One dies with Christ to the power of sin and lives in the Spirit, *which also concretely means* that one stops (and is acquitted of) sinning and produces the fruit of the Spirit. But we cannot understand Paul's thought the other way around: that one is forgiven for transgressions and thereby begins to participate in the life of the Spirit. This is why, as we said above, repentance and forgiveness are not substantial themes in Paul's writings: he did not begin with the problem to which they are a solution, namely, sin as transgression, but rather with the reality of the new life offered by Christ, which was first of all seen as accomplishing the beginning of the transfer of aeons, and not primarily as the accomplishment of atonement.

It should now be clear why I wrote above that the righteousness by faith terminology is not the most appropriate for grasping the essentials of Paul's thought, but that the dispute is in part a dispute about terms.[70] It seems necessary to follow Paul's own procedure and to define righteousness by faith by the other categories, those which we have called 'participatory'. Analysis of the history of 'righteousness' is not as revealing for understanding

[70] P. 438 above.

Paul as one might expect, since the term takes on the meaning, finally, of dying and rising with Christ and being one with him. It seems confusing to follow Käsemann's procedure of insisting that righteousness by faith is central but then to define it as a cosmic and corporate act.[71] Paul also had other terms for the cosmic and corporate significance of God's action in Christ, and terms which seem better to reflect that significance, such as dying and living with Christ, all being one in Christ, awaiting the full establishment of Christ's lordship, and the like. I agree with Käsemann that Paul's soteriology is basically cosmic and corporate or participatory. I do not agree that this is best expressed by the term 'righteousness', even though Paul himself sometimes used the term in this way.[72] It is precisely because he pressed the term into meanings which it does not easily bear that the exegesis of what he wrote has always been so difficult and confusing.

We thus conclude the consideration of what must be considered *the* problem of Pauline exegesis: the relationship among the various soteriological terms. We had first to present an overview of Paul's principal soteriological statements (section 3), in order to see the range and variety of terms and to begin where Paul began. We had then to consider Paul's view of the law, which led to a further consideration of the righteousness terminology; for it is especially addressed to the claims of the law. The inter-relationships of the various soteriological terms, however, could be seen only after noting Paul's description of man's plight. *Terminologically* the two main sets of soteriological terms, the 'juristic' and the 'participatory', respond to the two conceptions of man's plight, transgression and bondage. But *materially*, the two conceptions of man's plight go together – they are different ways of saying that man apart from Christ is condemned – and thus the two main sets of soteriological terms also go together. The more appropriate set is the participatory, as we have argued in this sub-section.

The varying definitions of man's plight

It is not my intention to enter into a detailed discussion of what Paul means by 'the flesh' and other similar terms, for I consider that they have been sufficiently treated elsewhere. Here we should only observe that Paul has a rich and well-developed conceptualization of man's plight. Although it was not the beginning point of his thought, he obviously reflected deeply on

---

[71] Above, p. 438 n. 41. Note Kümmel's statement that 'the doctrine of justification represents the basic and most highly personal form of expression of the Pauline message of God's eschatological saving action' (*Theology*, p. 195). If we have understood Paul correctly, the most personal (in the sense of related to the individual) cannot be the basic expression of Paul's thought.

[72] The question of what terminology best expresses Paul's thought has resulted in the effort to identify a one-verse summary of Paul's theology. I am inclined to agree with Robinson (*The Body*, p. 49) that it is Rom. 7.4 rather than Rom. 1.16f. (Conzelmann, *Theology*, p. 200 and many others) or Rom. 5.1 (Hunter, *Interpreting Paul's Gospel*, p. 22; slightly modified in *The Gospel According to St Paul*, p. 15).

man's plight in the light of the coming of Christ. We have been dealing with the basic distinction between the plight as transgression and as bondage to sin, and we have seen how they went together in Paul's own view. Paul had numerous ways of expressing the fact that everybody was in need of the salvation offered in Christ – whether because everybody transgressed, because all were under the power of sin, because all had been given over to their own lusts, all were under the condemnation of the law, all were under the fundamental spirits of the universe, all were 'in the flesh' and possibly others – but the point of real coherence is precisely that everybody had a plight from which only Christ could save him.[73] In Christ one is given sonship instead of slavery under the fundamental spirits of the universe, one is no longer condemned by the law, one is no longer 'in the flesh'. The very variety of conceptual terms helps us to see the centrality of the solution.

Since the coming of Christ, the basic distinction is between those who believe and those who do not believe. Just as 'believer' is one of Paul's two most characteristic terms for the Christian (the other is 'saint'), 'unbeliever', *apistos*, is one of the characteristic terms for the non-Christian. 'Believer' and 'unbeliever' play approximately the same role in Paul as do the terms 'righteous' and 'wicked' in most of Palestinian Jewish literature (and the latter term is occasionally used by Paul: 1 Cor. 6.1,9). Paul was not content, however, with merely these broad categories – all men are condemned and enslaved apart from Christ; since the coming of Christ men are either believers or unbelievers – but analysed *what it is* about man apart from Christ that is all wrong. It is this analysis which is one of the main reasons why Paul may be said to be a *theologian*; his analysis of the human predicament (anthropology) is his principal contribution to theological thought. From him we learn nothing new or remarkable about God. God is a God of wrath and mercy, who seeks to save rather than to condemn, but rejection of whom leads to death. One could, to be sure, list further statements made by Paul about God, but it is clear that Paul did not spend his time reflecting on the nature of the deity. His penetrating observations have to do with how it is that the man who does not have faith in Christ is not only lost in a formal and external sense – handed over to destruction – but is even lost to himself, being unable to achieve the goal which he so ardently desires. For that which is desired – life – can be received only as a gift, so that the effort to attain it is self-defeating.

The force and pathos of the human dilemma as seen by Paul, which is only pointed to at the end of the preceding paragraph, has been so powerful that it has arrested the attention of numerous Pauline exegetes. They have understandably considered it to be not only the main original contribution of Paul to theology, but the major element in Paul's own thinking and the

[73] See n. 2 above.

place at which to begin the analysis of his thought. I fully agree with Bultmann that Paul's theology is best expressed in his anthropology[74] in the
sense in which I described their relationship in the last paragraph. In
comparison with his analysis of the human plight, Paul's statements
directly about God are only a collection of standard opinions. I cannot,
however, agree that Paul *started* from an analysis of the human situation
as so desperate as to require a universal saviour or that Paul's thought can
be properly understood by choosing man's plight as the starting point.
It must be seen as the reflex of his soteriology; and Paul's soteriology is *not*
that a man is brought back to his true self (as Bultmann concludes on the
basis of his analysis of Paul's penetrating view of man's plight as involving,
among other things, self-estrangement),[75] but that one who believes in
Christ and the God who raised him from the dead belongs to Christ,
becomes a member of his body and will be completely transformed at the
eschaton.

Besides this essential disagreement with Bultmann's description of Paul's
view of man prior to faith, one could now also object to some other elements
of Bultmann's description, especially the consistent transformation of
Paul's categories into those of existentialism, which now seem somewhat
shopworn. To a large degree, these latter elements (though not the major
premise of beginning with man's plight) have been corrected by Bornkamm
and Conzelmann, and Käsemann in particular has corrected Bultmann's
over-emphasis of individualism.[76] Having noted my objections to the
analysis of Paul's anthropology by Bultmann and by his students – above all
the role which it is given in the total scheme – I must now say that otherwise
I do not think that it can be improved upon. For this reason I shall not repeat
what can readily be read there. The analysis of the existential aspects of
faith as accepting the gratuity of salvation, in distinction to human self-
assertion, whether in terms of wisdom or righteousness by the law,[77]
have never been more penetratingly described than by Bultmann, and I

---

[74] Bultmann, *Theology* I, p. 191.

[75] Bultmann, *Theology* I: man is 'no longer at one with himself' (p. 249). The solution to this problem
is obviously the offer of 'the new possibility of genuine, human life' (p. 336).

[76] See Käsemann, 'The Cry for Liberty in the Worship of the Church', *Perspectives*, p. 126; 'On
Paul's Anthropology', ibid., pp. 1–31. Some of the details of Bultmann's word studies on Paul's anthro-
pological terms have also been questioned. See e.g. Käsemann, 'Primitive Christian Apocalyptic',
Questions, p. 135; 'The Motif of the Body of Christ', *Perspectives*, p. 114 (both on *sōma*); Conzelmann,
Theology, pp. 173f. (on *sarx*).

[77] It has been correctly observed that the common denominator of Paul's objection to human wisdom
(I Corinthians) and righteousness by the law (Romans and Galatians) is that both involve 'boasting'. See
Conzelmann, *Theology*, p. 237, citing I Cor. 1.29 and Rom. 3.27. I would only observe that the objection
to boasting is part of Paul's analysis of the existential plight of man, and that this analysis in its entirety
is the result of Paul's soteriology rather than the basis of it. Thus soteriology does not consist in reversing
boasting, but in gaining the resurrection. Put another way: in I Corinthians the answer to boasting is not
righteousness by faith, but Jesus Christ crucified, the end of the age, the gift of the Spirit and life in
Christ. Against defining man's plight as being primarily his boasting, see also Stendahl, *HTR* 56, 1963,
p. 207.

close this discussion of man's plight by referring the reader to the work of
Bultmann and his students.

Addendum: Plight and soteriology in Paul according to S. Lyonnet

Instead of dealing with Lyonnet's view of sin and salvation in Paul piecemeal in the footnotes, it seems useful to give a short critique separately.
Lyonnet's many solid contributions to Pauline studies cannot be done justice
to here, where no more than a brief *Auseinandersetzung* on Paul's soteriology
is intended. We shall mention his view of man's sin, Christ's death and the
nature of salvation.[78]
   Although Lyonnet states that sin is a 'power' for Paul,[79] he still regards it
exclusively in terms of something committed by man in 'turning away from
God'.[80] Lyonnet never reconciles these notions, and consequently he does
not give a clear picture of man's plight. Rather, his description of man's
plight basically accords with the view that sin is transgression, from which
man must *return*.[81] He partially underplays and partially overlooks the
picture of man as in bondage to the law, the 'elemental spirits' and sin.
Thus salvation as liberation takes a secondary place to salvation as expiation
and 'returning'. Although Lyonnet does quote the passages on participating
in Christ's death from Rom. 6,[82] he does not seem to note other passages
which take the *purpose* of Christ's death to be that Christians may participate
in it, *not* that their sins may be atoned for (e.g. II Cor. 5.14f.; I Thess.
5.10). The death of Christ is called sacrificial and expiatory throughout.[83]
Thus basically sin and salvation are conceived nomistically: as transgression,
expiation and returning.

5. Covenantal nomism in Paul

Davies, it will be recalled, argued that Paul's theology is, in effect, to be
understood according to the Jewish pattern of covenantal nomism. There is
a new exodus ('redemption', 'being set free') which leads to a new covenant,
which entails a new Torah, to which obedience is required.[1] The weakest

---

[78] I shall deal here with his systematic treatment, 'Pauline Soteriology', in *Introduction to the New Testament*, ed. Robert and Feuillet, pp. 820–65.
[79] 'The force which sets man in opposition to God', ibid., p. 856; 'personified power', p. 862.
[80] Ibid., p. 865.
[81] Ibid., pp. 845, 851, 859–61.
[82] Ibid., p. 861.
[83] Ibid., pp. 845–63.

---

[1] Above, section 1 of the Introduction. See Davies, *Paul and Rabbinic Judaism*, pp. 216f.; 225; 250;
259f. ('Paul carried over into his interpretation of the Christian Dispensation the covenantal conceptions
of Judaism'); 323. Similarly Robinson, *The Body*, p. 72: the church is a covenant entered by baptism;

point in this series seems to me to be the first. I am not persuaded that in using the terms 'set free' and 'redemption' Paul was thinking of the exodus or describing life in the Spirit as resulting from a new exodus.[2] The term 'set free' seems rather to be connected with the change of aeons (from the old creation to the new creation), the change of lordship from the service of sin to the service of Christ (Paul's understanding of sin here is not reminiscent of the Israelites' bondage under Pharaoh), and the transformation of Christians, beginning in the present, from one stage of glory to the next. The last point in particular, which is crucial for Paul's understanding of redemption (the redemption of our bodies from corruption), does not derive from the exodus typology. In fact, the one time that Paul does discuss the wandering of Israel in the desert, it is not the exodus as such which is being pointed to, but eating and drinking as constituting participation (I Cor. 10).[3] We may further observe that while Paul may contrast *himself* with Moses, as the minister of the dispensation of life rather than the minister of the dispensation of death,[4] he does not compare Christ with Moses as the liberator of the elect. Moses is rather the representative of the law which bound everyone over to condemnation, not the liberator. Christ is called the second Adam, but not the new Moses. Further, participation in Christ, which Davies takes to be the central soteriological formulation, is not really contrasted with being 'in Israel', as Davies maintains[5] (despite the reference to 'the Israel of God' in Gal. 6.16), but is parallel with being 'in the Spirit', which is the opposite of being 'in the flesh' or 'under sin'. The primary antithesis, then, is not 'new Israel' versus 'old Israel' or 'Israel according to the flesh' (I Cor. 10.18).

When Davies writes that Paul was the herald 'not of a new mystery but of a new Exodus',[6] one must agree with the negative assertion, but not necessarily with the positive one. Davies's argument is that the Hellenistic theory does not account for the corporate aspects of Paul's thought, since the Hellenistic mystery religions (as far as we know) were concerned only with individual salvation. He wishes by contrast to derive Paul's conception of corporate participation from the corporateness involved in the idea of the covenant. But one must also observe that there is nothing in the exodus

---

Whiteley, *Theology of St Paul*, pp. 75f.: Paul thought in covenantal terms and his theology depends on them; van Unnik, 'La conception paulinienne de la nouvelle alliance', *Littérature et théologie pauliniennes* by A. Descamps et al., pp. 109–26. Of the contrary opinion was H. A. A. Kennedy, 'The Significance and Range of the Covenant-Conception in the New Testament', *The Expositor* 10, 1915, pp. 385–410: Paul focused on the notion of promise, but otherwise the covenant conception plays no role.

[2] Davies, op. cit., pp. 102–8. Whiteley notes the use in the LXX of *lutrousthai* in connection with the redemption from Egypt, but also as redemption from sin and death (*Theology of St Paul*, p. 142). The latter point seems more germane to Paul's thought.

[3] Contrast Davies, op. cit., p. 105.

[4] II Cor. 3.7–13. Cf. Munck, *Paul*, pp. 58–61.

[5] Davies, *Paul and Rabbinic Judaism*, pp. 85f., 102; *Invitation to the New Testament*, p. 349.

[6] *Paul and Rabbinic Judaism*, p. 108.

typology which would account for dying and rising with Christ and a union which forms one body, in which all, both Jews and Greeks, are one person. The appeal here to 'Israelite conceptions of personality and community' is not persuasive.[7] The Israelites were members of a group which God might collectively punish or reward, but passing through the waters of the Reed Sea did not make them members of one *body*. Further, ethics are not derived from anything which could be considered a new exodus, as they would have to be if the exodus-Torah analogy is to hold. Just as we earlier argued that Paul does not connect ethics with justification by faith, we must now observe that they are not connected with the references to a new covenant.[8] Ethics are connected above all to receiving the Spirit. Thus the exodus typology does not seem to have determined Paul's thinking.

Having made this caveat, we must grant that there is a good deal to be said for the view that Christianity is a new covenant which, once established (though not established by a new exodus), does function somewhat as does the old: for those in it there is salvation; for those outside condemnation and death, while remaining in it requires obedience, and disobedience leads to expulsion and condemnation. Further, Paul does once indicate that, for those who are *in* but who disobey, *repentance* is the required remedy of disobedience (II Cor. 12.21). What is to be obeyed may be presented as a word of the Lord or as the apostle's instructions; it is not a written code. Further, Paul considers that what constitutes proper behaviour is self-evident (cf. Gal. 5.19; Rom. 2.14f.). One may observe that the self-evident proper behaviour, the fruit of the Spirit, coincides materially with the ethical elements of the Old Testament.[9] That is, Paul seems *de facto* to accept the Jewish 'commandments between man and man', although he does not accept them by virtue of their being commandments.[10]

Thus one can see already in Paul how it is that Christianity is going to become a new form of covenantal nomism, a covenantal religion which one enters by baptism, membership in which provides salvation, which has a specific set of commandments, obedience to which (or repentance for the transgression of which) keeps one in the covenantal relationship, while repeated or heinous transgression removes one from membership.

On the other hand, we must note the inadequacy of the covenantal categories for understanding Paul. Although at one point he does view heinous immorality coupled with defiance of him as transgression which must be repented of if the offending member is to remain in the body of Christ, it seems more germane and natural to his thought when he grounds

---

[7] Ibid., p. 109.
[8] See ibid., pp. 250f.
[9] Cf. Bultmann, *Theology* I, p. 261.
[10] Cf. Bammel, 'Paul and Judaism', p. 282: 'Paul's ethics are indeed eschatological but as to their contents they are nothing special.'

his admonitions not on the threat of expulsion for unrepentant transgression, but on the fact that certain acts constitute a union which is mutually exclusive with the union with Christ (I Cor. 10.1–5). The fault of eating and drinking with idols and of fornication is not their character as transgression against the will of God (although Paul could have quoted the Bible to show that they are transgressions), nor their character as transgressions of the apostle's ordinances, but their result in forming a union which is antithetical to the union with Christ. This argument is not typical of covenantal nomism as we know it from Judaism.

Further, although Paul uses the term 'new covenant' to describe the community established by Christ's death, here doubtless following traditional Christian terminology (I Cor. 11.25; II Cor. 3.6), he can also speak of 'new creation' (II Cor. 5.17; Gal. 6.15).[11] What Christ has done is not, as we said just above, contrasted with what Moses did, but with what Adam did. Adam did not establish a covenant, but his transgression did determine the entire fate of mankind; and so has Christ's act determined the fate of the world. Here again we see the covenantal categories transcended.

But the primary reason for which it is inadequate to depict Paul's religion as a new covenantal nomism is that that term does not take account of his participationist transfer terms, which are the most significant terms for understanding his soteriology. The covenantal conception could readily encompass the discussion of Christ's dying for past transgression, but it is not adequate to take into account the believer's dying with Christ and thus to the old aeon and the power of sin. The heart of Paul's thought is not that one ratifies and agrees to a covenant offered by God, becoming a member of a group with a covenantal relation with God and remaining in it on the condition of proper behaviour; but that one dies with Christ, obtaining new life and the initial transformation which leads to the resurrection and ultimate transformation, that one is a member of the body of Christ and one Spirit with him, and that one remains so unless one breaks the participatory union by forming another.

Another way of responding to Davies's view is to argue that Paul's principal conviction was not that Jesus *as the Messiah* had come,[12] but that God had appointed Jesus Christ *as Lord* and that he would resurrect or transform those who were members of him by virtue of believing in him. Thus the conclusions which, in the view of Davies and many others, Paul must have drawn from the fact that Jesus was the Messiah, he need not and seems not to have drawn. It seems to me to be useless to speculate on what form of messianic hope was known to Paul (on the basis of an analysis of Jewish

[11] Käsemann (' "The Righteousness of God" in Paul', *Questions*, pp. 177f.) also opposes the covenantal interpretation of Paul on this ground.
[12] Davies, *Paul and Rabbinic Judaism*, p. 352; Whiteley, *Theology of St Paul*, pp. 124, 126. Against this view, see Conzelmann, *Theology*, p. 199.

apocalypses and other material) and to work out his theology by applying his hypothetical preconceived messianic theory to the fact that Jesus was the Messiah.[13] Paul repeatedly tells us what his dominating conviction was: that the end is at hand, that Christ is Lord and that only those who belong to the Lord will be saved on the Day of the Lord. This may be perceived as being only marginally different from the way Davies would state Paul's prime conviction. But the entire preceding chapter has shown how beginning with this starting point has led us to work out Paul's theology along lines different from those of Davies, just as the choice of starting point accounts for the differences between this description of Paul and those of Bultmann and others.

6. Judgment by works and salvation by grace

There are numerous other aspects of Paul's thought which a full theological treatment would take into consideration, but we have now dealt with the elements which are essential for our comparison. We can hardly conclude a discussion of Paul and Judaism, however, without taking some account of his statements to the effect that judgment is according to works.[1] The principal passages are these:

All who have sinned without the law will also perish without the law, and all who have sinned under the law will be judged by the law. For it is not the hearers of the law who are righteous before God, but the doers of the law who will be justified. When Gentiles who have not the law do by nature what the law requires, they are a law to themselves, even though they do not have the law. They show that what the law requires is written on their hearts, while their conscience also bears witness and their conflicting thoughts accuse or perhaps excuse them on that day when, according to my gospel, God judges the secrets of men by Christ Jesus. (Rom. 2.12–16)

We are of good courage, and we would rather be away from the body and at home with the Lord. So whether we are at home or away, we make it our aim to please him. For we must all appear before the judgment seat of Christ, so that each one may receive good or evil, according to what he has done in the body. (II Cor. 5.8–10)

---

[13] This argument applies more to Schweitzer's view than to Davies's, for Schweitzer applied a preconceived notion of Jewish apocalypticism very mechanically to Paul, while Davies allows Paul to speak more for himself. Davies nevertheless argues that certain consequences must have followed Paul's conviction that Jesus was the Messiah: thus *Paul and Rabbinic Judaism*, p. 216. Paul was more concerned with the parousia of Jesus as *Lord*. Against defining Paul in terms of pre-existing categories (in reply to Schoeps), see also Bammel, 'Paul and Judaism', *The Modern Churchman* n.s. 6, 1962–3, p. 281.

[1] The topic is the subject of several recent monographs. Most recently, see Calvin Roetzel, *Judgement in the Community*, 1972; Ernst Synofzik, *Die Gerichts- und Vergeltungsaussagen bei Paulus*, 1972.

According to the commission of God given to me, like a skilled master builder I laid a foundation, and another man is building upon it. Let each man take care how he build upon it. For no other foundation can anyone lay than that which is laid, which is Jesus Christ. Now if any one builds on the foundation with gold, silver, precious stones, wood, hay, stubble – each man's work will become manifest; for the Day will disclose it, because it will be revealed with fire, and the fire will test what sort of work each one has done. If the work which any man has built on the foundation survives, he will receive a reward. If any man's work is burned up, he will suffer loss, though he himself be saved, but only as through fire. (I Cor. 3.10–15)

For any one who eats and drinks without discerning the body eats and drinks judgment upon himself. That is why many of you are weak and ill, and some have died. But if we judged ourselves truly, we should not be judged. But when we are judged by the Lord, we are chastened so that we may not be condemned along with the world. (I Cor. 11.29–32)

If there is any passage in Paul that is aberrant, it is Rom. 2.12–16, but not because it mentions judgment on the basis of works. The curiosity is rather that it mentions *righteousness* by works, which Paul otherwise insists must be by faith and not by works. The solution to this difficulty seems to reside in the future tense of the verb, *will* be justified. This actually shows to what degree the theme of righteousness is not a theme with a single definition in Paul. When the question concerns righteousness as the goal of religion, Paul insists that Christians *have been* justified by faith in Christ. In the context of Rom. 2, however, Paul is arguing that Jews and Gentiles stand on an equal footing before God. This applies even to the day of judgment, when those, whether Jews or Gentiles, who have in fact sinned will be punished (as the result of the accusation of their deeds), while those who have not will escape punishment (be excused or 'justified'). Righteousness or being justified here has to do with whether or not one is punished on the day of judgment, and the term has here that forensic/eschatological meaning which Bultmann thinks it characteristically has. Once we see that here the righteousness terminology refers to the question of *punishment*, and not to whether or not one is *saved* (which is its more usual meaning in Paul), the difficulty vanishes; for Paul elsewhere mentions punishment according to deeds.

The distinction between being saved (by God's grace) and judged according to deeds, being rewarded for good deeds and punished for bad, is perfectly clear in the three passages from Corinthians. In I Cor. 3.10–15, Paul explicitly distinguishes between being saved and being punished or rewarded, referring to the work of himself and another apostle. 'Not discerning the body' in I Cor. 11.29 leads to the punishment of sickness or death, but this punishment *prevents* condemnation, in accordance with the

traditional Jewish view. When in II Cor. 5.8–10 Paul says that 'we' will be
punished or rewarded for deeds, the plural first person is probably not just
rhetorical; for Paul expected to be judged according to his work as an
apostle. No one could be surer than Paul of his own salvation. He knew that
if he died he would be with Christ (II Cor. 5.8; Phil. 1.23). Yet he hesitated
to pronounce judgment on his own work. He would not be so bold as to
decide whether he would be held completely innocent before God:

Moreover it is required of stewards that they be found trustworthy. But with me it
is a very small thing that I should be judged by you or by any human court. I
do not even judge myself. I am not aware of anything against myself, but I am not
thereby acquitted (*dedikaiōmai*). It is the Lord who judges. Therefore do not
pronounce judgment before the time, before the Lord comes, who will bring to
light the things now hidden in darkness and will disclose the purposes of the heart.
Then every man will receive his commendation from God. (I Cor. 4.2–5)

Thus Paul's assurance of salvation was not assurance that his work was
perfect nor that at the judgment nothing would be revealed against him
for which he could be punished. In all of this, Paul's view is typically Jewish.
As we saw above, the distinction between being *judged on the basis of deeds*
and punished or rewarded at the judgment (or in this life), on the one hand,
and being *saved by God's gracious election*, on the other, was the general view
in Rabbinic literature.[2] It is a very straightforward distinction, and it should
occasion no surprise when it meets us in Paul. Salvation by grace is not
incompatible with punishment and reward for deeds.[3]
     It agrees with this that in Paul, as in Jewish literature, good deeds are the
condition of remaining 'in', but they do not *earn* salvation. Thus Rom. 11.22:

Note then the kindness and the severity of God: severity towards those who have
fallen, but God's kindness to you, *provided you continue* in his kindness; otherwise
you too will be cut off.

Even clearer is I Cor. 6.9f.:

Do you not know that the unrighteous will not inherit the kingdom of God? Do
not be deceived; neither the immoral, nor idolaters, nor adulterers, nor homosexuals, nor thieves, nor the greedy, nor drunkards, nor revilers, nor robbers will
inherit the kingdom of God.

To the same effect is Gal. 5.21: 'I warn you, as I warned you before, that
those who do such things shall not inherit the kingdom of God.' Paul did
not mean that not sinning in the specified ways, but behaving correctly,
would earn salvation, just as the Rabbis and other Jewish authors whom we

---

[2] Chapter I, sections 6 and 7 above.
[3] Cf. Munck, *Paul*, p. 151. Whiteley (*Theology of St Paul*, p. 47) grants guilt some place in Paul's
thought, but denies to him the concept of merit entirely. What of reward and punishment in I Cor.
3.10–15?

studied did not mean that obedience earned salvation; but wilful or heinous disobedience would exclude one from salvation.[4] On both these points – punishment for transgression and reward for obedience as required by God's justice, but *not* as constituting soteriology, and correct behaviour as the condition of remaining 'in'[5] – Paul is in perfect agreement with what we found in Jewish literature.[6]

7. Coherence, relevance and sources

In taking the position that Paul was a coherent, but not systematic, thinker, we are taking the position most common among exegetes, and it needs little defence.[1] That Paul was a thinker is readily seen in the way he tried to work out solutions to problems by re-thinking the Christian tradition. This can be seen most clearly in the Corinthian correspondence, where Paul dealt with a succession of problems. He never simply answers with a formula or with a biblical quotation, although he makes use of both. Both are re-thought and applied to the particular question in what is probably a unique way. At any rate, it is a way which shows that Paul gave answers to practical problems on the basis of theological considerations. I would guess that the answer to the question of whether or not Christians should eat meat offered to idols, for example, is original with Paul. Or rather, the reasoning is original. Any Jew would answer 'no' to such a question. But Paul's 'no' is based on a particular application of his understanding of the Lord's Supper. Even if it is true that before Paul the Lord's Supper had the signifi-cance of participation in the body of Christ,[2] having already become more than a meal of commemoration and expectation, it is nevertheless likely that the application of this understanding to the practical life of the Christians in Corinth is Paul's original contribution. But original or not, the discussion shows that he thought, that he thought on the basis of theological convictions, and consequently that he thought coherently. It is frequently said that Paul's

---

[4] See the index, 'obedience as condition'.

[5] In Rabbinic Judaism especially, the term 'righteous' is used for those who behave correctly and stay 'in'. This is not Paul's terminology, although 'unrighteous' in I Cor. 6.9 might seem to imply it. Paul speaks of Christians remaining 'blameless and innocent' (e.g. Phil. 2.15). 'Become righteous' ('be justified') is one of Paul's 'transfer terms': see the Conclusion.

[6] We have noted above (p. 503) that when Paul analyses *why* he considers some actions to be wrong, he bases his argument on what is inappropriate for one who is in the body of Christ. This seems truer to his view of sin and salvation than the simple listing of deeds which, considered as transgressions, exclude one from salvation. He nevertheless does list such transgressions, and when he does so he con-siders avoiding them to be the condition of remaining 'in', in agreement with the general view in Judaism.

---

[1] See, for example, Bultmann, *Theology* I, pp. 190f.; Conzelmann, *Theology*, pp. 161f.; Bornkamm, *Paul*, pp. 117f.; Käsemann, 'The Spirit and the Letter', *Perspectives*, pp. 138, 160; Whiteley, *Theology of St Paul*, pp. xiv, 75; Kümmel, *Theology*, p. 139. Schweitzer (*Mysticism*, p. 139) viewed Paul as having a logical and complete system of thought, based on eschatology.

[2] Above, section 3 n. 18.

original contribution to Christianity is the doctrine of justification by faith.[3] I would take it that the general conception that one is saved by faith was completely common in early Christianity, and that Paul's original contribution lies in the antithetical formulation: by faith and not by works of law. It is possible that other apostles who worked among Gentiles exempted them from obedience to the law, but it was Paul who argued that obeying the law severed Gentile converts from Christ and who came to that conviction on the basis of his exclusivist soteriology: salvation is only in Christ and appropriated only by faith. Peter's behaviour in Antioch would seem to indicate that he could tolerate Gentile Christians' not observing the law, presumably on the ground that they were unable (it appears that Paul's charge in Gal. 2.14 that Peter would compel the Gentiles to Judaize was not quite accurate; apparently Peter himself Judaized and would 'compel' Gentiles to Judaize only if they wished to eat with him).[4] But for Paul it was not a question of ability or inability, but one of great theological moment. If salvation comes only in Christ, no one may follow any other way whatsoever. The rigour of the conclusion, again, marks Paul as a theological thinker with a coherent viewpoint.

The fact that Paul utilizes terms which we now identify as having different backgrounds does not do away with the claim that he thought coherently. I am by no means persuaded, for example, that Paul's view of the sacraments (or the view of the sacraments which appears in Paul; it may have originated before him) is derived from the Hellenistic mystery religions,[5] or that his discussions of the body of Christ derive from gnosticism.[6] Even if both theories are correct, however, the mixture of sources in no way points towards incoherence. What is most evident is that Paul was trying to express his religious convictions and that he employed a barrage of terminology to do so.[7] One may doubt that he was aware of the discrepancies in conceptualization which historical research would uncover by attributing the 'original' meaning of Paul's language to what he said.[8] The most conspicuous

---

[3] See, for example, Bornkamm, *Paul*, pp. 115f.

[4] On Peter in Antioch, cf. Munck, *Paul*, pp. 124f.

[5] See on the question, for example, Schweitzer, *Paul and his Interpreters*, ch. 7; Käsemann, 'The Lord's Supper', *Essays*, pp. 108f.; Davies, *Paul and Rabbinic Judaism*, pp. 89–98; G. Wagner, *Pauline Baptism and the Pagan Mysteries*.

[6] So Käsemann, *Leib und Leib Christi*, pp. 159–74. The various theories regarding the origin of the body of Christ terminology – none completely satisfying – are discussed by Conzelmann, *Theology*, p. 262; Robinson, *Body*, p. 55. Most recently, see J. Havet, 'La doctrine paulinienne du "Corps du Christ". Essai de mise au point', *Littérature et théologie pauliniennes*, by A. Descamps and others, pp. 185–216. For bibliography on the last Adam and the heavenly Man, see Whiteley, *Theology of St Paul*, pp. 114f.; see further Davies, *Paul and Rabbinic Judaism*, pp. 56f. (body of Christ based on Rabbinic speculation on Adam).

[7] Cf. Whiteley, *Theology of St Paul*, p. 102: it was Paul's 'Christology which called the language into use, rather than the words which gave rise to his Christology'.

[8] Compare Scrogg's discussion (*The Last Adam*, 1966, pp. xviii–xxiv) of Brandenburger's view that Paul partly but consciously accepts gnostic terminology in his debate with the Corinthians and corrects

case is the distinction between juristic and participationist terminology. Here is a distinction that will not go away. In brief, it is the distinction between saying that Christ dies *for* Christians and that they die *with* Christ, between saying that Christians are sanctified and justified from their past transgressions and that they have died with Christ to the power of sin, between saying that they should live 'blamelessly' and that they live 'in the Spirit'. These two series were not distinct in Paul's mind. He repeatedly stated them together, although it is also clear that the 'participationist' way of thinking brings one closer to the heart of Paul's thought than the juristic, once the two are distinguished. The two always serve to correct each other, so that the participationist language gives the depth of Paul's thought – a man is not merely acquitted for past trangressions, he is free from sin; he does not merely hang on to his blameless state, he lives in the Spirit – while the juristic terminology shows that Paul never lapsed into antinomianism in any form (works do matter and everyone will be judged; past transgressions must be expiated), nor into an ahistorical, 'gnostic' spirituality, nor into the mysticism of private experience and introspection.[9] There is a basic coherence in all this, but it is not *systematically* worked out. The precise relation, for example, between acquittal and death to the power of sin did not appear to Paul as a problem which required resolution.

In saying that the participationist language bring us closer than the juristic to the heart of Paul's thought and reveals the depth of it, we move away from one way of making Paul's thought relevant. Since the participationist way of thinking is less easily appropriated today than the language of acquittal and the like, or than the language of obedience versus boasting, it has not infrequently been dismissed or played down.[10] Thus, for example, Bultmann argued that Paul's discussion of 'the mythological notions of the spirit powers and Satan do not serve the purpose of cosmological speculation nor a need to explain terrifying or gruesome phenomena or to relieve men of responsibility and guilt'. When Paul speaks 'in naive mythology of the battle of the spirit powers against Christ or of his battle against them (I Cor. 2.6–8; 15.24–26)', he does not really mean that. 'In reality he is thereby only expressing a certain understanding of existence.' 'Through these mythological conceptions the insight is indirectly expressed that man does not have his life in his hand as if he were his own lord but that he is

---

it (E. Brandenburger, *Adam und Christus*). Paul unquestionably takes up his opponents' language and throws it back at them, but it may be doubted that he was conscious of the history-of-religions significance of all of his terminology.

[9] Conzelmann, for example, takes it that the juristic language interprets the 'mystical', and then that the juristic must give the real meaning (*Theology*, p. 209). It seems clear that the two sets of terminology interpret each other.

[10] On the modern difficulty with participationist language, cf. Käsemann, 'The Lord's Supper', *Essays*, pp. 111, 115f.

constantly confronted with the decision of choosing his lord.'[11] In a similar way Bultmann explained the meaning of the transfer from the old creation to the new: 'no magical or mysterious transformation of man' takes place. Rather, 'a new understanding of one's self takes the place of the old'.[12] Particularly striking is the interpretation of being one body with Christ:

The union of believers into one *soma* with Christ now has its basis not in their sharing the same supernatural substance, but in the fact that in the word of proclamation Christ's death-and-resurrection becomes a possibility of existence in regard to which a decision must be made, and in the fact that faith seizes this possibility and appropriates it as the power that determines the existence of the man of faith.[13]

The death of Christ is a 'cosmic' event in that 'it may no longer be considered as just the historical event of Jesus' crucifixion on Golgotha. For God made this event the eschatological occurrence, so that, lifted out of all temporal limitation, it continues to take place in any present moment . . .'[14] Similarly the incarnation is 'cosmic': 'i.e. in reality, *historic dimension* (a locus in the actual living of men, which is true "history"). The incarnation is present and active in the Christian proclamation.'[15] Jewish apocalypticism has been historicized. The eschatological salvation event is now present in the word which 'accosts each individual, throwing the person himself into question by rendering his self-understanding problematic, and demanding a decision of him.'[16] Receiving the Spirit does not mean receiving 'a mysterious power working with magical compulsion'. The Spirit, rather, is that which presents 'the new possibility of genuine, human life which opens up to him who has surrendered his old understanding of himself'.[17]

This way of interpreting Paul reaches its high point in Bultmann, and his successors have modified his consistent efforts to turn all of Paul's statements into existential demands which require a decision and which call into question the believer's self-understanding, thus opening the possibility of a new self-understanding. Similar points of view may nevertheless be seen in such scholars as Bornkamm and Conzelmann. Thus, for example, Conzelmann repeats the view that the receipt of the Spirit 'represents the real transference of the *word* of salvation'.[18] And Bornkamm, as

[11] Bultmann, *Theology* I, pp. 258f. Against this, note Bornkamm's statement that Paul 'does not begin with choices open to the Christian, but with powers and dominions from which he is delivered and for which he sets out' (*Paul*, p. 203).

[12] Bultmann, *Theology* I, pp. 268f.

[13] Ibid., p. 302.

[14] Ibid., p. 303.

[15] Ibid., p. 305.

[16] Ibid., p. 307.

[17] Ibid., p. 336.

[18] Conzelmann, *Theology*, p. 210. My emphasis.

did Conzelmann, argues that, although Paul used 'schemes of classification not directly stemming from his doctrine of justification', they are to be interpreted in terms of that doctrine. This guards 'against any naturalism or automatism in the understanding of salvation'.[19]

The seriousness of the position must be realized. Bultmann did not argue that the best we can now do in appropriating what Paul wrote is to translate it into existentialist categories, but that they represent what Paul *really* meant. This argument is buttressed by acute observations. Thus Bultmann noted correctly that even after a man is 'in Christ' he must still make decisions.[20] There is no magical transfer. In general, we may agree with what Bultmann and his successors wished to argue *against*: against magic, against viewing the soteriological event as taking place apart from man's will or as depriving him of it, against the possibility that Paul was interested in cosmological speculation for its own sake and the like. It must be wondered, however, whether the alternative as Bultmann proposed it – *either* cosmological speculation, magical transference and the like, *or* the ever-present demand to make a decision when faced with a demand which challenges one's self-understanding – does justice to Paul. Having agreed that Paul was not interested in cosmological speculation and did not believe in magical transference, are we then left with no choice but to interpret being one body with Christ as constantly accepting a revised self-understanding, or receiving the Spirit as accepting the word of grace? It would seem to me to be erroneous to deny the existential significance of what Paul wrote. That accepting the gospel was accepting the grace of God and that this resulted in a revised self-understanding of one's position before God is, I believe, true. But this seems to be the individual and internal consequence of Paul's theology rather than the exhaustive interpretation of it. The Spirit which works miracles and produces *charismata* is not simply 'the word of grace'. Being one body and one Spirit with Christ is not simply living out of a revised self-understanding, although that may also result. It seems to me best to understand Paul as saying what he meant and meaning what he said: Christians really are one body and Spirit with Christ, the form of the present world really is passing away, Christians really are being changed from one stage of glory to another, the end really will come and those who are in Christ will really be transformed.

But what does this mean? How are we to understand it? We seem to lack a category of 'reality' – real participation in Christ, real possession of the Spirit – which lies between naive cosmological speculation and belief in magical transference on the one hand and a revised self-understanding on the other. I must confess that I do not have a new category of perception to

---

[19] Bornkamm, *Paul*, pp. 151f. Cf. n. 9 above.
[20] Bultmann, *Theology* I, p. 259.

propose here.[21] This does not mean, however, that Paul did not have one. It must be emphasized that what Bultmann said against magical transference is correct. It is correct not only because it would lead to false theology today, but as a precise exegesis of Paul. The Christians whom he addressed had not been magically transferred, and he explicitly repudiated the notion when it cropped up in Corinth. On the other hand, he thought that a *real* change was at work in the world and that Christians were participating in it. Although it is difficult today to formulate a perceptual category which is not magic and is not self-understanding, we can at least assert that the realism of Paul's view indicates that he had one. To an appreciable degree, what Paul concretely thought cannot be directly appropriated by Christians today. The form of the present world did not pass away, the end did not come and believers were not caught up to meet the Lord in the heavens. Paul did express himself in terms which have proved more durable, and it is reasonable that those who wish to make Paul's gospel relevant today should emphasize them. That does not, however, mean that the more easily appropriated language of trust, obedience, renunciation of one's own striving, and the like, is the real and exhaustive interpretation of what Paul meant. What he really thought was just what he said: that Christ was appointed Lord by God for the salvation of all who believe, that those who believe belong to the Lord and become one with him, and that in virtue of their incorporation in the Lord they will be saved on the Day of the Lord.

Appendix

Perspectives on 'God's righteousness' in recent German discussion

Manfred T. Brauch

During the entire history of the church, but especially since the Reformation, Paul's concept of 'God's righteousness' and with it his doctrine of justification have been the source for a lively, diverse, and often heated exegetical and theological debate. The impetus for the voluminous literature and exegetical labour has not only, or primarily, been the recognition that Paul's teaching on the righteousness of God and the justification of the sinner is

---

[21] Whiteley (*Theology of St Paul*, p. 133) has proposed the term 'secondary literal sense' to indicate being a member of Christ: it is not precisely literal (as the hand is a member of one's body), nor simply metaphorical (as one is a member of a college). Whiteley shares with many British scholars the view that Paul's participationist language stems from the biblical view of human solidarity (cf. ibid., pp. 45f., 155f.), a view which seems to me not quite to account for Paul's view that Christians are one *person* with Christ. Cf. above, section 5.

an important, if not the most important, aspect of his thought, but the questions of (1) how the genitive construction *dikaiosynē theou* is to be interpreted, and (2) what the term *dikaiosynē theou* means contextually in the overall context of Pauline theology. Is *dikaiosynē theou* to be understood as an objective genitive, i.e. the righteousness given to man by God and which counts before God? Or are we to interpret the construction as a subjective genitive, referring to God's own righteousness, describing either his being (he is righteous) or his action (he acts righteously as Judge, Ruler and Redeemer), or both his being and action? Further, is Paul's use of the combination *dikaiosynē theou* to be interpreted from the common conception of *dikaiosynē* as 'justice' or 'righteous judgment' (in a legal sense), or does Paul describe a state of affairs which cannot be subsumed under the normal meaning of the term?

The history of interpretation[1] of the phenomenon characterized as *dikaiosynē theou* by Paul demonstrates that no agreement has been reached. The spectrum of alternatives, with its multiplicity of nuances and combinations, is undergirded by the work of reputable scholars. And one wonders whether anything approaching a consensus can ever be reached. But this same history also reveals points at which new insights opened up new interpretative possibilities and pointed in new directions for a clearer and more precise understanding of Paul's teaching on God's righteousness and the justification of man.

Such a turning-point in the history of interpretation must be seen in the publication of E. Käsemann's essay 'Gottesgerechtigkeit bei Paulus',[2] delivered at the Oxford Congress on 'The New Testament Today' in 1961. Käsemann's interpretation introduced a new terminology into the discussion. Such terms as 'Machtcharakter der Gabe' (power-character of the gift), 'Herrschaftswechsel' (change of Lordship) and 'Existenzwandel' (transformation of existence) provide new perspectives on the Pauline dialectic of God's action and man's existence under faith. Käsemann's essay provided the impetus and the direction for a renewed discussion[3] of the problems pointed out above. It is the purpose of this essay to present a summary

[1] The limited scope of this essay prevents a presentation of such a history. Excellent discussions are given in P. Stuhlmacher, *Gerechtigkeit Gottes bei Paulus*, 1965; C. Müller, *Gottes Gerechtigkeit und Gottes Volk*, 1964.

[2] *ZTK* 58, 1961, pp. 367–78 = *Exegetische Versuche und Besinnungen* II, 1964, pp. 181–193; ET in *The Bultmann School of Biblical Interpretation: New Directions?*, vol. I of *Journal for Theology and Church* (ed. R. W. Funk and G. Ebeling), 1965, and in *New Testament Questions of Today*, 1969, pp. 168–82. References in this appendix are to the *ZTK* article except where otherwise indicated.

[3] C. Müller, *Gottes Gerechtigkeit*; P. Stuhlmacher, *Gerechtigkeit Gottes*; R. Bultmann, 'ΔΙΚΑΙΟΣΥΝΗ ΘΕΟΥ', *JBL* 83, 1964, pp. 12–16; K. Kertelge, '*Rechtfertigung' bei Paulus*, 1967; H. Conzelmann, 'Die Rechtfertigungslehre des Paulus: Theologie oder Anthropologie?', *EvT* 28, 1968, pp. 389–404. M. Barth, *Justification. Pauline texts Interpreted in the Light of the Old and New Testaments*, 1970. Translated from the German 'Rechtfertigung. Versuch einer Auslegung Paulinischer Texte im Rahmen des Alten und Neuen Testaments', in *Foi et salut selon S. Paul* (ed. S. Agourides et al.), (*Analecta Biblica* 42, 1970, pp. 137–209).

analysis and evaluation of this recent debate on the German scene. To see this discussion in proper perspective, some representative interpretations from the prior debate must be briefly presented at the outset.

The prevailing pre-Reformation interpretation of *dikaiosynē theou* spoke of 'distributive justice' in the sense that God is the Judge who judges righteously, not haphazardly, but according to the norm of his own holiness and perfection.[4] Luther opened new interpretative possibilities. First, he took the construction *dikaiosynē theou* as an objective genitive throughout, translating the phrase with 'the Righteousness which counts before God', i.e., the righteousness which man possesses as a gift from God. Having emphasized the gift-character of God's righteousness over against his tradition, Luther went on to describe God's righteousness in terms which closely resemble the most recent discussion by describing it as God's gracious and creative and redemptive activity on behalf of man. Luther's contemporaries and Protestant scholastics were apparently not able to appropriate his insights.[5] A new turning point for the discussion was provided by H. Cremer[6] in that he pointed to the Old Testament as the historical presupposition for Paul's conception of 'God's righteousness'. Cremer demonstrated that *dikaiosynē theou* must be understood in terms of *tsedaqah*, a 'relational concept' which designates the action of partners in keeping with the covenant (i.e., covenant-faithfulness). As a result of this religio-historical understanding, many exegetes returned to an interpretation of *dikaiosynē theou* as a subjective genitive, not as a description of God's essence, but as designation of his action, his activity as Lord and Redeemer.[7] In this century, many exegetes became dissatisfied with the alternative of subjective genitive or objective genitive, and began to interpret the phrase as a 'genitive of the author', combining both the objective and subjective elements; i.e., God's righteousness is the righteousness which comes from God, which is given to man and which is the basis of man's relationship with God.[8] R. Bultmann is the most recent exponent of such an interpretation,[9] defending it again in answer to Käsemann's essay.[10] The main points of Bultmann's discussion

---

[4] Stuhlmacher (*Gerechtigkeit Gottes*, pp. 51–65) shows how this particular interpretation has raised its head again and again, even in the interpretation of the twentieth century.

[5] Cf. Stuhlmacher, op. cit., pp. 22–40. It is generally recognized today that the ethical-idealistic interpretation of nineteenth-century liberalism does not do justice to Paul, since his concept *dikaiosynē theou* is not derived from Greek moral philosophy, but from Hebraic thought patterns involving the divine-human relation.

[6] *Die Paulinische Rechtfertigungslehre im Zusammenhang ihrer geschichtlichen Voraussetzungen,*[2] 1900 (especially 33f.).

[7] Thus G. Schrenk in *TWNT* II, pp. 205–8 = *TDNT* II, pp. 203–5.

[8] See Kertelge ('*Rechtfertigung*', p. 8 n. 17) for those who have advocated such an interpretation. In this connection, H. Lietzmann (*An die Römer,*[4]1933, p. 95) speaks of a 'glittering double-meaning' of *dikaiosynē theou*: '. . . it designated a divine attribute which by grace is also given to the man of faith' (subjective genitive and genitive of author).

[9] *Theology* I, Paragraphs 28–31.

[10] 'ΔΙΚΑΙΟΣΥΝΗ ΘΕΟΥ', *JBL* 83, 1964, pp. 12–16.

will be outlined here, for Käsemann directs his new thesis specifically against the interpretation of his teacher.

In dependence on Rom. 10.3 and Phil. 3.9 (which he sees as the genuine interpretations of '*dikaiosynē theou*'),[11] Bultmann interprets *dikaiosynē theou* at Rom. 1.17; 3.21f., 26 as 'God-given, God-adjudicated righteousness', since 'its one and only foundation is God's grace.'[12] Bultmann arrives at this interpretation by a prior investigation of the term *dikaiosynē*, finding that when this term (as well as the adjective *dikaios*) denotes the condition (or essence) of salvation, it 'is a *forensic term*. It does not mean the ethical quality of a person . . . but a relationship. That is, *dikaiosynē* is not something a person has as his own; rather it is something he has in the verdict of the forum . . . "Righteousness" then is the "favourable standing" that a person has in the eyes of others.'[13] This forensic meaning of 'righteous' and 'being rightwised' is shared by Paul with his Judaistic tradition. Now in Paul's time, the forensic term 'righteousness' had also become an *eschatological* term, as Jewish piety more and more came to expect God's 'rightwising' verdict to come from his eschatological judgment. Thus, Bultmann sees 'complete agreement between them [Paul and Jews] as to the formal meaning of *dikaiosynē*: it is a forensic-eschatological term'.[14] What differentiates Paul's view from that of Jewish piety is that while the latter is concerned with the fulfilment of the conditions which are the presupposition for God's 'rightwising' verdict (i.e., keeping the law), the former asserts that this forensic-eschatological righteousness is already imputed in the present on the presupposition of faith.[15] Thus, the righteousness adjudicated to the believer is not 'sinlessness' in the sense of ethical perfection, but 'sinlessness' in the sense that God does not 'count' man's sin against him (II Cor. 5.19), i.e., he is placed in a new relation to God.[16]

Bultmann's interpretation throughout is dominated by an existentialist-anthropological perspective which is oriented around the individual. God meets the individual in the proclaimed kerygma (in which 'righteousness' as pure gift is present), as a result of which righteousness becomes a 'possibility' for the hearer of the kerygma, and a 'reality' for the hearer who responds in obedient faith.[17] This 'reality' of the rightwised sinner is what may be called a 'kerygmatic' reality: by constant appropriation of God's rightwising verdict in obedient existential decision he constantly 'becomes'

[11] Ibid., p. 13.
[12] *Theology* I, p. 285. Bultmann does not provide a uniform interpretation of *dikaiosynē theou*. In Rom. 3.5, the term is understood in terms of judicial justice (p. 288). In Rom. 3.24–25, the idea of the divine righteousness as demanding expiation (in the sense of distributive justice) is attributed by Bultmann to pre-Pauline tradition, which Paul seems to qualify and reinterpret by the additions of 'by his grace as a gift' and 'to be received by faith' (p. 46).
[13] Ibid., p. 272.
[14] Ibid., p. 273.
[15] Ibid., pp. 273f., 276.   [16] Ibid., pp. 276f.   [17] Ibid., pp. 274f.

what he is declared to be.[18] There is no transformation of essence or of willing here, but only a transformation of the historical situation, i.e., authentic decision has become a possibility.

Such an interpretation is the inevitable result when the Pauline *dikaiosynē theou* is understood from the general conception of *dikaiosynē*, when Cremer's insights into the 'relational' background of the conception of God's righteousness in the Old Testament are not taken seriously, and when the apocalyptic orientation[19] of Paul's view of history is reduced in favour of an understanding of God's righteousness which is guided by the question of the individual and his salvation. Over against Bultmann, A. Oepke[20] directed the attention of exegetes once again to the Old Testament and the literature of late Judaism, by asserting that *dikaiosynē theou* was a specific Jewish technical term which Paul used and filled with new content.[21]

Though Oepke's final interpretation did not go substantially beyond Bultmann, his pointer towards the Old Testament and late Jewish literature as the locus for the construction *dikaiosynē theou* was appropriated by E. Käsemann, whose formulations have dominated the discussion ever since.

Käsemann begins his own interpretation with the observation that the formulation *dikaiosynē theou* is not a creation of the apostle, but an independent technical term which, beginning with Deut. 33.21, and after a long history in the Old Testament tradition, has appeared again in the literature of apocalyptic Judaism.[22] This means that the meaning of the term can no longer be subsumed under the general conception of *dikaiosynē*, as a juridical-forensic concept, thus understood one-sidedly as a gift and robbed of its particularity. The formula as used in apocalyptic Judaism – and in conjunction with the Old Testament-Jewish conception of God's righteousness in terms of faithfulness to the covenant – signifies not an anthropologically oriented gift, but the theocentric-oriented concept of God's redemptive action.[23] What is significant for Paul's use of the formulation, according to Käsemann, is the fact that together with his emphasis on the 'gift-character' of God's righteousness, Paul clearly brings out the 'power-character', i.e., the power of God active in the gift. 'The gift can never be separated from the Giver; it participates in the power of God, since God steps on to the scene in the gift.'[24] Käsemann's interpretation results from a comparison of

---

[18] Ibid., Paragraph 38.

[19] Bultmann treats the problem of the 'final judgment according to works' (I Cor. 1.8; 3.12–15; 4.4f.; I Thess. 3.13; 5.23; II Cor. 5.10) as a Jewish remnant and virtually ignores it (*Theology* I, p. 262).

[20] A. Oepke, 'Δικαιοσύνη θεοῦ bei Paulus', *TLZ* 78, 1953, cols. 257–63.

[21] For Oepke this technical term in Judaism designated 'not God's activity (subjective genitive) but something attributed to man'. The term thus became useful for Paul, who qualified it with the emphatic *chōris nomou* and *dia pisteōs*.

[22] Test. Dan. 6.10; 1QS 11.12.   [23] Käsemann, 'Gottesgerechtigkeit bei Paulus', p. 370.

[24] Ibid., p. 371. This double aspect of God's righteousness as both 'gift' and 'power' in the context of God's redemptive action is for Käsemann the only satisfactory explanation of the subject-object orientation of the genitive construction.

'God's righteousness' with other central concepts of Pauline theology. Thus, *pneuma* is for Paul both the 'spirit which raises from the dead' and 'the gift of the *pneuma en hēmin*'. Again, Christ, whom Paul extols as Lord of the world, 'does not only give himself for us, but also dwells and lives in us'.[25] Similarly, *charis* is primarily God's gracious power as well as his gift, and the gospel is explicitly called *dynamis theou* in Rom. 1.16. The 'Lordship over our lives' is realized in the 'gift' as the 'presence of the giver' who demands obedience.[26] This may be called a 'transformation of existence', for when God's word brings about the 'new creation', what is implied is a 'change of Lordship'.[27] In such a context the tension in the relation between 'being declared righteous' and 'rightwised' is eliminated. For if God's righteousness is seen as an isolated gift, then it would seem as if God imputes something to us which we had to realize ourselves, or as if we had been transformed in essence. But if the 'power-character' of the gift is acknowledged and Christ's Lordship is seen as the essential content of the gift, then the relation between the Pauline indicative and imperative can be understood: 'remain with the Lord who has been given to you and in his Lordship';[28] for in such a relationship the Christian 'becomes what he is'.[29]

Käsemann goes on to demonstrate that Paul's designation of God's eschatological redemptive activity as *dikaiosynē theou* – already present in Old Testament-Jewish tradition, and seen in the pre-Pauline Jewish-Christian community in terms of God's renewed covenant-faithfulness (Rom. 3.25f.) – radically departed from his Jewish and Christian tradition, in that he saw in the revelation of God's righteousness in the Christ-event the faithfulness of God towards the entire creation.[30] Thus, 'since all have sinned' (Rom. 3.28), 'God's righteousness is what it must be as the power which rightwises the sinner, namely, God's victory over against the rebellion of the world. . . . For Paul it is God's dominion over this world revealed eschatologically in Christ.'[31] 'God's righteousness is his power which creates salvation . . . to be led back into God's Lordship is the world's redemption.'[32]

Käsemann's interpretation has brought a new perspective into the discussion. On the one hand, it avoids the one-sidedness of an anthropocentric perspective which sees *dikaiosynē* as pure gift or as the sinner's emancipa-

[25] Ibid., p. 371.
[26] Ibid., p. 372.
[27] Ibid., p. 373.
[28] Ibid., pp. 372f.
[29] Ibid.
[30] Ibid., pp. 374f. Käsemann points out that what separates Paul's use of *dikaiosynē theou* from that of his apocalyptic tradition is *not* the fact that it is already present (as Bultmann holds), for the eschatological 'now' of the manifestation of God's righteousness is to be found in the Thanksgiving Psalms of Qumran. See Käsemann's reply to Bultmann's criticism, *Exegetische Versuche und Besinnungen* II, p. 181.
[31] Ibid., p. 377.
[32] Ibid., p. 378.

tion-proclamation, and the attendant problem of the foundation of the new obedience. On the other hand, a one-sided theocentric perspective is also avoided in that the revelation of God's righteousness is not simply an external phenomenon in reference to man who must somehow rightly relate himself to it, but that the encounter takes place within man: the gift of righteousness demands response. The term 'power-character of the gift' designates this situation. It is also significant that Käsemann has provided a completely unified interpretation of the Pauline *dikaiosynē theou* in the context of Paul's 'universalizing' of God's covenant-faithfulness in terms of a 'new creation theology'. It will presently become evident how this interpretation has influenced the ensuing discussion.[33]

The title of C. Müller's work, *Gottes Gerechtigkeit und Gottes Volk: Eine Untersuchung zu Römer 9–11*,[34] reveals his immediate concern: to interpret the 'Israel problem' within the context of the Pauline understanding of God's righteousness and the justification of the sinner. The work attempts to show that Paul's discussion of the 'Israel problem' in Rom. 9–11 is permeated by an eschatological creation-tradition, in terms of the right of the Creator over against his Creation, and that this creation-tradition characterizes the essential nature of the Pauline doctrine of justification throughout.[35] Using the common image of the potter (Rom. 9), Paul underlines the unconditional sovereignty of the Creator in relation to his creation (i.e., his creatures) (p. 27). With this creation-tradition, the concept of God's *right* to act in sovereignty as Creator is everywhere connected. Thus, Paul speaks not only of the sovereign power of the Creator, but also of the *right* of the Creator to use this power as he wills (p. 30). According to Müller, Paul's understanding of *dikaiosynē theou* is dependent upon the Old Testament

---

[33] Bultmann in his short essay 'ΔΙΚΑΙΟΣΥΝΗ ΘΕΟΥ', *JBL* 83, 1964, pp. 12–16, reaffirms his own interpretation of *dikaiosynē theou* as 'gift' (pp. 12–13) over against Käsemann's interpretation, denies both the presence of a formalized use of *dikaiosynē theou* in Jewish apocalyptic, as also Paul's dependence upon such a technical term (pp. 15–16), and will not admit that Paul 'radicalized and universalized' the understanding of *dikaiosynē theou* – given in the tradition – as that power and activity of God which creates salvation (p. 16). Käsemann's reply to Bultmann's criticism (in the footnotes to the reprint of his essay in his *Exegetische Versuche und Besinnungen* II, 1964) centres upon the question whether context and Pauline theology permit the absolutizing of *dikaiosynē theou* as 'gift' – to which a purely conceptual analysis points – and whether it is then permissible to explain all occurrences of *dikaiosynē theou*, which do not conform to such an understanding, as 'rhetorical formulations' (as Bultmann seems to do). Though Käsemann admits again that Paul's emphasis in the use of *dikaiosynē theou* is on its gift-character, he reaffirms his contention that *dikaiosynē theou*, with the meaning 'power which creates salvation', influences Paul's usage from the background of the tradition, and everywhere qualifies the concept of *dikaiosynē theou* as gift, so that gift and Giver remain inseparable.

It seems to me that Bultmann's criticism has missed the central thrust of Käsemann's interpretation, and the latter's defence is quite convincing. It remained for his students to support and expand his insights with extensive religio-historical and exegetical foundations.

[34] C. Müller, *Gottes Gerechtigkeit*.

[35] From the viewpoint of a doctrine of justification interpreted in terms of a creation-tradition, Müller sees Rom. 9–11 no longer as simply an excursus to the 'Israel problem', but as an integral part of an overall unified theme, announced in Rom. 1.17, within which Rom. 9–11 represents a salvation-historical concretization (ibid., pp. 57, 104–6).

and apocalyptic-Jewish conceptions of the cosmic, juridical trial which pits Israel (and the nations) against God. The result of Müller's investigation of this 'trial' in the Old Testament and apocalyptic-Jewish tradition is as follows (p. 64): various groups within late Judaism saw 'God's righteousness' within the framework of a lawsuit (*Rechtsstreit*) which God brings against Israel (and the world), and in which God steps on to the scene as the victorious party. By means of the powerful assertion of his 'covenant-faithfulness' (i.e., his *tsedaqah*) or his claim over against the world, God judges the faithless party in this judicial process, be that Israel as a special community, or the representatives of the 'world'. Where *tsedaqah* appears in these contexts, it can be rendered by 'victory'; that is, God emerges as victor in the eschatological judgment-trial, his cause 'leads to victory' and must be 'acknowledged as victory' (p. 64). 'God's righteousness' is therefore the *victory* of God in which his universal claim *vis-à-vis* the world prevails (p. 62).

An analysis of Rom. 1.17; 3.1–22; 9–11 results for Müller in the same juxtaposition of *dikaiosynē theou* and trial-judgment: 'the observation that man's *adikia* "proves" God's *dikaiosynē* is only possible within the context of a trial, where the victory of one party involves the defeat of the other' (p. 65). Paul is concerned with God's being Lord and Judge over the *kosmos*, and in the context of Rom. 3.1–6 '*dikaiosynē theou* can only signify the *victory* of the *claim* of God over against the defeated, i.e., unrighteous, *kosmos*' (p. 67). *Dikaiosynē theou* in Rom. 3.21f. and 9–11 also designates the same reality. Paul's use of *martyresthai* (3.21) and *homologein* (10.9) clearly points to the situation of a trial, where legally binding testimony and confession serve to establish the right of the one party over against the other (pp. 68f.). However, the mere establishing of the guilt of the world does not comprise the total victory of the claim of God. The victory becomes complete only when the defeated party acknowledges the victory and submits to it in obedience. 'The *adikia anthrōpōn* "proves" the victory of God (3.5), but the victory of God is only complete when the defeated party acknowledges it by *pistis*. Thus, *dia pisteōs* is a necessary aspect of *dikaiosynē theou*' (p. 68). In Rom. 10.9f., Paul presents the historical concretization of this situation. The positive *homologein* (v. 9) corresponds to the negative *ouk hypotassesthai* (v. 3), and v. 9 proves that the *dikaiosynē tou theou* (v. 3) designates the victory of God's claim. 'In that the believing community submits to the demand of God's right, it helps to bring about the victory. The *confession* of the *community* is a part of the revelation of *dikaiosynē theou* in the Christ event' (pp. 68f.). As a result of this analysis, Müller describes the 'formal structure' of *dikaiosynē theou* as 'the eschatological realization of God's right in the world' (p. 72), for '*dikaiosynē ek nomou* and *ek pisteōs* (10.5) are not descriptions of the individual, but signs for the old and the new people of God, respectively' (p. 73). The fact that *dikaiosynē theou* is a 'relational concept'

(*Verhältnisbegriff*) underscores for Müller the observation that God's demand toward the world does not result in ultimate victory apart from the 'acknowledgment' on behalf of man. Thus, the 'realization of God's right' (*Rechtsverwirklichung*) among the 'new' people of God is not experienced in terms of an abstract norm or imputed idea, but in terms of a relationship in which God is *really* Lord and in which this Lordship is realized in the concrete life (pp. 74f.).

Let us summarize: Müller's interpretation of the Pauline *dikaiosynē theou* is guided by the thesis that Paul is operating with Old Testament-apocalyptic-Jewish traditions concerning God's sovereignty and prerogatives as Creator and the eschatological judicial process. On the basis of his unconditional claim over against his Creation, God emerges as victor in the trial. But as Creator, God is not vindicated, i.e., his right is not established, until man submits to the 'forensic' judgment. The concrete manifestation of the victory of God over the rebellious world is seen in the Christ-event (pp. 88f.), and in the believing community's obedient response. Thus, the right of the Creator over against the world has become an eschatological reality within the world: the believer acknowledges God's free and sovereign action in Christ, and in this acknowledgment becomes a new creation. This is justification. God's eschatological activity as Creator has reaffirmed his right over the rebellious world and has re-established it within the rebellious world.

Over against Müller's emphasis on the victory of God's right over the rebellious world, and in dependence on Käsemann's interpretation of *dikaiosynē theou* as 'salvation-creating power' (*Heilsetzende Macht*), Peter Stuhlmacher's work[36] emphasizes the soteriological aspect of *dikaiosynē theou* in the context of the faithfulness of God as Creator toward his creation (p. 236). This basic thesis is supported and expanded by an exegesis of all the relevant Pauline passages.[37] According to II Cor. 5.21, *'dikaiosynē theou* is the cosmic power and mode of manifestation of the Creator-God, which appears in the kerygma of the Apostle, calls into service, and contains within itself the judgment and the new creation' (p. 77). Rom. 1.17 shows *dikaiosynē theou* to be God's own creating-power which in the gospel moves through the world, creates faith and thus inaugurates God's new world (p. 83f.). In Rom. 3.4f., *dikaiosynē theou* is related more specifically to the covenant-people, and in parallel to *pistis theou* and *alētheia theou* signifies God's faithfulness to his covenant (p. 86). This faithfulness is then universalized by Paul to designate God's faithfulness to his creation-covenant in Rom. 3.21–26 (p. 91). Stuhlmacher sees the various aspects of the above interpretation of *dikaiosynē theou* coming together in Rom. 10.3: 'God's

[36] *Gottesgerechtigkeit bei Paulus*, 1965.
[37] II Cor. 5.21; Rom. 1.17; 3.4f.; 3.21–26; 10.3; Phil. 3.9.

righteousness is exclusively a redemptive event'; it is the creative activity of the Creator which overarches the aeons, is personified in Christ, and is realizing itself as 'word' in the kerygma (p. 98).

Stuhlmacher undergirds his interpretation of the relevant Pauline passages by an intensive religio-historical investigation, which reveals that the concept of God's righteousness has a long history in the Old Testament and apocalyptic-Jewish tradition. The roots (p. 144) of the concept *dikaiosynē theou* are to be located in the cultic understanding of God's righteousness in the Old Testament (p. 141). For at the centre of Israel's worship stood the proclamation of Yahweh's historically redemptive *tsedaqah*, the proof of his covenant faithfulness (p. 141). Yahweh's righteousness always denotes his salvation-creative activity on behalf of his covenant people (p. 115); thus *tsedaqah* denotes the power of the salvation-creating Word of God (p. 125). 'The juxtaposition of God's powerful word, creation, history, and Yahweh's future faithfulness are constitutive for the concept *tsedaqah* in the O.T.' (p. 141). Stuhlmacher considers this Old Testament conception of God's righteousness to belong to the pre-history of the Pauline term *dikaiosynē theou*, and locates the strictly terminological usage in apocalyptic Judaism, where the term has become a technical term.[38] It denotes throughout 'the power of the creating Word of God' in the context of God's right as Creator, his covenant faithfulness, his forgiving mercy, and his demand for obedience (p. 175). According to Stuhlmacher, this apocalyptic understanding of God's righteousness provides the relevant religio-historical presuppositions which are constitutive for the Pauline *dikaiosynē theou*: (1) the creation-tradition, (2) the concept of God's right over against his creation and (3) the word-structure of the divine creative activity.

Stuhlmacher sees *dikaiosynē theou* as the *Leitmotif* for the Pauline theology as a whole (pp. 203f.), but specifically for his doctrine of justification (pp. 217f.). 'How,' he asks, 'are verb (*dikaioun/dikaiousthai*) and *dikaiosynē theou* related to one another, i.e., how are forensic declaration and the concrete action of the Creator related?' An investigation of the use of the verb reveals that Paul speaks throughout of a very concrete justification, i.e., he does not distinguish between forensic judgment and the salvation-creating intervention of *dikaiosynē theou*. In both *dikaiosynē theou* and the verb *dikaioun/dikaiousthai*, there is a complete correlation between judicial and ontological conceptions (pp. 217–19). *Dikaiosynē theou* designates the Creator who in his *dikaioun* steps on to the scene and raises the dead (p. 219). Thus, 'justification' designates a divine-creative activity, the actualization of the *dikaiosynē theou* in terms of a word-event which creates new being.[39]

---

[38] IQS 10.25f.; 11.12; IQM 4.6; and Test. Dan. 6.10. In Eth. Enoch 71.14; 99.10; 101.3; IV Ezra 8.36, the term has been slightly altered according to textual needs (ibid., p. 175).

[39] Ibid., p. 236. The *Sitz im Leben* of this creative act of justification is baptism, and the gift of the

Yet, this creative work of God is not a mechanical intervention, but calls for man's response, and reaches its fulfilment when man acknowledges God as Judge and Creator. Both the creation of the new being and the faith-response of this being are word-event: 'The new free being of the creature which is founded in the act of justification is a being which both originates from, and has its existence in, the creative Word of God' (p. 227). Against the background of such an understanding of Paul's concept of justification and the new being, Stuhlmacher now sees the relationship of present justification to the still outstanding eschaton in Paul's thought. Just as God is present only in terms of the word in the old, disintegrating aeon, so it is with the new being; it too is present only in terms of the word. Thus, 'Paul's hope for the final coming of God is at the same time the necessary hope for the final vindication of God's right, because only then will God give to his own the new being in its fullness, which until then had been theirs only in terms of word-event' (p. 227). Paul knew all Christians to be endowed with God's Spirit, which meant to be subject to the creating power of the divine word. Yet the dialectic of *pneuma* and *sarx* remains and the final judgment is still outstanding. Paul's solution of the dilemma lies in the fact that the judgment according to works is for the Christian a judgment upon the *sarx* which still clings to him, while his pneumatic existence given him in the word of God is preserved. 'The faithfulness of the Creator towards his new creation outlasts the Judgment!' (pp. 230f.). 'Justification,' concludes Stuhlmacher, means for Paul 'the obligating, renewing calling of the individual, by the power of God, into the realm of encounter with God which has been opened by Christ. This renewing calling culminates in service' (p. 258).

A work which parallels Stuhlmacher's investigation within Catholic biblical scholarship is K. Kertelge's *'Rechtfertigung' bei Paulus*.[40] Kertelge is in substantial agreement with Stuhlmacher's location of the Pauline *dikaiosynē theou* in the religio-historical context of the Old Testament and specifically of apocalyptic Judaism. Though Kertelge recognizes that Paul has given the content of the formula new theological shape, its parentage in the Old Testament-late-Jewish usage is established by the fact that *dikaiosynē theou* is not descriptive of the essence of God, nor of the essence of man before God, but rather designates God's action in, and on behalf of, man (p. 305). And just as Stuhlmacher sees the 'righteousness of God' as 'signature and abbreviation' for the entire Pauline theology, so Kertelge

---

Spirit the means. For Paul, baptism, justification of the sinner, and creation are inseparable (II Cor. 5.17; Gal. 6.15). The initiate is justified, in that God's Spirit creates him anew. The Spirit is the new-creating power of the *dikaiosynē theou* and appears as the presence of Christ, for Christ is *dikaiosynē theou* in person (II Cor. 5.21).

[40] A comparison of Kertelge's Table of Contents with that of Stuhlmacher's work shows at once the same concerns.

sees *dikaiosynē theou* as the 'structural framework of the Pauline doctrine of justification', and this doctrine as a 'comprehensive theological presentation of Paul's concept of salvation' (p. 307).

Thus, the overall conceptions of these two works are quite similar, though in his interpretation of the Pauline *dikaiosynē theou* and the doctrine of justification, Kertelge represents a decided shift of emphasis. Yet he, as Müller and Stuhlmacher before him, reveals the influence of Käsemann's thesis that *dikaiosynē theou* is *'Heilsetzende Macht'*. Paul uses *dikaiosynē theou* for a new interpretation of the Christian salvation-event. In Paul, the pre-Pauline conception of *dikaiosynē theou* is transformed into an expression about *God's eschatological redemptive activity and the resulting redemptive situation of men*, on the basis of their faith in Jesus Christ. In Rom. 3.5, Paul's use of *dikaiosynē theou* is clearly reminiscent of the Old Testament covenant-relationship. The fundamental thought of this passage is that God's righteousness, as faithfulness to the covenant, is victorious over the unrighteousness of men, which in the old covenant revealed itself as faithlessness.[41] But Paul goes beyond this conception. Whereas late Judaism was waiting for the eschatological revelation of God's righteousness, and understood its presence in this world of unrighteousness as the support of the righteous (Test. Dan. 6.10), Paul understands *dikaiosynē theou* as the eschatological appearance of God's activity as judge of the sinful world (3.6). With this is given the specific Pauline orientation of the *dikaiosynē theou* towards all of mankind (pp. 67, 108), brought out concretely in Rom. 1.17 and 3.21–26. In these passages, *dikaiosynē theou* is unmistakably related to the eschatological revelation (or appearing) of God's redemption in Christ, and to the faith of all who accept it. The 'righteousness of God' which has appeared in Jesus Christ reaches far beyond what the Old Testament understood as God's covenant faithfulness. Its eschatological, creating power is evident in the fact that sinners are now declared righteous, and that by God's grace. Though *dikaiosynē theou* denotes God's redemptive activity and not God's gift of righteousness to man, it must not be overlooked that man is here the object, i.e., *dikaiosynē theou* implies a God-man relationship and is oriented towards the redemption of man (pp. 75f.). The *dikaiosynē theou* as redemptive activity would be nullified if its power did not bring about the *sōtēria* (1.16) of man. This 'direction-towards-man' of God's righteousness is clearly explicated in Rom. 3.22, 24–26, and is also at the centre of Rom. 1.16f. Here the gospel is called *dynamis* (clearly parallel to *dikaiosynē theou*), because in it God acts powerfully on behalf of man. *Dynamis* is not a designation of God's being, but a description of that action of God which results in *sōtēria* (pp. 85f.). Thus, the assertion

---

[41] Ibid., p. 107; cf. p. 67. *Dikaiosynē theou* in 3.5 is parallel and synonymous with *pistis tou theou* in 3.3.

about God's righteousness is oriented anthropologically, for *sōtēria* is concerned with the necessary salvation of men who are under sin.

Juxtaposed with the Christological-anthropological orientation of God's righteousness (i.e., his redemptive activity) Kertelge sees the eschatological orientation of *dikaiosynē theou* (especially in Rom. 10.4 and II Cor. 5.21). The assertion that Christ is the end of the law (Rom. 10.4) explains that in Christ the eschaton is already present. Christ is the end of the law in that he is the turning point from law to faith. This turning point is described (as in 1.17; 3.21f.) as the revelation of the righteousness of God. To reject Christ (who here appears as the personified *dikaiosynē theou*)[42] means not to submit to the righteousness of God, to refuse obedience (pp. 97f.). The same conception about the presence of the eschaton is underlined by II Cor. 5.21, where the identity between the eschatologically effective righteousness of God and Christ is presupposed (pp. 103–7). The presence of God's righteousness in Christ means for the believer that 'in Christ' he has begun a new existence, in which the old has passed away. For the *hamartia* which Christ becomes for us is the 'power of sin' under which man stands in the old aeon. Correspondingly, *dikaiosynē theou*, which we become, designates the redemptive power of God (operative in the new aeon) revealed in Christ (p. 104). The Pauline *dikaiosynē theou* thus reveals itself as a thoroughly eschatologically-oriented conception. With it Paul describes the situation of mankind 'in Christ' as a redemptive situation, which now amidst the disintegrating 'old aeon' has become a new possibility opened by God for all men (p. 107).

As the structural framework of Paul's doctrine of justification, *dikaiosynē theou* designates the decisive and final redemptive activity of God, in reference to which man is completely the receiver, the one who is redeemed and pardoned. The sinner is transferred into the sphere of God's righteousness and experiences his justification as a result of the action of God's grace (p. 112). But what happens to man when he submits to God's righteousness and is justified (rightwised)? When Paul speaks of a sinner as being 'declared righteous' or as 'having been justified', what happens in the process thus described? Kertelge attempts to answer that question by an analysis of the forensic and eschatological connotations of the terms *dikaiosynē* and *dikaioun/dikaiousthai* (pp. 112–60). Paul uses terms which have come to him out of the Old Testament-Jewish sphere of thought associated with definite conceptions of the judgment and the expectation of God's rightwising verdict at the end of time. How does Paul use and interpret the forensic and eschatological character of these terms?

---

[42] Ibid., p. 98. Kertelge maintains that on the basis of the overarching Christological tendency of Rom. 10, the *dikaiosynē theou* in v. 3 must be understood in the sense that Christ is its agent and representative.

The forensic character of the Pauline 'justification' consists in the fact that God's juridical verdict upon man, which is manifested in the death of Christ, is understood in faith as the self-realization of one's sinfulness and with it the experience of being grasped by the grace of God. By means of the verdict in which God declares the sinner righteous (*Rechtfertigungsurteil*), he freely absolves the sinner from his 'being-in-sin'. The forensic declaration of righteousness creates the sinner anew. Thus, the 'forensic' judgment is at the same time 'effective' judgment, because the judgment of God has creative power (p. 123). The forensic declaration therefore implies a new creation, so that the godlessness of the sinner is overcome in a newly created relationship to God. It is in this sense that the justified one is a 'new creation' in Christ (p. 159). God's action is not exhausted in simply an external decree (a purely forensic declaration), but signifies the effective creation of a new reality through God. But this new reality of the justified one, created by God, is not to be understood in terms of a static ontology, but rather as a 'relational reality' (*Beziehungsrealität*), i.e., a reality which consists of nothing except that new relationship between God and man created by God, the content of which is, from the side of God, Lordship, and from the side of man, obedience (p. 127). From this it becomes clear how Paul has transformed the forensic aspect of the terminology that has come to him from Judaism: 'justification' no longer designates the recognition of the righteousness which man has established himself in obedience to the Torah, nor simply the imputation of a foreign righteousness, that is, the righteousness of Christ. Rather, justification means for Paul that the sinner allows himself to be grasped and created anew by the grace of God. Justification finds its fullest expression in the relation between God and the justified one, in whose obedience the new relationship expresses itself, though this obedience would be impossible without the prior action of God's grace. Thus, the *reality* of justification is a *reality of relationship* (p. 159).

The eschatological character of 'justification' consists in the fact that 'justification' is experienced by faith as the eschatological action of God, grounded in the Christ event, in which Paul sees the final and decisive revelation of 'God's righteousness' as present: the eschaton has broken into the old aeon. The 'present' character of God's eschatological justifying action speaks of the presence of a redemption which was expected in the future and properly belongs to it. A *Heilsgeschichte* has literally been inaugurated, in the sense that the expected eschatological redemption has come, though its ultimate fulfilment is still outstanding (pp. 157f.). Yet for Paul, the 'present' character and the 'outstanding' character of God's eschatological redemption are essentially identical, because both have their basis in the Christ-event. For Kertelge, it is this forensic-eschatological structure of Paul's concept of justification which guards against a gnostic simplification of 'justification' in the sense of a purely present possession of salvation. Such a simplification is clearly seen in an interpretation of the Pauline concept of justification which sees it as a transformation of man's nature out of which the new ethical life results almost automatically (p. 159).

This leads to the question of how the act of justification, or rather the reality of justification, is related to the 'new obedience'. Kertelge locates this relationship in the Pauline 'justification by faith' (pp. 160–227). By his faith in Jesus Christ man experiences his justification. As such, faith is the beginning of salvation (on the side of the individual), the counterpart of grace and an essential aspect of the act of justification. But 'justification by faith' means more than this. For faith is the context in which the continuing existence of the justified one is related to the initial act of justification. 'Faith is for Paul always obedience to the redemptive will of God, and as such contains an active element' (p. 225). The freedom of the Christian from the bondage to sin is not experienced by him as an objective, natural reality, but as gift and demand at the same time. It is in faith that the tension between the continuing encroachments of 'the flesh' and the already present reality of the eschatological justification is abrogated.[43] The redemptive reality into which the believer has been placed must be allowed to become effective reality in the pragmatic life by obedience to the demand of grace. The justified one is called into service, and in this service he corresponds to the Lordship of grace. Thus, he not only receives, but is also obligated. Indeed, the justified one would invalidate for himself the gift of salvation if he were to sever himself from God's claim upon his life.

Ultimately, says, Kertelge, justification consists in this: that man is released from sin to obedience; the one does not exist without the other (p. 283). In the correspondence of grace and obedience, God's redemptive action comes to its intended goal. The universalism of God's redemptive will and the universal necessity for the salvation of men remains. But the actual success of God's redemptive activity is realized only in those who accept the offered grace and become obedient to it. This does not mean, however, that man's obedience has soteriological significance *beside* God's grace, but rather *within* it. The 'new obedience' of the Christian is not something which is added to God's grace; it is rather the historical form in which the success of God's redemptive action manifests itself (pp. 284f.).

H. Conzelmann's 'Die Rechtfertigungslehre des Paulus: Theologie oder Anthropologie?',[44] emphatically reaffirms Bultmann's interpretation and as such represents a decided retreat from the new insights of Käsemann, Stuhlmacher, Müller and Kertelge. In answering the question: 'The meaning of the doctrine of justification – theology or anthropology?' (p. 393),

[43] Ibid., p. 227; see further Part II, Ch. 4, 'Neuer Lebenswandel', pp. 250–85.
[44] *EvT* 28, 1968, pp. 389–404.

Conzelmann follows Bultmann's thesis that the Pauline theology must be interpreted anthropologically (pp. 391f.), since Christology and soteriology come tcgether in the salvation-event which is proclaimed *to man* in the kerygma (p. 392). The terminological analysis of *dikaiosynē theou* is now carried forward by means of the question, 'How is the relationship between God and man defined by this term?' (p. 398). Conzelmann rejects outright the subjective meaning of the genitive construction, in the sense of a description of God's character (i.e., that God is 'righteous'), without giving any consideration to the interpretation of the subjective genitive as a designation of God's action.[45] Where Paul uses the term, he speaks of man's own righteousness, given to him by God *sola gratia*. Paul, says Conzelmann, is concerned with the question of man's salvation, of how man can fulfil the condition of salvation, how he can get 'the righteousness which counts before God'.[46] By a brief analysis of various texts, Conzelmann seeks to underscore the anthropological concern of Paul. The *dikaiosynē theou . . . chōris nomou* of Rom. 3.21f. is said to prove that 'God's righteousness' is something which is given to and imputed to (*übereignet*) man, and the phrase *dikaiosynē de theou dia pisteōs . . . eis pantas tous pisteuontas* (3.22) is seen as 'the authentic definition of the term by Paul'.[47] In the interpretation of Rom. 1.16f., which Conzelmann understands as the central text for a subjective interpretation, the concept of the power-aspect of God's righteousness, so important for the recent discussion, is explicitly rejected: 'Because the content of the kerygma . . . is exclusively gospel, bearer of righteousness, Paul knows of no power-aspect of God which can be isolated' (p. 399). Conzelmann seems to have overlooked the fact that the Käsemann-oriented interpretation has not spoken of an isolated power, but of the powerful manifestation of God's redemptive activity. Again, Rom. 9.30f. is said to speak of the *proclaimed* righteousness of God appropriated by faith (p. 400), and II Cor. 5.21 'speaks for itself'; in one sentence, Conzelmann brushes aside any attempts to see here a subjective genitive (p. 401).

Conzelmann's attempt to inject new life into Bultmann's interpretation of the Pauline *dikaiosynē theou* and his conception of justification is not convincing, especially in the light of the exegetical and religio-historical labour which has been expended upon the elaboration and expansion of Käsemann's thesis. I am convinced that a step behind the 'new directions' and 'results' of the recent discussion is a step away from a clearer under-

[45] Conzelmann (op. cit., p. 398) asserts that where the subjective sense of the genitive is found, it is always in pre-Pauline tradition, and never Pauline.

[46] This was precisely Luther's question and, as in Bultmann, it is oriented upon the thoroughly objective interpretation of the genitive construction *dikaiosynē theou*.

[47] Conzelmann, op. cit., p. 399. The phrase *hysterountai tēs doxēs tou theou* in 3.23 is interpreted by Conzelmann as 'the glory which counts before God', and as shedding further light on the objective meaning of *dikaiosynē theou* in 3.22.

standing of Paul's doctrine of justification and from there, of his theology as a whole.[48]

Our survey of the recent German discussion has shown that Käsemann's interpretation of Paul's *dikaiosynē theou* as 'Heilsetzende Macht' (salvation-creating power) has thoroughly dominated the discussion, not only among his own students (Müller and Stuhlmacher), but even outside Protestant biblical scholarship (Kertelge). It has also become clear that those who have followed Käsemann's new directions have differed with him and among themselves at various points.[49] However, in terms of the comprehensive interpretation of Paul's doctrine of justification, the differences have been mainly in emphases,[50] rather than in substance. For this reason, it seems justifiable to speak of certain results which any interpretation of Pauline thought must take seriously if it is not to take a step backwards.[51]

We shall state below, in brief theses, the results of the analysed discussion, and conclude our study with some critical observations regarding the various emphases within the Käsemann-oriented line of interpretation.

1. The Old Testament conception of God's righteous acts on behalf of his people, seen in the context of God's covenant-faithfulness, is the theological presupposition for Paul's thinking on God's righteousness and the justification of man.

2. The religio-historical *Sitz im Leben* of the term *dikaiosynē theou* is apocalyptic Judaism, and especially the Qumran community. Thus, *dikaiosynē theou* is a technical term which has come to Paul with certain pre-formed associations.

3. Within pre-Pauline tradition, the concept of God's righteousness was associated with the following: (*a*) the creation-tradition, which sees God as the sovereign Lord over his creation; (*b*) the conception of the cosmos as a forum in which a judicial trial between God and Israel (the world) is staged; (*c*) the belief in the impending eschatological judgment in which God's faithfulness toward his own would once again manifest itself.[52]

4. These associational complexes of ideas have thoroughly determined

---

[48] Markus Barth's essay [see n. 3] is in agreement with the more recent trend in understanding justification against the background of the Old Testament (pp. 14–21). However, in his attempt to employ the plethora of concepts associated with 'God's righteousness' in the Old Testament, Barth too categorically subordinates the Pauline statements on justification to a dramatic, five-day judgment scene (pp. 25–82). In the process, 'justification' is seen almost exclusively as part of a juridical act (cf. this author's counter-proposal in *Set Free To Be*, 1975, pp. 11–31).

[49] See for example, Stuhlmacher, *Gerechtigkeit Gottes*, pp. 70, 77 n. 2; Kertelge, '*Rechtfertigung*', p. 68.

[50] See immediately below.

[51] Conzelmann's attempt did not take the religio-historical analysis of the Pauline *dikaiosynē theou* seriously, and must therefore be considered to have failed.

[52] Hans Heinrich Schmid's recent contribution to the understanding of the meaning of 'righteousness' in the Ancient Near East (*Gerechtigkeit als Weltordnung: Hintergrund und Geschichte des alttestamentlichen Gerechtigkeitsbegriffes*, 1968) is significant, but does not substantially affect the Pauline use of the concept 'righteousness of God'.

Paul's use of the term *dikaiosynē theou*, though he has transformed the term's content in keeping with his own Christological-soteriological kerygma.

5. For Paul, *dikaiosynē theou* is the redemptive action of God, not a description of God's essence, nor of man's essence before God. Over against his tradition, the term designated more than the renewal of the old covenant, but is universalized to include the entire creation: God acts redemptively on behalf of all men. Again, over against his tradition, Paul speaks of God's righteousness as present now in the Christ-event. In this eschatological redemptive intervention, God has broken into the old aeon and is creating the new aeon.

6. The manifestation of the 'righteousness of God' is that event in the context of which justification takes place. Though the juridical-forensic overtones are present in the Pauline use of the terms *dikaiosynē* and *dikaioun/ dikaiousthai*, they are not in the foreground. The forensic declaration is more than simply a proclamation; it is at the same time 'effective' declaration: The man who is 'declared righteous' by God stands under his sovereign, creative-redemptive disposal.

7. 'Justification' is not a possession over which the justified one can freely dispose. It is a state, an existence which is begun and continued in faith. God's redemptive action demands man's response. 'God's righteousness' is the powerful manifestation of his grace which calls to a life of obedience.

8. With Bultmann and Conzelmann, the newer interpretation affirms the anthropological 'orientation' of God's righteousness, but understands the content of the term *dikaiosynē theou* itself as qualifying the Christological-soteriological concern of Paul: the creative intervention of God in human history.

What has particularly distinguished the newer interpretation is the comprehensive and unified interpretation of Paul's conception of God's righteousness. This has been accomplished by a consistent application to Paul's use of terms that have come to him from the Old Testament-Jewish tradition of various aspects associated with those terms in the tradition. Now it is exactly the consistent and uniform interpretation of Paul's *dikaiosynē theou* from the background of his tradition which has distinguished the newer interpretation from most previous attempts to understand Paul's use of the term 'God's righteousness'. Yet it is also this consistent application of traditional associations to the Pauline use of the term which causes us to raise certain questions.

Müller has combined the creation-tradition (in its emphasis on the sovereign action of God) with the conception of God's right over against the world (expressed in the tradition about the cosmic trial) in his interpretation of Paul's conception of God's righteousness. With this emphasis on the juridical-forensic structure, '*dikaiosynē theou* can only signify the victory of the claim of God over the defeated, unrighteous cosmos' and 'the realization of God's right in the world'. It is highly questionable whether the concept of God's trial with the world can be used to explain *dikaiosynē theou* to the extent that Müller does. Can 'God's righteousness' really be rendered adequately by the word 'victory' as Müller does throughout? Is God's eschatological righteousness really the victory of God in which his universal claim *vis-à-vis* the world prevails? That 'victory' is the intended result of God's redemptive intervention is clear, but the action is not itself the victory, else the response of the defeated party (which Müller too sees as necessary) would be meaningless. God's righteousness is not so much the victory of God's right over the world, as it is the present revelation of God's longing for his creation to be reconciled to him.

Stuhlmacher too has used the creation-tradition as a basis for his interpretation, but has combined with this the 'word-structure' of the divine creative activity. And it is this combination which determines his interpretation throughout. Thus, the redemptive activity of God's righteousness 'is realizing itself as word in the kerygma'. In keeping with this understanding of 'God's righteousness', 'justification' designates 'a divine-creative activity, the actualization of the *dikaiosynē theou* in terms of a word-event'. To this corresponds the 'word-event' of the sinner's acknowledgment of God's redemptive intervention. Thus, 'justification' is only present in terms of the 'word'. The question which must be asked of this emphasis on the 'word-structure' of 'God's righteousness' is whether Paul's dynamic realism allows us to interpret him in terms of modern existentialist-linguistic categories. It is true that the Jewish tradition, and with it Paul, conceived of the Word of God as a creative power; but the powerful manifestation of this Word brought about *real* transformation and creation, which is far removed from the linguistic 'reality' of a *Sprachereignis*. For Paul, justification as the result of God's redemptive action was an 'existential reality', not simply a 'kerygmatic reality'.

In the context of his emphasis on the creation-tradition as an interpretative medium for Paul's *dikaiosynē theou*, Stuhlmacher brings out the 'faithfulness of the Creator toward his creation'. With Kertelge[53] we must ask whether Paul does not rather emphasize the 'new creation'. Does not the revelation of God's righteousness in the Christ-event (*nuni de*, Rom. 3.21) signify a break with the old, and a radically new beginning in the relation between God and the world? Is it really legitimate to speak of a Pauline transfer of God's faithfulness from the covenant-people to the entire creation? That Paul universalizes God's redemptive action is clear, but this is not a transfer of his faithfulness. It may be better to speak of God's judgment upon the 'old world' in the Christ-event, and at the same time of

[53] *'Rechtfertigung'*, p. 308.

God's sovereign, creative redemptive will which once again reaches into chaos to bring about the new creation. The overwhelming emphasis on God's creative action in the interpretation of Paul, which Stuhlmacher shares with Käsemann, must be seen as an over-emphasis. Where the expression *dikaiosynē theou* appears in Paul, the concept of his action as Creator is always in the background, but nowhere at the centre. It seems that Paul is primarily concerned with the *medium* (the Christ-event) and the *result* (the redemption of man) of that creative action of God, rather than with that action itself.

Whereas Müller and Stuhlmacher have emphasized the victory of God's right and the creative activity of God as interpretative structures, respectively, Kertelge has emphasized more the redemptive character of God's righteousness and the salvation of men which results from it. Thus he speaks of 'God's righteousness' as *Heilshandeln Gottes*, and of justification as *Heilsgeschehen*. In contrast to Stuhlmacher's interpretation of justification as 'word-event', Kertelge's interpretation of this Pauline phenomenon as *relational reality* is much more satisfying. For it avoids the extremes of either an idealistic transformation of man's essence or a reduction of the presence of redemption (i.e., justification) to the vagueness of a word-event. Paul is concerned with the *real* salvation of men, and this real salvation, in keeping with his tradition, consists in a relation, i.e., a new relation between man and God.

The questions asked above of the various emphases do not invalidate the results of this most fruitful discussion since Käsemann published his essay in 1961. They are meant as a word of caution against over-emphasis on particular insights, which so often in scholarship tend to overshadow the contributions of a work as a whole.

'God's power reaches for the world, and the world's salvation consists in the fact that it is led back under God's dominion. *Dikaiosynē theou* is *Heilsetzende Macht*.' This final observation in Käsemann's essay[54] may well be used as a summary of the recent German discussion of the Pauline *dikaiosynē theou*.

[54] *ZTK* 58, 1961, p. 378.

CONCLUSION

Paul and Palestinian Judaism

In section 5 of Chapter V, we drew one of the major conclusions of the study: Paul's 'pattern of religion' cannot be described as 'covenantal nomism', and therefore Paul presents an *essentially different type of religiousness from any found in Palestinian Jewish literature.*

This is true despite the fact that on the point at which many have found the decisive contrast between Paul and Judaism – grace and works – Paul is in agreement with Palestinian Judaism (Chapter V, section 6). There are two aspects of the relationship between grace and works: *salvation is by grace but judgment is according to works; works are the condition of remaining 'in', but they do not earn salvation.* The second aspect is found uniformly throughout Palestinian Judaism, even in IV Ezra, while the first aspect is present everywhere but in IV Ezra. The view that salvation is by grace but judgment is according to works may at first appear paradoxical, although it is not. The point is that God *saves* by grace, but that *within* the framework established by grace he rewards good deeds and punishes transgression. The last part of this formulation (judgment according to deeds) has often been held to be 'Jewish soteriology', but we have seen this nowhere to be the case, except in IV Ezra; and the compatibility between salvation by grace and reward and punishment on the basis of deeds is proved by the existence of both themes in Paul.

Paul's expectation of the imminent parousia of the Lord is in general to be explained as being in agreement with Palestinian Judaism, or at least some of it. Paul's expectation of the imminent end doubtless came from Christian tradition rather than directly from Judaism, but it nevertheless constitutes a similarity between Paul and Judaism. The similarity between Paul's view and apocalypticism is general rather than detailed. Paul did not, as has been observed, calculate the times and seasons, he did not couch his predictions of the end in visions involving beasts, and he observed none of the literary conventions of apocalyptic literature. Since the conventions of apocalypticism had so little influence on him, the hypothesis might be put forward that before his conversion and call Paul was not especially apocalyptically oriented. This is one more reason for not supposing that Paul began with a set apocalyptic view and fitted Christ into it. But if one is tallying differences and similarities, the expectation of the parousia counts as a general similarity between Paul and Palestinian Judaism.

Paul's attitude towards the law, with its basis in his exclusivist Christo-logical soteriology, cannot be paralleled in Judaism, but certain of his concrete ideas can be. He seems, for example, to work with an implicit distinction between the 'commandments which govern relations between man and man' and the 'commandments which govern relations between man and God'. It is especially the latter (sabbath, circumcision and the like) which Gentiles need not follow, while transgression of the former is invariably challenged – though again, not because the commandments are commandments, but on the ground of his soteriology, Christology and pneumatology.

The righteousness terminology is related to the righteousness terminology of Palestinian Judaism. One does not find in Paul any trace of the Greek and Hellenistic Jewish distinction between being righteous (man/man) and pious (man/God);[1] nor is righteousness in Paul one virtue among others.[2] Here, however, there is also a major shift; for to be righteous in Jewish literature means to obey the Torah and to repent of transgression, but in Paul it means to be saved by Christ. Most succinctly, righteousness in Judaism is a term which implies the *maintenance of status* among the group of the elect; in Paul it is a *transfer term*. In Judaism, that is, commitment to the covenant puts one 'in', while obedience (righteousness) subsequently keeps one in. In Paul's usage, 'be made righteous' ('be justified') is a term indicating getting in, not staying in the body of the saved. Thus when Paul says that one cannot be made righteous by works of law, he means that one cannot, by works of law, 'transfer to the body of the saved'. When Judaism said that one is righteous who obeys the law, the meaning is that one thereby stays in the covenant. The debate about righteousness by faith or by works of law thus turns out to result from the different usage of the 'righteous' word-group.

The difference in usage can be seen in part by noting the agreement on the point that correct behaviour is the condition of staying 'in'. In most of Judaism the principal term for one who behaves correctly is 'righteous' (the Dead Sea Scrolls are an exception, but there the usage does occur), while Paul never uses the term to refer to continuing correct behaviour. He refers rather to remaining 'blameless', 'innocent', 'steadfast', 'sound', 'guiltless' and the like (see the beginning of Chapter V, section 3), but never to being righteous, when speaking of the correct behaviour that keeps one 'in'.

The distinctiveness of Paul's usage of the *dik-* word-group can, however, best be seen in noting his use of the verb *dikaioō* and its passive forms. It is the adjective that is characteristically applied to the person in Hebrew

---

[1] Some examples are given by Schrenk, *TDNT* II, p. 182 (s.v. *dikaios*).
[2] See ibid., pp. 183, 192f., 210.

literature (one is righteous; usually collective: the righteous, *tsaddiqim*), while the verb simply means 'to declare one to be in the right who is in fact in the right'. God will not find innocent ('declare righteous', *yitsdaq*) a man who is in fact guilty,[3] for this would be a capricious miscarriage of justice. Only those who are innocent or righteous are said to be so. Similarly, when someone 'justifies God's judgment', he declares it to be just (which it is) and accepts it.[4] In Paul the verb often is used to mean 'become Christian' or 'be saved', and here one sees the 'transfer' use of the righteousness terminology fully at work.[5] There is no equivalent use in Hebrew. Thus in comparing 'righteousness' in Judaism and Paul, one must frequently shift from the adjective (in Judaism one who is righteous, *dikaios, tsaddiq*, is one who obeys the Torah) to the verb (in Paul one can be justified or made righteous, *dikaiousthai*, only by faith). Thus Paul contrasts with the biblical expression *ho dikaios ek pisteōs zēsetai* his own formulation: *en nomō oudeis dikaioutai* (Gal. 3.11). The adjective, which more readily implies the *status* of being among the righteous, tends to give way to the verb, which Paul can stretch to mean *being changed*. One is 'justified' from transgressions or from sin (I Cor. 6.9–11; Rom. 6.7); that is, one *transfers* from not being saved to being saved. This forces the righteousness terminology out of its customary meaning, and the shift helps show the distinctiveness of Paul's thought.[6]

There is a sense in which the righteousness terminology in Qumran is connected with the transfer from the non-saved to the saved state. By God's righteousness (= mercy) one is made to be righteous (= perfect of way). The similarity is probably connected with the fact that both in Qumran and in Paul one must 'be converted': join a group in which one was not born. Thus there is an element of the 'transfer' use also in Qumran. Neither the conception nor the use of terminology, however, is identical. The verb in Qumran means 'be righteous', that is, be upright or perfect of way, not 'be justified' in the sense of 'saved', as in Paul. Even when righteousness is conceived of as a gift of God, the verb 'to be righteous' means '*be* righteous', not 'be made righteous'. Further, human righteousness is conceived of as Torah obedience in Qumran, which is not the case in Paul. For Paul it may mean the general goal of religion, but that is not Torah obedience. Thus

---

[3] See Chapter I, section 8 n. 84; cf. IQH 9.14f.

[4] Sifra Shemini Milu'im 23 (to Lev. 9.22).

[5] See Gal. 2.15–17, and especially 2.17: 'seeking *to be made* righteous (justified)'; i.e. saved; Rom. 4.5: 'justifies the ungodly'; i.e. forgives and saves them. In Phil. 3.9 the noun has a similar meaning: what one gets who is in Christ.

[6] For the meaning 'set free' or 'made pure' from sin, Bauer (*Lexicon*, ET by Arndt and Gingrich) cites from originally Hebrew literature Ben Sirach 26.29 and Testament of Simeon 6.1, where *dikaioō* in the passive governs *apo* [*tēs*] *hamartias*. In both cases, however, the meaning is probably 'be innocent of' or 'be declared innocent of', rather than 'be set free from'. On Hermetica 13.9, also cited by Bauer (from Reitzenstein's *Hellenistische Mysterienreligionen*, p. 258), see Dodd's better explanation, *The Bible and the Greeks*, pp. 58f.

despite some similarities one still sees that Paul extends the terminology to cover meanings not present in Jewish literature.

There is not even a material equivalence between the Qumran statements that no one is righteous (*yitsdaq*) before God or in his judgment (IQH 9.14f.; cf. 7.28) and Paul's statement that no one is made righteous or justified (*dikaioutai*) by works of law (Gal. 2.16). What Paul means is that the right kind of righteousness ('life'; cf. Gal. 3.21) does not come by works of law, no matter how numerous. The statements in the Scrolls mean that, in comparison with God or in God's sight, no one is *perfect* by his own endeavour. The Qumran statements point towards the inadequacy and frailty of humans in comparison with God. They do not refer to how one is saved; for those who are not 'righteous' before God are the members of the sect. Even they, judged in comparison with God, will *never* be righteous in the sense of perfect. (Thus one does not have in the Qumran statements a forensic/eschatological declaration of the righteousness of some on the basis of deeds. From God's point of view, no one is ever really righteous; although from another perspective the sectarians can be called the righteous, as in IQH 1.36.)

In Judaism, being righteous and thus maintaining one's status in the covenant implies repentance, and repentance is in fact essential to the pattern. If repentance virtually disappears (as in Paul) or is so reduced as to have no scope and force (as in IV Ezra) covenantal nomism will either disappear or not work. In the dialogues of IV Ezra, the form of covenantal nomism was retained, but the reduction of repentance and the consequent requirement of perfection in obedience rendered the religion effectively non-operative. Only the perfectly obedient could be saved. In Paul, on the other hand, the absence of one of the essential motifs of the Jewish pattern is a clue to a change in the overall pattern. The author of the dialogues in IV Ezra is pessimistic about man's ability to obey the law. He does not seem to see repentance as providing a means to remain righteous despite disobedience, or else he is pessimistic about the likelihood of repentance. He is in any case pessimistic about the possibility of salvation, and this pessimism is connected with the reduction in the role accorded repentance. Paul's pessimism concerns life in 'the flesh'. He is not pessimistic about being able to obey the law, nor about the possibility of salvation; and he is thus not pessimistic in the way the author of the dialogues is. Repentance is not part of his scheme, not because he is pessimistic, but because he has a different scheme.

Another point at which the difference in the overall pattern becomes obvious is the definition of sin. In Judaism sin is uniformly transgression. We saw this to be the case even in the Dead Sea Scrolls, despite the connection of sin and the flesh (human frailty). Paul certainly held the conception of sin as transgression, and he made extensive use of it in Rom. 1–3. The dominant conception, however, is of sin as a power from which one must be freed in order to be saved. One must transfer from the lordship of sin to the lordship of Christ. In Qumran the weakness of sinful flesh is not a power out of the hands of which the elect were transferred; even the elect remain in the weakness of flesh. Salvation consists of remaining properly in the covenant, not in escaping the power of 'the flesh'. Further, the flesh is primarily weak, not a power at all. Thus despite surface similarity between Paul and Qumran on the nature of sin, the ideas are fundamentally different.[7]

It agrees with the basic difference on the definition of sin that *dying* does not have the same significance for Paul as it does, for example, in Rabbinic Judaism. Many have seen a 'Rabbinic' idea in Paul's view that one who is in Christ dies to the law.[8] In Paul the theme is connected with the transfer of lordships ('you have died to the law through the body of Christ, so that you may belong to another', Rom. 7.4) and implies the abrogation of the law, ideas which are quite foreign to Jewish literature. The Rabbinic statements have to do with death as *atoning for transgression*, not death to a *power* so that one may live to another power. The difference is between saying that one dies on account of transgression and that one dies to an enslaving power as a means of gaining liberty.

It perhaps goes without saying that the formulation of being among the saved is different. There is, to be sure, an important similarity: *both Judaism and Paul take full account of the individual and the group.*[9] In Judaism God's covenant is with *Israel*, but this in no way removes the individual's personal relation with God. He must be pious before God, remain right with God, and thus retain his membership in the group of the saved. In Paul one comes to be among the saved by the act of faith which results in participating *in Christ*. One *shares* the inheritance by becoming a 'joint heir' and *participates* in Christ's resurrection. The conception, as we have seen, is difficult to define positively. Negatively, it is neither simply personal mysticism nor external-istic group membership (like being a member of a college, to use Whiteley's example). It is the second negative which distinguishes Paul's view from that of Judaism. However close the feeling of corporate unity in Judaism, there are no expressions parallel to Paul's statement that Christians become one person in Christ (Gal. 3.28), just as one could not imagine a parallel formula to 'Christ is in you' (Israel is in you?). Here the *nature* of the group identity is different. The body of Christ is not analogous to Israel, and being in Christ is not formally the same as being in the covenant between God and Israel.

It is most striking that Paul thought that everyone – whether Jew or

---

[7] Cf. above, p. 281; Brandenburger, *Fleisch und Geist*, pp. 96–102.

[8] For example Schrenk, *TDNT* II, p. 218; see the Introduction, n.5.

[9] On the individual and the group in Paul, see Davies, *The Land*, p. 218; Käsemann, 'Anthropology', *Perspectives*, pp. 2–5, 10, 17, 29.

Gentile – must *transfer* from the group of those who are perishing to the group of those who are being saved. The only possible parallel to this view in Jewish literature is found in the insistence in the Qumran scrolls that, to be saved, the other Israelites must join the 'new covenant'. Even here, however, the *means* of transfer is conceived completely differently. The 'conversion' required at Qumran is 'repentance' and adherence to the sect's understanding of the covenant and the Torah, not death to sin and participation in one body, as is the case with Paul.

Thus in all these essential points – the meaning of 'righteousness', the role of repentance, the nature of sin, the nature of the saved 'group' and, most important, the necessity of transferring from the damned to the saved – Paul's thought can be sharply distinguished from anything to be found in Palestinian Judaism. Despite agreements, there is a fundamental difference. We thus in a way agree with one of the conclusions of previous comparisons of Paul and Judaism, that there are peripheral agreements and a basic disagreement.[10] I should say, however, that there are *substantial* agreements and a basic difference. Further, the difference is not located in a supposed antithesis of grace and works (on grace and works there is in fact agreement, and an agreement which can hardly be called 'peripheral'), but in the total type of religion.

The types are identified by what we have called 'patterns', referring to the sequence of steps from the logical starting-point to the logical conclusion of the religion. The term 'pattern' refers both to how one would think through the religion on its own terms (thus 'pattern' or 'structure' rather than 'systematic theology') and to the course which a participant or convert might follow in his own apprehension of and engagement with the religion (thus 'pattern' is sometimes more useful than 'structure': it refers more readily to the course which one follows in getting in and staying in). The logical steps are clearer in Judaism than in Paul. In Judaism, for example, transgression and obedience must precede reward and punishment. It was a major point of inquiry whether election was *perceived* to precede the requirement of obedience, and we concluded that it was. Here the relationship of the sequential steps to each other was crucial. The conclusion was that the participants themselves (at least those who left literary remains) saw the sequence or pattern as it has been described here. With regard to Paul the basic question was the sequence of his own thought and how the parts were related to one another. We can know far less about how Paul's converts perceived the gospel to 'work'. There seemed good reason to think that the sequence of Paul's thought was from solution to plight, with individual commandments being understood to be implied in the solution. One enters by becoming one with Christ Jesus and one stays in by remaining 'pure and

---

[10] See the Introduction.

blameless' and by not engaging in unions which are destructive of the union with Christ. Paul then thought through man's non-Christian position as the opposite of belonging to Christ or of being one with him. Thus one meets in Paul's thought a series of polarities rather than the smooth sequence of covenantal nomism: in Christ/in the flesh; under grace/under law; and the like. The basic insight was that the believer becomes one with Christ Jesus and that this effects a transfer of lordship and the beginning of a transformation which will be completed with the coming of the Lord. The sequence of thought, and thus the pattern of Paul's religious thought, is this: God has sent Christ to be the saviour of all, both Jew and Gentile (and has called Paul to be the apostle to the Gentiles); one participates in salvation by becoming one person with Christ, dying with him to sin and sharing the promise of his resurrection; the transformation, however, will not be completed until the Lord returns; meanwhile one who is in Christ has been freed from the power of sin and the uncleanness of transgression, and his behaviour should be determined by his new situation; since Christ died to save all, all men must have been under the dominion of sin, 'in the flesh' as opposed to being in the Spirit. It seems reasonable to call this way of thinking 'participationist eschatology'.

While the differences between Paul and Judaism have been determined by analysing the pattern, sequence or structure of religious *thinking*, it is not necessarily the case that we are dealing only with intellectual differences. Behind the differences of scheme, motif and formulation there may lie differences of religious experience. One may hazard the guess that the experience of being 'in Christ' was not the same as the experience of being 'in Israel'. This is a matter which is much more opaque to research than is thought, and we must be content with analysing how religion appears in Jewish and Pauline thought.

One of the basic questions posed by the history of research on Paul and Judaism, as was pointed out in the Introduction, is that of the accuracy of Paul's polemics. We noted that Montefiore and Schoeps, among others, supposed that the Judaism criticized by Paul must have been Hellenistic Judaism, since Rabbinic Judaism was better than one would gather from Paul's attacks. Others (we gave Bultmann as an example) have supposed that Paul's criticisms were perfectly accurate, and the criticism of Judaism given by Paul was held to be supported by Rabbinic literature. To assess this question we must carefully note what Paul's attack has been held to be and what it actually was. It is generally taken to be the case that Paul's criticism was that Judaism was a religion of legalistic works-righteousness; that is, that he criticized the means (works of law) while agreeing with the goal (righteousness). His failure to mention the significance of the covenant as indicating God's grace and of repentance as providing continuing access to forgiveness has been held either accurately to represent Judaism (the covenant conception receded in late Judaism) or to reveal ignorance of it. Jewish arrogance may be seen as under attack by Paul in the discussion of boasting in Rom. 3.27–4.5, and it has been maintained that smug self-satisfaction (as well as uncertainty of salvation) is evidenced in Rabbinic literature.

Our analysis of Rabbinic and other Palestinian Jewish literature did not reveal the kind of religion best characterized as legalistic works-righteousness. But more important for the present point is the observation that in any case that charge is not the heart of Paul's critique. As we argued in the discussion of Paul's attitude toward the law (Chapter V, section 4), the basis for Paul's polemic against the law, and consequently against doing the law, was his exclusivist soteriology. Since salvation is only by Christ, the following of *any* other path is wrong. Paul does say that faith excludes boasting, and he does warn the Jews against boasting (Rom. 2.17), but the warning is not against a self-righteousness which is based on the view that works earn merit before God. The warning is against boasting of the relationship to God which is *evidenced* by *possession* of the law and against being smug about the *knowledge* of God's will while in fact transgressing. Paul regarded zeal for the law itself as a good thing (Rom. 10.2; Phil. 3.6). What is wrong with it is not that it implies petty obedience and minimization of important matters, nor that it results in the tabulation of merit points before God, but *that it is not worth anything in comparison with being in Christ* (Phil. 3.4–11). The fundamental critique of the law is that following the law does not result in being found in Christ; for salvation and the gift of the Spirit come only by faith (Rom. 10.10; Gal. 3.1–5). Doing the law, in short, is wrong only because it is not faith. In itself obedience to the law is a good thing (Rom. 2.13), just as circumcision in itself is a good thing (2.25–3.2) and is faulted only when it seems to threaten the exclusiveness of salvation by faith in Christ (Galatians). What is wrong with Judaism is not that Jews seek to save themselves and become self-righteous about it, but that their seeking is not directed toward the right goal. They are not enlightened. They do not know that, as far as salvation goes, Christ has put an end to the law and provides a different righteousness from that provided by Torah obedience (Rom. 10.2–4).

In the heat of the argument Paul does say worse things than this about the law (Gal. 3.19), but the soberer reflection evident in Romans, as well as what he says about the law in Phil. 3 and elsewhere, shows the thrust of his argument. The law is good, even *doing* the law is good, but salvation is only by Christ; therefore the entire system represented by the law is worthless for salvation. *It is the change of 'entire systems' which makes it unnecessary for him to speak about repentance or the grace of God shown in the giving of the covenant.* These fade into the background because of the surpassing glory of the new dispensation (II Cor. 3.9f.). Paul was not trying accurately to represent Judaism on its own terms, nor need we suppose that he was ignorant on essential points. He simply saw the old dispensation as worthless in comparison with the new.

Paul himself often formulated his critique of Judaism (or Judaizing) as having to do with the *means* of attaining righteousness, 'by faith and not by works of law', and this formulation has been held to be accurate: Paul agreed on the *goal*, righteousness, but saw that it should be received by grace through faith, not achieved by works. But this formulation, though it is Paul's own, actually misstates the fundamental point of disagreement. Just as what is wrong with the law is that it is not Christ, so what is wrong with 'righteousness based on the law' (Phil. 3.9) is that it is not *the* righteousness from God which depends on faith, which is received when one is 'found in Christ', shares his suffering and is placed among those who will share his resurrection. That is, 'righteousness' itself is a different righteousness. It is, in effect, the salvation which comes from belonging to Christ and that alone. Thus Paul does not differ only on the means. Means and end correspond. The *real* righteousness is being saved by Christ, and it comes only through faith. This implies, again, that it is not the activity of doing the law which is wrong as an activity. Rather, such a means leads to the wrong end (righteousness based on the law); and the end itself is wrong, since it is not salvation in Christ.

The actual basis of Paul's critique of Judaism can be seen in one other way. Paul seems to ignore (and by implication deny) the grace of God toward Israel as evidenced by the election and the covenant. But this is neither because of ignorance of the significance of the covenant within Jewish thought nor because of the demise of the covenant conception in late Judaism. *Paul in fact explicitly denies that the Jewish covenant can be effective for salvation, thus consciously denying the basis of Judaism.* Circumcision without complete obedience is worthless or worse (Rom. 2.25–3.2; Gal. 3.10). More important, *the covenantal promises to Abraham do not apply to his descendants, but to Christians* (Rom. 4.13–25; Gal. 3.15–29). The discussions of 'law' and 'faith' are very concrete; they are designed to show that not those who keep the covenant, but only those who have faith in Christ and are 'in' him, receive the biblical promises. Thus Gal. 3.29: 'And *if* you are Christ's, *then* you are Abraham's offspring, heirs according to promise'; Rom. 4.24f.: 'It will be reckoned to us who believe in him that raised from the dead Jesus our Lord, who was put to death for our trespasses and raised for our justification.' It is thus not first of all against the *means* of being properly religious which are appropriate to Judaism that Paul polemicizes ('by works of law'), but against the prior fundamentals of Judaism: the election, the covenant and the law; and it is because these are wrong that the means appropriate to 'righteousness according to the law' (Torah observance and repentance) are held to be wrong or are not mentioned. In short, *this is what Paul finds wrong in Judaism: it is not Christianity.*

It is not one of the conclusions of this study that one of the patterns which we have described is superior to the other. I am not completely opposed to passing value judgments on ancient religions, although one must always be wary of using as the criteria for judgment only the values of modern humanism. One may detect a tone of self-righteous bigotry in Qumran and decry it, as one may regret some of Paul's vain gloriousness. With regard to the main lines of covenantal nomism and participationist eschatology, however, there seems to be no reason for thinking one is superior to another. Paul's view could hardly be maintained, and it was not maintained. Christianity rapidly became a new covenantal nomism, but Paulinism is not thereby proved inferior or superior. In saying that participationist eschatology is different from covenantal nomism, I mean only to say that it is different, not that the difference is instructive for seeing the error of Judaism's way.

Rather than coming to a theological judgment on the inferiority or superiority of either Paul or Judaism, I hope only to have presented a study which will be helpful for understanding. Throughout, difficult cases have been argued: that Rabbinic Judaism was not as it has been depicted by many scholars; that, despite differences important enough to make the Qumran community a sect, there is an underlying agreement of religious type between Qumran and other forms of Judaism known from the period; that the main theme of Paul's theology is found in his participationist language rather than in the theme of righteousness by faith; that despite agreements Paul's type of religion is basically different from anything known from Palestinian Judaism. The conclusions which involve a comparison were arrived at on the basis of a study of religious patterns. Their soundness depends on the soundness of the general view that it is possible to compare 'whole' with 'whole', that there is *significance* to a basic agreement or disagreement with regard to a whole pattern, and that basic agreement can exist despite differences on even important elements, while basic disagreement can exist despite agreement on important elements. This general view is the supposition on which the two principal conclusions rest: there was a generally prevailing religious type in Palestinian Judaism (covenantal nomism); Paul's pattern of religious thought was basically different (participationist eschatology).

Paul, Hellenism and Hellenistic Judaism

If the pattern of Paul's religious thought cannot be explained satisfactorily as having been derived from Palestinian Judaism, the question of where it comes from naturally arises. It would be presumptuous to pretend to treat this question in the last half of the conclusion to a book on something else, but the question cannot be simply ignored. I shall try to sketch how an answer might go, without pretending to completeness or certainty.

The question can perhaps best be put by focusing on Paul's conception of man's plight. The notion of enslavement, bondage, immediately suggests the possibility of a Hellenistic origin. It is this point which has served as a major element in the comparison drawn between Paul and Philo by Goodenough[11] and Sandmel.[12] Thus Sandmel has argued that Paul's approach to the human predicament was Hellenistic, and this is his description of the Greek view:

> To the Greeks, the world was a place of sorrows, man was an unhappy mixture of the soul, which was spirit and good, and of the body, which was material and evil; and life was a burden. The goal of Greek religion, indeed, its leitmotif, was that of escape: escape from the inevitable end, death, escape from bondage to the body.[13]

Sandmel makes the comparison between Paul and Philo thus:

> . . . Paul and Philo have many elements in common. Both of them view the Bible as a vehicle for individual salvation. Both are preoccupied with the question of how the individual can enable his mind (or soul; the words are interchangeable) to triumph over his body. For both of them, man, the mixture of the material and the immaterial, plays host to the struggle within him between the enlightened mind and the aggressive senses and passions. Both of them ask similar questions: Will the appetites of the body conquer man's reason? Or will man, through his reason, regiment his bodily desires?[14]

This seems accurately to describe Philo but not Paul. When Paul speaks of the conflict between 'spirit' and 'flesh' (Gal. 5.16–25) it would be better to capitalize the two words. The conflict is between God's Spirit and the Flesh, the power which opposes God (see especially v. 25). The Spirit which is here engaged in struggle is the same Spirit which Christians have, which dwells in them; it is not the human spirit at war against corporeality. Paul does sometimes relate the Flesh to human lusts and desires in a way reminiscent of Philo's *sōma/sēma* conception,[15] but the similarity is not profound. Paul does not present the human aspiration as being the liberation of one's own spirit from the bodily tomb. The human need is rather to become one with Christ Jesus and to have the Spirit of God. The war, in other words, is not within one's self, but has to do with which power one – body and soul –

---

[11] E. R. Goodenough, 'Paul and the Hellenization of Christianity', *Religions in Antiquity*, ed. J. Neusner, pp. 23–68.

[12] See specially *The Genius of Paul*, pp. 8–14.

[13] Ibid., p. 22.

[14] Ibid., p. 53.

[15] Note 'passions and desires' in Gal. 5.24, the phrase 'sinful body' in Rom. 6.6, and the conflict between the body and the mind in Rom. 7.23. Cf. Goodenough, op. cit. in n. 11, p. 53.

belongs to. Paul's 'flesh' is not the equivalent of Philo's 'body', nor is the
'spirit' in Paul the equivalent of 'soul' in Philo. The depiction of the 'real
person' sojourning in the body is possible for Philo (*Conf.* 77), but not for
Paul; and Paul can speak of a definite transfer from the flesh, and therefore
not from the body (Rom. 7.5), whereas Philo could not. Put another way,
Paul's view seems to owe as much to the apocalyptic theory of two aeons as to
the Hellenistic theory of the struggle between body and soul.

This reply to the proposal that man's plight in Paul can be seen as parallel
to man's plight in Philo should not be taken as denying all similarity. The
difference in conceptualization is vast; yet in addition to Paul's occasional
connection of the Flesh with human corporeality, there is a basic similarity
which is represented by the word *bondage.* The individual who is in the
covenant is not considered *enslaved* in Palestinian Jewish literature. In
apocalyptic literature he may be seen as *oppressed* during the evil aeon and as
unable to vindicate himself and become victorious until the eschaton,[16]
but this does not have quite the tone of slavery which meets us in Paul. I
should thus hesitate to explain man's plight in Paul's view as having been
simply taken over from apocalypticism, despite the pronounced similarities
(the two aeons, the opposing world powers, the resolution with God's
victory at the eschaton). One finds, in a way, the Hellenistic tone of slavery
and the apocalyptic scheme of opposing world powers. It might at first be
thought that the combination of these two conceptions (slavery and opposing
powers) is found in astrology, and it is noteworthy that in Galatians Paul
explicitly formulates the plight of the non-Christian in terms of bondage to
the astrological deities (Gal. 4.3). Yet astrology cannot offer the exhaustive
explanation of Paul's view, since it does not consider escape to be effected
by the change of aeons ('when the time had fully come', Gal. 4.4). Thus on
the basis of the traditional lines of history-of-religions research Paul appears
to have held to a curious combination of conceptions concerning man's
plight.

The explanation for this is probably that Paul did not begin with a definite
conception of a universal plight to which he sought a solution. If he had
begun with the Hellenistic (or Hellenistic Jewish, as seen in Philo) plight of
the human soul entrapped in the body/tomb, we should expect to see the
problem more fully articulated in those terms. Similarly, had he begun with
the plight of apocalypticism – the oppression of the righteous by the wicked,
perhaps representing the power of Belial[17] – we should expect to see that
more closely articulated and to find more of the apocalyptic conventions.
Man's plight, rather, is that he is *not in Christ*. He is in bondage to the
fundamental spirits of the universe (cf. astrology), 'in the Flesh' (cf. Philo's

[16] See, for example, I Enoch 95–7.
[17] Cf. IQM 1.1.

use of 'body' as the enemy), unable not to transgress (cf. Palestinian Judaism), and the like. Paul does not have simply a 'Jewish' or a 'Hellenistic' or a 'Hellenistic Jewish' conception of man's plight. It appears that Paul's thought was not simply taken over from any one scheme pre-existing in the ancient world.[18]

In claiming a measure of uniqueness for Paul we should be cautious on two points. One is that we must agree with the common observation that nothing is totally unique. Indeed, with respect to man's plight, one can see relationships between what Paul thought and various other conceptions in the ancient world. What is lacking is a precise parallel which accounts exhaustively for Paul's thought, and this has partly to do with Paul's making use of so many different schemes of thought, ranging from unrighteousness to slavery to the astral powers. These schemes are employed to describe the reverse of his soteriology, and they derive their meaning in Paul's thought from their context in his own theology, and not primarily from their meaning in their own thought-worlds. It is in the soteriological and Christological determination of his thought that Paul's uniqueness lies, not in the ingenuity of the concepts he employs. Secondly, we should note that saying that Paul's thought is to some degree unique is not a value judgment. It is not thereby made more profound. The basis of our tentative conclusion that Paul's conception of man's plight is not precisely paralleled in the ancient world is not the conviction that Christianity, to be true, must be novel. I simply do not know a precise parallel to Paul's thought, and it seems unlikely that one will appear, since his thought on man's plight seems to have been determined by his solution to it.

To summarize this part of the conclusion: Having noted that Paul, in essential ways, is different from Palestinian Judaism, we inquired whether or not the difference could be explained from Hellenism or Hellenistic Judaism, and we focused on the conception of man's plight. Although we could not perform a detailed analysis on this point, it seems that there is not any one simple source for Paul's view of the human dilemma. The explanation for this appears to lie in the fact that his view of the human plight was derived from his soteriology, although he made use of various conceptions in expressing it and when comparing man without Christ to one who lives in Christ. We cannot give an account here of Paul's relationship to all the contemporary religious movements, but it does appear that it may be just as difficult to peg him as a Hellenistic Jew who thought that Christ presented the true mystery or true *gnosis* as it is to characterize him as a Rabbinic Jew who thought that Jesus was the Messiah. In his letters Paul appears as one

---

[18] We should note that Sandmel, while finding close agreement between Paul and Philo, has also argued that Paul is best understood on his own terms, not on the basis of parallels. See *The Genius of Paul.*

who bases the explanations of his gospel, his theology, on the meaning of the death and resurrection of Jesus, not as one who has fitted the death and resurrection into a pre-existing scheme, where they take the place of other motifs with similar functions.

BIBLIOGRAPHY
AND SYSTEM OF REFERENCES

I TEXT AND TRANSLATIONS

A. RABBINIC LITERATURE

Since Rabbinic references are often complex and difficult to find, especially since they are often incorrectly or incompletely given (usually because of reliance on Billerbeck), I give here both a list of editions and translations used and an explanation of the reference system.[1]

1. The Mishnah

The principal edition used is that of H. Albeck, *Shishshah Sidre Mishnah* (The six orders of the Mishnah), 6 vols., Jerusalem/Tel Aviv 1958 and subsequent years.

Except where otherwise noted, the translation quoted is that of H. Danby, *The Mishnah*, Oxford 1933. For Pirke Aboth, I have also consulted the editions of R. T. Herford, *Pirke Aboth. The Ethics of the Talmud: Sayings of the Fathers*, New York 1962 (= 1945), and Charles Taylor, *Sayings of the Jewish Fathers*, Cambridge 1897 (repr. New York 1969).

The Mishnah is quoted by tractate, chapter and mishnah (paragraph), with no preceding M. Thus Berakoth 2.1 = Mishnah Berakoth, chapter 2, mishnah 1.

2. The Tosefta

The text used for the first three orders (covering the tractates from Berakoth to Kiddushin) is that of Saul Lieberman, *The Tosefta*, 4 vols., New York 1955–73. For the rest of the tractates I have used the edition of M. S. Zuckermandel, *Tosephta*, Jerusalem 1963 (= 1875). For selected tractates (referred to in the notes), I have used G. Kittel and K. H. Rengstorf, eds., *Die Tosefta. Text, Übersetzung, Erklärung* (Rabbinische Texte), Stuttgart 1934 and subsequent years.

A few tractates are translated into German, and fewer into English. The only translation cited is H. Danby, *Tractate Sanhedrin. Mishnah and Tosefta*, London 1919.

The Tosefta is cited by tractate, chapter and halakah, preceded by T. Thus T. Berakoth 2.1 = Tosefta, tractate Berakoth, chapter 2, halakah 1. Alternative

---

[1] The works listed in this Bibliography are only those referred to in the text and footnotes. For discussion of the contents of these and other Rabbinic materials and for longer lists of Midrashim, see H. L. Strack, *Introduction to the Talmud and Midrash*; G. F. Moore, *Judaism* I, pp. 135–73 (still the best general discussion of the literature in short compass); *JE*, *s.v.* 'Midrash' and 'Midrashim'; J. Bowker, *The Targums and Rabbinic Literature*, pp. 53–92.

enumeration systems for the chapters and halakot (as conveniently noted in the editions) are given in parentheses.

3. The Babylonian Talmud (*Talmud Babli*)

All of the editions of the Babylonian Talmud are identical with regard to the text (differing only in the number of commentaries printed, and the like). I have used a four-volume edition, published in New York, by E. Grossman, 1963.

Except where otherwise noted, the translations from the Babylonian Talmud are quoted from the Soncino edition: *The Babylonian Talmud*, general ed. I. Epstein, 35 vols., repr. in 18, London 1935–52 (repr. 1961).

The Babylonian Talmud is cited without the prefatory b or B sometimes employed, by tractate, folio and side of the standard edition. The folio and side numbers are also carried in the English translation. Thus Berakoth 4b = Babylonian Talmud, tractate Berakoth, folio 4, side 2. The English page number is frequently given.

4. The Palestinian Talmud (*Talmud Yerushalmi*)

For the Palestinian Talmud I have used two editions, the Venetian edition of 1522 (repr. New York, no date) and the Krotoshin edition of 1866 (repr. Jerusalem 1969).

There is a French translation by M. Schwab, *Le Talmud de Jérusalem*, Paris 1871–90 (repr., n.d.). There is an English translation of one tractate: M. Schwab, *The Talmud of Jerusalem*, vol. I: *Berakhoth*, New York 1969 (= 1886). Schwab's translations are often paraphrastic or worse, and they are only seldom cited. They should not be used without consulting the original. Further, use of the volumes is hindered by the fact that the folio and column numbers, by which the originals are most conveniently cited, are not printed.

As indicated, the Palestinian Talmud is cited by tractate, folio and column (four columns to each folio).[2] The tractate is prefaced by the letter p. After the folio and column, the chapter and halakah numbers (which generally correspond to the chapter and mishnah numbers of the mishnah being commented on) are given in parentheses. Thus p. Kiddushin 61d (1.10) = Palestinian Talmud, tractate Kiddushin, folio 61, column 4, chapter 1, halakah 10 (a comment on Kiddushin 1.10). The folio and column numbers in the two editions used are usually identical or virtually identical, but discrepancies are cited in the notes.

5. The Mekilta of R. Ishmael

Three editions have been used:

Mechilta d'Rabbi Ismael, ed. H. S. Horovitz; 2nd ed. by I. A. Rabin, Jerusalem 1960 (= 1930).

Mekilta d'Rabbi Ishmael, ed. M. Friedmann (Meir Ish Shalom), Vienna 1870 (repr. Jerusalem 1968).

Mekilta de-Rabbi Ishmael, 3 vols., ed. and transl. by J. Z. Lauterbach, Philadelphia 1933–35.

---

[2] The Palestinian Talmud is never cited 'by folio, front or back, exactly as in the Babylonian talmud' (Bowker, *Targums and Rabbinic Literature*, p. 67), but always by column.

I have relied on Lauterbach and Horovitz, citing Friedmann only when his text is significantly different. The English translation is that of Lauterbach, except where noted to the contrary.

The editions of the Mekilta, like those of most other Tannaitic midrashim, do *not* carry in the margins the chapter and verse number of the biblical passage being commented on, and for that reason it is awkward to find a reference such as Mek. Exod. 16.1, which is the most frequent form of citation, presumably since it is the form employed by Billerbeck.[3] (Billerbeck did give folio and side numbers for the edition he used, listed as Wien 1865; but this appears to be an edition which has not remained in use.) The proper way of referring to the Mekilta is by tractate and chapter. There are, however, difficulties and confusions. Some tractates are identical with biblical sections and some not. Authors sometimes cite the name of the biblical section being commented on rather than the name of the tractate (e.g. Bo' for Pisḥa). When a tractate overlaps two biblical sections, most, but not all, editors begin to renumber the chapters when the new biblical section starts. It is in these cases best to cite both the section and the tractate (thus Beshallaḥ Amalek and Jethro Amalek). Further, the chapters themselves are too long to render references to passages in them easy to locate. To make matters still worse, Lauterbach renumbered some of the chapters and in other ways did not always follow the principles which he himself gave in his article on 'The Arrangement and the Divisions of the Mekilta', *HUCA* I, 1924, pp. 452f.

To facilitate finding references to the Mekilta, I have cited tractate (and biblical section where necessary), chapter, page numbers in Horovitz's edition, volume and page numbers in Lauterbach's edition (*in that order*), and the passage in Exodus being commented on. The folio and side of Friedmann's edition are cited when his reading differs substantially. When Lauterbach differs from Horovitz in name of tractate or chapter number, I give first Horovitz and then Lauterbach in brackets. Thus Mek. Jethro Amalek 1 (195–6; II, 178 [Amalek 3]; to 18.12) = Mekilta, tractate Amalek (of the part that falls within the biblical section Jethro), ch. 1 (ch. 3 in Lauterbach's enumeration); pp. 195f. in Horovitz; vol. II, p. 178 in Lauterbach; commenting on Exod. 18.12.

6. Sifra (*Torat Kohanim*)

Three editions have been used:

Sifra d'Be Rab, ed. M. Friedmann (Meir Ish Shalom), Breslau 1915 (repr. Jerusalem 1967). This edition, the only critical text of Sifra, covers the commentary only to Lev. 3.9.

Sifra d'Be Rab. Hu' Sefer Torat Kohanim, ed. I. H. Weiss, Wien 1862.

Sifra d'Be Rab. Hu' Sefer Torat Kohanim, Jerusalem 1959 (a reprinting of the traditional text).

There is a German translation which has occasionally been employed:

Sifra. Halachischer Midrasch zu Leviticus, transl. by J. Winter. Breslau 1938.

Editions of Sifra do not carry in the margin the biblical chapter and verse being

---

[3] This form of reference is regrettably still recommended by Bowker (op. cit., pp. 71f.) for the Mekilta, Sifra and Sifre. It is equally inconvenient for all three Midrashim, except for the Finkelstein-Horovitz edition of Sifre Deut.

commented on. References are by biblical section, *either* pereq or parasha, and halakah. It is to be noted that two systems of division are employed which are not related to each other. There are pereqs and there are parashas, but one is not a sub-division of another. Both begin to be renumbered with the beginning of each biblical section, but they do not fall in any regular sequence in relation to each other. Thus Sifra Behuqqotai parasha 8.1 (to 27.26) = Sifra, biblical section Behuqqotai, parasha 8, halakah 1, commenting on Lev. 27.26.

7. Sifre Numbers (*Sifre Bemidbar*)

Sifre d'Be Rab, ed. M. Friedmann (Meir Ish Shalom), Vienna 1864 (repr. Jerusalem 1968).

Siphre d'Be Rab, Fasciculus primus: *Siphre ad Numeros adjecto Siphre zutta*, ed. H. S. Horovitz, Leipzig 1917 (repr. Jerusalem 1966).

I have also consulted the German translation:

Sifre zu Numeri, ed. K. G. Kuhn (Rabbinische Texte, zweite Reihe, 3. Band), Stuttgart 1959.

References to Sifre Num. are by paragraph (pisqa'), numbered consecutively without regard to biblical section, page number in Horovitz (Friedmann being cited only in case of disagreement), and passage commented on. Thus Sifre Num. 40 (43f.; to 6.24) = Sifre Numbers, pisqa' 40; Horovitz, pp. 43f.; commenting on Num. 6.24.

8. Sifre Deuteronomy (*Sifre Debarim*)

The principal text is:

Sifre on Deuteronomy, ed. L. Finkelstein and H. S. Horovitz, New York 1969 (= 1939).

I have also consulted Friedmann's text (see Sifre Num.).

The following partial translations were consulted:

Sifre zu Deuteronomium, erste Lieferung, ed. G. Kittel (Rabbinische Texte), Stuttgart 1922.

Sifre Deuteronomium, ed. Henrik Ljungman (Rabbinische Texte, zweite Reihe, Band 4, 1. Lieferung), Stuttgart 1964.

Citations of Sifre Deut. follow the same pattern as those of Sifre Num. Page numbers in the Finkelstein-Horovitz edition are cited.

9. Reconstructed Tannaitic Midrashim

Mekhilta d'Rabbi Sim'on b. Jochai, ed. J. N. Epstein and E. Z. Melamed, Jerusalem 1955. Cited by passage in Exodus (carried in margin) and page number.

Sifre Zuṭa. See Horovitz's ed. of Sifre Num. above. Cited by passage in Numbers (carried in margin) and page number.

Midrasch Tannaïm zum Deuteronomium, 2 vols., ed. D. Hoffmann, 1909. Repr. Jerusalem, n.d. Cited by passage in Deuteronomy (carried in margin) and page number.

10. The Fathers According to R. Nathan (*Aboth de Rabbi Nathan*). Abbreviated as ARN

Text:
Aboth de Rabbi Nathan, ed. by S. Schechter. Corrected edition, New York 1967
 (orig. publ. 1887).
Translation:
The Fathers According to Rabbi Nathan, trans. by Judah Goldin (YJS 10), New
 Haven 1955.
 References are given by chapter only. Page numbers are given as necessary.

11. Later Midrashim
(*a*) Midrash Rabbah[4]
Text:
Midrash Rabbah on the Five Books of the Torah and the Five Megillot, Wilna ed.,
 2 vols., 1878 (repr. Jerusalem 1961).
English translation:
Midrash Rabbah, general eds. H. Freedman and Maurice Simon, 10 vols., London
 1939.
 Citations are according to the Wilna edition, which divides the chapters into
paragraphs. The passage commented on and the page numbers of the ET are also
given.
(*b*) *Midrash Haggadol on the Pentateuch: Exodus*, ed. Mordecai Margulies,
 Jerusalem 1967. (Cited by biblical chapter and verse.)
(*c*) *Midrash Haggadol on the Pentateuch: Numbers*, ed. Z. M. Rabinowitz,
 Jerusalem 1967. (Cited by biblical chapter and verse.)
 Ibid., ed. S. Fisch, Manchester 1940.
(*d*) *Midrash Tanḥuma on the five books of the Torah*. Traditional text, repr.
 Jerusalem 1965.
(*e*) Ibid., ed. S. Buber, Wilna 1883 (repr. Jerusalem 1964).
 The Tanḥuma is cited by biblical section, chapter and paragraph (given in the
text). Where useful, I have cited page numbers of Buber's edition.
(*f*) *Yalqut Shim'oni: Midrash on the Torah, the Prophets and the Writings*,
 traditional text, repr. in 2 vols., Jerusalem 1960.
 The Yalqut is divided into long sections (each section is called a remez) which
are numbered consecutively through each of the two principal divisions: Torah/
Prophets and Writings. Each principal division contains approximately 1,000
sections or remezim, the enumeration starting over at the beginning of the second
division. The margin also carries the biblical section and chapter number, the
citing of which facilitates finding the reference.
(*g*) *The Midrash on Psalms*, transl. W. G. Braude, 2 vols. (YJS 13), New Haven
 1959.
(*h*) *Bet ha-Midrasch*, ed. A. Jellinek, 6 vols. in 2,[3] 1853 (repr. Jerusalem 1967).
(*i*) Translation anthologies cited:
   Joseph Bonsirven, *Textes Rabbiniques des deux premiers siècles chrétiens:
   pour servir à l'intelligence du Nouveau Testament*, Rome 1955.
   C. G. Montefiore, and H. Loewe, *A Rabbinic Anthology*, ca. 1938 (repr.
   New York, n.d.).

---

[4] A collection of diverse Midrashim. The title of the Wilna ed. is misleading. See *JE* 8, p. 558.

B. DEAD SEA SCROLLS

The Scrolls are all cited by column and line. Where line enumerations differ, I have followed those of Lohse. Except where otherwise noted, the text and translation of CD are those of Rabin; the text and translation of IQM are those of Yadin; and the translations of the other Scrolls are those of Vermes. For the text of the other Scrolls, I have always had Lohse's edition at hand, but where there are doubts I have also consulted the editions of IQS and IQH by Licht, the relevant passage in DJD, and Habermann's text. The other editions and translations cited below have been both consulted and cited. Editions consulted but not cited do not appear in the Bibliography.

1. General Texts

D. Barthélemy and J. T. Milik, eds., *Discoveries in the Judaean Desert* I: *Qumran Cave I*, Oxford 1955. (Cited as DJD I.)

A. M. Habermann, ed., *Megillot Midbar Yehuda* (The Scrolls from the Judean Desert), Israel 1959.

E. Lohse, ed., *Die Texte aus Qumran, Hebräisch und Deutsch*, Darmstadt ^{2}1971.

2. General Translations

J. Carmignac and P. Guilbert, *Les Textes de Qumran. Traduits et annotés*, vol. I: *La règle de la communauté; la règle de la guerre; les hymnes*, Paris 1961.

A. Dupont-Sommer, *The Essene Writings from Qumran*, ET by G. Vermes, Oxford and Cleveland 1962.

G. Vermes, *The Dead Sea Scrolls in English*, Harmondsworth 1962. (Later editions have been compared.)

3. The Manual of Discipline (IQS)

W. H. Brownlee, *The Dead Sea Manual of Discipline* (BASOR Supplementary Studies 10–12), New Haven 1951.

A. R. C. Leaney, *The Rule of Qumran and its Meaning*, London and Philadelphia 1966.

Jacob Licht, *Megillat ha-Serakim*, Jerusalem 1965.

P. Wernberg-Møller, *The Manual of Discipline*, Leiden 1957.

4. The Hymn Scroll (IQH)

M. Delcor, *Les Hymnes de Qumran* (*Hodayot*), Paris 1962.

Svend Holm-Nielsen, *Hodayot: Psalms from Qumran*, Aarhus 1960.

Jacob Licht, *Megillat ha-Hodayot*, Jerusalem 1957.

M. Mansoor, *The Thanksgiving Hymns* (STDJ III), Grand Rapids 1961.

5. The War Scroll (IQM)

Yigael Yadin, *The Scroll of the War of the Sons of Light against the Sons of Darkness*, ET by Batya and Chaim Rabin, Oxford 1962.

6. The Covenant of Damascus (CD)

Chaim Rabin, *The Zadokite Documents*, Oxford 1958.

C. APOCRYPHA AND PSEUDEPIGRAPHA

The texts and translations which are used and the method of citation are given in the footnotes to each section. I give here only the bibliographical references, omitting, however, the standard biblical texts and versions.

1. General Translations
R. H. Charles, ed., *The Apocrypha and Pseudepigrapha of the Old Testament*, 2 vols., Oxford 1913 (repr. 1963).
A. Kahana, ed., *Ha-Sepherim ha-Hestsonim*, 2 vols., rev. ed., Jerusalem 1970.

2. Ben Sirach
Israel Lévi, *The Hebrew Text of the Book of Ecclesiasticus*, Leiden 1904 (repr. 1951).
S. Schechter and C. Taylor, *The Wisdom of Ben Sira. Portions of the Book Ecclesiasticus from Hebrew Manuscripts in the Cairo Genizah Collection*, Cambridge 1899.
M. S. Segal, *Sefer Ben Sira Ha-Shalem*, Jerusalem ²1959.
Yigael Yadin, *The Ben Sira Scroll from Masada*, ET by A. Newman, Jerusalem 1965.

3. I Enoch
Matthew Black, ed., *Apocalypsis Henochi Graece*, Leiden 1970.
Campbell Bonner, *The Last Chapters of Enoch in Greek* (Studies and Documents 8), London 1937 (repr. Darmstadt 1968).
R. H. Charles, *The Book of Enoch or I Enoch, translated from the editor's Ethiopic text*, Oxford ²1912. (Cited as *I Enoch*.)
Adolphe Lods, *Le livre d'Hénoch. Fragments grecs découverts à Akhmîm (Haute-Egypte)*, Paris 1892.

4. Jubilees
R. H. Charles, *The Book of Jubilees or the Little Genesis, translated from the editor's Ethiopic text*, London 1902.

5. The Psalms of Solomon
Wilhelm Frankenberg, *Die Datierung der Psalmen Salomos*, Giessen 1896.
O. von Gebhardt, Ψαλμοὶ Σολομῶντος: *Die Psalmen Salomo's zum ersten Male ... herausgegeben* (TU XIII 2), Leipzig 1895.
R. Harris and A. Mingana, *The Odes and Psalms of Solomon*, 2 vols., Manchester 1916.
H. E. Ryle and M. R. James, ΨΑΛΜΟΙ ΣΟΛΟΜΩΝΤΟΣ. *Psalms of the Pharisees, commonly called The Psalms of Solomon*, Cambridge 1891.

6. IV Ezra
G. H. Box, *The Ezra-Apocalypse*, London 1912.

D. BIBLE

It does not seem necessary give bibliographical data for the standard biblical texts and translations. Quotations are generally according to the RSV, *except* when biblical passages are contained in a passage being quoted from another source, when a Rabbinic comment requires a special rendering of the biblical text, and when otherwise indicated. I have also consulted the Jerusalem Bible and the New English Bible. The Hebrew Old Testament text is that of Kittel; the Greek New Testament text is that of Nestle-Aland, 25th ed. I have relied on the short LXX texts published by Rahlfs and by Swete for the Greek Old Testament.

II REFERENCE WORKS

Again, the standard reference works familiar to all students of the Bible and related subjects are cited in the notes without full bibliographical information: Arndt and Gingrich's ed. of Bauer's Greek lexicon; Jastrow's dictionary of Rabbinic and related literature; the Hebrew lexicon edited by Brown, Driver and Briggs; Segal's grammar of Mishnaic Hebrew; Thackeray's grammar of the LXX. Used, but not cited in the notes are the following: Hatch and Redpath's concordance to the LXX; Moulton and Geden's concordance to the NT; the concordances to the OT by both Lisowski and Mandelkern; the concordances to the DSS by Kuhn and by Habermann.

Of dictionaries and encyclopedias, principal use has been made of the *Jewish Encyclopedia* (ed. Singer, 1901), the *Interpreter's Dictionary of the Bible* (ed. Buttrick and others, 1962), and Kittel's *Wörterbuch*. It should be explained that the latter is generally cited in the English translation (*TDNT*, ed. G. W. Bromily, 1964 and subsequent years).

The following reference works have proved most useful in the study and are probably less familiar to biblical students:

M. Haiman, *Sefer Torah, Ha-Ketubah, ve-Ha-Massorah 'al Torah, Nebi'im ve-Ketubim*, 3 vols., Tel Aviv 1965 (= 1936). This is an index, by biblical passage, of comments on that biblical passage in Rabbinic literature. There are many errors, both of omission and commission, but the work nevertheless proves very valuable, especially since many Rabbinic works do not have indices to biblical passages.

C. Y. Kasovsky, *'Otsar Leshon Ha-Mishnah: Thesaurus Mishnae: Concordantiae quae in sex Mishnae ordinibus reperiuntur*, rev. ed. by Moshe Kasovsky, 4 vols., Tel Aviv 1967.

C. J. Kasowski (the same as above), *'Otsar Leshon Ha-Tosefta: Thesaurus Thosephthae: Concordantiae, etc.*, ed. by Moshe Kasovsky, 6 vols., Jerusalem, concluding in 1961.

Biniamin Kosovsky, *Otzar Leshon Hatanna'im: Concordantiae verborum quae in Mechilta d'Rabbi Ismael reperiuntur*, 4 vols., Jerusalem 1965–66.

— *Otzar Leshon Hatanna'im: Concordantiae verborum quae in Sifra ... reperiuntur*, 4 vols., Jerusalem 1967–69.

— *Otzar Leshon Hatanna'im: Thesaurus "Sifrei": Concordantiae verborum quae in ("Sifrei" Numeri et Deuteronomium) reperiuntur*, 5 vols., Jerusalem 1970–74.

III GENERAL

Abelson, J., *The Immanence of God in Rabbinical Literature*, New York 1969 (= 1912).

Aleksandrov, G. S., 'The Role of 'Aqiba in the Bar Kokhba Rebellion', ET by Sam Driver in Neusner's *Eliezer* II, pp. 422–36.

Alon, G., *Meḥqarim Be-Toldot Yisra'el* I (Studies in Jewish History), Tel Aviv ²1967.

Amiot, F., *The Key Concepts of St. Paul*, ET by J. Dingle, New York 1962.

Andrews, Mary Z., 'Paul and Repentance', *JBL* 54, 1935, p. 125.

Bacher, W., *Die Agada der Tannaiten*, 2 vols., Strassburg ²1903 and 1890 (repr. 1965, 1966).

Baltzer, Klaus, *The Covenant Formulary*, ET by David E. Green, Philadelphia 1971.

Bamberger, B. J., *Proselytism in the Talmudic Period*, Cincinnati 1939 (repr. 1968).

Bammel E.,'Gottes ΔIAΘHKH (Gal. III. 15–17) und das jüdische Rechtsdenken', *NTS* 6, 1959–60, pp. 313–19.

— 'Νόμος Χριστοῦ', *Studia Evangelica* III (TU 88), Berlin 1964, pp. 120–8.

— 'Paul and Judaism', *The Modern Churchman* n.s. 6, 1962–3, pp. 279–85.

Banks, Robert, *Jesus and the Law in the Synoptic Tradition* (SNTSMS 28), Cambridge 1975.

Bardtke, H., 'Considérations sur les cantiques de Qumrân', *RB* 63, 1956, pp. 220–33.

— (ed.), *Qumran-Probleme. Vorträge des leipziger Symposions über Qumran-Probleme vom 9. bis 14. Oktober 1961*, Berlin 1963.

Baron, S. W., and others, *Yitzhak F. Baer Jubilee Volume*, Jerusalem 1960 [in Hebrew].

Barrett, C. K., *A Commentary on the Epistle to the Romans* (Black/Harper), London and New York 1957.

Barth, M., *Justification. Pauline Texts Interpreted in the Light of the Old and New Testaments*, Grand Rapids 1970.

— 'The Kerygma of Galatians', *Interpretation* 21, 1967, pp. 131–46.

Barthélemy, D., 'La sainteté selon la communauté de Qumrân et selon l'Évangile', *La secte de Qumrân et les origines du Christianisme* (ed. van der Ploeg), pp. 203–16.

Becker, J., *Das Heil Gottes. Heils- und Sündenbegriffe in den Qumrantexten und im Neuen Testament* (SUNT 3), Göttingen 1964.

— *Untersuchungen zur Entstehungsgeschichte der Testamente der zwölf Patriarchen*, Leiden 1970.

Beilner, Wolfgang, 'Der Ursprung des Pharisäismus', *BZ* 3, 1959, pp. 235–51.

Belkin, Samuel, 'The Problem of Paul's Background', *JBL* 54, 1935, pp. 41–60.

Berkovits, E., 'The Centrality of Halakhah', *Understanding Rabbinic Judaism* (ed. Neusner), pp. 65–70.

Betz, O., 'Le ministère cultuel dans la secte de Qumrân et dans le Christianisme primitif', *La secte de Qumrân et les origines du Christianisme* (ed. van der Ploeg), pp. 163–202.
— *What do we know about Jesus?* London 1968.
Bietenhardt, Hans, 'Sabbatvorschriften von Qumrān im Lichte des rabbinischen Rechts und der Evangelien', *Qumran-Probleme* (ed. Bardtke), pp. 53–74.
Black, Matthew, 'Pharisees', *IDB*, vol. 3, pp. 774–81.
— *The Scrolls and Christian Origins*, New York 1961.
— (ed.), *The Scrolls and Christianity* (Theological Collections II), London 1969.
Blackman, E. C., *Marcion and his Influence*, London 1948.
Bloch, Renée, 'Midrash', *Supplément au Dictionnaire de la Bible* 5, Paris 1957, cols. 1263–81.
— 'Note méthodologique pour l'étude de la littérature rabbinique', *RSR* 43, 1955, pp. 194–227.
Bogaert, P. *Apocalypse de Baruch*, 2 vols. (Sources Chrétiennes 144), Paris 1969.
Bokser, B. M., 'Jacob N. Epstein's *Introduction to the Text of the Mishnah*' and 'Jacob N. Epstein on the Formation of the Mishnah', *The Modern Study of the Mishnah* (ed. J. Neusner), pp. 13–36 and 37–55.
Bokser, Ben Zion, *Pharisaic Judaism in Transition: R. Eliezer the Great and Jewish Reconstruction after the War with Rome*, New York 1935.
Bonsirven, J., *Le judaïsme Palestinien au temps de Jésus-Christ*, 2 vols., Paris 1934.
Bornkamm, Günther, *Geschichte und Glaube* II (Gesammelte Aufsätze Band IV), Munich 1971.
— *Paul*, ET by D. M. G. Stalker, London 1971.
Bousset, W., *Die Religion des Judentums im neutestamentlichen Zeitalter*, Berlin 1903.
— *Die Religion des Judentums im späthellenistischen Zeitalter* (ed. H. Gressmann) (HNT 21), Tübingen [4]1966. (Repr. of 1925 ed.).
— *Jesu Predigt in ihrem Gegensatz zum Judentum*, Göttingen 1892.
Bouttier, M., *Christianity According to Paul*, ET by Frank Clarke (SBT 49), London 1966.
— *En Christ*, Paris 1962.
Bowker, John, *Jesus and the Pharisees*, Cambridge 1973.
— *The Targums and Rabbinic Literature*, Cambridge 1969.
Box, G. H., 'The Idea of Intermediation in Jewish Theology', *JQR* 23, 1932–33, pp. 103–19.
Brandenburger, Egon, *Adam und Christus. Exegetisch-religionsgeschichtliche Untersuchung zu Röm. 5,12–21 (1. Kor. 15)* (WMANT 7), Neukirchen 1962.
— *Fleisch und Geist. Paulus und die dualistische Weisheit* (WMANT 29), Neukirchen 1968.
Brauch, M., *Set Free To Be*, Valley Forge 1975.
Braun, H., 'Beobachtungen zur Tora-Verschärfung im häretischen Spätjudentum', *TLZ* 79, 1954, cols. 347–52.
— *Gesammelte Studien zum Neuen Testament und seiner Umwelt*, Tübingen [2]1967. The following articles:
'Römer 7, 7–25 und das Selbstverständnis des Qumran-Frommen', pp.

100–19 = *ZTK* 56, 1959, pp. 1–18.

'"Umkehr" in spätjüdisch-häretischer und in frühchristlicher Sicht', pp. 70–85 = *ZTK* 50, 1953, pp. 243–58.

'Vom Erbarmen Gottes über den Gerechten: zur Theologie der Psalmen Salomos', pp. 8–69 = *ZNW* 43, 1950–51, pp. 1–54.

— *Spätjüdisch-häretischer und frühchristlicher Radikalismus I: Das Spätjudentum*, Tübingen 1957.

Breech, Earl, 'These Fragments I Have Shored Against My Ruins: The Form and Function of 4 Ezra', *JBL* 92, 1973, pp. 267–74.

Brocke, M., 'Tun und Lohn im nachbiblischen Judentum', *Bibel und Leben* 8, 1967, pp. 166–78.

Bröker, G., *Die Lehre von der Sünde bei Paulus und im Schrifttum der Sekte von Qumrān*, Diss. Leipzig 1959, Report in *TLZ* 87, 1962, cols. 709f. Thesis not seen.

Brown, R. E., 'The Qumran Scrolls and the Johannine Gospel and Epistles', *The Scrolls and the New Testament* (ed. Stendahl), pp. 183–207.

Brownlee, W. H., 'Light on the Manual of Discipline from the Book of Jubilees', *BASOR* 132, October 1951, pp. 30–2.

Buchanan, G. W., *The Consequences of the Covenant* (SNT 20), Leiden 1970.

Buck, C. and Taylor, G., *Saint Paul, a Study of the Development of his Thought*, New York 1969.

Büchler, A., 'Ben Sira's Conception of Sin and Atonement', *JQR*, n.s. 13, 1922–23, pp. 303–35, 461–502; 14, 1923–24, pp. 53–83.

— *Der galiläische ʿAm-haʾareṣ des zweiten Jahrhunderts*, Hildesheim 1968 (= 1906).

— 'The Law of Purification in Mark VII. 1–23', *ExpT* 21, 1909–10, pp. 34–40.

— *Studies in Sin and Atonement in the Rabbinic Literature of the First Century*, New York 1967 (= 1939).

— *Types of Jewish-Palestinian Piety From 70 B.C.E. to 70 C.E.*, New York 1968 (= 1922).

Bultmann, R., 'Δικαιοσύνη Θεοῦ', *JBL* 83, 1964, pp. 12–16.

— *Jesus and the Word*, ET by L. P. Smith and E. H. Lantero, New York 1934 (repr. New York and London 1958).

—— 'The πίστις Group in the New Testament, πιστεύω κτλ.', *TDNT* VI, pp. 203–22.

— 'Romans 7 and the Anthropology of Paul', *Existence and Faith* (ed. S. M. Ogden), New York 1960, pp. 147–57 (first published 1932).

— *Theology of the New Testament* I, ET by K. Grobel, New York and London 1952.

— *Das Urchristentum im Rahmen der antiken Religionen*, Zürich 1949. ET by R. H. Fuller, *Primitive Christianity in Its Contemporary Setting*, London and New York 1956.

Burchard, Christoph, *Bibliographie zu den Handschriften vom toten Meer*, 2 vols. (BZAW 76, 89), Berlin 1957, 1965.

Burkill, T. A., 'Theological Antinomies: Ben Sira and St Mark', *New Light on the Earliest Gospel*, Ithaca 1972.

Burrows, Millar, *The Dead Sea Scrolls*, New York and London 1955.

— *More Light on the Dead Sea Scrolls*, New York and London 1958.

Burton, E. de Witt, *A Critical and Exegetical Commentary on the Epistle to the Galatians* (ICC), Edinburgh 1921 (repr. 1959).

Cambier, J., 'Justice de Dieu, salut de tous les hommes et foi', *RB* 71, 1964, pp. 537–83.

Carmignac, J., 'La théologie de la souffrance dans les Hymnes de Qumrân', *RQ* 3, 1961–2, pp. 365–86.

— 'L'utilité ou l'inutilité des sacrifices sanglants dans la "Règle de la Communauté" de Qumrân', *RB* 63, 1956, pp. 524–32. With a postscript by J. T. Milik.

Cerfaux, L., *The Christian in the Theology of St Paul*, New York 1967.

Chamberlain, J. V., 'Toward a Qumran Soteriology', *NT* 3, 1959, pp. 305–13.

Conzelmann, H., 'Current Problems in Pauline Research', *Interpretation* 22, 1968, pp. 171–86 (= *Der Evangelische Erzieher* 18, 1966, pp. 241–52).

— *An Outline of the Theology of the New Testament*, ET by John Bowden, London and New York 1969.

— 'Die Rechtfertigungslehre des Paulus: Theologie oder Anthropologie?', *EvT* 28, 1968, pp. 389–404.

Coppens, J., *L'état présent des études pauliniennes*, Bruges 1956.

Cranfield, C. E. B., *A Critical and Exegetical Commentary on the Epistle to the Romans* I (ICC, new ed.), Edinburgh 1975.

— 'St Paul and the Law', *SJT* 17, 1964, pp. 43–68.

Crenshaw, James L., 'The Problem of Theodicy in Sirach: On Human Bondage', *JBL* 94, 1975, pp. 47–64.

Cross, F. M. Jr, *The Ancient Library of Qumran*, New York 1961.

Dahl, N. A., 'The Atonement – An Adequate Reward for the Akedah? (Rom. 8.32)', *Neotestamentica et Semitica: Studies in honour of Matthew Black* (ed. E. E. Ellis and M. Wilcox), Edinburgh 1969.

Daniélou, J., *The Dead Sea Scrolls and Primitive Christianity*, ET by S. Attanasio, Baltimore 1958.

Daube, David, *Wine in the Bible*, St Paul's Lecture 1974.

Davenport, G. L., *The Eschatology of the Book of Jubilees* (SPB 20), Leiden 1971.

Davies, W. D., 'Apocalyptic and Pharisaism', *Christian Origins and Judaism*, Philadelphia 1962, pp. 19–30.

— *The Gospel and the Land*, Berkeley 1974.

— *Invitation to the New Testament*, New York 1966.

— 'Paul and Judaism', *The Bible and Modern Scholarship* (ed. P. Hyatt), pp. 178–86.

— *Paul and Rabbinic Judaism*, London ²1958.

— 'Paul: from the Semitic Point of View', *Cambridge History of Judaism* (forthcoming).

— *Torah in the Messianic Age and/or the Age to Come* (JBL Monograph Series 7), Philadelphia 1952.

Deissmann, Adolf, *Paul*, ET by W. E. Wilson, New York 1957 (= ²1927).

de Jonge, M., 'Christian Influence in the Testaments of the Twelve Patriarchs', *NT* 4, 1960, pp. 182–235.

— 'Once More: Christian Influence in the Testaments of the Twelve Patriarchs', *NT* 5, 1962, pp. 311–19.

— *The Testaments of the Twelve Patriarchs*, Leiden 1953.

Delcor, M., 'Le sacerdoce, les lieux de culte, les rites et les fêtes dans les documents de Khirbet Qumrân', *RHR* 144, 1953, pp. 5–41.

— 'Le vocabulaire juridique, cultuel et mystique de l'"initiation" dans la secte de Qumrân', *Qumran-Probleme* (ed. Bardtke), pp. 109–34.

Denis, A. M., *Introduction aux Pseudépigraphes grecs d'Ancien Testament* (Studia in Veteris Testamenti Pseudepigrapha I), Leiden 1970.

Descamps, A. and others, *Littérature et théologie pauliniennes* (Recherches Bibliques 5), Bruges and Paris 1960.

DiLella, A. A., *The Hebrew Text of Sirach*, The Hague 1966.

Dinkler, Erich, 'Prädestination bei Paulus. Exegetische Bemerkungen zum Römerbrief', *Festschrift für Günther Dehn* (ed. W. Schneemelcher), Neukirchen 1957, pp. 81–102.

Dodd, C. H., *The Bible and the Greeks*, London 1935.

— 'The Mind of Paul II', *New Testament Studies*, Manchester 1953.

Dodds, E. R., *The Greeks and the Irrational*, Berkeley and Los Angeles 1966 (= 1951).

Donfried, K. P., 'False Presuppositions in the Study of Romans', *CBQ* 36, 1974, pp. 332–55.

Driver, G. R., 'Hebrew Notes on the "Wisdom of Jesus Ben Sirach"', *JBL* 53, 1934, pp. 273–90.

van Dülmen, Andrea, *Die Theologie des Gesetzes bei Paulus*, Stuttgart 1968.

Dupont, Jacques, 'La conversion de Paul et son influence sur la conception du salut par la foi', *Foi et Salut selon S. Paul*, by M. Barth and others (AB 42), Rome 1970, pp. 67–88.

— *La réconciliation dans la théologie de sant Paul*, Bruges and Paris 1953.

— ΣΥΝ ΧΡΙΣΤΩΙ. *L'union avec le Christ suivant saint Paul*, Bruges 1952.

Dupont-Sommer, A., '"Elus de Dieu" et "Elu de Dieu" dans le Commentaire d'Habacuc', *Proceedings of the twenty-second Congress of Orientalists* II (ed. Z. V. Togan), Leiden 1957, pp. 568–72.

— 'Le Problème des influences étrangères sur la secte juive de Qoumrân', *RHPhR* 35, 1955, pp. 75–92.

Elbogen, I., *Geschichte des Achtzehngebets*, Breslau 1903.

Ellis, E. E., *Paul and His Recent Interpreters*, Grand Rapids 1961.

— Review of Whiteley, *Theology of St Paul*, *JBL* 84, 1965, pp. 454–6.

Epp, Eldon J., Review of Samuel Sandmel, *The First Christian Century in Judaism and Christianity*, *Central Conference of American Rabbis Journal* 18, 1971, pp. 72–4.

Eppstein, Victor, 'When and How the Sadducees were Excommunicated', *JBL* 85, 1966, pp. 213–24.

Epstein, J. N., *Mabo' le-Nosah ha-Mishnah*, 2 vols. (*Introduction to the Mishnah*), Jerusalem 1964.

— *Mebo'ot le-Sifrut ha-Tannaim* (Introduction to Tannaitic Literature), ed. E. Z. Melamed, Jerusalem 1957.

Farmer, W. R., Moule, C. F. D., and Niebuhr, R. R., eds., *Christian History and Interpretation: Studies presented to John Knox*, Cambridge 1967.

Finkelstein, Louis, *Akiba: Scholar, Saint and Martyr*, New York 1962 (= 1936).
— 'The Book of Jubilees and the Rabbinic Halaka', *HTR* 16, 1928, pp. 39–61 (reprinted in *Pharisaism in the Making*, pp. 199–221).
— 'The Development of the Amidah', *JQR* n.s. 16, 1925–6, pp. 1–43; 127–70 (reprinted in *Pharisaism in the Making*, pp. 245–332).
— 'Introductory Study to *Pirke Abot*', *JBL* 57, 1938, pp. 13–50 (reprinted in *Pharisaism in the Making*, pp. 121–58).
— *Mabo le-Massektot Abot ve-Abot d'Rabbi Natan* (Introduction to the Treatises Abot and Abot of Rabbi Nathan), New York 1950.
— *New Light from the Prophets*, London 1969.
— *Pharisaism in the Making* (Selected Essays), New York 1972.
— *The Pharisees: The Sociological Background of Their Faith*, 2 vols., Philadelphia ³1962.
— 'Studies in the Tannaitic Midrashim', *Proceedings of the American Academy of Jewish Research* VI, 1934–5, pp. 189–228.
Fitzmyer, J. A., 'The Contribution of Qumran Aramaic to the Study of the New Testament', *NTS* 20, 1974, pp. 382–407.
— 'The Languages of Palestine in the First Century A.D.', *CBQ* 32, 1970, pp. 501–31.
— *Pauline Theology*, Englewood Cliffs 1967.
— Review of A. D. Macho's edition of *Targum Neofiti*, *CBQ* 32, 1970, pp. 107–12.
— Review of M. McNamara, *The New Testament and the Palestinian Targum to the Pentateuch*, *Theological Studies* 29, 1968, pp. 321–6.
— 'Saint Paul and the Law', *The Jurist* 27, 1967, pp. 18–36.
Flusser, D., 'The Dead Sea Sect and Pre-Pauline Christianity', *Aspects* (ed. Rabin and Yadin), pp. 215–66.
— 'The Jewish Origin of Christianity', *Yitzhak F. Baer Jubilee Volume* (ed. Baron), pp. 75–98 [in Hebrew].
— 'Scholem's recent book on Merkabah Literature', *JJS* 11, 1960, pp. 59–68.
— 'Two notes on the Midrash on 2 Sam. VII', *IEJ* 9, 1959, pp. 99–109.
Ford, J. M., '"Hast Thou Tithed thy Meal?" and "Is thy Child Kosher?"', *JTS* n.s. 17, 1966, pp. 71–9.
Forkman, Göran, *The Limits of the Religious Community*, Lund 1972.
Furnish, V. P., 'The Place and Purpose of Philippians iii', *NTS* 10, 1963, pp. 80–5.
— *Theology and Ethics in Paul*, New York 1968.
Gärtner, Bertil, *The Temple and the Community in Qumran and the New Testament* (SNTSMS 1), Cambridge 1965.
Gaston, Lloyd, Review of F. W. Danker, *Jesus and the New Age According to St Luke*, *JBL* 94, 1975, pp. 140f.
Gélin, Albert, *Les Pauvres de Yahvé* (Témoins de Dieu 14), Paris 1953.
Gibbs, John G., *Creation and Redemption*, Leiden 1971.
Giblin, C. H., *In Hope of God's Glory*, New York 1970.
Ginzberg, Louis, *On Jewish Law and Lore*, Cleveland and New York 1962.
The following articles:
'An Introduction to the Palestinian Talmud' (repr. from *Commentary on the*

Jerusalem Talmud, New York 1941).
'The Significance of the Halachah for Jewish History' (trans. by Arthur Hertz-
berg from a Hebrew address given in 1929–30).
Goguel, M., 'Remarques sur un aspect de la conversion de Paul', *JBL* 53, 1934,
pp. 257–67.
Goldberg, A. M., *Untersuchungen über die Vorstellung von der Schekhinah in der
frühen rabbinischen Literatur* (SJ 5), Berlin 1969.
Goldin, Judah, *The Song at the Sea*, New Haven and London 1971.
— 'The Thinking of the Rabbis', *Judaism* 5, 1956, pp. 3–12.
Goodenough, E. R., *Jewish Symbols in the Greco-Roman Period*, 12 vols., New
York 1953–65.
— 'Paul and the Hellenization of Christianity' (completed by A. T. Kraabel),
Religions in Antiquity. Essays in Memory of Erwin Ramsdell Goodenough (ed.
J. Neusner) (Studies in the History of Religions 14), Leiden 1968, pp. 23–68.
Goodspeed, E. J., *The Meaning of Ephesians*, Chicago 1933.
— 'Some Greek Notes: III Justification', *JBL* 73, 1954, pp. 86–91.
Greenfield, J., Review of *The Targums of Onkelos and Jonathan ben Uzziel on the
Pentateuch*, ET by J. W. Etheridge, *JBL* 89, 1970, pp. 238f.
Guilbert, P., 'Plan de la "Règle de la Communauté"', *RQ* 1, 1958–9, pp. 323–44.
Hanhart, Karel, 'Paul's Hope in the Face of Death', *JBL* 88, 1969, pp. 445–57.
Harnisch, Wolfgang, *Verhängnis und Verheissung der Geschichte. Untersuchungen
zum Zeit- und Geschichtsverständnis im 4. Buch Esra und in der syr. Baruch-
apokalypse* (FRLANT 97), Göttingen 1969.
Harrison, P. N., *Paulines and Pastorals*, London 1964.
Harrison, R. K., 'The Rites and Customs of the Qumran Sect', *The Scroll's and
Christianity* (ed. M. Black), pp. 22–36.
Haspecker, J., *Gottesfurcht bei Jesus Sirach*, Rome 1967.
Havet, J., 'La doctrine paulinienne du "Corps du Christ". Essai de mise au point',
Littérature et théologie pauliniennes, by A. Descamps and others, pp. 185–216.
Heinemann, J., 'Birkath Ha-Zimmun and Havurah-Meals', *JJS* 13, 1962, pp.
23–9.
— *Ha-Tefillah bi-Tequfat ha-Tanna'im ve-ha-Amora'im* (Prayer in the Period
of the Tanna'im and the Amora'im: its Nature and Patterns), Jerusalem ²1966.
Helfgott, B. W., *The Doctrine of Election in Tannaitic Literature*, New York 1954
(= 1952).
Helfmeyer, F. J., '"Gott Nachfolgen" in den Qumrantexten', *RQ* 7, 1969, pp.
81–104.
Hengel, M., *Judaism and Hellenism*, 2 vols., ET of German ²1973 by John Bowden,
London and Philadelphia 1974.
Herford, R. Travers, *The Pharisees*, New York 1924.
Hill, David, 'Δίκαιοι as a Quasi-Technical Term', *NTS* 11, 1965, pp. 296–302.
Hillers, Delbert R., *Covenant: The History of a Biblical Idea*, Baltimore 1969.
Hindley, J. C., 'Towards a Date for the Similitudes of Enoch', *NTS* 14, 1968,
pp. 551–65.
Hirsch, E. G., 'Gentile', *JE* V, pp. 615–26.
— 'Shemoneh 'Esreh', *JE* XI, pp. 270–282.

Holm-Nielsen, S., 'Erwägungen zu dem Verhältnis zwischen den Hodajot und den Psalmen Salomos', *Bibel und Qumran* (ed. S. Wagner), pp. 112–31.
— '"Ich" in den Hodajoth und die Qumrāngemeinde', *Qumran-Probleme* (ed. Bardtke), pp. 217–29.
Howard, George, 'Romans 3.21–31 and the Inclusion of the Gentiles', *HTR* 63, 1970, pp. 223–33.
Hruby, K., 'Le concept de Révélation dans la théologie rabbinique', *Orient Syrien* 11, 1966, pp. 17–50; 169–98.
Hübner, Hans, 'Anthropologischer Dualismus in den Hodayoth?', *NTS* 18, 1972, pp. 268–84.
— 'Existentiale Interpretation der paulinischen "Gerechtigkeit Gottes". Zur Kontroverse Rudolf Bultmann-Ernst Käsemann', *NTS* 21, 1975, pp. 462–88.
— 'Gal. 3,10 und die Herkunft des Paulus', *KD* 19, 1973, pp. 215–31.
Hunter, A. M., *The Gospel According to St Paul*, London and Philadelphia 1966.
— *Interpreting Paul's Gospel*, London and Philadelphia 1954.
Hunzinger, C.-H., 'Beobachtungen zur Entwicklung der Disziplinarordnung der Gemeinde von Qumrān', *Qumran-Probleme* (ed. Bardtke), pp. 231–45.
— 'Fragmente einer älteren Fassung des Buches Milḥamā aus Höhle 4 von Qumrān', *ZAW* 69, 1957, pp. 131–51.
Huppenbauer, H., 'בשר "Fleisch" in den Texten von Qumran (Höhle I)', *TZ* 13, 1957, pp. 298–300.
— *Der Mensch zwischen zwei Welten. Der Dualismus der Texte von Qumran (Höhle I) und der Damaskus Fragmente* (ATANT 34), Zürich 1959.
Hurd, J. C., *The Origin of First Corinthians*, London 1965.
— 'Pauline Chronology and Pauline Theology', *Christian History and Interpretation* (ed. W. R. Farmer and others), pp. 225–48.
Hyatt, J. P., ed., *The Bible in Modern Scholarship* (Papers Read at the 100th Meeting of the Society of Biblical Literature, December 28–30, 1964), Nashville, New York and London 1965.
Jacobs, L., 'The Concept of Ḥasid in the Biblical and Rabbinic Literatures', *JJS* 8, 1957, pp. 149–54.
Jaubert, A., *La notion d'alliance dans le judaïsme*, Paris 1963.
Jeremias, Gert, *Der Lehrer der Gerechtigkeit* (SUNT 2), Göttingen 1963.
Jeremias, J., *Jerusalem in the Time of Jesus*, ET by F. H. and C. H. Cave, London and Philadelphia 1969.
— 'Justification by Faith', *The Central Message of the New Testament*, London and New York 1965, pp. 51–70.
— *New Testament Theology* I, ET by John Bowden, London and New York 1971.
— 'πολλοί', *TDNT* VI, pp. 540f.
Jervell, J., 'Die offenbarte und die verborgene Tora. Zur Vorstellung über die neue Tora im Rabbinismus', *ST* 25, 1971, pp. 90–108.
Jewett, R., 'The Epistolary Thanksgiving and the Integrity of Philippians', *NT* 12, 1970, pp. 40–53.
— *Paul's Anthropological Terms. A Study of their Use in Conflict Settings.* (AGJU 10), Leiden 1971.
Kadushin, Max, *A Conceptual Approach to the Mekilta*, New York 1969.

— *Organic Thinking. A Study in Rabbinic Thought*, New York 1938.
— 'The Rabbinic Concept of Israel', *HUCA* 19, 1945–46, pp. 71–80.
— *The Rabbinic Mind*, New York ²1965.
Käsemann, Ernst, *An die Römer* (HNT 8a), Tübingen 1974 (ET forthcoming).
— *Exegetische Versuch und Besinnungen*, 2 vols., Göttingen 1960, 1964. Selected essays from Vol. I translated in *Essays on New Testament Themes*, ET by W. J. Montague (SBT 41), London 1964.
The following articles:
'Ministry and Community in the New Testament', pp. 63–94 = paper, 1949.
'The Pauline Doctrine of the Lord's Supper', pp. 108–35 = *EvT* 7, 1947–8, pp. 50ff.
Selected essays from Vol. II translated in *New Testament Questions of Today*, ET by W. J. Montague, London and Philadelphia 1969.
'The Beginnings of Christian Theology', pp. 82–107 = *ZTK* 57, 1960, pp. 162–85.
'On the Subject of Primitive Christian Apocalyptic', pp. 108–37 = *ZTK* 59, 1962, pp. 257–84.
'"The Righteousness of God" in Paul', pp. 168–82 = *ZTK* 58, 1961, pp. 367–78.
— *Leib und Leib Christi*, Tübingen 1933.
— *Perspectives on Paul*, by Margaret Kohl, London and Philadelphia 1971.
Kapelrud, A. S., 'Der Bund in den Qumran-Schriften', *Bibel und Qumran* (ed. S. Wagner), pp. 137–49.
Karris, R. J., 'The Occasion of Romans: A response to Professor Donfried', *CBQ* 36, 1974, pp. 356–8.
Kennedy, H. A. A., 'The Significance and Range of the Covenant-Conception in the New Testament', *Exp* 10, 1915, pp. 385–410.
Kertelge, K., '*Rechtfertigung*' *bei Paulus*, Münster 1967.
Klinzing, Georg, *Die Umdeutung des Kultus in der Qumrangemeinde und im Neuen Testament* (SUNT 7), Göttingen 1971.
Knox, John, *Chapters in a Life of Paul*, New York 1950.
— *Marcion and the New Testament*, Chicago 1942.
Koch, K., *The Rediscovery of Apocalyptic* (SBT II 22), ET by Margaret Kohl, London 1972.
Köberle, J., *Sünde und Gnade im religiösen Leben des Volkes Israel bis auf Christum. Eine Geschichte des vorchristlichen Heilsbewusstseins*, München 1905.
Kümmel, W. G., *Introduction to the New Testament*, rev. ed., ET by H. C. Kee, Nashville, New York and London 1975.
— 'πάρεσις and ἔνδειξις. A Contribution to the Understanding of the Pauline Doctrine of Justification', *JTC* 3, 1967, pp. 1–13 (= *ZTK* 49, 1952, pp. 154–67).
— 'Das Problem der Entwicklung in der Theologie des Paulus', *NTS* 18, 1972, pp. 457f.
— *The Theology of the New Testament*, ET by J. E. Steely, Nashville, New York and London 1974.
— *Römer 7 und die Bekehrung des Paulus*, Leipzig 1929.

Kuhn, H.-W., *Enderwartung und gegenwärtiges Heil. Untersuchungen zu den Gemeindeliedern von Qumran* (SUNT 4), Göttingen 1966.

Kuhn, K. G., 'New Light on Temptation, Sin, and Flesh in the New Testament', *The Scrolls and the New Testament* (ed. Stendahl), pp. 94–113.

Kuhn, Peter, *Gottes Selbsterniedrigung in der Theologie der Rabbinen* (SANT 17), München 1968.

Lauterbach, J. Z., 'Midrash halakah', *JE* 8, pp. 569–72.

— *Rabbinic Essays*, Cincinnati 1951.

Le Déaut, R., 'Apropos a Definition of Midrash', ET in *Interpretation* 26, 1971, pp. 259–82.

— 'Aspects de l'intercession dans la Judaïsme ancien', *JSJ* 1, 1970, pp. 35–57.

— *La nuit Pascale. Essai sur la signification de la Pâque juive à partir du Targum d'Exode XII 42* (AB 22), Rome 1963.

— 'Targumic Literature and New Testament Interpretation', *Biblical Theology Bulletin* 4, 1974, pp. 243–89.

Légasse, Simon, 'Les Pauvres en Esprit et les "Volontaires" de Qumran', *NTS* 8, 1962, pp. 336–45.

Lévi-Strauss, Claude, *Structural Anthropology*, ET by C. Jacobson and B. G. Schoepf, New York and London 1963.

Lewandowski, G. A., 'An Introduction to Ernst Käsemann's Theology', *Encounter* 35, 1974, pp. 222–42.

Licht, J., 'An Analysis of the Treatise on the Two Spirits in DSD', *Aspects* (ed. Rabin and Yadin), pp. 88–99.

— 'The Doctrine of the Thanksgiving Scroll', *IEJ* 6, 1956, pp. 1–13, 89–101.

— 'Mussag ha-Nedabah Biktabeha shel Kat Midbar Yehuda' (The Concept of *Nedabah* in the Dead Sea Scrolls), *'Iyyunim Bimgillah Midbar Yehudah* (Studies in the DSS in memory of E. L. Sukenik) (ed. J. Liver), Jerusalem 1957, pp. 77–84.

Lieberman, Saul, 'The Discipline in the So-Called Dead Sea Manual of Discipline', *JBL* 71, 1952, pp. 199–206.

— *Greek in Jewish Palestine*, New York ²1965.

— 'Light on the Cave Scrolls from Rabbinic Sources', *PAAJR* 20, 1951, pp. 395–404.

— *Tosefeth Rishonim*, 4 vols., Jerusalem 1937–9.

— *Tosefta Ki-Fshuṭah*, 9 vols., New York 1955–73.

Lietzmann, H., *An die Römer* (HNT 8), Tübingen ⁴1933.

Limbeck, Meinrad, *Die Ordnung des Heils. Untersuchungen zum Gesetzesverständnis des Frühjudentums*, Düsseldorf 1971.

Loewe, H., 'Pharisaism', *Judaism and Christianity I: The Age of Transition* (ed. W. O. E. Oesterley), pp. 105–90.

Lohse, Eduard, *Märtyrer und Gottesknecht. Untersuchungen zur urchristlichen Verkündigung vom Sühntod Jesu Christi* (FRLANT 64, NF 46), Göttingen ²1963.

— 'Vorwort', *Die Religion des Judentums* by W. Bousset, 1966, pp. V–X.

Longenecker, R. N., *Paul: Apostle of Liberty*, New York 1964.

Luther, M., *A Commentary on St Paul's Epistle to the Galatians*, ET ed. by Philip S. Watson, London 1953 (repr. 1961).

Luz, Ulrich, *Das Geschichtsverständnis des Paulus*, Munich 1968.

Lyonnet, Stanislav, 'Pauline Soteriology', *Introduction to the New Testament* (ed. A. Robert and A. Feuillet), ET by Patrick Skehan and others, New York 1965, pp. 821–65.

— 'St Paul: Liberty and Law', *The Bridge. A Yearbook of Judaeo-Christian Studies* IV (ed. J. M. Oesterreicher), Newark, NJ 1962, pp. 229–51.

Mach, R., *Der Zaddik in Talmud und Midrasch*, Leiden 1957.

MacRae, G. W., 'The Colossian Heresy and Modern Gnostic Scholarship', a paper read at the 1972 *SNTS* Meeting.

Maier, G., *Mensch und freier Wille*, Tübingen 1971.

Maier, J., *Zum Gottesvolk- und Gemeinschaftsbegriff in den Schriften vom Toten Meer* (Diss. Wien, 1958). Report in *TLZ* 85, 1960, cols. 705f.

Marböck, Johann, *Weisheit im Wandel. Untersuchungen zur Weisheitstheologie bei Ben Sira* (BBB 37), Bonn 1971.

Marcus, R., 'The Pharisees in the Light of Modern Scholarship', *JR* 32, 1952, pp. 153–64.

Marmorstein, A., *The Doctrine of Merits in Old Rabbinical Literature*, New York 1968 (= 1920).

— *The Old Rabbinic Doctrine of God: The Names and Attributes of God* and *Essays in Anthropomorphism*, New York 1968 (= 1927 and 1937).

Martin, Ralph, Review of *Creation and Redemption* by J. Gibbs, *JBL* 91, 1972, pp. 429–31.

Marx, A., 'Y a-t-il une prédestination à Qumrân?', *RQ* 6, 1967–9, pp. 163–82.

McNamara, Martin, *The New Testament and the Palestinian Targum to the Pentateuch* (AB 27), Rome 1966.

— *Targum and Testament*, Grand Rapids 1972.

Melamed, E. Z., *Ha-Yahas sh-ben Midrashe-Halakah le-Mishnah ve-le-Tosefta* (The Relationship between the Halakhic Midrashim and the Mishna and Tosefta), Jerusalem 1967.

Mihaly, E., 'A Rabbinic Defense of the Election of Israel', *HUCA* 25, 1964, pp. 103–35.

Milik, J. T., 'Problèmes de la Littérature Hénochique à la Lumière des Fragments Araméens de Qumrân', *HTR* 64, 1971, pp. 333–378.

— *Ten Years of Discovery in the Wilderness of Judaea*, ET by J. Strugnell (SBT 26), London 1959.

Miller, Gene, 'ΑΡΧΟΝΤΩΝ ΤΟΥ ΑΙΩΝΟΣ – A New Look at I Corinthians 2.6–8', *JBL* 91, 1972, pp. 522–8.

Miller, Merrill, 'Targum, Midrash and the use of the Old Testament in the New Testament', *JSJ* 2, 1971, pp. 29–82.

Mitton, C. L., *The Epistle to the Ephesians*, Oxford 1951.

Montefiore, C. G., *Judaism and St Paul: Two Essays*, London 1914.

Moore, G. F., 'Christian Writers on Judaism', *HTR* 14, 1921, pp. 197–254.

— 'Intermediaries in Jewish Theology', *HTR* 15, 1922, pp. 41–61.

— *Judaism in the First Centuries of the Christian Era: The Age of the Tannaim*, 3 vols., Cambridge, Mass. 1927–30.

Morawe, G., *Aufbau und Abgrenzung der Loblieder von Qumrān*, Berlin ca. 1961.

Morgenstern, J., 'The Calendar of the Book of Jubilees, its Origins and its Character', *VT* 5, 1955, pp. 34–76.
— 'The Mythological Background of Psalm 82', *HUCA* 14, 1939, pp. 29–126.
Moule, C. F. D., ' "Justification": in its relation to the condition κατὰ πνεῦμα (Rom. 8.1–11)', *Battesimo e Giustizia in Rom 6 e 8* (ed. Lorenzo de Lorenzi), Rome 1974, pp. 176–201.
— 'Obligation in the ethic of Paul', *Christian History and Interpretation* (ed. W. R. Farmer and others), pp. 389–406.
— 'St Paul and Dualism: The Pauline Conception of Resurrection', *NTS* 12, 1966, pp. 106–23.
Müller, C., *Gottes Gerechtigkeit und Gottes Volk* (FRLANT 86), Göttingen 1964.
Müller, H., 'Der rabbinische Qal-Wachomer-Schluss in paulinischer Typologie: zur Adam-Christus-Typologie in Rm 5', *ZNW* 58, 1967, pp. 73–92.
Munck, J., *Paul and the Salvation of Mankind*, ET by F. Clarke, London 1959.
— 'Pauline Research Since Schweitzer', *The Bible in Modern Scholarship* (ed. Hyatt), pp. 166–77.
Mundle, W., 'Das religiöse Problem des IV. Esrabuches', *ZAW* 47, 1929, pp. 222–49.
Murphy, Roland, 'BSR in the Qumrân Literature and Sarks in the Epistle to the Romans', *Sacra Pagina: Miscellanea Biblica Congressus Internationalis Catholici de Re Biblica (1958)* (ed. J. Coppens and others), 2 vols., Brussels 1959, vol. II, pp. 60–76.
Murphy-O'Connor, J., 'The Critique of the Princes of Judah', *RB* 79, 1972, pp. 200–16.
— 'La genèse littéraire de la *Règle de la Communauté*', *RB* 76, 1969, pp. 528–49.
Neill, Stephen, *The Interpretation of the New Testament*, London 1964.
Neusner, J., *Development of a Legend*, Leiden 1970.
— *Eliezer Ben Hyrcanus*, 2 vols., Leiden 1973.
— 'The Fellowship (חבורה) in the Second Jewish Commonwealth', *HTR* 53, 1960, pp. 125–42.
— *From Politics to Piety*, New Jersey 1973.
— *A Life of Yohanan ben Zakkai*, Leiden 1962; rev. ed. 1970.
— ed., *The Modern Study of the Mishnah*, Leiden 1973.
— *The Rabbinic Traditions about the Pharisees Before 70*, 3 vols, Leiden 1971.
— ed., *Understanding Rabbinic Judaism*, New York 1974.
Nielsen, E., 'The Righteous and the Wicked in Habaqquq', *ST* 6, 1952, pp. 54–78.
Nissen, Andreas, 'Tora und Geschichte im Spätjudentum', *NT* 9, 1967, pp. 241–77.
Nötscher, Friedrich, 'Schicksalsglaube in Qumran und Umwelt', *Vom alten zum neuen Testament* (BBB 17), Bonn 1962, pp. 17–71 (= *BZ* 3, 1959, pp. 205–34; 4, 1960, pp. 98–121).
— *Zur Theologischen Terminologie der Qumran-Texte*, Bonn 1956.
Obermann, J., 'Calendaric Elements in the Dead Sea Scrolls', *JBL* 75, 1956, pp. 285–97.
O'Dell, Jerry, 'The Religious Background of the Psalms of Solomon (Re-evaluated in the light of the Qumran Texts)', *RQ* 3, 1961–2, pp. 241–57.

Oepke, A., 'Δικαιοσύνη Θεοῦ bei Paulus', *TLZ* 78, 1953, cols. 257–63.

Oesterley, W. O. E., ed., *Judaism and Christianity*. Vol. I: *The Age of Transition*, London 1937. Vol. II: *The Contact of Pharisaism with other Cultures* (ed. H. Loewe), London 1937. Vol. III: *Law and Religion* (ed. E. I. J. Rosenthal), London 1938.

Repr. in one vol., New York 1969, with Prolegomenon by Ellis Rivkin.

O'Rourke, J. J., '*Pistis* in Romans', *CBQ* 35, 1973, pp. 188–94.

von der Osten-Sacken, P., *Gott und Belial* (SUNT 6), Göttingen 1969.

Parkes, James, *The Foundations of Judaism and Christianity*, Chicago 1960.

— *Jesus, Paul and the Jews*, London 1936.

Petuchowski, J. J., 'The Concept of "Teshuvah" ', *Judaism* 17, 1968, pp. 175–85.

— ed., *Contributions to the Scientific Study of Jewish Liturgy*, New York 1970.

Pfleiderer, Otto, *Paulinism: A Contribution to the History of Primitive Christian Theology*, ET by E. Peters, 2 vols., London 1877.

— *Primitive Christianity* I, ET by W. Montgomery, 4 vols., London 1906.

Podro, Joshua, *The Last Pharisee: The Life and Times of Rabbi Joshua Ben Hananyah*, London 1959.

Pollard, T. E., 'The Integrity of Philippians', *NTS* 13, 1966, pp. 57–66.

Pryke, J., ' "Spirit" and "Flesh" in the Qumran Documents and Some New Testament Texts', *RQ* 5, 1965, pp. 345–60.

Przybylski, Benno, *The Meaning and Significance of the Concept of Righteousness in the Gospel of Matthew: With Special Reference to the Use of this Concept in the Dead Sea Scrolls and the Tannaitic Literature*, Unpublished PhD Thesis, McMaster University 1975.

Rabin, C., *Qumran Studies*, London 1957.

— and Y. Yadin, eds., *Scripta Hierosolymitana* IV: *Aspects of the Dead Sea Scrolls*, Jerusalem ²1965.

Rabinowitz, I., 'Sequence and Dates of the Extra-Biblical Dead Sea Scrolls and "Damascus" Fragments', *VT* 3, 1953, pp. 175–85.

Rabinowitz, L. I., 'The Halakha as Reflected in Ben-Sira', *Papers of the Fourth World Congress of Jewish Studies* I, Jerusalem 1967, pp. 145–8; English summary, p. 264.

von Rad, Gerhard, 'The Wisdom of Jesus Sirach', *Wisdom in Israel*, London, Nashville and New York 1972, pp. 240–62.

Reicke, Bo, 'The Constitution of the Primitive Church in the Light of Jewish Documents', *The Scrolls and the New Testament* (ed. Stendahl), pp. 143–56.

— 'The Law and this World According to Paul', *JBL* 70, 1951, pp. 259–76.

— 'Official and Pietistic Elements of Jewish Apocalypticism', *JBL* 74, 1960, pp. 137–50.

Reitzenstein, Richard, *Die hellenistischen Mysterienreligionen*, Darmstadt 1956 (= 1927).

Rengstorf, K. H., 'ἐλπίς, ἐλπίζω', Sect. C, *TDNT* II, pp. 523–9.

— ed., *Das Paulusbild in der neueren deutschen Forschung*, Darmstadt 1964.

Reumann, J., 'The Gospel of the Righteousness of God', *Interpretation* 20, 1966, pp. 432–52.

Rigaux, B., 'L'interprétation du paulinisme dans l'exégèse récente', *Littérature et théologie pauliniennes*, by A. Descamps and others, 1960.

— 'Révélation des Mystères et Perfection à Qumran et dans le Nouveau Testament', *NTS* 4, 1957–58, pp. 237–62.

Ringgren, H., *The Faith of Qumran*, ET by Emilie T. Sander, Philadelphia 1963.

Rivkin, E., 'Defining the Pharisees: the Tannaitic Sources', *HUCA* 40–41, 1969–70, pp. 234–8.

Robinson, J. A. T., *The Body* (SBT 5), London 1952.

Robinson, J. M., 'Introduction: The Dismantling and Reassembling of the Categories of New Testament Scholarship', *Trajectories through Early Christianity* by J. M. Robinson and H. Koester, Philadelphia 1971, pp. 1–19.

— 'The Johannine Trajectory', *Trajectories through Early Christianity*, by J. M. Robinson and H. Koester, pp. 232–68.

— 'The Problem of History in Mark, Reconsidered', *USQR* 20, 1965, pp. 131–47.

— ed., *Zeit und Geschichte: Dankesgabe an Rudolf Bultmann*, Tübingen 1964; ET *The Future of our Religious Past*, by C. Carlston and R. P. Scharlemann, London and New York 1971.

Rössler, Dietrich, *Gesetz und Geschichte. Untersuchungen zur Theologie der jüdischen Apokalyptik und der pharisäischen Orthodoxie* (WMANT 3), Neukirchen [2]1962 ([1]1960).

Roetzel, Calvin J., *Judgement in the Community. A Study in the Relationship between Eschatology and Ecclesiology in Paul*, Leiden 1972.

Rohde, E., *Psyche*, ET by W. B. Hillis, London 1950 (= 1925).

Rollins, W. G., 'The New Testament and Apocalyptic', *NTS* 17, 1971, pp. 454–76.

Rosenthal, F., *Vier apokryphische Bücher aus der Zeit und Schule R. Akiba's*, Leipzig 1885.

Rost, Leonhard, *Einleitung in die alttestamentlichen Apokryphen und Pseudepigraphen*, Heidelberg 1971.

— 'Zum "Buch der Kriege der Söhne des Lichts gegen die Söhne der Finsternis" ', *TLZ* 80, 1955, cols. 205–8.

Rowley, H. H., *The Relevance of Apocalyptic*, London and New York [3]1963.

Russell, D. S., *The Method and Message of Jewish Apocalyptic*, London and Philadelphia 1964.

Saldarini, A. J., 'The End of the Rabbinic Chain of Tradition', *JBL* 93, 1974, pp. 97–106.

Sanday, W. and Headlam, A. C., *A Critical and Exegetical Commentary on the Epistle to the Romans* (ICC), Edinburgh 1895 (repr. 1914).

Sanders, E. P., 'Chiasmus and the Translation of *IQ Hodayot* VII, 26–27', *RQ* 6, 1968, pp. 427–31.

— 'The Covenant as a Soteriological Category and the Nature of Salvation in Palestinian and Hellenistic Judaism', *Jews, Greeks and Christians: Studies in Honor of W. D. Davies* (ed. Hamerton-Kelly and Scroggs), Leiden 1976, pp. 11–44.

— 'Literary Dependence in Colossians', *JBL* 85, 1966, pp. 28–45.

— 'On the Question of Fulfilling the Law in Paul and Rabbinic Judaism', *Donum Gentilicium: New Testament Studies in Honour of David Daube* (ed. E. Bammel, C. K. Barrett and W. D. Davies), Oxford 1977, pp. 103–26.

— 'Patterns of Religion in Paul and Rabbinic Judaism: A Holistic Method of Comparison', *HTR* 66, 1973, pp. 455–78.
— 'R. Akiba's View of Suffering', *JQR* n.s. 63, 1973, pp. 332–51.
Sanders, J. A., 'The Old Testament in 11Q Melchizedek', *The Journal of the Ancient Near Eastern Society of Columbia University* 5, 1973 (The Gaster Festschrift), pp. 373–82.
Sanders, J. T., *The New Testament Christological Hymns* (SNTSMS 15), Cambridge 1971.
Sandmel, Samuel, *The First Christian Century in Judaism and Christianity: Certainties and Uncertainties*, New York 1969.
— *The Genius of Paul*, New York 1958.
— 'The Jewish Scholar and Early Christianity', *The Seventy-Fifth Anniversary Volume of the Jewish Quarterly Review* (ed. A. A. Neuman and S. Zeitlin), Philadelphia 1967, pp. 473–81.
— 'The Need of Cooperative Study', *Theological Soundings: Notre Dame Seminary Jubilee Studies 1923–1973* (ed. I. Mihalik), New Orleans 1973, pp. 30–5.
—— 'Parallelomania', *JBL* 81, 1962, pp. 1–13.
— *Philo's Place in Judaism*, New York 1971 (= 1956).
Schechter, S., *Aspects of Rabbinic Theology*, New York 1961 (= 1909).
Schlatter, A., *Der Evangelist Matthäus*, Stuttgart 1959 (= 1948).
— *Der Glaube im Neuen Testament*, Darmstadt 1963 (= ⁴1924).
Schmid, H. H., *Gerechtigkeit als Weltordnung: Hintergrund und Geschichte des alttestamentlichen Gerechtigkeitsbegriffes*, Tübingen 1968.
Schmid, J., 'Sünde und Sühne im Judentum', *Bibel und Leben* 6, 1965, pp. 16–26.
Schmidt, K. L., 'Der Apostel Paulus und die antike Welt', *Das Paulusbild* (ed. Rengstorf), pp. 214–45.
Schneider, J., *Die Passionsmystik des Paulus*, Leipzig 1929.
Schoeps, H. J., 'Haggadisches zur Auserwählung Israels', *Aus frühchristlicher Zeit*, Tübingen 1950, pp. 184–211.
— *Paul: The Theology of the Apostle in the Light of Jewish Religious History*, ET by H. Knight, London 1961.
Scholem, G., *Jewish Gnosticism, Merkabah Mysticism, and Talmudic Tradition*, New York 1965.
— *Major Trends in Jewish Mysticism*, New York 1961 (= 1941).
Schrenk, G., 'δίκη κτλ.', *TDNT* II, pp. 178–225.
Schubert, K., *The Dead Sea Community*, ET by J. W. Doberstein, New York 1959.
Schubert, P., 'Paul and the New Testament Ethic in the Thought of John Knox', *Christian History and Interpretation* (ed. W. R. Farmer and others), pp. 363–88.
Schürer, E., *Lehrbuch der Neutestamentlichen Zeitgeschichte*, 1874; revised as *Geschichte des jüdischen Volkes im Zeitalter Jesu Christi*, 1886–90. ET by John Macpherson and others, *A History of the Jewish People in the Time of Jesus Christ*, 5 vols., Edinburgh 1885–91; rev. ed. by G. Vermes and F. Millar, vol. I, 1973.
Schulz, Siegfried, 'Zur Rechtfertigung aus Gnaden in Qumran und bei Paulus', *ZTK* 56, 1959, pp. 155–85.
Schweitzer, A., *The Mysticism of Paul the Apostle*, ET by W. Montgomery,

London 1956 (= 1931).

— *Paul and His Interpreters*, ET by W. Montgomery, London 1956 (= 1912).

Schweizer, E., 'Dying and Rising with Christ', *NTS* 14, 1967, pp. 1–14.

Jesus, ET by David E. Green, Atlanta, Ga and London 1971.

Scroggs, R., *The Last Adam*, Philadelphia 1966.

— 'Romans vi.7 ὁ γὰρ ἀποθανὼν δεδικαίωται ἀπὸ τῆς ἁμαρτίας', *NTS* 10, 1963, pp. 104–8.

Segal, M. H., 'The Qumran War Scroll and the Date of its Composition', *Aspects* (ed. Rabin and Yadin), pp. 138–43.

Simon, M., and Benoit, A., *Le Judaïsme et le Christianisme antique*, Paris 1968.

Sjöberg, Erik, *Gott und die Sünder im palästinischen Judentum nach dem Zeugnis der Tannaiten und der apocryphisch-pseudepigraphischen Literatur* (BWANT 27), Stuttgart 1939.

— 'Wiedergeburt und Neuschöpfung im palästinischen Judentum', *ST* 4, 1951–2, pp. 44–85.

Smith, D. M., Jr, 'Ὁ ΔΕ ΔΙΚΑΙΟΣ ΕΚ ΠΙΣΤΕΩΣ ΖΗΣΕΤΑΙ', *Studies in the History and Text of the New Testament in Honor of Kenneth Willis Clark* (ed. B. L. Daniels and J. Suggs), Salt Lake City 1967, pp. 13–25.

Smith, Morton, 'The Dead Sea Sect in Relation to Ancient Judaism', *NTS* 7, 1960–61, pp. 347–60.

— 'On the Problem of Method in the Study of Rabbinic Literature', *JBL* 92, 1973, pp. 112–13.

Smolar, L. and Aberbach, Moshe, 'The Golden Calf Episode in Postbiblical Literature', *HUCA* 39, 1968, pp. 91–116.

Spivey, R. A., 'Structuralism and Biblical Studies: The Uninvited Guest', *Interpretation* 28, 1974, pp. 133–45.

Stanley, D. M., *Christ's Resurrection in Pauline Soteriology* (AB 13), Rome 1961.

Stendahl, K., 'The Apostle Paul and the Introspective Conscience of the West', *HTR* 56, 1963, pp. 199–215.

— ed., *The Scrolls and the New Testament*, London 1958.

Strack, H., *Introduction to the Talmud and Midrash*, ET of 5th German ed., New York and Philadelphia 1959 (= 1931).

— and P. Billerbeck, *Kommentar zum Neuen Testament aus Talmud und Midrasch*, 4 vols., München 1924 and subsequent years (cited as S.-B.).

Stuhlmacher, P., *Gerechtigkeit Gottes bei Paulus*, Göttingen 1966.

Styler, G. M., 'The basis of obligation in Paul's christology and ethics', *Christ and Spirit in the New Testament. Festschrift C. F. D. Moule* (ed. B. Lindars and S. S. Smalley), Cambridge 1973, pp. 175–87.

Sutcliffe, E. F., 'The First Fifteen Members of the Qumran Community: A Note on IQS 8.1ff.', *JSS* 4, 1959, pp. 134–8.

Swete, H. B., *An Introduction to the Old Testament in Greek*, rev. by R. R. Ottley, New York 1968 (= 1902).

Synofzik, Ernst, *Die Gerichts- und Vergeltungsaussagen bei Paulus. Eine Traditionsgeschichtliche Untersuchung*, Göttingen 1972.

Talbert, C. H., 'A Non-Pauline Fragment at Romans 3.24–26?', *JBL* 85, 1966, pp. 287–96.

Talmon, S., 'The Calendar Reckoning of the Sect from the Judaean Desert', *Aspects* (ed. Rabin and Yadin), pp. 162–99.

Tannehill, R. C., *Dying and Rising with Christ. A Study in Pauline Theology*, Berlin 1967.

Taylor, G. M., 'The Function of ΠΙΣΤΙΣ ΧΡΙΣΤΟΥ in Galatians', *JBL* 85, 1966, pp. 58–76.

Testuz, Michel, *Les idées religieuses du Livre des Jubilés*, Geneva and Paris 1960.

Thackeray, Henry St John, *The Relation of St Paul to Contemporary Jewish Thought*, London 1900.

Thüsing, W., *Per Christum in Deum. Studien zum Verhältnis von Christozentrik und Theozentrik in den paulinischen Hauptbriefen*, Münster 1965.

Thyen, Hartwig, *Studien zur Sündenvergebung im Neuen Testament und seinen alttestamentlichen und jüdischen Voraussetzungen* (FRLANT 96), Göttingen 1970.

Towner, W. S., 'Form-Criticism of Rabbinic Literature', *JJS* 24, 1973, pp. 101–18.

— *The Rabbinic 'Enumeration of Scriptural Examples'*, Leiden 1973.

Urbach, E. E., *Hazal. Pirqe 'Emunot ve-De'ot*, Jerusalem 1969; ET *The Sages: Their Concepts and Beliefs*, 1975.

— 'Ha-Masorot 'al Torat ha-Sod bi-Tequfat ha-Tannaim' (The Traditions about Merkabah Mysticism in the Tannaitic Period), *Studies in Mysticism and Religion. Festschrift Gershom Scholem* (ed. Urbach and others), Jerusalem 1967, pp. 1–28.

van Unnik, W. C., 'La conception paulinienne de la nouvelle alliance', *Littérature et théologie pauliniennes*, by A. Descamps and others, pp. 109–26.

van der Ploeg, J., *The Excavations at Qumran*, ET by Kevin Smyth, SJ, London 1958.

— and others, *La secte de Qumrân et les origines du Christianisme. Recherches Bibliques* IV, Louvain 1959.

Vermes, G., *Discovery in the Judean Desert*, New York 1956.

— *Scripture and Tradition in Judaism* (SPB 4), Leiden 1961.

Via, Dan O., Jr, 'Justification and Deliverance: Existential Dialectic', *Studies in Religion/Sciences Religieuses* 1, 1971, pp. 204–12.

Volz, Paul, *Die Eschatologie der jüdischen Gemeinde im Neutestamentlichen Zeitalter*, Hildesheim 1966 (= 1924).

Wacholder, Ben Zion, 'The Date of the Mekilta de-Rabbi Ishmael', *HUCA* 39, 1968, pp. 117–44.

— 'A Reply' [to Morton Smith], *JBL* 92, 1973, pp. 114f.

— Review of M. McNamara, *Targum and Testament*, *JBL* 93, 1974, pp. 132f.

— Review of J. Neusner, *Development of a Legend*, *JBL* 91, 1972, pp. 123f.

Wagner, G., *Pauline Baptism and the Pagan Mysteries*, ET by J. P. Smith, Edinburgh and London 1967 (orig. Zürich 1962).

Wagner, S., ed., *Bibel und Qumran*, Berlin 1968.

Waugh, Evelyn, *Unconditional Surrender*, London 1961.

Weber, Ferdinand, *Jüdische Theologie auf Grund des Talmud und verwandter Schriften*, Leipzig 1897 (*System der altsynagogalen palästinischen Theologie*, ed.

F. Delitzsch and G. Schnedermann, ²1880).

Wellhausen, J., *Die Pharisäer und die Sadducäer*, Greifswald 1874.

West, J. K., *Justification in the Qumran Scrolls*, Unpublished diss. Vanderbilt 1961.

Whiteley, D. E. H., *The Theology of St Paul*, Oxford 1964.

Wicks, H. J., *The Doctrine of God in the Jewish Apocryphal and Apocalyptic Literature*, New York 1971 (= 1915).

Wikenhauser, Alfred, *Pauline Mysticism*, ET by J. Cunningham, Freiburg 1960.

Wilckens, U., *Rechtfertigung als Freiheit. Paulusstudien*, Neukirchen 1974.

Windisch, Hans, *Paulus und das Judentum*, Stuttgart 1935.

Winter, P., 'Psalms of Solomon', *IDB* III, pp. 958–60.

Worrell, John, 'עצה: "Counsel" or "Council" at Qumran', *VT* 20, 1970, pp. 65–74.

Wrede, W., *Paulus*, 1904, reissued in *Das Paulusbild* (ed. Rengstorf), pp. 1–97.

Wright, Addison G., *The Literary Genre Midrash*, Staten Island 1967.

Wright, G. E. and Reginald Fuller, *The Book of the Acts of God*, London and New York 1960.

Yadin, Y., 'The Dead Sea Scrolls and the Epistle to the Hebrews', *Aspects* (ed. Rabin and Yadin), pp. 36–55.

York, Anthony D., 'The Dating of Targumic Literature', *JSJ* 5, 1974, pp. 49–62.

Young, Jung, 'Interpreting the Demonic Powers in Pauline Thought', *NT* 12, 1970, pp. 54–69.

Zeitlin, Solomon, *The Rise and Fall of the Judaean State* II, Philadelphia 1962.

Zerwick, M., *The Epistle to the Ephesians*, London 1969.

Ziesler, J. A., *The Meaning of Righteousness in Paul* (SNTSMS 20), Cambridge 1972.

INDEX OF PASSAGES

BIBLE

583

RABBINIC LITERATURE

MISHNAH

TOSEFTA

MEKILTA

MEKILTA OF R. SIMEON b. YOHAI

SIFRA

PALESTINIAN TALMUD

MIDRASH RABBAH

TANHUMA

ABOTH D'R. NATHAN

DEAD SEA SCROLLS

APOCRYPHA AND PSEUDEPIGRAPHA

OTHER ANCIENT LITERATURE

JOSEPHUS

PHILO
De Confusione

CORPUS HERMETICUM

INDEX OF NAMES

INDEX OF SUBJECTS

Chastisements, in Rabbinic literature, *see* Suffering; in DSS, 253f., 286f.; in Pss. Sol., sign of the pious, 390f., as atoning, 397f.; in Paul, as obviating condemnation, 516

Cleanse, *see* Purity

Commandments, Rabbinic concern to define, 76–81; motives for fulfilment of, 81–4, 92f., 106, 120–22; Rabbinic insistence on obedience of, 107–10; obedience to indicates acceptance of covenant, 94, 135; represented as blessing, 110f., 114, 231; relation of ethical and cultic, 112; relation of many commandments to 'core' commandments, 112–14; commandments concerning man and God and man and man, 114, 168, 168 n. 104, 179, 341, 364; definition of in DSS, 270f.; requirement to obey, 270f.; commandments for which there is no atonement in DSS, 285; in Ben Sirach, compared with Rabbis, 341; definition of in Jubilees, 364–66; for which there is no atonement in Jubilees, 368f.; in Pss. Sol., implied but not itemized, 390; to be obeyed in IV Ezra, 416, 424; 'between man and man' in Paul, 513, 544; *see also* Obedience, Law

Compensation, of sin by fulfilment, 39, 52, 143–7, 197; neither in DSS nor Rabbinic literature, 300, 300 n. 176.

Confessing, and denying, 92–6, 134f., 234, 422, 425; confessing Exodus indicates covenant conception, 236; *see also* Intention, Denial of God

Corporate conception, in Rabbinic literature, combined with individualism, 237f.; in Jubilees, 367; in Paul contrasted with Judaism, 512f., 547f.; *see also* Participationist aspects of Paul's thought

Cosmic aspects of Paul's thought, 435, 435 n. 25, 437, 446, 473f., 508, 514; interpreted in existential categories, 521

Covenant, conception of in Rabbinic Judaism, 50, 236f.; relation to commandments, 81–4, 84–98, 205; as enduring, 101–4, 223, 236; kept by God, 105; provides promises and blessings, as well as commandments, 101–5; requires suffering, 105f.; as soteriological category in Tannaitic literature, 135, 149, 181f., 205, 206, 211f., 236, 297; presupposed by view of repentance and atonement as return, 182; as God's merciful gift, 231; terminology in Rabbinic literature for, 236f.; conception of in DSS, 240–42, 245; new covenant, 240f., 269; 'secrets' in convenant, 241f., 269; membership in, in DSS, 242f.; in IQM, 251; as soteriological category in DSS, 257, 270, 281, 283, 295, 297, 320; entered by individual adults in DSS, 260f., 270; determined by God, 258–61; determined by free choice, 262–4, 267; not mutually exclusive, 264–9, 320; regulations for entry and expulsion, 263f.; in Ben Sirach, 329–33, compared with Rabbis, 341; soteriological category in Jubilees, 367, 370f.; no new covenant in Jubilees, 372–4; in Pss. Sol., 389f.; soteriological category in Pss. Sol., 408; loses traditional efficacy in IV Ezra, 409, 418; and law in Palestinian Judaism, 419–22; degeneration of view of relation of covenant and law attributed to late Judaism, 419; covenant in late Judaism as based on God's grace and requiring obedience as consequence, 420; significance of scant use of term, 420f.; new, in Paul, 511, 514; Jewish, Paul's attitude toward, 550–52

Covenantal nomism, defined, 75, 236; collapses in IV Ezra, 409; common in Judaism, except IV Ezra, 422f.; typical of Judaism before 70 c.e., 426–8; elements of in Paul, 511–13; Christianity is to adopt covenantal nomism, 513, 552; limitations of for understanding Paul, 513–15, 543; depends on repentance, 546

Covenants, between God and Israel, 94f.

Credit and debit, system of attributed to Judaism, 366, 388 n. 24; *see also* Book-keeping, Merit, Weighing, Works-righteousness

Day of Atonement, 37, 151, 163, 303, 339, 379f.; passages regarding, 157–9, 379

Dead Sea Scrolls, divergences and similarities in, 239 n. 1, 319f.

Death and dying, as atoning, 158f., 172–4, 204; view fully developed after fall of Temple, 173; caused by sin, 173 n. 128, 360; accompanied by repentance, 174; time of expression of humility, 225f., 228f.; in Ben Sirach, as time for reward and punishment, 335f.; with

and Qumranian, 239; attitude of, differs from prayer, 224, 266f., 292f., 376; cannot be self-contradictory, 325; little interest in Pss. Sol., 390

Ḥasid, ḥasidim, 155, 202, 244, 244 n. 16 (not title in Qumran); 342 (not title in Ben Sirach), 350, 398

Hasmoneans, in Pss. Sol., 403f., 408

Heilsgewissheit, Heilsbewusstsein, see Uncertainty of salvation, Anxiety

Hellenism, relation to Paul not dealt with, 1; relation to Palestinian Judaism and Paul, scholarly views on, 7, 23, 23 n. 21, 512

Hellenistic Judaism, relation to Palestinian, 1f., 7; relation to Paul, 2, 4, 6, 7 n. 22, 11, 552–6

Hope, in Rabbinic literature, 225–7, 235; *see also* Uncertainty of salvation

Hymns, as appropriate for emphasizing grace of God, 297; use of, in Qumran, 321–23; *see also* Halakah, prayer

Idolatry, 134f., 354, 358, 365, 455f., 503, 518

'In Christ', 441, 453, 453 n. 19, 454 nn. 23, 25, 458–61

Individuals, transfer of from damned to saved state not described in apocalyptic literature, 348, 357; hopeless plight of in IV Ezra, 415f.; in Paul, 435–8, 446; in mystery religions, 512; in Paul and Judaism, 547; *see also* Corporate conception, Individualism

Individualism, 237f.

Innocence and innocent, 198f., *see also* Guilt

Intention, in Tannaitic literature, 70, 107–9, 147f.: indicated by 'confessing', 94, 134f., 141; rather than perfection required, 93, 138; indicated by study, 219f.

Intermediaries, as indicating God's remoteness, 212–15, 314; hypostases or not, 214f.; indicate God's presence, 214f.; *see also* Shekinah

Intermediate state, in Rabbinic literature, 43, 142f.

Israel, sons of God, 95f., 362; God's love for, 104–6, 362; members of, have share in world to come, 147–50, 182, 236, 368, 406; a planting not to be plucked up, 103, cf. 301 (of sect), 391; use of title in DSS, 244–55; 'true Israel', 245, 361, 371, 378, 408; eschatological Israel, relation of sect to, 247f., 250; to be saved at end-time, 331, 333; conception of in I Enoch compared with Rabbis, 361; conception of in Jubilees, 362–4; use of title in Pss. Sol., 399, 404f.; expectation of gathering of in Pss. Sol., 406, 408, in IV Ezra, 417; question of salvation of in IV Ezra, 412f.; victory of over the Gentiles in IV Ezra, 417f.; old and new, in Paul, 512; as salvific corporate body, but not analogous to body of Christ, 547; *see also* Commandments, Covenant, Election

Judgment by mercy and according to deeds, 293f., 307–9, 371f., in IV Ezra, according to deeds, 422, in Paul, according to deeds, 515–18, *see also* Mercy to the righteous, Reward and punishment

Juridical terminology in Paul, 441, 460, 472, 487, 501f.; compared with participationist, 502–8, 520

Justification, *see* Righteousness

Kingship of God, 85f.; covenantal conception, 236f.; in Paul, 450

Knowledge, in DSS, 259f., 261, 269, 271, 312, 313f., 317f.

Land, atoned for in DSS, 302f.

Law, fulfilment of in Paul and Qumran, 281; attitude toward in Paul and Qumran, 306, 306 n. 206, 328 n. 2; consequence of election in Judaism, 422; Paul's attitude toward, 441, 475–85, 488–97, determined by Christology and soteriology, 482–5, 488–91, 496, 544, 550f.; Jewish attitude toward, *see* Commandments, Confessing, Covenant, Denial, Intention, Obedience

Logos, see Intermediaries

Lord's Supper, 455, 518

Lordship of Christ, in Paul, 435, 435 n. 25, 441, 442 n. 55, 445, 462, 467f., 497, 499, 507, 512, 514f.

Lostness, not indicated by 'in sin' in DSS, 279; no view of fundamental lostness in Judaism, 397; *see also* Flesh, Salvation, Sin

Love, and fear, as reasons for obedience, 120–22

Mekilta, date of, 67f.; tractates of, 67 n. 53

Memra, see Intermediaries

Mercy, God's, greater than his justice, *see* God as just

Mercy to the righteous (and strict justice for the wicked), 224, 293f., 334f., 350f., 356, 358, 360, 375f., 392–97, 421f., 423

Merit(s), 37–41, 43, 45, 47, 49–52, 54, 57f., 87, 89–92, 97f., 100f., 102, 104, 106, 110, 141, 143f., 183–98, 338 n. 24; whether or not transferable at judgment, 183, 185, 197; not soteriological concept, 198; in IV Ezra, 422; in Paul, 517 n. 3

Messiah, Jesus as, 9, 496f., 514f.

Methodology, 12–18, 29, *see also* Pattern of religion

Midrash, 26–29

Mysticism, visionary, 220 n. 50; 'normal', 220f.; use of term for Paul's thought, 434, 434 n. 19, 440, 460

Name, God's name's sake, 99; pronunciation of Tetragrammaton, 148; taken in vain, atonement for, 159f.

Noachian commandments, 210, 210 n. 28.

Nothingness of man, in DSS, 289f.

Normative Judaism, 34, 34 n. 11

Obedience, as Israel's response to covenant, 82, 84, 106, 420; as *condition* of staying in covenant or of being saved, 92–7, 107, 135, 141, 146f., 177, 180, 234, 236f.; required, 107–10, 232; and intention to obey, 107–9; not burdensome, 110f.; to one commandment as fulfilling whole law, 113–14; as within man's competence, 115; of one commandment as 'saving', 133f., 138–41, 189; required is DSS, 271f.; in DSS as consequence of election, 295f.; in DSS as *condition* of salvation, 295f., 312, 320; requirement heightened in DSS, 297; required in Ben Sirach, 334; in I Enoch as *condition* of salvation, 362; in Jubilees as *condition* of salvation, 371; in Jubilees as consequence of election, 383; in Pss. Sol. as *condition* of remaining in covenant, 397; in IV Ezra purported to be condition of salvation, 410, perfect obedience required, 416f., 422; in Old Testament as *condition* of remaining in covenant, 419, persistence of that view in late Judaism, 420; degree required to prove basic loyalty, 422; as consequence of election in Judaism, 422; as *condition* of salvation in Judaism, 422f.; demonstrates basic loyalty, 424; as *condition* of remaining in Christ in Paul, 451f., 503, 513, 517f.; limitation of this view, 455f., 503, 514, 518 n. 6; as *condition* in Paul and Judaism, 543; *see also* Commandments, Denial, Intention

Parenesis, in Paul, connected with participatory language, 456f., 459; connected with Spirit, 458; *see also* Ethics

Participationist aspects of Paul's thought, 435, 439, 440, 440 n. 49, 453–63, 463–72, 487, 498, 501f.; compared with juristic, 502–8, 520; significance of participationist transfer terms, 514; interpretation of, 522f.

Participationist eschatology, as Paul's pattern of religion, 549

Pattern of religion, definition, 16–18, 24, 70; in Rabbic literature, 180f., 236; elements of in DSS, 239, 286; in DSS, 316–20, compared with Rabbinic, 320; in Ben Sirach, 341; in I Enoch, 362; in Jubilees, 370f.; in Pss. Sol., 388f., 408f.; in Judaism, 422f.;

in Paul, 433; in Judaism and Paul, 548f.

Paul, polemics against Jews and Judaizers, 1, 4, 7, 8, 11f.; *see also* Polemics; relation to Palestinian Judaism: scholarly views, 2–11; as Hillelite or Shammaite, 138 n. 61; authentic letters of, 431–33; as theologian and thinker, 433, 518–23; theology, centre of, 434–42

Perfection, not required by Rabbis, 93, 137f., 175f., 203; aimed for, but not actually required, in DSS, 286, 286 n. 142, 287f., 297; man not able to achieve, 288–91; given by grace of God, 290f., 293; not expected in Ben Sirach, 343–6; required in IV Ezra, 414, 416f.; *see also* Intention, Sin, universality of

Perushim, not 'Pharisees' in second-century texts, 61 n. 12, 153f.

Pessimism, in Paul, 5, 7; in IV Ezra, 416, 418, 427; in Paul and IV Ezra, 546

Pharisaism and Pharisees, 51, 57; relation to Rabbis and to Rabbinic literature, 60–62, 63f.; not defined by second-century discussion of *ḥaberim* and *perushim*, 152–5; not alone in belief in resurrection, 151 n. 19, 354 n. 18, 388 n. 4; relation to Jubilees, 373; relation to Pss. Sol., 388, 388 nn. 4,5, 402–4; works previously attributed to, 425; lack of knowledge of, 426

Plight, human, in Paul, used as basis of soteriology, 442f., 474 n. 1; depends on soteriology, 443, 446, 474f., 497, 499, 510, 555; variation of descriptions of, 474, 474f. n. 2, 509; as transgression and bondage, 497–502, 507f.; existential dimensions of, 508–11; compared with Philo, 553f.; compared with apocalypticism and astrology, 554f.; various conceptions in, 555; *see also* Sin

Polemics in Paul, connected with participatory language, 456f., 459; against Judaism, 1, against 'works of law', 7, explanation of, 549–52; *see also* Law

'Poor' as designation for the righteous, 244, 251, 399, 399 n. 36

Prayer, Rabbinic, 217f., 220f., 223f.; connected with presence of God, 223–9, 230–33; indicates humility and reliance on God, 178, 224, 232; confident prayer at time of death, 229; *Sitz im Leben* of types of prayer, 230; the Eighteen Benedictions, 231f.; in DSS, expresses unworthiness, 266f., 292, 328; expresses human inadequacy in both Rabbinic literature and DSS, 298; for forgiveness in Ben Sirach, 341; in Jubilees, indicates reliance on mercy, 375f.; in Pss. Sol., indicates hope for mercy, 395; *see also* Halakah

Preaching, Paul's, content of, 444–6

Predestination, in Qumran and Paul, 15; in DSS, 257–70; not exclusive of free will, 261, 264f., 268; insisted on to explain election, 266, 267f.; connected with confessions of unworthiness in prayer, 267; expresses grace of God, 267f.; and sin, 282f.; in Paul, 434, 446f.

Presence of God with Israel, despite uncleanness, 81f.; as God's promise, 105; as experienced in 'studying' and 'doing', 217–23; experienced in prayer and at the time of death, 223–9, 230–33; in DSS, 314–16; *see also* Accessibility, Shekinah

Promise, God's promises to Israel, 102–4, 227f., 235; trusted in, 229; held to be forfeited in IV Ezra, 412; to maintain the election, 422; *see also* Faithfulness

Proselytes, 84; like Israelites, accept and keep covenant, 206f., 211; in DSS, 243 n. 11

Psalms of Solomon, idea of mercy in, 52f.; *see also* Mercy to the righteous

Punishment, of wicked in DSS, 272; corresponds to deserts of the wicked, 272f.; in DSS of intra-covenantal transgression, 284–7, 323–5; of the wicked in I Enoch, 350, 357 (by the righteous), 358 (after death); of both righteous and wicked in Pss. Sol., indicates justice of God, 407f.; for disobedience in Paul, 461f.; *see also* Judgment, Reward and Punishment, Reward

Purity, concern of the Pharisees for, 62; and impurity, 81; terminology of indicates moral innocence and guilt, 115f., 278f., 313, 349, 364, 365, 378, 381, 451–3, 468; concern of *ḥaberim* for, 153; terminology of indicates forgiveness, 161 n. 66, 275–7, 298f., 307, 309, 365, 367, 397f., 450–53, 463, 499f.; connected with joining covenant, 278f., 318f.

Rabbinic Judaism, contrasted with other forms of Judaism, 47f.; used as source for legalistic Judaism, 57

Rabbinic literature, point of departure for comparison with Paul, 7, 24f.; importance of for studying Judaism, 34; works used, 59f.; date and reliability of, 60, 63–9; *see also* Tannaitic literature

Reconciliation, 441, 469f., 471f., 498

Religious experience, 212; of the Jew, alienation and separation, 215f.; of the presence of God, 217–23; not remote and alienated, 222; reliance on God's grace, 224, 229, 232f.; *see also* Anxiety, Self-righteousness, Uncertainty

Remnant, use of terminology in DSS, 250f., 250f. n. 35, 268; in I Enoch, 351

Repentance, importance of in Judaism, 5, 6, 7; as achievement, 36, 46, 53, 216; removes blemish, 96; encouraged by suffering, 106; cure for disobedience, 112, 175, 203; as explanation of why one lives, 128; as soteriology, 141, 175, 204; whether or not required for redemption, 150; indicates intention to remain in covenant, 157; 236; as atoning, 158f., 174–80; not a 'work', 176–9; as 'status maintaining', 178f.; as appropriate to restore relationship, 216; prayer for, 178, 232; of wicked Israelites hoped for, 247; required for entry to DSS sect, 270, 276, 284, 548; relation of DSS and Rabbinic literature with regard to, 284; not cure for man's plight in Paul, 284; not major theme of atonement in DSS, 305, but implied, 316; as 'turning back' in Ben Sirach, 340f.; in I Enoch, 356f., 360; in Jubilees, 376–8; in Pss. Sol., 397f.; in IV Ezra, 415; in Paul, 452, 470, 513; reason for virtual absence from Paul, 499–501, 503, 507, 550; in Paul and Judaism, 546

Resurrection, not exclusively Pharisaic belief, 151 n. 19, 354 n. 18, 388 n. 4; not mentioned in Pss. Sol. as point of dispute, 403; in Paul, 434; future expectation, 448–50, 498

Reward, corresponding to justice of God, 83; given before commandments, 86; appropriate to obedience, 89f.; in this world or in the world to come, 125–8, 335–7, 390f.; in DSS, seldom stated, 287; long life and salvation, 294; for deeds in Paul, 451; *see also* Reward and punishment

Reward and punishment, as reflecting the justice of God, 106, 117–19, 198; as fitting the deed, 118f.; not always in strict accord with deserts, 119f., 122f.; exhortative function of, 119f., 124; meted out in this world, 125; meted out in the world to come, 125–8; not soteriology, but reflects justice of God, 128; intra-covenantal behaviour of God, not basis of soteriology, 181f., 234; former by mercy, latter in accord with justice, 293f.; in DSS, 320; in Ben Sirach, 334–7, 346; in I Enoch, 356f.; in Jubilees, 366f.; in Pss. Sol., 389–91; in Pss. Sol., DSS, Rabbinic literature, Paul, 395, 395 n. 29; not alternative to mercy in Judaism, reflects God's justice, 421f.; in Judaism, 422; corresponding to deeds in Paul, 515–18; in Paul and Judaism, 543; *see also* Grace, Judgment, Mercy to Righteous, Punishment, Reward

The Righteous, 142f., 149, 210–5; in Tannaitic literature, those who obey and atone and maintain status, 205; rely on God, 224; designations of in DSS, 244; conception of in DSS, 310–12: those who obey, atone and maintain status, 312, compared with Rabbinic view, 312; in Ben Sirach, 333f., 342–6: those who obey, atone and maintain status, 346; in I Enoch, 350, 355, 357f., saved: 358, 359, 360; the loyal and obedient, 361f., compared with Rabbinic view, 361; in Jubilees, 366, 380–83: those who obey and atone, 381; in Pss. Sol., 389–97, remain among the elect, 396, 398–406; titles for, 399: those who fear and love God and do not betray the covenant, 405, remain in covenant unless they sin heinously, 408; in IV Ezra, those who avoid sin and are saved, 414, very few righteous, 415, 418; not used as title in Paul, 452; in Judaism, those who obey and atone, not those declared righteous in the future, 494; status-maintaining title in Judaism, not in Paul, 518 n. 5, 544f.; *see also* Righteousness, Righteousness of God

Righteousness, in Paul, contrasted with Judaism, 2–4, 9, 544–6; in Paul, relation to DSS sect, 8, 240, 305f., 545f.; in DSS, = perfection, 311f.; gift of God, 311f.; in Paul, significance of 'righteousness by faith', 435–41, 482–7, 488–95; as 'transfer term', 470–72, 501, 518 n. 5, 544; verb ('justify') used to indicate moral cleansing or forgiveness, 451, 471f., 491f., 492 n. 57, 493f., 495, 503; *see also* Forensic declaration; verb ('justify') as equivalent to 'set free', 472, 503, 506, 545 n. 6; as preliminary to life, 471f., 491, 494f., 502f.: as term for Paul's soteriology = life, 492, 494f., 502f., 545; varying meanings of righteousness, 491f., 492–5, 502; as 'imputed', 470 n. 55, 492 n. 57, 494; as determined by works, 491, 495, 516; terms paralleled with, 493; as present not peculiar to Paul, 494; in Paul, righteousness indicates different goal from that of Judaism, 494, 505f., 546, 551; relation to participationist terminology, 495–508; righteousness terminology interpreted by participationist, 503–5, or yields to it, 504; equals life in Christ, 506; not systematically the preliminary to 'life', 506f., 506 n. 68; by the law, reason for Paul's opposition to, 551f.; *see also* Forensic, The Righteous, Righteousness of God, Status-maintenance, Works-righteousness

Righteousness of God, in DSS, 305–10; God's righteousness contrasted with human inability, 306f.; God's 'righteousness' as his mercy, 307–10; as his distributive justice, 310; in Pss. Sol., 407f., his justice, 407; in Paul, 436; varying meanings of, 491; not technical term in Judaism, 494, nor in Paul, 495; scholarly views on, 523–42; *see also* God as just, God as merciful, Righteousness, the Righteous

Romans, purpose and occasion of, 488

Sacraments, in Judaism, 39; Bousset's view that they are needed but missing, 216; not needed, 222; in Paul, 519; *see also* Baptism, Lord's Supper

Sacrifices, 37; Tractate Zebahim, 80; substitutes for in Rabbinic literature, 109; as atoning, 162–4; Rabbinic attitude toward, 163f.; not externalistic fulfilment, 164f.; not mechanistic 167f.; and repentance, 165–7; in DSS, 164, 299f.; substitutes for in DSS, 299f., 302–4, 303–4 nn. 194f.; in Ben Sirach, 338–40; in Jubilees, 379f.; in Pss. Sol., 398

Sadducees, 149f., 354 n. 18, 426; view of Rabbis (and Pharisees) toward, 150–52; in Pss. Sol., 402f., 408

Saints, as title in Paul, 452; *see also* Purity

Salvation, way to in Judaism, 5,7; God as salvation for Israelites, both as group and as individuals, 104–6; provided by election, 220; for those who trust God, 232; for faithful members of Israel, 236; forfeited by transgression, but not earned by obedience, 293, 371, 517f.; way to in DSS, 317; of the righteous in I Enoch, 358; in I Enoch compared with Rabbis, 361; in Jubilees, for all but apostate Israelites, 367–71; in IV Ezra, for the few perfectly obedient, 413, 415, 418, 420; depends on grace in Judaism, 422; in Paul by Christ, 441f.; for all who believe, 442, 445; assurance of, 460, coupled with anxiety about judgment, 517; in Paul, scope of, 472–4; for Jews and Gentiles on same ground, 488–91; by faith and not by law, reasons for, 489f.; for all those 'in', 513; *see also* Obedience as condition, Soteriology

Salvation history (*Heilsgeschichte*), 437f.

Saviour, Jesus as, 443; *see also* Lordship of Christ, Messiah, Soteriology of Paul, summaries

Sect, different from 'party', 267, 267 n. 74; and parties, 425f.; and parties, assignment of literature to, 425f.

Sects and sectarians, Rabbis (and Pharisees) not sectarians, 156f., 425; Jubilees not sectarian, 373f., 383–5, 425; Pss. Sol. not sectarian, 405f., 408f.; DSS sectarian, 314, 425

Self-righteousness, as typical of Jewish piety, 40, 45, 48, 51, 54, 212f.; not typical of Rabbis, 87, 101; whether or not implied by death-bed prayers, 229f.; attributed to authors of Pss. Sol., 394f.; *see also* Anxiety, Religious experience, Uncertainty, Works-righteousness

Separation, in DSS, indicates concern for ritual and moral purity, 312f.

Shekinah, 82, 105; indicates God's presence, 214f.

Trust, of Israelites in God, 103, 227
Truth, ultimate, 30, 32, 430
Tsadaq, tsaddiq, tsedaqah, etc.; *see also* 'Righteous', 'Charity'; 198–205, 305–12, 342–4,
    350, 357, 361, 399

Unbeliever, term for non-Christian in Paul, 445, 452, 463; destruction of, 446, 473
Uncertainty of salvation, 38, 41, 45, 49, 52, 54, 216, 225–9, 298, 394f.; in Paul, combined
    with assurance of salvation, 517; *see also* Anxiety

Visions, in IV Ezra, *see* Apocalypses

War, eschatological, 248, 250f., 417
War Scroll (IQM), history of, 251f.
Weighing, 37–9, 41, 43, 45, 50, 52, 54, 58, 128–32, 138–43, 143–5, 225, 227, 229; not
    Rabbinic soteriology, 146f., 149f., 172, 176, 181, 205, 213, 233, 236; connected to view
    of Rabbinic religion as arid and sterile, 213, 215; *see also* Book-keeping, Credit and
    debit
The Wicked, 142f., 149, 199; did not accept the Torah, 203; designations of in DSS, 243;
    as non-Essene Israelites, 244f.; all those outside the covenant, 247; destruction or
    conversion of, 250, 254f.; destruction of, 257, 272; in Ben Sirach, 333f., 342–5; in
    I Enoch, 350, 351 n. 16, 351–5, 357f., 360, 361, compared with Rabbinic view, 361; in
    Pss. Sol., destruction of, 391, forfeit place in covenant, 396, titles for, 399, identity of,
    400–4, those who sinned in such a way as to be excluded from covenant, 404, sin worse
    than Gentiles, 405; in IV Ezra, those who transgress and are damned, 414; in Paul, 452
Wisdom, motifs in Ben Sirach, 329, 329 n. 2, equated with law, 330–33; in Paul, 505f.
Works-righteousness, scholarly views on Judaism as a religion of, 2f., 9, 33–59, 220, 297
    n. 164, 409f., 419, 419 n. 1; in Qumran, 291f.; context of gratuity, 293, 295; in Jubilees,
    382f.; in Pss. Sol., 395; in IV Ezra, 409, 418, 420, 427; not revealed by Jewish literature,
    550
World to come, locale of reward and punishment, 125–8; promised to Israelites, 147–50,
    177; ambiguity of the nature of, 148; promised to the righteous, 204f.; patriarchs would
    have share in, 227; whether or not envisaged in Pss. Sol., 391 n. 11

Zakah, zekut, 91, 183–98; translation of, 187f.
Zekut 'abot, 47, 58, 90f., 103, 183–98, *see also* Merits